WATER PUBLICATIONS
OF STATE AGENCIES

WATER INFORMATION CENTER

PERIODICALS

Water Newsletter
Research and Development News
Ground Water Newsletter

BOOKS

Geraghty and Miller   *Water Atlas of the United States*

Todd   *The Water Encyclopedia*

van der Leeden   *Ground Water – A Selected Bibliography*

Giefer and Todd   *Water Publications of State Agencies*

WATER PUBLICATIONS
OF STATE AGENCIES

*A Bibliography of Publications on Water Resources
and Their Management Published by the States
of the United States.*

Edited by

GERALD J. GIEFER
  Librarian, Water Resources Center Archives
  University of California, Berkeley

DAVID K. TODD
  Professor of Civil Engineering
  University of California, Berkeley

with the assistance of
MARY LOUISE QUINN

WATER INFORMATION CENTER
Port Washington, New York

Library of Congress Catalog Card Number: 72-75672

ISBN: 0-912394-04-8

Printed in the United States of America

Set in Cold-type Composition and Designed by: *Trotta Composition, Inc.*
Printed and Bound by: *The Maple Press Company*

PREFACE

Water resources publications by Federal government agencies are generally widely distributed and are included in various Federal publication listings. The inquiring public thus knows that this material exists. This is not true for the numerous water resources publications of agencies at the state level for which there is no unified reference source. We have endeavored to meet this need by compiling in this book a listing of water resources publications issued by 335 state agencies in the 50 states of the United States. Information is listed by state with publications grouped under the issuing agencies of each state.

In compiling this bibliography we wrote to every state agency which might have some connection with water resources and asked them for a complete and up-to-date list of their publications, both those currently available and those out of print. Some agencies were unable to comply. Either they did not publish, did not maintain a listing of their publications, or, due to organizational changes, no longer kept a record of the published work of their predecessor agencies. Where possible, these gaps were filled by independent research in the libraries of the University of California, Berkeley.

The publication information given here is largely that supplied by the agencies themselves. The bibliographic format employed by each agency has been retained. An address is given for every state agency listed. Brief introductory statements with information as to availability and price of publications have been included where they were supplied. Where this information is not given, it is suggested that readers apply to the agency involved.

The water resources research centers established in each state under Public Law 88-376 have been included. Agricultural experiment stations, agricultural extension service agencies, and interstate agencies are omitted.

In those cases where the orientation of an agency includes water as only one element in a broader spectrum (e. g., the state geological surveys), we included from their publication lists only those titles which were directly related to water resources. This accounts for the nonsequential numbering appearing in many of the lists. In the case of State Departments of Fisheries (or Fish and Game), we listed titles which reflect a close association between the fishery resource and the water resource. Thus, for example, an article on a fish kill resulting from pollution was included but not one on regulation of commercial fishing gear. The same criterion was applied in regard to wildlife.

State agencies sometimes include in their lists of publications the titles of pertinent Federal studies concerning their state's water resources. Reports by the U. S. Geological Survey and the U. S. Army Corps of Engineers are two examples. Unless it was noted that the Federal and stage agencies produced a report "cooperatively", we deleted the title. Similarly, "reprint" series were generally omitted; these titles, in many instances, have appeared in one or another of the well-known journals in the water resources field and are readily located in standard indices such as *Engineering Index, Science and Technology Index,* and *Selected Water Resources Abstracts.* An exception was made where the reprint was published in a technical series, or where the originating journal was relatively obscure, such as the proceedings of a local society.

Consideration was given to adding area, author, and subject indices, but these would have increased the size and cost of the volume substantially. With all state agencies listed in the Table of Contents, we believe that pertinent information within a given state can be readily located.

We make no claim that this book is complete. Undoubtedly, publications have been overlooked and perhaps some agencies have been omitted. Readers are encouraged to inform us of oversights and errors so that subsequent editions can be improved.

Acknowledgment is due to the hundreds of state agencies that generously cooperated with us by supplying information so that this bibliographic compilation could become a reality.

Gerald J. Giefer
David K. Todd

Berkeley
February 1972

HOW TO OBTAIN PUBLICATIONS

Many of the publications cited in this book are available for loan at major public libraries, the libraries of leading educational institutions, or at the State Library of the state in which the document was produced. The name and address of each State Library is listed below for the reader's convenience.

Publications also can be obtained directly from their source. Information regarding price, photocopy fees, and policy on lending material is often included in the textual material preceding each agency listing. In the absence of this information, it is suggested the researcher write directly to the agency.

An asterisk (*) has been used throughout this book to designate those publications which are out-of-print.

Some contract reports are noted in the text as being available from the "Clearinghouse" or "National Technical Information Service." The address to be used to obtain these titles is: National Technical Information Service, U. S. Department of Commerce, Springfield, Virginia 22151.

STATE PUBLIC LIBRARIES

ALABAMA PUBLIC LIBRARY SERVICE
155 Administrative Building
Montgomery, Alabama 36104

ALASKA STATE LIBRARY
State Capitol Building
Pouch G
Juneau, Alaska 99801

ARIZONA DEPARTMENT OF LIBRARY AND ARCHIVES
3rd Floor, Capitol Building
Phoenix, Arizona 85007

ARKANSAS LIBRARY COMMISSION
506–1/2 Center Street
Little Rock, Arkansas 72201

STATE PUBLIC LIBRARIES (continued)

CALIFORNIA STATE LIBRARY
Library-Courts Building
Sacramento, California 95809

COLORADO STATE LIBRARY
Department of Education
1362 Lincoln Street
Denver, Colorado 80203

CONNECTICUT STATE LIBRARY
Division of Library Development
231 Capitol Avenue
Hartford, Connecticut 06115

LIBRARY COMMISSION FOR THE STATE OF DELAWARE
West Loockerman Street
Box 635
Dover, Delaware 19901

FLORIDA DEPARTMENT OF STATE
Division of State Library Services
Supreme Court Building
Tallahassee, Florida 32304

GEORGIA STATE DEPARTMENT OF EDUCATION
Public Library Service
156 Trinity Avenue, S.W.
Atlanta, Georgia 30303

HAWAII OFFICE OF THE STATE LIBRARIAN
Department of Education
Office of Library Service
Box 2360
Honolulu, Hawaii 96804

IDAHO STATE LIBRARY
615 Fulton Street
Boise, Idaho 83706

ILLINOIS STATE LIBRARY
Centennial Building
Springfield, Illinois 62706

INDIANA STATE LIBRARY
140 N. Senate Avenue
Indianapolis, Indiana 46204

IOWA STATE TRAVELING LIBRARY
Historical Building
Des Moines, Iowa 50319

STATE PUBLIC LIBRARIES (continued)

STATE LIBRARY OF KANSAS
3rd Floor, State House
Topeka, Kansas 66612

KENTUCKY STATE DEPARTMENT OF LIBRARIES
Berry Hill
P. O. Box 537
Frankfort, Kentucky 40601

LOUISIANA STATE LIBRARY
State Capitol Grounds
Box 131
Baton Rouge, Louisiana 70821

MAINE STATE LIBRARY
State House
Augusta, Maine 04330

MARYLAND STATE DEPARTMENT OF EDUCATION
Division of Library Development & Services
600 Wyndhurst Avenue
Baltimore, Maryland 21210

MASSACHUSETTS STATE DEPARTMENT OF EDUCATION
Bureau of Library Extension
648 Beacon Street
Boston, Massachusetts 02215

MICHIGAN STATE LIBRARY
735 E. Michigan Avenue
Lansing, Michigan 48913

MINNESOTA STATE DEPARTMENT OF EDUCATION
Library Division
117 University Avenue
St. Paul, Minnesota 55101

MISSISSIPPI LIBRARY COMMISSION
405 State Office Building
Jackson, Mississippi 39201

MISSOURI STATE LIBRARY
308 E. High Street
Jefferson City, Missouri 65101

MONTANA STATE LIBRARY
930 E. Lyndale Avenue
Helena, Montana 59601

STATE PUBLIC LIBRARIES (continued)

NEBRASKA PUBLIC LIBRARY COMMISSION
State Capitol
Lincoln, Nebraska   68509

NEVADA STATE LIBRARY
Carson City
Nevada   89701

NEW HAMPSHIRE STATE LIBRARY
20 Park Street
Concord, New Hampshire   03301

NEW JERSEY DEPARTMENT OF EDUCATION
New Jersey State Library
Public & School Library Services Bureau
185 W. State Street
Box 1898
Trenton, New Jersey   08625

NEW MEXICO STATE LIBRARY COMMISSION
State Library
Box 1529
Santa Fe, New Mexico   87501

NEW YORK STATE DEPARTMENT OF EDUCATION
New York State Library
Albany, New York   12224

NORTH CAROLINA STATE LIBRARY
Archive & History
State Library Building
Raleigh, North Carolina   27601

NORTH DAKOTA STATE LIBRARY COMMISSION
Bismarck
North Dakota   58501

THE STATE LIBRARY OF OHIO
State Office Building
65 S. Front Street
Columbus, Ohio   43215

OKLAHOMA DEPARTMENT OF LIBRARIES
109 State Capitol
Box 53344
Oklahoma City, Oklahoma   73105

OREGON STATE LIBRARY
Salem
Oregon   97310

STATE PUBLIC LIBRARIES (continued)

PENNSYLVANIA DEPARTMENT OF EDUCATION
State Library
Box 1601
Harrisburg, Pennsylvania   17126

RHODE ISLAND DEPARTMENT OF STATE LIBRARY SERVICES
95 Davis Street
Providence, Rhode Island   02908

SOUTH CAROLINA STATE LIBRARY
1500 Senate Street
Columbia, South Carolina   29201

SOUTH DAKOTA STATE LIBRARY COMMISSION
322 South Fort Street
Pierre, South Dakota   57501

TENNESSEE STATE LIBRARY AND ARCHIVES
Nashville
Tennessee   37219

TEXAS STATE LIBRARY
Box 12927 Capitol Station
Austin, Texas   78711

UTAH STATE LIBRARY COMMISSION
2150 South Second West
Salt Lake City, Utah   84115

VERMONT DEPARTMENT OF LIBRARIES
State Library Building
Montpelier, Vermont   05602

VIRGINIA STATE LIBRARY
Extension Branch
Richmond, Virginia   23219

WASHINGTON STATE LIBRARY
Olympia
Washington   98501

WEST VIRGINIA LIBRARY COMMISSION
2004 Quarrier Street
Charleston, West Virginia   25311

WISCONSIN DEPARTMENT OF PUBLIC INSTRUCTION
Division of Library Services
State of Wisconsin
126 Langdon Street
Madison, Wisconsin   53702

STATE PUBLIC LIBRARIES (continued)

WYOMING STATE LIBRARY
Supreme Court Building
Cheyenne, Wyoming 82001

CONTENTS

ALABAMA

ALABAMA DEVELOPMENT OFFICE
State Office Building
Montgomery, Alabama 36104

*Water Planning & Management for Alabama. November 1968. 15 p.

*A Guide for Reducing Flood Damage. 1969. 14 p.

*A Comprehensive Planning for Water and Related Land Resources in Alabama. 1970. 47 p.

*Design and Cost for Liquid-Waste Disposal Systems. December 1969. 98 p.

Alabama Agencies with Water-Resources and Related Land Use Responsibilities. October 1970. 75 p.

Status of Water-Resources Management in Alabama. October 1970. 103 p.

Land Use Regulations in Flood-Prone Areas. November 1970. 110 p.

Development of Water Resources in Non-Appalachian Alabama (10 volumes, one of which is a section on water resources and pollution). 1969.

*Water for Alabama—Water Situation. August 1970. 28 p.

Alabama Industrial Guide (Section on Natural Resources which covers water aspects of Alabama's industrial and economic development). 1970.

Various up-to-date maps showing rivers and other miscellaneous data.

ALABAMA GEOLOGICAL SURVEY
P. O. Drawer O
University, Alabama 35486

These publications may be obtained from the Geological Survey of Alabama, at the above address. Remittance must accompany orders for reports and maps. Please make checks and money orders payable to Map Fund, Geological Survey of Alabama.

REPORTS OF PROGRESS AND ANNUAL REPORTS

*Report of progress for 1874, by Eugene A. Smith. 139 p. 1875.

Report of progress for 1875, by Eugene A. Smith. 220 p. 1876. $0.10.

Report of progress for 1876, by Eugene A. Smith. 99 p. 1876. $0.10.

*Report of progress for 1877 and 1878, by Eugene A. Smith. 138 p. 4 maps. 1879.

*Report of progress for 1879-1880, by Eugene A. Smith. 158 p. 2 maps. 1881.

Report of the years 1881 and 1882.

*Report of progress for 1884-88, by Eugene A. Smith. 24 p. Map. 1888.

*Biennial report of the State Geologist (1889-90), by Eugene A. Smith. 18 p. 1890.

*Report for fiscal years ending September 30, 1891-92, by Eugene A. Smith. 22 p. 1892.

*Report of progress for the years ending September 30, 1895 and September 30, 1896, by Eugene A. Smith. 18 p. 1896.

*Report of progress for the years ending September 30, 1897 and September 30, 1898, by Eugene A. Smith. 21 p. 1898.

*Reports of progress for the fiscal years 1898-99 and 1899-1900 and 1900-01 and 1901-02. 26 p. 1902.

*Report of progress for the fiscal years 1902-06, by Eugene A. Smith. 19 p. 1907.

Report of progress for the fiscal years 1906-10, by Eugene A. Smith. 19 p. 1911. $0.10.

*Report of progress for the fiscal years 1910-14, by Eugene A. Smith. 24 p. 1914.

Report of progress for the fiscal years 1914-18, by Eugene A. Smith. 14 p. 1918. $0.10.

Report of progress for the fiscal years 1918-22, by Eugene A. Smith. 16 p. 1922. $0.10.

Report of progress for the fiscal years 1923-26, by Eugene A. Smith. 16 p. 1926. $0.10.

Report of progress for the fiscal years 1926-30, by Walter B. Jones. 29 p. 1931. $0.10.

Report of progress for the fiscal years 1930-34, by Walter B. Jones. 12 p. 1937. $0.10.

Report of progress for the fiscal years 1934-38, by Stewart J. Lloyd. 11 p. 1942. $0.10.

Report of progress for the fiscal years 1938-42, by Stewart J. Lloyd and Lyman D. Toulmin. 69 p. 1943. $0.10.

Annual report for the fiscal year 1942-43, by Stewart J. Lloyd and Lyman D. Toulmin. 13 p. 1944. $0.10.

Annual report for the fiscal year 1943-44, by Stewart J. Lloyd and Lyman D. Toulmin. 31 p. 1944. $0.10.

Annual report for the fiscal year 1944-45, by Walter B. Jones. 32 p. 1945. $0.10.

Annual report for the fiscal year 1945-46, by Walter B. Jones. 26 p. 1947. $0.10.

Annual report for the fiscal year 1946-47, by Walter B. Jones. 28 p. 1948. $0.10.

Annual report for the fiscal year 1947-48, by Walter B. Jones. 32 p. 1949. $0.10.

Annual report for the fiscal year 1948-49, by Walter B. Jones. 32 p. 1950. $0.10.

Annual report for the fiscal year 1949-50, by Walter B. Jones. 21 p. 1951. $0.10.

Annual report for the fiscal year 1950-51, by Walter B. Jones. 23 p. 1952. $0.10.

Annual report for the fiscal year 1951-52, by Walter B. Jones. 22 p. 1953. $0.10.

Annual report for the fiscal year 1952-53, by Walter B. Jones. 37 p. 1954. $0.10.

Annual report for the fiscal year 1953-54, by Walter B. Jones. 29 p. 1955. $0.10.

Annual report for the fiscal year 1954-55, by Walter B. Jones. 37 p. 1956. $0.10.

Annual report for the fiscal year 1955-56, by Walter B. Jones. 44 p. 1957. $0.10.

Annual report for the fiscal year 1956-57, by Walter B. Jones. 59 p. 1958. $0.10.

Annual report for the fiscal year 1957-58, by Walter B. Jones. 41 p. 1959. $0.10.

Annual report for the fiscal year 1958-59, by Walter B. Jones. 46 p. 1960. $0.10.

Annual report for the fiscal year 1959-60, by Walter B. Jones. 34 p. 1961. $0.10.

Annual report for the fiscal year 1960-61, by Walter B. Jones and Philip E. LaMoreaux. 17 p. 1962. $0.10.

Annual report for the fiscal year 1961-62, by Philip E. LaMoreaux. 18 p. 1964. $0.10.

Annual report for the fiscal year 1962-63, by Philip E. LaMoreaux. 16 p. 1966. $0.10.

Annual report for the fiscal year 1963-64, by Philip E. LaMoreaux. 11 p. 1968. $0.10.

Annual report for the fiscal year 1964-65, by Philip E. LaMoreaux. 11 p. 1968. $0.10.

Annual report for the fiscal year 1965-66, by Philip E. LaMoreaux. 11 p. 1968. $0.10.

SPECIAL REPORTS

16 Ground water in the Paleozoic rocks of northern Alabama, by W. D. Johnson, Jr. Part 1, 414 p., 54 figs., 23 pls., 2 folded tables. Part 2, 48 well and spring tables, folded map. 1933. $1.50.

17 Natural resources of the Tennessee Valley Region in Alabama, by R. M. Harper. 93 p., 3 figs. 1942. $0.50.

18 Ground-water resources of the Cretaceous area of Alabama, by C. W. Carlston. 203 p. 1944. $2.50.

20 Water resources and hydrology of southeastern Alabama, by R. W. Carter and others. 265 p. 1949. $0.50.

22 Hydrology and surface-water resources of east-central Alabama, by L. B. Peirce. 318 p. 1955. $0.75.

23 Geology and ground water of the Piedmont area of Alabama, by Jack Baker. 99 p. 1957. $0.50.

24 Surface-water resources and hydrology of west-central Alabama, by L. B. Peirce. 236 p. 1959. $0.50.

This series was discontinued October 1, 1963. The last publication in this series was SPECIAL REPORT 24. Publications formerly issued as Special Reports are now issued as Bulletins.

COUNTY REPORTS

2 Geology and ground-water resources of Choctaw County, Alabama, by L. D. Toulmin, P. E. LaMoreaux, and C. R. Lanphere. (Also issued as Special Report 21.) 197 p. 1951. $1.50. (Paper bound, $0.50.)

3 Geology and ground-water resources of Madison County, Alabama, by G. T. Malmberg and H. T. Downing. 225 p. 1957. $1.00.

4 Geology and ground-water resources of Wilcox County, Alabama, by P. E. LaMoreaux and L. D. Toulmin. 280 p. 1959. $2.00.

5 Geology and ground-water resources of Marengo County, Alabama, by J. G. Newton, Horace Sutcliffe, Jr., and P. E. LaMoreaux. 443 p., 46 figs., 11 pls. 1961. $2.00.

6 Ground-water resources and geology of Tuscaloosa County, Alabama, by Quentin F. Paulson, J. D. Miller, Jr., and C. W. Drennen. 97 p., 15 figs., 3 pls. 1962. $1.00.

7 Geology and ground-water resources of Calhoun County, Alabama, by J. C. Warman and L. V. Causey. 77 p., 19 figs., 6 pls. 1962. $1.00.

8 Geology and ground-water resources of Lauderdale County, Alabama, by H. B. Harris, R. R. Peace, Jr., and W. F. Harris, Jr. 178 p., 26 figs., 5 pls. 1963. $1.00.

9 Surface water in Tuscaloosa County, Alabama, by L. B. Peirce. 89 p., 18 figs., 1 pl. 1962. $0.50.

10 Geology and ground-water resources of Colbert County, Alabama, by H. B. Harris, G. K. Moore, and L. R. West. 71 p., 17 figs., 6 pls. 1963. $0.75.

11 General geology and ground-water resources of Limestone County, Alabama, a reconnaissance report, by W. M. McMaster and W. F. Harris, Jr. 43 p., 4 figs., 4 pls. 1963. $0.50.

This series was discontinued October 1, 1963. The last publication in this series was COUNTY REPORT

11. Publications formerly issued as County Reports are now issued as Bulletins.

MONOGRAPHS

*2   List of the fresh-water and marine Crustacea of Alabama, with descriptions of the new species and synoptical keys for identification, by C. L. Herrick. 56 p., 8 pls. 1887.

*6   The underground water resources of Alabama, by Eugene A. Smith. 388 p., 30 pls. 1907.

BULLETINS

*7   A preliminary report on a part of the water powers of Alabama, by B. M. Hall. 185 p., 4 pls. 1903. (See Bull. 17)

17   Second report on the water powers of Alabama, 2d ed., by B. M. Hall and M. R. Hall. 448 p. 1916. $1.00.

50   Well logs of Alabama, by Edgar Bowles. 357 p. 1941. $1.00

52   Fluoride in the ground water of the Cretaceous area of Alabama, with map, by C. W. Carlston. 67 p. 1942. $0.50.

56   Natural water losses from selected drainage basins in Alabama, by E. B. Rice and C. H. Hardison. 35 p. 1945. $0.50.

57   Well logs of Alabama, 1940-45, by L. D. Toulmin. 177 p. 1945. $2.00.

58   Ground-water investigations in the Mobile area, Alabama, by C. G. Peterson. 32 p. 1947. $0.50.

59   Fluoride in the ground water of the Tertiary area of Alabama, by P. E. LaMoreaux. 77 p. 1948. $0.50.

62   Ground-water resources of the Huntsville area, Alabama, by P. E. LaMoreaux, G. W. Swindel, Jr., and C. R. Lanphere. 82 p. 1950. $0.50.

66   Geology and ground water in the Monroeville area, Alabama, by J. B. Ivey. 109 p. 1957. $0.50.

68A   Geology and ground-water resources of Montgomery County, Alabama, with special reference to the Montgomery area, by D. B. Knowles, H. L. Reade, Jr., and J. C. Scott. 76 p., 22 figs., 15 pls. 1963. $1.50.

68B   Geology and ground-water resources of Montgomery County, Alabama, with special reference to the Montgomery area, basic data, by D. B. Knowles, H. L. Reade, Jr., and J. C. Scott. 493 p., 1 pl. 1960. $1.50.

71   Geology and ground-water resources of the Athens area, Alabama, by W. M. McMaster. 45 p., 8 figs., 8 pls. 1963. $0.50.

72   Geology and ground-water resources of Franklin County, Alabama, a reconnaissance report, by R. R. Peace, Jr. 55 p., 5 figs., 2 pls. 1963. $0.75.

73   Geology and ground-water resources of St. Clair County, Alabama, a reconnaissance report, by L. V. Causey. 84 p., 9 figs., 2 pls. 1963. $1.25.

74   Geology and ground-water resources of Escambia County, Alabama, by J. W. Cagle, Jr., and J. G. Newton. 205 p., 17 figs., 2 pls. 1963. $1.00.

75   Ground-water resources of Russell County, Alabama, a reconnaissance, by J. C. Scott. 77 p., 17 figs., 4 pls. 1964. $0.75.

76   Geology and ground-water resources of Morgan County, Alabama, by C. L. Dodson and W. F. Harris, Jr. 90 p., 19 figs., 4 pls. 1965. $1.00.

77   Geology and ground-water resources of the Russellville area, Alabama, by R. R. Peace, Jr. 83 p., 23 figs., 3 pls. 1964. $0.75.

78   Geology and ground-water resources of Lawrence County, Alabama, by W. F. Harris, Jr., and W. M. McMaster. 70 p., 8 figs., 3 pls. 1965. $1.00

79   Geology and ground-water resources of Cherokee County, Alabama, a reconnaissance by L. V. Causey. 63 p., 5 figs., 2 pls. 1965. $1.00.

81   Availability of ground water in Talladega County, Alabama, a reconnaissance, by L. V. Causey. 63 p., 4 figs., 2 pls. 1965. $1.00.

82   Reservoir temperatures in north-central Alabama, by L. B. Peirce. 103 p., 30 figs. 1964. $0.50.

83   Ground-water resources of Pickens County, Alabama, a reconnaissance, by K. D. Wahl. 34 p., 8 figs., 2 pls. 1965. $1.25.

84   Surface water in southwestern Alabama, by L. B. Peirce, with a section on chemical quality of surface water, by S. M. Rogers. 182 p., 36 figs., 2 pls. 1966. $1.00.

85   Ground water in Marshall County, Alabama, a reconnaissance, by Thomas H. Sanford, Jr. 66 p., 2 pls. 1966. $1.00.

86   Geology and ground-water resources of Greene County, Alabama, by K. D. Wahl. 93 p., 11 figs., 2 pls. 1966. $1.00.

87   7-Day low flows and flow duration of Alabama streams, by L. B. Peirce. 114 p., 8 figs., 3 pls. 1967. $0.75.

89   Water laws of Alabama, by A. J. Harris and W. T. Watson. 155 p. 1968. $2.00.

94C   Hydrology of limestone terranes, photogeologic investigations, by J. L. Sonderegger. 26 p., 9 figs., 5 pls. 1970. $1.00.

94D   Hydrology of limestone terranes, geophysical investigations, by T. J. Joiner and W. L. Scarbrough. 43 p., 23 figs., 9 pls. 1969. $1.00.

CIRCULARS

11   Conservation of our natural and wildlife resources, by W. B. Jones. 12 p. 1938. $0.25.

18   Ground-water geology of Tennessee Valley area in Alabama, with reference to vertical drainage, by P. E. LaMoreaux. 13 p. 1949. $0.50.

22   Water problems associated with oil production in Alabama, by W. J. Powell, L. E. Carroon, and J. R. Avrett. 63 p. 1964. $0.50.

23   Ground-water levels in Alabama in 1959 and 1960, by D. M. O'Rear. 123 p., 56 figs. 1964. $0.50.

24   Ground-water conditions in the Huntsville area, Alabama, January 1960 through June 1961, by T. H. Sanford, Jr. 46 p., 17 figs., 1 pl. 1965. $0.50

25   Ground water in the vicinity of Bryce State Hospital, Negro Colony, Tuscaloosa County, Alabama, by K. D. Wahl. 38 p., 6 figs., 2 pls. 1965. $0.50.

32   Flow characteristics of Alabama streams, a basic data report, compiled by C. F. Hains. 382 p. 1968. $3.00.

33   Surface water resources of Calhoun County, Alabama, by J. R. Harkins, with a section on quality of water by R. G. Grantham. 75 p., 11 figs., 1 pl. 1965. $0.50.

36   A compilation of surface water quality data in Alabama, by J. R. Avrett. 574 p., 1 fig., 1 pl. 1966. $3.00.

37   A compilation of ground water quality data in Alabama, by J. R. Avrett. 336 p., 2 figs. 1968. $3.00.

40   Water, minerals and oil in the South — a frontier of our nation's resources, by P. E. LaMoreaux. 24 p., 8 figs. 1967. No Charge.

42   Geophysical prospecting for ground water in the Piedmont area, Alabama, by T. J. Joiner, J. C. Warman, W. L. Scarbrough, and D. B. Moore. 48 p., 17 figs., 3 pls. 1967. $0.50.

56   A problem of subsidence in a limestone terrane at Columbiana, Alabama, by W. J. Powell and P. E. LaMoreaux. 30 p., 20 figs., 1969. $0.50.

58   Deep-well disposal study for Baldwin, Escambia, and Mobile Counties, Alabama, by R. M. Alverson. 49 p., 8 figs., 10 pls., 1 table, appendix. 1970. $0.50.

INFORMATION SERIES

*1   Progress report on ground-water studies in the Huntsville area, Alabama, by T. H. Sanford. 4 p., 7 figs. 1955.

2   Water levels and artesian pressures in Alabama, 1954, by D. M. O'Rear and D. B. Knowles. 49 p., 5 figs. 1955. $0.50.

3   Interim report on the geology and ground-water resources of Montgomery, Alabama and vicinity, by W. J. Powell, H. L. Reade, and J. C. Scott. 108 p., 4 figs., 10 pls. 1957. $0.50.

4   Interim report on the geology and ground-water resources of Marengo County, Alabama, by Horace Sutcliffe, Jr., and J. G. Newton. 64 p., 11 figs., 4 pls. 1957. $0.50.

5   Water levels and artesian pressures in Alabama, 1955, by D. M. O'Rear. 49 p., 6 figs. 1957. $0.50.

6   Ground-water resources of Lowndes County, Alabama, a reconnaissance report, by J. C. Scott. 80 p., 6 figs., 4 pls. 1957. $0.50.

7   Interim report on ground water in Escambia County, Alabama, with special reference to the Brewton area, by J. W. Cagle, Jr., and B. L. Floyd. 30 p., 7 figs. 1957. (See Bull. 74). $0.50.

8   Interim report on the geology and ground-water resources of Wilcox County, Alabama, by P. E. LaMoreaux and Horace Sutcliffe, Jr. 17 p., 6 figs., 1 pl. 1957. $0.50.

9   Interim report on ground-water studies in the Huntsville area, Alabama, to February 1957, by T. H. Sanford, Jr. 131 p., 15 figs., 7 pls. 1957. $0.50.

10   Springs in Colbert and Lauderdale Counties, Alabama, by H. B. Harris. 16 p., 1 fig., 1 pl. 1957. $0.50.

11   Ground-water levels in Alabama in 1956, by D. M. O'Rear and D. B. Knowles. 46 p., 4 figs. 1957. $0.50.

12   Ground water in the vicinity of Bryce State Hospital, Tuscaloosa County, Alabama, by J. D. Miller, Jr., 8 figs., 16 pls. 1958. $0.25.

14   Geology and ground-water resources of Tuscaloosa County, Alabama, an interim report, by J. D. Miller, Jr., and L. V. Causey. 71 p., 5 figs., 3 pls. 1958. $0.50.

15   Ground-water investigations in Alabama with a selected bibliography, by W. J. Powell and P. E. LaMoreaux. 2 figs. 1959. $0.25.

16   Ground-water resources of Macon County, Alabama, a reconnaissance report, by J. C. Scott. 97 p., 10 figs., 4 pls. 1960. $0.50.

17   Geology and ground-water resources of Calhoun County, Alabama, an interim report, by J. C. Warman, L.V. Causey, J. H. Burks, and H. W. Ziemand. 67 p., 2 figs., 1 pl. 1960. $0.50.

19   Ground-water levels in Alabama in 1957 and 1958, by D. M. O'Rear. 81 p., 28 figs. 1960. $0.50.

20   Interim report on ground-water study in Colbert County, Alabama, by H. B. Harris, G. K. Moore, and L. V. Causey. 59 p., 4 figs., 1 pl. 1960. $0.50.

21   Ground-water resources of Autauga County, Alabama, a reconnaissance report, by J. C. Scott. 92 p., 8 figs., 4 pls. 1960. $0.50.

22   Ground-water levels in Madison County, Alabama, July 1956 to July 1959, by T. H. Sanford, Jr., and L. R. West. 42 p., 7 figs. 1960. $0.50.

23   Interim report on ground-water studies in the Athens area, Alabama, through January 1960, by W. M. McMaster. 72 p., 18 figs., 4 pls. 1960. $0.50.

24   Interim report on the geology and ground-water resources of Morgan County, Alabama, by C. L. Dodson and W. F. Harris, Jr. 129 p., 3 figs., 1 pl. 1961. $0.50.

25   Ground-water resources of Etowah County, Alabama, a reconnaissance report, by L. V. Causey. 63 p., 7 figs., 2 pls. 1961. $0.50.

27   Chemical quality of water of Alabama streams, 1960, a reconnaissance study, by R. N. Cherry. 95 p., 16 figs., i pl. 1963. $0.50.

28   Geology and ground-water resources of the Russellville area, Alabama, an interim report, by R. R. Peace, Jr. 29 p., 4 figs., 1 pl. 1962. $0.50.

29 Ground-water resources of Bullock County, Alabama, a reconnaissance report, by J. C. Scott. 120 p., 12 figs., 4 pls. 1962. $0.50.

35 Temperature of Alabama streams, by J. R. Avrett and L. E. Carroon. 165 p., 1 fig. 1964. $0.50.

36 Mineral and water resources, Butler County, Alabama. 37 p., 13 figs. 1967. $1.00.

37 Mineral and water resources of Barbour County, Alabama, by P. E. LaMoreaux and others. 41 p., 11 figs., 5 tables. 1968. $1.00.

38 Mineral and water resources of Houston County, Alabama, by P. E. LaMoreaux and others. 36 p., 8 figs., 4 tables. 1969. $1.00.

39 Mineral and water resources of Geneva County, Alabama, by P. E. LaMoreaux and others. 34 p., 9 figs., 4 tables. 1969. $1.00.

40 Mineral, water, and energy resources of Wilcox County, Alabama, by P. E. LaMoreaux and others. 49 p., 17 figs., 8 tables. 1969. $1.00.

41 Geologic and hydrologic research through space-acquired data for Alabama, delineation of linear features and application to reservoir engineering using Apollo 9 multi-spectral photography, by W. J. Powell, C. W. Copeland, and J. A. Drahovzal. 37 p., 13 figs., 3 tables. 1970. $2.00.

SPECIAL MAPS

29 Water-level fluctuations and chemical quality of ground water in Alabama, by W. J. Powell and A. C. Duncan. 29 x 44 inches. $0.50.

34 Water availability, Barbour County, Alabama, by J. G. Newton, W. J. Powell, H. G. Golden, and J. R. Avrett. 42 x 51 inches. Colored. 1966. $1.00.

55 Water availability map of Geneva County, Alabama, by J. C. Scott, H. G. Golden, and J. R. Avrett. 30 x 48 inches. Colored. 1967. $1.00.

57 Water availability map of Butler County, Alabama, by P. C. Reed, J. C. Scott, H. G. Golden, and J. R. Avrett. 38 x 44 inches. Colored. 1967. $1.00.

59 Water availability map of Houston County, Alabama, by J. C. Scott, J. F. McCain, and J. R. Avrett. 32 x 48 inches. Colored. 1967. $1.00.

64 Water availability map of Dale County, Alabama, by J. G. Newton, H. G. Golden, J. R. Avrett and J. C. Scott. 18 x 21 inches. Colored. Basic data, 26 p., 7 tables. 1968. $1.00.

67 Water availability map of Covington County, Alabama, by J. D. Turner, J. C. Scott, J. F. McCain, and J. R. Avrett. 22 x 24 inches. Colored. Basic data, 9 p., 4 tables. 1968. $1.00.

69 Water availability map of Crenshaw County, Alabama, by R. G. McWilliams, J. C. Scott, H. G. Golden, and J. R. Avrett. 17 x 24 inches. Colored. Basic data, 19 p., 6 tables. 1968. $1.00.

71 Water availability map of Henry County, Alabama, by J. G. Newton, J. F. McCain, and J. R. Avrett. 20 x 22 inches. Colored. Basic data, 14 p., 4 tables. 1968. $1.00.

73 Water availability map of Pike County, Alabama, by V. M. Shamburger, Jr., J. C. Scott, H. G. Golden, and J. R. Avrett. 20 x 23 inches. Colored. Basic data, 30 p., 5 tables. 1968. $1.00.

75 Water availability map of Conecuh County, Alabama, by P. C. Reed, J. C. Scott, H. G. Golden, and J. R. Avrett. 23 x 25 inches. Colored. Basic data, 24 p., 4 tables. 1968. $1.00.

76 Water availability map of Coffee County, Alabama, by J. D. Turner, J. C. Scott, H. G. Golden, and J. R. Avrett. 19 x 22 inches. Colored. Basic data, 12 p., 4 tables. 1968. $1.00.

ALABAMA WATER IMPROVEMENT COMMISSION
Rooms 324–326
State Office Building
Montgomery, Alabama 36104

Water Pollution Progress Report for the Years 1967-1968 (Publication of 1969-1970 pending) 100 p.

Water Quality Criteria. 21 p.

Some Aspects of the Alabama Water Improvement Commission's Program for Water Pollution Control. 12 p.

Act No. 574, Acts of Alabama, Regular Session, 1965. 7 p.

Studies of Pollution in Streams of Alabama. 1949. 298 p.

NATURAL RESOURCES CENTER
Water Resources Program
University of Alabama
P. O. Box 6171
University, Alabama 35486

Alabama Agencies with Water-Resource and Related Land-Use Responsibilities. Natural Resources Center Report 691, August 1969, by David M. Grubbs.

Design and Cost of Liquid-Waste Disposal Systems. Natural Resources Center Report 692, December 1969, by Charles D. Haynes and David M. Grubbs.

Status of Water-Resources Management in Alabama. Natural Resources Center Report 702, October 1970, by David M. Grubbs and Harry Cohen.

Land-Use Regulations in Flood-Prone Areas, A Summary of the Wisconsin Study and An Analysis of Alabama Land-Use Law. Natural Resources Center Report 703, November 1970, by Harry Cohen.

Conservation of Fresh-Water Resources by Deep-Well Disposal of Liquid Wastes. University of Alabama, Natural Resources Center and Geological Survey of Alabama, 119 pages, by David M. Grubbs, Charles D. Haynes, and William E. Tucker. Also includes Appendices A, B and C, as follows:

Appendix A: by Charles D. Haynes and David M. Grubbs. Design and Cost of Liquid-Waste Disposal Systems. 90 pages, 30 pages print-out.

Appendix B: Part 1 by Travis H. Hughes. Chemical Reactions Between Acid Industrial Wastes, Formation Waters, and Minerals in Salaquifers of Alabama, pages 1-12. Part 2 by David M. Grubbs. Laboratory Study of Selected Reservoir Rocks, pages 13–23.

Appendix C: by Donald B. Moore. Stratigraphy of Alabama, with a section on Physiography, by James Daniel Moore. 56 pages. (Project B–019–ALA).

WATER RESOURCES
RESEARCH INSTITUTE
Auburn University
Auburn, Alabama 36830

"Studies on the Interactions of Aquatic Bacteria and Aquatic Nematodes", by Gerald R. Wilt and Roger E. Smith. WRRI BULLETIN 701.

"Soil Surface Characteristics and Rainfall-Runoff-Moisture Relationships on Coastal Plain Soils", by Ronald E. Hermanson. WRRI BULLETIN 702.

"Evaluation of Earthy Materials for Use in Decontamination of Water", by Joe B. Dixon. WRRI BULLETIN 703.

"Identification and Interrelationships of Secondary Benefits in Waterways Development", by Rex K. Rainer and Charles R. White. WRRI BULLETIN 711.

Reports published by the School of Business of Auburn University in cooperation with the Water Resources Research Institute include:

"Industrial Use and Community Supplies of Water in Alabama, Economic and Legal Aspects", by Donald R. Street, Robert R. Criss, Robert L. Burks and James H. Baker, School of Business Research Series 1.

"Socio-Economic Problems in Water Resources Use and Control", by Donald R. Street, School of Business Report Series 1.

ALASKA

DEPARTMENT OF ENVIRONMENTAL CONSERVATION
Pouch O
Juneau, Alaska 99801

Note: A number of the publications listed below are out of print. However, copies will be made available upon request by interested parties.

HYDROLOGICAL DATA REPORTS

*1   Ground Water Reconnaissance and Drilled Wells Studies in the Gastineau Channel Area. 1957.

*2   Ground Water and Permafrost at Bethel, Alaska. 1957.

*3   Ground Water Reconnaissance and Drilled Wells Studies in the Ketchikan Area. 1957.

*4   Ground Water Reconnaissance of six Eskimo Villages in the Kobuk-Noatak Area, Alaska. 1957.

*5   Ground Water Reconnaissance in five Eskimo Villages in the Lower Kuskokwim-Yukon River Area, Alaska. 1955.

*6   Water Resources Reconnaissance of Gambell and Savoonga Villages, St. Lawrence Island, Alaska. 1957.

*7   Ground Water Reconnaissance of Koyuk and Shaktolik Villages, Alaska. 1958.

*8   Summary of Test Drilling Results in Last Chance Basin, Juneau, Alaska. 1959.

*9   Ground Water Data for Fairbanks, Alaska. 1959.

*10   Data on Water Wells and Springs in the Chugiak Area, Alaska. 1960.

*11   Summary of Ground Water Conditions in Alaska as they Affect Private Water Supplies. 1961.

*12   Water Utilization in the Anchorage Area, 1958-1959. 1961.

*13   Data on Wells at Ladd Airforce Base, Alaska. 1961.

*14   Data on Wells in the Anchorage Area, Alaska. 1961.

*15   Data on Wells and Springs along the Glenn Highway (State 1), Alaska. 1962.

*16   Data on Wells and Springs along the Richardson (State 4) Highway, Alaska. 1962.

*17   Data on Water Supplies at Nome, Alaska. 1962.

*18   Data on Wells along the Alaska Highway (State 2), Alaska. 1962.

*19   Data on Ground Water Exploration and Development in Southeastern Alaska. 1962.

*20   Anchorage Water Pollution Survey. 1963.

*21   Fairbanks Water Pollution Survey. (This data has never been published and therefore is not available.)

*22   Water Supply Potential in the Ohlson Mountain Area, Kenai Peninsula, Alaska. 1963.

*23   Data on Wells in the Homer Area, Alaska. 1963.

*24   Data on Wells in the King Salmon Area, Alaska. 1963.

*25   Data on Water Resources in Umiat Area, Northern Alaska. 1964.

DEPARTMENT OF HEALTH & WELFARE PUBLICATIONS

Note: As of July 1, 1971, the Dept. of Environmental Conservation assumed the water resources duties formerly handled by the Department of Health and Welfare.

Cold Regions Science and Engineering Monograph III-C5a, Water Supply in Cold Regions, by Amos J. Alter. January 1969. 85 p.

Scientific Research Data and Reports, Current Investigations in Alaska. April 1969. 102 p.

Scientific Research Data and Reports, Solid Waste Management in Cold Regions. August 1969. 46 p. and appendices.

Cold Regions Science and Engineering Monograph III-C5b, Sewerage and Sewage Disposal in Cold Regions, by Amos J. Alter. October 1969. 107 p.

Cold Region Environmental Health Practices. August 1970. 7 p.

DEPARTMENT OF NATURAL RESOURCES
Division of Mines and Minerals
Juneau, Alaska 99801

GEOCHEMICAL REPORTS

11   A Geochemical Investigation of Stream Sediments in the Elliott Highway Area, Alaska, by W. M. Burand. 16 p. Price: $1.00.

12   A Geochemical Investigation of Minook Creek, Rampart District, Alaska, by W. M. Burand and R. H. Saunders. 15 p. Price: $1.00.

DEPARTMENT OF NATURAL RESOURCES
Inter-Agency Technical Committee for Alaska
Juneau, Alaska 99801

Alaska Ten-Year Comprehensive Plan for Climatologic and Hydrologic Data. 2nd edition. Anchorage, 1967. Various pagings.

DEPARTMENT OF PUBLIC WORKS
Division of Water and Harbors
Pouch Z
Juneau, Alaska 99801

Note: Copies of the publications listed below are available on a limited basis at no charge to other public or quasi-public agencies.

Directory, State Harbors & Boating Facilities. 60 p.

Planning Study for a Small Boat Harbor at Whittier, Alaska. 44 p.

Needs Study for Harbor Facilities at Unalaska, Alaska.

Feasibility Study, Eyak Lake Water Level Stabilization, Cordova, Alaska. (Available through the Alaska Department of Fish & Game.)

INSTITUTE OF WATER RESOURCES
University of Alaska
College, Alaska 99701

IWR SERIES

*IWR-1 Saline Conversion and Ice Structures from Artificially Grown Sea Ice, by H. R. Peyton and P. R. Johnson. 1967. 30 p.

*IWR-2 The Biochemical Bases of Psychrophily in Microorganisms, by Ann P. Miller. 1967. 35 p.

*IWR-3 Evaluation of Water Research Needs in Alaska, by Charles E. Behlke. 1968. 9 p.

*IWR-4 Inherent and Maximum Microbiological Activity in Smith Lake, by S. Burton. 1968. 8 p.

*IWR-5 Treatment of Low Quality Water by Foam Fractionation, by R. Sage Murphy. 1968. 12 p.

*IWR-6 Reconnaissance of the Distribution and Abundance of *Schistosomatium Douthitti*, A Possible Human Disease Agent in Surface Waters in Alaska, by L. G. Swartz. 1968. 17 p.

*IWR-7 A Program for Cook Inlet Alaska for the Collection, Storage and Analysis of Baseline Environmental Data, by David G. Wagner, R. Sage Murphy, and Charles E. Behlke.

*IWR-8 A Water Distribution System for Cold Regions — The Single Main Recirculating Method — An Historical Review, Field Evaluation, and Suggested Design Procedures, by R. Sage Murphy and Charles W. Hartman. March 1969. 78 p.

*IWR-9 Practical Application of Foam Fractionation Treatment of Low Quality Water, by R. Sage Murphy. 1969. 11 p.

*IWR-10 A Ground Water Quality Summary for Alaska, by Steve W. Kim, Phillip R. Johnson, and R. Sage Murphy. 1969. 32 p.

*IWR-11 Bibliography of Arctic Water Resources, by Charles W. Hartman and Robert F. Carlson. November 1970. 538 p.

*IWR-12 The Influence of Decomposing Salmon on Water Chemistry, by David C. Brickell and John J. Goering.

IWR-13 The Effectiveness of a Contact Filter for the Removal of Iron from Ground Water, by Steve W. Kim. 1971.

IWR-14 The Effects of Extreme Floods and Placer Mining on the Basic Productivity of SubArctic Streams, by James E. Morrow. (The data contained herein is only partial as most records were lost in the 1967 Fairbanks flood.)

IWR-15 The Effects of Water Quality and Quantity on the Fauna of a Non-Glacial Alaskan River, by James E. Morrow. (The data contained herein is only partial as most records were lost in the 1967 Fairbanks flood.)

ARIZONA

ARIZONA BUREAU OF MINES

The University of Arizona
Tucson, Arizona 85721

Note: Prices quoted apply to all non-residents of Arizona. Payment must accompany all requests for publications.

BULLETINS

180   Mineral and Water Resources of Arizona. Price: $3.00.

MAPS

12   Map of Arizona Showing Principal Power and Transportation Facilities. 1963. In color with scale 1:1,000,000. Price: $0.50.

ARIZONA COLORADO RIVER COMMISSION

This Commission is no longer in existence.

Annual Report. 1927 to 1945.

The Colorado River Question. 1928. 16 p.

Explanation of Terms in the Colorado River Controversy Between Arizona and California. 1929. 12 p.

Colorado River International Problem. 1938. 36 p.

Arizona Stream Flow Summary. 1940.

ARIZONA STATE DEPARTMENT OF HEALTH

Arizona State Office Building
1624 West Adams Street
Phoenix, Arizona 85007

Rules and Regulations for Public Water Supply Systems, Article 2, Part 2.

Water Quality Standards for Surface Waters in Arizona.

Oak Creek Water Quality Report.

Wastes from Watercraft in Arizona. 1968. 17 p.

ARIZONA STATE LAND DEPARTMENT

422 State Office Building
Phoenix, Arizona 85007

Note: These studies have been prepared cooperatively with the U. S. Geological Survey. Copies may be secured by writing to either the above address or to the U. S. Geological Survey offices at: 5017 Federal Building, 230 North First Avenue, Phoenix; or 2555 East First Street, Tucson. Reports indicated as being out of print are available on loan only from the U. S. Geological Survey, 2555 East First Street, Tucson, Arizona.

WATER-RESOURCES REPORTS

*1   Pumpage and ground-water levels in Arizona in 1955, by P. W. Johnson, N. D. White, and J. M. Cahill: 69 p., 30 figs., 1956.

*2   Annual report on ground water in Arizona, spring 1956 to spring 1957, by J. W. Harshbarger and others: 42 p., 18 figs., 1957.

*3   Geology and ground-water resources of the Harquahala Plains area, Maricopa and Yuma Counties, Arizona, by D. G. Metzger: 40 p., 2 pls., 7 figs., 1957.

*4   Geology and ground-water resources of the Palomas Plain-Dendora Valley area, Maricopa and Yuma Counties, Arizona, by C. A. Armstrong and C. B. Yost, Jr.: 49 p., 3 pls., 4 figs., 1958.

*5   Annual report on ground water in Arizona, spring 1957 to spring 1958, by W. F. Hardt, J. M. Cahill, and M. B. Booher: 60 p., 19 figs., 1958.

*6   Annual report on ground water in Arizona, spring 1958 to spring 1959, by W. F. Hardt, R. S. Stulik, and M. B. Booher: 61 p., 18 figs., 1959.

*7   Annual report on ground water in Arizona, spring 1959 to spring 1960, by W. F. Hardt, R. S. Stulik, and M. B. Booher: 89 p., 22 figs., 1960.

*8   Geology and ground-water resources of the McMullen Valley, Maricopa, Yavapai, and Yuma Counties, Arizona, by William Kam: 72 p., 17 figs., 1961.

9   Hydrologic data and drillers' logs, Papago Indian Reservation, Arizona, by L. A. Heindl and O. J. Cosner, with a section on chemical quality of the water by L. R. Kister: 116 p., 3 figs., 1961.

*10   Annual report on ground water in Arizona, spring 1960 to spring 1961, by N. D. White, R. S. Stulik, E. K. Morse, and others: 93 p., 32 figs., 1961.

*11   Annual report on ground water in Arizona, spring 1961 to spring 1962, by N. D. White, R. S. Stulik, and others: 116 p., 35 figs., 1962.

*12A   Geohydrologic data in the Navajo and Hopi Indian Reservations, Arizona, New Mexico, and Utah—Part I, Records of ground-water supplies, by G. E. Davis, W. F. Hardt, L. K. Thompson, and M. E. Cooley: 159 p., 3 figs., 1963.

*12B   Geohydrologic data in the Navajo and Hopi Indian Reservations, Arizona, New Mexico, and Utah—Part II, Selected chemical analyses of the ground water, by L. R. Kister and J. L. Hatchett: 58 p., 2 figs., 1963.

12C   Geohydrologic data in the Navajo and Hopi Indian Reservations, Arizona, New Mexico, and Utah—Part III, Selected lithologic logs, drillers' logs, and stratigraphic sections, by M. E. Cooley, J. P. Akers, and P. R. Stevens: 157 p., 3 figs., 1964.

12D   Geohydrologic data in the Navajo and Hopi Indian Reservations, Arizona, New Mexico, and Utah—Part IV, Maps showing locations of wells, springs, and stratigraphic sections, by M. E. Cooley and others: 2 sheets, 1966.

12E   Geohydrologic data in the Navajo and Hopi Indian Reservations, Arizona, New Mexico, and Utah—Part I-A, Supplemental records of ground-water supplies, by E. H. McGavock, R. J. Edmonds, E. L. Gillespie, and P. C. Halpenny: 55 p., 4 figs., 1966.

13   Desert floods—a report on southern Arizona floods of September 1962, by D. D. Lewis: 13 p., 18 figs., 1963.

*14   Basic ground-water data of the Willcox basin, Graham and Cochise Counties, Arizona, by S. G. Brown, H. H. Schumann, L. R. Kister, and P. W. Johnson: 93 p., 15 figs., 1963.

*15   Annual report on ground water in Arizona, spring 1962 to spring 1963, by N. D. White, R. S. Stulik, E. K. Morse, and others: 136 p., 47 figs., 1963.

16   Effects of ground-water withdrawal in part of central Arizona projected to 1969, by N. D. White, R. S. Stulik, and C. L. Rauh: 25 p., 7 figs., 1964.

17   Effects of ground-water withdrawal, 1954-63, in the lower Harquahala Plains, Maricopa County, Arizona, by R. S. Stulik: 8 p., 5 figs., 1964.

18   Basic ground-water data for western Pinal County, Arizona, by W. F. Hardt, R. E. Cattany, and L. R. Kister: 59 p., 4 figs., 1964.

19   Annual report on ground water in Arizona, spring 1963 to spring 1964, by N. D. White, R. S. Stulik, E. K. Morse, and others: 60 p., 27 figs., 1964.

20   Hydrologic and drill-hole data, San Xavier Indian Reservation and vicinity, Pima County, Arizona, by L. A. Heindl and N. D. White: 48 p., 3 figs., 1965.

21   Basic hydrologic data for San Simon basin, Cochise and Graham Counties, Arizona, and Hidalgo County, New Mexico, by N. D. White and C. R. Smith: 42 p., 4 figs., 1965.

22   Bibliography of U. S. Geological Survey water-resources reports, Arizona, 1891 to 1965, compiled by the Arizona District, Water Resources Division, U. S. Geological Survey: 59 p., 1965.

*23   Geohydrology of the Dateland-Hyder area, Maricopa and Yuma Counties, Arizona, by W. G. Weist, Jr.: 46 p., 8 figs., 1965.

*24   Annual report on ground water in Arizona, spring 1964 to spring 1965, by N. D. White and others: 62 p., 22 figs., 1965.

25   An appraisal of the ground-water resources of Avra and Altar Valleys, Pima County, Arizona, by N. D. White, W. G. Matlock, and H. C. Schwalen: 66 p., 12 figs., 1966.

26   Basic hydrologic data of the Hualapai, Sacramento, and Big Sandy Valleys, Mohave County, Arizona, by J. B. Gillespie, C. B. Bentley, and William Kam: 39 p., 6 figs., 1966.

27   Basic ground-water data for western Salt River Valley, Maricopa County, Arizona, by William Kam, H. H. Schumann, L. R. Kister, and F. E. Arteaga: 72 p., 11 figs., 1966.

28   Anticipated changes in the flow regimen caused by the addition of water to the East Verde River, Arizona, by H. W. Hjalmarson and E. S. Davidson: 10 p., 3 figs., 1966.

29   Infiltration and recharge from the flow of April 1965 in the Salt River near Phoenix, Arizona, by P. C. Briggs and L. L. Werho: 12 p., 7 figs., 1966.

30   Hydrologic conditions in the Douglas basin, Cochise County, Arizona, by N. D. White and Dallas Childers: 26 p., 9 figs., 1967.

31   Compilation of flood data for Maricopa County, Arizona, through September 1965, by L. L. Werho: 36 p., 1 fig., 1967.

*32   Annual report on ground water in Arizona, spring 1965 to spring 1966, by E. B. Hodges and others: 61 p., 22 figs., 1967.

33   Basic ground-water data for southern Coconino County, Arizona, by E. H. McGavock: 49 p., 4 figs., 1968.

34   Spring flow into the Colorado River—Lees Ferry to Lake Mead, Arizona, by P. W. Johnson and R. B. Sanderson: 26 p., 5 figs., 1968.

35   Ground water in Paradise Valley, Maricopa County, Arizona, by F. E. Arteaga, N. D. White, M. E. Cooley, and A. F. Sutheimer: 76 p., 15 figs., 1968.

36   Annual report on ground water in Arizona, spring 1966 to spring 1967, by C. J. Cox and others: 43 p., 30 figs., 1968.

37   Ground-water conditions in the Waterman Wash area, Maricopa and Pinal Counties, Arizona, by E. E. Denis: 23 p., 9 figs., 1968.

38   Annual report on ground water in Arizona, spring 1967 to spring 1968, prepared under the direction of H. M. Babcock, District Chief, Arizona District, Water Resources Division, U. S. Geological Survey: 54 p., 32 figs., 1969.

39   Hydrologic conditions in the Gila Bend basin, Maricopa County, Arizona, by R. S. Stulik and Otto Moosburner: 63 p., 10 figs., 1969.

40   Ground-water conditions in McMullen Valley, Maricopa, Yuma, and Yavapai Counties, Arizona, by P. C. Briggs: 31 p., 9 figs., 1969.

41   Ground-water conditions in the Ranegras Plain, Yuma County, Arizona, by P. C. Briggs: 28 p., 7 figs., 1969.

42   Annual report on ground water in Arizona, spring 1968 to spring 1969, prepared under the direction of H. M. Babcock, District Chief, Arizona District, Water Resources Division, U. S. Geological Survey: 46 p., 33 figs., 1969.

43 Annual report on ground water in Arizona, spring 1969 to spring 1970, prepared under the direction of H. M. Babcock, District Chief, Arizona District, Water Resources Division, U. S. Geological Survey: 44 p., 30 figs., 1970.

ARIZONA STATE LAND DEPARTMENT
Watershed Management Division
Phoenix, Arizona 85007

Arizona Watershed Symposium Proceedings, 1957 – to date. Annual.

ARIZONA WATER COMMISSION
34 West Monroe Street – Suite 707
Phoenix, Arizona 85003

formerly Arizona Interstate Stream Commission

Annual Report: First, 1948 through Twenty-Second, 1969. (First, Nineteenth, and Twentieth not available).

Reports to the Arizona Interstate Stream Commission:

Report on Cooperative Water Resource Inventory, 1965. Vol. I – State of Arizona. Bureau of Reclamation, Boulder City, Nevada.

Report on Cooperative Water Resource Inventory, 1965. Vol. II – Hydrologic Study Areas, Arizona. Bureau of Reclamation, Boulder City, Nevada.

Arizona-Colorado River Diversion Projects: Little Colorado River Colorado River Basin and Adjacent Counties, Reconnaissance Investigations. September 1966, revised June 1968. Bureau of Reclamation, Boulder City, Nevada.

Water Resources, State of Arizona. October 1967.

Efficiency Analysis of Water Utilization in the Central Area of Arizona, Technical Report No. 2, December 1968.

*Impact of Declining Water Levels on Rural Communities in Pinal County, Arizona, June 1969. Dunlap & Associates, Manhattan, Kansas.

An Approach to Maximizing Returns from the Use of Central Arizona Project Water, June 1969. Dunlap & Associates, Manhattan, Kansas.

WATER RESOURCES RESEARCH CENTER
The University of Arizona
Tucson, Arizona 85721

Annual Report. 1965 to date.

ARKANSAS

ARKANSAS STATE BOARD OF HEALTH

State Capitol
Little Rock, Arkansas 72201

Rural Water Supplies. Bureau of Sanitary Engineering Bulletin No. 12. (no date).

Chemical Data on Arkansas Public Water Supplies. Bureaus of Sanitary Engineering and Laboratories. 1954.

Chemical Data on Arkansas Public Water Supplies. Bureau of Sanitary Engineering. 1958.

Arkansas Municipal Water Supplies Chemical Data 1961. Bureau of Sanitary Engineering. 1961.

Public Water Supplies. Bureau of Sanitary Engineering. January 1963.

ARKANSAS GEOLOGICAL COMMISSION

State Capitol
Little Rock, Arkansas 72201

BULLETINS

17   Surface Water Resources of Arkansas, by John L. Saunders and G. A. Billingsley. 1950, 181 p., paper. Price: $1.00, mailing $0.15, total $1.15.

WATER RESOURCES CIRCULARS

1   Arkansas's Ground-Water Resources, by R. C. Baker. 1955, 16 p., 8 figs., cardboard. Price: $0.25, mailing $0.10, total $0.35.

2   Ground-Water Resources in a Part of Southern Arkansas, by H. B. Counts, D. B. Tait, Howard Klein, and G. A. Billingsley. 1955, 35 p., 6 pls., 8 figs., 12 tables, cardboard. Price: $0.50, mailing $0.15, total $0.65.

3   Ground-Water Resources of Chicot County, Arkansas, by Frank E. Onellion and James H. Criner, Jr. 1955, 32 p., 8 figs., 11 tables, cardboard. Price: $0.50, mailing $0.15, total $0.65.

4   Geology and Ground Water Resources of Drew County, Arkansas, by Frank E. Onellion. 1956, 43 p., 10 figs., 6 tables, cardboard. Price: $0.50, mailing $0.15, total $0.65.

5   Ground-Water Resources of Parts of Lonoke, Prairie, and White Counties, Arkansas, by Harlan B. Counts. 1957. 65 p., 7 pls., 8 figs., 8 tables, cardboard. Price: $0.50, mailing $0.15, total $0.65.

6   Geology and Ground-Water Resources of Desha and Lincoln Counties, Arkansas, by M. S. Bedinger and J. E. Reed. 1961, 129 p., 19 pls., 23 figs., 10 tables, cardboard. Price: $0.50, mailing $0.20, total $0.70.

7   Ground-Water Potential of Mississippi County, Arkansas, by Roy W. Tyling. 1960, 87 p., 21 figs., 15 tables, cardboard. Price: $0.50, mailing $0.15, total $0.65.

8   Fresh-Water Aquifers of Crittenden County, Arkansas, by Raymond O. Plebuch. 1961, 65 p., 19 figs., 5 tables, cardboard. Price: $0.50, mailing $0.15, total $0.65.

9   Water-Supply Characteristics of Selected Arkansas Streams, by Marion S. Hines. 1965, 43 p., 11 figs., 3 tables, cardboard. Price: $0.50, mailing $0.15, total $0.65.

10   Storage Requirements for Arkansas Streams, by James L. Patterson. 1967, 35 p., 16 figs., 2 tables, cardboard. Price: $0.50, mailing $0.15, total $0.65.

WATER RESOURCES SUMMARY

1   Resume of the Ground-Water Resources of Bradley, Calhoun, and Ouachita Counties, Arkansas, by Donald R. Albin. 1962, 4 p., 1 fig., 2 tables, paper. Price: $0.25, mailing $0.10, total $0.35.

2   Ground-Water Temperatures in the Coastal Plain of Arkansas, by Raymond O. Plebuch, 1962, 2 p., 3 figs., cardboard. Price: $0.25, mailing $0.15, total $0.40.

3   Changes in Ground-Water Levels in Deposits of Quaternary Age in Northeastern Arkansas, by Raymond O. Plebuch. 1962, 2 p., 5 figs., paper. Price: $0.25, mailing $0.10, total $0.35.

4   Ground-Water Levels in Deposits of Quaternary and Tertiary Age, Spring 1965, by Donald R. Albin, J. W. Stephens, and Joe Edds. 1967, 10 p., 3 figs., cardboard. Price: $0.25, mailing $0.10, total $0.35.

5   Use of Water in Arkansas, 1965, by H. N. Halberg and J. W. Stephens. 1966, 12 p., 3 figs., 4 tables, cardboard. Price: $0.25, mailing $0.15, total $0.40.

6   Index of Water Resources Data for Arkansas, 1968, by L. D. Reid and B. W. Vines. Cardboard. Price: $0.25, mailing $0.15, total $0.40.

SPECIAL WATER REPORTS

Murfreesboro Area. Special Ground-Water Report No. 1, by D. R. Albin. 1960.

Use of Water in Arkansas, 1960. Special Ground-Water Report No. 4, by J. W. Stephens and H. N. Halberg (U. S. Geol. Survey cooperation). 1961.

Water Resources of Lincoln County, Arkansas. Special Water Report No. 5, by D. R. Albin, Marion S. Hines and A. G. Lamonds. 1965.

Water Resources of Ouachita County, Arkansas. Special Water Report No. 6, by D. R. Albin and Marion S. Hines. 1966.

Water Resources of Randolph County, Arkansas. Special Water Report No. 7, by D. R. Albin, Marion S. Hines and C. T. Taylor. 1965.

MISCELLANEOUS PUBLICATIONS

Arkansas Valley Well-Location Maps. Scale 1/4" equals 1 mile. Various dates.

Eastern Arkansas Well-Location Maps. County maps, scale of 1/2" equals 1 mile. Various dates.

The Mineral Waters of Arkansas. John C. Branner. Annual Report, Vol. 1. 1891.

Water Powers of Arkansas—a preliminary report on White River and some of its tributaries. W. N. Gladson. 1911.

Stream Gaging in Arkansas from 1857 to 1928. W. A. Frame. Published jointly by the U. S. Geol. Survey and the Ark. Geol. and Conserv. Comm. 1930. 149 p., 2 pls., cloth. Price: $0.50, mailing $0.10, total $0.60.

List of Arkansas Water Wells. Information Circular 11, by G. C. Branner. 1937.

Floods of July 16-17, 1963 in Vicinity of Hot Springs, Arkansas. R. C. Gilstrap and R. C. Christensen (U. S. Geol. Survey cooperation). Open-file report. 1964.

Water for Arkansas. A comprehensive nontechnical discussion of water resources, abundantly illustrated in color. including 11 figs., 12 pls. 1970. Price: $0.50, mailing $0.15, total $0.65.

ARKANSAS STATE HIGHWAY COMMISSION
State Capitol
Little Rock, Arkansas 72201

Floods in Arkansas, Magnitude and Frequency. James L. Patterson (U. S. Geol. Survey cooperation). Open-file report. 1961.

Floodflow Characteristics of Arkansas River at Interstate Highway 540 at Van Buren, Arkansas. R. C. Christensen and R. C. Gilstrap (U. S. Geol. Survey cooperation). Open-file report. 1965.

ARKANSAS LEGISLATIVE COUNCIL
State Capitol
Little Rock, Arkansas 72201

Sub-surface Water Study. Research Memorandum 2, to Committee on Agr. and Conserv., Robert Harvey, Chairman, Little Rock, Arkansas. February 2, 1954.

Public Recreation on Private Lands. The Council Research Report No. 129. 1964.

ARKANSAS STATE PLANNING COMMISSION
State Capitol
Little Rock, Arkansas 72201

Note: Also listed here are several publications from the Arkansas State Planning Board.

State Planning for Arkansas. A Report on the Land and Water Resources of Arkansas. Ark. State Planning Board. 2nd Report. March 1935.

Progress Report — Arkansas. Ark. State Planning Board. November 1936.

Arkansas Water Resources. Ark. State Planning Board. June 1939.

State Plan Inventory:
    Section 2 — Land Characteristics Climate and Land Use. Jan. 1964.
    Section 5 — Water and Other Natural Resources. April 1964.
Prepared for the Ark. Planning Commission by the College of Business Adm., Industrial Research and Extension Center, Little Rock, Ark.; and Div. of Agriculture, Department of Agr. Econ. and Rural Sociology, University of Arkansas, Fayetteville, Arkansas.

Arkansas: A Preliminary Plan, 1980. Prepared for Ark. Planning Commission by Associated Planners. 1964.

A Preliminary Statewide Comprehensive Outdoor Recreation Plan for Arkansas. 1965.

ARKANSAS POLLUTION CONTROL COMMISSION
1100 Harrington Avenue
Little Rock, Arkansas 72202

REPORTS AND REGULATIONS — BY YEAR:

1957

Sources of Pollution — Ouachita River Basin.

Summary Report — Sources of Pollution in the Lapile Creek Drainage Basin.

Summary Report — Sources of Pollution in West Two Bayou Drainage Basin.

Transcript of Lapile Creek Drainage Basin Public Hearing at El Dorado.

Annual Progress Report — Arkansas Water Pollution Control Commission, 1956-7.

1958

Transcript of Allied Chemical Corporation — "Show Cause" Hearing.

Transcript of City of Camden — "Show Cause" Hearing.

Transcript of International Paper Company — "Show Cause" Hearing.

Summary Report of Smackover Creek Drainage Basin.

Transcript of Smackover Creek Drainage Basin — Public Hearing; Part I — Camden; 6-23-58. Part II — El Dorado; 6-25-58.

Sources of Pollution in Mill Creek Drainage Basin.

Summary of Sources of Pollution in Mill Creek Drainage Basin.

Transcript of Mill Creek Drainage Basin Public Hearing at El Dorado.

Annual Progress Report — Arkansas Water Pollution Control Commission, 1957-58.

Sources of Pollution in Dorcheat Bayou Basin.

Summary Report — Sources of Pollution in Dorcheat Bayou Drainage Basin.

Summary Report — Sources of Pollution in Caney Creek Drainage Basin.

Order No. 1-58 — In the Matter of the Pollution of the Lower Ouachita River and Tributaries by Salt Water and Other Oil Field Wastes.

Regulation No. 1 — Regulation for the Prevention of Pollution by Salt Water and Other Oil Field Wastes Produced by Wells in New Fields or Pools.

Order — In the Matter of the Pollution of West Two Bayou and the Ouachita River by the City of Camden.

1959

Dorcheat Bayou Basin — Transcript of Arkansas–Louisiana Gas Company — "Show Cause" Hearing.

Transcript of the Public Hearing — Including Bodcaw Creek Drainage Basin, Dorcheat Bayou Drainage Basin, Caney Creek Drainage Basin at Lewisville.

Transcript of the City of El Dorado — "Show Cause" Hearing.

Dorcheat Bayou Basin — City of Waldo, "Show Cause" Hearing.

Dorcheat Bayou Basin — City of Taylor, "Show Cause" Hearing.

Transcript of "Show Cause" Hearing — City of Stephens.

Transcript of "Show Cause" Hearing — City of Smackover.

Transcript of Lower Red River Drainage Basin — Public Hearing at Texarkana — Part I.

Sources of Pollution in Lower Red River Basin — Part I.

Summary Report — Sources of Pollution in Lower Red River Basin — Part I.

Transcript of Hearing on Ouachita River Fish Kill.

Dorcheat Bayou Basin — Transcript of "Show Cause" Hearing — City of Magnolia.

Bodcaw Creek Basin — Transcript of "Show Cause" Hearing — City of Lewisville.

A List of Biological Indicators of Pollution including Plankton, Bottom Organisms and Larger Aquatic Plants and Animals.

Annual Progress Report — Arkansas Water Pollution Control Commission — 1958-59.

Summary Report — Sources of Brine Pollution — Moro Creek, Champagnolle Creek, Two Bayou Drainage Basin.

Summary Report — Sources of Pollution in Champagnolle Drainage Basin.

Summary Report — Sources of Pollution in Bodcaw Creek Basin.

Order No. 1-59 — "In the Matter of the Pollution of the Drainage Basins of the Lower Red River, Loutre Bayou, Moro Creek, Champagnolle Creek, Two Bayou, Bodcaw Creek, Caney Creek, and Dorcheat Bayou by Salt Water and Other Oil Field Wastes."

Order No. 2-59 — "In the Matter of the Pollution of the Corney Creek Drainage Basin (Including Big Corney, Little Corney, and Three Creeks) by Salt Water and Other Oil Field Wastes."

1960

Lower Red River Drainage Basin, Part II — Transcript of Public Hearing at Texarkana.

Upper Red River Drainage Basin — Transcript of Public Hearing at DeQueen.

Sources of Pollution in Grand (Neosho) River Basin — Part I.

Summary Report — Sources of Pollution in Grand (Neosho) River Basin — Part I.

Sources of Pollution in Upper Red River Basin & Lower Red Basin, Part II.

Summary Report — Sources of Pollution in Lower Red River Basin, Part II, 1960.

Transcript of Public Hearing for Grand (Neosho) River Basin — Part I at Bentonville.

Resurvey of Cornie Creek Basin.

Coliform Density of The White River near Clarendon.

Survey of "New" Oil Fields.

Annual Progress Report — Arkansas Water Pollution Control Commission — 1959-60.

Poultry Processing and Slaughterhouse Wastes.

1961

Sources of Pollution in Grand (Neosho) River Basin — Part II.

Summary Report — Sources of Pollution in Grand (Neosho) River Basin — Part II.

Grand (Neosho) River Basin — Part II — Transcript of Public Hearing at Bentonville.

Annual Progress Report — Arkansas Water Pollution Control Commission — 1960-61.

1962

Water Pollution Control Survey of The Upper Ouachita River Basin — Part I Mena to Malvern.

Summary of The Upper Ouachita River Basin — Part I — Mena to Malvern.

Water Pollution Control Survey of The Lower Arkansas River Basin — Pine Bluff to Mississippi River.

Sources of Pollution in Upper White River Basin.

Water Pollution Control Survey of Monticello Wastewaters

Plankton Indicator Organisms

Annual Progress Report — Arkansas Water Pollution Control Commission — 1961-62.

1963

Water Pollution Control Survey of The Little Missouri River Basin.

Oil Field Survey — Order 2-59.

Water Pollution Control Survey of Burlington Industries Wastewaters, Monticello.

Upper Ouachita River Basin — Part I — Transcript of Public Hearing.

Oil Field Survey — Order 1-58.

Oil Field Survey — Order 1-59.

Bayou Meto Basin — Transcript of Hercules Powder Company — "Show Cause" Hearing.

Annual Progress Report — Arkansas Water Pollution Control Commission — 1962-63.

Progress Report on a Compendium of the Insecticides, Herbicides, and Related Compounds Currently Used in Arkansas, 1962-63.

Research Needs in the Field of Water Supply and Pollution Control in Arkansas.

Transcript of Minark Corp. Barite Mill — "Show Cause" Hearing.

Transcript of Dierks Forests, Inc. Wood Treating Plant — "Show Cause" Hearing.

Statement of Arkansas Water Pollution Control Commission Before the Sub-Committee on Natural Resources and Power, Washington, D. C.

Water Pollution Control Survey of the Upper Ouachita River Basin — Part II — Arkadelphia to Camden.

Stream Flow Quantity and Quality Correlations and Statistical Analyses — U. of A. Report No. 3.

1964

Water Pollution Control Survey of Arkansas Grain Corporation, Stuttgart.

Water Pollution Control Survey of Elk Roofing Company, Stephens.

Water Pollution Control Survey of Saline River Basin.

Water Pollution Control Survey of Moro-Champagnolle Creek Basin.

Annual Progress Report — Arkansas Pollution Control Commission — 1963-64.

Transcript of City of Monticello, Charm Tred Mills, Inc. & Burlington Industries, Inc. — "Show Cause" Hearing.

Transcript of City of Prairie Grove — "Show Cause" Hearing.

Transcript of City of Fayetteville — "Show Cause" Hearing.

General Order No. 1-64 — In the Matter of the Pollution of Lake Hamilton and Lake Catherine.

1965

Transcript of "Show Cause" Hearing for the City of Danville.

Transcript of Berry Asphalt Company — "Show Cause" Hearing.

Annual Progress Report — Arkansas Pollution Control Commission — 1964-65.

Bacteriological Survey of Maddox Bay Monroe County.

Water Pollution Control Survey of Little Rock Industrial District and Twin City Transit Shops.

Water Pollution Control Survey of Landers, Norge, Forgecraft Plants — Fort Smith.

Arkansas Water and Air Pollution Control Acts (Act 472 of 1949 as amended by Act 183 of the 1965 Legislature.)

Water Pollution Control Survey of Bayou Macon and Boeuf River Basins.

Water Pollution Control Survey of Bayou Bartholomew Basin.

Transcript of Elk Roofing Co. (Stephens) — "Show Cause" Hearing.

1966

Transcript of Public Hearing, Lower Ouachita River Basin (Oil Fields Only).

Annual Progress Report — Arkansas Pollution Control Commission — 1965-66.

Bacteriological Resurvey of Lake Hamilton and Lake Catherine.

Field Survey Procedures for the Determination of Air Pollution Damage to Vegetation.

Transcript of "Show Cause" Hearing on O. G. Kukendall Laundromat — Gravel Ridge.

Transcript of "Show Cause" Hearing for Arkansas Rock & Gravel Company and Malvern Sand and Gravel Company.

1967

Water Quality Criteria for Interstate Streams and Plan for Implementation.

Regulation No. 2 (Water Quality Criteria for Interstate Streams).

Transcript of "Show Cause" Hearing for Lee's Landing, Lake Hamilton.

Transcript of "Show Cause" Hearing for Dulin Gravel Washer, Hot Springs.

Transcript of General Public Hearing on proposed Water Quality Criteria for Interstate Streams.

Transcript of Specific Public Hearings on Proposed Water Quality Criteria for Interstate Streams.

Microscopic Analyses of Airborne Particulates.

Bacteriological Resurvey of Lake Hamilton and Lake Catherine.

Water Quality Studies for Arkansas Streams of U. of A. Report No. 11.

Special Survey in Upper Bayou Meto Basin.

Transcript of "Show Cause" Hearing for Missouri Pacific Shops, North Little Rock.

Survey of Cherokee Carpet Mills, Inc., Lewisville.

Transcript of "Show Cause" Hearing for Lane Poultry Farms, Grannis.

Survey of Booneville Sewage Treatment Plant.

Annual Progress Report — Arkansas Pollution Control Commission — 1966-67.

1968

Survey of Clarendon STP and Stoddard-Quirk Electroplating Plant.

Transcript of M. P. Cotton Felt, Inc. "Show Cause" Hearing at Fort Smith.

Transcript of Mountain Pine Pressure Treating Company "Show Cause" Hearing at Plainview.

South Pulaski County Air Survey — June — July 1966.

Booneville Air Survey — September 1966.

East Arkansas Air Quality Surveys — August — October 1966.

Airport Industrial District Survey — May 1967.

Little Rock City Dump Source Evaluation — April 1967.

Pine Bluff Air Survey — August — September 1967.

Annual Progress Report — 1968/1969 to date.

ARKANSAS RESOURCES AND DEVELOPMENT COMMISSION

This Commission is no longer in existence.

Arkansas' Natural Resources, Their Conservation and Use, by R. P. Bartholomew and others. 1942. 452 p.

Ground Water Possibilities, Pulaski and Jefferson Counties, Arkansas, by Norman F. Williams, Harold B. Foxhall and Roger C. Baker. January 1948.

ARKANSAS SOIL AND WATER CONSERVATION COMMISSION
151 State Capitol
Little Rock, Arkansas 72201

Bibliography: Water and Land Resources of Arkansas, by Charles Finger. 1967. 90 p.

Lakes of Arkansas, Reins for Raindrops. 1968. 30 p.

The national Flood Insurance Program. A community flood-plain management proposal with flood insurance for property owners. A brochure.

ARKANSAS WATER STUDY COMMISSION

This Commission is no longer in existence.

Water in Arkansas: A Report on the Surface Water Resources in Arkansas, November 1956. 55 p. (Prepared at the direction of the General Assembly of Arkansas.)

ARKANSAS WATER RESOURCES RESEARCH CENTER
University of Arkansas
Fayetteville, Arkansas 72701

1   Quantitative Analysis of Stream Flow Rate Extremes. Hugh M. Jeffus. 1967.

2   Arkansas Water Resources: Supply, Use, and Research Needs. Jared Sparks. 1967.

3   Subsurface Irrigation Research in Arkansas. John P. Hoskyn and Billy B. Bryan. 1969.

4   Virus Movement in Groundwater Systems. William A. Drewry. 1969.

5   Environmental Changes Produced by Cold-Water Outlets from Three Arkansas Reservoirs. Carl Hoffmann and Raj Kilambi. 1970.

6   Distribution of Trace Elements in Impoundments. Joe F. Nix. In press.

7   Water Resources Planning Studies — Arkansas and Oklahoma. Loren Heiple. In press.

CALIFORNIA

CALIFORNIA ADVISORY COMMISSION ON MARINE AND COASTAL RESOURCES

714 P Street, 7th Floor
Sacramento, California 95814

Defining the California public interest in the marine environment. 1969. 71 p. (1st annual report).

Proceedings of meetings. Published irregularly. First, April 1968 — to date.

Transcript of proceedings; hearing ... on the public interest in the shoreline, and coordinated marine resource development, December 13, 1968, San Diego, California. 154 p.

Compilation of recommendations ... , January 1965 — January 1967. 48 p.

COLORADO RIVER BOARD OF CALIFORNIA

217 West First Street
Room 302
Los Angeles, California 90012

California's stake in the Colorado River. (Appears irregularly in up-dated editions.)

*The Colorado River case: Arizona vs. California — in the Supreme Court of the United States. [1956 ?]. 61 p.

*Comments on questions addressed by the House Committee on Public Lands to the Secretary of the Interior and the Director of the Bureau of the Budget re S. 75, 31st Congress. 1st Session. 1950. 80 p.

*Comments on questions ... Supplemental answers ... , 1950.

Need for controlling salinity of the Colorado River. 1970. 89 p.

*Official statement on behalf of California in opposition to proposed treaty with Mexico for Colorado River water, by Evan T. Hewes. Los Angeles, Colorado River Board of California, March 1, 1944. 18 p.

*Pacific Southwest water plan; preliminary compilation of information and comments by Colorado River Board Staff on January 1964 report. 1964. 28 p.

Report. Annual since 1963-64.

*Salinity problems in the Lower Colorado River area, by C. W. Lee and R. H. Figuero. September 1962. 28 p.

*Statement on behalf of California summarizing some of the reasons for opposition to proposed treaty with Mexico relating to the Colorado River. 1944.

*Statement to the President's Water Resources Policy Commission; summary of recommendations and supporting data. 1950. 27 p.

*Why the Upper Colorado River Basin and the Fryingpan-Arkansas Projects are opposed. [1955 ?]. 84 p.

CALIFORNIA STATE CONTROLLER'S OFFICE

Room 1114, State Capitol
Sacramento, California 95814

*Report of financial transactions concerning irrigation districts of California. Annual. 1951-1967.

Report of financial transactions concerning special districts of California. Annual. 1956-57 — to date.

Report of financial transactions concerning water utility operations of special districts of California. Annual. 1968-69 — to date.

CALIFORNIA STATE DEPARTMENT OF CONSERVATION

Division of Mines and Geology
1416 Ninth Street
Sacramento, California 95814

BULLETINS

170 Geology of Southern California. Richard H. Jahns, editor. 1954. Reprint, 1960, in 2 clothbound volumes. Price: $13.00.

Volume 1. Contains 10 chapters.

Chapter VI. Hydrology. 1954, 28 p., 10 pls., 13 figs.

(1) Hydrology of the Los Angeles region, by Harold C. Troxell and Walter Hofmann, p. 5-12, 8 figs.

(2) Hydrology of the Mojave Desert, by Harold C. Troxell and Walter Hofmann, p. 13-17, 5 figs.

(3) Geology and hydrology of Ventura County, by R. G. Thomas, E. C. Marliave, L. B. James, and R. T. Bean, p. 19-28, pls. 1-10. Price: $1.00.

SPECIAL REPORTS

2 Geology of part of the Delta-Mendota Canal near Tracy, California, by Parry Reiche. 1950. 12 p., 5 figs. Price: $0.25.

44 Bibliography of marine geology and oceanography, California coast. By Richard D. Terry. 146 p., 2 figs. Price: $0.75.

70 Sand and gravel resources of the Kern River near Bakersfield, California. By Harold B. Goldman and Ira E. Klein. 1961. 33 p., 2 pls., 3 figs., 20 photos, 7 tables. Price: $1.00.

75 Exploration and development of geothermal power in California. By James R. McNitt. 1963. Second printing (revised) 1965. 45 p., frontis., 11 photos, 15 figs. Price: $1.00.

97 Geologic and engineering aspects of San Francisco Bay fill. By Harold B. Goldman, editor. 130 p., 4 maps. Price: $3.00.

MISCELLANEOUS

Field Trip D: Hydrology field trip to East Bay area and northern Santa Clara Valley, by S. N. Davis. Price: $0.50.

CALIFORNIA STATE DEPARTMENT OF CONSERVATION

Division of Soil Conservation
1416 Ninth Street
Sacramento, California 95814

Economic analysis of the January-February 1969 floods in the Carpinteria Valley Watershed. [n.p., 1969]. 52 p.

Laws relating to soil conservation and soil conservation districts [by] the Resources Agency of California, Department of Conservation, Division of Soil Conservation and State Soil Conservation Commission. 1963. 78 p. (Division 9, Public Resources Code.)

New Jerusalem Watershed, San Joaquin and Alameda Counties, California. Prepared by Tracy Soil Conservation District and New Jerusalem Drainage District. 1967. 37 p.

A preliminary investigation of the feasibility of providing works of improvement within Burch-Rice Watershed, Tehama County, California. 1969. 24 p.

A preliminary investigation of the feasibility of providing works of improvement within Goose Lake Watershed, Modoc County, California, for construction under the Watershed Protection and Flood Prevention Act. 1968. 14 p.

A preliminary investigation of the feasibility of providing works of improvement within Mayfork Watershed, Trinity County, California, for construction under the Watershed Protection and Flood Prevention Act (Public Law 566 as amended). 1969. 10 p.

A preliminary investigation of the feasibility of providing works of improvement within Los Alamos Watershed, Santa Barbara County, California. 1969. 15 p.

A preliminary investigation of the feasibility of providing works of improvement within Surprise Valley Watershed, Modoc County, California, for construction under the Watershed Protection and Flood Prevention Act. 1969. 13 p.

A preliminary investigation of the feasibility of providing works of improvement within McCoy Wash Watershed, Riverside County, California. 1968. 12 p.

A preliminary investigation of the feasibility of providing works of improvement within the Anderson Valley Watershed, Mendocino County, California. 1968. 13 p.

A preliminary investigation of the feasibility of providing works of improvement within the Butte Valley Watershed, Siskiyou County, California. 1967. 13 p.

A preliminary investigation of the feasibility of providing works of improvement within the Tynan Lake Watershed, Santa Cruz County, California. 1967. 10 p.

A preliminary investigation to determine the feasibility of the installation of works of improvement within Mt. Diablo-Seal Creek Watershed, Contra Costa County, California. 1967. 13 p.

A reconnaissance study to investigate the feasibility for the installation of works of improvement within the Orchard Drive Watershed (Orange County, California). 1966. 8 p.

A reconnaissance study to investigate the feasibility of the Anderson Valley Watershed project (Mendocino County, California). 1964. 12 p.

A reconnaissance study to investigate the feasibility of the Arroyo Seco Watershed Project (Monterey County, California). 1965. 12 p.

A reconnaissance study to investigate the feasibility of the Dos Palos drainage project (Fresno and Merced Counties, Calif.) under the Federal Watershed Protection and Flood Prevention Act. 1963. 10 p.

A reconnaissance study to investigate the feasibility of the El Estero and Carpinteria Creek watershed project, Santa Barbara County, California, for construction under the Federal Watershed Protection and Flood Prevention Act. 1964. 6 p.

A reconnaissance study to investigate the feasibility of the Hungry Hollow Watershed Project. 1967. 7 p.

A reconnaissance study to investigate the feasibility of the New Jerusalem drainage project (San Joaquin County, California). 1964. 12 p.

A reconnaissance study to investigate the feasibility of the Pup Creek watershed project (Fresno County, California). 1964. 8 p.

A reconnaissance study to investigate the feasibility of the Stone Corral watershed project (Tulare County, California). 1964. 9 p.

A reconnaissance study to investigate the feasibility of the Stone's Canyon Creek watershed project (Modoc and Lassen Counties, California). 1964. 9 p.

A reconnaissance study to investigate the feasibility of the Willow Creek watershed project (Lassen County, California). 1963. 11 p.

A reconnaissance study to investigate the feasibility of Upper Stony Creek watershed project) (Glenn and Colusa Counties, California) for construction under the Federal Watershed Projection and Flood Prevention Act. 1964. 14 p.

Sedimentation and erosion in the Upper Truckee River and Trout Creek Watershed, Lake Tahoe, California. 1969. 43 p.

Work plan for Buttonwillow water management project, Kern County, California, by M. L. Engineering Inc., Bakersfield, California. 1967. 69 p.

Watershed work plan; Patterson Watershed, Stanislaus County, California. 1970. 39 p.

CALIFORNIA STATE DEPARTMENT OF ENGINEERING

Note: Organization succeeded by the California Department of Water Resources, 1416 Ninth Street, Sacramento, California 95814.

BULLETINS

*1 Progress report of co-operative irrigation investigations in California, 1912-1914, by Frank Adams. 1915. 74 p.

*2 Irrigation districts in California, 1887-1915, by Frank Adams. 1916 (republished 1917 as an appendix to the biennial report). 148 p.

*3 Investigations of the economical duty of water for alfalfa in Sacramento Valley, California, 1910-1915, by Frank Adams, Ralph D. Robertson, Samuel H. Beckett, Wells A. Hutchins and O. W. Israelsen. 1917. 78 p.

*4 Preliminary report on conservation and control of flood water in Coachella Valley, California, by C. E. Tait. 1917. 31 p.

*5 Report on the utilization of Mojave River for irrigation in Victor Valley, California, by Mojave River Commission: W. F. McClure, J. A. Sourwine, and C. E. Tait. 1918. 93 p.

*6 California Irrigation District Laws as amended 1919, compiled by the California State Library. 1919. 176 p.

*7 Use of water from Kings River, California, 1918, by Harry Barnes. 1920. 119 p.

*8 Flood problems of Calaveras River, October 31, 1919, by Harry Barnes. 1919. 57 p.

*9 Water resources of Kern River and adjacent streams and their utilization, 1920, by S. T. Harding. 1921. 209 p.

CALIFORNIA STATE DEPARTMENT OF FISH AND GAME

1416 Ninth Street
Sacramento, California 95814

California fish and wildlife plan. 1966. 5 vol.

Delta fish and wildlife protection study; report. Annual, 1962-1967.

The effects of Middle Fork Eel River development on wildlife resources. 1969. 12, 59 p.

Effects on fish and wildlife resources of proposed water development on Middle Fork Feather River. 1961. 35, 19 p. (Water Projects report no. 2).

Feasibility and desirability of designating the Middle Fork Feather River a wild river. 1966. 44 p.

Fish and wildlife problems and study requirements in relation to North Coast water development. 1965. 229 p. (Water Projects Branch report no. 5).

Fish and wildlife losses due to pesticides and pollution from 1965 to 1969. 1970. 1 vol. (unpaged).

Fish and wildlife resource planning guide. 3rd edition. 1970. 124 p.

Fish and wildlife resources of San Francisco Bay and Delta: description, environmental requirements, problems, opportunities and the future. 1968. 338 p.

An historical review of the fish and wildlife resources of the San Francisco Bay Area, by John E. Skinner. 1962. 22 p. (Water Projects Branch report no. 1).

The natural resources of Bolinas Lagoon: their status and future, by Paul E. Giguere [and others.] 1970. 107 p.

The natural resources of Goleta Slough and recommendations for use and development, by John Speth [and others.] 1970. 42 p.

Recommendations on thermal objectives for water quality control policies on the interstate waters of California, by Lloyd R. Dunham. 1968. 155 p. (Water Projects Branch report no. 7).

Report on Phase I development of a preliminary plan and program for a study of toxicity and biostimulation in San Francisco Bay — Delta waters, by the Department of Water Resources and Department of Fish and Game. 1970. 1 vol.

Report on proposed water appropriations affecting the fish and game resources of Eagle Lake, Lassen County, by Region I Staff. 1961. 38 p.

Report to the State Water Resources Control Board on the impact of water development on the fish and wildlife resources of the Sacramento-San Joaquin Delta and Suisun Marsh. 1969. 1 vol.

Santa Barbara oil leak; interim report. 1969. 50 p.

Some effects of potential water projects on the fish and wildlife of San Mateo County coastal streams, by Emil J. Smith Jr. 1964. 43 p.

A summarized report of the federal aid in fish and wildlife programs in California. 1962. 211 p.

A survey of the marine environment from Fort Ross, Sonoma County to Point Lobos, Monterey County. Prepared by Melvyn W. Odemar, Paul W. Wild and Kenneth C. Wilson. 1968. 238 p.

Upper Sacramento River Basin investigation, fish and wildlife evaluation of tributary developments and Butte Basin flood control. Prepared by Howard R. Leach [and] William F. Van Woert. 1968. 132 p.

Water development and the Delta environment. December 1967. 30 p. (Delta fish and wildlife protection study. Report no. 7).

Water requirements for the waterfowl of Butte Basin, California, by Philip H. Arend. 1967. 73 p. (Water Projects Branch report no. 6).

CALIFORNIA STATE DEPARTMENT OF PUBLIC HEALTH

2151 Berkeley Way
Berkeley, California 94704

California domestic water supplies. 1962. 76 p.

California water supply statistics. 1941. 32 p. (Special bulletin no. 63).

Directory of wastewater reclamation operations in California. 1969. 45 p.

Instrumentation and control of wastewater reclamation plants. 1970. 41 p.

Recreation on domestic water supply reservoirs: a study of recreational use and water quality of reservoirs, 1959-1961. 1961. 62 p.

CALIFORNIA STATE DEPARTMENT OF PUBLIC WORKS

Division of Water Rights

Note: Organization succeeded by the California Department of Water Resources, 1416 Ninth Street, Sacramento, California 95814.

BULLETINS

*1 Hydrographic investigation of San Joaquin River. 1923. 120 p.

*2 Kings River investigation — present and proposed use of water for irrigation and power development — Water Masters reports, 1918-1923, by Harold Conkling and Charles L. Kaupke. 1923. 240 p.

*3 Proceedings of Sacramento River Problems Conference held under the auspices of the Sacramento Chamber of Commerce and the Division of Water Rights, State Department of Public Works at Sacramento, California, on January 25 and 26, 1924. March 1924. 182 p.

*4 Proceedings of the Second Sacramento-San Joaquin River Problems Conference and Water Supervisor's Report, 1924, by Harlowe M. Stafford. 1925. 233 p.

*5 San Gabriel investigation. Report for the period July 1, 1923 to September 30, 1926, by Harold Conkling. 1927. 640 p.

*6 San Gabriel investigation. Report for the period October 1, 1926 to September 30, 1928. 1929. 200 p.

*7 San Gabriel investigation; analysis and conclusion, by Harold Conkling. 1929. 155 p.

CALIFORNIA DEPARTMENT OF WATER RESOURCES

1416 Ninth Street
Sacramento, California 95814

Note: Title of issuing agency on individual bulletins varies as follows:

Department of Public Works. Division of Engineering and Irrigation. Bulletins 1-14, 18 (Basic volume), 19, 20, 21 (Basic volume).

Department of Public Works. Division of Water Resources. Bulletins 18 (1929-1948), 21A-P, 22, 23, (Basic volume), 24-29, 31-38, 39A-W, 40, 40A, 41-45, 46, 46A, 47 and supplement, 48, 49, 49A-B, 50, 51, 52, 52A and first supplement, 52B, 53-57.

Department of Water Resources. Division of Resources Planning. Bulletins 21:51-58, 23:55-60, 49C, 52A supplements 5-7, 58, 59-63, 64 (Preliminary), 65-58 through 65-59 Pt I, 66 through 66-58, 67, 68, 73, 75, 77-58, 79, 81 through 83, 86 (Preliminary), 87 (Preliminary), 89, 90 (Preliminary), 93.

Department of Water Resources. Division of Design and Construction. Bulletins 16, 88.

Department of Water Resources. Bulletins 16-62 through 16-69, 17, 21-59 through 21-64, 23-61, 23-62, 24-60 through 39-62, 40-57, 63-3, 64, 65-59 Pt II through 65-62, 68-62, 69-63 through 69-68, 70, 71, 72, 74, 74-2 through 74-6, 74-8, 74-9, 76, 77-59 through 77-62, 78, 79-64, 80, 83, 84, 86 (Final), 87 (Final), 91, 92, 94 through 180.

State Water Resources Board. Bulletins 52A supplements 2-4. (See also its Bulletin series.)

BULLETINS

*1 California irrigation district laws as amended 1921, compiled by California State Library and revised by Legislative Counsel Bureau. 1922. 163 p.

*2 Procedure for securing State approval of formation of irrigation districts, issuance of bonds by irrigation districts, expenditure of construction funds by irrigation districts, construction of dams. 1922. 14 p.

*3 Water resources of Tulare County and their utilization, by S. T. Harding, Chester Marliave and G. H. Russell. 1922. 155 p., 7 maps.

*4 Water resources of California — A report to the Legislature of 1923, by Paul Bailey. 1923. 55 p.

*5 Flow in California streams, being Appendix "A" to report to the Legislature of 1923 on the water resources of California, by Paul Bailey. 1923. 557 p.. 54 pls., in pocket.

*6 Irrigation requirements of California lands, being Appendix "B" to report to the Legislature of 1923 on the water resources of California, by Paul Bailey. 1923. 196 p., 7 pls.

*7 California irrigation district laws as amended 1923, compiled by California State Library and revised by Legislative Counsel Bureau. 1923. 183 p.

*8 Cost of water to irrigators in California, by Harry F. Blaney. 1925. 66 p.

*9   Supplemental report on water resources of California: A report to the Legislature of 1925, by Paul Bailey. 1926. 51 p., maps.

*10   California irrigation district laws, compiled by Legislative Counsel Bureau. 1925. 273 p.

*11   Groundwater resources of the Southern San Joaquin Valley, by S. T. Harding. 1927. 146 p.

*12   Summary report on the water resources of California and a coordinated plan for their development: a report to the Legislature of 1927, by Paul Bailey. 1927. 49 p.

*13   The development of the Upper Sacramento River, an appendix to the summary report to the Legislature of 1927 on the water resources of California and a coordinated plan for their development, by Paul Bailey. 1928. 209 p.

*14   The control of floods by reservoirs, an appendix to the summary report to the Legislature of 1927 on the water resources of California and a coordinated plan for their development, by Paul Bailey. 1928. 463 p.

15   Not published.

*16   Flood flows and stages in Sacramento and Northern San Joaquin Valleys, 1954-1956. 1957. 92 p., appendices. *See notes under Bulletin 23.*

*16-62 Weather modification operations in California, October 1, 1961 – September 30, 1962. February 1963. 6 p. *See also Bulletin 16, "Weather modification operations in California," June 1955, by the State Water Resources Board.*

16-63 Weather modification ... October 1962 – September 1963. June 1964. 22 p. Price: $0.75.

16-64 Weather modification ... October 1963 – September 1964. May 1965. 24 p. Price: $0.50.

16-65 Weather modification ... October 1964 – September 1965. August 1966. 72 p. Price: $1.00.

16-66 Weather modification ... October 1965 – September 1966. August 1967. 32 p. Price: $0.50.

16-67 Weather modification ... October 1966 – September 1967. August 1968. 32 p. Price: $0.50.

16-68 Weather modification ... October 1967 – September 1968. July 1969. 24 p. Price: $1.00.

16-69 Weather modification ... October 1968 – September 1969. June 1970. 14 p. Price: $1.00.

*17-58 Dams within jurisdiction of the State of California. 1958. 58 p.

*17-62 Dams within jurisdiction of the State of California. January 1962. 108 p.

*17-65 Dams within jurisdiction of the State of California. August 1965. 130 p.

*17-67 Dams within jurisdiction of the State of California. July 1967. 122 p.

*17-68 Dams within jurisdiction of the State of California. June 1968. 120 p.

17-69 Dams within jurisdiction of the State of California. January 1970. 66 p. Price: $2.00.

*18   Irrigation District Laws, 1927-1948, compiled by Legislative Counsel Bureau. (Basic volume and no's A thru I.) 10 vol.

*19   Santa Ana Investigation, flood control and conservation, by William S. Post. 1929. 2 vol.

*20   Report on Kennett Reservoir development, an analysis of methods and extent of financing by electric power revenue, by Lester S. Ready. 1929. 65 p.

21   Report on irrigation and water storage districts in California. 1929 – current.
Title varies: Bulletin 21, 1929, "Irrigation districts in California," by Frank Adams. – Bulletin 21A – 21P, 1930-1950, "Report on irrigation districts in California." – Bulletin 21-55 – to-date, "Report on irrigation and water storage districts in California."

Complete series is as follows:

Bulletin No.	Year(s) Reported	Publication Date	Pages	Price
*21	1928	1929	422	
*21A	1929	1930	42	
*21B	1930	1931	80	
*21C	1931	1932	36	
*21D	1932	1933	34	
*21E	1933	1934	42	
*21F	1934	1935	38	
*21G	1935	1936	38	
*21H	1936	1937	44	
*21I	1937	1938	62	
*21J	1938	1939	34	
*21K	1939	1940	38	
*21L	1940	1941	44	
*21M	1941	1942	46	
*21N	1942	1943	44	
*21O	1943	1944	38	
*21P	1944-50	1951	106	
21-55	1951-55	Jan 1958	94	$1.50
21-58	1956-58	Mar 1960	72	$3.00
21-59	1959	Dec 1960	24	$1.00
*21-60	1960	Jan 1962	16	
21-61	1961	Jan 1963	20	$0.75
21-62	1962	Mar 1964	30	$1.00
*21-63	1963	Oct 1964	20	
21-64	1964	Dec 1965	20	$0.50

*22   Report on salt water barrier below confluence of Sacramento and San Joaquin Rivers, California, by Walker R. Young. 1929. 2 vol.

23   Surface water flow for 1924 – 1962. 1930-1965. 38 vol.

Title varies: 1924 – 1955, "Report of Sacramento – San Joaquin Water Supervision."

Superseded by Bulletin 130.

Complete series is as follows:

Bulletin or Item No.	Year(s) Reported	Publication Date	Pages	Price
*23	1924-28	1930	432	
*23-29	1929	July 1930	–	
*23-30	1930	July 1931	186	
*23-31	1931	Aug 1932	228	
*23-32	1932	June 1933	156	
*23-33	1933-34	June 1935	236	
*23-35	1935	June 1936	122	
*23-36	1936	May 1937	130	
*23-37	1937	July 1938	132	
*23-38	1938	April 1939	142	

Bulletin or Item No.	Year(s) Reported	Publication Date	Pages	Price
*23-39	1939	June 1940	194	
*23-40	1940	June 1941	198	
*23-41	1941	June 1942	202	
*23-42	1942	June 1943	310	
*23-43	1943	June 1944	264	
*23-44	1944	June 1945	162	
*23-45	1945	June 1946	158	
*23-46	1946	June 1947	162	
*23-47	1947	June 1948	146	
*23-48	1948	May 1949	158	
*23-49	1949	June 1950	194	
23-50	1950	Oct 1951	188	$2.00
23-51	1951	Oct 1952	194	$2.00
23-52	1952	Nov 1953	210	$2.00
23-53	1953	Oct 1954	212	$2.00
23-54	1954	Aug 1955	218	$2.00
23-55	1955	June 1957	232	$2.00
23-56	1956	Jan 1959	206	$2.00
23-57	1957	Feb 1960	314	$3.00
23-58	1958	Dec 1960	358	$3.00
23-59	1959	May 1961	306	$3.00
23-60	1960	Sept 1961	324	$3.00
23-61	1961	Aug 1963	322	$4.00
23-62	1962	July 1965	416	$4.50

*24   A proposed major development on American River: An analysis of its utility in the coordinated plan for the development of the water resources of California – A report to the Joint Legislative Committee of 1927 on water resources and to the State Department of Finance, 1929, by A. D. Edmonston. 1930. 190 p.

24-60 Coastal Los Angeles County land and water use survey, 1960. 1964. 51 p. Price: $2.00.

*25   Report to Legislature of 1931 on State Water Plan, by A. D. Edmonston and Harold Conkling. 1930. 204 p.

*26   Sacramento River Basin, 1931, by T. B. Waddell. 1933. 583 p.

*27   Variation and control of salinity in Sacramento-San Joaquin Delta and upper San Francisco Bay, 1931, by Raymond Matthew. 1932. 440 p.

*28   Economic aspects of a salt water barrier below confluence of Sacramento and San Joaquin Rivers, 1931, by Raymond Matthew. 1932. 450 p.

*29   San Joaquin River Basin, 1931, by G. H. Jones, 1934. 656 p.

30   Not published.

*31   Santa Ana River Basin – A plan for flood control and control and conservation of waste water; present and future importation requirements; sources of outside supply and salinity intrusion, by Harold Conkling. 1930. 73 p.

*32   South Coastal Basin: A cooperative symposium of activities and plans of public agencies in Los Angeles, Orange, San Bernardino and Riverside Counties leading to conservation of local water supplies and management of underground reservoirs, 1930, by Harold Conkling. 1930. 79 p.

*33   Rainfall penetration and consumptive use of water in Santa Ana River Valley and coastal plain-1930, by Harry F. Blaney, C. A. Taylor and A. A. Young. 1931. 162 p.

*34   Permissible annual charges for irrigation water in Upper San Joaquin Valley, 1930, by Frank Adams and Martin R. Huberty. 1930. 89 p.

*35   Permissible economic rate of irrigation development in California, 1930, by David Weeks. 1930. 205 p.

*36   Cost of irrigation water in California, 1930, by Harry F. Blaney and Martin R. Huberty. 1930. 146 p.

*37   Financial and general data pertaining to irrigation, reclamation and other public districts in California, prepared under the direction of California Irrigation and Reclamation Financing and Refinancing Commission, 1930, by Harmon S. Bonte. 1931. 255 p.

*38   Report of the Kings River Water Master for the period 1918-1930, by Charles L. Kaupke. 1931. 426 p.

39   Water supply conditions in Southern California during [1931]-1962. 1932-1964. 42 vol.

Title varies: 1932-1940, "South Coastal investigation, records of ground water levels at wells." 1941-1947, "South Coastal Basin investigation including San Jacinto Valley and Antelope Valley ... ground water levels ... precipitation records." 1948-1955, "South Coastal Basin investigation, ground water levels and precipitation records in Los Angeles, San Gabriel, and Santa Ana River Basins and Antelope Valley and water supply summary for southern portion of California." 1955-1962, "Water supply conditions in Southern California."

Superseded by Bulletin 130.

Complete series is as follows:

Bulletin No.	Year(s) Reported	Publication Date	Pages	Price
*39	1900-1931	1932	590	
*39A	1932	1933	162	
*39B	1933	1934	156	
*39C	1934	1935	150	
*39D	1935	1936	154	
*39E	1936	1937	178	
*39F	1937	1938	118	
*39G	1938	1939	116	
*39H	1939	1941	114	
*39I	1940	1941	108	
*39J	1941	1944	480	
*39K	1942	1945	138	
*39L	1943	1946	132	
*39M	1944	1948	124	
*39N	1945	Sept 1948	120	
*39O	1946	1949	118	
*39P	1947	1950	118	
*39Q	1948	1953	166	
*39R	1949	1954	130	
*39S	1950	1955	150	
*39T	1951	June 1955	142	
*39U	1952	Aug 1955	142	
*39V	1953	Aug 1955	130	
*39W	1954	June 1956	142	
39-56	1955-56	Mar 1957	178	$2.00
39-57I	1956-57	June 1958	100	$2.00
39-57II	1956-57	June 1958	874	$4.00
39-57III	1956-57	June 1958	672	$3.50
39-57IV	1956-57	June 1958	354	$2.00
39-58I	1957-58	Aug 1960	90	$3.00
39-58II	1957-58	Aug 1960	490	$2.50
39-58III	1957-58	Aug 1960	376	$2.50
39-59I	1958-59	May 1961	90	$3.00
39-59II	1958-59	May 1961	398	$2.50

Bulletin No.	Year(s) Reported	Publication Date	Pages	Price
39-59III	1958-59	May 1961	258	$2.50
39-60I	1959-60	Dec 1961	98	$3.00
39-60II	1959-60	Dec 1961	430	$2.50
39-60III	1959-60	Dec 1961	358	$2.50
39-61I	1960-61	Feb 1963	104	$3.50
39-61II	1960-61	Feb 1963	381	$3.00
39-61III	1960-61	Feb 1963	260	$3.50
39-62I	1961-62	July 1964	106	$3.00
39-62II	1961-62	July 1964	386	$3.50
39-62III	1961-62	July 1964	284	$3.00

*40   South Coastal Basin investigation: Quality of irrigation waters, 1933, by Carl S. Scofield. 1933. 95 p.

40-57 Quality of surface and ground waters in Upper Santa Ana Valley, by Jack C. Coe and Frank S. Floriun. June 1, 1957. 140 p., Price: $2.00.

*41   Pit River investigation 1933, by Gordon Zander. 1933. 152 p.

*42   Santa Clara investigation, 1933, by Everett N. Bryan. 1933. 271 p.

*43   South Coastal Basin investigation: Value and cost of water for irrigation in Coastal Plain of Southern California, 1933, by Frank Adams and Martin R. Huberty. 1934. 189 p.

*44   South Coastal Basin investigation: Water losses under natural conditions from wet areas in Southern California, 1933, by Harry F. Blaney and Harold C. Troxell. 1934. 176 p.

*45   South Coastal Basin investigation: Geology and ground water storage capacity of valley fill, by Rollin Eckis. 1934. 279 p.

*46   Ventura County investigation, 1933. 1934. 244 p.

*46-A Ventura County investigation – 1933. Basic data for the period 1927 to 1932, inclusive. 1934. 594 p.

*47   Mojave River investigation, 1934, by Harold Conkling. [1934]. 249 p.

*48   San Diego County investigation, 1935, by P. H. Van Etten. [1935]. 252 p.

*48-A San Luis Rey River investigation, 1936, by Robert I. Wing. 1937. 49 p.

*49   Kaweah River flows, diversions, and service areas, 1940. 1940. 348 p.

*49-A Kaweah River flows, diversions, and service areas, 1939-1949. 1950. 210 p.

49-B   Kaweah River flows, diversions, and service areas, 1949-1955. 1956. 158 p. Price: $1.50.

49-C   Kaweah River flows, diversions, and service areas, 1955-1960. 1961. 132 p. Price: $2.00.

*50   Use of water by native vegetation, 1942, by Arthur A. Young and Harry F. Blaney. 1942. 160 p.

*51   Irrigation requirements of California crops, 1945, by Arthur A. Young. 1946. 132 p.

*52   Salinas Basin investigation. 1946. 230 p.

*52-A Salinas Basin investigation, basic data. 1949. 426 p.

       – – – – Supplements 1948 – 1958. 7 vol.

*52-B Salinas Basin investigation, summary report. 1946. 46 p.

*53   South Coastal Basin investigation, overdraft on ground water basins, 1947, by George B. Gleason. 1947. 256 p.

*54   Evaporation from water surfaces in California, a summary of pan records and coefficients, 1881 to 1946, by Arthur A. Young. 1947. 68 p.

*54-A Evaporation from water surfaces in California, basic data, by Arthur A. Young. 1948. 205 p.

*54-B Evaporation from water surfaces in California, by Harry F. Blaney and Gilbert L. Corey, 1955. 98 p.

*55   San Dieguito and San Diego Rivers investigation, by P. H. Van Etten. 1949. 245 p.

56   Survey of mountainous areas, December 1955, by R. G. Eiland. 1955. 150 p. Price: $5.00.

57   Santa Margarita River investigation, June 1956, by L. R. Illingworth. 1956. 2 vol. Price: $7.50.

58   Northeastern Counties investigation, June 1960, by John R. Teerink, Stuart T. Pyle and John W. Shannon. 1960. 312 p. Price: $7.50.

*59   Investigation of Upper Feather River Basin development; interim report on engineering, economic and financial feasibility of initial units. 1957. 2 vol. (appendices in separate vol.).

59-2   Investigation of upper Feather River Basin development. 1960. 2 vol. (appendices in separate vol.). Price: $5.00.

60   Interim report to the California State Legislature on the salinity control barrier investigation, March 1957, by Herbert A. Howlett. 1957. 79 p. Price: $1.50.

61   Feather River Project – Investigation of alternative aqueduct routes to San Diego County, by Robert M. Edmonston and Lucian J. Meyers. 1957. 181 p. Price: $7.50.

62   Recommended water well construction and sealing standards, Mendocino County, by Richard W. Kretsinger, James L. Welsh, Harley R. Woodworth, and Donald H. Neudeck. 1958. 169 p. Price: $3.00.

63   Sea-water intrusion in California. 1958. 92 p.

       – – – – Appendix A, never published.

       – – – – Appendix B, "Report by Los Angeles County Flood Control District on investigational work for prevention and control of sea water intrusion, West Coast Basin experimental project ... ", 1957. 142 p. Price: $5.00.

       *– – – – Appendices C, D, and E, "Laboratory and model studies, an abstract of literature, review of formulas and derivations; An investigation of some problems in preventing sea-water intrusion by creating a fresh water barrier; Preliminary chemical-quality study in the Manhattan Beach area, California," 1960. 265 p.

63-1   Sea-water intrusion, Oxnard Plain of Ventura County. 1965. 100 p. Price: $2.50.

63-2   Sea-water intrusion: Bolsa-Sunset Area, Orange County. 1968. 167 p. Price: $3.50.

63-3   Sea-water intrusion: Pismo-Guadalupe area. 1970. 76 p. Price: $3.50.

64   West Walker River investigation. 1964. 144 p. Price: $4.00.

65   Quality of surface waters in California, 1955-1956 to 1962. 1957-1965. 9 vols.

Superseded by Bulletin 130.

Complete series is as follows:

Bulletin No.	Year(s) Reported	Publication Date	Pages	Price
*65	1955-56	Dec 1957	464	
65-57	1957	Dec 1960	352	$3.50
65-58	1958	Dec 1960	526	$3.50
65-59	1959			
Part I: Northern and Central California		July 1961	442	$6.00
Part II: Southern California		Nov 1962	296	$4.00
65-61	1961			
Vol. I: Northern and Central California				
Part I: Text		Aug 1963	454	$5.00
Part II: Appendices		Aug 1963	478	$3.50
Vol. II: Southern California		Jan 1964	178	$6.00
65-62	1962	June 1965	420	$3.50

66   Quality of ground waters in California, 1955-56 to 1961-1962. 1958-1964. 9 vols.

Superseded by Bulletin 130.

Complete series is as follows:

Bulletin No.	Year(s) Reported	Publication Date	Pages	Price
*66	1955-56	June 1958	242	
66	1957	April 1960	242	$4.00
66-58	1958	Nov 1960	334	$3.00
66-59	1959			
* Part I: Northern and Central California		Feb 1963	322	
Part II: Southern California		Feb 1963	200	$4.50
66-60	1960			
Part I: Northern and Southern California		Mar 1964	374	$6.00
Part II: Southern California		Mar 1964	96	$4.00
66-62	1961-62			
Part I: Northern and Central California		Aug 1964	444	$6.00
Part II: Southern California		Sept 1964	180	$4.00

67   Reclamation of water from sewage and industrial wastes, Watsonville Area, Santa Cruz and Monterey Counties, by Charles F. Kleine and Harry G. Behrens. August 1959. 32 p.

*68   Reclamation of water from sewage and industrial wastes. Progress report, July 1, 1953–June 30, 1955, by Claude W. Hewitt and others. January 1958. 24 p.

68-62   Reclamation of water from sewage and industrial wastes in California, July 1, 1955 – June 30, 1962. 1963. 197 p. Price: $3.00.

69-63   California high water, 1962-1963. 1964. 82 p. Price: $3.00.

69-64   California high water, 1963-1964. 1965. 42 p. Price: $1.00.

69-65   California high water, 1964-1965. 1966. 194 p. Price: $3.75

69-66   California high water, 1965-1966. 1967. 70 p. Price: $3.75.

69-67   California high water, 1966-1967. 1968. 96 p. Price: $1.00.

69-68   California high water, 1967-1968. 1969. 42 p. Price: $1.50.

*70   Orange County land and water use survey, 1957. 1959. 84 p.

70-64   Orange County land and water use survey, 1964. 1967. 78 p. Price: $1.25.

71   Upper Santa Ana River drainage area land and water use survey, 1957. 1960. 92 p. Price: $3.00.

71-64   Upper Santa Ana River drainage area land and water use survey, 1964. 1966. 90 p. Price: $2.00.

72   San Dieguito River investigation. 1959. 2 vols. Price: $8.50.

73   Evaporation from water surfaces in California. 1959. 81 p. Available free of charge.

*74   Water well standards: State of California. 1968. 224 p.

74-2   Water well standards: Alameda County. 1964. 94 p. Price: $2.00.

74-3   Water well standards: Del Norte County. 1966. 118 p. Price: $1.75.

*74-4   Water well standards: Central, Hollywood, Santa Monica Basins, Los Angeles County. Preliminary edition. 1965. 62 p.

    –––– Supplement. 1968. 16 p. Price: $0.25.

74-5   Water well standards: San Joaquin County. Preliminary edition. 1965. 2 vols. Price: Text and appendices A-D, $2.50; Appendix E, $0.50.

    –––– Final supplement. 1969. 30 p. Price: $1.00.

74-6   Water well standards: Fresno County. 1968. 16 p. Price: $0.25.

74-8   Water well standards: Shasta County. 1968. 148 p. Price: $1.75.

74-9   Water well standards: Ventura County, 1968. 73 p. Price: $1.25.

*75   Water quality and water quality problems, Ventura County, by Robert F. Clauson and others. February 1959. 2 vol.

76   Delta water facilities as an integral feature of the State water resources development system. Preliminary edition. 1960. 60 p. Price: free of charge.

Appendices

Delta water requirements. 1962. 150 p. Price: $3.00.

Economic aspects. 1961. 198 p. Price: $3.00.

*Salinity incursions and water resources. 1962. 186 p.

Recreation. 1962. 78 p. Price: $2.00.

77 Ground water conditions in Central and Northern California, 1957-58 to 1961-62. 1959-1964. 5 vols.

Superseded by Bulletin 130.

Complete series is as follows:

Bulletin No.	Year(s) Reported	Publication Date	Pages	Price
77-58	1957-58	Oct 1959	218	$7.00
77-59	1958-59	Feb 1962	234	$3.00
77-60	1959-60	Jan 1963	188	$3.50
77-61	1960-61	June 1964	178	$2.50
77-62	1962	Aug 1964	176	$2.50

78 Investigation of alternative aqueduct systems to serve Southern California. 1959. 160 p. Price: $5.00.

Appendices

*Long range economic potential of the Antelope Valley-Mojave River. 1959. 218 p.

Effects of differences in water quality, Upper Santa Ana Valley and coastal San Diego County. 1959. 174 p. Price: $3.00.

*Procedure for estimating costs of tunnel construction. 1959. 84 p.

Economic demand for imported water. 1960. 368 p. Price: $7.00.

*Financial and economic analyses. 1960. 72 p.

*Conveyance and distribution of imported water within service areas. 1960. 196 p.

*79 Index of topographic mapping in California. 1958. 126 p.

79-64 Index of topographic mapping in California. 1965. 164 p. Price: $2.00.

*80 Feasibility of reclamation of water from wastes in the Los Angeles Metropolitan area. 1961. 155 p.

80-2 Reclamation of water from wastes: coastal San Diego County. 1968. 157 p. Price: $2.00.

80-3 Reclamation of water from wastes: Coachella Valley. 1966. 82 p. Price: $1.25.

81 Intrusion of salt water into ground water basins of southern Alameda County. 1960. 44 p. Price: $2.00.

82 Upper Tule River reconnaissance investigation. 1960. 60 p. Price: $2.00.

83 Klamath River Basin investigation. 1964. 210 p. Price: $4.50.

84 Mojave River ground water basins investigation. 1967. 151 p. Price: $3.50.

85 Not published.

86 Upper Pit River investigation. 1964. 158 p. Price: $4.50.

87 Shasta Valley investigation. 1964. 170 p. Price: $3.50.

*88 Procedures for estimating maximum possible precipitation. 1960. 29 p.

89 Lower San Joaquin Valley water quality investigation. 1960. 189 p. Price: $5.00.

*90 Clear Lake-Cache Creek Basin investigation. 1961. 267 p.

91 Water wells and springs.

Complete series is as follows:

No.	Data on Water Wells and Springs in	Date	Pages	Price
*91-1	West Part of the Middle Mojave Valley Area, San Bernardino County	6/60	126	
*91-2	Yucca Valley-Twentynine Palms Area, San Bernardino and Riverside Counties	6/60	164	
*91-3	Eastern Part of the Middle Mojave Valley Area, San Bernardino County	8/60	224	
91-4	Willow Springs, Gloster, and Chaffee Areas, Kern County	9/60	90	$1.50
91-5	Dale Valley Area, San Bernardino and Riverside Counties	3/61	60	$1.50
91-6	Edwards Air Force Base Area	6/62	212	$3.00
*91-7	Chuckwalla Valley Area, Riverside County	5/63	78	
*91-8	Rice and Vidal Valley Areas, Riverside and San Bernardino Counties	5/63	36	
91-9	Indian Wells Valley Area, Inyo, Kern, and San Bernardino Counties	5/63	246	$4.00
91-10	Lower Mojave Valley Area, San Bernardino County	12/63	212	$3.00
91-11	Western Part of the Antelope Valley Area, Los Angeles and Kern Counties	5/65	278	$1.50
91-12	Eastern Part of the Antelope Valley Area, Los Angeles County	12/66	448	$4.75
91-13	Soda, Silver, and Cronise Valleys, San Bernardino County	8/67	80	$1.00
91-14	Bristol, Broadwell, Cadiz, Danby, and Lavic Valleys and Vicinity, San Bernardino and Riverside Counties	8/67	80	$1.50
91-15	Borrego, Carrizo, and San Felipe Valley Areas, San Diego and Imperial Counties	1/68	140	$2.00
91-16	Fremont Valley Area, Kern County	2/69	160	$2.00
91-17	Panamint, Searles, and Knob Valleys, San Bernardino and Inyo Counties	12/69	110	$2.00

92 Branscomb Project investigation. 1965. 132 p. Price: $2.25.

93 Saline water demineralization and nuclear energy in the California Water Plan. 1960. 145 p. Price: $2.25.

94-1 Land and water use in the Tule River hydrographic unit. 1964. 89 p. Price: $4.50.

94-2 Land and water use in Trinity River hydrographic unit. 1964. 2 vol. Price: $7.00.

94-3 Land and water use in Yuba-Bear Rivers hydrographic unit. 1965. 2 vol. Price: $8.00.

*94-4 Land and water use in Smith River hydrographic unit. 1965. 120 p.

94-5 Land and water use in Shasta-Scott Valleys hydrographic unit. 1965. 2 vol. Price: $8.75.

94-6 Land and water use in Klamath River hydrographic unit. 1965. 2 vol. Price: $13.25.

94-7 Land and water use in Mad River-Redwood Creek hydrographic unit. 1965. 120 p. Price: $1.50.

94-8 Land and water use in Eel River hydrographic unit. 1965. 3 vol. Price: $16.00.

94-9 Land and water use in Lost River-Butte Valley hydrographic unit. 1965. 98 p. Price: $5.25.

      Final supplement, 1967. 26 p. Price: $0.75.

94-10 Land and water use in Mendocino coast hydrographic unit. 1964. 2 vol. Price: $7.00.

      Final supplement, 1967. 26 p. Price: $0.75.

94-11 Land and water use in Russian River hydrographic unit. 1964. 2 vol. Price: $10.00.

      Final supplement, 1967. 26 p. Price: $0.75.

94-12 Land and water use in Sacramento Valley west hydrographic unit. 1967. 2 vol. Price: $2.75.

94-13 Land and water use in Putah-Cache Creeks hydrographic unit. 1965. 2 vol. Price: $8.75.

94-14 Land and water use in American River hydrographic unit. 1965. 2 vol. Price: $9.50.

94-15 Not published.

94-16 Land and water use in Sacramento Valley northeast hydrographic unit. 1966. 2 vol. Price: $2.75.

      Final supplement, 1967. 26 p. Price: $0.75.

94-17 Land and water use in Feather River hydrographic unit. 1967. 318 p. Price: $3.50.

*95   Tuolumne County Water District No. 2 investigation. 1962. 207 p.

      Summary edition, 1967. 11 p. Price: $0.25.

96   Southern Tuolumne County investigation. 1965. 140 p. Price: $3.50.

*97   Calaveras area investigation reconnaissance report. 1963. 228 p.

98   Northeastern Counties Ground water investigation. 1963. 2 vol. Price: $9.00.

      *Appendix C: Geology, 1965. 210 p.

99   Reconnaissance report on upper Putah Creek Basin investigation. 1962. 254 p. Price: $4.00.

99-1 Upper Putah Creek basin investigation, Dry Creek project. 1965. 284 p. Price: $3.00.

100   Mt. Shasta City-Dunsmuir area investigation. 1964. 130 p. Price: $3.00.

101   Desert areas of southeastern California, land and water use survey, 1958. 1963. 74 p. Price: $3.50.

102   San Diego County land and water use survey, 1958. 1963. 55 p. Price: $2.00.

103   San Luis Obispo and Santa Barbara Counties land and water use survey, 1959. 1964. 50 p. Price: $2.00.

104   Planned utilization of ground water basins, coastal plain of Los Angeles County. 1968. 32 p. Price: $0.50.

      Appendix A: Ground water geology. 1961. 196 p. Price: $4.00.

      Appendix B: Safe yield determinations. 1962. 142 p. Price: $3.00.

      Appendix C: Operations and economics. 1966. 454 p. Price: $5.75.

104-2 [Basic volume never published.]

      Planned utilization of ground water basins, San Gabriel Valley, Appendix A: Geohydrology. 1966. 248 p. $4.00.

105-1 Developing the North Coast, an action program. Progress report. 1966. 58 p. Price: $0.75.

105-2 North Coastal Area action program; a study of the McKinleyville-Trinidad Area. 1969. 42 p. Price: $1.50.

106-1 Ground water occurrence and quality Lahontan region. 1964. 439 p. Price: $4.50.

106-2 Ground water occurrence and quality: San Diego region. 1967. 2 vol. Price: $8.00.

107   Recommended well construction and sealing standards for protection of ground water quality in West Coast Basin, Los Angeles County. 1962. 86 p. Price: $3.00.

*108 Coachella Valley investigation. 1964. 145 p.

109   Colusa Basin investigation. 1964. 126 p. Price: $3.50.

110   North Bay Aqueduct. 1961. 74 p. Price: $1.50.

111   Sacramento River water pollution survey. 1962. 112 p. Price: $2.00.

      Appendix A: Hydrography, hydrology, and water utilization. 1962. 138 p. Price: $2.50.

      Appendix B: Water quality. 1962. 384 p. Price: $4.00.

      Appendix C: Public health aspects. 1962. 186 p. Price: $2.00.

      Appendix D: Benthic biology. 1962. 88 p. $1.50.

*112 San Diego County flood hazard investigation. 1964. 44 p.

      *Appendix A: Regional flood frequency analysis. 1963. 72 p.

113   Vegetative water use studies, 1954-1960 (Interim Report). 1963. 132 p. Price: $2.50.

113-2 Vegetative water use. 1967. 94 p. Price: $1.25.

114   Directory of water service agencies in California. 1962. 72 p. Price: $2.00.

115   Yuba and Bear Rivers Basin investigation. 1964-65. 2 vols. Price: $4.25.

116-1 Crustal strain and fault movement investigation. Progress report. 1963. 37 p. Price: $1.00.

116-2 Crustal strain and fault movement investigation; faults and earthquake epicenters in California. 1964. 96 p. Price: $4.00.

116-3 Earthquake damage to hydraulic structures in California. 1967. 200 p. Price: $2.25.

116-4   Earthquake engineering programs. 1968. 149 p. Price: $2.75.

116-5   The Alaskan earthquake. 1965. 64 p. Price: $1.00.

116-6   Geodimeter fault movement investigations in California. 1968. 183 p. Price: $2.00.

117   Recreation and fish and wildlife program for the State Water Project. 1968. 31 p. Price: Free of charge.

117-1   Not published.

117-2   Del Valle Reservoir, recreation development plan. 1966. 15 p. Price: $0.25.

117-3   Lake Davis recreation development plan. 1965. 80 p. Price: $1.75.

117-4   Abbey Bridge Reservoir; water resources recreation report. 1966. 31 p. Price: $0.50.

117-5   Not published.

117-6   Oroville Reservoir, Thermalito Forebay, Thermalito Afterbay; water resources recreation report. 1966. 48 p. Price: $0.75.

117-7   San Luis Reservoir and Forebay recreation development plan. 1965. 58 p. Price: $1.00.

         *Appendix C: Fish and wildlife development plan. 1966. 38 p.

117-8   Not published.

117-9   Castaic Lake area, recreation development plan. 1970. 15 p. Price: $0.25.

117-10   Silverwood Lake recreation development plan. 1970. 14 p. Price: $0.25.

117-11   Not published.

117-12   Not published.

117-13   Not published.

117-14   Not published.

117-15   Not published.

117-16   Not published.

117-17   Not published.

117-18   Oroville borrow area, water resources recreation report. 1968. 30 p. Price: $0.50.

117-19   Kettleman City Aquatic Recreation Area, recreation development plan. 1966. 94 p. Price: $1.25.

117-20   Ingram Creek Aquatic Recreation Area, recreation development plan. 1966. 16 p. Price: $0.50.

118-1   Evaluation of ground water resources in the South Bay, Volume I: Fremont study area. 1968. 136 p. Price: $1.50.

         Appendix A: Geology. 1967. 168 p. Price: $3.00.

         (Volume II will not be published.)

118-2   Livermore and Sunol Valleys, evaluation of ground water resources; Appendix A: Geology. 1966. 92 p. Price: $1.75.

         (Basic volume is not to be published.)

*119-1   Feasibility of serving the Desert Water Agency service area from the state water facilities. 1962. 92 p.

*119-2   Feasibility of serving the San Gorgonio Pass Water Agency from the state water facilities. 1963. 80 p.

*119-3   Feasibility of serving the Coachella Valley County Water District from the state water facilities. 1963. 94 p.

*119-4   Feasibility of serving the Palmdale Irrigation District and the Pearland area from the state water facilities. 1963. 56 p.

*119-5   Feasibility of serving the Solano County Flood Control and Water Conservation District from the State Water Project. 1964. 88 p.

119-6   Feasibility of serving the San Gabriel Valley Municipal Water District from the State Water Project. 1964. 54 p. Price: $1.00.

*119-7   Feasibility of serving the San Luis Obispo County Flood Control and Water Conservation District from the state water facilities. 1963. 40 p.

119-8   Feasibility of serving the Kern County Water Agency from the State Water Project. 1963. 61 p. Price: $2.00.

*119-9   Feasibility of serving the Napa County Flood Control and Water Conservation District from the State Water Project. 1965. 63 p.

119-10   Feasibility of serving the Hacienda Water District from the State Water Project. 1964. 47 p. Price: $2.00.

119-11   Feasibility of serving the Tulare Lake Basin Water Storage District from the State Water Project. 1965. 40 p. Price: $0.75.

119-12   Feasibility of serving the Mojave Water Agency from the State Water Project. 1965. 77 p. Price: $1.25.

119-13   Feasibility of serving the Devil's Den Water District from the State Water Project. 1965. 40 p. Price: $0.75.

*119-14 Feasibility of serving the Dudley Ridge Water District from the State Water Project. 1964. 44 p.

119-15   Feasibility of serving the Oak Flat Water District from the State Water Project. 1965. 38 p. Price: $0.75.

119-16   Feasibility of serving the Plumas County Flood Control and Water Conservation District from the State Water Project. 1965. 35 p. Price: $0.75.

*119-17 Feasibility of serving the Ventura County Flood Control District from the State Water Project. 1965. 56 p.

*119-18 Feasibility of serving the Upper Santa Clara Valley Water Agency from the State Water Project. 1964. 58 p.

119-19   Feasibility of serving the Crestline-Lake Arrowhead Water Agency area from the State Water Project. 1965. 52 p. Price: $1.25.

119-20   Feasibility of serving the Littlerock Creek Irrigation District from the State Water Project. 1965. 64 p. Price: $1.00.

*119-21   Feasibility of serving the Santa Barbara County Flood Control and Water Conservation District from the state water facilities. 1963. 44 p.

119-22   Feasibility of serving the city of Yuba City from the State Water Project. 1964. 50 p. Price: $0.75.

119-23   Feasibility of serving Butte County from the State Water Project. 1966. 52 p. Price: $0.75.

119-24   Not published.

119-25   Feasibility of serving the Empire West Side Irrigation District from the State Water Project. 1965. 42 p. Price: $0.75.

119-26   Not published.

119-27   Not published.

119-28   Feasibility of serving Kings County from the State Water Project. 1968. 31 p. Price: $0.50.

119-29   Feasibility of serving the South Bay contractors from the State Water Project. 1968. 31 p. Price: $0.50.

120-63 through 120-69   Water conditions in California. Issued in five numbers a year (February, March, April, May and October). First four issues in two parts: basic report and basic data supplement. Price: Free of charge.

121   Southern Lahontan area land and water use survey, 1961. 1965. 77 p. Price: $2.00.

122   Ventura County and Upper Santa Clara River drainage area land and water use survey, 1961. 1965. 100 p. Price: $1.75.

123   Delta and Suisun Bay water quality investigation. 1967. 166 p. Price: $2.00.

124   Water use by manufacturing industries in California 1957-59. 1964. 137 p. Price: $2.50.

125   Sacramento Valley seepage investigation. 1967. 128 p. Price: $4.50.

126   Fish Slough Dam and Reservoir, feasibility investigation. 1964. 63 p. Price: $2.50.

127   San Joaquin Master Drain: San Joaquin Valley drainage investigation. Preliminary edition. 1965. 50 p. Price: $1.00.

    *Appendix A: Proposed San Joaquin drainage Act. 1965. 40 p.

    Appendix D: Waste water quality, treatment and disposal. 1969. 64 p. Price: $1.50.

128   Lake Davis, advance planning report. 1965. 69 p. Price: $1.75.

*129   Snow survey measurements through 1964. 1965. 366 p.

130   Hydrologic data, 1963 — to date.

    The complete series to date is as follows:

130-63   (for the 1963 water year):

    Volume I: North Coastal area, May 1965. 112 p. 5 pls. Price: $1.50.

    Volume II: Northeastern California. Text and Appendices A, Climatology, and B, Surface water flow, April 1965. 394 p., 9 pls. Price: $5.25.

Appendix C: Ground water measurements, November 1964. 190 p., 13 pls. Price: $4.00.

Appendices D, Surface water quality, and E, Ground water quality, April 1965. 220 p., 6 pls. Price: $2.50.

Volume III: Central Coastal area, September 1965, 220 p., 7 pls. Price: $2.75.

Volume IV: San Joaquin Valley, May 1965. 368 p., 21 pls. Price: $5.00.

Volume V: Southern California. Text and Appendices A, Climatology, and B, Surface water flow, November 1965. 192 p., 14 pls. Price: $2.75.

Appendix C, Ground water measurements, July 1965.

Part 1, Central Coastal and Los Angeles drainage provinces, 544 p., 2 pls. Price: $5.75.

Part 2, Lahontan, Colorado River Basin, Santa Ana, and San Diego drainage provinces, 290 p., 4 pls. Price: $3.25.

Appendices D, Surface water quality, and E, Ground water quality, April 1965. 118 p., 2 pls. Price: $1.75.

130-64   (for the 1964 water year):

Volume I: North Coastal area, March 1966. 110 p., 2 pls. Price: $1.25.

Volume II: Northeastern California. Text and Appendices A, Climate, and B, Surface water flow, May 1966. 396 p., 9 pls. Price: $5.00.

Appendix C, Ground water measurements, September 1965. 172 p., 11 pls. Price: $3.50.

Appendices D, Surface water quality, and E, Ground water quality, June 1966. 230 p. Price: $2.50.

Volume III: Central Coastal area, June 1966. 232 p., 5 pls. Price: $3.00.

Volume IV: San Joaquin Valley, December 1965, 396 p., 19 pls. Price: $5.00.

Volume V: Southern California. Text and Appendices A, Climate, and B, Surface water flow, August 1966. 72 p., 7 pls. Price: $1.25.

Appendix C, Ground water measurements, July 1966.

Part 1, Central Coastal and Los Angeles drainage provinces, 492 p., 2 pls. Price: $5.00.

Part 2, Lahontan, Colorado River Basin, Santa Ana, and San Diego drainage provinces, 308 p., 4 pls. Price: $3.50.

130-65   (for the 1965 water year):

Volume I: North Coastal area, December 1966. 94 p., 1 pl. Price: $1.25.

Volume II: Northeastern California. Text and Appendix A, Climate, December 1966. 64 p., 3 pls. Price: $1.00.

Appendix B: Surface water flow, December 1966. 332 p., 6 pls. Price: $3.50.

Appendix C: Ground water measurements, December 1966. 142 p., 6 pls. Price: $2.00.

Appendices D, Surface water quality, and E, Ground water quality, December 1966. 196 p. Price: $2.50.

Volume III: Central Coastal area, July 1967. 256 p., 5 pls. Price: $3.00.

Volume IV: San Joaquin Valley, December 1966. 342 p., 16 pls. Price: $4.75.

Volume V: Southern California. Text and Appendices A, Climate, and B, Surface water flow, April 1967. 90 p., 7 pls. Price: $1.25.

Appendix C, Ground water measurements, April 1967. 485 p., 6 pls. Price: $5.25.

Appendix D, Surface water quality, December 1966. 192 p., 1 pl. Price: $2.00.

Appendix E, Ground water quality, December 1966. 572 p., 6 pls. Price: $5.25.

130-66   (for the 1966 water year):

Volume I: North Coastal area, January 1968. 118 p., 1 pl. Price: $1.50.

Volume II: Northeastern California. Appendix A, Climatological data, January 1968. 72 p., 3 pls. Price: $1.00.

Appendix B, Surface water flow, February 1968. 310 p., 6 pls. Price: $3.50.

Appendix C, Ground water measurements, December 1967. 140 p., 5 pls. Price: $2.25.

Appendices D, Surface water quality, and E, Ground water quality, December 1967. 160 p. Price: $1.75.

Volume III: Central Coastal area, May 1968. 206 p., 3 pls. Price: $2.50.

Volume IV: San Joaquin Valley, November 1967. 466 p., 4 pls. Price: $5.00.

Volume V: Southern California. Appendices A, Climatological data, B, Surface water measurements, and C, Ground water measurements, April 1968. 496 p. Price: $5.00.

Appendices D, Surface water quality, and E, Ground water quality, May 1968. 214 p. Price: $2.25.

130-67   (for the 1967 water year):

Volume I: North Coastal area, November 1968. 88 p. Price: $1.00.

Volume II: Northeastern California, May 1969. 678 p., 10 pls. Price: $10.00.

Volume III: Central Coastal area, June 1969. 230 p., 3 pls. Price: $3.00.

Volume IV: San Joaquin Valley, September 1968. 332 p., 4 pls. Price: $3.75.

Volume V: Southern California. Appendices A, Climatological data, B, Surface water measurements, and C, Ground water measurements, July 1969. 460 p. Price: $4.00.

Appendices D, Surface water quality, E, Ground water quality, and F, Waste water data, January 1969. 170 p., Price: $2.00.

130-68   (for the 1968 water year):

Volume I: North Coastal area, 1970. 73 p. Price: $2.00.

Volume II: Not yet published.

Volume III: Central Coastal area, Aug. 1970. 143 p. Price: $3.50.

Volume IV: San Joaquin Valley, Oct. 1969. 222 p. Price: $4.00.

Volume V: Southern California. Appendices A, Climatological data; B, Surface water measurements; and C, Ground water measurements, March 1970. 423 p. Price: $5.00.

Appendices D, Surface water quality; E, Ground water quality; and F, Waste water data, January 1970, 207 p. Price: $6.00.

131   Mariposa area investigation. Preliminary edition. 1965. 219 p. Price: $3.00.

Final supplement. Summary of Public Hearing comments and changes to the preliminary edition of Bulletin No. 131, dated November 1965. July 1967. 22 p. Price: $0.25.

*132-63   California State Water Project in 1963. April 1963. 306 p.

*Supplement A: Monthly Distribution of Annual Project Electric Power Requirements and Generation. September 1963. 108 p.

132-64   California State Water Project in 1964. June 1964. 438 p. Price: $6.00.

Appendix D: Financial Statements. June 1964.
Part I: 76 p. Price: Free of charge.
Part II: 40 p. Price: Free of charge.

Appendix E: Monthly Distribution of Annual Project Electric Power Requirements and Generation. August 1964. 86 p. Price: Free of charge.

132-65   California State Water Project in 1965. June 1965. 368 p. Price: $4.50.

Appendix C: State Water Project Statistics. November 1965. 46 p. Price: Free of charge.

132-66   California State Water Project in 1966. June 1966. 400 p. Price: $4.50.

Appendix C: Facility Descriptions. June 1966. 32 p. Price: Free of charge.

132-67   California State Water Project in 1967. June 1967. 334 p. Price: $3.50.

Appendix C: Development and Status. June 1967. 32 p. Price: Free of charge.

132-68   California State Water Project in 1968. June 1968. 368 p. Price: $4.25.

*Appendix C: Description and Status. October 1968. 32 p.

132-69   California State Water Project in 1969. June 1969. 268 p. Price: $3.50.

Appendix C: Description and Status. June 1969. 32 p. Price: Free of charge.

Appendix D: Costs of Recreation and Fish and Wildlife Enhancement. March 1969. 12 p. Price: Free of charge.

132-70 California State Water Project in 1970. June 1970. 234 p. Price: $5.00.

Appendix C: Summary 1969. 31 p. Price: Free of charge.

Appendix D: Costs of Recreation and Fish and Wildlife Enhancement. May 1970. 32 p. Price: Free of charge.

133 Folsom-East Sacramento ground water quality investigation. 1964. 156 p. Price: $4.00.

*134-62 Saline water conversion activities in California. 1963. 60 p.

134-69 Desalting – state of the art. 1969. 56 p. Price: $1.00.

*135 Madera Area investigation. Preliminary edition. 1966. 226 p.

135-1 Madera Area investigation. Progress report. 1964. 55 p. Price: $1.50.

136 North Coastal Area investigation. 1964. 182 p. Price: $2.00.

Appendix A: Watershed management in the Eel River Basin. 1964. 160 p. Price: $2.50.

Appendix B: Recreation. 1965. 282 p. Price: $3.50.

Appendix C: Fish and wildlife. 1965. 250 p. Price: $4.50.

Appendix D: (Printed in basic volume).

Appendix E: Engineering Geology. 1965. 2 vols. Price: $9.75.

Final supplement. 1966. 32 p. Price: $0.50.

137 Sacramento Valley East Side investigation. August 1967. 304 p. Price: $3.00.

Final supplement. 1969. 32 p. Price: $1.50.

*138 Coastal San Mateo County investigation. March 1966. 322 p.

139 Abbey Bridge Reservoir; advanced planning report. 1966. 63 p. Price: $1.00.

140 Water rights data and estimated entitlements to the flow of the Feather River. 1965. 289 p. Price: $5.25.

141 The California State Water Project, water supply contracts. 1965. 2 vol. Price: $13.50.

142-1 Water resources and future water requirements, North Coastal hydrographic area: Volume I: Southern portion. Preliminary edition. 1965. 482 p. Price: $5.00.

(Volume II will not be published).

143-1 San Lorenzo River Watershed water quality investigation. 1966. 198 p. Price: $2.50.

*143-2 Clear Lake water quality investigation. 1966. 202 p.

*143-3 Fresno-Clovis metropolitan area water quality investigation. 1965. 76 p.

143-4 Russian River watershed water quality investigation. 1968. 282 p. Price: $3.50.

143-5 Lower San Joaquin River water quality investigation. 1969. 207 p. Price: $3.50.

143-6 Delano nitrate investigation. 1968. 42 p. Price: $0.50.

143-7 Geothermal wastes and the water resources of the Salton Sea Area. 1970. 123 p. Price: $3.50.

144-68 Radiological Applications Program: Annual Report for Fiscal Year 1967-68. 1968. 64 p. Price: $0.75.

144-69 Radiological Applications Program: Annual Report for Fiscal Year 1968-69. 1969. 26 p. Price: $2.00.

*145 Agua Fria investigation. Feasibility study. 1964. 99 p.

146 San Joaquin County ground water investigation. 1967. 177 p. Price: $2.50.

147-1 Ground Water Basin Protection Projects: Santa Ana Gap Salinity Barrier, Orange County. (Final Edition). December 1966. 194 p. Price: $4.00.

147-2 Not published.

147-3 Not published.

147-4 Not published.

147-5 Sanitary Landfill Studies: Appendix A: Summary of Selected Previous Investigations. July 1969. 122 p. Price: $3.00.

147-6 Ground water basin protection projects: Oxnard basin experimental extraction-type barrier. September 1970. 157 p. Price: $3.00.

148 Not published.

*149-65 Project levee maintenance and repair: 1965 inspection report. May 1966. 86 p.

149-66 Project levee maintenance and repair: 1966 inspection report. March 1967. 102 p.

*149-67 Project levee maintenance and repair: 1967 inspection report. April 1968. 74 p.

149-68 Flood control project maintenance and repair: 1968 inspection report. July 1969. 16 p. Price: $1.00.

150 Upper Sacramento River basin investigation (Preliminary Edition). March 1965. 300 p. Price: $4.50.

150-1 Upper Sacramento River basin investigation. February 1969. 112 p. Price: $1.50.

151-65 Water progress in California, July 1, 1962–June 30, 1965. October 1965. 24 p. Price: Free of charge.

151-67 Water: A Progress Report. September 1968. 32 p. Price: Free of charge.

Progress reports in the 151 Series preceding 1962-65 were issued without Bulletin number. These are as follows:

Water: Key to California's Future (First Annual Progress Report). January 1958. 32 p. Price: Free of charge.

Water for California (Second Annual Progress Report). November 1958. 48 p. Price: Free of charge.

Water – White Gold of California (Biennial Progress Report). February 1961. 54 p. Price: Free of charge.

Water: Number One Resource of the Number One State (Biennial Progress Report). January 1963. 32 p. Price: Free of charge.

152 Ewing project. Feasibility study. 1965. 73 p. Price: $1.25.

153-66 Allocations of costs among purposes of the California State Water Project. January 1966. 82 p. Price: $1.00.

153-67 Allocations of costs among purposes of the California State Water Project. December 1966. 104 p. Price: $1.25.

153-68 Allocations of costs among purposes of the California State Water Project. February 1968. 74 p. Price: $1.00.

*154 Potential recreation areas along the California Aqueduct. 1965. 70 p.

154-66 Recreation areas along the California Aqueduct in the San Joaquin Valley. 1966. 30 p. Price: $0.50.

155 General comparison of California water district acts. 1965. 343 p. Price: $3.75.

156 Not published.

157 Not published.

158-66 Flood control funds: Biennial report to the Legislature, January 1, 1965–December 31, 1966. January 1967. 25 p. Price: Free of charge.

158-67 Flood control funds: 1967 report to the Legislature. January 1968. 16 p. Price: Free of charge.

158-68 Flood control funds: 1968 report to the Legislature. January 1969. 16 p. Price: Free of charge.

159-65 California flood control program, 1965. 1965. 178 p. Price: $2.00.

160-66 Implementation of the California Water Plan, 1966-67. 1966. 2 vols. Price: $5.50.

161 Flood! December 1964–January 1965. 1965. 48 p. Price: $2.50.

162 Box Canyon project; feasibility study. 1965. 110 p. Price: $2.00.

163 West Side Crop Adaptability Study. 1970. 83 p. Price: $3.00.

164 Tehachapi Crossing design studies. 1965-1968. Studies are as follows:

Book I: Tehachapi pump lift system, May 1965. 330 p. Price: $2.50.

Book II: Technical studies, May 1965. 496 p. Price: $5.00.

Book III: Investigations of high speed pumping practices in Europe and the United States, May 1965. 556 p. Price: $5.75.

Book IV: Program management, May 1965. 264 p. 12 pls. Price: $3.25.

Book V: Considerations relating to a single lift for the Tehachapi crossing, August 1965. 380 p. Price: $3.25.

Book VI: Contractors prequalification for furnishing and installing four-stage centrifugal pumps for the Tehachapi pumping plant, August 1968. 384 p. Price: $3.50.

165 Not published.

166-1 Municipal and industrial water use. 1968. 106 p. Price: $1.25.

167 Pilot Levee Maintenance Study; Sacramento-San Joaquin Delta. Preview edition. 1966. 31 p. Price: $0.50.

Another edition. 1967. 24 p. Price: $0.50.

168 Not published.

169 Southern Tuolumne County water resources development. 1968. 103 p. Price: $1.25.

170 Abstracts of Department of Water Resources Publications. Series is as follows:

Bulletin No.	Publication Date	Pages	Price
170-65	March 1966	32	Free
*170-66 I	September 1966	32	
170-66 II	March 1967	32	Free
170-67 I	September 1967	32	Free
170-67 II	April 1968	32	Free
170-68 I	September 1968	48	Free
170-68 II	March 1969	56	Free
170-79	July 1970	207	5.00

171 Upper Eel River development investigation of alternative conveyance routes. 1967. 75 p. Price: $1.00.

172 Eel River development alternatives. 1969. 36 p. Price: Free of charge.

Appendix: Supporting studies. January 1970. 120 p. Price: Free of charge.

173 South Fork Eel River study. Preliminary edition. 1968. 183 p. Price: $2.00.

Final supplement. 1969. 20 p. Price: Free of charge.

174-1 Bio-engineering aspects of agricultural drainage: the fate of pesticides applied to irrigated agricultural land. 1964. 52 p. Price: $0.50.

174-2 Bio-engineering aspects of agricultural drainage: San Joaquin Valley drainage investigation quality and treatment studies: progress report through December 31, 1967. 1968. 16 p. Price: $0.25.

174-3 Bio-engineering aspects of agricultural drainage: field evaluation of anaerobic denitrification in simulated deep ponds. May 1969. 32 p. Price: $1.00.

175   Not published.

176   Not published.

*177   Watermaster service in Northern California, for the period 1966-67, to date. Series is as follows:

Bulletin No.	Year Reported (October-September)	Publication Date	Pages
None	1958-1959	November 1961	156
None	1959-1960	January 1962	152
None	1960-1961	February 1963	120
None	1961-1962	November 1963	162
None	1962-1963	May 1964	164
None	1963-1964	August 1965	248
None	1964-1965	June 1966	240
None	1965-1966	June 1967	284
177-67	1966-1967	August 1968	206
177-68	1967-1968	August 1969	144

*178-69   Watermaster service in the Raymond Basin, Los Angeles County, for the period July 1, 1967 to date. Series is as follows:

Bulletin No.	Year Reported (July-June)	Publication Date	Pages
None	1944-1945	August 1945	52
None	1945-1946	August 1946	52
None	1946-1947	August 1947	54
None	1947-1948	August 1948	54
None	1948-1949	August 1949	60
None	1949-1950	August 1950	54
None	1950-1951	August 1951	60
None	1951-1952	August 1952	58
None	1952-1953	August 1953	58
None	1953-1954	August 1954	68
None	1954-1955	August 1955	80
None	1955-1956	August 1956	76
None	1956-1957	August 1957	84
None	1957-1958	August 1958	178
None	1958-1959	August 1959	140
None	1959-1960	August 1960	107
None	1960-1961	August 1961	115
None	1961-1962	August 1962	100
None	1962-1963	August 1963	98
None	1963-1964	August 1964	100
None	1964-1965	August 1965	100
None	1965-1966	August 1966	76
None	1966-1967	August 1967	70
178-68	1967-1968	August 1968	66
178-69	1968-1969	August 1969	66

*179   Watermaster service in the West Coast Basin, Los Angeles County, for the period October 1, 1967 to date. Series is as follows:

Bulletin No.	Year Reported	Publication Date	Pages
None	1955-1956	August 1956	62
None	1956-1957	August 1957	150
None	1957-1958	August 1958	126
None	1958-1959	August 1959	80
None	1959-1960	August 1960	94
None	1960-1961	August 1961	112
None	1961-1962	August 1962	50
None	1962-1963	December 1963	92
None	1963-1964	December 1964	86
None	1964-1965	December 1965	112
None	1965-1966	December 1966	142
None	1966-1967	December 1967	108
179-68	1967-1968	December 1968	96
179-68	1968-1969	December 1969	96

*180   Watermaster service in the Central Basin, Los Angeles County, for period October 1, 1967, to date. Series is as follows:

Bulletin No.	Year Reported (October-September)	Publication Date	Pages
None	1962-1963	December 1963	89
None	1963-1964	December 1964	102
None	1964-1965	December 1965	124
None	1965-1966	December 1966	156
None	1966-1967	January 1968	208
180-68	1967-1968	January 1969	146

181-69   Watermaster service in the Upper Los Angeles River area, Los Angeles County, for period October 1, 1968 through September 30, 1969. 1970. 75 p. Price: Free of charge.

CALIFORNIA DEPARTMENT OF WATER RESOURCES

Division of Resources Planning
1416 Ninth Street
Sacramento, California 95814

WATER QUALITY INVESTIGATIONS REPORTS

*1   Sea-water intrusion into ground water basins bordering the California coast and inland bays, by Harvey O. Banks, George B. Gleason and Raymond C. Richter. December 1950. 23 p.

*2   Flow and quality characteristics of the Russian River, report to North Coastal Regional Water Pollution Control Board, by Harvey O. Banks and Jack H. Lawrence. January 1951. 24 p.

*3   Ground water basins in California, by Raymond C. Richter and Elmer C. Marliave. November 1952. 44 p.

*4   Ground water occurrence and quality, Colorado River Basin region, by David B. Willets. May 1954. 59 p.

5 Never published.

6 Never published.

*7 Quality of groundwater in the Stockton area, San Joaquin County, by James March, James L. Welsh and Earl Molander. March 1955. 57 p.

8 Never published.

*9 Abstract of laws and recommendations concerning water well construction and sealing in the United States, by C. E. Plumb and James L. Welsh. April 1955. 391 p.

*10 Geology, hydrology and water quality of alluviated areas in Mendocino County and recommended standards of water well construction and sealing, by James L. Welsh and Donald H. Neudeck. June 1956. 211 p.

11 Never published.

12 Never published.

13 Never published.

*14 Groundwater quality monitoring program in California, by Carl B. Meyer. June 1956. 198 p.

*15 Quality of surface waters in California, 1951-54, by Carleton E. Plumb, Jack H. Lawrence, and Richard W. Kretsinger. November 1956. 519 p.

CALIFORNIA STATE WATER RESOURCES BOARD

Note: Organization succeeded by the California Department of Water Resources, 1416 Ninth Street, Sacramento, California 95814.

BULLETINS

*1 Water resources of California, by Carl B. Meyer. 1951. 648 p.

*2 Water utilization and requirements of California, by C. B. Meyer and W. L. Horn. June 1955. 2 vols. Vol I: Text. Vol. II: Appendices and plates.

3 The California water plan, by Albert J. Dolcini, Oswald Speir and others. May 1957. 245 p. Price: $5.00.

4 Never published.

*5 Santa Cruz-Monterey Counties investigation, by J. M. Haley. August 1953. 230 p.

*6 Sutter-Yuba Counties investigation, by J. M. Haley, September 1952. 174 p.

*7 Santa Clara Valley investigation, by J. M. Haley, June 1955. 154 p.

*8 Central Valley investigation: Lower Los Angeles and San Gabriel Rivers area, County of Los Angeles, by H. C. Kelly. March 1952. 32 p.

*9 Elsinore Basin investigation, by Wayne MacRostie and D. W. Sabiston. February 1953. 105 p.

10 Placer County investigation, by J. M. Haley. June 1955. 270 p. Price: $5.00.

*11 San Joaquin County investigation, by J. M. Haley. June 1955. 294 p.

*12 Ventura County investigation, by R. M. Edmonston. Revised April 1956. 2 vols.

13 Alameda County investigation, by M. Reed Wilson. March 1963. 196 p. Price: $5.00.

14 Lake County investigation, by T. M. Stetson. July 1957. 191 p. Price: $6.00.

15 Santa Ana River investigation, by Wayne MacRostie and A. J. Dolcini. February 1959. 207 p. Price: $7.50.

16 Weather modification operations in California, by R. R. Reynolds and E. P. Warren. June 1955. 271 p. Price: $3.00.

17 Klamath River Basin Investigation. (Published as Bulletin No. 83 of the California Department of Water Resources.)

18 San Luis Obispo County investigation, by Robert M. Edmonston and Lucian J. Meyers. May 1958. 2 vols. Vol. I (text). Price: $5.00. *Vol. II (appendices).

*19 Salinas River Basin investigation, by A. J. Dolcini and T. M. Stetson. March 1955. (Preliminary edition subject to revision). 225 p.

*20 Interim report Cache Creek investigation – Comparison of alternative Wilson Valley and Guinda Projects on Cache Creek, by M. Guy Fairchild and Frederick A. Maynard. April 1958. 81 p.

*21 American River Basin investigation – Report on development proposed for the California Water Plan, by Myer Samuel. June 1955. 2 vols.

22 Shasta County investigation. July 1964. 2 vols. Price: $11.00.

23 Never published.

*24 Los Angeles County land and water use survey, 1955, by Lucian J. Meyers and Robert H. Born. June 1956. 56 p.

CALIFORNIA STATE WATER RESOURCES CONTROL BOARD
1416 Ninth Street
Sacramento, California 95814

*1 Digest of sewerage enabling acts of the State of California. Sacramento, State Water Pollution Control Board, rev. 1955. 68 p.

*2 Report on the investigation of leaching of ash dumps. Sacramento, State Water Pollution Control Board, 1952. 100 p.

3-A Water quality criteria. Second edition, edited by Jack Edward McKee and Harold W. Wolf. Sacramento, State Water Quality Control Board, 1963. 548 p. Price: $6.85.

*4 Preliminary statement of objective and policy and report on water-quality evaluation. Sacramento, State Water Pollution Control Board, 1952. 9 p.

*5   Water pollution control progress report for 1950 through 1952. Sacramento, California State and Regional Water Pollution Control Boards, 1952. 55 p.

*6   Field investigation of waste water reclamation in relation to ground water pollution. Sacramento, State Water Pollution Control Board, 1953. 124 p.

*7   Report on a systematic study of the algae of sewage oxidation ponds by Paul C. Silva and George F. Papenfuss. Sacramento, State Water Pollution Control Board, 1953. 35 p.

*8   Map of California water pollution control regions. Sacramento, State Water Pollution Control Board, 1954. 1 folding sheet.

*9   Studies of waste water reclamation and utilization by A. F. Bush and S. F. Mulford. Sacramento, State Water Pollution Control Board, 1954. 82 p.

10   Final report on the investigation of leaching of a sanitary landfill. Sacramento, State Water Pollution Control Board, 1954. 91 p. Price: $1.75.

*11 Report on the investigation of travel of pollution. Sacramento, State Water Pollution Control Board, 1954. 218 p.

12   A survey of direct utilization of waste waters. Sacramento, State Water Pollution Control Board, 1955. 80 p. Price: $1.65.

*13 General features of algal growth in sewage oxidation ponds by M. B. Allen. Sacramento, State Water Pollution Control Board, 1955. 46 p.

*14 An investigation of the efficiency of submarine outfall disposal of sewage and sludge by Erman A. Pearson. Sacramento, State Water Pollution Control Board, 1956. 154 p.

15   Report on continued study of waste water reclamation and utilization. Sacramento, State Water Pollution Control Board, 1956. 90 p. Price: $2.00.

16   Report on oily substances and their effects on the beneficial uses of water, by Jack Edward McKee. Sacramento, State Water Pollution Control Board, 1956. 71 p. Price: $1.65.

*17 Waste treatment and disposal aspects to development of California's pulp and paper resources. Sacramento, State Water Pollution Control Board, 1957. 102 p.

18   Third report on the study of waste water reclamation and utilization. Sacramento, State Water Pollution Control Board, 1957. 102 p. Price: $1.90.

19   Investigation of current measurement in estuarine and coastal waters, by J. W. Johnson and R. L. Wiegel. Sacramento, State Water Pollution Control Board, 1959. 233 p. Price: $2.25.

20   Oceanographic survey of the continental shelf area of Southern California. Sacramento, State Water Pollution Control Board, 1959. 560 p. Price: $4.25.

21   Determination of the quantity of oily substances on beaches and in nearshore water, Part I, by Sanitary Engineering Research Lab., University of So. Calif. Characterization of coastal oil pollution by submarine seeps, Part II, by A. A. Rosen, L. R. Musgrave and J. J. Lichtenberg. Sacramento State Water Pollution Control Board, 1959. 61 p. Price: $2.10.

22   Summary of marine waste disposal research program in California, by Erman A. Pearson, Richard D. Pomeroy and Jack E. McKee. Sacramento, State Water Pollution Control Board, 1960. 77 p. Price: $1.65.

23   Tracer studies and pollutional analyses of estuaries, by Robert E. Selleck and Erman A. Pearson. Sacramento, State Water Pollution Control Board, 1961. 139 p. Price: $1.65.

*24 Effects of refuse dumps on ground water quality. Sacramento, State Water Pollution Control Board, 1961. 107 p.

25   An oceanographic study between the points of Trinidad Head and the Eel River. Sacramento, State Water Quality Control Board, 1964. 135 p. Price: $2.90.

26   An investigation of the effects of discharged wastes on kelp. Sacramento, State Water Quality Control Board, 1964. 124 p. Price: $4.25.

27   An oceanographic and biological survey of the Southern California mainland shelf. Sacramento, State Water Quality Control Board, 1965. 232 p. Price: including Appendix 27a, $6.30.

28   Digest of sewerage enabling acts of the State of California. Sacramento, State Water Quality Control Board, 1964. 67 p. Price: $1.65.

29   An investigation on the fate of organic and inorganic wastes discharged into the marine environment and their effects on biological productivity. Sacramento, State Water Quality Control Board, 1965. 116 p. Price: $3.95.

30   Dispersion and persistence of synthetic detergents in ground water, San Bernardino and Riverside Counties. Sacramento, State Water Quality Control Board, 1965. 97 p. Price: $5.25.

31   In-situ investigation of movements of gases produced from decomposing refuse. Sacramento, State Water Quality Control Board, 1965. 211 p. Price: $4.25.

32   Microbiological content of domestic waste waters used for recreational purposes. Sacramento, State Water Quality Control Board, 1965. 50 p. Price: $2.15.

33   Wastewater reclamation at Whittier Narrows by Francis Clay McMichael and Jack Edward McKee. Sacramento, State Water Quality Control Board, 1966. 99 p. Price: $2.90.

34   Eutrophication – a review, by Kenton M. Stewart and Gerard A. Rohlich. Sacramento, State Water Quality Control, 1967. 188 p. Price: $2.90.

35   In-situ investigation of movements of gases produced from decomposing refuse. Sacramento, State Water Quality Control Board, 1967. 1 vol. (various pagings). Price: $2.80.

36   Problems of setting standards and of surveillance for water quality control, by Richard D. Pomeroy and Gerald T. Orlob. Sacramento, State Water Quality Control Board, 1967. 123 p. Price: $2.90.

37   Useful waters for California. Sacramento, State Water Quality Control Board, 1967. 72 p.

38   In-plant treatment of cannery wastes: a guide for cannery waste treatment, utilization and disposal. Sacramento, State Water Resources Control Board, 1968. 78 p.

39 Cannery waste treatment, utilization and disposal. Sacramento, State Water Resources Control Board, 1968. 395 p.

UNNUMBERED PUBLICATIONS

*Design of standard record system for water pollution control, a report prepared for the State Water Pollution Control Board by Brown and Caldwell, 1952. 47 p.

*A plan for the biological phases of the periodic stream sampling program, by Robert L. Usinger and Paul R. Heedham, State Department of Fish and Game, 1954.

*Engineering evaluation and development of bioassay kinetics, by John W. Klock and Erman A. Pearson, Sanitary Engineering Research Laboratory, University of California, Berkeley, 1961. 160 p.

An interagency system for water quality management, by Water Resources Engineers, Inc. 1962.

*Investigation to determine the quantity and quality of gases produced during refuse decomposition, by the Department of Civil Engineering, University of Southern California, Los Angeles, 1964.

Collation, evaluation, and presentation of scientific and technical data relative to the marine disposal of liquid wastes, by Engineering-Science Inc., Arcadia, California, 1964.

*Physical and chemical characterization of the fresh water intake, separate in-plant waste streams, and composite waste flows originating in a cannery processing peaches and tomatoes, by the National Canners Association Research Foundation Division, Berkeley, California. 1965.

A study of detergents in California; the effects of synthetic detergent residuals in waters of the state, by the State Water Quality Control Board, the State Department of Water Resources, and the State Department of Public Health, 1965. 55 p.

*A reconnaissance study and preliminary report on a water quality control plan for Salton Sea, by Richard D. Pomeroy and Henry Cruse, Pasadena, California, 1965.

WATER RESOURCES CENTER
University of California
Los Angeles, California 90024

The following is a list of the publications issued under sponsorship of the Water Resources Center. These reports, unless otherwise indicated, are distributed by the Water Resources Center, University of California, Los Angeles, California, 90024. Loan copies of reports out of print can be made available.

CONTRIBUTIONS

1 Conference on sediment problems in California, Berkeley, California, November 26-27, 1956. Proceedings, edited by Hans A. Einstein and Joe W. Johnson. Univ. of Calif. Committee on Research in Water Resources. [1956]. 142 p.

2 Conference on the California groundwater situation, Berkeley, California, December 3-4, 1956. Proceedings, edited by David K. Todd and Frank B. Clendenen. Univ. of Calif. Committee on Research in Water Resources. [1956]. 212 p.

3 Conference on industrial uses of water in California, Los Angeles, California, December 10-11, 1956. Proceedings, edited by Edward H. Taylor and Martin R. Huberty. Univ. of Calif. Committee on Research in Water Resources. [1957]. 129 p.

*4 Conference on recreational use of impounded water, Richmond, California, December 13-14, 1956. Proceedings. Univ. of Calif. Committee on Research in Water Resources. [1956]. 115 p.

5 Conference on new research methods in hydrology, Scripps Institution of Oceanography, La Jolla, California, February 2-3, 1957. Proceedings, edited by Harmon Craig. Univ. of Calif. Committee on Research in Water Resources. [1957]. 37 p.

6 Conference on geological engineering problems of water in California, Berkeley, California, March 18-19, 1957. Proceedings, edited by Parker D. Trask. Univ. of Calif. Committee on Research in Water Resources. [1957]. 162 p.

7 Conference on water spreading for ground-water recharge, Davis, California, March 19, 1957. Proceedings, edited by Leonard Schiff. Univ. of Calif. Committee on Research in Water Resources. [1957]. 80 p.

8 Conference on recent research in climatology, Scripps Institution of Oceanography, La Jolla, California, March 25-26, 1957. Proceedings, edited by Harmon Craig. Univ. of Calif. Committee on Research in Water Resources. [1957]. 121 p.

9 Conference on legal problems in water resources, Berkeley, California, May 15, 16 and 17, 1957. Proceedings, edited by Leland O. Graham. Univ. of Calif. Committee on Research in Water Resources. 1957. 262 p. (Published in *California Law Review*, vol. 45, no. 5, Dec. 1957. Available in this form for $2.00 from the School of Law, Univ. of Calif., Berkeley.)

10 Conference on water resources research in the University of California. Ambassador Hotel, Los Angeles, California, June 28, 1957. Proceedings, edited by Edward H. Taylor and Martin R. Huberty. Univ. of Calif. Water Resources Center. [1957]. 78 p.

*11 Conference on economics of California's water development, Lake Arrowhead, California, August 12, 13, 1957. Proceedings, edited by S. V. Ciriacy-Wantrup and Stephen C. Smith. Univ. of Calif. Committee on Research in Water Resources. 1958. 180 p.

*12 Recent and current research in water resources, University of California. Univ. of Calif. Committee on Research in Water Resources. 1957. 90 p.

*13 Economic evaluation of water, Part I: A search for criteria, by P. H. McGauhey and Harry Erlich. Berkeley, Univ. of Calif. Sanitary Engineering Research Laboratory. 1957. 237 p.

14 Conference on quality of water for irrigation, Davis, California, January 21-22, 1958. Proceedings, edited by Lloyd D. Doneen, Univ. of Calif. Committee on Research in Water Resources. [1958]. 206 p.

15 Drainage problems in the San Joaquin Valley, by Lorne G. Wilson, James N. Luthin, Frank B. Clendenen, Martin

R. Huberty, and Arthur F. Pillsbury. Univ. of Calif. Water Resources Center. [1958]. 137 p.

*16 Water resources reports and data in the Bernard A. Etcheverry collection. Compiled by Morill G. Folsom and Wilma J. Woodward. Berkeley, Univ. of Calif. Water Resources Center Archives. 1958. 107 p.
(Also appeared in the series Water Resources Center Archives, Report no. 1).

*17 Engineering, economic, social and legal aspects of water: theses presented for higher degrees, University of California ... 1900-1957. Berkeley, Univ. of Calif. Water Resources Center Archives. 1958. 73 p.
(Also appeared in the series Water Resources Center Archives, Report no. 2.)

18 Report on suggestions for research in water resources. Univ. of Calif. Water Resources Center. 1958. 48 p.

19 Eddy diffusion in open channel flow, by Gerald T. Orlob. Berkeley, Univ. of Calif., Sanitary Engineering Research Laboratory. 1958. 144 p.

20 River seepage investigation, by David K. Todd and Jacob Bear. Berkeley, Univ. of Calif. Hydraulics Laboratory. 1959. 163 p.

21 Measurement of helium on ground water tracing, by Ralf C. Carter, David K. Todd, Gerald T. Orlob and Warren J. Kaufman. Berkeley, Univ. of Calif. Sanitary Engineering Research Laboratory. 1959. 56 p.

*22 Waste water reclamation through production of algae, by William J. Oswald, Clarence G. Golueke and Henry K. Gee. Berkeley, Univ. of Calif. Sanitary Engineering Research Laboratory. 1959. 89 p.

23 Vortex theory for multiple phase flow through porous media, by G. de Josselin de Jong. Berkeley, Univ. of Calif. Hydraulic Laboratory. 1959. 80 p.
(Published in Journal of Geophysical Research, vol. 65, no. 11, Nov. 1960.)

24 Flood control analogs, by James A. Harder, Lyle Mockros and Ray Nishizaki. Berkeley, Univ. of Calif. Hydraulic Laboratory. 1960. 40 p.

*25 Series staging of vapor compression distillation, by John T. Chambers and Paul S. Larsen. Berkeley, Univ. of Calif. Institute of Engineering Research. Sea Water Conversion Program. 1960. 39 p.

*26 Current and potential methods for demineralizing water, by Everett D. Howe. Berkeley, Univ. of Calif. Institute of Engineering Research. Sea Water Conversion Program. 1960. 13 p.

*27 Ionite membranes and their characteristics, by V. A. Klachko, translated by Andre Kusubov. Berkeley, Univ. of Calif. Institute of Engineering Research. Sea Water Conversion Program. 1960. 34 p.

*28 Progress report, ending June 1960. Berkeley, Univ. of Calif. Institute of Engineering Research. Sea Water Conversion Program. 1960. 29 p.

29 The transition zone between fresh and salt waters in coastal aquifers, by Jacob Bear and David K. Todd. Berkeley, Univ. of Calif. Hydraulics Laboratory. 1960. 156 p.
(Theoretical aspects of this report were published in the Journal of Geophysical Research, April and August, 1961.)

*30 Thermodynamic and economic considerations in the preparation of fresh water from the sea, by Myron Tribus (and others). Los Angeles, Univ. of Calif. Dept. of Engineering. 1960.

31 Directional permeability in anisotropic porous media, by H. Marcus and D. E. Evenson. Berkeley, Univ. of Calif. Hydraulics Laboratory. 1961. 105 p.

32 Saline water research: Progress summary. Los Angeles, Univ. of Calif. Dept. of Engineering. 1960. 103 p.

33 A study on meandering and other bed patterns in straight alluvial channels, by Hsieh Wen Shen. Berkeley, Univ. of Calif. Hydraulics Laboratory. 1961. 68 p.

34 Sea water demineralization by means of a semipermeable membrane, by S. Loeb and S. Sourirajan. Los Angeles, Univ. of Calif. Dept. of Engineering. 1960. 35 p.
(Also available from Engineering Research, Univ. of Calif., Los Angeles.)

*35 Transient behavior of the electrical double-layer of stressed metals in electrolytes, by Ken Nobe. Los Angeles, Univ. of Calif. Dept. of Engineering. 1961. 22 p.

*36 Sea water demineralization by means of a semipermeable membrane, progress report, July 1, 1960 to December 31, 1960, by S. Loeb. Los Angeles, Univ. of Calif. Dept. of Engineering. 1961. 45 p.

37 Saline water demineralization — A review and bibliography, by J. W. McCutchan. Los Angeles, Univ. of Calif. Dept. of Engineering. 1961. 94 p.
(Also available from Engineering Research, Univ. of Calif., Los Angeles.)

38 Saline water research, June 1961, progress summary. Los Angeles, Univ. of Calif. Dept. of Engineering. 1961. 56 p.
(Also available from Engineering Research, Univ. of Calif., Los Angeles.)

*39 Sea water conversion research program. Berkeley progress report for the year ending June 30, 1961. Berkeley, Univ. of Calif. Institute of Engineering Research. 1961. 32 p.

40 Nonlinear analysis of hydrologic systems, by J. Amorocho and G. T. Orlob. Berkeley, Univ. of Calif. Sanitary Engineering Research Laboratory. 1962. 147 p.

41 An evaluation of the inflow-runoff relationships in hydrologic studies, by J. Amorocho and G. T. Orlob. Berkeley, Univ. of Calif. Sanitary Engineering Research Laboratory. 1961. 61 p.

*42 Economic evaluation of water, Part II: Jurisdictional considerations in water resources management, by Harry Erlich and P. H. McGauhey. Berkeley, Univ. of Calif. Sanitary Engineering Research Laboratory. 1964. 377 p.

43 Studies of liquid film flow and evaporation with reference to saline water distillation, by Walter Unterberg. Los Angeles, Univ. of Calif. Dept. of Engineering. 1961. 84 p.

44 Determination of coefficients for thermodynamic equations for determining the properties of sea water, particularly vapor pressure, by Charles Gastaldo. Los Angeles, Univ. of Calif. Dept. of Engineering. 1962. 149 p.

*45 Condensing heat transfer in steam-air mixtures in turbulent flow, by Paul B. Stewart, Benigno Loya, James L. Clayton and Donald R. Burnett. Berkeley, Univ. of Calif. Institute of Engineering Research. Sea Water Conversion Program. 1961. 33 p.

*46 Performance of greenhouse solar stills, by Lester H. MacLeod and Horace W. McCracken. Berkeley, Univ. of Calif. Institute of Engineering Research. Sea Water Conversion Program. 1961. 57 p.

*47 Correlation of the effects of temperature, geometry, and heat capacity on the performance of a single-effect solar distiller, by Lester H. MacLeod and Horace W. McCracken. Berkeley, Univ. of Calif. Institute of Engineering Research. Sea Water Conversion Program. 1961. 26 p.

48 Hydraulics of artificial recharge in non-homogeneous formations, by Keith Marmion. Berkeley, Univ. of Calif. Hydraulic Laboratory. 1962. 88 p.

*49 Effect of stress on the electrode potential of silver, steel and brass in aqueous solutions, by Ken Nobe and Swie-In Tan. Los Angeles, Univ. of Calif. Dept. of Engineering. 1962. 31 p.

50 Quality of percolating waters: No. 1, Development of a computer program for calculating the ionic composition of percolating waters, by Gordon Dutt. Davis, Univ. of Calif., [n.d.] 35 p.

*51 Salt water demineralization with a modified aquafresh electrodialytic stack by Pascal M. Rapier, Susan Weiner and Walter K. Baker. Berkeley, Univ. of Calif. Institute of Engineering Research. Sea Water Conversion Program. 1962. 24 p.

52 Sea water demineralization by means of a semipermeable membrane. Progress report, Jan. 1, 1961 – June 30, 1961, by S. Loeb. Los Angeles, Univ. of Calif. Dept. of Engineering. 1962. 31 p.

53 Seepage of saline water in Delta lowlands, by Hendrikus Marcus, Donald E. Evenson and David K. Todd. Berkeley, Univ. of Calif. Hydraulics Laboratory. 1962. 70 p.

54 Saline water research: June 1962 progress summary. Los Angeles, Univ. of Calif. Dept. of Engineering. 1962. 71 p. (Also available from Engineering Research, Univ. of Calif., Los Angeles.)

55 Effect of illumination on the electrode potential of copper and silver single crystals in aqueous solutions, by Ken Nobe and D. A. Chance. Los Angeles, Univ. of Calif. Dept. of Engineering. 1962. 33 p.

56 A contribution to the theory of thermo-economics, by Robert Evans. Los Angeles, Univ. of Calif. Dept. of Engineering. 1962. 125 p. (Also available from Engineering Research, Univ. of Calif., Los Angeles.)

*57 Effect of monochromatic illumination on the electrode potential of copper and tin in aqueous solutions, by H. A. Arbit and K. Nobe. Los Angeles, Univ. of Calif. Dept. of Engineering. 1962. 55 p.

58 Sea water demineralization by means of a semi-permeable membrane. Progress report July 1, 1961 – December 31, 1961, by S. Loeb. Los Angeles, Univ. of Calif. Dept. of Engineering. 1962. 29 p. (Also available from Engineering Research, Univ. of Calif., Los Angeles.)

*59 Saline water demineralization by electrodialysis with components manufactured by Ionics, Inc., by Pascal M. Rapier, Walter K. Baker and Susan W. Weiner. Berkeley, Univ. of Calif. Institute of Engineering Research. Sea Water Conversion Program. 1962. 29 p.

60 Sea water conversion program. Berkeley progress report for the year ending June 30, 1962. Berkeley, Univ. of Calif. Sea Water Conversion Program. 1962. 42 p. (Available from Sea Water Conversion Laboratory, Univ. of Calif., Berkeley.)

61 The thermo-economics of sea-water conversion, by Myron Tribus and Robert Evans. Los Angeles, Univ. of Calif. Dept. of Engineering. 1963. 241 p. (Also available from Engineering Research, Univ. of Calif., Los Angeles.)

62 Condensation coefficient of water, by Khosrow Nabavian and LeRoy A. Bromley. Berkeley, Univ. of Calif. Dept. of Chemical Engineering. Sea Water Conversion Program. 1962. 23 p. (Available from Sea Water Conversion Laboratory, Univ. of Calif., Berkeley.)

63 Design, development, and testing of a 500 gallon per day osmotic sea water desalination cell, by S. Loeb and F. Milstein. Univ. of Calif., Dept. of Engineering, Los Angeles. 1962. 63 p.

*64 The optimum temperature for the operation of nonsealing multi-stage flash evaporator plant, by Lester H. MacLeod, Abraham Gendel, Ahemd F. El Sahrigi. Berkeley, Univ. of Calif. Sea Water Conversion Laboratory. 42 p.

*65 Removal of scale-forming constituents from saline water by ion exchange-equilibrium conditions, by Gerhard Klein, Milagros Villena and Theodore Vermeulen. Berkeley, Univ. of Calif. Sea Water Conversion Laboratory. 1963. 66 p.

*66 Sea water demineralization by means of a semi-permeable membrane. Progress report January 1, 1962 – June 30, 1962, by S. Loeb. Los Angeles, Univ. of Calif. Dept. of Engineering. 1962. 26 p.

67 Economic evaluation of water, Part III: An interindustry analysis of the California water economy, by E. M. Lofting and P. H. McGauhey. Berkeley, Univ. of Calif. 1963. 83 p. (Also available from the Sanitary Engineering Research Laboratory, Univ. of Calif., Berkeley.)

68 The Lost River system: a water quality management investigation, by Phillip C. Woods and Gerald T. Orlob. Berkeley, Univ. of Calif. 1963. 54 p. (Also available from the Sanitary Engineering Research Laboratory, Univ. of Calif., Berkeley.)

*69 Saline water conversion research: Berkeley progress report for the six-month period ending December 31, 1962. Berkeley, Univ. of Calif. Sea Water Conversion Laboratory. 1963.

*70 Experimental study of some basic parameters in electrodialysis, by Pascal M. Rapier, Susan A. Weiner and Walter K. Baker. Berkeley, Univ. of Calif. Sea Water Conversion Laboratory. 1963. 43 p.

*71 Condensing heat transfer in steam-air mixtures in turbulent flow – Reynolds number relationships, by Paul B. Stewart and Stanley E. Hurd. Berkeley, Univ. of Calif. Sea Water Conversion Laboratory. 1963. 43 p.

72 Investigation of the hydraulics of flow near recharge wells, by Fereidoun Mobasheri and David K. Todd. Berkeley, Univ. of Calif. 1963. 32 p.

*73 Saline water research: progress summary, July 1, 1962 – December 31, 1962. Los Angeles, Univ. of Calif. Dept. of Engineering. 1963. 71 p.

*74 Brackish water desalination by an osmotic membrane: progress report October 1962 – December 1962, by

S. Loeb and S. Manjikian. Los Angeles, Univ. of Calif. Dept. of Engineering. 1963. 11 p.

*75 Aqueous oxygen corrosion of iron. Transient and steady state galvanostatic phenomena in H_2SO_4, by F. M. Donahue and K. Nobe. Los Angeles, Univ. of Calif. Dept. of Engineering. 1963. 43 p.

76 Specific yield of unconsolidated alluvium, by Franklin A. Preuss and David K. Todd. Berkeley, Univ. of Calif. 1963. 22 p.

77 Sea water demineralization by means of a semi-permeable membrane; progress report July 1, 1962 – December 1962, by S. Loeb. Los Angeles, Univ. of Calif. Dept. of Engineering. 1963. 28 p.

78 Brackish water desalination by an osmotic membrane; progress report December 1962 – March 1963, by S. Loeb and S. Manjikian. Los Angeles, Univ. of Calif. Dept. of Engineering. 1963. 24 p.
(Also available from Engineering Research, Univ. of Calif., Los Angeles.)

*79 Sea water evaporation by direct contact heat transfer, by C. R. Wilke, C. T. Cheng, V. L. Ledesma and J. W. Porter. Berkeley, Univ. of Calif. Sea Water Conversion Laboratory. 1963. 34 p.

80 Electrochemical and surface studies of Zn and InSb single crystals, by D. Chance and K. Nobe. Los Angeles, Univ. of Calif. Dept. of Engineering. 1963. 79 p.
(Also available from Engineering Research, Univ. of Calif., Los Angeles.)

81 The use of thin, capillarity controlled, gaseous diffusion gaps in saline water demineralization, by Thomas Thorsen. Los Angeles, Univ. of Calif. Dept. of Engineering. 1963. 105 p.
(Also available from Engineering Research, Univ. of Calif., Los Angeles.)

82 Preliminary economic study U.C.L.A. reverse osmosis process for brackish water desalination, by J. W. McCutchan, S. Loeb, P. A. Buckingham and A. W. Ayers. Los Angeles, Univ. of Calif. Dept. of Engineering. 1963. 60 p.
(Also available from Engineering Research, Univ. of Calif., Los Angeles).

83 Saline water research, progress summary January 1, 1963 – December 31, 1963. Los Angeles, Univ. of Calif. Dept. of Engineering. 1964. 63 p.
(Also available from Engineering Research, Univ. of Calif., Los Angeles.)

84 Scale formation in saline water evaporators; progress report January 1 – December 31, 1963, by J. W. McCutchan and J. Glater. Los Angeles, Univ. of Calif. Dept. of Engineering. 1964. 72 p.
(Also available from Engineering Research, Univ. of Calif., Los Angeles.)

*85 Saline water research: 1963 progress report Berkeley and San Diego campuses. Berkeley, Univ. of Calif. Sea Water Conversion Laboratory. 1964. 55 p.
(Microfilm copies available for purchase from the Library Photographic Service, Univ. of Calif., Berkeley.)

86 Thermophysical properties of aqueous sodium chloride solutions, by Walter Unterberg. Los Angeles, Univ. of Calif. Dept. of Engineering. 1964. 41 p.
(Also available from Engineering Research, Univ. of Calif., Los Angeles.)

87 Review and analysis of evaporation from falling and wiped saline water films, by Walter Unterberg, D. K. Edwards. Los Angeles, Univ. of Calif. Dept. of Engineering. 1964. 140 p.
(Also available from Engineering Research, Univ. of Calif., Los Angeles.)

88 Study of criteria for the semipermeability of cellulose acetate membranes to aqueous solutions, by Rodney Blunk. Los Angeles, Univ. of Calif. Dept. of Engineering. 1964. 72 p.
(Also available from Engineering Research, Univ. of Calif., Los Angeles.)

89 Electrodialytic treatment of irrigation drainage water, preliminary study, by W. K. Baker, S. A. Weiner and E. D. Howe. Berkeley, Univ. of Calif. Sea Water Conversion Laboratory. 1964. 34 p.

90 Sea water entrainment in low temperature flash evaporators, by E. I. Ewoldsen, P. Dattani, A. F. Mills and E. M. Stocking. Berkeley, Univ. of Calif. Sea Water Conversion Laboratory. 1964. 42 p.
(Available from Sea Water Conversion Laboratory, Univ. of Calif., Berkeley.)

91 Evaporation experiments with wiped and falling saline water films, by R. Webb., W. Unterberg and W. Gregson, Jr. Los Angeles, Univ. of Calif. Dept. of Engineering. 1964. 137 p.
(Also available from Engineering Research, Univ. of Calif., Los Angeles.)

92 Field tests on osmotic desalination membranes by S. Loeb and S. Manjikian. Los Angeles, Univ. of Calif. Dept. of Engineering. 1964. 28 p.
(Also available from Engineering Research, Univ. of Calif., Los Angeles.)

93 Determination of aquifer permeability by slug tests of wells, by Kuo-Toh and David K. Todd. Berkeley, Univ. of Calif., Hydraulics Laboratory. 1964. 41 p.

94 Saline water research: 1964 progress report, Berkeley and San Diego campuses. Berkeley, Univ. of Calif. Sea Water Conversion Laboratory. 1965. 51 p.
(Available from Sea Water Conversion Laboratory, Univ. of Calif., Berkeley.)

95 Saline water research progress summary, Jan. – Dec. 1964. Los Angeles, Univ. of Calif. Dept. of Engineering. 1965. 78 p.
(Also available from Engineering Research, Univ. of Calif., Los Angeles.)

96 Appropriate electrolytic additives in cellulose acetate casting solutions for reverse osmosis desalination membranes, by Sidney Loeb. Los Angeles, Univ. of Calif. Dept. of Engineering. 1965. 178 p.
(Also available from Engineering Research, Univ. of Calif., Los Angeles.)

97 Tile drainage in the San Joaquin Valley of California, by Arthur F. Pillsbury and William R. Johnston. Los Angeles, Univ. of Calif. Dept. of Irrigation and Soil Science. 1965. 245 p.

98 Saline-water softening by fixed-bed ion exchange, equilibrium-stage computation method for multicomponent systems, by Punit J. Pandya, Gerhard Klein and Theodore Vermeulen. Berkeley, Univ. of Calif. Sea Water Conversion Laboratory. 1965. 40 p.
(Available from Sea Water Conversion Laboratory, Univ. of Calif., Berkeley.)

99   Condensation on and evaporation from radially grooved
      rotating disks, by L. A. Bromley, R. F. Humphreys, and
      William Murray. Berkeley, Univ. of Calif. Sea Water
      Conversion Laboratory, 1965. 25 p.
      (Available from Sea Water Conversion Laboratory, Univ.
      of Calif., Berkeley.)

*100 Multiple-effect rotating evaporator, by LeRoy A. Bromley.
      Berkeley, Univ. of Calif. Sea Water Conversion Labora-
      tory. 1965. 111 p.

101   Semipermeable desalination membranes from organic
      casting solutions, by S. Manjikian. Los Angeles, Univ.
      of Calif., Dept. of Engineering. 1965. 41 p.
      (Also available from Engineering Research, Univ. of
      Calif., Los Angeles.)

102   Corrosion studies, Parts I and II, by Francis M. Donahue
      and Ken Nobe. Los Angeles, Univ. of Calif. Dept. of
      Engineering. 1965. 19 p.

103   Turbulent flow through porous media, by Daniel K.
      Sunada. Berkeley, Univ. of Calif. Hydraulic Laboratory.
      1965. 47 p.

104   The polarization and selective transport characteristics
      of perselective membranes, by Susan A. Weiner. Berke-
      ley, Univ. of Calif. Sea Water Conversion Laboratory.
      1965. 25 p.
      (Available from Sea Water Conversion Laboratory, Univ.
      of Calif., Berkeley.)

105   Nocturnal production of solar distillers, by Badawi W.
      Thieimat and Everett D. Howe. Berkeley, Univ. of Calif.
      Sea Water Conversion Laboratory. 1965. 19 p.
      (Available from Sea Water Conversion Laboratory, Univ.
      of Calif., Berkeley.)

*106 Lateral movement of water through the unsaturated zone
      of an unconfined aquifer, by F. Mobasheri, M. Shahbazi
      and David K. Todd. Berkeley, Univ. of Calif. Hydraulics
      Laboratory. 1965. 39 p.

107   The optimum use of a ground-water and surface water
      system: a parametric linear programming approach, by
      John A. Dracup. Berkeley, Univ. of Calif. Hydraulics
      Laboratory. 1966. 134 p.

108   Gradients in temperature and density across a vapor-liq-
      uid interface undergoing steady-state evaporation, by
      J. L. Dyer and R. L. Perrine. Los Angeles, Univ. of
      Calif. Dept. of Engineering. 1965. 59 p.

109   Corrosion studies, Part III – Anodic polarization of im-
      pure and higher purity nickel in H_2SO_4, by R. R. Sayano
      and Ken Nobe. Los Angeles, Univ. of Calif. Dept. of
      Engineering. 1965. 35 p.
      (Also available from Engineering Research, Univ. of
      Calif., Los Angeles.)

110   Corrosion studies, Part IV – Kinetics of uninhabited
      iron, by F. M. Donahue and Ken Nobe. Los Angeles,
      Univ. of Calif., Dept. of Engineering. 1965. 46 p.
      (Also available from Engineering Research, Univ. of
      Calif., Los Angeles.)

111   Corrosion studies, Part V – Kinetics of consecutive elec-
      trode reactions on iron, by F. M. Donahue and Ken
      Nobe. Los Angeles, Univ. of Calif., Dept. of Engineer-
      ing. 1965. 25 p.
      (Also available from Engineering Research, Univ. of
      Calif., Los Angeles.)

112   Corrosion studies, Part VI – Passivity of inconel in acid-
      ic chloride solutions, by E. P. Koutsoukos and Ken
      Nobe. Los Angeles, Univ. of Calif., Dept. of Engineer-

ing. 1965. 15 p.
(Also available from Engineering Research, Univ. of
Calif., Los Angeles.)

*113 Corrosion studies, Part VII – Corrosion inhibition of
      iron with aniline and substituted aniline compounds, by
      F. M. Donahue, A. Akiyama and Ken Nobe. Los An-
      geles, Univ. of Calif. Dept. of Engineering. 1965. 44 p.

*114 Theoretical analysis of groundwater basin operations, by
      William D. McMillan. Berkeley, Univ. of Calif. Hydrau-
      lics Laboratory. 1966. 167 p.

115   Corrosion studies, Part VIII – Corrosion kinetics of
      molybdenum in H_2SO_4, by L. L. Wikstrom and Ken
      Nobe. Part IX, Effect of chloride ions on the corrosion
      of nickel and niobium (Columbium), by D. L. Piron and
      Ken Nobe. Los Angeles, Univ. of Calif. Dept. of Engi-
      neering. 1966. 63 p., 30 p.
      (Also available from Engineering Research, Univ. of
      Calif., Los Angeles.)

*116 Economic evaluation of water, Part IV, an input-output
      and linear programming analysis of California water re-
      quirements, by E. M. Lofting and P. H. McGauhey.
      Berkeley, Univ. of Calif. Sanitary Engineering Research
      Laboratory and School of Public Health. 1968. 187 p.

117   Analytic techniques for determining ground water flow
      fields, by M. Shahbazi and D. K. Todd. Berkeley, Univ.
      of Calif. Hydraulics Laboratory. 1967. 139 p.

*118 The effect of loose blocks on the rate of sediment trans-
      port, by D. L. Aramayo. Berkeley, Univ. of Calif. Hy-
      draulics Laboratory. 1967. 39 p.

119   An investigation of meteorological conditions during a
      California rainfall period. I. A study of mid-tropospheric
      phenomena during a propagation of a Hovinoller im-
      pulse, by T. N. Krishnamurti. II. Tropospheric long-
      wave behavior during downstream amplification of
      troughs and ridges, by Lt. Bobby J. Higgins. Los An-
      geles, Univ. of Calif. Water Resources Center. 1967. 1
      v. (various pagings).

120   Cost, precision, and value relationships of data collection
      and design activities in water development planning, by
      Stephen V. Allison. Berkeley, Univ. of Calif. Hydraulics
      Laboratory. 1967. 142 p.

*121 Management of hydrologic systems for water quality
      control, by Philip C. Woods. Berkeley, Univ. of Calif.
      Sanitary Engineering Research Laboratory and School of
      Public Health. 1967. 121 p.

122   Optimum operations for planning of a complex wa-
      ter resources system [by] W. A. Hall and R. W. Shep-
      hard. Univ. of Calif. Water Resources Center. 1967.
      75 p.

*123 Identification of aquifer parameters by decomposition
      and multilevel optimization, by Y. Y. Haimes, P. L.
      Perrine, and D. A. Wismer. Los Angeles, Univ. of Calif.
      Dept. of Engineering. 1968. 53 p.

124   Analysis of transient fluid flow in multi-layered systems,
      by Iraj Javendel and Paul A. Witherspoon. Berkeley,
      Univ. of Calif. Dept. of Civil Engineering. 1968. 119 p.

125   Economic evaluation of water: Part V, multiregional in-
      put-output techniques and western water resources de-
      velopment, by H. Craig Davis. Berkeley, Univ. of Calif.
      Sanitary Engineering Research Laboratory. 1968.
      142 p.

126 Economic evaluation of water resources development project in a developing economy, by F. Mobasheri. Berkeley, Univ. of Calif. Hydraulics Laboratory. 1968. 191 p.

127 Mineral taste in domestic water; a technical report and record, by William H. Bruvold. Univ. of Calif. Water Resources Center. 1968. 128 p.

128 Economic evaluation of water; Part VI, a dynamic inter-regional input-output programming model of the California and Western States water economy, by Jona Bargur. Berkeley, Univ. of Calif. Sanitary Engineering Research Laboratory and School of Public Health, 1969. 116 p.

*129 Optimization of conjunctively managed surface and ground water resources by dynamic programming, by Gert Aron. Davis, Univ. of Calif., Dept. of Water Science and Engineering. 1969. 157 p.

130 Optimum firm power output from a two reservoir system by incremental dynamic programming, by Warren A. Hall, Ricardo C. Harboe, Wm. Yeh, and A. J. Askew. Los Angeles, Univ. of Calif., School of Engineering and Applied Science, Engineering Systems Department. 1969. 65 p.

131 Streamflow generating techniques: a comparison of their abilities to stimulate critical periods of drought, by Arthur J. Askew, Wm. W. G. Yeh, and Warren A. Hall. Los Angeles, Univ. of Calif. School of Engineering and Applied Science. 1970. 1 v. (various pagings).

132 A method of predicting pollutant transport in tidal waters, by Hugo B. Fischer. Berkeley, Univ. of Calif. Hydraulics Laboratory. 1970. 143 p.

133 Mechanized surface irrigation systems for rolling lands, by William E. Hart and John Borrelli. Davis, Univ. of Calif. Dept. of Water Science and Engineering. 1970. 93 p.

134 An annotated bibliography on the design of water resources systems, by Hani Asfur and William W-B. Yeh. Los Angeles, Univ. of Calif. School of Engineering and Applied Science. 1971. 85 p.

ARCHIVES SERIES

The following publications are available from the Water Resources Center Archives, University of California, Berkeley, California, 94720. (Numbers 1 and 2 also carried Contribution numbers 16 and 17.)

*1 Water resources reports and data in the Bernard A. Etcheverry collection. Compiled June 1958, by Morrill G. Folsom and Wilma J. Woodward. 107 p.

*2 Engineering, economic, social and legal aspects of water. Theses presented for higher degrees [Berkeley, Davis and Los Angeles] 1900-1957, by Emily O. Lumbard. 1958. 73 p.

*3 Watershed management research data, U. S. Department of Agriculture, Forest Service, California. Forest and Range Experiment Station, Berkeley and Glendora, California. Compiled by Morrill G. Folsom and Cynthia Barnes. 1959. 127 p.

*4 Publications and reports of Charles Gilman Hyde. Compiled by Gerald Giefer, Cynthia Barnes and Morrill G. Folsom. 1959. 38 p.

*5 Water pollution data. Regional Water Pollution Control Boards, State of California. Compiled by Gerald J. Giefer and Cynthia Barnes. 1959. 79 p.

*6 Bachelor of science theses on water resources engineering, University of California, Berkeley. Compiled by Gerald J. Giefer and Cynthia Barnes. 1959. 93 p.

*7 Theses on water resources, Stanford University, California Institute of Technology and University of Southern California. Compiled by Gerald J. Giefer, Lois Judd, and Cynthia Barnes. 1959. 81 p.

*8 The early Pacific Coast photographs of Carlton E. Watkins, by J. W. Johnson. 1960. 64 p.

*9 Water resources reports and data: Los Angeles County Flood Control District. 1960. 77 p.

*10 Reports and data in the water resources collection, Honnold Library, Claremont Colleges, Claremont, California. Compiled by Gerald J. Giefer and Cynthia Barnes. 1960. 66 p.

*11 A bibliography of the reports and publications of James Dix Schuyler, by Lois Judd. 1961. 60 p.

*12 Water resources reports by Walter LeRoy Huber: an annotated listing. Compiled by Lois Judd and Clare Bullitt. 1962. 103 p.

*13 Water wells, an annotated bibliography, by Gerald J. Giefer. 1963. 141 p.

*14 Index to periodical literature on aspects of water in California. Compiled by Cynthia Barnes and Gerald J. Giefer. 1963. 337 p.

*15 Bulletins and reports of California State water agencies. 1962. 157 p.

*16 Recent variations in the water supply of the Western Great Basin, by S. T. Harding. 1965. 226 p.

17 The flow of water in commercially smooth pipes: introducing a general formula, by Fred C. Scobey. 1966. 1 v. (various pagings).

*18 Water: a subject heading list. Compiled by Gerald J. Giefer and staff. 1967. 217 p.

19 Water: a classification scheme. Compiled by Gerald J. Giefer and staff. 1967. 88 p.

*20 Index to "Proceedings of the International Conference on Water for Peace, Washington, D.C., 1967." Compiled by Gerald J. Giefer and staff. 1969. 65 p.

21 Water resources reports and papers in the J. B. Lippincott collection. Compiled by Gerald J. Giefer and Anelle McCarty Kloski. 1970. 301 p.

22 Theses on water submitted to Universities in California through June 1969. Compiled by Mary Deane. 1971. 152 p.

REPORTS

The following reports are distributed by the Water Resources Center, University of California, Los Angeles, California, 90024. Where price is indicated, make checks payable to the Water Resources Center.

1 Water Resources Center Progress Report No. 1.

2 Proceedings of Conference on Water Research in the University of California, Davis, May 25-26, 1960. Edited by M. R. Huberty and Vincent Lawton.

3 Proceedings of Conference on Water Decisions in the Critical 60's, University of California, Davis, California, January 11-13, 1961. Edited by Robert M. Hagan and Vincent Lawton.

4 Proceedings of the Water Resources Economics Conference, 1963. Edited by Warren A. Hall.

5   Agricultural water quality research conference, August 12-14, 1963. Lake Arrowhead, California. Edited by O. R. Lunt. 1964.

6   Proceedings, [First] Western Interstate Conference, Las Vegas, Nevada, September 16-17, 1964. Edited by Warren A. Hall and M. A. Keller. Price: $1.50.

    Although not in numbered series, the proceedings of the second Western Interstate Water Conference, entitled "Strategies for Western Regional Water Development" have been published in book form. Price: $3.00 (paperbound), $4.00 (hardbound).

7   Water Resources Center Annual report, 1964.

8   Water Resources Center Annual Report, 1965.

9   Impact of water on land, proceedings of the San Joaquin Study Group Conference, Solvang, California, March 9-11, 1966. Edited by David K. Todd. 140 p.

10 Agricultural waste waters; proceedings, symposium on agricultural waste waters, Davis, California, April 6-8, 1966. Edited by L. D. Doneen. Los Angeles, University of California, Water Resources Center, 1966. 568 p. Price: $5.00.

11 Proceedings of a two day conference at University of California, Los Angeles, March 22-23, 1967; Man and his total environment. Sponsored by Environmental Systems and Resources Division, Dept. of Engineering, University of California, Los Angeles. 114 p.

12 Water Resources Center Annual report (1 Jan. 1966 – 30 June 1967).

13 Proceedings, Water pricing policy conference, University of California, Los Angeles, California, March 19, 1968. Edited by A. F. Pillsbury. 109 p. Price: $2.00.

14 Water Resources Center Annual report, 1 July 1967 – 30 June 1968. 160 p.

15 Proceedings of tile drainage research conference, held at Imperial Valley Field Station, University of California, El Centro, California ... 18 to 20 November 1968. Edited by Arthur F. Pillsbury. 1969. 59 p.

16 Proceedings: Water quality management symposium, University of California, Davis, California, June 9-10, 1969. Edited by Arthur F. Pillsbury. 148 p. Price: $3.00.

17 Water Resources Center Annual report (1 July 1968 – 30 June 1969), by A. F. Pillsbury. 143 p.

18 Proceedings, Seventh biennial conference on ground water, University of California, Los Angeles, September 10 and 11, 1969. 1970. 235 p. Price: $3.00.

19 Research on water quality. Edited by Ray Coppock. 1970. 36 p.

20 Information for the future: the West Side San Joaquin Valley Project. Edited by the Public Policy Research Organization, University of California, Irvine. 1970.

21 Water Resources Center Annual report (1 July 1969 – 30 June 1970). 203 p.

DESALINATION REPORT SERIES

1   1965 Progress report, Berkeley campus; Riverside campus; San Diego campus. Sea Water Conversion Laboratory, Univ. of Calif., Richmond. 1966. 59 p.

(Available from Sea Water Conversion Laboratory, Univ. of Calif., Berkeley.)

2   Saline water research progress summary, January 1, 1965 – December 31, 1965. Los Angeles, Univ. of Calif. Dept. of Engineering. 1966. 62 p.

3   Cellulose acetate membranes as a means of removing scale forming ions of natural saline waters, by David Leif Erickson. Los Angeles, Univ. of Calif. Dept. of Engineering. 1966. 108 p.

4   Mass transport of binary electrolyte solutions in membranes, by Douglas N. Bennion. Los Angeles, Univ. of Calif. Dept. of Engineering. 1966. 29 p.

5   A composite tubular assembly for reverse osmosis desalination, by Sidney Loeb. Los Angeles, Univ. of Calif. Dept. of Engineering. 1966. 18 p.

6   Variation of the heat transfer with length pressure, flow rate and temperature difference in an LTV falling film evaporator, by John Ernest Kroll. Los Angeles, Univ. of Calif. Dept. of Engineering. 1966. 98 p.

7   Reverse osmosis desalination at the Coalinga Pilot Plant; progress report January 1, 1966 to June 30, 1966, by J. S. Johnson and S. Loeb. Los Angeles, Univ. of Calif. Dept. of Engineering. 1966. 16 p.

8   Further studies on thin wiped film heat transfer, by V. J. Jusionis and R. L. Perrine. Los Angeles, Univ. of Calif. Dept. of Engineering. 1966. 38 p.

9   Fouling problems encountered in a reverse osmosis desalination pilot plant, by S. Loeb and J. S. Johnson. Los Angeles, Univ. of Calif. Dept. of Engineering. 1966. 26 p.

10 Turbulent region performance of reverse osmosis desalination tubes. Experience at Coalinga Pilot Plant, by Judy Rosenfeld and Sidney Loeb. Los Angeles, Univ. of Calif. Dept. of Engineering. 1966. 20 p.

11 Ion transport inside charged membranes, by Richard A. Wallace. Richmond, Univ. of Calif. Sea Water Conversion Laboratory. 1966. 48 p. (Available from Sea Water Conversion Laboratory, Univ. of Calif. Berkeley.)

12 Saline water research progress summary January 1, 1966 – December 31, 1966 [Los Angeles campus]. Los Angeles, Univ. of Calif. Dept. of Engineering. 1967. 83 p.

13 Reverse osmosis desalination costs derived from the Coalinga Pilot Plant operation. Los Angeles, Univ. of Calif. Dept. of Engineering. 1967. 31 p.

*14 1966 Progress report: Berkeley campus; Riverside campus; San Diego campus. Berkeley Sea Water Conversion Laboratory, Univ. of Calif. 1967. 63 p.

15 Corrosion studies:
    Part X   Corrosion kinetics of iron-nickel alloys.
    Part XI   Corrosion kinetics of antimony.
    Part XII   Corrosion kinetics of copper.
    Part XIII Potentiodynamic studies of antimony.
    Part XIV   Corrosion kinetics of iron.

    By Ken Nobe and Staff. Los Angeles, Univ. of Calif. Dept. of Engineering. 1967. 1 v. (various pagings).

16 Performance of cellulose acetate semipermeable membranes under brackish water field conditions, by James Stephen Johnson. Los Angeles, Univ. of Calif. Dept. of Engineering. 1967. 115 p.

17 Solar distillation, by Everett D. Howe, Badawi W. Tleimat, Alan D. K. Laird. Richmond, Univ. of Calif. Sea Water Conversion Laboratory [1967] 52 p. (Available from Sea Water Conversion Laboratory, Univ. of Calif. Berkeley.)

18 Vapor-compression distillation. Richmond, Univ. of Calif. Sea Water Conversion Laboratory. [1967]. 61 p. (Available from Sea Water Conversion Laboratory, Univ. of Calif., Berkeley.)

*19 Multicomponent diffusion: generalized theory with ion-exchange applications by Ronald N. Clazie, Gerhard Klein, Theodore Vermeulen. Richmond, Univ. of Calif. Sea Water Conversion Laboratory. 1967. 258 p.

20 Corrosion studies, pts. 15-19, by K. Nobe. Los Angeles, Univ. of Calif. Dept. of Engineering. 1967. 1 v. (various pagings).

21 Mass transport of binary electrolytes in membranes: concentration dependence for NaCl transport in cellulose acetate. Los Angeles, Univ. of Calif., Dept. of Engineering. 1967. 35 p.

22 Saline water research progress summary, January 1, 1967 – December 31, 1967. Los Angeles, Univ. of Calif. Dept. of Engineering. 1968. 79 p.

*23 1967 Progress report: [Berkeley, Riverside, and San Diego] Berkeley, Univ. of Calif. Sea Water Conversion Laboratory. 1968. 71 p.

24 Uncertainty cost of new systems with special consideration to desalting, by Nabil A. El-Ramly and J. Morley English. Los Angeles, Univ. of Calif. School of Engineering and Applied Science. 1970. 39 p.

25 Design and cost of ion-exchange softening for a 50-MGD sea-water evaporation plant, by Gerhard Klein, Kamel M. Makar, Badawi W. Tleimat, and Theodore Vermeulen. Berkeley, Univ. of Calif. Sea Water Conversion Laboratory. 1968. 59 p. (Available from Sea Water Conversion Laboratory, Univ. of Calif., Berkeley.)

26 Electrical properties of electrodialysis membranes, by Richard A. Wallace. Berkeley, Univ. of Calif. Sea Water Conversion Laboratory. 1968. 41 p. (Available from Sea Water Conversion Laboratory, Univ. of Calif., Berkeley.)

*27 Multiple effect flash (MEF) evaporator, by LeRoy A. Bromley and Stanley M. Read. Berkeley, Univ. of Calif. Dept. of Chemical Engineering. 1968. 86 p.

28 1968 Progress report: [Berkeley, Riverside, and San Diego] Berkeley, Univ. of Calif. Sea Water Conversion Laboratory. 1969. 69 p.

(Available from Sea Water Conversion Laboratory, Univ. of Calif., Berkeley.)

29 Saline water research progress summary, January 1, 1968 – December 31, 1968. Los Angeles, Univ. of Calif. Dept. of Engineering. 1969. 74 p.

30 The solubility of carbon dioxide in distilled water, synthetic sea water and synthetic sea-water concentrates, by Paul B. Stewart and Prem K. Munjal. Berkeley, Univ. of Calif. Sea Water Conversion Laboratory. 1969. 43 p. (Available from Sea Water Conversion Laboratory, Univ. of Calif., Berkeley.)

31 Three and one-half years experience with reverse osmosis at Coalinga, California, by J. S. Johnson, J. W. McCutchan and D. N. Bennion. Los Angeles, Univ. of Calif. School of Engineering and Applied Science. 1969. 50 p.

32 Mass transfer of binary electrolytes in membranes: concentration dependence, by J. C. Osborn and D. N. Bennion. Los Angeles, Univ. of Calif. School of Engineering and Applied Science. 1969. 98 p.

33 Condensation on and evaporation from a rotating flat-disk wiped-film evaporator, by Badawi W. Tleimat. Berkeley, Univ. of Calif. Sea Water Conversion Laboratory. 1969. 20 p. (Available from Sea Water Conversion Laboratory, Univ. of Calif., Berkeley.)

34 Scale abatement in saline water distillation by injection of carbon dioxide, by R. D. Ellis. Los Angeles, Univ. of Calif. School of Engineering and Applied Science. 1969. 113 p.

35 1969 Progress report: Berkeley campus; Riverside campus. Berkeley, Univ. of Calif. Sea Water Conversion Laboratory. 1970. 51 p. (Available from Sea Water Conversion Laboratory, Univ. of Calif., Berkeley.)

36 Saline water research progress summary: January 1, 1969 – December 31, 1969. Los Angeles, Univ. of Calif. School of Engineering and Applied Science. 1970. 80 p.

37 Submerged combustion, by P. A. Iyer and Chieh Chu. Los Angeles, Univ. of Calif. School of Engineering and Applied Science. 1970. 15 p.

40 Saline water research progress summary, January 1, 1970 – December 31, 1970. Los Angeles, Univ. of Calif. School of Engineering and Applied Science. 1971. 75 p.

COLORADO

ARKANSAS RIVER COMPACT ADMINISTRATION
Court House
Lamar, Colorado 81052

Annual Report. 1948 – to date. Data on daily discharges from the Arkansas and Purgatoire Rivers, the daily content of reservoirs, outflow from reservoirs, water demands by Colorado and Kansas, and diversion of flows by ditches.

COLORADO DEPARTMENT OF HEALTH
Water Pollution Control Commission
4210 East 11th Avenue
Denver, Colorado 80220

Guidelines for Control of Water Pollution from Mine Drainage. 1970. 10 pages. Price: $0.15.

Water Pollution Control in Colorado. 25 p.

Rules and Guidelines for Water Pollution Control at Livestock Confinement Areas. 1970. 11 p.

Water Pollution Control. Chapter 66, Article 28. 17 p.

Water Quality Standards for Colorado. 1968. 6 p.

Classification of Interstate and Intrastate Streams in Colorado by River Basins. 1969. 25 pages. Includes the following river basins and sub-basins: Arkansas, North Platte, Colorado, South Platte, San Juan, Dolores, White, Green-Yampa, and Rio Grande.

COLORADO DIVISION OF WATER RESOURCES
101 Columbine Building
1845 Sherman Street
Denver, Colorado 80203

GROUND WATER

A *Basic Information:*

  *1 Manual of Ground Water Laws (as amended)

  *2 Basic Data Report 17 (Listing of all Fee Wells)

  3 Water Well Drillers and Pump Installation Contractors – Rules & Regulations. Free of charge

  4 List of Colorado Licensed Well Drillers and Pump Installation Contractors. Free of charge

B *Studies*

  *1 Northern High Plains (Woodward, Clyde, Sherard & Associates)

  2 Black Squirrel (Erker & Romero) Price: $2.00

  *3 Kiowa-Bijou (Colorado State University)

  *4 Prowers-Baca-Las Animas (R. W. Beck & Associates)

  5 Lost Creek (Will Owens) Price: $4.00

SURFACE WATER

A *Basic Information*

  1 Manual of Rules & Regulations for Filing Claims to Water. Free of charge

  2 Manual of Livestock Water Tank Act. Free of charge

  3 Map of Irrigation Division by Water District (change pending due to SB 81) Free of charge

B *Studies:*

  1 Water Adjudications in Irrigation Division I – thru 1920. (check payable to: Mrs. C. C. Hezmalhalck). Price: $5.00

  2 Engineering Water Code Studies for the South Platte River (M. W. Bittinger & Associates and Wright Water Engineers)

  3 South Platte River – State Line Study (M. W. Bittinger & Assoc. and Wright Water Engineers)

  4 Water Utilization – Water District #2 (M. W. Bittinger & Assoc.)

  5 Water Investigations for the Arkansas River Basin in Colorado (W. W. Wheeler & Associates)

  6 Report on Colorado Water Administration (Clyde-Criddle-Woodward, Inc.)

DAMS & RESERVOIRS

Basic Information:

A *Current:*

  1 Plans and Specifications for the Construction of Reservoir Dams. Free of charge

2 Specimen Plans and Specifications for Small (Under 10 feet) Earth Dams (Revision Pending) Free of charge

B *Future:*

1 Listing of Dams in the State of Colorado.

MISCELLANEOUS

Any and all Basic Water Diversions Reports, Hydrographic Reports, Reservoirs Reports in this office. Price: $0.50 a sheet.

Any and all Basic Ground Water Well Applications, Permits, etc., in this office. Price: $0.50 a sheet.

COLORADO GEOLOGICAL SURVEY

This is an inactive organization. Those publications still available are sold by the Department of Geology, Room 205, Geology Building, University of Colorado, Boulder, Colorado.

BULLETINS

11 Mineral Waters of Colorado, by R. D. George, Harry A. Curtis, O. C. Lester, J. A. Crook, J. B. Yeo, and others. 1920. Price: $1.00.

*26 Preliminary Report on the Underground Waters of a Part of Southeastern Colorado, by Coffin and A. J. Tieje. 1921.

*27 Underground Water Possibilities for Stock and Domestic Purposes in the LaJunta Area, Colorado, by Horace B. Patton.

Underground Water Resources of Parts of Crowley and Otero Counties, by W. C. Toepelman. 1924. Price: $0.50.

28 Oil and Water Possibilities of Parts of Delta and Mesa Counties, Colorado, by Herbert J. Weeks. 1925. Price: $0.25.

COLORADO WATER CONSERVATION BOARD

102 Columbine Building
1845 Sherman Street
Denver, Colorado 80203

GROUND WATER SERIES

BULLETINS

I Geology and Ground Water Resources of parts of Lincoln, Elbert, and El Paso Counties; November, 1946. Price: $0.50.

II Geology and Ground Water Resources of Baca County Colorado; Water Supply Paper #1256 USGS. 1954. Price: $1.50.

III Ground Water Resources of the San Luis Valley, Colorado; June, 1958. Water Supply Paper #1379 USGS. Price: $3.50.

CIRCULARS

1 Ground Water in the Julesburg Area, Colorado; July, 1948. Price: $0.50.

4 Ground Water in Colorado and the Status of Investigations; Second Printing, January, 1956. Price: $0.50.

5 Ground Water in the Ogallala and several Consolidated Formations in Colorado; December, 1960. Price: $0.50.

6 Legal and Management Problems Related to the Development of an Artesian Ground-Water Reservoir; 1962. Price: $0.50.

7 Ground Water – Prospects for Irrigation in Eastern Cheyenne and Kiowa Counties, Colorado – 1963. Price: $0.50.

8 Potential Ground-Water Development in the Northern Part of the Colorado High Plains – 1963. Price: $0.50.

9 Ground Water in Colorado – Its Importance during an Emergency – 1963. Price: $0.50.

10 Effects of Water Management on a Reach of the Arkansas Valley, La Junta to Las Animas, Colorado – 1963. Price: $0.50.

11 Pumping Tests in Colorado – 1965. Price: $1.00.

12 Geohydrologic Data from the Piceance Creek Basin between the White and Colorado Rivers, Northwestern Colorado – 1968. Prices: $0.50.

13 Availability of Water for Artificial Recharge, Plains Groundwater Management Dist., Colorado – 1970. Price: $0.50.

BASIC DATA GROUND WATER REPORTS

Basic Data Reports will be supplemented by U.S.G.S. Water Supply Papers when printed by the U.S. Government Printing Office. "W.S.P." in the following citations indicate Water Supply Papers.

1 Prowers County, 1960. W. S. P. 1772. Price: $0.50.

2 Yuma County, 1960. W.S.P. 1539J. Price: $0.50.

3 El Paso County, Fountain, Jimmy Camp, and Black Squirrel Valleys, 1961. W.S.P. 1583. Price: $0.50.

4 Huerfano County, 1961. W.S.P. 1805. Price: $0.50.

5 Boulder County, Boulder Area, Colorado, 1961. Price: $0.50.

6 Washington County, 1961. W.S.P. 1777. Price: $0.50.

7 Radiochemical Analyses of Water in Colorado, 1961. Price: $0.50.

8 Lower Cache La Poudre River Basin, Colorado, 1961. W.S.P. 1669X. Price: $0.50.

9 South Platte River Basin in Western Adams and Southwestern Weld Counties, Colorado, 1962. W.S.P. 1658. Price: $0.50.

10 Kit Carson County, 1962. Price: $0.50.

11   Otero and the Southern Part of Crowley Counties, Colorado, 1962. W.S.P. 1799. Price: $0.50.

12   Big Sandy Creek Valley in Lincoln, Cheyenne, and Kiowa Counties, Colorado, 1962. W.S.P. 1843. Price: $0.50.

13   Eastern Parts of Cheyenne and Kiowa Counties, Colorado, 1962. W.S.P. 1779N. Price: $0.50.

14   Bent County, 1963. Price: $0.50.

15   Hydrogeologic Data of the Denver Basin, Colorado, 1964. Price: $0.50.

16   Hydrogeologic Data from Parts of Larimer, Logan, Morgan, Sedgwick and Weld Counties, Colorado, 1964. W.S.P. 1809L. Price: $0.50.

18   Hydrogeological Data of Alluvial Deposits in Pueblo and Fremont Counties, Colorado, 1965. Price: $0.50.

19   Hydrogeologic Data for Baca and Southern Prowers Counties, Colorado, 1968. W.S.P. 1772. Price: $1.00.

20   Water Level Records for the Northern High Plains of Colorado, 1969. Price: $1.00.

21   Hydrogeologic Data for the Lower Arkansas Valley, Colorado, 1970. Price: $1.00.

RIVER BASIN AND RELATED REPORTS

Water and Related Land Resources, Yampa River Basin. (CWCB and SCS) 1969. Price: $3.00.

Water and Related Land Resources, Gunnison River Basin. (CWCB and SCS) 1962. Price: $3.00.

Water and Related Land Resources, White River Basin. (CWCB and SCS) 1966. Price: $3.00.

Water and Related Land Resources, Colorado River Basin. (CWCB and SCS) 1965. Price: $3.00.

Geo-Hydrologic Study of the Closed Basin, San Luis Valley, Woodward-Clyde-Sherard & Associates, 1967. Price: $3.00.

Evaluation Report on Closed Basin Division, San Luis Valley Project. Woodward-Clyde-Sherard & Associates, 1967. Price: $2.00.

Engineering Water Code Studies for the South Platte River, Vol. I. Bittinger and Associates, 1968. Price: $0.50.

Water Legislation Investigation for the Arkansas River Basin in Colorado. W. W. Wheeler and Woodward-Clyde & Associates, 1968. Price: $0.50.

MISCELLANEOUS

Federal-State Water Resources Planning and Development in Colorado — a summary of potential projects in Colorado, costs, present status, and priority of development (CWCB). 1959. Price: $5.00.

Water Conservation and Conservancy Districts of the State of Colorado — a compilation of applicable state laws and all conservancy and conservation districts presently organized with a current list of all Board members, officers, employees, etc. (Fourth Edition — CWCB). 1968. Price: $5.00.

Water Supplies of the Colorado River — Upper Colorado River Commission, Parts I and II, 1965, by Tipton and Kalmbach, Inc. Price: $10.00.

Ground Water Statutes of Selected Western States (CWCB). Price: $10.00.

Evaluation of Water Resources in Kiowa and Bijou Creek Basins, Colorado, by Civil Engineering Department, Eng. Research, Colorado State University, May 1966. Price: $2.00.

A Hundred Years of Irrigation in Colorado, 1852–1952, by Colorado State University, 1952. Price: $0.50.

Report on the Economic Potential of Western Colorado, by the University of Colorado, 1953. Price: $0.50.

Water Requirements for Oil Shale, 1960–1975, by Cameron and Jones, Inc. (1959). Price: $2.00.

Report on Colorado Water Administration, by Clyde-Criddle-Woodward, Inc., 1968. Price: $1.00.

Public Water Supplies of Colorado (USGS and CSU). Price: $1.50.

Ground Water in Colorado 504-S (CSU). Price: $0.25.

Ground Water — The Law 505-S (CSU). Price: $0.25.

Ground Water — The Economic Picture 506-S (CSU). Price: $0.25.

CONNECTICUT

CONNECTICUT STATE BOARD OF FISHERIES AND GAME

Room 243 State Office Building
Hartford, Connecticut 06115

Fishes of Connecticut Lakes and Neighboring Waters; with Notes on Plankton Environment, by W. C. Kendall and E. L. Goldsborough. 1908. Doc. 633.

A Report of Investigations Concerning Shad in the Rivers of Connecticut, by P. H. Mitchell. 1925.

Report of Fish and Game Conditions in Connecticut and Six Year Program for State Board of Fisheries and Game to Hon. Wilbur L. Cross, Governor of Connecticut, by T. H. Beck. 1931. 33 p.

Connecticut Wetlands in the Town Plan, by J. S. Bishop and Ruth Billard. 1960.

A History of the Connecticut River and its Fisheries, by D. D. Moss. 1960.

OTHER MISCELLANEOUS LITERATURE

Guide to Public Access to Connecticut Fishing Waters.

Lake and Pond Surveys, Nos. 1-8.

DEPARTMENT OF AGRICULTURE & NATURAL RESOURCES

State Office Building
Hartford, Connecticut 06115

Connecticut's Natural Resources—A Proposal for Action, by William H. Whyte. June 1962. 64 p.

CONNECTICUT STATE DEPARTMENT OF HEALTH

79 Elm Street
Hartford, Connecticut 06103

Report on the Investigation of the Pollution of Streams. 1915. Presented to the General Assembly of 1915. 144 p.

Analyses of Connecticut Public Water Supplies. 1936. (Bureau of Sanitary Engineering).

Water Supply and Sewage Disposal at Realty Subdivisions, by D. C. Wiggin. 1956.

Sewage Disposal in Connecticut, by C. A. Jaworski. 1962. Health Bull. 76.

Analyses of Connecticut Public Water Supplies. 1962. 6th Edition.

CONNECTICUT DEVELOPMENT COMMISSION

State Office Building
Hartford, Connecticut 06115

Beach Erosion Committee: A Report of Shore Erosion Problems, with Recommendations for Remedial Measures. August 15, 1946.

Water Resources Conservation Through Planning and Zoning. 1952. (Research and Planning Division).

The Economic Outlook for the Naugatuck and Farmington-River Valleys in the State of Connecticut, by J. P. Miller and G. Sirkin. 1956. HHFA 701:2.

Regional Planning Study – Farmington River Valley Region, by Adams, Howard and Greeley. 1957.

Economic Development and Competitive Position of the State of Connecticut, 1959-1975. Vol. 1, by Booz, Allen and Hamilton. 1959.

Resume of Flood Control Measures, Connecticut. 1960. (Planning Division).

Connecticut's Shoreline. 1962. Tech. Bull. (Connecticut Interregional Planning Program).

Public Water Supplies. 1962. Tech. Bull. (Connecticut Interregional Planning Program).

Community Services: Part I. A Survey of Public Water Supplies, Sewerage Systems, Gas, Electricity and Telephones. 1963. Tech. Rept. 150.

Inland Water Bodies. 1963. Tech. Bull.

Resource Industries: an analysis of Connecticut's Agriculture, Forestry, Mining and Fisheries, by J. E. Hickey. 1963. Tech. Rept. 141. (Connecticut Interregional Planning Program).

Water: A Resource Inventory. 1963. Tech. Rept. 124. (Connecticut Interregional Planning Program).

Connecticut Takes Stock for Action. 1964. 145 p. (Connecticut Interregional Planning Program).

CONNECTICUT STATE FLOOD CONTROL AND WATER POLICY COMMISSION

Hartford
Connecticut 06115

Experiences in Establishing Stream Channel Encroachment in Connecticut, by W. S. Wise. 1957.

CONNECTICUT GEOLOGICAL AND NATURAL HISTORY SURVEY

Wesleyan Station
Middletown, Connecticut 06457

Please note: Available publications should be ordered from the Survey's Distribution and Exchange Agent: State Librarian, State Library, Hartford, Connecticut 06115. Payment must accompany order, and please make checks payable to Connecticut State Library.

BULLETINS

*2   A Preliminary Report on the Protozoa of the Fresh Waters of Connecticut, by Herbert William Conn; 69 p., 34 pls., 1905.

*10   A Preliminary Report on the Algae of the Fresh Waters of Connecticut, by Herbert William Conn and Lucia Washburn (Hazen) Webster; 78 p., 44 pls., 1908.

*30   Drainage Modifications and Glaciation in the Danbury Region, Connecticut, by Ruth Sawyer Harvey; 59 p., 5 pls., 10 figs., 1920.

42   The Algae of Connecticut, by Clarence John Hylander; 245 p., 28 pls., 1928. Price: $2.00.

*44   Report on the Water Resources of Connecticut, by Roscoe Henry Suttie; 168 p., 7 figs., 1928.

*46   The Physical History of the Connecticut Shoreline, by Henry Staats Sharp; 97 p., 8 pls., 28 figs., 1929.

*61   The Weather and Climate of Connecticut, by Joseph Milton Kirk; 253 p., 12 figs., 1939. (Superseded by Bulletin 99).

*63   A Fishery Survey of Important Connecticut Lakes by a Survey Unit of the State Board of Fisheries and Game. Introduction and Section I: Fishery Management, by Lyle M. Thorpe; Section II: Limnology, by E. S. Deevey, Jr., and J. S. Bishop; Section III: Life Histories of Certain Fishes, by D. A. Webster; Section IV: Parasites of Fresh Water Fishes, by G. W. Hunter III; 339 p., 128 figs., 1942.

*   Supplement to Bulletin 63: 60 maps showing bottom contours of important Connecticut lakes, scale 1 inch to 600 inches.

94   Marine Sedimentary Environments in the Vicinity of the Norwalk Islands, Connecticut, by Charles W. Ellis; 89 p., 44 figs., 1 pl., 1962. Price: $1.00.

99   The Climate of Connecticut, by Joseph J. Brumbach; 215 p., 13 figs., 1965. Price: $1.50.

101   Freshwater Fishes of Connecticut, by Walter R. Whitworth, Peter L. Berrien, and Walter T. Keller; 134 p., 139 figs., 1968. Price: $1.50.

MISCELLANEOUS PUBLICATIONS

Post Glacial Stratigraphy and Morphology of Coastal Connecticut. A. L. Bloom and C. W. Ellis. 1965. 10 p. Guidebook 1.

Geological and Economic Aspects of Beach Erosion along the Connecticut Coast. J. E. Sanders and C. W. Ellis. 1961. 14 p. Rept. Inv. 1.

Ground Water in the Hartford, Stamford, Salisbury, Willimantic and Saybrook Areas, Connecticut. H. E. Gregory and A. J. Ellis. 1916. 150 p. (A cooperative work between the Conn. Geol. & Nat. Hist. Survey and the Conn. Board of Agriculture.)

CONNECTICUT INTERREGIONAL PLANNING PROGRAM

State Office Building
Hartford, Connecticut 06115

Note: See also Connecticut Development Commission.

Connecticut: Choices for Action. The Green Land. 1966. 85 p. This is one of a series of six planning reports. The other five do not deal directly with water resources, and therefore are not cited here. The four state agencies involved in this study are: State Highway Department, Department of Agriculture and Natural Resources, Development Commission, and Department of Finance and Control.

CONNECTICUT WATER RESOURCES COMMISSION

225 State Office Building
Hartford, Connecticut 06115

Note: The publications which are known to be out of print may be consulted at the Hartford, Connecticut office of the U. S. Geological Survey.

First through Fifth Biennial Reports. 1924-1934.

Report on the Water Resources of Connecticut pursuant to Special Act 427, Chapter 413, 1929. 54 p. 1930.

A Report on the Great Flood of March 1936 in Connecticut with Supplementary Data on the Farmington River Valley Flood of March, 1936. 1938.

Bibliography of Publications Relating to Ground Water in Connecticut. R. V. Cushman. 1950. 12 p.

Conservation and Development of the Water Resources of Connecticut and New England. R. Martin. 1950.

An Act Creating the State Water Commission and Bearing on Pollution of Waterways. 1953.

An Act Concerning the Supervision of Dams and Reservoirs. 1953. 9 p.

State Flood Control and Water Policy Commission; an Act Creating a Flood Control and Water Policy Commission. 1953. 6 p.

Connecticut's Water – Wealth or Waste? 1953. 14 p. Prepared in cooperation with the Connecticut State Department of Health.

Pollution in the Farmington River Watershed. (unpubl. report). 1955.

Water Resources of Connecticut. A Report to the 1957 Connecticut General Assembly. 1957. 189 p.

*Chemical and Physical Quality of Water Resources in Connecticut, 1955-1958. F. H. Pauszek. 1958. Bulletin 1.

Classification and Standards of Quality for Interstate Waters – Farmington Basin. Adopted October 1959. Interstate Water Pollution Control Survey. 1959.

*Ground Water Levels in Connecticut, 1956-1959. A. M. LaSala, Jr. 1959. Bulletin 2.

Report on Flood Control Improvements for Mad River, Winsted, Connecticut. Dewey & Kropper, Engineers. 1961.

Report on Flood Control Improvements for Pequabuck River and North Creek, Bristol, Connecticut. Dewey & Kropper, Engineers. 1961.

Farmington River, Flood Control Study, Collinsville, Connecticut. J. J. Mozzochi. 1962.

Method of Removing Accumulated Deposits from the Oxoboxo River, Town of Montville, Connecticut. 1962.

Report on Flood Control Improvements for Highland Lake Stream, Winsted, Connecticut. Dewey & Kropper, Engineers. 1962.

Feasibility Report, Local Flood Protection, Nepaug River, New Hartford, Connecticut. Dewey & Kropper, Engineers. 1963.

Flood Control Improvements, Pequabuck River, Bristol to Plainville, Connecticut. Dewey & Kropper, Engineers. 1963.

A Hydrographic Survey of New Haven Harbor, 1962-63. A. C. Duxbury. 1963. Bulletin 3A.

Report on Flood Control, Farmington River, Unionville, Connecticut. R. C. Brown. 1963.

Report on Flood Control, West Branch Farmington River, New Hartford, Connecticut. R. C. Brown. 1963.

Records and Logs of Selected Wells and Test Borings, Records of Springs, and Chemical Analyses of Water in the Farmington-Granby Area, Connecticut. A. D. Randall. 1964. Bulletin 3.

*Records and Logs of Selected Wells and Test Borings and Chemical Analyses of Water in North-central Connecticut. R. V. Cushman, J. A. Baker and R. L. Meikle. 1964. Bulletin 4.

Records and Logs of Selected Wells and Test Borings and Chemical Analyses of Water in the Bristol-Lainville-Southington Area, Connecticut. A. M. LaSala and R. L. Meikle. 1964. Bulletin 5.

Effects of Loss of Valley Storage Due to Encroachment – Connecticut River. Dewey & Kropper, Engineers. 1964.

Public Hearing on July 20, 1964 Concerning an Application Received from the Connecticut Yankee Atomic Power Co. entitled, "Proposed Dredging and Screenwell Structure in the Connecticut River". 1964. 157 p.

Waste Water Disposal by Connecticut Industries. Inventory as of January 1, 1961, compiled from Basic Data Files. 1964.

A Preliminary Appraisal of Water Quality in the Housatonic River Basin in Connecticut. F. H. Pauszek and R. J. Edmonds. 1965. Bulletin 6.

Ground Water Levels in Connecticut, 1960-1964. R. L. Meikle and J. A. Baker. 1965. Bulletin 7.

Waste Water Disposal by Connecticut Industries, Inventory as of January 1, 1961, compiled from basic data files of Connecticut Water Resources Commission, Division of Water Supply and Pollution Control. 1965.

Water Resources Inventory of Connecticut, Part I – Quinebaug River Basin. A. D. Randall, M. P. Thomas; C. E. Thomas, Jr. and J. A. Baker. 1966. Bulletin 8.

Hydrogeologic Data in the Quinebaug River Basin, Connecticut. C. E. Thomas, Jr., A. D. Randall and M. P. Thomas. 1966. Bulletin 9.

Survey of Federal Aids. Inst. of Public Service, Univ. of Connecticut. Nov. 3, 1966. 1966.

Water Resources Inventory of Connecticut, Part 2 – Shetucket River Basin. M. P. Thomas, G. A. Bednar, C. E. Thomas and W. E. Wilson. 1967. Bulletin 11.

Hydrogeologic Data for the Shetucket River Basin, Connecticut. C. E. Thomas, Jr., G. A. Bednar, M. P. Thomas and W. E. Wilson. 1967. Bulletin 12.

Ground Water Levels in Connecticut, 1965-1966. R. L. Meikle. 1967. Bulletin 13.

Connecticut's Clean Water Act of 1967. An Analysis of Public Act 57. Prepared by the Clean Water Task Force. 1967. 13 p.

*Records and Logs of Selected Wells and Test Borings, Ground Water Levels in Selected Observation Wells, and Freshwater Inflow into the Connecticut River at the CANEL Site, Middletown, Connecticut. J. A. Baker. 1968. Bulletin 10.

Ground Water Resources of the Hamden-Wallingford Area, Connecticut. A. M. LaSala, Jr. 1968. Bulletin 14.

Water Resources Inventory of Connecticut, Part III – Lower Thames and Southeastern Coastal River Basins. C. E. Thomas, Jr., M. A. Cervione, Jr., and I. G. Grossman. 1968. Bulletin 15.

Hydrogeologic Data for the Lower Thames and Southeastern Coastal River Basins, Connecticut. M. A. Cervione, Jr., I. G. Grossman and C. E. Thomas, Jr. 1968. Bulletin 16. 65 p.

Hydrogeologic Data for the Southwestern Coastal River Basins, Connecticut. M. P. Thomas, R. B. Ryder, and C. E. Thomas, Jr. 1969. Bulletin 18.

An Act Concerning the Oil Pollution of Connecticut Waters. Public Act No. 765. 1969. 4 p.

Water Resources Inventory of Connecticut, Part IV – Southwestern Coastal River Basins. R. B. Ryder, M. A. Cervione, Jr., C. E. Thomas, Jr., and M. P. Thomas. 1970. Bulletin 17.

Water Resources Inventory of Connecticut, Part V – Lower Housatonic River Basin. W. E. Wilson, E. L. Burke and C. E. Thomas, Jr. 1970. Bulletin 19.

Hydrogeologic Data for the Lower Housatonic River Basin, Connecticut. I. G. Grossman and W. E. Wilson. 1970. Bulletin 20.

Hydrogeologic Data for the Upper Housatonic River Basin, Connecticut. R. L. Melvin. 1970. Bulletin 22.

A Proposed Streamflow Data Program for Connecticut. M. P. Thomas and M. A. Cervione, Jr. 1970. Bulletin 23.

Water Quality Standards. 1970. 41 p.

Clean Water by 1974. 1970. 13 p.

Water Resources Inventory of Connecticut, Part VI — Upper Housatonic River Basin. M. A. Cervione, Jr., D. L. Mazzaferro and R. L. Melvin. 1971. Bulletin 21.

SOUTHEASTERN CONNECTICUT WATER AUTHORITY

257 Main Street
Norwich, Connecticut 06360

Water Supply Plan for the Southeastern Connecticut Region, Volume I — Inventory. 1969. 167 p.

Water Supply Plan for the Southeastern Connecticut Region, Volume II — Recommended Plan. 1970. 100 p.

Summary of the Water Supply Plan for the Southeastern Connecticut Region. 1970. 9 p.

INSTITUTE OF WATER RESOURCES

University of Connecticut
Storrs, Connecticut 06268

REPORT SERIES

*1 Water Resources Research at the University of Connecticut, Proceedings of the Water Resources Conference. William C. Kennard (ed.). May 1966, 20 p.

*2 Lectures on Law in Relation to Water Resources Use and Development. William C. Kennard (ed.). March 1967, 27 p.

*3 Analysis of Quasi-Periodic Weather Data. Chesley J. Posey. June 1967, 20 p.

4 Connecticut Water Law: Judicial Allocation of Water Resources. Robert I. Reis. August 1967, 215 p. Price: $3.00.

5 Political Organization and the Planning of Water Resource Development in the Farmington Valley: A Preliminary Profile. Roger E. Kasperson. October 1967, 20 p.

6 The Quality of Connecticut's Surface Waters — Water Quality and Environment. Chester E. Thomas, Jr. July 1968, 11p.

7 Lectures on Water Conservation. William C. Kennard (ed.). October 1968, 36 p.

8 Connecticut's Administrative Control of Water Pollution — The Fluid Administrative Process. Theodore H. Focht. April 1969, 44 p.

9 A Limnological Study of the Lower Farmington River with Special Reference to the Ability of the River to Support American Shad. Walter R. Whitworth. February 1970, 57 p.

10 A Bibliography of Publications Relating to Water Resources in Connecticut 1900-1970. William C. Kennard and Jane S. Fisher. May 1970, 125 p.

11 An Economic Evaluation of Connecticut Water Law: Water Rights, Public Water Supply and Pollution Control. Robert L. Leonard. July 1970, 67 p.

12 Water Resources Research Activities and Interests at the University of Connecticut. William C. Kennard and Jane S. Fisher. September 1970, 55 p.

13 Water Resources Research 1970. William C. Kennard. September 1970, 20 p.

DELAWARE

DELAWARE GEOLOGICAL SURVEY
101 Penny Hall
University of Delaware
Newark, Delaware 19711

BULLETINS

No. 1 Ground-water problems in highway construction and maintenance: W. C. Rasmussen and L. B. Haigler, 1953.

*No. 2 Geology and ground-water resources of the Newark area, Delaware: J. J. Groot and W. C. Rasmussen, 1954.

*No. 4 Preliminary report on the geology and ground-water resources of Delaware: I. W. Marine and W. C. Rasmussen, 1955.

*No. 6 The water resources of northern Delaware: W. C. Rasmussen, J. J. Groot, R. O. R. Martin, E. F. McCarren, V. C. Behn and others, 1956.

*No. 8 Water resources of Sussex County, Delaware – A progress report: W. C. Rasmussen, R. A. Wilkens, and R. M. Beall, 1960.

No. 10 Salinity of the Delaware Estuary: B. Cohen and L. T. McCarthy, Jr., 1963.

No. 11 Ground-water resources of southern New Castle County, Delaware: D. R. Rima, O. J. Coskery, and P. W. Anderson, 1964.

No. 13 Geology and hydrology of Columbia sediments in Middletown-Odessa area, Delaware: N. Spoljaric and K. D. Woodruff, 1970 (in press).

REPORTS OF INVESTIGATIONS

*No. 1 Salinity of the Delaware estuary: B. Cohen, 1957.

*No. 2 High-capacity test well developed at the Dover Air Force Base: W. C. Rasmussen, J. J. Groot, and A. J. Depman, 1958.

*No. 3 Wells for the observation of chloride and water levels in aquifers that cross the Chesapeake and Delaware Canal: W. C. Rasmussen, J. J. Groot, and N. H. Beamer, 1958.

No. 6 Some observations on the sediments of the Delaware River south of Wilmington: R. R. Jordan and J. J. Groot, 1962.

*No. 8 Evaluation of the water resources of Delaware: W. W. Baker, R. D. Varrin, J. J. Groot, and R. R. Jordan, 1966.

No. 9 Ground-water levels in Delaware, January 1962 – June 1966: K. D. Woodruff, 1967.

No. 10 Pleistocene channels of New Castle County, Delaware: N. Spoljaric, 1967.

No. 13 The occurrence of saline ground water in Delaware aquifers: K. D. Woodruff, 1969.

No. 15 General ground-water quality in fresh-water aquifers of Delaware: K. D. Woodruff, 1970 (in press).

WATER LEVEL REPORTS

*No. 1 Water levels and artesian pressures in Delaware – 1952: I. W. Marine, 1954.

*No. 2 Water levels and artesian pressures in Delaware – 1953: D. H. Boggess and O. J. Coskery, 1954.

*No. 3 Water levels and artesian pressures in Delaware – 1954: D. H. Boggess and O. J. Coskery, 1955.

*No. 4 Water levels and artesian pressures in Delaware – 1955: O. J. Coskery, 1956.

No. 5 Water levels in Delaware – 1956: O. J. Coskery, 1958.

No. 6 Water levels in Delaware – 1957: O. J. Coskery, 1961.

No. 7 Water levels in Delaware – 1958: O. J. Coskery, 1961.

SPECIAL PUBLICATIONS

Summary of Water Conditions in Delaware: K. D. Woodruff (Issued monthly starting Nov., 1966).

*Long Range Plan for Water Resources Investigations in Delaware, 1961.

The Story of Your State Geological Survey's SEARCH FOR WATER.

REPORTS PREPARED FOR PUBLICATION BY COOPERATING AGENCIES

Water Resources Evaluation Map of Delaware: Del. Geol. Survey staff, 1964 (Prepared for the Del. State Planning Office).

The Natural Resources of Delaware (Published by the Del. State Soil and Water Conservation Commission), 1966.

Geology Section, The Availability of Ground Water from the Potomac Formation in the Chesapeake and Delaware Canal Area, Delaware: Water Resources Center, University of Delaware. J. J. Groot, R. R. Jordan, T. E. Pickett, N. Spoljaric, and K. D. Woodruff, 1967.

Geology Section, The Availability of Ground Water in Kent County, Delaware with special reference to the Dover area: Water Resources Center, University of Delaware. T. E. Pickett, 1968 (Supported by Del. Water and Air Resources Commission).

Geology Section, The Availability of Ground Water in Eastern Sussex County, Delaware: Water Resources Center, University of Delaware. T. E. Pickett, 1969 (Supported by Del. Water and Air Resources Commission).

Geology Section, Environmental Study of the Rehoboth, Indian River and Assawoman Bays: T. E. Pickett, 1969 (Published by Del. State Planning Office).

Geology Section, The Availability of Ground Water in Western Sussex County, Delaware: Water Resources Center, University of Delaware. T. E. Pickett, 1970 (Supported by Del. Water and Air Resources Commission). In press.

Hydrologic Investigations Atlases prepared cooperatively by U.S. Geological Survey, Delaware Geological Survey, and Delaware State Highway Department (Published by U.S. Geological Survey).

Water-table, surface-drainage, and engineering soils map of:

HA-60 St. Georges area, Delaware: J. K. Adams and D. H. Boggess, 1963.

HA-64 Newark area, Delaware: D. H. Boggess and J. K. Adams, 1963.

HA-79 Wilmington area, Delaware: J. K. Adams and D. H. Boggess, 1964.

HA-80 Taylors Bridge area, Delaware: J. K. Adams and D. H. Boggess, 1964.

HA-81 Smyrna area, Delaware: D. H. Boggess, J. K. Adams, and C. F. Davis, 1964.

HA-82 Middletown area, Delaware: D. H. Boggess and J. K. Adams, 1964.

HA-83 Clayton area, Delaware: J. K. Adams, D. H. Boggess, and O. J. Coskery, 1964.

HA-84 Sharptown area, Delaware: J. K. Adams and D. H. Boggess, 1964.

HA-89 Greenwood Quadrangle, Delaware: D. H. Boggess and J. K. Adams, 1964.

HA-100 Hickman Quadrangle, Delaware: J. K. Adams and D. H. Boggess, 1964.

HA-101 Ellendale Quadrangle, Delaware: J. K. Adams and D. H. Boggess, 1964.

HA-102 Milton Quadrangle, Delaware: D. H. Boggess, J. K. Adams, and O. J. Coskery, 1964.

HA-103 Lewes area, Delaware: J. K. Adams, D. H. Boggess, and C. F. Davis, 1964.

HA-105 Seaford West area, Delaware: D. H. Boggess and J. K. Adams, 1964.

HA-106 Seaford East Quadrangle, Delaware: J. K. Adams, D. H. Boggess, and O. J. Coskery, 1964.

HA-107 Georgetown Quadrangle, Delaware: D. H. Boggess, J. K. Adams, and C. F. Davis, 1964.

HA-108 Harbeson Quadrangle, Delaware: J. K. Adams and D. H. Boggess, 1964.

HA-109 Rehoboth Beach area, Delaware: D. H. Boggess, J. K. Adams, and C. F. Davis, 1964.

HA-119 Frankford area, Delaware: J. K. Adams, D. H. Boggess, and O. J. Coskery, 1964.

HA-120 Trap Pond area, Delaware: J. K. Adams and D. H. Boggess, 1964.

HA-121 Millsboro area, Delaware: D. H. Boggess and J. K. Adams, 1965.

HA-122 Bethany Beach area, Delaware: D. H. Boggess and J. K. Adams, 1964.

HA-123 Laurel area, Delaware: D. H. Boggess and J. K. Adams, 1964.

HA-132 Marydel area, Delaware: D. H. Boggess and J. K. Adams, 1964.

HA-133 Milford Quadrangle, Delaware: D. H. Boggess, C. F. Davis, and O. J. Coskery, 1964.

HA-134 Little Creek Quadrangle, Delaware: D. H. Boggess and J. K. Adams, 1965.

HA-135 Burrsville area, Delaware: D. H. Boggess, C. F. Davis, and O. J. Coskery, 1965.

HA-136 Harrington Quadrangle, Delaware: C. F. Davis and D. H. Boggess, 1964.

HA-137 Mispillion River Quadrangle, Delaware: C. F. Davis and D. H. Boggess, 1964.

HA-138 Kenton area, Delaware: D. H. Boggess and J. K. Adams, 1965.

HA-139 Dover Quadrangle, Delaware: J. K. Adams, D. H. Boggess, and C. F. Davis, 1964.

HA-140 Frederica area, Delaware: C. F. Davis, D. H. Boggess, and O. J. Coskery, 1965.

HA-141 Wyoming Quadrangle, Delaware: D. H. Boggess, C. F. Davis, and O. J. Coskery, 1965.

DEPARTMENT OF NATURAL RESOURCES AND ENVIRONMENTAL CONTROL

P. O. Box 916
Dover, Delaware 19901

Water and Air Resources Act, 1966. Title 7, Part VII, Delaware Code. 30 p.

Guidelines for Septic Tank Systems. Prepared by the Delaware Water and Air Resources Commission. 13 p.

Water Quality Standards Submitted to the Department of the Interior, June 1967. Prepared by Delaware Water and Air Resources Commission. Approved by the Department of Interior, March 1968. 33 p.

Water Pollution Control Regulation #2: Governing the Installation and Operation of Septic Tank Sewage Disposal Systems. Prepared by the Delaware Water and Air Resources Commission, October 1968. 24 p.

Regulations Governing the Use of Water Resources and Public Subaqueous Lands. Prepared by the Delaware Water and Air Resources Commission. Adopted July 14, 1969. 34 p.

Annual Report of the Delaware Water and Air Resources Commission. 1966 to date.

WATER RESOURCES CENTER

University of Delaware
Newark, Delaware 19711

1966

DeWiest, R. J. M. Hydraulic Model Study of Non-Steady Flow to Multi-aquifer Wells. Journal of Geophysical Research, v. 71, no. 20, October, pp. 4799-4810.

Fieldhouse, D. J., P. E. Read, and J. C. Ryder. Growth Retardants for Use on Tomato Transplants. Transactions of the Peninsula Horticultural Society, v. 56, no. 5, pp. 33-35.

Fieldhouse, D. J., J. C. Ryder, and E. L. Ratledge. A Wax Base Transpiration Suppressant for Use on Tomato and Pepper Transplants. Transactions of the Peninsula Horticultural Society, v. 56, no. 5, pp. 23-28.

Fieldhouse, D. J. and P. E. Read. Pepper and Lima Bean Response with Alar and Cycocel. Proc. XVII Int. Hort. Cong., v. 1, Abstr. no. 183.

Hoeh, Roger Smith. Water Resources Administration in Delaware. Division of Urban Affairs, University of Delaware, August, 175 p.

Read, P. E. and D. J. Fieldhouse. Effects of Growth Retardants on Flowering, Yield, and Quality of Tomatoes. Proc. XVII Hort. Cong., v. 1, Abstr. no. 68.

Seidenstat, Paul. The Market for Water Based Outdoor Recreation Services in New Castle County, Delaware. Water Resources Center, University of Delaware, July, 70 p.

1967

Astarita, G. Two Dimensionless Groups Relevant in the Analysis of Steady Flows of Viscoelastic Materials. Ind. & Eng. Chem. Fundamentals, v. 6.

Marshall, R. J. and A. B. Metzner. Flow of Viscoelastic Fluids Through Porous Media. Ind. & Eng. Chem. Fundamentals, v. 6, August, pp. 393-400.

Sundstrom, R. W. and others. The Availability of Ground Water From the Potomac Formation in the Chesapeake and Delaware Canal Area, Delaware. Water Resources Center, Univ. of Delaware, June, 95 p.

Tannian, Francis X., Charles Chandler, and Nancy Wilson. City of Wilmington Water System. Division of Urban Affairs, University of Delaware, 53 p.

1968

Banerji, S. K., B. D. Bracken, and B. M. Garg. Effect of Boron on Aerobic Biological Waste Treatment. Paper presented at 23rd Purdue Industrial Waste Conference, Purdue University, Lafayette, Indiana, May.

Crosswhite, William M. Use of Water for Supplemental Irrigation in Delaware. Delaware Experiment Station Bulletin.

Fang, H. Y., and Robert D. Varrin. Model Analysis of Hydraulic Conductivity of an Aquifer. Fritz Engineering Lab. Report No. 341.2, Lehigh University, 21 p.

Kraft, John C., and Marilyn Maisano. Geologic Cross Section of Delaware Showing Stratigraphic Correlation, Aquifer Distribution and Geologic Setting within the Atlantic Coastal Plain — Continental Shelf Geosyncline. Water Resources Center, University of Delaware.

Schaftlein, R. W., and T. W. F. Russell. Two Phase Reactor Design, Part I, Tank Type Reactors. Industrial and Engineering Chemistry, v. 60, no. 5, May, 14 p.

Sundstrom, R. W. and T. E. Pickett. The Availability of Ground Water in Kent County, Delaware, with Special Reference to the Dover Area. Water Resources Center, University of Delaware, 123 p.

1969

Anderson, R. J., and T. W. F. Russell. Circumferential Variation of Interchange in Horizontal Annular Flow. Ind. & Eng. Chem. Fundamentals Quarterly, April.

Banerji, S. K. Boron Adsorption on Soils and Biological Sludges and its Effect on Endogeneous Respiration of Sludges. Paper presented at the 24th Purdue Industrial Waste Conference, Purdue University, Lafayette, Indiana, May.

Brams, M. R., C. Chandler, and N. Wilson. The Economic and Engineering Feasibility of a Unified Water System for Northern New Castle County, Delaware. Division of Urban Affairs, University of Delaware, 166 p.

Cichy, P. T., J. J. Ultman, T. W. F. Russell. Two-Phase Reactor Design — Tubular Reactions — Reactor Model Development. Ind. & Eng. Chemistry, v. 61, no. 7, August, pages 6-14.

Cichy, P. T., T. W. F. Russell. Two-Phase Reactor Design — Tubular Reactors — Reactor Model Parameters. Ind. & Eng. Chemistry, v. 61, no. 7, August, pages 15-26.

Fieldhouse, D. J. and E. L. Ratledge. Wax Dips for Tomato Transplants. Trans. Pen. Hort. Society, pp. 16-18.

Krimgold, D. Aspects of a Climatic Water Balance — Delmarva Peninsula. Water Resources Center, University of Delaware, 26 p.

Mather, J. R. Factors of the Climatic Water Balance over the Delmarva Peninsula, Water Resources Center, University of Delaware.

Russell, T. W. F. Gas-Liquid Flow. McGraw Hill Yearbook of Science & Technology.

Stevens, Thomas H. and Gerald L. Cole. Economics of Water Use and Waste Disposal in Delaware Vegetable Processing. Agricultural Experiment Station Bulletin #380, July.

Sundstrom, R. W. and T. E. Pickett. The Availability of Ground Water in Eastern Sussex County, Water Resources Center, Univ. of Delaware, 136 p.

1970

Hudson, B. L., G. L. Cole, and R. C. Smith. An Economic Analysis of Poultry Processing Wastewater in Delaware. Agricultural Experiment Station Bulletin #383, University of Delaware, December.

Read, Paul E. and D. J. Fieldhouse. Use of Growth Retardants for Increasing Tomato Yields and Adaptation for Mechanical Harvest. J. Amer. Soc. Hort. Sci., v. 95, no. 1, pages 73-78.

Sundstrum, R. W. and T. E. Pickett. The Availability of Ground Water in Western Sussex County. Water Resources Center, University of Delaware, July.

FLORIDA

CENTRAL AND SOUTHERN FLORIDA FLOOD CONTROL DISTRICT
P. O. Box 1671
West Palm Beach, Florida 33402

Water Management Bulletin, a bi-monthly publication. Vol. 1 No. 1, Oct.-Nov. 1967 to Vol. 4 No. 4, Feb.-March 1971.

Annual Report, 1949-1950 to date.

Central and Southern Florida Flood Control Project — Eight Years of Progress, 1949-1957. 45 p.

Fifteen Years of Progress, 1949-1964. 24 p.

An Act Establishing the Upper St. Johns River Flood Plain. Unabridged Text of Chapter 30542, Laws of Florida 1955 with Maps of Flood Plain Boundaries. September 1955.

The Proposed Water Control Project for Kissimmee River Between Lake Kissimmee and Lake Okeechobee-Project Canal C-38. July 1958. 5 p. and 2 figures.

Report on Flood Conditions in the Central and Southern Florida Flood Control District in September 1960. 26 p. and 8 plates.

Hydraulic Study of The North New River Canal. October 1960. 13 p. and 12 plates.

The Plan for Water Control in the Upper St. Johns River Basin Described in the Corps of Engineers Report of February 1962. March 1962. 12 p. and 7 plates.

Benefits of a Water Control Project in the Upper St. Johns Basin to Lands in and Adjacent to the Existing Floodway. October 1963. 10 p. and 5 plates.

Freddy's Hurricane Guide, booklet. June 1970, 35 p.

A River in Distress, booklet. 24 p.

Alligator!!, descriptive pamphlet.

Central and Southern Florida Flood Control District, descriptive pamphlet.

Silent Intruder, descriptive pamphlet.

Conservation in Action, descriptive pamphlet.

So - - - - You Think You Have W - E - E - D Problems, descriptive pamphlet.

A Few Facts & Figures About the Flood Control District, March 1971. 5 p.

Pumping Stations of the FCD.

Recreation in the Everglades, booklet. 36 p.

Million Acre Playground, descriptive pamphlet.

Flood Fighters, descriptive pamphlet.

A Map of The Everglades.

A Map of the Recreation Areas.

FLORIDA DEPARTMENT OF AIR & WATER POLLUTION CONTROL
300 Tallahassee Bank Building
Tallahassee, Florida

Water Pollution Control in Florida. 17 p.

Florida Air and Water Pollution Control Act, Chapter 403.

Rules of the Department of Air and Water Pollution Control. Chapter 17-2 Air Pollution.

Rules of the Florida Air and Water Pollution Control Commission. Chapter 17-3 Pollution of Waters.

FLORIDA DEPARTMENT OF NATURAL RESOURCES
Tallahassee, Florida 32304

Water Resources Investigations in Florida — 1965, conducted by U. S. Geological Survey in cooperation with the State of Florida.

Florida Water and Related Land Resources: St. Johns River Basin. Report on water and related land resources availability and use in the St. Johns River Basin and adjoining coastal area. 1970. 205 p.

Map — Generalized Cross Section Through Peninsular Florida, 11 inches by 17 inches.

OTHER MISCELLANEOUS PUBLICATIONS

Water Education for Teachers.

Are You Concerned About Water?

Water Conservation Quiz for Teachers.

Water Conservation Quiz for Students.

The Effects of Human Attitudes on Conservation of Natural Resources.

Conservation Primer.

The History of the Florida Board of Conservation.

Water Education and Water Conservation – Aids to Teachers.

Conservation of Florida's Resources – (Water) with Problems and Suggestions.

Historical Development of Conservation in America.

FLORIDA DEPARTMENT OF NATURAL RESOURCES

Division of Interior Resources
Bureau of Geology
P. O. Drawer 631
Tallahassee, Florida 32302

Note: When ordering publications, please specify series heading and publication number.

ANNUAL REPORTS

*Third, 1910, 397 p., 30 text fig.
This report contains: (1) a preliminary paper on the Florida phosphate deposits; (2) some Florida lakes and lake basins; (3) the artesian water supply of eastern Florida; (4) a preliminary report on the Florida peat deposits.

*Fourth, 1912, 175 p., 16 pl., 15 text fig., 1 map.
This report contains: (1) the soils and other surface residual materials of Florida, their origin, character, and the formations from which derived; (2) the underground water supply of west central and west Florida; (3) the production of phosphate rock in Florida during 1910 and 1911.

*Fifth, 1913, 306 p., 14 pl., 17 text fig., 2 maps.
This report contains: (1) origin of the hard rock phosphate deposits of Florida; (2) list of elevations in Florida; (3) artesian water supply of eastern and southern Florida; (4) production of phosphate in Florida during 1912; (5) statistics on public roads in Florida.

*Sixth, 1914, 451 p., 90 fig., 1 map.
This report contains: (1) mineral industries and resources of Florida; (2) some Florida lakes and lake basins; (3) relation between the Dunnellon formation and the Alachua clays; (4) geography and vegetation of northern Florida.

Twenty-first and Twenty-second, 1931, 129 p., 39 fig.
This report contains: (1) administrative report and statistics of mineral production, 1928-1929; (2) need for conservation and protection of our water supply; (3) the possibility of petroleum in Florida; (4) beaches of Florida; (5) a palm nut of *Attalea* from the upper Eocene of Florida. [Separates 2, 3, 4, and 5 available.]

Twenty-third and Twenty-fourth, 1933, 227 p., 11 pl., 23 fig., 3 tables.
This report contains: (1) administrative report and statistics on mineral production, 1930-1931; (2) northern disjuncts in northern Florida and cypress domes; (3) notes on the geology and the occurrence of some diatomaceous earth deposits of Florida and diatoms of the Florida peat deposits; (4) ground-water resources of Sarasota County, Florida, and exploration of artesian wells in Sarasota County, Florida. [Separate 2 available.]

BIENNIAL REPORTS

Note: F. G. S. Biennial Reports discontinued with Fourteenth Biennial Report. They are now included in State Board of Conservation Biennial Reports.

*First-Administrative report, 1933-34; including economic investigation of water and mineral resources. 1935, 25 p., 4 fig.

Sixth-Administrative report, 1943-44; water resources, discovery of oil; mineral industry and summaries of production, 1942-43. 1945, 29 p., 3 fig. No charge.

*Twelfth-Administrative report, 1955-56; duties of the Survey personnel of the Florida and U. S. Geological Surveys; cooperative activities with other agencies; study of proposed Cross-Florida Barge Canal and Sanford Titusville Canal; Florida mineral industry – and producers during 1954-55. 1957, 86 p., 12 fig., 2 tables.

BULLETINS

*1   The underground water supply of central Florida, 1908, 103 p., 6 pl., 6 text fig.
This bulletin contains: (1) underground water, general discussion; (2) the underground water of central Florida, deep and shallow wells, spring and artesian prospects; (3) effects of underground solution, cavities, sinkholes, disappearing streams, and solution basins; (4) drainage of lakes, ponds, and swamp lands and disposal of sewage by bored wells; (5) water analyses and tables giving general water resources, public water supplies, spring, and well records.

*11   Ground water investigations in Florida, 1933, 33 p.

*27   Late Cenozoic geology of southern Florida, with a discussion of the ground water, 1944, 119 p., 26 pl., 4 fig.

31   Springs of Florida, 1947, 198 p., frontispiece, (spring location map in pocket), 37 fig., 4 tables. $1.00.

47   Geology and ground-water resources of Leon County, Florida, 1966, 171 p., 37 fig., 1 pl., 8 tables. $1.00.

REPORT OF INVESTIGATIONS
(Nos. 1-6 Mimeographed)

1   Ground water in Seminole County, Florida, 1934, 14 p. $1.00.

2   Ground water in Lake Okeechobee area, Florida, 1933, 31 p. $1.00.

4   Interim report on the investigations of water resources in southeastern Florida with special reference to the Miami area in Dade County, 1944, 39 p., 9 pl. $1.00.

5   Ground water conditions in Orlando and vicinity, 1944, 61 p., 11 fig., 2 tables. $1.00.

6   Geology and ground water of the Fort Lauderdale area, Florida, 1948, 32 p., 12 pl. $1.00.

7   Water resource studies, 1951, 84 p., 10 fig., 3 tables. Part I: Potential yield of ground water of the Fair Point peninsula, Santa Rosa County, 1951, 66 p., 10 fig., 3 tables. Part II: Geology and hydrologic features of an artesian submarine spring east of Florida, 1951, 16 p., 6 fig. Part III: Cessation of flow of Kissengen Spring in Polk County, 1951, 12 p., 5 fig. $1.00.

9 Miscellaneous studies, 1953. Part I: Dissolved phosphorus in Florida waters, 40 p., 9 fig., 7 tables. Part II: Petrology of Eocene limestones in and around the Citrus-Levy County area, Florida, 70 p., 15 fig., 6 tables. $1.00.

10 Ground water of central and northern Florida, 1953, 37 p., 23 fig. $1.00.

11 Ground water resources of the Naples area, Collier County, Florida, 1954, 64 p., 15 fig., 7 tables. $1.00.

12 Ground-water resources of Pinellas County, Florida, 1954, 139 p., 21 fig., 5 tables. $1.00.

13 Water resources of Palm Beach County, Florida, 1954, 63 p., 21 fig., 10 tables. $1.00.

15 Geology and ground-water resources of Highlands County, Florida, 1956, 115p., 12 fig., 11 tables. $1.00.

16 Miscellaneous studies, 1958. Part I: Geology of the area in and around the Jim Woodruff Reservoir, 52 p., 8 fig. Part II: Phosphate concentrations near bird rookeries in south Florida, 16 p., 1 fig., 5 tables. Part III: An analysis of Ochlockonee River channel sediments, 9 p., 3 tables. $1.00.

17 Biscayne aquifer of Dade and Broward counties, Florida, 1958, 56 p., 24 fig. $1.00.

18 Ground-water resources of Manatee County, Florida, 1958, 99 p., 1 pl., 46 fig., 7 tables. $1.00.

19 Hydrologic features of the Lake Istokpoga and Lake Placid areas, Highlands County, Florida, 1959, 73 p. $1.00.

20 Ground-water resources of the Oakland Park area of eastern Broward County, Florida, 1959, 40 p., 23 fig., 2 tables. $1.00.

21 The artesian water of the Ruskin area of Hillsborough County, Florida, 1959, 96 p., 1 pl., 47 fig., 7 tables. $1.00.

22 The ground-water resources of Volusia County, Florida, 1960, 65 p., 30 fig., 3 tables. $1.00.

23 Geology and ground-water resources of Martin County, Florida, 1960, 149 p., 26 fig., 8 tables. $1.00.

24 Part 1: Hydraulic conditions in the vicinity of Levee 30, northern Dade County, Florida, 1961, 24 p., 11 fig., Part 2: Hydrologic studies in the Snapper Creek Canal area, Dade County, Florida, 1962, 32 p., 18 fig. Part 3: Hydrologic studies in the Snake Creek Canal area, Dade County, Florida, 1963, 33 p., 19 fig. Part 4: Salt-water movement caused by Control-dam operations in the Snake Creek Canal, Miami, Florida, 1964, 49 p., 22 fig. Each part $1.00.

25 Water resources of Hillsborough County, Florida, 1961, 101 p., 52 fig., 6 tables. $1.00.

26 The drought of 1954-56 - its effect on Florida's surface-water resources, 1962, 65 p., 9 fig., 5 tables. $1.00.

27 Ground-water resources of Seminole County, Florida, 1962, 91 p., 45 fig., 7 tables. $1.00.

28 Water resources of Brevard County, Florida, 1962, 104 p., 45 fig., 10 tables. $1.00.

29 Aquifers and quality of ground water along the gulf coast of western Florida, 1962, 28 p., 12 fig. $1.00.

30 Reconnaissance of the geology and ground-water resources of Columbia County, Florida, 1962, 73 p., 19 fig., 8 tables. $1.00.

31 Ground-water resources of Collier County, Florida, 1962, 82 p., 29 fig., 5 tables. $1.00.

32 Geology and ground-water resources of Flagler, Putnam and St. Johns counties, Florida, 1963, 97 p., 38 fig., 7 tables. $1.00.

33 Hydrology of Brooklyn Lake near Keystone Heights, Florida, 1963, 43 p., 26 fig., 2 tables. $1.00.

34 Hydrologic reconnaissance of Pasco and southern Hernando counties, Florida. $1.00.

35 Water resources of Alachua, Bradford, Clay, and Union counties, Florida. $1.00.

36 Hydrology of the Biscayne aquifer in the Pompano Beach area, Broward County, Florida. $1.00.

37 Geology and ground-water resources of Glades and Hendry counties, Florida, 1964, 101 p., 33 fig., 8 tables. $1.00.

38 Possibility of salt-water leakage from proposed intracoastal waterway near Venice, Florida well field. $1.00.

39 Reconnaissance of springs and sinks in west-central Florida, 1965, 5 fig. $1.00.

40 Water resources of Escambia and Santa Rosa counties, Florida, 1965, 46 fig., 1 table. $1.00.

41 Water resources of the Econfina Creek Basin, 1965, 51 p., 2 tables, 28 fig. $1.00.

42 Hydrology of the Green Swamp Area in Central Florida, 1966, 137 p., 58 fig., 18 tables. $1.00.

43 Ground Water in Duval and Nassau counties, Florida, 1966, 91 p., 22 fig., 8 tables. $1.00.

44 Ground-water resources of Polk County, 1966, 170 p., 36 fig., 14 tables. $1.00.

45 Salt-water study of the Miami River and its tributaries, Dade County, Florida, 1966, 36 p., 21 fig. $1.00.

46 Fluoride in Water in the Alafia and Peace River Basins, Florida, 1967, 46 p., 20 fig., 2 tables. $1.00.

47 Hydrologic Effects of Area B Flood Control Plan on Urbanization of Dade County, Florida, 1967, 61 p., 24 fig., 7 tables. $1.00.

48 Analysis of the Water Level Fluctuations of Lake Jackson near Tallahassee, Florida. $1.00.

49 Hydrologic Effects of Gound-Water Pumpage in the Peace and Alafia River Basins, Florida, 1934-1965, 32 p., 10 fig., 1 table. $1.00.

50 Water Resources of Orange County, Florida, 62 fig., 14 tables. $1.00.

51 Chemical Quality of Waters of Broward County, Florida, 1968, 52 p., 16 fig., 3 tables. $1.00.

52 Reconnaissance of the Ground-Water Resources of Baker County, Florida, 1968, 24 p., 9 fig., 3 tables. $1.00.

53 Low Streamflow in the Myakka River Basin Area in Florida, 1968, 34 p., 5 fig., 6 tables. $1.00.

54 Water Resources of Northeast Florida, 1970. $1.00.

55 Ground Water Resources of the Lower Hillsboro Canal Area, Southeastern Florida, 1970. $1.00.

56 General Hydrology of the Middle Gulf Area, Florida. $1.00.

INFORMATION CIRCULARS
(Nos. 1-6 Mimeographed)

*3   Ground water in Florida, 1950, 6 p., 5 fig.

*4   The artesian water of the Ruskin area of Hillsborough County, Florida-Interim report, 1953, 22 p., 7 fig.

*5   Interim report on the ground-water resources of Manatee County, Florida, 1955, 38 p., 10 fig.

*6   Interim report on the ground-water resources of Manatee County, Florida, 1955, 38 p., 10 fig.

*7   Interim report on surface-water resources and quality of waters in Lee County, Florida, 1956, 69 p., 9 fig., 3 tables.

*8   Interim report on ground-water resources of the northeastern part of Volusia County, Florida, 1956, 68 p., 14 fig., 4 tables.

*9   Interim report on salt-water encroachment in Dade County, Florida, 1957, 5 p., 12 fig.

*10   Interim report on the progress of an inventory of artesian wells in Florida, 1957, 178 p., 27 fig., 3 tables.

*11   Interim report on the water resources of Brevard County, Florida, 1957, 109 p., 30 fig., 15 tables.

*12   Ground-water resources of the Stuart area, Martin County, Florida, 1957, 47 p., 9 fig., 4 tables.

*13   Interim report on the ground-water resources of Flagler County, Florida, 1958, 32 p., 11 fig., 1 table.

*14   Interim report of the ground-water resources of St. Johns County, Florida, 1958, 35 p., 13 fig., 1 table.

*15   Interim report on the ground-water resources of Putnam County, Florida, 1958, 32 p., 11 fig., 1 table.

*16   Interim report on the changes in the chloride content of ground-water in Pinellas County, Florida, between 1947 and 1956; 1958, 11 p., 4 fig., 1 table.

*17   Interim report on the flood of June 9, 1957, at Perry, Florida, 1958, 12 p., 8 fig.

*18   Interim report on geology and ground-water resources of Indian River County, Florida, 1958, 74 p., 12 fig., 4 tables.

*19   Interim report on records of wells in Manatee County, Florida, 1958, 199 p., 3 fig., 1 table.

*20   Interim report on surface-water resources, Baker County, Florida, 1958, 32 p., 7 fig., 2 tables.

*21   Final report on an inventory of flowing artesian wells in Florida, 1959, 30 p., 9 fig., 3 tables.

*22   Record of wells in Ruskin area, Hillsborough County, Florida, 1959, 85 p., 2 fig., 2 tables.

*23   The geology and ground-water resources of northwestern Polk County, Florida, 1959, 83 p., 19 fig., 9 tables.

24   Record of wells in Volusia County, Florida, 1961, 96 p., 2 fig., 1 pl., 1 table. $1.00.

*25   Surface-water resources of Polk County, Florida, 1961, 123 p., 50 fig., 9 tables.

*26   Interim report on the hydrologic features of the Green Swamp area in central Florida, 1961, 96 p., 22 fig., 3 tables. $1.00.

*27   Preliminary investigation of the ground-water resources of northeast Florida, 1961, 28 p., 11 fig., 2 tables.

*28   Reconnaissance of the ground-water resources of the Fernandina area, Nassau County, Florida, 1961, 24 p., 7 fig., 2 tables.

*29   Ground-water resources of northwest Collier County, Florida, 1961, 44 p., 17 fig., 2 tables.

*30   Interim report on the water resources of Escambia and Santa Rosa counties, Florida, 1961, 89 p., 30 fig., 1 table.

*31   Stage characteristics of Florida lakes, 1961, 82 p., 62 fig.

*32   Water-resource records of Brevard County, Florida, 1962, 180 p., 7 fig., 16 tables.

*33   Water levels in artesian and nonartesian aquifers of Florida in 1960; 1962, 19 p., 3 fig., 3 tables.

*34   Ground-water records of Seminole County, Florida, 1962, 148 p., 3 fig., 3 tables.

*35   Well design as a factor contributing to loss of water from the Floridan aquifer - eastern Clay County, Florida, 1962, 10 p., 4 fig.

*36   Interim report on the water resources of Alachua, Bradford, Clay and Union counties, Florida, 1962, 92 p., 46 fig., 6 tables.

37   Ground-water records of Flagler, Putnam, and St. Johns counties, Florida, 1963, 89 p., 5 fig., 3 tables. $1.00.

38   Records of wells and water resources data in Polk County, Florida, 1963, 144 p., 4 fig., 9 tables. $1.00.

39   Surface-water resources of St. Johns, Flagler, and Putnam counties, 1963, 44 p., 10 fig., 16 tables. $1.00.

40   Maps showing depths of selected lakes in Florida 1964, 82 p., 76 fig., 2 tables. $1.00.

*41   Interim report on the water resources of Orange County, Florida, 1964, 50 p., 13 fig., 6 tables.

43   Water-resources data for Alachua, Bradford, Clay, and Union counties, Florida, 1964, 154 p., 4 fig., 8 tables. $1.00.

44   Water-resources records of Hillsborough County, Florida, 1964, 95 p., 4 fig., 13 tables. $1.00.

47   Control of lake levels in Orange County, Florida, 1965, 15 p., 7 fig. $1.00.

48   Water levels in Artesian and Non-artesian aquifers in Florida, 1961-62, 53 p., 53 fig., 1966. $1.00.

50   Water resource records of Escambia and Santa Rosa counties, Florida; 1966, 106 p., 4 fig., 8 tables. $1.00.

*51   Groundwater in the Immokalee area, Collier County, Florida, 1967, 31 p., 11 fig., 1 table.

52   Water Levels in Artesian and Non-Artesian Aquifers in Florida, 1963-64, 1968, 68 p., 46 fig., 1 table. $1.00.

53   Groundwater Resource Data of Charlotte, DeSoto and Hardee counties, Florida, 1968, 24 p., 4 fig., 4 tables. $1.00.

56   Test Well Exploration in the Myakka River Basin Area, Florida, 1968, 61 p., 15 fig., 3 tables. $1.00.

57   Water Resource Records of the Econfina Creek Basin Area, Florida, 1968, 127 p., 9 fig., 14 tables. $1.00.

58   Production and Utilization of Water in the Metropolitan Area of Jacksonville, Florida, 1969, 37 p., 9 fig., 14 tables. $1.00.

59   Seepage Tests in L-D1 Borrow Canal at Lake Okeechobee, Florida, 1969, 31 p., 13 fig., 1 table. $1.00.

61   Water Levels in Artesian and Nonartesian Aquifers of Florida, 1965-66, 55 p., 47 fig., 1 table. $1.00.

62A   Test of Flushing Procedures to Control Salt-Water Intrusion at the W.P. Franklin Dam near Ft Myers, Florida and The Magnitude & Extent of Salt-Water Contamination in the Caloosahatchee River Between La Belle and Olga, Florida. $1.00.

64   Report on geophysical and television explorations in City of Jacksonville Water Wells, 1970, 15 p., 9 fig., $1.00.

67   Selected Water Resources of Okaloosa County, Florida. In press.

68   Water Levels in Artesian and Non-Artesian Aquifers of Florida, 1967-68, 1970. In press.

69   Selected Flow Characteristics of Florida Streams and Canals. In press.

SPECIAL PUBLICATIONS

*4   Bibliography and index of articles relating to the ground-water resources of Florida-1861-1955, 1959, 104 p.

*7   Investigation of Darby and Hornsby Springs, Alachua County, Florida, 1961, 124 p., 10 fig., 16 pl., 1 table.

11   Index to water resources data collection stations 1963, 168 p., 3 fig., 2 tables. $1.00.

LEAFLETS

1   Your water resources, 1953 revision, 35 p., 22 fig. No charge.

2   Water for thirsty industry - it's your problem, 9 p., 7 fig. No charge.

3   The Pensacola area's water, 1965, 13 p., 16 fig. No charge.

4   Chronological bibliography of principal published ground water reports in Florida, prepared by the U.S. Geological Survey or the Florida Geological Survey, 1908-1963, 1965, 18 p., 5 fig. No charge.

5   Water control versus sea-water intrusion in Broward County, Florida, 1965, 13 p., 9 fig. No charge.

*6   Jacksonville's water, 1965, 12 p., 3 fig., 2 tables.

7   Salt intrusion can be controlled, 1966, 6 p., 3 fig. No charge.

8   Water in Orange County, Florida, 1968, 17 p., 12 fig. No charge.

9   Large Springs of Florida's Sun Coast. No charge.

MAP SERIES

4   Piezometric map with the area of artesian flow of the Floridan aquifer. Prepared by the U.S. Geological Survey in cooperation with the Florida Geological Survey. Size 15 x 15 inches. Scale approximately 30 miles to

1 inch. No charge. Wall size map of above, 42 inches wide, $1.00. Mailed in tube, $1.75.

5   Hydrologic map showing features of the Floridan aquifer in Seminole County, Florida. January, 1963. Map prepared by the U.S. Geological Survey in cooperation with the Florida Geological Survey, in five colors. Size: 19 x 25 inches. Scale approximately 2 miles to 1 inch. No charge.

7   Generalized water-table contours in southern Florida. May, 1964. Map prepared by the U.S. Geological Survey in cooperation with the Florida Geological Survey. Size: 10 x 15 inches. Scale approximately 25 miles to 1 inch. No charge.

9   Quality of water from the Floridan aquifer in Hillsborough County, Florida, 1963. Compiled by Donald E. Shattles, U.S. Geological Survey. Prepared by the U.S. Geological Survey in cooperation with the Florida Geological Survey. Size: 19 x 25 inches. Scale approximately 4 miles to 1 inch. No charge.

10   Quality of water from the Floridan aquifer in the Econfina Creek Basin area, Florida, 1962. Compiled by L.G. Toler and W.J. Shampine, U.S. Geological Survey. Prepared by the U.S. Geological Survey in cooperation with the Florida Geological Survey. Size: 19 x 25 inches. Scale approximately 3 miles to 1 inch. No charge.

12   Chloride concentration in water from the upper part of the Floridan aquifer in Florida. Compiled by William J. Shampine, U.S. Geological Survey. Prepared by the U.S. Geological Survey in cooperation with the Florida Geological Survey. Size: 19 x 25 inches. Scale approximately 30 miles to 1 inch. No charge.

13   Hardness of water from the upper part of the Floridan aquifer in Florida. Compiled by William J. Shampine, U.S. Geological Survey. Prepared by the U.S. Geological Survey in cooperation with the Florida Geological Survey. Size: 19 x 25 inches. Scale approximately 30 miles to 1 inch. No charge.

14   Dissolved solids in water from the upper part of the Floridan aquifer in Florida. Compiled by William J. Shampine, U.S. Geological Survey. Prepared by the U.S. Geological Survey in cooperation with the Florida Geological Survey. Size: 19 x 25 inches. Scale approximately 30 miles to 1 inch. No charge.

15   Sulfate concentration in water from the upper part of the Floridan aquifer in Florida. Compiled by William J. Shampine, U.S. Geological Survey. Prepared by the U.S. Geological Survey in cooperation with the Florida Geological Survey. Size: 19 x 25 inches. Scale approximately 30 miles to 1 inch. No charge.

16   Principal aquifers in Florida. Compiled by Luther W. Hyde, U.S. Geological Survey. Prepared by the U.S. Geological Survey in cooperation with the Florida Geological Survey. Size: 19 x 25 inches. Scale approximately 30 miles to 1 inch. No charge.

17   Quality of water from the Floridan aquifer in Brevard County, Florida, 1963. Compiled by William J. Shampine, U.S. Geological Survey. Prepared by the U.S. Geological Survey in cooperation with the Florida Geological Survey. Size: 19 x 25 inches. No charge.

20   Chloride content of ground water in Pinellas County, Florida in 1950 and 1963; 1966. Size 20½ x 27 inches. Scale approximately 4½ miles to 1 inch. No charge.

21 Availability of ground water in Orange County, Florida, 1966. Size: 24-3/4 x 36-3/4 inches. No charge.

22 Runoff in Florida, 1966. Size: 16 x 20 inches. Scale approximately 30 miles to 1 inch. No charge.

23 Fluoride content of water from the Floridan Aquifer in northwestern Florida, 1966. Size: 16-3/4 x 24 inches. Scale approximately 15 miles to 1 inch. No charge.

24 Availability and quality of surface water in Orange County, Florida, 1966. Size: 22-3/4 x 34-1/2 inches. No charge.

25 Temperature and chemical characteristics - St. Johns River, 1967. Size: 25 x 18-3/4 inches. No charge.

26 Groundwater-Escambia and Santa Rosa counties, Florida, 1967. Size: 24 x 38 inches. No charge.

27 Chemical character of water in the Floridan Aquifer in Southern Peace River Basin, Florida, 1968. Size: 26 x 31 inches. No charge.

28 Drainage Basins in Florida, 1967. Size: 19 x 25 inches. No charge.

29 Water in Broward County, Florida. Compiled by H. J. McCoy and C. B. Sherwood. Prepared by the U. S. Geological Survey in cooperation with the Bureau of Geology, Florida Department of Natural Resources. Size: 25 x 38 inches. No charge.

30 Surface Water Characteristics in Volusia County, Florida. Compiled by Darwin D. Knochenmus. Prepared by the U. S. Geological Survey in cooperation with the Bureau of Geology, Florida Department of Natural Resources. Size: 25½ x 32 inches. No charge.

31 Seasonal Variation of Streamflow in Florida. Compiled by W. E. Kenner. Prepared by the U. S. Geological Survey in cooperation with the Bureau of Geology, Florida Department of Natural Resources. Size: 18 x 22 inches. No charge.

32 The Difference between Rainfall and Potential Evaporation in Florida. Compiled by F. N. Vischer and G. H. Hughes. Prepared by the U. S. Geological Survey in cooperation with the Bureau of Geology, Florida Department of Natural Resources. Size: 18 x 22 inches. No charge.

33 Generalized Distribution and Concentration of Orthophosphate in Florida Streams. Compiled by Matthew I. Kaufman. Prepared by the U. S. Geological Survey in cooperation with the Bureau of Geology, Florida Department of Natural Resources. Size: 18 x 22 inches. No charge.

34 Average Flow of Major Streams in Florida. Compiled by W. E. Kenner, E. R. Hampton, and C. S. Canover. Prepared by the U. S. Geological Survey in cooperation with the Bureau of Geology, Florida Department of Natural Resources. Size: 18 x 22 inches. No charge.

35 Color of Water in Florida Streams and Canals. Compiled by Matthew I. Kaufman. Prepared by the U. S. Geological Survey in cooperation with the Bureau of Geology, Florida Department of Natural Resources. Size: 18 x 22 inches. No charge.

36 Estimated Water Use in Florida, 1965. Compiled by R. W. Pride. Prepared by the U. S. Geological Survey in cooperation with the Bureau of Geology, Florida Department of Natural Resources. Size: 18 x 22 inches. No charge.

37 pH of Water in Florida Streams and Canals. Compiled by Matthew I. Kaufman. Prepared by the U. S. Geological Survey in cooperation with the Bureau of Geology, Florida Department of Natural Resources. Size: 18 x 22 inches. No charge.

38 Hydrologic Setting of Deer Point Lake near Panama City, Florida. Compiled by G. H. Hughes. Prepared by the U. S. Geological Survey in cooperation with the Bureau of Geology, Florida Department of Natural Resources. Size: 34 x 23 inches. No charge.

FLORIDA DEPARTMENT OF NATURAL RESOURCES

Division of Interior Resources
Bureau of Water Resources
107 W. Gaines Street
Tallahassee, Florida 32304

First Biennial Report of the Florida Department of Water Resources, October 1957 - December 1958, Florida Department of Water Resources, 1959, 37 p.

*Second Biennial Report of the Department of Water Resources, January 1959, December 1960, Florida Department of Water Resources, 1961, 44 p.

*Preliminary Investigation and Report on Proposed Impoundment Areas in Southeast Green Swamp, Polk County, Florida, by Lamar Johnson, February 1961, 58 p.

*Preliminary Report on Flood Control Problems, Withlacoochee River, Florida, by Maurice H. Connell and Associates, March 1961, 59 p.

Anclote River Basin Pilot Study, by Frank C. Mohler, Division of Water Resources and Conservation, Florida Board of Conservation, February 1962, 44 p.

Third Biennial Report, 1961 - 1962, Division of Water Resources and Conservation, 1963.

Control of Salt Water Intrusion in Dade County for Protection of the Biscayne Aquifer, by E. W. Bishop and Ney C. Landrum, reprinted by the Division of Water Resources, June 30, 1963, 19 p.

*Biennial Report, 1963 - 1964, Florida Board of Conservation, 1965.

High Points in the Development of Florida's Water Resources and the Role of the Florida Board of Conservation, by Donald P. Schiesswohl, Division of Water Resources and Conservation, Florida Board of Conservation, October 1965, 7 p.

Controlling Wild Flowing Wells in Florida, by H. J. Woodard, Division of Water Resources and Conservation, Florida Board of Conservation, November 1965, 11 p.

*Recommended Procedure for Plugging Water Wells in Florida, Florida Board of Conservation, 1966, 2 p.

*Gazetteer of Florida Streams, Florida Board of Conservation, Division of Water Resources, June 1966, 88 p.

Surface and Sub-Surface Water Availability, by Frank C. Mohler, Florida Board of Conservation, Division of Water Resources, June 1966, 18 p.

Florida Land and Water Resources, Southwest Florida. Florida Board of Conservation, Division of Water Resources, September 1966, 181 p. $1.00 a copy.

Summary Report, Florida Land and Water Resources, Southwest Florida. Florida Board of Conservation, Division of Water Resources, September 1966, 19p.

Florida Statutes, Chapter 373, 1967, Water Resources.

Florida Statutes, Chapter 378, 1967, Flood Control.

Florida Lakes: Part 1, A study of the High Water Lines of Some Florida Lakes; Part 2, A Tentative Classification of Lake Shorelines. Florida Board of Conservation, Division of Water Resources, March 1967, 75 p. $1.00 a copy.

Water Use by Florida Golf Courses, by Frank C. Mohler, Division of Water Resources and Conservation, Florida Board of Conservation, Revised November 1967, 35 p.

FLORIDA GAME AND FRESH WATER FISH COMMISSION

Information Education Division
Tallahassee, Florida 32304

What is Conservation?

*Suwannee River Watershed.

*St. Johns River Report.

FLORIDA WATER RESOURCES RESEARCH CENTER

220 Environmental Engineering Building
University of Florida
Gainesville, Florida 32601

Note: Single copies available at no cost unless otherwise stated.

Research Highlights—Florida Water Resources Research Center. by John E. Kiker, Jr., Director, and William H. Morgan, Assistant Director. Published as Leaflet No. 187, December 1966, Engineering Progress at the University of Florida, Engineering and Industrial Experiment Station, College of Engineering. 13 p.

Urban Environmental Problems—A Graduate Interdisciplinary Seminar, organized by Edwin E. Pyatt, Dr. Eng., Professor of Environmental Engineering, edited by Rachel Albertson, Editor, Engineering and Industrial Experiment Station. Published as Bulletin Series No. 128, June 1967, Engineering Progress at the University of Florida. 98 p.

A Partial Checklist of Florida Fresh-Water Algae and Protozoa with Reference to McCloud and Cue Lakes, by James B. Lackey, Professor Emeritus, Earle B. Phelps Laboratory for Sanitary Engineering Research and Elsie W. Lackey, Consultant. Published as Bulletin Series No. 131, November 1967, Engineering Progress at the University of Florida. 28 p.

Water Law and Administration—The Florida Experience, by Frank E. Maloney, Dean, Sheldon J. Plager, Professor, and Fletcher N. Baldwin, Jr., Professor, College of Law, University of Florida, Gainesville, University of Florida Press, 1968. Price: $25.00.

Eutrophication Factors in North Central Florida Lakes, by P. L. Brezonik, W. H. Morgan, E. E. Shannon and H. D. Putnam, Department of Environmental Engineering, University of Florida. Published as Bulletin Series No. 134, August 1969, Engineering Progress at the University of Florida. 101 p.

Rate of Solution of Limestone in the Karst Terrane of Florida, by H. K. Brooks, Associate Professor of Geology, University of Florida, 1967. 16 p.

The Net Effect of Wind on Recreation Tidal Streams in Florida, by D. H. Moreau, Assistant Professor of Environmental Engineering, University of Florida, 1967. 11 p.

GEORGIA

BUREAU OF STATE PLANNING AND COMMUNITY AFFAIRS
270 Washington Street, S. W.
Atlanta, Georgia 30334

*Georgia Water Resources Planning. November 1968. (A six-part preliminary report):

Part I — Social—Economic Implications, 41 p.

Part II — Water Quantity—Quality—Pollution, 37 p.

Part III — Uses and Interests, 64 p.

Part IV — Laws—Regulations—Policies, 42 p.

Part V — Information System, 38 p.

Part VI — Needs and Recommendations, 21 p.

ENVIRONMENTAL RESOURCES CENTER
Georgia Institute of Technology
Atlanta, Georgia 30332

Carstens, M. R. and George D. May, Seepage flow through an earth dam. 1966. Various pagings. (WRC-0466).

Carstens, M. R. and George D. May, Salt-water intrusion effect of a fresh-water canal. 1967. 41 p. (WRC-0567).

Champlin, Jerry B. F., The movement of micron-size particles through a sand bed. 1967. 106 p. (WRC-0867).

Champlin, Jerry B. F., The transport of radioisotopes by fine particulate matter in aquifers. 1969. 187 p. (WRC-1169).

Champlin, Jerry B. F., The relation of ion movement to fine particle displacement in a sand bed. 1969. 22 p.

Charmonman, Srisakdi, M. R. Carstens and George D. May, A fresh-water canal as a barrier to salt-water intrusion. 1967. 7 p. (WRC-0367.5).

Craft, Thomas Fisher Jr., Radiotracer study of rapid sand filtration. 1969. 179 p. (WRC-0469).

Edge, Billy L. and Paul G. Mayer, A stochastic model for the response of permanent offshore structures subject to soil restraints and wave forces. 1969. 203 p.

Elmore, George Roy, Jr., Georgia laws, policies and programs pertaining to water and related land resources. 1967. 112 p. (WRC-0667).

Flege, R. K., Determination, evaluation and abatement of color in textile plant effluents. A. French Textile School, 1968. 59 p.

Flege, R. K., Determination of degraded dyes and auxiliary chemicals in effluents from textile dyeing processes. A. French Textile School, 1970. 42 p.

Gates, William E. and Shun-Dar Lin, Pilot plant studies on the anaerobic treatment of tannery effluents. 1967. (WRC-0267.5).

Ghosh, Sambhunath, Kinetics of aerobic utilization of mixed sugars by heterogeneous microbial populations. 1969. 467 p. (WRC-0969).

Hyden, William L., Douglas F. Becknell and Telford E. Elders, Survey of the nature and magnitude of the water research needs of the textile industry of Georgia; final report. 1966. 27 p. (WRC-0366).

Jackson, Henry C. and Paul G. Mayer, Unsteady flow of dilute aqueous polymer solutions in pipe networks - a method to improve water distribution. 1970. 134 p. (WRC-0170).

Jones, Leonard D. and William L. Hyden, The state of the art of water use and waste disposal in the textile industry (1950-66). 1966. 61 p. (WRC-0166).

Kelnhofer, Guy J. Jr., Metropolitan planning and river basin planning: some interrelationships. July 1968. 218 p.

Majumdar, Hirendra and M. R. Carstens, Diffusion of particles by turbulence: effect of particle size. 1967. 102 p. (WRC-0967).

Marlar, John T., The effect of turbulence on bacterial substrate utilization. 1968. 110 p.

Martin, Charles Samuel and Mustafa M. Aral, The effect of a permeable sand bed on sediment motion. 1969. 97 p. (WRC-0869).

Martin, Charles Samuel, The effect of a permeable bed on sediment motion; Phase I: Seepage force on bed particles, final report. 1966. 60 1. (WRC-0266).

Mayer, Paul G. and Bruce R. Olmstead, Hydraulic investigations of tainter gates as flow measuring devices. 1968. 103 p.

Mussalli, Yusuf G. and M. R. Carstens, A study of flow conditions in shaft spillways. 1969. 158 p. (WRC-0669).

Olinger, Lawrence W., The effect of induced turbulence on the growth of algae. 1968. 81 p.

Sturrock, Peter E. and Robert L. Poole, Jr., The application of phase selective alternating current polarography to the analysis of heavy metals in water. 1970. 55 p. (ERC-0470).

Weaver, Charles E. and Kevin C. Beck, Changes in the clay-water system with depth, temperature, and time. 1969. 95 p. (WRC-0769).

York, C. Michael, Instruments for measuring attitude toward a community water issue. 1969. 35 p. (WRC-0569).

Zovne, Jerome Joseph, The numerical solution of transient supercritical flow by the method of characteristics with a technique for simulating bore propagation. 1970. 165 p. (ERC-0370).

GEOLOGICAL SURVEY OF GEORGIA
Department of Mines, Mining and Geology
19 Hunter Street S.W.
Atlanta, Georgia 30303

BULLETINS

*3 The Water-Powers of Georgia, by C. C. Anderson and B. M. Hall, 1896, 150 p., 10 pl., 2 maps.

7 Artesian-Well System of Georgia, by S. W. McCallie, 1898, 214 p., 7 pl., 2 maps. Price: $5.00.

15 Underground Waters of Georgia, by S. W. McCallie, 1908, 376 p., 29 pl., 2 maps. Price: $2.00.

16 Water-Powers of Georgia, 2nd report, by B. M. Hall and M. R. Hall, 1908, 424 p., 14 pl., 1 map. Price: $1.00.

20 Mineral Springs of Georgia, by S. W. McCallie, 1913, 190 p., 24 pl., 1 map. Price: $2.00.

*25 Drainage Investigations in Georgia, by S. W. McCallie and U.S. Department of Agriculture, 1911, 123 p., 7 pl., 5 maps.

32 Agricultural Drainage in Georgia, by J. E. Brantly and U.S. Department of Agriculture, 1917, 117 p., 6 maps. Price: $1.00.

38 Water-Powers of Georgia, 3rd report, by B. M. Hall and M. R. Hall, 1921, 316 p., 11 pl., 4 maps. Price: $2.00.

42 Physical Geography of Georgia, by Laurence LaForge, C. W. Cooke, and others, 1925, 189 p., 43 pl. Price: $4.00.

49 Artesian Water in Southeastern Georgia, with Special Reference to the Coastal Area—Well Records, by M. A. Warren, 1945, 83 p., 1 map. Price: $1.00.

49-A Artesian Water in Southeastern Georgia, with Special Reference to the Coastal Area—Well Records, by M. A. Warren, 1945, 83 p., 1 map. Price: $3.00.

*52 Geology and Ground-Water Resources of the Coastal Plain of East-Central Georgia, by P. E. LaMoreaux, 1946, 173 p., 2 pl., 21 fig.

55 Geology and Ground-Water Resources of the Atlanta Area, Georgia, by S. M. Herrick and H. E. LeGrand, 1949, 124 p., 2 pl., 9 fig. Price: $1.00.

64 Geology and Ground-Water Resources of Central East Georgia, by A. S. Furcron and H. E. LeGrand, 1956, 164 p., 1 map. Price: $2.00.

65 The Availability and Use of Water in Georgia, by M. T. Thomson, S. M. Herrick, Eugene Brown and others, 1956, 316 p., 3 pl., 74 fig., 19 tables. Price: $1.00.

69 Reconnaissance of Chemical Quality of Georgia Streams, by R. N. Cherry, 1961, 100 p., 52 engravings. Price: $1.00.

70 Well Logs of the Coastal Plain of Georgia, by S. M. Herrick, 1961, 470 p., 1 map. Price: $5.00.

72 Geology and Ground-Water Resources of the Macon Area, Georgia, by H. E. LeGrand, 1962, 68 p., 3 maps. Price: $2.00.

73 Effect of a Severe Drought, 1954, on Stream Flow in Georgia, by M. T. Thomson and R. F. Carter, 1963, 98 p. 1 map. Price: $1.00.

78 Specific Cations in Ground Waters Related to Geologic Formations in the Broad Quadrangle, Georgia, by C. A. Salotti and J. A. Fouts, 1967, 34 p., 1 map. Price: $1.00.

INFORMATION CIRCULARS
(Price: $1.50 each)

8 Water, Georgia's Unknown Natural Resource, by R. W. Smith, 1936.

16 The Characteristics of Georgia's Water Resources and Factors Related to Their Use and Control, by Garland Peyton, 1954.

17 Surface Water Resources of Georgia During the Drought of 1954, Part I, Streamflow, by M. T. Thomson and R. F. Carter, 1955.

18 Source and Quality of Ground Water in Southwestern Georgia, by R. L. Wait, 1960.

20 Relation of Salty Ground Water to Fresh Artesian Water in the Brunswick Area, Glynn County, Georgia, by J. W. Stewart, 1960.

21 Streamflow Maps of Georgia's Major Rivers, by M. T. Thomson, 1960.

22 Yellow River Area, by R. S. Carter and W. B. Gannon, 1963.

23 Interim Report on Test Drilling and Water Sampling in the Brunswick Area, Glynn County, Georgia, by R. L. Wait, 1962.

24 Geology and Ground-Water Resources of Mitchell County, Georgia, by Vaux Owen, Jr., 1963.

26 Geology and Ground-Water Resources of Dade County, Georgia, by M. G. Croft, 1964.

27 Geology and Ground-Water Resources of the Paleozoic Rock Area, Chattooga County, Georgia, by C. W. Cressler, 1964.

28 Geology and Ground-Water Resources of Catoosa County, Georgia, by C. W. Cressler, 1963.

29 Geology and Ground-Water Resources of Walker County, Georgia, by C. W. Cressler, 1964.

30 Geology and Ground-Water Resources of Crystalline Rocks, Dawson County, Georgia, by C. W. Sever, 1964.

32 Ground-Water Resources of Bainbridge, Georgia, by C. W. Sever, 1965.

33 Ground-Water Resources and Geology of Rockdale County, Georgia, by M. J. McCollum, 1966.

34   Reconnaissance of the Ground Water and Geology of Thomas County, Georgia, by C. W. Sever, 1966.

36   Hydraulics of Aquifers at Alapaha, Collidge, Fitzgerald, Montezuma, and Thomasville, Georgia, by C. W. Sever, 1969.

SPECIAL PUBLICATIONS

1   Emergency Water Supplies for the Atlanta Area in a National Emergency, by J. W. Stewart and S. M. Herrick, 1963. $2.00.

GEORGIA WATER AND POLLUTION CONTROL ASSOCIATION

Rt. 3, Mars Hill Road
Acworth, Georgia 30101

Georgia Operator, a quarterly magazine which is the official news organ of the Georgia Water & Pollution Control Association.

GEORGIA WATER QUALITY CONTROL BOARD

47 Trinity Avenue, S. W.
Atlanta, Georgia 30334

Rules of the Georgia Water Quality Control Board; Chapter 730. 34 p.

Georgia Water Quality Control Act. Act No. 870 as amended through 1966. 17 p.

Water Pollution Control in Georgia. A 7-page report.

Annual Progress Report — 1965 to date.

Technical Report No. 1, Water Quality of Tobesofkee Creek, 1966. 112 p.

Technical Report No. 2, Water Quality Study of Chatham County Waters, with Recommendations for Pollution Abatement and Prevention, 1966. 256 p.

HAWAII

DEPARTMENT OF LAND AND NATURAL RESOURCES

Division of Water and Land Development
P. O. Box 373
Honolulu, Hawaii 96809

The publications listed herein include those published under several former agencies which were eventually succeeded by the Division of Water and Land Development, Department of Land and Natural Resources. These agencies were the Hawaii Division of Hydrography, the Hawaii Irrigation Authority, and the Hawaii Water Authority.

In consolidating its own publications with those issued by the above former agencies, the Division of Water and Land Development has assigned new publication numbers in the following categories: Bulletins, Reports and Circulars. Generally:

Bulletins *refer to publications whose subject matter is general and comprehensive, for example, island-wide or state-wide in scope:*

Reports *refer to publications whose subject matter is specific and limited, for example, project study, research paper, or basic data compilation;*

Circulars *refer to those publications whose subject matter is preliminary, introductory, or brief.*

New publication numbers have been assigned to all publications except the former Hawaii Division of Hydrography Bulletins 1 through 13 which have been revised by including the prefix letter "B" to their original numbers.

Many of the publications are either out of print or in short supply due to limited publication runs.

BULLETINS

*B1 Geology and Ground-Water Resources of the Island of Oahu, Hawaii. Harold T. Stearns and Knute N. Vaksvik, Hawaii Division of Hydrography, 1935.

*B2 Geologic Map and Guide of the Island of Oahu, Hawaii. Harold T. Stearns, Hawaii Division of Hydrography, 1939.

*B3 Annotated Bibliography and Index of Geology and Water Supply of the Island of Oahu, Hawaii. Norah D. Stearns, Hawaii Division of Hydrography, 1935.

*B4 Records of the Drilled Wells on the Island of Oahu, Hawaii. Harold T. Stearns and Knute N. Vaksvik, Hawaii Division of Hydrography, 1938.

*B5 Supplement to the Geology and Ground-Water Resources of the Island of Oahu, Hawaii. (Includes chapters on geophysical investigations by Joel H. Swartz, and petrography by Gordon A. MacDonald.) Harold T. Stearns, Hawaii Division of Hydrography, 1940.

*B6 Geology and Ground-Water Resources of the Islands of Lanai and Kahoolawe, Hawaii. (Includes chapters on geophysical investigations by Joel H. Swartz, and petrography by Gordon A. MacDonald.) Harold T. Stearns, Hawaii Division of Hydrography, 1940.

*B7 Geology and Ground-Water Resources of the Island of Maui, Hawaii. Harold T. Stearns and Gordon A. MacDonald, Hawaii Division of Hydrography, 1942.

*B8 Geology of the Hawaiian Islands. Harold T. Stearns, Hawaii Division of Hydrography, 1946.

*B9 Geology and Ground-Water Resources of the Island of Hawaii. Harold T. Stearns and Gordon A. MacDonald, Hawaii Division of Hydrography, 1946.

*B10 Bibliography of the Geology and Ground-Water Resources of the Island of Hawaii. Annotated and Indexed. Gordon A. MacDonald, Hawaii Division of Hydrography, 1947.

*B11 Geology and Ground-Water Resources of the Island of Molokai, Hawaii. Harold T. Stearns and Gordon A. MacDonald, Hawaii Division of Hydrography, 1947.

*B12 Geology and Ground-Water Resources of the Island of Niihau, Hawaii. (Includes chapters on petrography by Gordon A. MacDonald.) Harold T. Stearns, Hawaii Division of Hydrography, 1947.

B13 Geology and Ground-Water Resources of the Island of Kauai, Hawaii. Gordon A. MacDonald, Dan A. Davis, and Doak C. Cox, Hawaii Division of Hydrography, 1960.

B14 Water Resources in Hawaii. Hawaii Water Authority, March, 1959.

B15 Flood Control and Flood Water Conservation in Hawaii. Division of Water and Land Development. Volume I. Floods and Flood Control. January 1963. Volume II. General Flood Control Plan for Hawaii. January 1963. Volume III. (In preparation)

*B16 Water Resources Development: Molokai. Division of Water & Land Development, February 1966.

REPORTS

*R1 Methods for Development and Delivery of Water for Irrigation of Hawaiian Homes Commission Lands at Hoolehua, Island of Molokai. (Prepared by H. A. R. Austin and Harold T. Stearns), Hawaii Water Authority, May 1954.

*R2 General Reference Guide for Irrigation Project Planning in Hawaii. Hawaii Water Authority, March 1957.

*R3 Kokee Irrigation Project Progress Report, Island of Kauai. Hawaii Water Authority, April 1957.

*R4 Kula Irrigation Project Feasibility Report, Island of Maui. Hawaii Water Authority, March 1957.

*R5 Waianae Irrigation Project Feasibility Report, Island of Oahu. Hawaii Water Authority, April 1957.

*R6 Growth of Population in the Kona District, Island of Hawaii. (Prepared by Stanford Research Institute), Hawaii Water Authority, January 1958.

*R7 Report on Estimated Costs of Operating the Waimanalo Irrigation System to Serve the Existing Farm Lots Subdivision and the University of Hawaii Experimental Farm. L. H. Herschler, Hawaii Water Authority, January 1958.

*R8 Kona Rainfall. William J. Taliaferro, Hawaii Water Authority, September 1958.

*R9 Kona Rainfall (supplement). William J. Taliaferro, Hawaii Water Authority, September 1959.

*R10 Kona Irrigation Project Feasibility Report, Island of Hawaii. Hawaii Water Authority, March 1959.

*R11 Progress Report on Hawaii Water Authority's Plans for the Kona Water System. Hawaii Water Authority, June 1959.

*R12 Rainfall of the Hawaiian Islands. William J. Taliaferro, Hawaii Water Authority, September 1959.

*R13 Rainfall, Tanks, Catchment and Family Use of Water. Chester K. Wentworth, Hawaii Water Authority, December 1959.

*R14 A Report on a Water Supply for the Proposed Ahuamoa Camp, Island of Hawaii. Hawaii Water Authority, February 1960.

*R15 An Inventory of Basic Water Resources Data: Molokai. Division of Water and Land Development, January 1961.

*R16 Molokai Project, Loan Application Report. Division of Water and Land Development, April 1961.

R17 Pan Evaporation Data, State of Hawaii. Division of Water and Land Development, September 1961.

R18 A Domestic Water Plan for Kaunakakai-Pukoo, Island of Molokai. Division of Water and Land Development, January 1962.

*R19 Relationship of the State Water Program and the U. S. Geological Survey. Division of Water and Land Development, January 1962.

R20 Report on Lihue Water System, Island of Kauai. Division of Water and Land Development, June 1962.

R21 Improvements to County Water System, Lahaina District, Maui. Division of Water and Land Development, August 1963.

R22 Kokee Water Project, Island of Kauai, Hawaii. A Report on the Feasibility of Water Development. Division of Water and Land Development, 1964.

R22a Kokee Water Project, Island of Kauai, Hawaii-Geology Supplement. Division of Water and Land Development, May 1966.

*R23 Ocean Outfall Report, Waimanalo Core Development. (Prepared by R. M. Towill Corp.), Division of Water and Land Development, April 1964.

*R24 Report on Oceanographic Study for Kapaa Ocean Sewer Outfall, Kapaa, Kauai. (Prepared by Sunn, Low, Tom & Hara, Inc.). Division of Water and Land Development, November 1964.

R25 A Water Development Plan for South Kohala-Hamakua, Island of Hawaii. Division of Water and Land Development, January 1965.

R26 Floods of December 1964 – February 1965 in Hawaii. Stuart Hoffard (Prepared by U.S. Geological Survey). Division of Water and Land Development, June 1965.

R27 Flow Characteristics of Selected Streams in Hawaii. George T. Hirashima (Prepared by U. S. Geological Survey). Division of Water and Land Development, September 1965.

*R28 Effects of Water Withdrawals by Tunnels, Waihee Valley, Oahu, Hawaii. George T. Hirashima (Prepared by U. S. Geological Survey). Division of Water and Land Development, November 1965.

R29 Water Supply Investigations for Laupahoehoe Water System, South Hamakua, Island of Hawaii. Division of Water and Land Development, July 1966.

R30 Flood of March 24, 1967, Kihei and Olowalu Areas, Island of Maui. Stuart H. Hoffard (Prepared by U.S. Geological Survey). Division of Water and Land Development, July 1968.

R31 Geologic-Hydrologic Investigations for Deep-Well Disposal, Waimanalo, Oahu, Hawaii. Daniel Lum, Division of Water and Land Development, (In preparation).

R32 Waikolu and Pelekunu Valleys Water Resources Feasibility Study, Island of Molokai. (Prepared by Parsons, Brinckerhoff and Hirota, Assoc.). Division of Water and Land Development, January 1969.

R33 A Water Source Development Plan for the Lahaina District, Island of Maui. (Prepared by Belt, Collins & Assoc.). Division of Water & Land Development, November 1969.

R34 An Inventory of Basic Water Resources Data, Island of Hawaii. Division of Water and Land Development, February 1970.

R35 Kohakohau Dam Engineering Feasibility, South Kohala Water Project, Hawaii. (Prepared by Parsons, Brinckerhoff, Hirota Associate). Division of Water and Land Development. February 1970.

R36 Flood Frequencies for Selected Streams in Hawaii. Division of Water and Land Development, July 1970.

R37 Flood Hazard Information Island of Hawaii. Division of Water and Land Development, (In cooperation with the U.S. Geological Survey) September 1970.

CIRCULARS

*C1 Rights in Ground Water. (Prepared by Legislative Reference Bureau). Hawaii Water Authority, September 1957.

*C2 Ground Water Legislation. Wells A. Hutchins, Hawaii Water Authority, June 1958.

*C3 Summary of Drilling Logs and Pumping Test for Kawaihae Exploratory Well No. 1, South Kohala, Hawaii. Job No. 15-H-1. Division of Water and Land Development, March 1961.

*C4 Summary of Drilling Logs and Pumping Test for Exploratory Well No. 1, Waikapu, Maui, Hawaii. Job No. 17-H-1. Division of Water and Land Development, March 1961.

*C5   Summary of Drilling Logs and Pumping Test for Exploratory Well No. 2, Hanapepe, Kauai, Hawaii. Job No. 17-H-1. Division of Water and Land Development, May 1961.

*C6   Summary of Drilling Logs and Pumping Test for Kawaihae Exploratory Well No. 2, South Kohala, Hawaii. Job No. 15-H-1. Division of Water and Land Development, June 1961.

*C7   Summary of Drilling Logs and Pumping Test for Exploratory Well No. 4 (USGS Well No. 73), Maka Ridge, Hanalei Kauai. Job No. 17-H-1. Division of Water and Land Development, November 1961.

*C8   Summary of Drilling Logs and Pumping Test for Exploratory Well No. 3 (USGS Well No. 11), Lihue, Kauai, Hawaii. Job No. 17-H-1. Division of Water and Land Development, January 1962.

*C9   Summary of Drilling Logs and Pumping Tests for Lahaina Exploratory Well (USGS Well No. 291), Lahaina, Maui, Hawaii. Job No. 26-I-2. Division of Water and Land Development May, 1962.

*C10   Preliminary Summary of Findings in Water Resources studies of Windward Oahu, Hawaii. K. J. Takasaki, George Yamanaga, and R. R. Lubke. Division of Water and Land Development, (In cooperation with the U. S. Geological Survey) March 1962.

*C11   Summary of Drilling Logs and Pumping Test for Kamalo Exploratory Well (USGS Well No. 31), Kamalo, Molokai, Hawaii. Job No. 17-I-2. Division of Water and Land Development, August 1962.

*C12   Summary of Drilling Logs and Pumping Test for Malama-Ki Well 9-9, Malama-Ki, Puna, Hawaii. Job No. 17-J-3, Exploratory Well Drilling. Division of Water and Land Development, October 1962.

*C13   Interim Report on Hamakua-Kohala Water Study. Division of Water and Land Development, January 1963.

*C14   Preliminary Report on the Water Resources of Kohala Mountain and Mauna Kea, Hawaii. Dan A. Davis and George Yamanaga (Prepared by U. S. Geological Survey). Division of Water and Land Development, January 1963.

*C15   Investigations of Ferruginous Bauxite and Plastic Clay Deposits on Kauai and a Reconnaissance of Ferruginous Bauxite Deposits on Maui, Hawaii. Sam H. Patterson (Prepared by U. S. Geological Survey). Division of Water and Land Development, February 1963.

C16   Preliminary Report on the Ground Water Resources of the Waianae Area, Oahu. C. P. Zones (Prepared by U. S. Geological Survey). Division of Water and Land Development, 1963.

C17   Preliminary Report on Legal Problems to be Studied in Connection with the Hamakua-Kohala Water Study, Island of Hawaii. Division of Water and Land Development, March 1963.

*C18   A Brief Description of the Upper Hamakua Ditch, Waimea, Island of Hawaii. Division of Water and Land Development, March 1963.

*C19   Reconnaissance Geologic Report on Proposed Penstock Alinement and Afterbay Reservoir Site, Kokee Project, Hawaii. Daniel Lum, Division of Water and Land Development, March 1963.

C20   Aspects of Ground-water Storage and Depletion Along the Molokai Irrigation Tunnel, Molokai, Hawaii. George

T. Hirashima (Prepared by U. S. Geological Survey). Division of Water and Land Development, 1963.

C21   Influence of Water-Development Tunnels on Streamflow-Groundwater Relations in Haiku-Kahaluu Area, Oahu, Hawaii. George T. Hirashima (Prepared by U. S. Geological Survey). Division of Water and Land Development, 1963.

*C22   Summary of Drilling Logs and Pumping Test for Kamiloloa Well 19, Kamiloloa, Molokai. Job No. 17-I-2, Exploratory Well Drilling, Division of Water & Land Development, August 1963.

*C23   Summary of Drilling Logs and Pumping Test for Keei Well 12-8, Keei, South Kona, Hawaii. Job No. 8-I-16. Division of Water and Land Development, September 1963.

*C24   Summary of Drilling Logs and Pumping Test for Kawaihae Well 16, Kawaihae, South Kohala, Hawaii. Job No. 17-K-7, Exploratory Well Drilling. Division of Water and Land Development, September 1963.

*C25   Summary of Drilling Logs and Pumping Test for Kalaheo Well 24, Kalaheo, Kauai, Hawaii. Job No. 17-K-8, Exploratory Well Drilling. Division of Water and Land Development, December 1963.

*C26   Summary of Drilling Logs and Pumping Test for Pulama Well 9-10, Pulama, Puna, Hawaii. Division of Water and Land Development, May 1964.

*C27   Water Resources of the Kau District, Hawaii. Dan A. Davis and George Yamanaga (Prepared by U. S. Geological Survey). Division of Water and Land Development, October 1966.

*C28   Summary of Drilling Logs and Pumping Test for Makena Well 68, Makena, Maui, Hawaii. Division of Water and Land Development, November 1964.

C29   Summary of Drilling Logs for Pohakuloa Test Hole 20, Pohakuloa, Hamakua, Hawaii. Division of Water and Land Development, March 1965.

C30   (In preparation).

C31   (In preparation).

C32   Flood Prevention by Soil Conservation Service. Division of Water & Land Development, June 1965.

C33   (In preparation).

C34   Summary of Drilling Logs and Pumping Test for Maui High School Well 35, Hamakuapoko, Maui, Hawaii. Division of Water and Land Development, May 1965.

C35   Summary of Drilling Logs and Pumping Test for Alaeloa Well 318, Alaeloa, Maui, Hawaii. Division of Water and Land Development, May 1965.

C36   Summary of Drilling Logs for Waimea Test Hole T-19, Waimea, South Kohala, Hawaii. Division of Water and Land Development, May 1965.

C37   Summary of Drilling Logs for Lahaina Well 292, Lahaina, Maui, Hawaii. Division of Water and Land Development, May 1965.

C38   Application for Grant Under Water Resources Planning Act of 1965. Department of Land and Natural Resources, September 1966.

C39   Preliminary Report on the Water Resources of the Kahuku Area, Oahu, Hawaii. K. J. Takasaki, S. Valenciano, and A. M. Ho (Prepared by U. S. Geological Survey). Division of Water and Land Development, November 1966.

*C40 Drainage Criteria Meeting. Division of Water and Land Development, November 1966.

C41 Summary of Drilling Log and Pumping Test for Haena Well 66, Haena, Kauai. Division of Water and Land Development, June 1967.

C42 Summary of Drilling Log and Pumping Test for Hanapepe Well 25-1, Hanapepe, Kauai. Division of Water and Land Development, June 1967.

C43 Summary of Drilling Log and Pumping Test for Maalaea Well 272, Maalaea, Maui. Division of Water and Land Development, July 1967.

C44 Summary of Drilling Log and Pumping Test for Waimea Well 26, Waimea, Kauai. Division of Water and Land Development, July 1967.

*C45 Preliminary Report on the Water Resources of the Hilo-Puna Area, Hawaii. Dan A. Davis and George Yamanaga (Prepared by U. S. Geological Survey). Division of Water and Land Development, April 1968.

C46 Preliminary Report on the Water Resources of the Kona Area, Hawaii. Dan A. Davis and George Yamanaga (Prepared by U. S. Geological Survey). Division of Water and Land Development, June 1968.

C47 Post Flood Report, Storm of 17 and 18 December 1967, Islands of Kauai and Oahu. (Prepared by Department of the Army, Honolulu District, Corps of Engineers). Division of Water and Land Development, October 1968.

C48 Summary of Drilling Log and Pumping Test for Kalaoa Well 12-11 (Near Keahole), North Kona, Hawaii. Division of Water and Land Development, November 1968.

C49 Post Flood Report, Storm of 5 January 1968, Island of Oahu. (Prepared by Department of the Army, Honolulu District, Corps of Engineers). Division of Water and Land Development, November 1968.

C50 Post Flood Report, Storm of 15-16 April 1968, Island of Maui. (Prepared by the Department of the Army, Honolulu District, Corps of Engineers). Division of Water and Land Development, December 1968.

C51 Preliminary Report on the Water Resources of the Lahaina District, Maui. George Yamanaga and C. J. Huxel (Prepared by U. S. Geological Survey). Division of Water and Land Development, February 1969.

C52 Post Flood Report, Storm of 3-4 October 1968, Island of Hawaii. (Prepared by Department of the Army, Honolulu District, Corps of Engineers). Division of Water and Land Development, March 1969.

C53 Interim Report on Kahena Ditch Water Study, Island of Hawaii. Division of Water and Land Development, March 1969.

C54 Preliminary Report on Geohydrologic Exploration for Deep Well Disposal of Effluent, Waimanalo Sewage Treatment Plant, Waimanalo, Oahu. Daniel Lum, Division of Water and Land Development, May 1969.

C55 Post Flood Report, Storms of November 28 to December 1, 1968 and January 5, 1969, Island of Kauai, Hawaii. (Prepared by U. S. Department of the Army, Honolulu District, Corps of Engineers). Division of Water and Land Development, August, 1969.

C56 Post Flood Report, Storm of 1 February 1969, Island of Oahu, Hawaii. (Prepared by U. S. Department of the Army, Honolulu District, Corps of Engineers.) Division of Water and Land Development, September 1969.

C57 Post Flood Report, Storm of 1-2 & 4 December 1969, Hawaiian Islands. (Prepared U. S. Department of the Army, Honolulu District, Corps of Engineers.) Division of Water and Land Development, March 1970.

C58 (In preparation)

C59 Hydrologic Data Networks, Island of Molokai. Rainfall Stations, Stream Gage Stations & Ground Water. Division of Water and Land Development, May 1970.

C60 Preliminary Report on the Water Resources of Northeast Maui. (Prepared by the U. S. Geological Survey.) Division of Water and Land Development, August 1970.

WATER RESOURCES RESEARCH CENTER

University of Hawaii
2525 Correa Road
Honolulu, Hawaii 96822

TECHNICAL REPORTS

*1 Reginald H. F. Young, L. Stephen Lau & Nathan C. Burbank, Travel of ABS and ammonia nitrogen with percolating water through saturated Oahu soils. January 1967. 54 p.

*2 Melvin K. Koizumi, Nathan C. Burbank & L. Stephen Lau, Infiltration and percolation of sewage through Oahu soils in simulated cesspool lysimeters. August 1966. 49 p.

*3 L. Stephen Lau, Dynamic and static studies of seawater intrusion. February 1967. 31 p.

*4 Doak C. Cox & Chester Lao, Development of deep monitoring stations in the Pearl Harbor ground water area on Oahu. March 1967. 34 p.

*5 James S. Kumagai, A survey of literature on ground water recharge and sulfide generation. March 1967. 41 p.

*6 Leonard A. Palmer, Instrumentation for seismic exploration for ground water in Hawaii. April 1967. 26 p.

*7 James S. Kumagai, Infiltration and percolation studies of sulfides and sewage carbonaceous matter. June 1967. 58 p.

*8 David von Seggern & William M. Adams, Electro-magnetic mapping of Hawaiian lava tubes. August 1967. 27 p.

*9 Marshall A. Eto, Nathan C. Burbank, Jr., Howard W. Klemmer & L. Stephen Lau, Behavior of selected pesticides with percolating water in Oahu soils. August 1967. 35 p.

*10 George R. Jiracek, Feasibility of radio sounding to the ground-water table in Hawaii. August 1967. 47 p.

*11 Cornelius Joziasse & William M. Adams, Some seismic techniques for mapping small scale shallow structures. August 1967. 15 p.

*12 K. R. Gundersen & D. B. Stroupe, Bacterial pollution of Kaneohe Bay, Oahu (June through August 1967). December 1967. 24 p.

*13 Paul C. Ekern, Pilot evapotranspiration studies: lysimeter design. August 1967. 26 p.

*14 Nathan C. Burbank, Jr., Po Lau Chan & Reginald H. F. Young, Removal of color from South Kohala water: island of Hawaii. August 1967. 22 p.

*15 I-pai Wu, Hydrological data and peak discharge determination of small Hawaiian watersheds: Island of Oahu. December 1967. 97 p.

*16 Kenneth Ishizaki, Nathan C. Burbank, Jr. & L. Stephen Lau, Effects of soluble organics on flow through thin cracks of basaltic lava. August 1967. 56 p.

*17 Donald M. Hussong & Doak C. Cox, Estimation of ground water configuration near Pahala, Hawaii using electrical resistivity techniques. August 1967. 35 p.

*18 Larry K. Lepley & Leonard A. Palmer, Remote sensing of Hawaiian coastal springs using multi-spectral and infrared techniques. August 1967. 39 p.

19 Chester Lao & William M. Adams, Potential water development of the Kahua area, Kohala, Hawaii. April 1968. 16 p.

20 Richard M. Tanimoto, Nathan C. Burbank, Jr., Reginald H. F. Young, & L. Stephen Lau, Migration of bacteriophage T_4 in percolating water through selected Oahu soils. January 1968. 45 p.

21 Chester Lao & Frank L. Peterson, Electric well logging and other well logging methods in Hawaii. November 1969. 108 p.

22 L. Stephen Lau & Tsegaye Hailu, Tritium measurements in natural Hawaiian waters: instrumentation. November 1968. 36 p.

23 William M. Adams, An electrical resistivity profile from Mahukona to Kawaihae, Hawaii. November 1968. 32 p.

24 Doak C. Cox, Frank L. Peterson, William M. Adams, Chester Lao, John F. Campbell & Richie D. Huber, Coastal evidences of ground water conditions in the vicinity of Anaehoomalu and Lalamilo, South Kohala, Hawaii. March 1969. 53 p.

25 Larry K. Lepley & William M. Adams, Reflectivity of electromagnetic waves at an air-water interface for pure and sea water. December 1968. 15 p.

26 William M. Adams & Larry K. Lepley, Infrared images of the Kau and Puna coastlines on Hawaii. December 1968. 51 p.

27 Martin J. K. McMorrow, Reginald H. F. Young, Nathan C. Burbank, Jr., L. Stephen Lau & Howard W. Klemmer, Anaerobic digestion of pineapple mill wastes. January 1969. 33 p.

28 William M. Adams, Surendra P. Mathur & Richie D. Huber, Aeromagnetic, gravity, and electrical resistivity exploration between Pahala and Punaluu, Hawaii. February 1970. 62 p.

29 Stanley N. Davis, Silica in streams and ground water of Hawaii. January 1969. 31 p.

30 I-pai Wu, Hydrograph study and peak discharge determination of small Hawaiian watersheds: Island of Oahu. March 1969. 85 p.

31 Doak C. Cox & Lawrence C. Gordon, Jr., Estuarine pollution in the State of Hawaii — volume 1: statewide study. March 1970. 151 p. Volume II: Kaneohe Bay (In press).

32 William M. Adams, Frank L. Peterson, Surendra P. Mathur, Larry K. Lepley, Clifton Warren & Richie D. Huber, A hydrogeophysical survey from Kawaihae to Kailua-Kona, Hawaii. September 1969. 156 p.

33 Pedro A. Tenorio, Reginald H. F. Young & H. Collins Whitehead, Identification of return irrigation water in the subsurface: water quality. October 1969. 90 p.

34 Theodorus H. Hufen, Robert A. Duce & L. Stephen Lau, Some measurements of the tritium content in the natural water of southern Oahu, Hawaii. November 1969. 32 p.

35 Edison L. Quan, Reginald H. F. Young, Nathan C. Burbank, Jr. & L. Stephen Lau, Effects of surface runoff and waste discharge into the southern sector of Kaneohe Bay: January — April 1968. January 1970. 39 p.

36 Daniel H. Hori, Nathan C. Burbank, Jr., Reginald H. F. Young, L. Stephen Lau & Howard W. Klemmer, Migration of poliovirus type 2 in percolating water through selected Oahu soils. January 1970. 40 p.

37 Paul C. Ekern, Consumptive use of water by sugarcane. February 1970. 63 p.

38 Nathan C. Burbank, Jr., Po Lau Chan & Reginald H. F. Young, Removal of color from the water of Waikoloa Stream, South Kohala district, Island of Hawaii. March 1970. 21 p.

39 John A. Williams, Ronald N. Wada & Ru-yih Wang, Model studies of tidal effects on ground water hydraulics. May 1970. 77 p.

40 Jerry H. Nunogawa, Nathan C. Burbank, Jr., Reginald H. F. Young & L. Stephen Lau, Relative toxicities of selected chemicals to several species of tropical fish. August 1970. 37 p.

41 L. Stephen Lau & James C. S. Chou, Electrodialysis for desalting Hawaiian brackish ground water: a field study. July 1970. 20 p.

42 Ru-yih Wang, I-pai Wu & L. Stephen Lau, Instantaneous unit hydrograph analysis of Hawaiian small watersheds, also HAES Journal Series No. 1259. August 1970. 54 p.

43 David R. Hargis & Frank L. Peterson, Artificial recharge practices in Hawaii. October 1970. 33 p.

COOPERATIVE REPORTS

Requests for these publications should be directed to the cooperating institution.

1 Paul C. Ekern & L. E. Worthley, Annotated bibliography of publications and papers relevant to Hawaiian weather. Data Report No. 11 (HIG-68-11), Hawaii Institute of Geophysics, University of Hawaii. July 1968.

2 William M. Adams & Alexander Malahoff, Evaluation of some geophysical techniques applied to the environment of a Maui well. HIG-68-23, Hawaii Institute of Geophysics, University of Hawaii. November 1968.

ANNUAL REPORTS

Brief reviews of progress on individual projects.

Annual Report 1965-66. Unpaginated.

Annual Report 1966-67. 73 p.

Annual Report 1967-68. 126 p.

Annual Report 1968-69. 121 p.

Annual Report 1969-70. (In press).

IDAHO

IDAHO BUREAU OF MINES AND GEOLOGY

University of Idaho
Mines Building
Moscow, Idaho 83843

PAMPHLETS

103 A Survey of the Groundwater of the State of Idaho, by P. T. Kinnison. 1955. Price: $1.00.

137 Interpretation of Short Term Water Fluctuations in the Moscow Basin, Latah County, Idaho. By D. Sokol. 1966. Price: $1.00.

141 Ground-Water Flow Systems and the Origin of Evaporite Deposits. By Roy E. Williams. 1968. Price: $.75.

143 Feasibility of Re-Use of Treated Wastewater for Irrigation, Fertilization and Ground-Water Recharge in Idaho. By Roy E. Williams, Douglas D. Eier and Alfred T. Wallace. 1969. Price: $1.00.

OTHER PUBLICATIONS

Special Report No. 1. Mineral and Water Resources of Idaho. (A reprint of a report prepared cooperatively by several agencies for the U. S. Senate Committee on Interior and Insular Affairs.). 1964. Price: $1.00.

Earth Science Series No. 1. Idaho Earth Science, Geology, Fossils, Climate, Water and Soils. By S. H. Ross & C. N. Savage. 1967. Price: $4.00.

IDAHO DEPARTMENT OF HEALTH

Capitol Building
Boise, Idaho 83707

Implementation, Enforcement and Surveillance Plan for the Rules and Regulations for Standards of Water Quality for the Interstate Waters of Idaho. June 1967. 44 p.

Rules and Regulations for Standards of Water Quality for the Interstate Waters of Idaho and Disposal Therein of Sewage and Industrial Wastes. June 1967. 10 p.

Rules and Regulations for the Establishment of Standards of Water Quality and for Waste Water Treatment Requirements for Waters of the State of Idaho. September 1968. 7 p.

Cleaner Water for Idaho. January 1971. 16 p.

STATE OF IDAHO DEPARTMENT OF WATER ADMINISTRATION

Statehouse — Annex 2
Boise, Idaho 83707

WATER BULLETINS

*1 Ground-Water Conditions in Idaho, 1966.

*2 A Ground-Water Monitoring Network for Southwestern Idaho.

*3 Ground-Water Development in Idaho, 1967.

4 Ground-Water Resources of the Mountain Home Area, Elmore County, Idaho.

5 Ground-Water Levels in Idaho, 1968.

6 Record of North-Side Springs and Other Inflow to the Snake River Between Milner and King Hill, Idaho 1948-1967.

7 Water Level Changes in the Mud Lake Area, Idaho 1958-68.

8 Water Resources of the Goose Creek-Rock Creek Area-Idaho, Utah, and Nevada.

9 Inflow to the Snake River Between Milner and King Hill, Idaho.

10 Ground-Water Development in Idaho, 1968.

11 Ground-Water Levels in Idaho, 1969.

12 Artificial Recharge to Snake Plain Aquifer: An Evaluation of Potential and Effect. August 1969.

13 Hydrologic Reconnaissance of the Bear River Basin in Southeastern Idaho, October 1969.

14 Ground-Water Resources of Northern Owyhee County, Idaho, November 1969.

15 Ground-Water Resources of Southern Ada and Western Elmore Counties, Idaho, February 1970.

16 Reconnaissance of the Water Resources of the Portneuf River Basin, Idaho, June 1970.

17 Ground-Water Development in Idaho. 1969.

18 Ground-Water Levels in Idaho, 1970.

19 The Raft River Basin, Idaho-Utah, as of 1966: A Reappraisal of the Water Resources and Effects of Ground-Water Development.

20 Water Resources of the Blue Gulch Area, Eastern Owyhee and Western Twin Falls Counties, Idaho.

MISCELLANEOUS REPORTS

Twenty-Sixth Biennial Report of the Idaho Department of Reclamation, 1968-1970.

Idaho Water Law and Regulations, 1970. Price: $10.00.

IDAHO FISH AND GAME DEPARTMENT

Fisheries Division
Box 25, 600 South Walnut Street
Boise, Idaho 83707

Publications listed are bound and available for review in the Department's Library. Please request by Volume and Number.
SH – Publications marked "SH" indicate a "Supply on Hand" for distribution through the Information and Education Division of the Department and will be supplied free of charge.
LC – "Library Copy" only. The publication marked "LC" indicates the only available copy is in a bound volume and can be used for reference in the Department's Library only.

Andriano, Donald, Twin Lakes Reservoir Reclaimed. Idaho Wildlife Review. March-April, 1953. LC. 1 p.

Andriano, Donald, Fisheries Management Plans for the Palisades Reservoir Area. Idaho Wildlife Review. May-June, 1956. LC. 2 p.

Bachmann, Roger W., The Ecology of Four North Idaho Trout Streams with Reference to the Influence of Forest Road Construction. 1958. Ms Thesis, University of Idaho. LC.

Bell, Robert J., Timing of Runs of Anadromous Species of Fish and Resident Fishery Studies in the Pleasant Valley – Mountain Sheep Section of the Middle Snake River. Progress Report. 1957. LC. Vol. 3, No. 30. 20 p.

Bell Robert J., Summary of Operations on the Wildhorse River Weir, May, 1958. LC. Vol. 19, No. 5. 5 p.

Bell, Robert J., Summary of Trapping of Downstream Migrant Steelhead Trout and Chinook Salmon at Wildhorse River Weir during 1958. 1959. LC. Vol. 6, No. 68. 8 p.

Bell, Robert J., Summary of Trapping of Downstream Migrant Steelhead Trout and Chinook Salmon at Wildhorse River Weir during 1959. 1960. LC. Vol. 7, No. 84. 10 p.

Bell, Robert J., Catches of Downstream Migrating Chinook Salmon and Steelhead Trout in Barge Traps below Brownlee Dam, 1959. 1960. Annual Report. SH. Vol. 7, No. 83. 19 p.

Bell, Robert J., Mormon Reservoir – 1967. Idaho Wildlife Review, September-October, 1967. LC. 1 p.

Bjornn, Ted C., and Jerry Mallet, Movements of Planted and Wild Trout in an Idaho River System. Trans. Am. Fish. Soc., 93(1): 70-76. 1964. SH. Vol. 13, No. 160. 20 p.

Casey, Osborne E., Water Quality Investigations - Job 1 - General Investigations in Water Quality; Job 2 - The Heavy Metal Ions in Bear Lake Waters as Factors Limiting Plankton Production: Job 3 - The Effects of Placer Mining (Dredging) on a Trout Stream. Annual Progress Report, Project F-34-R-1. 1959. LC. Vol. 6, No. 72. 27 p.

Casey, Osborne E., and William E. Webb, Water Quality Investigations - Job 1 - General Investigations in Water Quality; Job 2 - The Heavy Metal Ions in Bear Lake Water as a Factor in Limiting Plankton Production; Job 3 - The Effects of Placer Mining (Dredging) on a Trout Stream; Job 4 - Toxicity of Four Pesticides to Rainbow Trout Fingerlings. Annual Progress Report, Project F-34-R-2. 1960. LC. Vol. 7, No. 88. 89 p.

Casey, Osborne E., and William E. Webb, General Investigations in Water Quality. Annual Progress Report, Project F-34-R-3. 1960. LC. Vol. 8, No. 109. 98 p.

Corley, Donald R., Salmon, Steelhead ... and Fish Screens. Idaho Wildlife Review, May-June, 1963. LC. Vol. 12, No. 144-A. 5 p.

Corley, Donald R., Effects of Forest Spraying on Aquatic Organisms. Presented at PMFC Meeting at Boise, Idaho, November 19, 1965. SH. Vol. 15, No. 7. 5 p.

Corley, Donald R., Biological Sampling of Panther Creek Above and Below the Introduction of Mining Wastes, 1967. LC. Vol. 21, No. 4. 22 p.

Cuplin, Paul E., and Robert B. Irving, The Effect of Hydroelectric Developments on the Fishery Resources of the Snake River, November 15, 1952 to July 1, 1953. Narrative Progress Report, Project F-8-R-1. LC. Vol. 19, No. 8. 3 p.

Cuplin, Paul E., and Robert B. Irving, The Effect of Hydroelectric Developments on the Fishery Resources of Snake River. Final Report, Project F-8-R. 1956. LC. Vol. 2, No. 21. 172 p.

Davis, Sterling P., A Limnological Survey of the Backwater of the Lower St. Joe River, Idaho. 1961. Ms Thesis, University of Idaho. LC.

Fisher, Jack G., Dagger Falls Fishway. Closing Report, BCF Contract Nos. 14-17-001-181 and 14-17-001-220. 1961. LC. Vol. 19, No. 13. 18 p.

Fisher, Jack G., Stream Clearance and Minor Falls Correction, Phase II. Project Closing Report, Project No. 221.1C-IDA-4; Contract No. 14-17-0001-1056. 1967. SH. Vol. 21, No. 6. 4 p.

Fisher, Jack G., The Construction of Selway Falls Fishway, Selway River, Idaho. Project Closing Report, Project No. 221.1C-IDA-2; Contract No. 14-17-0007-144. 1967. SH. Vol. 21, No. 7. 25 p.

Gebhards, Stacy V., Fish Loss in Irrigation Canals on the Salmon River Drainage as Determined by Electrical Shocker. Special Report. 1958. LC. Vol. 4, No. 45. 9 p.

Gebhards, Stacy V., Stage Reduction and Channel Relocation on the Lemhi River and the Effects on Fish Production. 1958. LC. Vol. 4, No. 46. 42 p.

Gebhards, Stacy V., The Effects of Irrigation on the Natural Production of Chinook Salmon (*Oncorhynchus tschawytscha*) in the Lemhi River, Idaho. 1959. Ms Thesis, Utah State University. LC.

Gebhards, Stacy V., Mountain Lakes ... A Challenge to Man, Beast, and Machines. Idaho Wildlife Review, March-April, 1965. LC. 5 p.

Hauck, Forrest R., Background in History and Management Policies of the Salmon and Steelhead Fisheries of the Columbia River Basin. 1962. LC. Vol. 19, No. 30. 11 p.

Hazzard, A. S., A Preliminary Limnological Study of Bear Lake, Utah-Idaho (with Particular Reference to Its Fish Producing Possibilities). 1935. LC. Vol. 19, No. 31. 28 p.

Heimer, John T., Lake and Reservoir Investigations - Job A5 - Survival of Various Species and Strains of Trout in a Reservoir Environment, June 1, 1965 to March 31, 1966. Job Completion Report, Project F-53-R-1. 1967. SH. Vol. 21, No. 8D. pp. 58-60.

Heimer, John T. and David Heiser, Lake and Reservoir Investigations - Job A4b - Limnological Investigations of Anderson Ranch Reservoir & Appendix A. Job Completion Report, Project F-53-R-1. 1967. SH. Vol. 21, No. 8C. pp. 32-57.

Heiser, David, Lake and Reservoir Investigations - Job A4a - Limnological Investigations of Arrowrock Reservoir, July 1, 1965 to December 31, 1965 and Appendix. Job Completion Report, Project F-53-R-1. 1967. SH. Vol. 21, No. 8F. pp. 17-31.

Holmes, Harlan B., A Study of Fish Passage at Lewiston Dam, Clearwater River, Idaho, with Recommendations for Improvement in Fish Passage Facilities. 1961. LC. Vol. 8, No. 113. 111 p.

Irizarry, Richard A., The Effects of Stream Alteration in Idaho - Job 1 - Inventory of Amount, Type and Location of Channel Alterations; Job 2 - Physical Changes in Stream Habitat Following Channel Alterations. Annual Progress Report, Project F-55-R-1. 1968. SH. Vol. 23, No. 3A, B. 15 p.

Irving Robert B., Roseworth Reservoir Treated. Idaho Wildlife Review. January-February, 1954. LC. 2 p.

Irving Robert B., Rehabilitation of Roseworth Reservoir. Completion Report, Project F-11-D. 1955. LC. Vol. 20, No. 1, 3 p.

Irving, Robert B., Physical and Chemical Aspects of Lakes. Idaho Wildlife Review. January-February, 1958. LC. 3 p.

Jeppson, Paul, A report on the Effects of Log Driving in the St. Joe River, Idaho. 1953. LC. Vol. 20, No. 3. 3 p.

Jeppson, Paul, North Idaho Lake Development. Annual Progress Report, Project F-17-D-1. 1955. LC. Vol. 20, No. 6. 4 p.

Jeppson, Paul, Palisades Reservoir Fishery Investigations, 1963. Annual Report. 1964. LC. Vol. 14, No. 171. 11 p.

Keating, James F., and Ralph B. Pirtle, The Size and Timing of Runs of Anadromous Species of Fish in the Columbia and Snake Rivers and Their Tributaries above the Confluence of the Snake River. 1954. LC. Vol. 1, No. 14. 95 p.

Keating, James, Effects of Aerial Spraying of DDT on Fish and Fish Foods in the Palouse River Drainage, Idaho, 1965. LC. Vol. 15, No. 11. 4 p.

Marcuson, Patrick E., Limnology and Fish Food Abundance in Round Lake, Idaho. Ms Thesis, University of Idaho. 1966. LC.

Metsker, Howard E., Investigation of Steelhead Passage at Selway Falls, 1958-59. SH. Vol. 20, No. 12. 30 pp.

Murphy, Leon W., Screening Irrigation Diversions. Project 7061B-IDA-SCR-1; Contract 14-19-008-3142. 1962. SH. Vol. 10, No. 134. 15 p.

Oein, Waine E., A Prelogging Inventory of Four Trout Streams in Northern Idaho. 1957. Ms Thesis, University of Idaho. LC.

Pirtle, Ralph B., The Size and Timing of Runs of Blueback Salmon in the Columbia and Snake Rivers and Their Tributaries above the Confluence of the Snake River. Prepared for U. S. Army Corps of Engineers. 1955. LC. Vol. 1, No. 15. 24 p.

Pirtle, Ralph B., The Size and Timing of Runs of Adult Spring Chinook Salmon in the Columbia and Snake Rivers and Their Tributaries above the Confluence of the Snake River. Prepared

for U. S. Army Corps of Engineers. 1955. LC. Vol. 20, No. 17. 37 p.

Pirtle, Ralph B., Fish Counts at the Lewiston Dam. Idaho Wildlife Review, July-August, 1956. LC. 2 p.

Pirtle, Ralph B., Field Studies to Estimate the Size and Timing of Runs of Anadromous Species of Fish in the Columbia and Snake Rivers and Their Tributaries above the Confluence of the Snake River. Final Report to the U. S. Army Corps of Engineers. 1957. LC. Vol. 3, No. 37. 75 p.

Platts, William S., A Comparison of Limnological Data Collected from Lake Pend Oreille During and After Dam Construction, with Food Habits of the Kokanee. Progress Report, Project F-3-R-8. 1958. LC. Vol. 5, No. 56. 74 p.

Platts, William S., It Takes Water. Idaho Wildlife Review. March-April, 1962. LC. Vol. 11, No. 136. 2 p.

Platts, William S., The Aquatic Cycle of Life. Idaho Wildlife Review, May-June, 1963. LC. Vol. 12, No. 144-B. 2 p.

Platts, William S., High Dams Against the Sturgeon ... Battle of the Century. Idaho Wildlife Review, September-October, 1965. LC. 3 p.

Reingold, Melvin, Fisheries Studies in Connection with Dworshak (Bruces Eddy) Dam and Reservoir. Completion Report. (Idaho Fish & Game and Corps of Engineers Publication). Corps of Engineers CIVENG-62-294. 1964. SH. Vol. 14, No. 177. 47 p.

Rich, Willis H., The Probable Effect of Albeni Falls Dam on the Kokanee Fishery of Lake Pend Oreille, Idaho. 1954. LC. Vol. 20, No. 18. 20 p.

Richards, Monte R., Operation, Repair, and Maintenance of Fish Screens, Fiscal Year, 1963. Annual Project Closing Report, Project 161.ID-IDA, Contract No. 14-17-0001-634. 1964. LC. Vol. 20, No. 22. 3 p.

Richards, Monte R., Operation, Repair, and Maintenance of Fish Screens in the Upper Salmon River Drainage, Fiscal Year, 1964. Annual Project Closing Report, Project 161.ID-IDA; Contract No. 14-17-0001-783. 1964. LC. Vol. 20, No. 23. 3 p.

Richards, Monte R., The Construction and Installation of Fish Screens in Irrigation Diversions in the Salmon River. Annual Project Closing Report, Project 221. IB-IDA-1; Contract No. 14-17-0001-886. LC. 1964. Vol. 20, No. 24. 8 p.

Richards, Monte R., The Construction and Installation of Fish Screens in Irrigation Diversions Located in the Salmon River and Its Tributaries, Fiscal Year 1965. Annual Project Closing Report, Project 221.IB-IDA-1; Contract No. 14-17-0001-1001. 1965. LC. Vol. 16, No. 3. 5 p.

Richards, Monte R., Operation, Repair, and Maintenance of Fish Screens in the Salmon River Drainage, Fiscal Year, 1965. Annual Project Closing Report, Project 161.ID-IDA; Contract No. 14-17-0001-1002. 1965. LC. Vol. 16, No. 4. 3 p.

Richards, Monte R., Investigation of Flood Damage to Stream Habitat. Project Closing Report. Project 221.1C-IDA-4; Contract No. 14-17-0001-1039. 1967. SH. Vol. 21, No. 21. 7 p.

Richards, Monte R., Repair of Flood Damage to Hatching Channels in the Clearwater River Drainage. Project Closing Report, Project 221.1F-IDA; Contract No. 14-17-0001-1052. 1967. SH. Vol. 21, No. 18. 4 p.

Richards, Monte R., Operation, Repair, and Maintenance of Fish Screens in the Salmon River Drainage, Fiscal Year 1966.

Annual Project Closing Report. Project 161.1D-IDA; Contract No. 14-17-0001-1265. 1967. SH. Vol. 21, No. 19. 4 p.

Richards, Monte R., Stream Improvement Operation and Maintenance, Dagger Falls and Selway Falls Fishways. Annual Project Closing Report, Project 161.1C-IDA; Contract No. 14-17-0001-1264. 1967. SH. Vol. 21, No. 20. 3 p.

Richards, Monte R., Operation, Repair, and Maintenance of Fish Screens in the Salmon River Drainage, Fiscal Year 1967. Project No. 161.1D-IDA; Contract No. 14-17-0001-1420. 1967. SH. Vol. 21, No. 22. 3 p.

Richards, Monte R., Stream Improvement Operation and Maintenance, Dagger Falls and Selway Falls Fishways. Annual Project Closing Report, Project No. 161.1C-IDA; Contract No. 14-17-0001-1421. 1968. SH. Vol. 23, No. 17. 2 p.

Simpson, James C., Relationship of Dams and River Development to the Anadromous Fishery of the Columbia River Basin. Paper presented at Utah Academy of Science, Utah State Agricultural College, Logan, Utah, May 14, 1955. 1955. LC. 4 p.

Simpson, James C., Pesticides in Relation to Fish and Wildlife in Idaho. Paper included in Pesticides, People, & Problems (A Collection of Papers) presented at Idaho Annual Health Conference at Sun Valley, Idaho, May 25-27, 1965. LC. 1965. Vol. 20, No. 27. 6 p.

Simpson, James C., Pesticides, Fish and Wildlife. Idaho Wildlife Review, July-August, 1966. LC. 4 p.

Simpson, James C., Idaho Streams—A Vanishing Heritage. Presented at 48th Annual Conference of Western Association of State Game and Fish Commissioners, Reno, Nevada, July, 1968. LC. 2 p.

Smith, Graydon W., and T. J. Jones, Before the Federal Power Commission. In the Matter of Application for License for Mountain Sheep-Pleasant Valley Hydroelectric Project on the Middle Snake River in the States of Idaho and Oregon by Pacific Northwest Power Company. 1957. LC. Vol. 3, No. 39. 33 p.

Stross, Ray G., A Limnological Study of Lake Pend Oreille. Job Completion Report, Project F-3-R-2, Work Plan 1. 1953. LC. Vol. 1, No. 4. 26 p.

Stross, Ray G., A Limnological Study of Lake Pend Oreille, Idaho with Special Consideration of the Ecology of the Kokanee. Ms Thesis, University of Idaho. 1954. LC.

Webb, William E., The Use of Pesticides in Relation to Fish and Wildlife. Idaho Wildlife Review. March-April, 1960. LC. 2 p.

Webb, William E., Toxicity of Certain Pesticides to Fish. Project F-34-R-2. 1961. SH. Vol. 9, No. 122. 14 p.

Webb, William E., Water Quality Investigations, November 1, 1960 - October 31, 1961 - Job 1 - General Investigations in Water Quality; Job 4 - Toxicity Tests on Insecticides and Herbicides. Annual Progress Report, Project F-34-R-4. 1962. LC. Vol. 11, No. 139. 74 p.

Webb, William E., Water Quality Investigations, November 1, 1961 - October 31, 1962 - Job 1 - General Investigations in Water Quality; Job 2 - Toxicity Studies on the Effects of Pesticides and Other Chemicals on Fish and Fish-food Organisms. Job Completion Report, Project F-34-R-5. 1964. LC. Vol. 14, No. 179. 85 p.

Webb, William E., The Boise River ... A Problem Stream. Idaho Wildlife Review, September-October, 1964. LC. 4 p.

Webb, William E., Water Quality Investigations, November 1, 1962 - October 31, 1963 - Job 1 - General Investigations in Water Quality; Job 2 - Toxicity Studies on the Effects of Pesticides and Other Chemicals. Job Completion Report, Project F-34-R-6. 1965. LC. Vol. 16, No. 5. 45 p.

Webb, William E., Water Pollution Problems in Idaho in Relation to the Aquatic Resource. Presented at PMFC in Boise, Idaho, November 19, 1965. SH. Vol. 16, No. 6. 9 p.

Webb, William E., Water Quality Investigations, November 1, 1963 - October 31, 1964 - Job 1 - General Investigations in Water Quality; Job 2 - Toxicity Studies on the Effects of Pesticides and Other Chemicals on Fish and Fish-food Organisms. Job Completion Report, Project F-34-R-7. 1966. SH. Vol. 18, No. 14. 66 p.

Webb, William E., Idaho Water Pollution. Idaho Wildlife Review, May-June, 1966. LC. 5 p.

Webb, William E., Water Quality Investigations, November 1, 1964 - October 31, 1965. Job 1 - General Investigations in Water Quality. Job 2 - Toxicity Studies on the Effects of Pesticides and Other Chemicals on Fish and Fish-food Organisms. Annual Completion Report, Project F-34-R-8. 1968. SH. Vol. 23, No. 18-A & B. 29 p.

Welch, Donald J., Lake and Reservoir Investigations, 1966-1967 and 1967-1968 - Jobs A6 (F-53-R-2, 1966-1967) and A5 (F-53-R-3, 1967-1968) - Limnological Investigations of Arrowrock and Lucky Peak Reservoirs. Job Completion Report, Projects F-53-R-2 and F-53-R-3. 1968. SH. Vol. 23, No. 19-B. p. 13-30.

Welsh, Thomas L., Raymond Corning, Stacy Gebhards, and Howard Metsker, Inventory of Idaho Streams Containing Anadromous Fish ... Part 1, Snake, Salmon, Weiser, Payette, and Boise River Drainages. Contract 14-19-001-431. 1965. SH. Vol. 16, No. 7. 181 p.

Whitt, Charles R., The Clearwater River Pollution Tests. 1952. LC. Vol. 20, No. 26. 13 p.

Whitt, Charles R., Evaluation of Spawning Areas in Lake Pend Oreille, Idaho and Tributaries Upstream from Albeni Falls Dam, June 1, 1957 to May 31, 1958. Annual Summary Report, Project F-3-R-7 and F-3-R-8. Work Plan II. 1958. LC. Vol. 5, No. 66. 34 p.

WATER RESOURCES RESEARCH INSTITUTE
University of Idaho
Moscow, Idaho 83843

1963-67

*Water Resources Committee (1963), Research in Water Resources for Idaho. Water Resources Committee, University of Idaho, 24 p.

Water Resources Research Institute (no date), Descriptive Brochure: Water Resources Research Institute, University of Idaho, 16 p.

*Walenta, T. R., Warnick, C. C., and Folz, W. E. (1965), Analysis of the Water Resources Planning Act, PL 89-80. University of Idaho, Report of the Water Resources Research Institute to Idaho Water Resource Board, 10 p.

Coffing, A. L. and Lindeborg, K. H. (1966), Relationship Between Farm Size and Ability to Pay for Irrigation Water. University of Idaho, Agr. Expt. Sta., Progress Report 112, 29 p.

*Walenta, T. R. (1966), Summary Report on Title to Beds and Use of Water of Navigable Streams and Lakes in Idaho. University of Idaho, Water Resources Research Institute, Report to the Subcommittee on High Water Mark Legislation of the Idaho Legislative Council, 35 p.

McKean, G. A. (1967), A Nuclear Radiation Snow Gage. University of Idaho, Engr. Expt. Sta. Bulletin No. 13, 48 p.

1968

*Belt, G. H. (1968), The Influence of Microclimate on the Water Exchange Processes of Selected Forest and Range Communities. University of Idaho, Water Resources Research Institute, Progress Report, Project A-014-Ida, 28 p.

Bloomsburg, G. L. and Brockway, C. E. (1968), Movement of Water from Canals to Ground Water Table. University of Idaho, Water Resources Research Institute, Research Technical Completion Report, Project A-009-Ida, 7 p.

Cheline, R. J. and Haynes, R. G. (1968), Relationship of Pumping Lift to Economic Use of Groundwater for Irrigation. University of Idaho, Agr. Expt. Sta., Progress Report No. 130, 24 p.

*Day, R. L. (1968), A Microclimatic Profile Between the Snake River Canyon and Clearwater Mountains, Idaho. University of Idaho, Water Resources Research Institute, Research Technical Completion Report, Project A-012-Ida, 60 p.

Hagen, J. I. (1968), Studies on Methods of Soil Water Determination. University of Idaho, Water Resources Research Institute, Research Technical Completion Report, Project A-019-Ida.

*Idaho Water Resources Board (1968), Idaho Water Resources Inventory. University of Idaho, Water Resources Research Institute, 2 Volumes, 50 maps, 598 p.

Jones, R. W. (1968), Hydrology of Some Small Groundwater Basins in Idaho. University of Idaho, Water Resources Research Institute, R.P.T.T.R., Project A-020-Ida, 6 p.

Jones, R. W., Ross, S. H. and Williams, R. E. (1968), Feasibility of Artificial Recharge of a Small Ground Water Basin by Utilizing Seasonal Runoff from Intermittent Streams. Proceedings of Sixth Annual Symposium on Engineering Geology and Soils Engineering, April 17-19, 1968, Boise, (A-011-Ida), p. 258-282.

*Lindeborg, K. H. (1968), Economic Value of Water in Different Uses within Agriculture. University of Idaho, Water Resources Research Institute, Research Technical Completion Report, Project A-017-Ida.

Walenta, T. R. (1968), A Critical Study of the Idaho Code of Laws Together with Various Agencies and their Functions in the Field of Water Resources. University of Idaho, Water Resources Research Institute, Research Technical Completion Report, Project A-010-Ida, 12 p.

*Walenta, T. R. (1968), Legal Problems Concerned with Ground Water. Proceedings of the Ground Water Symposium, American Water Resources Association, San Francisco.

Warnick, C. C. (1968), Social Problems Needing Solution — State Agencies. Utah State University, Social Science Institute Series, Proceedings of the Workshop for Sociological Aspects of Water Resources Research, Report No. 1.

Williams, R. E. (1968), Ground Water Flow Systems and the Origin of Evaporite Deposits. Pamphlet No. 141 of Idaho Bureau of Mines and Geology, 15 p. (A-021-Ida).

1969

Brusven, M. A., and Gilpin, B. R. (1969), Aquatic Environment and Food Habits of Mayflies. University of Idaho, Water Resources Research Institute, Research Technical Completion Report, Project A-022-Ida, 86 p.

Gilpin, B. R., Brusven, M. A., and McMullen, J. L. (1969), Algae of the St. Maries River in Idaho. Northwest Science.

Jones, R. W. and Ross, S. H. (1969), Detailed Ground Water Investigation of Moscow Basin. University of Idaho, Water Resources Research Institute, R.P.T.T.R., Project A-011-Ida, 11 p.

Lindeborg, K. A., (1969), Economic Values of Irrigation Water in Four Areas Along the Snake River in Idaho. Idaho Agricultural Experiment Station, Bulletin 513, January, 1970.

MacPhee, C. and Norman, D. (1969), A Lethal Index for Classifying Chemicals which Affect Water Quality of Aquatic Life. University of Idaho, Water Resources Research Institute, Research Technical Completion Report, Project A-013-Ida, 38 p.

MacPhee, C. and R. Ruelle, (1969), Lethal Effects of 1888 Chemicals upon Four Species of Fish from Western North America. Forest Wildlife and Range Experiment Station, University of Idaho, Bulletin No. 3, November, 1969.

McKean, G. A. and Read, J. C. (1969), Physical State Properties of Precipitation. University of Idaho, Water Resources Research Institute, Research Technical Completion Report, Project A-008-Ida, 19 p.

Peebles, J. J. (1969), Problems in Preparing a State Water Inventory. University of Idaho, Water Resources Research Institute, Information Circular No. 1.

Warnick, C. C. (1969), Historical Background and Philosophical Basis of Regional Water Transfer. Arid Lands in Perspective, American Association for the Advancement of Science, University of Arizona Press, p. 340-352.

Watts, F. J., (1969), Preliminary Report on Investigation of Culverts and Hydraulic Structures Used for Fishways. University of Idaho, Water Resources Research Institute, Moscow, Idaho, September, 1969.

1970

Belt, G. A., (1970), Spring Evapotranspiration from Low Sagebrush Range in Southern Idaho. Research Technical Completion Report, Projection A-014-Ida, University of Idaho, Water Resources Research Institute, Moscow, Idaho.

Brockway, C. E. and Herbig, A. E., (1970), Operations and Maintenance Costs of Irrigation Distribution Systems. Engineering Experiment Station, Progress Report No. 1, University of Idaho, Moscow, Idaho.

Gordon, D., (1970), An Economic Analysis of Idaho Sport Fisheries. Statewide Fishing Harvest Survey, Idaho Cooperative Fishery Unit, April, 1970.

Gordon, D., Haber, D., Michalson, E. L., Peebles, J., (1970), An Environmental Survey of the Lower Clearwater River in Idaho. University of Idaho, Water Resources Research Institute, Information Bulletin No. 5. (In Press).

Gordon, D., (1970), A Survey of Angler Preferences, Behavior, and Opinions. Statewide Fishing Harvest Survey, Idaho Cooperative Fishery Unit, February, 1970.

Herbst, J. and E. L. Michalson, (1970), Symposia on Wild and Scenic Rivers. University of Idaho, Water Resources Research Institute, Information Bulletin No. 6.

Holte, K. E., F. L. Rose, and C. H. Trost, (1970), An Environmental Survey of the Big and Little Wood Rivers in Idaho. University of Idaho, Water Resources Research Institute, Bulletin No. 4, June, 1970.

Michalson, E. L., (1970), Economics of Water Quality Control. University of Idaho, Water Resources Research Institute, Information Bulletin No. 3, January, 1970.

Michalson, E. L. and Larry Kirkland, (1970), A Methodology Study to Develop Evaluative Criteria for Wild and Scenic Rivers.

University of Idaho, Water Resources Research Institute, Progress Report No. 1, January 31, 1970.

Peebles, John J., (1970), Report of Flood Control Subproject. For a Methodology Study to Develop Evaluative Criteria for Wild and Scenic Rivers; University of Idaho, Water Resources Research Institute, February, 1970.

Watts, F. J., (1970), Water for Municipal and Industrial Use Subproject. For a Methodology Study to Develop Evaluative Criteria for Wild and Scenic Rivers; University of Idaho, Water Resources Research Institute, 1970.

Williams R. E. and A. T. Wallace, Hydrological Aspects of the Selection of Refuse Disposal Sites in Idaho. Idaho Bureau of Mines and Geology (In press).

ILLINOIS

ILLINOIS DEPARTMENT OF BUSINESS AND ECONOMIC DEVELOPMENT

State Office Building
222 South College Street
Springfield, Illinois 62706

*Water for Illinois, A Plan for Action. 1967. 452 p.

Priority and Planning Elements for Developing Illinois Water Resources. 1970. 53 p., 28 illustrations, 13 tables. Available at no cost but supply is limited.

Technical Appendix. 1970. 137 p., 42 tables, 31 figs. Available at no cost but supply is limited.

ILLINOIS DEPARTMENT OF CONSERVATION

Division of Education
113 State Office Building
Springfield, Illinois 62706

Note: These publications are available free of charge.

Illinois Department of Conservation Fishing Waters.

Aquatic Weeds — Their Identification and Control.

Small Lakes and Ponds — Their Construction and Care.

Horseshoe Lake Wildlife Refuge and Union County Wildlife Refuge Folder.

Teaching Water Conservation.

Boating Regulations.

ILLINOIS STATE GEOLOGICAL SURVEY

Natural Resources Building
Urbana, Illinois 61801

Note: Checks and money orders should be made payable to: Chief, Illinois State Geological Survey. Items bearing a charge are subject to the 5% State Retailers' Occupation Tax. When no price is indicated, the publication is free of charge.

BULLETINS

*B 5   Water Resources of the East St. Louis District: Isaiah Bowman, assisted by C. A. Reeds. 1907. 128 p., 4 pls., 11 figs.

*B 7   Physical Geography of the Evanston-Waukegan Region: W. W. Atwood and J. W. Goldthwait. 1908. Reprinted 1925. 102 p., 14 pls., 52 figs.

B10   Mineral Content of Illinois Waters: Edward Bartow, J. A. Udden, S. W. Parr, and G. T. Palmer. 1909. 192 p., 9 pls., 1 fig. $0.50.

*B 11   Physical Features of the DesPlaines Valley: J. W. Goldthwait. 1909. 103 p., 9 pls., 21 figs.

*B 15   Geography of the Middle Illinois Valley: H. H. Barrows. 1910. Reprinted 1925. 128 p., 16 pls., 47 figs. $0.50.

*B 19   Geology and Geography of the Wheaton Quadrangle: A. C. Trowbridge. 1912. 79 p., 12 pls., 17 figs.

*B 24   Some Deep Borings in Illinois: Johan A. Udden. 1914. 141 p., 4 pls.

B 25   Report and Plans for Reclamation of Lands Subject to Overflow in the Embarrass River Valley: J. A. Harman. 1913. 61 p., 9 maps and profiles. $0.50.

*B 26   Geology and Geography of the Galena and Elizabeth Quadrangles: A. C. Trowbridge, E. W. Shaw, and B. H. Schockel. In cooperation with U. S. Geol. Survey. 1916. 233 p., 25 pls., 50 figs. $0.50.

B 27   Geography of the Upper Illinois Valley and History of Development: C. O. Sauer. 1916. 208 p., 2 pls., 69 figs. $0.50.

*B 32   Report and Plans for Reclamation of Lands Subject to Overflow in the Spoon River Valley: J. A. Harman. 1916. 57 p., 6 maps and profiles.

B 34   Artesian Waters of Northeastern Illinois: C. B. Anderson. 1919. 326 p., 4 pls., 3 figs. $1.00.

B 42   Engineering and Legal Aspects of Land Drainage in Illinois: G. W. Pickels and F. B. Leonard, Jr. 1921. Revised 1928. 334 p., 1 map. $1.00.

*B 68   Some Addresses and Papers Presented on the Occasion of the Dedication of the State Natural Resources Building and the 1940 Illinois Mineral Industries Conference. 1944. 305 p., 92 figs.

*B 75   Groundwater in the Peoria Region: Leland Horberg, T. E. Larson, and Max Suter. 1950. In cooperation with the Illinois State Water Survey. 128 p., 4 pls., 53 figs. $1.00.

B 80   Symposium on Waterflooding. 1957. 163 p., 78 figs. $0.50.
Contents:
1. Input well completion practices in the Illinois Basin: Ray R. Vincent.
2. Increasing the intake rate of input wells in waterflooding: Robert B. Bossler.
3. Water-injection-well fracture treatments, Benton field, Franklin County, Illinois: H. R. Parkison.
4. Sources of ground-water for waterflooding in Illinois: W. A. Pryor, G. B. Maxey, and R. R. Parizek.

5. Use of sewage effluent as a waterflood medium, Mattoon pool, Illinois: J. D. Simmons.
6. Recent trends in treating waters for injection into oil-productive formations: J. Wade Watkins.
7. Effect of reactions between interstitial and injected waters on permeability of reservoir rocks: G. G. Bernard.
8. Some field results on selective plugging of input wells: H. G. Botset and P. F. Fulton.
9. Profiling water injection wells by the brine-freshwater interface method: Don R. Holbert.
10. Gas injection as an adjunct to waterflooding: J. C. Calhoun, Jr.
11. Studies of waterflood performance—I.—Causes and character of residual oil: Walter Rose.

B 81 Petroleum Industry in Illinois in 1955. Part I—Oil and Gas Developments: A. H. Bell and Virginia Kline. Part II—Waterflood Operations: P. A. Witherspoon and D. A. Pierre. 1957. 195 p., 30 figs., 16 tables. $0.50.

B 83 Petroleum Industry in Illinois in 1956: A. H. Bell, Virginia Kline, and D. A. Pierre. Part I—Oil and Gas Developments. Part II—Waterflood Operations. 1958. 173 p., 29 figs., 16 tables. $0.50.

B 85 Petroleum Industry in Illinois in 1957. Part I—Oil and Gas Developments. Part II—Waterflood Operations: Alfred H. Bell, Virginia Kline, Carl W. Sherman. 1959. 115 p., 8 figs., 15 tables. $0.50.

B 87 Petroleum Industry in Illinois, 1958. Part I—Oil and Gas Developments. Part II—Waterflood Operations: A. H. Bell, R. F. Mast, M. O. Oros, C. W. Sherman, J. Van Den Berg. 117 p., 2 pls., 5 figs., 17 tables. $0.50.

B 88 Petroleum Industry in Illinois, 1959. Part I—Oil and Gas Developments. Part II—Waterflood Operations: A. H. Bell, R. F. Mast, M. O. Oros, C. W. Sherman, and J. Van Den Berg. 1960. 127 p., 1 pl., 5 figs., 17 tables. $0.50.

REPORTS OF INVESTIGATIONS

RI 12 Limestone for Sewage Filter Beds—Causes of Disintegration, Desirable Properties, and Methods of Testing: J. E. Lamar. 1927. 21 p., 5 figs. $0.25.

RI 13 Stratigraphy and Geologic Structure of Northern Illinois, with Special Reference to Underground Water Supplies: F. T. Thwaites. 1927. 49 p., 2 pls., 2 figs. $0.25.

*RI 58 A Study of the Equilibration Method of Determining Moisture in Coal for Classification by Rank: O. W. Rees, F. H. Reed, and G. W. Land. 1939. 34 p., 14 figs.

RI 67 Porosity, Total Liquid Saturation, and Permeability of Illinois Oil Sands: R. J. Piersol, L. E. Workman, and M. C. Watson. 1940. 72 p., 39 figs., 53 tables. $0.25.

RI 73 Moisture Relations of Banded Ingredients in an Illinois Coal: O. W. Rees, G. W. Land, and F. H. Reed. 1941. (Reprinted from Ind. Eng. Chem., v. 33, no. 3, p. 416, 1941.) 10 p., 3 figs.

RI 89 Water Flooding of Oil Sands in Illinois: Frederick Squires and A. H. Bell. 1943. 101 p., 76 figs. $0.25.

RI 103 Some Clay-Water Properties of Certain Clay Minerals: R. E. Grim and F. L. Cuthbert. 1945. (Reprinted from Am. Ceramic Soc. Jour., v. 28, no. 3, 1945.) 15 p., 6 figs.

RI 155 An Integrated Geophysical and Geological Investigation of Aquifers in Glacial Drift near Champaign-Urbana, Illinois: John W. Foster and Merlyn B. Buhle. 1951. (Reprinted from Econ. Geology, v. 46, no. 4, June-July 1951.) 31 p., 14 figs.

RI 191 Groundwater Geology of the East St. Louis Area, Illinois: R. E. Bergstrom and T. R. Walker. 1956. 44 p., 4 pls., 6 figs., 2 tables. $0.25.

RI 194 Groundwater Geology of Lee and Whiteside Counties, Illinois: John W. Foster. 1956. 67 p., 9 figs. $0.25.

RI 196 Groundwater Geology of White County, Illinois: Wayne A. Pryor. 1956. 50 p., 4 pls., 21 figs. $0.25.

RI 208 Water Sorption Properties of Homoionic Clay Minerals: W. Arthur White. 1958. 46 p., 16 figs., 4 tables. $0.25.

*RI 213 Ground-water Geology of Winnebago County, Illinois: J. E. Hackett. 1960. 63 p., 2 pls., 11 figs., app. $0.25.

RI 221 Ground-Water Geology of the Rock Island, Monmouth, Galesburg, and Kewanee Area, Illinois: J. E. Brueckmann and R. E. Bergstrom. 1968. 56 p., 14 figs., 3 tables.

CIRCULARS

*C 1 Effects of Water Flooding on Oil Production from the McClosky Sand, Dennison Township, Lawrence County: A. H. Bell and R. J. Piersol. 1932. 4 p.

*C 25 Systematic Water Flood May Revive Older Illinois Fields: Frederick Squires. 1938. (Reprinted from the Weekly Derrick, Feb. 3, 1938.) 2 p., 4 figs.

C 34 Engineering Aspects of the Geology of the Vienna City Reservoir: G. E. Ekblaw. 1938. (Reprinted from Illinois Acad. Sci. Trans., v. 30, no. 2, p. 229-31, 1937.) 3 p., 1 fig.

*C 36 The Preglacial Rock River Valley as a Source of Groundwater for Rockford: L. E. Workman. 1938. (Reprinted from Illinois Acad. Sci. Trans., v. 30, no. 2, p. 245-47, 1937.) 3 p., 1 fig.

C 41 Potential Markets for Illinois Coal on the Upper Mississippi Waterway: W. H. Voskuil. 1938. 19 p., 2 figs.

C 85 Map of the State of Illinois Showing Areal Type Classification for Wells in the Illinois Coal Basin: E. F. Taylor and G. H. Cady. Aug. 1942. First revision, Dec. 1942. 2 p., 1 map.

*C 95 Buried Bedrock Valleys East of Joliet and Their Relation to Water Supply: Leland Horberg and K. O. Emery. 1943. 6 p., 3 pls.

*C 98 New Developments in Groundwater Exploration: C. A. Bays. 1943. (Reprinted from Am. Water Works Assoc. Jour., v. 35, no. 7, p. 911-20, 1943.) 10 p., 6 figs.

*C 101 Oil-Field Flooding Streamlined for War—A Suggestion: Frederick Squires. 1943. (Reprinted from Oil and Gas Jour., v. 42, no. 30, Dec. 2, 1943.) 10 p., 10 figs.

*C 103 Pressure Maintenance by Conjoint Injection of Gas and Water—A Wartime Suggestion: Frederick Squires. 1944. (Reprinted from Oil and Gas Jour., v. 42, no. 42, 1944.) 14 p., 13 figs.

C 108 Developments in the Application of Geophysics to Groundwater Problems: C. A. Bays and Stewart Folk. 1944. (Reprinted from Eng. Soc. of West. Pennsylvania. Nov. 1943.) 25 p., 19 figs.

C 113 Geophysical Logging of Water Wells in Northeastern Illinois: C. A. Bays and S. H. Folk. 1944. (Reprinted from West. Soc. Eng. Jour., v. 49, no. 3, p. 248-66, Sept. 1944.) 19 p., 7 figs.

*C 122 Use of Electrical Geophysical Methods in Groundwater Supply: C. A. Bays. 1946. (Reprinted from Jour. Missouri Water and Sewage Conf., v. 16, no. 4, p. 22-35, Oct. 1945.) 14 p., 10 figs.

*C 125 Flood Tide in Illinois: Frederick Squires. 1946. (Reprinted from Producers Monthly, July 1946.) 10 p., 23 figs.

*C 130 Designs for Oil Field Tools to Aid in Water Flooding: Frederick Squires. 1947. (Reprinted from Oil Weekly, p. 50-53. May 5, 1947.) 4 p., 3 figs.

*C 137 Transparent Model of Reservoir Showing Displacement of Oil by Conjoint Use of Gas and Water: Frederick Squires. 1947. (Reprinted from World Oil, p. 145-48, Oct. 1947.) 4 p., 8 figs.

*C 145 Water-Flooding Opportunities Explored by Gas Injection: Frederick Squires. 1948. (Reprinted from World Oil, p. 136-40, April, 1948.) 6 p., 6 figs.

*C 153 Flooding with Re-Used Water: Frederick Squires. 1949. (Reprinted from World Oil, p. 152-54, April 1949.) 4 p., 2 figs.

*C 154 Illinois Fluid Injection Reviewed: Frederick Squires. 1949. (Reprinted from Producers Monthly, v. 13, no. 9, p. 32-43, 1949.) 11 p., 35 figs.

*C 163 Flooding Prospects of Illinois Basin Oil Sands: Frederick Squires and P. G. Luckhardt. 1950. (Reprinted from World Oil, p. 146-148, 150, 152, 154, March 1950.) 6 p., 10 figs.

*C 165 Summary of Water-Flooding Operations in Illinois: Frederick Squires and members of the Secondary Recovery Study Committee for Illinois. 1951. (Reprinted from Interstate Oil Compact Commission Rept., September 1950.) 40 p., 27 figs., 1 table.

C 173 Illinois Water Floods—A Summary: Frederick Squires et al. 1951. (Reprinted from Oil and Gas Jour., v. 49, no. 43, p. 42-48, 66, March 1, 1951.) 8 p., 11 figs., 1 table.

*C 174 Natural Resources and Geological Surveys: M. M. Leighton. 1951. (Reprinted from Econ. Geology, v. 46, no. 6, p. 563-577, September-October, 1951.) 15 p., 1 fig.

*C 176 Summary of Water-Flooding Operations in Illinois Oil Pools to 1951: Frederick Squires et al. 1951. (Reprinted from Interstate Oil Compact Commission Rept., 1951.) 42 p., 27 figs., 1 table.

*C 179 Short Papers on Geologic Subjects. 1952. (Reprinted from Illinois Acad. Sci. Trans., v. 44, 1951.) 59 p., illustrated.
    1. Major Aquifers in Glacial Drift Near Mattoon, Illinois: John Foster.

2. Notes on the Illinois "Lafayette" Gravel: J. E. Lamar and R. R. Reynolds.
3. Cambrian and Lower Ordovician Exposures in Northern Illinois: H. B. Willman and J. S. Templeton.
4. Revision of Croixan Dikelocephalidae: G. O. Raasch.

*C 180 Some Important Aspects of Water Flooding in Illinois: Paul A. Witherspoon. 1952. (Reprint of paper presented at the Spring Meeting of the Eastern Dist., Div. of Prod., Am. Petroleum Inst., Pittsburgh, Pa., April 4, 1952.) 14 p., 11 figs., 1 table.

C 182 Summary of Water Flood Operations in Illinois Oil Pools During 1951: P. A. Witherspoon and P. J. Shanor et al. 1953. (Joint publication with the Illinois Secondary Recovery and Pressure Maintenance Study Committee.) 17 p., 4 figs., 2 tables.

C 185 Summary of Water Flood Operations in Illinois Oil Pools During 1952: Paul A. Witherspoon et al. 1953. (Reprinted from Interstate Oil Compact Commission Rept., 1953.) 23 p., 5 figs., 2 tables.

C 191 Filter Cake Formation and Water Losses in Deep Drilling Muds. Wolf von Engelhardt, transl. by Paul A. Witherspoon. 1954. (Originally published in Erdoel und Kohle, April and May, 1953.) 24 p., 12 figs., 6 tables.

C 192 Water Wells for Farm Supply in Central and Eastern Illinois: John W. Foster and Lidia F. Selkregg. 1954. 8 p., 1 pl. Second edition. 1955. (See C 248.)

*C 193 Summary of Water Flood Operations in Illinois Oil Pools During 1953: Paul A. Witherspoon et al. 1954. (Reprinted from Interstate Oil Compact Commission Rept., 1954.) 27 p., 5 figs., 3 tables.

*C 194 The Flow of Fluids through Sandstones: Wolf von Engelhardt and W. L. M. Tunn, transl. by Paul A. Witherspoon. 1955. (Originally published in Heidelberger Beiträge zur Mineralogie und Petrographie, 1954.) 17 p., 2 figs., 7 tables.

C 198 Groundwater Possibilities in Northeastern Illinois: R. E. Bergstrom et al. 1955. 24 p., 4 figs.

C 207 Groundwater in Northwestern Illinois: J. E. Hackett and R. E. Bergstrom. 1956. 25 p., 8 figs.

C 210 Unpublished Reports on Open File. III. Groundwater Geology and Geophysics: G. B. Maxey and J. W. Foster. 1956. 14 p.

C 212 Groundwater Geology in Southern Illinois—A Preliminary Geologic Report: W. A. Pryor. 1956. 25 p., 7 figs.

C 215 Quality of Groundwater Estimated from Electric Resistivity Logs: W. A. Pryor. 1956. 15 p., 6 figs.

C 222 Groundwater Geology in Western Illinois, North Part: Robert E. Bergstrom. 24 p., 6 figs., 1956.

C 224 Studies in Waterflood Performance: II. Trapping Oil in a Pore Doublet: Walter Rose and Paul Witherspoon. 13 p., 4 figs., 1956. (See B 80, C's 237, 262.)

C 225 Groundwater Geology in South-Central Illinois: L. F. Selkregg, W. A. Pryor, and J. P. Kampton. 30 p., 7 figs., 1957.

C 232 Groundwater Geology in Western Illinois, South Part: R. E. Bergstrom and A. J. Zeizel. 1957. 28 p., 7 figs.

*C 237   Studies of Waterflood Performance. Part III—Use of
         Network Models: Walter Rose. 1957. 31 p., 11 figs.
         (See C's 224, 262.)

C 248   Groundwater Geology in East-Central Illinois. A Pre-
         liminary Geologic Report: L. F. Selkregg and J. P.
         Kempton. 1958. 36 p., 7 figs. (See C 192.)

C 262   Studies of Waterflood Performance. IV—Influence of
         Curtailments on Recovery: Walter Rose. 1958. 32 p.,
         8 figs., 1 table. (See B 80, C's 224, 237.)

C 266   Water Sorption Characteristics of Clay Minerals: W.
         Arthur White and Ernesto Pichler. 1959. 20 p., 22
         figs.

C 344   Earthquakes and Crustal Movement as Related to Wa-
         ter Load in the Mississippi Valley Region: L. D.
         McGinnis. 1963. 20 p., 8 figs., 1 table.

C 393   The Origin of Saline Formation Waters. II—Iosotopic
         Fractionation by Shale Micropore Systems: D. L.
         Graf, Irving Friedman, and W. F. Meents. 1965. 32
         p., 8 figs., 2 tables.

C 397   The Origin of Saline Formation Waters. III—Calcium
         Chloride Waters: D. L. Graf, W. F. Meents, Irving
         Friedman, and N. F. Shimp. 1966. 60 p., 15 figs.,
         6 tables.

C 406   Bedrock Aquifers in Northeastern Illinois: G. M.
         Hughes, Paul Kraatz, and R. A. Landon. 1966. 16
         p., 1 pl., 5 figs., 1 table.

C 426   Feasibility of Subsurface Disposal of Industrial Wastes
         in Illinois: R. E. Bergstrom. 1968. 18 p., 4 figs., 1
         table.

C 433   Temperature Prospecting for Shallow Glacial and Al-
         luvial Aquifers in Illinois: Keros Cartwright. 1968.
         41 p., 27 figs., 4 tables.

ENVIRONMENTAL GEOLOGY NOTES

EGN 4   Geological and Geophysical Investigations for a
         Ground-Water Supply at Macomb, Illinois: Keros Cart-
         wright and D. A. Stephenson. 1965. 11 p., 5 figs.

EGN 11   Ground-Water Supplies Along the Interstate Highway
         System in Illinois: Keros Cartwright. 1966. 20 p., 3
         figs., 2 tables.

EGN 12   Effects of a Soap, a Detergent, and a Water Softener
         on the Plasticity of Earth Materials: W. A. White and
         Shirley M. Bremser. 1966. 14 p., 2 figs.

EGN 13   Geologic Factors in Dam and Reservoir Planning. W.
         C. Smith. 1966. 10 p.

*EGN 14 Geologic Studies as an Aid to Ground-Water Manage-
         ment: R. A. Landon. 1967. 9 p., 2 figs.

*EGN 15 Hydrogeology at Shelbyville, Illinois—A Basis for Wa-
         ter Resources Planning: Keros Cartwright and Paul
         Kraatz. 1967. 15 p., 4 figs.

EGN 23   Effects of Waste Effluents on the Plasticity of Earth
         Materials: W. A. White and M. K. Kyriazis. 1968.
         23 p., 2 figs., 6 tables.

*EGN 25 Preliminary Geological Evaluation of Dam and Reser-
         voir Sites in McHenry County, Illinois: W. C. Smith.
         1969. 33 p., 5 figs.

*EGN 26 Hydrogeologic Data from Four Landfills in Northeast-
         ern Illinois: G. M. Hughes, R. A. Landon, and R. N.
         Farvolden. 1969. 42 p., 5 figs., 8 tables.

ILLINOIS PETROLEUM SERIES

*III Pet 22   Effects of Water-Flooding on Oil Production from
              the McClosky Sand, Dennison Township, Lawrence
              County, Illinois: A. H. Bell and R. J. Piersol. June
              18, 1932. 26 p., 9 figs.

III Pet 66   Illinois Oil-Field Brines—Their Geologic Occurrence
              and Chemical Composition: W. F. Meents, A. H.
              Bell, O. W. Rees, and W. G. Tilbury. 1952. 38 p.,
              13 figs., 1 table. $0.25.

*III Pet 73   Summary of Water Flood Operations in Illinois Oil
              Pools During 1954: P. A. Witherspoon et al. 1955.
              (Reprint from Interstate Oil Compact Commission
              Rept. 1955.) 63 p., 24 figs.

GROUND-WATER REPORTS

*Prepared and published in cooperation with Illinois State
Water Survey.*

1   Preliminary Report on Ground-Water Resources of the Chi-
    cago Region, Illinois: Max Suter, Robert E. Bergstrom, H. F.
    Smith, Grover H. Emrich, W. C. Walton, and T. E. Larson.
    1959. 89 p., 50 figs., 26 tables. $0.50.

    Summary of Preliminary Report on Ground-Water Resources
    of the Chicago Region, Illinois. 1959. 18 p., 4 figs.

2   Ground-Water Resources of DuPage County, Illinois: A. J.
    Zeizel, W. C. Walton, R. T. Sasman, T. A. Prickett. 1962.
    103 p., 1 pl., 79 figs., 27 tables. $0.75.

ILLINOIS DEPARTMENT OF PUBLIC HEALTH

Bureau of Environmental Health
535 West Jefferson Street
Springfield, Illinois 62706

Illinois Water Well Construction Code Rules and Regulations.

Illinois Water Well Construction Code Law.

Illinois Pump Installation Code Rules and Regulations.

Illinois Pump Installation Code Law.

Water Well Form Letters:
    Instructions for Completing the Well Construction Report.
    Letter indicating Construction Reports we have not
        Received.
    Water Well Construction Report Form.

Pump Installation Report Form.

Private Water Analysis Report Form MW 61 Pvt.

Multiple Public Water Analysis Form MW-61R.

Explanation of Water Analysis.

Collecting a Sample of Water for Sanitary Analysis. SE-1
6-60.

Mineral Analysis-Fluoride or Chemical Form MW-63.

ILLINOIS DEPARTMENT OF PUBLIC WORKS AND BUILDINGS

Division of Waterways
201 W. Monroe Street
Springfield, Illinois 62706

Note: These publications are free of charge where available.

Survey Report for Flood Control, Addison Creek. 1950.

*Report for Flood Control and Drainage Development, Arlington Heights, Branch of Salt Creek, Cook County, Illinois. 1965.

*Report on Plan for Flood Control and Drainage Development, Cook and DuPage Counties, Bensonville Ditch. 1965.

Summary Report for Flood Control and Drainage Development, Big Ditch at West Frankfort, Franklin County, Illinois. 1962.
Addenda – 1964.

*Survey Report for Flood Control and Drainage Development, Blackberry Creek, Kane and Kendall County. 1962.

*Survey Report for Small Boat Harbor, Boat Harbor at Henry, Harshall County. 1962.

*Survey Report for Small Boat Harbor, Boat Harbor at Pekin, Tazwell County. 1962.

*Survey Report for Flood Control, Bureau Creek near Bureau, Illinois. 1948.

Report on Plan for Flood Control and Drainage Development; DesPlaines River, Cook, Lake and DuPage Counties. 1961.
Appendix – 1961.
  Errata – 1961.
    Addendum – 1962.

Interim Plan of Flood Protection for North Libertyville Estate Sub-Division, Lake County, Desplaines River. 1962.

Survey Report for Flood Control; DePage River, DuPage and Will Counties. 1962.
Addendum – 1965.
  Appendix G–Maps – 1962.

Survey Report for Flood Control; Embarrass River and Tributaries, Villa Grove and Vicinity, Douglas County, Illinois. 1960.

Interim Report for Flood Control and Drainage Development; Embarrass River, Lawrence, Crawford, Richland, Jasper, Cumberland, Coles, Douglas and Champaign Counties. 1963.
Appendix–Maps – 1963.

*Survey Report for Flood Control; Flag Creek, Cook and DuPage Counties. 1948.

Flow Duration of Illinois Streams. 1957.

Survey Report for Development; Fox River, Ottawa to McHenry Dam – LaSalle, Kane, Kendall, McHenry and Lake Counties. 1962.
Appendix D–Maps – 1962.

*Survey Report for Flood Control; Gimlet Creek at Sparland, Marshall County. 1955.

*Flood Protection, City of Joliet and Environs; Hickory Creek and Tributaries. 1950.

Survey Report for Flood Control; I & M Canal and Tributaries, Joliet to Calumet Sag Channel. 1951.

*Rehabilitation; I & M Canal – Marseilles to Ottawa in LaSalle County for Conservation and Recreational Purposes. 1962.

Interim Report for Erosion Control; Illinois Shore of Lake Michigan. 1952.
*Appendix – 1952.

Interim Report for Erosion Control; Illinois Shore of Lake Michigan. 1958.

Survey Report for Flood Control; Indian Creek and Tributaries, Aurora and Vicinity, Kane County, Illinois. 1960.

Survey Report for Flood Control and Drainage Development; Iroquois River, Iroquois and Kankakee Counties. 1962.

*Survey Report for Flood Control; Jacksonville Branch, Sangamon County, Illinois. 1965.

*Preliminary Report for Recreational Navigation; Kankakee River – near Aroma Park, Kankakee County. 1964.

A Comprehensive Plan for Water Resource Development; Kankakee River Basin. 1967.

*Survey Report for Flood Control; Kent Creek at Rockford, Winnebago County. 1953.
*Appendix – 1953.

*Preliminary Survey Report; Kinkaid Creek. 1964.

Survey Report for Flood Control and Drainage Development; Lucas Ditch, Cook County, Illinois. 1961.

Meandered Lakes in Illinois. 1962.
Appendix – Maps.

*Interim Report for Flood Control; Midlothian Creek, Cook and Will Counties. 1963.

Piles Fork Creek and Freeman Storm Drain, City of Carbondale, Jackson County. 1950.

Survey Report for Recreational Navigation; Quincy Bay, Adams County. 1952.

Report Survey; Rend Lake Reservoir, Jefferson and Franklin Counties. 1957.
Appendix III

Report on Plan for Flood Control Drainage Development; Salt Creek, Cook and DuPage Counties. 1958.
Appendix E–Maps – 1958.

*Survey Report for Flood Control; Salt Creek, Cook and DuPage Counties. 1955.

*Survey Report; Siltation Control, Vermilion River, Livingston. 1965.

Survey Report for Flood Control; Silver Creek, Cook County. 1955.

Survey Report for Flood Control and Drainage Development; Soldier Creek, Kankakee County. 1962.
Appendix–Maps – 1962.

Survey Report for Flood Control; St. Joseph Creek, DuPage County, Illinois. 1961.

Survey Report for Recreational Navigation and Sedimentation Control; Sturgeon Bay and Tributaries, Mercer County, Illinois. 1961.

*Spoon River – near London Hills. 1965.

*Survey Report for Flood Control; Thorn Creek, Cook and Will Counties. 1948.

Unit Hydrograph in Illinois. 1948.

Survey Report for Flood and Drainage Control; Utica and Vicinity, LaSalle County. 1960.

A Comprehensive Plan for Water Resource Development; Vermillion River Study. 1967.

A Comprehensive Plan for Water Resource Development; Little Wabash River Basin Study. 1967.

*Report on Water Levels; McHenry Dam and Fox Chain-of-Lakes Region, McHenry and Lake Counties. 1962.

Water Supply Characteristics of Illinois Streams. 1950.

Report on Plan for Flood Control and Drainage Development; Weller Creek, Cook County. 1961.
Appendix E—Maps – 1961.

Report on Plan for Flood Control and Drainage Development; Willow-Higgins Creek, Cook and DuPage County. 1961.
Appendix E—Maps.

*Report on Illinois Interstate Drainage; Yellowhead Singleton Ditch System. 1954.

COUNTY DRAINAGE MAPS

Boone County, 1958
Cass County, 1958
Christian County, 1964
Cook County, 1958
*Kankakee County, 1955
Logan County, 1960
Mason County, 1959
Menard County, 1958
Piatt County, 1964
Will County, 1956
Winnebago County, 1956
*Drainage Map of Illinois, 1964

FOX CHAIN OF LAKES MAPS

Chain-of-Lakes Region Index Map, 1964.

Chain-of-Lakes Region, Grass Lake, Fox River Area, 1958.

Chain-of-Lakes Region, Nippersink, Fox Lakes Area, 1956.

Chain-of-Lakes Region, Pistakee Lake Area, 1956.

Chain-of-Lakes Region, Petite Lake Area, 1956.

Low Flow Frequencies of Illinois Streams, 1970.

ILLINOIS ENVIRONMENTAL PROTECTION AGENCY

525 West Jefferson Street
Springfield, Illinois 62706

Note: This agency was created as of July 1, 1970. It is a separate agency from the Illinois Department of Public Health

and handles matters pertaining to air, water, land and noise pollution control. To be found here also are various publications of the Sanitary Water Board.

SWB 1-6 Rules and regulations.

SWB-7 "Water Quality Standards: Interstate Waters, Lake Michigan and Little Calumet River, Grand Calumet River and Wolf Lake."

SWB-8 "Water Quality Standards: Illinois River and Lower Sec. Des Plaines River."

SWB-9 "Water Quality Standards: Interstate Waters, Wabash River and Tributary Streams Crossing into Indiana."

SWB-10 "Water Quality Standards: Interstate Waters, Ohio River and Saline River."

SWB-11 "Water Quality Standards: Interstate Waters, Rock River, Fox River, DesPlaines River, Kankakee River and certain named interstate tributaries."

SWB-12 "Water Quality Standards: Interstate Waters, Mississippi River Common Boundary Between Illinois and Iowa."

SWB-13 "Water Quality Standards: Interstate Waters, Mississippi River Between Illinois and Missouri."

SWB-14 "Water Quality Standards: Intrastate Waters, Exclusive of Interstate Waters."

SWB-15 "Water Quality Standards: Interstate Waters, Chicago River and Calumet River System and Calumet Harbor Basin."

SWB-16 Rules and regulations. Use of Sanitary Water Board seal. 1967. 4 p.

SWB-17 Rules and regulations. Criteria for project priorities, construction grants for municipal sewage treatment works. (1967 ?). 5 p.

SWB-18 Rules and regulations. Certification of Water Pollution Control Facilities for Property Tax Treatment.

SWB-19 Rules and regulations. Disposal of Sewage and Wastes from Watercraft.

Water Quality Sampling Form: Part 1, Application – Location Property Tax Treatment. Part 2, Application – Facility Property Tax Treatment.

Sanitary Water Board Certification of Pollution Control Facility.

Sanitary Water Board Act.

Public Water Supply Control Law.

Technical Release 20-8a: Animal Waste Treatment Requirements.

Pamphlet No. 840: Rules and Regulations Governing Submission of Plan Documents and the Design of Sewage Works.

Technical Release 20-24: Proprietary Treatment Plants and Treatment of Sewer Overflow.

75th General Assembly (1967). Amendments to Sanitary Water Board Act.

Public Water Supply Systems – Rules and Regulations.

Public Water Supply Data Book.

Public Water Supplies Facility Characteristics Inventory Form.

Public Water Supply Operator Directory.

Public Water Supply Operator Certification Law.

Public Water Supply Operation Certification Application Form.

Public Water Supply Operator Certification Examination.

Public Water Supply Operator Certification Data Sheet.

Water Plant Operator Introductory Short Course.

Responsibilities of Cities, Water Companies, and Individuals for Illness Caused by Water.

Over the Spillway.

Waste treatment works completed and put into operation, January 1 – December 31, 1967. 1968. n.p.

A report on water quality surveillance during 1968, Chicago and Calumet River systems in the Metropolitan Sanitary District of Greater Chicago. 1969. 37 p.

Environment: Illinois. October 1970.

Municipal Waste Treatment Works – Construction Needs. April 1970.

A report on water quality surveillance during 1969. March 1970.

1968 Lake Michigan beach survey of water quality, report to the 76th General Assembly. 1969. 40 p.

Report to the Governor and 76th General Assembly: Lake Michigan Open Water and Lake Bed Survey 1969. June 1970. 35 p.

Report to the Governor and 76th General Assembly: Lake Michigan Shore Water Survey 1969. May 1970.

Data book, waste water treatment works. Annual.

The Digester. Quarterly (irregular). Vol. 1 (1936) – to date.

Illinois water quality network, compilation of data. Annual.

NORTHEASTERN ILLINOIS PLANNING COMMISSION

400 West Madison Street
Chicago, Illinois 60606

Water Resources Planning:

1 "The Water Resource in Northeastern Illinois: Planning Its Use", Technical Report No. 4, 1966, 182 p. No charge.

*2 "Ground-Water Pollution Problems in Northeastern Illinois", Metropolitan Planning Paper No. 8.

*3 "Toward Comprehensive Water Resources Management in the Calumet Union Drainage System", 1966, 16 p.

Wastewater Planning:

1 "Sewage Treatment", Metropolitan Planning Guideline, 1965, 27 p. with maps. No charge.

*2 "Preliminary Wastewater Plan for the Inner Area", Metropolitan Planning Guideline, phase two, 1969.

3 "Supplement No. 1, "Preliminary Wastewater Plan for the Inner Area, Recommended Plan for DuPage County", Metropolitan Planning Guideline, Phase Two, 1969, limited distribution.

4 "Regional Wastewater Plan", Metropolitan Planning Guideline, Phase Two, 1970, limited distribution.

5 "Suggested Flood Damage Prevention Ordinance", Local Planning Aid No. 9, 1964, 22 p. Price: $1.00.

*6 "Flood Control on Weller Creek: A Planning Policy Statement", Metropolitan Planning Paper No. 7.

7 "Simulation of Continuous Discharge and Stage Hydrographs in the North Branch of the Chicago River", 1970, 56 p. Price: $4.00.

ILLINOIS STATE WATER SURVEY
Box 232
Urbana, Illinois 61801

Water Survey publications are distributed without charge, and the number is generally limited to one copy per request. Water Survey publications may be reproduced in whole or part, giving proper credit. To avoid delay when ordering, please give both the number of the publication and the complete title. Out-of-print publications are available for loan upon request.

BULLETINS

*1 Chemical survey of water supplies of Illinois, preliminary report. 98 p. 1897.

*2 Chemical survey of the waters of Illinois, 1897-1902. 254 p. 1903.

*3 Chemical and biological survey of the waters of Illinois. 30 p. 1906.

*4 The mineral content of Illinois waters. 192 p. 1908.

*5 Municipal water supplies of Illinois. 123 p. 1907.

*6 Chemical and biological survey of the waters of Illinois, 1906-1907. 88 p. 1908.

*7 Chemical and biological survey of the waters of Illinois, 1908. 204 p. 1909.

*8 Chemical and biological survey of the waters of Illinois, 1909-1910. 148 p. 1911.

*9 Chemical and biological survey of the waters of Illinois, 1911. 173 p. 1912.

*10 Chemical and biological survey of the waters of Illinois, 1912. 198 p. 1913.

*11 Chemical and biological survey of the waters of Illinois, 1913. 478 p. 1914.

*12 Chemical and biological survey of the waters of Illinois, 1914. 261 p. 1916.

*13 Chemical and biological survey of the waters of Illinois, 1915. 381 p. 1916.

*14 Chemical and biological survey of the waters of Illinois, 1916. 190 p. 1917.

15 Chemical and biological survey of the waters of Illinois, 1917. 133 p. 1918.

*16 Chemical and biological survey of the waters of Illinois, 1918-1919. 280 p. 1920.

*17 Index to bulletins 1-16. 17 p. 1921.

*18 Activated-sludge studies, 1920-1922. By A. A. Brensky, S. L. Neave, H. L. Long, C. C. Larson and A. M. Buswell. 150 p. 1923.

*19 Solubility and rate of solution of gases, bibliography. By S. L. Neave. 49 p. 1924.

20 Comparison of chemical and bacteriological examinations made on the Illinois river during a season of low and a season of high water, 1923-1924, AND a preliminary notice of a survey of the sources of pollution of the streams of Illinois. By R. E. Greenfield, G. A. Weinhold with A. M. Buswell. 59 p. 1924.

21 Public ground-water supplies in Illinois. 710 p. 1925.
Supplement I, 378 p. 1938.
Supplement II, 44 p. 1940.

22 Investigations of chemical reactions involved in water purification, 1920-1925. By R. E. Greenfield, G. P. Edwards, W. U. Gallaher, L. H. McRoberts with A. M. Buswell. 133 p. 1926.

23 The disposal of the sewage of the sanitary district of Chicago. U. S. Corps Engineers report. 195 p. 1927.

24 Pollution of streams in Illinois. With State Dept. Conserv. 35 p. 1927.

25 Bioprecipitation studies, 1921-1927. By R. A. Shive, S. L. Neave and A. M. Buswell. 94 p. 1928.

26 Depth of sewage filters and degree of purification. By S. I. Strickhouser et al. 100 p. 1928.

27 A study of factors affecting the efficiency and design of farm septic tanks. By E. W. Lehmann, R. C. Kelleher and A. M. Buswell. With Ill. Agric. Experiment Sta. 45 p. 1928.

28 Illinois river studies, 1925-1928. By C. S. Boruff and A. M. Buswell. 127 p. 1929.

29 Studies on two-stage sludge digestion, 1928-1929. By A. M. Buswell, H. L. White, H. E. Schlenz, G. E. Symons et al. 92 p. 1930.

30 Laboratory studies of sludge digestion. By A. M. Buswell and S. L. Neave. 84 p. 1930.

*31 Preliminary data on surface-water resources. By W. D. Gerber. 157 p. 1937.

*32 Anaerobic fermentations. 193 p. 1939.

33 Water resources in Peoria-Pekin district. 114 p. 1940.

34 Sandstone water supplies of the Joliet area. By W. D. Gerber, T. E. Larson et al. 128 p. 1941.

35 Ground-water supplies of the Chicago-Joliet-Chicago Heights area. By Ross Hanson, W. D. Gerber and T. E. Larson. 285 p. 1943.

36 Ground-water supplies in northern Cook and northern DuPage counties. By Ross Hanson and T. E. Larson. 119 p. 1945.

37 The causes and effects of sedimentation in Lake Decatur. By C. B. Brown, J. B. Stall and E. E. DeTurk. With U.S. Soil Conserv. Serv., Ill. Agric. Experiment Sta. 62 p. 1947.

38 Hydrology of five Illinois water-supply reservoirs. By W. J. Roberts. With U. S. Geol. Survey. 260 p. 1948.

39 Ground water in the Peoria region. By Leland Horberg, Max Suter and T. E. Larson. With Ill. State Geol. Survey. 128 p. 1950.

*40 Public ground-water supplies in Illinois. By Ross Hanson. 1036 p. 1950.
Supplement 1, New public ground-water supplies in Illinois, 1950-1957. By Ross Hanson. 260 p. 1958.
Supplement 2, Additions to public ground-water supplies in Illinois. By Ross Hanson. 656 p. 1961.

41 Proceedings conference on water resources, 1951. 335 p. 1952.

42 Water and land resources of the Crab Orchard Lake basin. By J. B. Stall, J. B. Fehrenbacher, L. J. Bartelli, G. O. Walker, E. L. Sauer and S. W. Melsted. With U. S. Fish and Wildlife Serv., U. S. Soil Conserv. Serv., Southern Ill. Univ., Ill. Agric. Experiment Sta. 53 p. 1954.

*43 1952-55 Illinois drought with special reference to impounding reservoir design. By H. E. Hudson Jr. and W. J. Roberts. 52 p. 1955.

*44 Rainfall relations on small areas in Illinois. By F. A. Huff and J. C. Neill. 54 p. 1957.

45 Quality of surface waters in Illinois. By T. E. Larson and B. O. Larson. 135 p. 1957.

*46 Frequency relations for storm rainfall in Illinois. By F. A. Huff and J. C. Neill. 65 p. 1959.

*47 Summary of weather conditions at Champaign-Urbana, Illinois. By S. A. Changnon Jr. 95 p. 1959.

48 Artificial ground-water recharge at Peoria, Illinois. By Max Suter and Robert H. Harmeson. 48 p. 1960.

49 Selected analytical methods for well and aquifer evaluation. By W. C. Walton. 82 p. 1962.

50 Drought climatology of Illinois. By F. A. Huff and S. A. Changnon Jr. 68 p. 1963.

51 Low flows of Illinois streams for impounding reservoir design. By John B. Stall. 395 p. 1964.

52 Precipitation climatology of Lake Michigan basin. by Stanley A. Changnon Jr. 46 p. 1968.

53 Climatology of severe winter storms in Illinois. By Stanley A. Changnon Jr. 45 p. 1969.

54 Quality of surface water in Illinois, 1956-1966. By Robert H. Harmeson and T. E. Larson. 184 p. 1969.

REPORTS OF INVESTIGATION

1 Temperature and turbidity of some river waters in Illinois. By Max Suter. 14 p. 1948.

2 Ground-water resources in Winnebago county with specific reference to conditions at Rockford. By H. F. Smith and T. E. Larson. 35 p. 1948.

*3 Radar and rainfall. By G. E. Stout and F. A. Huff. With Pfister Hybrid Corn Co. 71 p. 1949.

*4 The silt problem of Spring Lake, Macomb, Illinois. By J. B. Stall, L. C. Gottschalk, A. A. Klingebiel, E. L. Sauer and E. E. DeTurk. With U. S. Soil Conserv. Serv., Ill. Agric. Experiment Sta. 87 p. 1949.

5   Infiltration of soils in the Peoria area. By R. S. Stauffer. With Ill. Agric. Experiment Sta. 24 p. 1949.

6   Ground-water resources in Champaign county. By H. F. Smith. 44 p. 1950.

*7   The silting of Ridge Lake, Fox Ridge State Park, Charleston, Illinois. By J. B. Stall, L. C. Gottschalk, A. A. Klingebiel, E. L. Sauer and S. W. Melsted. With U. S. Soil Conserv. Serv., Ill. Agric. Experiment Sta. 35 p. 1951.

8   The silting of Lake Chautauqua, Havana, Illinois. By J. B. Stall and S. W. Melsted. With Ill. Agric. Experiment Sta. 15 p. 1951.

*9   The silting of Carbondale Reservoir, Carbondale, Illinois. By B. O. Larson, A. A. Klingebiel, E. L. Sauer, S. W. Melsted and R. C. Hay. With U. S. Soil Conserv. Serv., Ill. Agric. Experiment Sta. 29 p. 1951.

10   The silting of Lake Bracken, Galesburg, Illinois. By B. O. Larson, H. M. Smith, E. L. Sauer and S. W. Melsted. With U. S. Soil Conserv. Serv., Ill. Agric. Experiment Sta. 27 p. 1951.

*11   Irrigation in Illinois. By W. J. Roberts. 11p. 1951.

*12   The silting of West Frankfort reservoir, West Frankfort, Illinois. By J. B. Stall, A. A. Klingebiel, S. W. Melsted and E. L. Sauer. With U. S. Soil Conserv. Serv., Ill. Agric. Experiment Sta. 29 p. 1951.

*13   Studies of thunderstorm rainfall with dense rain-gage networks and radar. By H. E. Hudson Jr., G. E. Stout and F. A. Huff. 30 p. 1952.

*14   The storm of July 8, 1951, in north central Illinois. With U. S. Geol. Survey, U. S. Soil Conserv. Serv. 45 p. 1952.

15   The silting of Lake Calhoun, Galva, Illinois. By J. B. Stall, A. A. Klingebiel, S. W. Melsted and E. L. Sauer. With U. S. Soil Conserv. Serv., Ill. Agric. Experiment Sta. 26 p. 1952.

16   The silting of Lake Springfield, Springfield, Illinois. By J. B. Stall, L. C. Gottschalk and H. M. Smith. With U. S. Soil Conserv. Serv. 28 p. 1953.

*17   Preliminary investigation of ground-water resources in the American bottom in Madison and St. Clair counties, Illinois. By J. Bruin and H. F. Smith. 28 p. 1953.

18   The silting of Lake Carthage, Carthage, Illinois. By J. B. Stall, G. R. Hall, S. W. Melsted and E. L. Sauer. With U. S. Soil Conserv. Serv., Ill. Agric. Experiment Sta. 21 p. 1953.

19   Rainfall-radar studies of 1951. By G. E. Stout, J. C. Neill and G. W. Farnsworth. Under contract DA-36-039 SC42446. 41 p. 1953.

20   Precipitation measurements study, bibliography. By J. C. Kurtyka. Under contract DA-36-039 SC794C-0. 178 p. 1953.

*21   Analysis of 1952 radar and rain-gage data. By J. C. Neill. Under contract DA-36-039 SC42446. 22 p. 1953.

22   Study of an Illinois tornado using radar, synoptic weather and field survey data. By F. A. Huff, H. W. Hiser and S. G. Bigler. 73 p. 1954.

23   Bubbler system instrumentation for water level measurement. By G. H. Nelson. 30 p. 1954.

24   The storm of July 18-19, 1952 Rockford, Illinois and vicinity. By B. O. Larson, H. W. Hiser and W. S. Daniels. With U. S. Geol. Survey. 14 p. 1955.

*25   Selected methods for pumping test analysis. By J. Bruin and H. E. Hudson Jr. 54 p. 1955. Third printing 1961.

26   Ground-water resources in Lee and Whiteside counties. By Ross Hanson. 67 p. 1955.

*27   The October 1954 storm in northern Illinois. By F. A. Huff, H. W. Hiser and G. E. Stout. 23 p. 1955.

*28   Radar back-scattering from non-spherical scatterers. By P. Mathur and E. A. Mueller. 85 p. 1955.

*29   Evaluation of a low-powered 3-cm radar for quantitative rainfall measurements. By F. A. Huff, J. C. Neill and M. Spock Jr. Under contract DA-36-039 SC64723. 35 p. 1956.

30   Trends in residential water use. By Ross Hanson and H. E. Hudson Jr. 32 p. 1956.

31   Potential water resources of southern Illinois. By W. J. Roberts, Ross Hanson, F. A. Huff, S. A. Changnon Jr., T. E. Larson et al. 100 p. 1957. Reprinted 1962.

*32   The water level problem at Crystal Lake, McHenry county. By R. T. Sasman. 28 p. 1957.

*33   Cloud distribution and correlation with precipitation in Illinois. By S. A. Changnon Jr. and F. A. Huff. 44 p. 1957.

*34   Thunderstorm-precipitation relations in Illinois. By S. A. Changnon Jr. 24 p. 1957.

*35   Hydrometeorological analysis of severe rain-storms in Illinois, 1956-1957, with summary of previous storms. By F. A. Huff, R. G. Semonin, S. A. Changnon Jr. and D. M. A. Jones. 79 p. 1958.

*36   Three-dimensional mesoanalysis of a squall line. By T. Fujita. Under contract DA-36-039 SC64656. 80 p. 1958.

*37   Correlation of reservoir sedimentation and water-shed factors, Springfield Plain, Illinois. By J. B. Stall and L. J. Bartelli. With U. S. Soil Conserv. Serv. and Agric. Research Serv., and Ill. Agric. Experiment Sta. 21 p. 1959.

*38   Hail climatology of Illinois. By F. A. Huff and S. A. Changnon Jr. 46 p. 1959.

39   Leaky artesian aquifer conditions in Illinois. By W. C. Walton. 27 p. 1960.

40   Hydrologic budgets for three small watersheds in Illinois. By R. J. Schicht and W. C. Walton. 40 p. 1961.

41   Ground-water development in three areas of central Illinois. By W. H. Walker and W. C. Walton. 43 p. 1961.

42   Severe rainstorms in Illinois, 1958-1959. By F. A. Huff and S. A. Changnon Jr. 70 p. 1961.

43   Yields of deep sandstone wells in northern Illinois. By W. C. Walton and Sandor Csallany. 47 p. 1962.

44   Ground-water levels and pumpage in East St. Louis area, Illinois, 1890-1961. By R. J. Schicht and E. G. Jones. 40 p. 1962.

45   Ground-water levels in Illinois through 1961. By R. R. Russell. 51 p. 1963.

46   Yields of shallow dolomite wells in northern Illinois. By Sandor Csallany and W. C. Walton. 44 p. 1963.

47   Ground-water development in several areas of northeastern Illinois. By T. A. Prickett, L. R. Hoover, W. H. Baker and R. T. Sasman. 93 p. 1964.

48   Ground-water recharge and runoff in Illinois. By William C. Walton. 55 p. 1965.

49   Temperatures of surface waters in Illinois. By Robert H. Harmeson and Virginia M. Schnepper. 45 p. 1965.

50   Ground-water pumpage in northeastern Illinois through 1962. By R. T. Sasman. 31 p. 1965.

51   Ground-water development in East St. Louis area, Illinois. By R. J. Schicht. 70 p. 1965.

52   Ground-water pumpage in Northwestern Illinois through 1963. By R. T. Sasman and W. H. Baker. 33 p. 1966.

*53   Potential yields of aquifers in Embarrass River basin, Illinois. By W. C. Walton and Sandor Csallany. Open file report. 1965.

54   Potential surface water reservoirs of south-central Illinois. By Julius H. Dawes and Michael L. Terstriep. 119 p. 1966.

55   Yields of wells in Pennsylvanian and Mississippian rocks in Illinois. By Sandor Csallany. 42 p. 1966.

56   Potential surface water reservoirs of north-central Illinois. By Julius H. Dawes and Michael L. Terstriep. 144 p. 1966.

57   Lake evaporation in Illinois. By Wyndham J. Roberts and John B. Stall. 44 p. 1967.

58   Potential surface water reservoirs of northern Illinois. By Julius H. Dawes and Michael L. Terstriep. 86 p. 1967.

59   Development in deep sandstone aquifer along the Illinois River in LaSalle County. By L. R. Hoover and R. J. Schicht. 1967.

60   Coarse filter media for artificial recharge. By Roger L. Thomas. 23 p. 1968.

61   Groundwater levels and pumpage in the Peoria-Pekin area, Illinois, 1890-1966. By Miguel A. Marino and Richard J. Schicht. 29 p. 1969.

62   Groundwater resources of the buried Mahomet bedrock valley. By Adrian P. Visocky and Richard J. Schicht. 52 p. 1969.

63   Provisional time-of-travel for Illinois streams. By John B. Stall and Douglas W. Heistand. 31 p. 1969.

64   Dissolved oxygen resources and waste assimilative capacity of the La Grange pool, Illinois River. By T. A. Butts, D. H. Schnepper, and R. L. Evans. 28 p. 1970.

65   Model test results of circular, square, and rectangular forms of drop Inlet entrance to closed conduit spillways. By Harold W. Humphreys, Gunnar Sigurdsson, and H. James Owen.

CIRCULARS

*1   Well-water recessions in Illinois. By G. C. Habermeyer. Jour. AWWA, 18(6):694-702, 1927.

*2   The effect of certain Illinois waters on lead. By O. W. Rees and A. L. Elder. Jour. AWWA, 19(6):714-24, 1928.

3   Removal of colloids from sewage. By A. M. Buswell, R. A. Shive and S. L. Neave. Ill. Engr., 4(4):6-8; 4(5):4-7, 1928.

*4   Control of scum in sewage tanks. By A. M. Buswell. Indus. and Engr. Chem., 21(4):322-26, 1929.

*5   The biology of a sewage treatment plant, a preliminary survey, Decatur, Illinois. By H. P. K. Agersborg and W. D. Hatfield. Sew. Wks. Jour., 1(4):411-24, 1929.

*6   Some idiosyncrasies of ground waters. By W. D. Gerber. Jour. AWWA, 22(1):110-16, 1930.

7   Fermentation products of cellulose. By C. S. Boruff with A. M. Buswell. Indus. and Engr. Chem., 21(12) - 1181-86, 1929.

*8   Chemical studies on sludge digestion. By S. L. Neave with A. M. Buswell. 9 p. 1930.

*9   Illinois river studies, 1929-1930. By C. S. Boruff. Indus and Engr. Chem., 22(11):1252-60, 1930.

10   Production of fuel gas by anaerobic fermentations. By A. M. Buswell. Indus. and Engr. Chem., 22(11):1168-78, 1930.

*11   The hydrology of industrial and municipal water supplies in Illinois. By W. D. Gerber. Trans. Ill. Acad. Science, 23(3):1-13, 1931.

*12   Some economic problems of the Illinois river valley. Papers presented before Ill. State Acad. Science. 72 p. 1931.

*13   Soap usage and water hardness. By H. W. Hudson. Water Wks. Engr., Jan., 1934.

14   A carbon study of sludge digestion. By T. E. Larson, C. S. Boruff and A. M. Buswell. Sew. Wks. Jour., 6(1):- 24-35, 1934.

15   The determination of free chlorine. By D. Tarvin, H. R. Todd and A. M. Buswell. Jour. AWWA, 26(11):1645-62, 1934.

16   The treatment of "beer slop" and similar wastes. By A. M. Buswell. Water Wks. and Sewerage, April, 1935.

17   Data on the ground waters of Lake county, Illinois. By W. D. Gerber, S. M. McClure, D. Tarvin and A. M. Buswell. 65 p. 1935.

18   A survey of the ground-water resources of Illinois. By W. D. Gerber, S. M. McClure, D. Tarvin and A. M. Buswell. 47 p. 1935.

19   Water quality for fire fighting. By A. M. Buswell and W. V. Upton. 12 p. 1937.

20   Model study of spillway characteristics, West Frankfort, Illinois, 1935-1937. By J. J. Doland, T. E. Larson and C. O. Reinhardt. With Univ. Ill. Engr. Experiment Sta. 22 p. 1937.

21   Collected papers on water softening, by T. E. Larson and A. M. Buswell. Indus. and Engr. Chem., 32:130, 132, 1240, 1940.

22   Calcium carbonate saturation index and alkalinity interpretations. By T. E. Larson and A. M. Buswell. Jour. AWWA, 34(11):1667-78, 1942.

*23   Rehabilitation of sandstone wells. By J. B. Millis. Jour. AWWA, 38(1):31-40, 1946.

24   Corrosion in vertical turbine pumps. By T. E. Larson. Water and Sew. Wks., 94(4):117-21, 1947.

*25 Water treatment for the small homes or farms. By T. E. Larson and H. A. Spafford. Ill. Well Driller, 16(1):15-19, 1947.

26   Interpretation of soap savings data. By T. E. Larson. Jour. AWWA, 40(3):296-300. 1948.

*27 Geologic correlation and hydrologic interpretation of water analyses. By T. E. Larson. Water and Sew. Wks., 96-(2):67-74, 1949.

*28 Rainfall intensity-frequency data for Champaign-Urbana, Illinois. By F. A. Huff. 3 p. 1949.

29   Chicago area water supply. Midwest Engr., 2(6):3-12, 1950.

30   Annual report for 1948-1949. Dept. Regis. and Educ. Ann. Rep. 1948-49:129-42, 1950.

*31 Mineral content of public ground-water supplies in Illinois. By T. E. Larson. 19 p. 1951 (revised 1954).

32   Water resource conservation in Illinois. By H. E. Hudson Jr. Trans. Ill. Acad. Science, 43:101-109, 1950.

33   Residential water use and family income. By B. O. Larson and H. E. Hudson Jr. Jour. AWWA, 43(8):603-11, 1951.

*34 A preliminary study of atmospheric moisture-precipitation relationships over Illinois. By F. A. Huff and G. E. Stout. Bull. AMS, 32(8):295-7, 1951.

35   The ideal lime-softened water. By T. E. Larson. Jour. AWWA, 43(8):649-64, 1951.

*36 Getting the facts through surveys and investigations. From panel on the watershed—using it as a basis for soil and water conservation. By H. E. Hudson Jr. and J. B. Stall. Jour. Soil and Water Conserv., 7(1):11-15, 1952.

37   Mortality experience with Illinois municipal wells. By H. E. Hudson Jr. and J. L. Geils. Jour. AWWA, 44(3):-193-207, 1952.

*38 On the determination of transmissibility and storage coefficients from pumping test data. By V. T. Chow. Trans. AGU, 33(3):397-404, 1952.

*39 Area-depth studies for thunderstorm rainfall in Illinois. By F. A. Huff and G. E. Stout. Trans. AGU, 33(4):495-8, 1952.

*40 Hardness reduction vs. removal: a critical evaluation. By T. E. Larson. Water and Sew. Wks., 99(6):226-9, 1952.

41   Feed water treatment at the Illinois state institutions. By R. W. Lane. Proc. Amer. Power Conf., 14:473-83, 1952.

*42 Municipal and home water softening. By T. E. Larson. Jour. AWWA, 45(6):557-61, 1953.

43   Evaporation records in Illinois. By W. J. Roberts. Trans. Ill. Acad. Science, 46:104-108, 1953.

44   Gravel packing water wells. By H. F. Smith. Water Well Jour., 8(1):15-18, 1954.

45   Corrosion by water at low flow velocity. By T. E. Larson and R. M. King. Jour. AWWA, 46(1):1-9, 1954.

*46 Quantitative measurement of rainfall by radar. By A. M. Buswell, G. E. Stout and J. C. Neill. Jour. AWWA, 46-(9):837-52, 1954.

47   Hydrogen exchange resin for steam purity analysis. By R. W. Lane, T. E. Larson and J. W. Pankey. Indus. and Engr. Chem., 47(1):47-50, 1955.

*48 Hydraulic laboratory research facilities of the Illinois State Water Survey. 15 p. 1955.

*49 Comparison between standard and small orifice rain gages. By F. A. Huff. Trans. AGU, 36(4):689-94, 1955.

50   Report on loss in carrying capacity of water mains. By T. E. Larson. Jour. AWWA, 47(11):1061-72, 1955.

*51 Illinois cooperative project in climatology, first progress report. By S. A. Changnon Jr. 44 p. 1955.

52   Radar scope interpretations of wind, hail and heavy rain storms between May 27 and June 8, 1954. By G. E. Stout and H. W. Hiser. Bull. AMS, 36(10):519-27, 1955.

53   Corrosion of brass by chloramine. By T. E. Larson, R. M. King and L. M. Henley. Jour. AWWA, 48(1):84-8, 1956.

54   High-rate recharge of ground water by infiltration. By Max Suter. Jour. AWWA, 48(4):355-60, 1956.

55   Chromatographic determination of volatile acids. By H. F. Mueller, A. M. Buswell and T. E. Larson. Sew. and Indus. Wastes, 28(3):255-59, 1956.

56   Mineral composition of rainwater. By T. E. Larson and Irene Hettick. Tellus, 8(2):191-201, 1956.

*57 Illinois cooperative project in climatology, second progress report. By S. A. Changnon Jr. 24 p. 1956.

58   Tuberculation of tar-coated cast iron in Great Lakes water. By T. E. Larson, R. V. Skold and E. Savinelli. Jour. AWWA, 48(10):1274-78, 1956.

59   A method for determining permeability and specific capacity from effective grain size. By H. G. Rose and H. F. Smith. Water Well Jour., 11(3):10, 1957.

*60 Frequency of point and areal mean rainfall rates. By F. A. Huff and J. C. Neill. Trans. AGU, 37(6):679-81, 1956.

61   Measurement of the instantaneous corrosion rate by means of polarization data. By R. V. Skold and T. E. Larson. Corrosion, 13(2):139-42, 1957.

*62 Construction and operation of Larson-Lane steam purity and condensate analyzers. By A. B. Sisson, F. G. Straub and R. W. Lane. Symp. Steam Quality, ASTM, Sp. Tech. Pub. 192, p. 37-49, 1956.

*63 Tornadoes in Illinois. By S. A. Changnon Jr. and G. E. Stout. 12 p. 1957.

*64 Illinois cooperative project in climatology, third progress report. By S. A. Changnon Jr. 12 p. 1957.

65   Evaluation of use of polyphosphates in water industry. By T. E. Larson. Jour. AWWA, 49(12):1581-86, 1957.

66   Corrosion and tuberculation of cast iron. By T. E. Larson and R. V. Skold. Jour. AWWA, 49(10):1294-1302, 1957.

67   Mineral quality of Illinois rivers. By T. E. Larson and B. O. Larson. Jour. AWWA, 49(9):1213-22, 1957.

*68 Evaporation suppression from water surfaces. By W. J. Roberts. Trans. AGU, 38(5):740-44, 1957.

69   Chromatographic identification and determination of organic acids in water. By H. F. Mueller, T. E. Larson and W. J. Lennarz. Anal. Chem., 30(1):41-44, 1958.

*70 RHI radar observations of a tornado. By J. Schuetz and G. E. Stout. Bull. AMS, 38(10):591-95, 1957.

71 Laboratory studies relating mineral quality to corrosion of steel and iron. By T. E. Larson and R. V. Skold. Corrosion, 14(6):285-88, 1958.

72 Sediment transport in Money Creek. By J. B. Stall, N. L. Rupani and P. K. Kandaswamy. Proc. ASCE, 84-(HYI):1531-1 to 27, 1958.

*73 Water resources of Illinois. By S. M. Bartell. 11 p. 1958.

74 Corrosion and tuberculation of cast iron, fourth report. By T. E. Larson and R. V. Skold. Jour. AWWA, 50(11):-1429-32, 1958.

75 Effect of metal grating deck on drop-inlet spillway performance. By H. W. Humphreys and G. Sigurdsson. 8 p. 1959.

*76 Reducing lake evaporation in the midwest. By W. J. Roberts. Jour. Geophys. Research, 64(10):1605-10, 1959.

*77 The shape of raindrops. By D. M. A. Jones. Jour. Meteor., 16(5):504-10, 1959.

78 Stabilization of magnesium hydroxide in solids-contact process. By T. E. Larson, R. W. Lane and C. H. Neff. Jour. AWWA, 51(12):1551-58, 1959.

*79 Water-level decline and pumpage during 1959 in deep wells in the Chicago region, Illinois. By W. C. Walton, R. T. Sasman and R. R. Russell. 39 p. 1960.

80 Chromatographic separation and identification of organic acids. By H. F. Mueller, T. E. Larson and M. Ferretti. Anal. Chem., 32(6):687-90, 1960.

81 Natural radioactivity in Illinois water resources. By T. E. Larson and R. L. Weatherford. Jour. AWWA, 52(6):769-78, 1960.

82 Loss in pipeline carrying capacity due to corrosion and tuberculation. By T. E. Larson. Jour. AWWA, 52(10):-1263-70, 1960.

*83 Water-level decline and pumpage during 1960 in deep wells in the Chicago region, Illinois. By R. T. Sasman, T. A. Prickett and R. R. Russell. 43 p. 1961.

84 Water hardness and domestic use of detergents. By L. M. DeBoer and T. E. Larson. Jour. AWWA, 53(7):809-822. July 1961.

85 Water-level decline and pumpage during 1961 in deep wells in the Chicago region, Illinois. By R. T. Sasman, W. H. Baker Jr., and W. P. Patzer. 32 p. 1962.

86 Water use and related costs with cooling towers. By Brian Berg, R. W. Lane, and T. E. Larson. 18 p. 1963.

*87 Illinois cooperative project in climatology, fourth progress report. By S. A. Changnon Jr. 9 p. 1963.

*88 History of Urbana weather station, 1888-1963. By S. A. Changnon Jr. and G. R. Boyd. 37 p. 1963.

89 Range of evapotranspiration in Illinois. By Douglas M. A. Jones. 13 p. 1966.

90 Mineral content of public ground-water supplies in Illinois. By T. E. Larson. 28 p. 1963.

91 Selected papers on cooling tower water treatment. Compiled by R. W. Lane. 120 p. 1966.

92 Groundwater availability in Shelby County, Illinois. By E. W. Sanderson. 42 p. 1967.

93 Climatology of hourly occurrences of selected atmospheric phenomena in Illinois. By S. A. Changnon Jr. 1967.

94 Water-level decline and pumpage in deep wells in northeastern Illinois 1962-1966. By R. T. Sasman, C. K. McDonald, and W. R. Randall. 36 p. 1967.

95 Groundwater levels and pumpage in the East St. Louis area, Illinois, 1962-1966. By G. E. Reitz Jr. 30 p. 1968.

96 Cost of reservoirs in Illinois. By J. H. Dawes and Magne Wathne. 22 p. 1968.

97 Groundwater availability in Ford County. By J. P. Gibb. In press. 1970.

98 Cost of municipal and industrial wells in Illinois, 1964-1966. By J. P. Gibb and E. W. Sanderson. 22 p. 1969.

CONTRACT PUBLICATIONS

*1 Wind data from radar echoes. By H. W. Hiser and S. G. Bigler. Technical report 1. Contract N189s-88164. 18 p. Mar. 1953.

*2 Rainfall-radar studies of 1951. By G. E. Stout, J. C. Neill and G. W. Farnsworth. Research report 1. Contract DA-36-039 SC-42446. 41 p. May 1953.

*3 Analysis of 1952 radar and raingage data. By J. C. Neill. Research report 2. Contract DA-36-039 SC42446. 22 p. July 1953. (Same as Report of Investigation 21).

*4 Utilization of radar in short-range weather forecasting. By H. W. Hiser and S. G. Bigler. Final report. Contract N189s-88164. 46 p. Aug. 1953.

*5 A raindrop camera. By D. M. A. Jones and L. A. Dean. Research report 3. Contract DA-36-039 SC42446. 19 p. Dec. 1953.

*6 Precipitation measurement study. By H. W. Hiser and F. A. Huff. Final report. Contract DA-36-039 SC15484. 76 p. Feb. 1954.

*7 Evaluation of a low-powered 3-cm radar for quantitative rainfall measurements. By F. A. Huff, J. C. Neill and Michael Spock Jr. Research report 4. Contract DA-36-039 SC64723. 35 p. 1956. (Same as Report of Investigation 29).

*8 The theory and operations of the area integrator. By G. W. Farnsworth and E. A. Mueller. Research report 5. Contract DA-36-039 SC64723. 31 p. Jan. 1956.

*9 Rainfall drop size-distribution and radar reflectivity. By D. M. A. Jones. Research report 6. Contract DA-36-039 SC64723. 20 p. Apr. 1956.

*10 An evaluation of raindrop sizing and counting techniques. By J. E. Pearson and G. E. Martin. Scientific report 1. Contract AF 19(604)-1900. 116 p. Nov. 1957.

*11 Study as to merits of various rapid raindrop counting and sorting techniques. By G. E. Stout. Final report. Contract AF 19(604)-1900. 28 p. May 1956—Mar. 1958.

*12 Evaluation of the AN/APQ-39(XA-3) cloud detector radar. By K. E. Wilk. Final report. Contract AF 19-(604)-1395. 39 p. Mar. 1955—Mar. 1958.

*13   Study on intensity of surface precipitation using radar instrumentation. By E. A. Mueller. Final report. Contract DA-36-039 SC64723. 33 p. July 1955–Mar. 1958.

*14   Mesometeorological analysis of atmospheric phenomena. By R. H. Blackmer Jr., J. B. Holleyman and H. M. Gibson. Final report. Contract DA-36-039 SC64656. 107 p. May 1955–May 1958.

*15   An evaluation of the area integrator. By E. A. Mueller. Research report 7. Contract DA-36-039 SC75055. 34 p. Dec. 1958.

*16   The hail hazard in Illinois. By G. E. Stout, R. H. Blackmer Jr., S. A. Changnon Jr. and F. A. Huff. Preliminary report. Contract 44-26-84-314 (CHIAA). 33 p. Jan. 1959.

*17   25 most severe summer hailstorms in Illinois during 1915-59. By S. A. Changnon Jr. CHIAA Research report 4. 18 p. Dec. 12, 1960.

*18   Relations between summer hailstorms in Illinois and associated synoptic weather. By F. A. Huff. CHIAA Research report 5. 35 p. Dec. 15, 1960.

*19   A detailed study of a severe Illinois hailstorm on June 22, 1960. By S. A. Changnon Jr. CHIAA Research report 6. 36 p. Sept. 30, 1960.

*20   Radar investigations of Illinois hailstorms. By K. E. Wilk. Scientific report 1. Contract AF 19(604)-4940. 42 p. Jan. 15, 1961.

*21   Studies of radar-depicted precipitation lines. By S. A. Changnon Jr. and F. A. Huff. Scientific report 2. Contract AF 19(604)-4940. 63 p. Feb. 15, 1961.

*22   Atmospheric particulates in precipitation physics. By R. G. Semonin and G. E. Stout. Final report, National Science Foundation G-6352. 18 p. July 19, 1961.

*23   Study on intensity of surface precipitation using radar instrumentation. By R. M. Johnson and E. A. Mueller. Contract DA-36-039 SC75055. Final report. 37 p. Apr. 1958–Sept. 1961.

*24   Evaluation of electric charges induced in the atmosphere. By G. E. Stout and W. E. Bradley. National Science Foundation G-11970. Final report. 34 p. Dec. 1, 1961.

*25   Correlation between summer hail patterns in Illinois and associated climatological events. By F. A. Huff. CHIAA Research report 10. 17 p. Dec. 15, 1961.

*26   Research concerning analysis of severe thunderstorms. By K. E. Wilk. Contract AF 19 (604)-4940. Final report. 68 p. Dec. 1961.

*27   Investigation of the quantitative determination of point and areal precipitation by radar echo measurements: first quarterly technical report (1 Oct.–31 Dec. 1961). By E. A. Mueller. Contract DA-36-039 SC87280. 18 p.

*28   Investigation of the quantitative determination of point and areal precipitation by radar echo measurements: second quarterly technical report (1 Jan.–31 Mar. 1962). By E. A. Mueller. Contract DA-36-039 SC-87280. 33 p.

*29   Cloud electrification studies in Illinois. By R. G. Semonin, D. W. Staggs, and G. E. Stout. National Science Foundation G-17038. Annual report. 13 p. Apr. 1, 1962.

*30   Investigation of the quantitative determination of point and areal precipitation by radar echo measurements: third quarterly technical report (1 Apr.–30 June 1962). By E. A. Mueller. Contract DA-36-039 SC-87280. 17 p.

*31   Investigation of the quantitative determination of point and areal precipitation by radar echo measurements: fourth quarterly technical report (1 July–30 Sept. 1962). By E. A. Mueller. Contract DA-36-039 SC87280. 13 p.

*32   Raindrop size distributions with rainfall types and weather conditions. By Miyuki Fujiwara. Contract DA-36-039 SC87280. Research report 8. 67 p. 1961.

*33   Singularities in severe weather events in Illinois. By S. A. Changnon Jr. CHIAA Research report 13. 19 p. Oct. 22, 1962.

*34   Regional characteristics of severe summer hailstorms in Illinois. By S. A. Changnon Jr. CHIAA Research report 14. 19 p. Dec. 15, 1962.

*35   Summary of research on hailstones in Illinois during 1962. By G. E. Stout. CHIAA Research report 15. 15 p. Dec. 15, 1962.

*36   Investigation of the quantitative determination of point and areal precipitation by radar echo measurements: fifth quarterly technical report (1 Oct.–31 Dec. 1962). By E. A. Mueller. Contract DA-36-039 SC87280. 19 p.

*37   Raindrop distributions at Miami Florida. By E. A. Mueller. Contract DA-36-039 SC-87280. Research report 9b. 281 p. June 1962.

*38   Investigation of water droplet coalescence. By C. D. Hendricks and R. G. Semonin. Contract DA-SIG-36-039-62-G19. Final report. 29 p. 1962.

*39   Study of rainout of radioactivity in Illinois. By F. A. Huff. Contract AT(11-1)-1199. First progress report. 58 p. Jan. 31, 1963.

*40   Investigation of the quantitative determination of point and areal precipitation by radar echo measurements: sixth quarterly technical report (1 Jan.–31 Mar. 1963). By E. A. Mueller. Contract DA-36-039 SC-87280. 17 p.

*41   Investigation of water droplet coalescence; third quarterly technical report (April 1 – June 30, 1963). By C. D. Hendricks and R. G. Semonin. Contract DA-SIG-36-039-63-G2. 4 p.

*42   Investigation of the quantitative determination of point and areal precipitation by radar echo measurements: seventh quarterly technical report (1 April–30 June 1963). By E. A. Mueller. Contract DA-36-039 SC-87280. 10 p.

*43   Investigation of the quantitative determination of point and areal precipitation by radar echo measurements: eighth quarterly technical report (1 July–30 Sept. 1963). By E. A. Mueller and A. L. Sims. Contract DA-36-039 SC87280. 20 p.

*44   Monthly and semi-monthly distributions of hail days in Illinois. By S. A. Changnon Jr. CHIAA Research report 17. 21 p. Dec. 30, 1963.

*45   A detailed investigation of an Illinois hailstorm on August 8, 1963. By S. A. Changnon Jr. and G. E. Stout. CHIAA Research report 18. 33 p. Jan. 10, 1964.

*46   Study of rainout of radioactivity in Illinois. By F. A. Huff. Contract AT(11-1)-1199. Second progress report. 61 p. Jan. 31, 1964.

*47   Cloud electrification studies in Illinois. By R. G. Semonin, D. W. Staggs and G. E. Stout. National Science Foundation G-17038. Final report. 76 p. 1964.

*48   Investigation of water droplet coalescence. By C. D. Hendricks and R. G. Semonin. Final report (1 Nov. 1962–31 Oct. 1963). Contract DA-AMC-36-039-63-G2. 61 p.

*49 Investigation of the quantitative determination of point and areal precipitation by radar echo measurements: ninth technical report. (1 Oct. 1963–31 Mar. 1964). By E. A. Mueller and A. L. Sims. 45 p.

*50 Study of rainout of radioactivity in Illinois. By F. A. Huff. Contract AT(11-1)-1199. Third progress report. 66 p. Jan. 31, 1965.

*51 Prediction of corn and soybean yields using weather data. By S. A. Changnon Jr. CHIAA Research report 22. 29 p. Feb. 5, 1965.

*52 Summary of 1964 research on hail in Illinois. By S. A. Changnon Jr. CHIAA Research report 23. 23 p. Feb. 24, 1965.

*53 Radioactive rainout relations in convective rainstorms. By F. A. Huff. Contract AT (11-1)-1199. Research report 1. 131 p. March 1965.

*54 Investigation of the quantitative determination of point and areal precipitation by radar echo measurements: interim report 1 (Oct. 1964–31 Mar. 1965). By A. L. Sims and E. A. Mueller. Contract DA-28-043 AMC-00032(E). 22 p.

*55 Evaluation of the maser-equipped radar set AN/MPS-34 and area precipitation measurement indicator: first quarterly progress report (1 April–30 June 1965). By R. E. Rinehart and D. M. A. Jones. Contract DA-28-043 AMC-01257(E). 9 p.

*56 Determination of free chlorine residuals in water: final report (15 Feb. 1963–31 Aug. 1965). By T. E. Larson and F. W. Sollo. Contract DA-49-193-MD-2399. 43 p.

*57 1964 project Springfield studies. By Pieter J. Feteris. Contract AT(11-1)-1199. Research report 2. 20 p. Oct. 1965.

*58 Evaluation of the maser-equipped radar set AN/MPS-34 and area precipitation measurement indicator: second quarterly progress report (1 July–30 Sept. 1965). By R. E. Rinehart and D. M. A. Jones. Contract DA-28-043 AMC-01257(E). 14 p.

*59 Investigation of the quantitative determination of point and areal precipitation by radar echo measurements: interim report 2 (1 Apr.–30 Sept. 1965). By A. L. Sims and E. A. Mueller. Contract DA-28-043 AMC-00032(E). 17 p.

*60 Investigation of the quantitative determination of point and areal precipitation by radar echo measurements: final report (1 Oct. 1961–30 Sept. 1964). By A. L. Sims, E. A. Mueller, and G. E. Stout. Contract DA-36-039 SC-87280. 197 p.

*61 Study of rainout of radioactivity in Illinois: fourth progress report (Oct. 1965). By Floyd A. Huff and Wayne E. Bradley. Contract AT (11-1)-1199. 20 p.

*62 Evaluation of the maser-equipped radar set AN/MPS-34 and area precipitation measurement indicator: third quarterly progress report (1 Oct.–31 Dec. 1965). By R. E. Rinehart, D. M. A. Jones, and E. A. Mueller. Contract DA-28-043 AMC-01257(E). 31 p.

*63 Summary of 1965 hail research in Illinois. By Stanley A. Changnon Jr. CHIAA Research report 30. 39 p. 1966.

*64 Disastrous hailstorms on June 19-20, 1964, in Illinois. By Stanley A. Changnon Jr. CHIAA Research report 31. 37 p. Feb. 3, 1966.

*65 Relationship of weather factors and crop yields in Illinois. By Stanley A. Changnon Jr. CHIAA Research report 32. 23 p. Mar. 25, 1966.

*66 Investigation of the quantitative determination of point and areal precipitation by radar echo measurements: interim report 3 (1 Oct. 1965–31 Mar. 1966). By E. A. Mueller and A. L. Sims. Contract DA-28-043 AMC-00032(E). 22 p.

*67 Feasibility study of quantitative radar measurement of precipitation on Lake Michigan. By Stanley A. Changnon Jr. and Floyd A. Huff. Univ. of Ill. Water Resources Center. Final report. Contract 6666-04G (26-84). 18 p. June 20, 1966.

*68 Evaluation of the maser-equipped radar set AN/MPS-34 and area precipitation measurement indicator: fourth quarterly progress report (1 Jan. 1966–31 Mar. 1966). By R. E. Rinehart, E. A. Mueller, and D. W. Staggs. Technical report ECOM-01257-4. Contract DA-28-043 AMC-01257(E). 16 p.

*69 Relation of lightning, rainfall, and hail to the properties of mesoscale meteorological patterns. By Pieter J. Feteris. National Science Foundation GP-5196. First progress report. 34 p. Nov. 1966.

*70 Atmospheric electrical soundings and their relation to precipitation. By Wayne E. Bradley. National Science Foundation GP-3479. Final report. 22 p. Nov. 15, 1966.

*71 Study of rainout of radioactivity in Illinois. By Wayne E. Bradley and Pieter J. Feteris. Contract AT(11-1)-1199. Fifth progress report. 26 p. Dec. 1966.

*72 Investigation of the quantitative determination of point and areal precipitation by radar echo measurements. By E. A. Mueller and A. L. Sims. Technical report ECOM-00032-F. Contract DA-28-043 AMC-00032(E). Final report. 88 p. Dec. 1966.

*73 Evaluation of the maser-equipped radar set AN/MPS-34 and area precipitation measurement indicator: fifth quarterly progress report (1 Apr.–30 June 1966). By R. E. Rinehart. Technical report ECOM-01257-4. Contract DA-28-043 AMC-01257(E). 20 p.

*74 Radar analysis of project warm rain, Hilo, Hawaii–Summer, 1965. By R. G. Semonin, E. A. Mueller, G. E. Stout, and D. W. Staggs. National Science Foundation GP-194. Final report. 17 p. Feb. 17, 1967.

*75 Occurrence of nitrate in well waters. By T. E. Larson and Laurel Henley. Univ. of Ill. Water Resources Center. Project 65-05G. Final report. 15 p. June 1966.

*76 Experimental and theoretical investigation of the coalescence of liquid drops. By Richard G. Semonin. National Science Foundation GP-2528. Final report. 117 p. Feb. 23, 1967.

*77 Raindrop distributions at Majuro Atoll, Marshall Islands. By E. A. Mueller and A. L. Sims. Contract DA-28-043 AMC-02071(E). Technical report. 93 p. March 1967.

*78 Summary of 1966 hail research in Illinois. By S. A. Changnon Jr. CHIAA Research report 33. 37 p. Dec. 1966.

*79 Evaluation of the maser-equipped radar set AN/MPS-34 and area precipitation measurement indicator. By D. M. A. Jones, R. E. Rinehart, E. A. Mueller, and D. W. Staggs. Contract DA-28-043 AMC-01257(E). Final report. 54 p. Dec. 31, 1966.

*80 Investigation of the quantitative determination of precipitation by radar: interim report 1 (1 Oct. 1966–31 Mar. 1967). By E. A. Mueller, A. L. Sims, and R. Cataneo. Technical report ECOM-02071-1. Contract DA-28-043 AMC-02071(E). 52 p. June 1967.

*81 Determination of free chlorine residuals in water. By T. E. Larson and F. W. Sollo Jr. Contract DA-49-193-MD-2399. Annual progress report. (1 Mar. 1964–28 Feb. 1965) 48 p.

*82 Raindrop distributions at Island Beach, New Jersey. By E. A. Mueller and A. L. Sims. Contract DA-28-043 AMC-02701(E). Technical report. 108 p. Sept. 1967.

*83 The effect of artificially produced space charge on the electrification of clouds. By W. E. Bradley and R. G. Semonin. National Science Foundation G-3479. Final report. 24 p. September 1967.

*84 Raindrop distributions at Franklin, North Carolina. By E. A. Mueller and A. L. Sims. Contract DA-28-043 AMC-02071(E). Technical report ECOM-02071-RR3. 157 p. September 1967.

*85 Study of rainout of radioactivity in Illinois. By F. A. Huff, W. E. Bradley, and P. J. Feteris. Contract AT(11-1)-1199. Sixth progress report. 19 p. November 1967.

*86 Investigation of the quantitative determination of precipitation by radar: Interim report 2. By E. A. Mueller, A. L. Sims, and R. Cantaneo. Contract DA-28-043 AMC-02071(E). 23 p. December 1967.

*87 Raindrop distributions at Woody Island, Alaska. By E. A. Mueller and A. L. Sims. Contract DA-28-043 AMC-02071(E). Technical report ECOM-02071-4. 93 p. November 1967.

*88 Raindrop distributions at Bogor, Indonesia. By E. A. Mueller and A. L. Sims. Contract DA-28-043 AMC-02071(E). Technical report ECOM-02071-RR5. 72 p. January 1968.

*89 Raindrop distributions at Corvallis, Oregon. By E. A. Mueller and A. L. Sims. Contract DA-28-043 AMC-02071(E). Technical report ECOM-02071-RR6. 69 p. February 1968.

*90 Program in atmospheric electricity and cloud modification, Flagstaff, 1966. Edited by D. M. A. Jones. Contract DA-28-043 AMC-02376(E). Technical report ECOM-02376-F. 112 p. June 1967.

*91 Summary of 1967 hail research in Illinois. By Stanley A. Changnon Jr. CHIAA research report 39. 50 p. January 1968.

92 Hydraulic geometry of Illinois streams. By John B. Stall and Yu-Si Fok. University of Illinois Water Resources Center, Project B-005-Ill. Research report 15. 47 p. July 1968.

*93 Tracing tropospheric radioactive debris by isentropic trajectories. By John W. Wilson and Parker T. Jones III. Contract AT(11-1)-1199. 33 p. Research report 3. July 1968.

*94 Determination of free bromine in water (U). By T. E. Larson and F. W. Sollo Jr. Contract DA-49-193 MD-2909. Annual progress report. 38 p. August 1968.

*95 Statistical analysis of sub-synoptic meteorological patterns. By Pieter J. Feteris. National Science Foundation GA-1321. Final report. 75 p. October 1968.

*96 Summary of radar-rainfall research. By G. E. Stout, E. A. Mueller, A. L. Sims, R. Cataneo, and F. A. Huff. Contract DA-28-043 AMC-02071(E). Interim report 3. 47 p. October 1968.

*97 Study of rainout of radioactivity in Illinois. By J. W. Wilson and W. E. Bradley. Contract AT(11-1)-1199. Seventh progress report. 64 p. November 1968.

*98 Effects of rainfall and drop size on the M564 fuze. By E. A. Mueller and A. L. Sims. Contract DAAG 11-68-C-1342. Final report. 50 p. October 1968.

*99 Raindrop distributions near Flagstaff, Arizona. By D. M. A. Jones. Contract DA-ARO-D-31-124-G-937. Final report. 50 p. January 1969.

*100 Relationships between reflectivity, attenuation, and rainfall rate derived from drop size spectra. By E. A. Mueller and A. L. Sims. Contract DA-28-043 AMS-02071(E). Final report. 112 p. May 1969.

*101 A study of holography for spherical particle size analysis. By Daniel J. Stigliani Jr. National Science Foundation GP-2528, GA-630, and GA-4576. Research report. 105 p. May 1969.

*102 Insurance-related hail research in Illinois during 1968. By Stanley A. Changnon Jr. CHIAA research report 40. 47 p. February 1969.

*103 Hail evaluation techniques. By Stanley A. Changnon Jr. National Science Foundation GA-482. Part 1 of final report. 97 p. April 1969.

*104 A statistical methodology for the planning and evaluation of hail suppression experiments in Illinois. By Paul T. Schickedanz, Stanley A. Changnon Jr., and Carl G. Lonnquist. National Science Foundation GA-482. Part 2 of final report. 140 p. April 1969.

*105 Effects of rainfall and drop size spectra on the standard and modified MTSQ M564 fuze. By E. A. Mueller and A. L. Sims. Contract DAAG 11-69-C-0178. Final report. 40 p. June 1969.

*106 Evaluation of precipitation modification experiments from precipitation rate measurements. By F. A. Huff, W. L. Shipp, and P. T. Schickedanz. Contract INT-14-06-D-6575. Final report. 122 p. April 1969.

*107 Determination of free bromine in water (U). By T. E. Larson and F. W. Sollo. Contract DA-49-193 MD-2909. Annual progress report. 30 p. July 1969.

*108 Study of rainout of radioactivity in Illinois. Project Director, G. E. Stout. AEC Contract AT(11-1)-1199. Eighth progress report. 49 p. November 1969.

*109 Recording hailgage evaluation. By Stanley A. Changnon Jr. and Donald W. Staggs. National Science Foundation GA-1520. Final report. 47 p. December 1969.

*110 Investigations of crop-hail loss measurement techniques. By N. A. Barron, S. A. Changnon Jr., and J. Hornaday. CHIAA research report 42. 67 p. January 1970.

COOPERATIVE REPORTS
WITH STATE GEOLOGICAL SURVEY

1 Preliminary report on ground-water resources of the Chicago region, Illinois. By Max Suter, R. E. Bergstrom, H. F. Smith, G. H. Emrich, W. C. Walton and T. E. Larson. 1959.

   1-S Summary of preliminary report on ground-water resources of the Chicago region, Illinois. 1959.

2 Ground-water resources of DuPage County, Illinois. By A. J. Zeizel, W. C. Walton, R. T. Sasman, and T. A. Prickett. 104 p. 1962.

3 Preliminary report on ground-water resources of the Havana region in west-central Illinois. By W. H. Walker, R. E. Bergstrom and W. C. Walton. 61 p. 1965.

MISCELLANEOUS PUBLICATIONS

*1 Summary of statement on water policy. Prepared for Illinois Water Resources and Flood Control Board in response to request from President's National Water Policy Commission. Mimeo. 1950.

*2 An act to provide for the establishment of water authorities and to define their powers and duties. Mimeo. 1951.

*3 Local climatological data. Mt. Vernon, 1901-1954. 4 p. 1955.

*4 Local climatological data. Urbana. 1901-1954. 4 p. 1955.

*5 Local climatological data. Monmouth, 1901-1954. 4 p. 1955.

6 Local climatological data, Rockford, 1905-1954. 4 p. 1955.

7 Publications of the Illinois State Water Survey. 30 p. 1967.

8 History and activities of Illinois State Water Survey. 24 p. 1965.

9 Technical letter 1. Point rainfall frequencies in Illinois for periods of one hour to ten days. 5 p. 1959.

10 Technical letter 2. Reducing reservoir evaporation. 1 p. 1959.

11 Technical letter 3. Reservoir sedimentation. 4 p. 1959.

12 Technical letter 4. Rainfall frequencies for five to sixty minutes. 3 p. 1960.

*13 Technical letter 5. Lake evaporation in Illinois. 3 p. 1960.

14 Local climatological data. Havana, 1901-1962. 6 p. 1964.

15 Local climatological data. Bloomington-Normal, 1901-1962. 6 p. 1964.

16 Local climatological data. Danville, 1901-1962. 6 p. 1964.

*17 Local climatological data. Aurora, 1901-1962. 6 p. 1964.

18 Local climatological data. Charleston, 1901-1962. 6 p. 1964.

19 Local climatological data. Carbondale, 1910-1962. 6 p. 1964.

*20 Local climatological data. Decatur. 1901-1962. 6 p. 1964.

21 Local climatological data. Hillsboro, 1901-1962. 6 p. 1964.

22 Local climatological data. Kankakee, 1917-1962. 6 p. 1964.

23 Local climatological data. Ottawa, 1901-1962. 6 p. 1964.

24 Local climatological data. Rushville, 1901-1962. 6 p. 1964.

*25 Local climatological data. Quincy, 1901-1962. 6 p. 1964.

26 Technical letter 6. Nitrate in water supplies. 4 p. 1966.

27 Technical letter 7. Water transmission costs. 4 p. 1967.

28 Technical letter 8. Cost of reservoirs in Illinois. 4 p. 1968.

29 Technical letter 9. Cost of pumping water. 4 p. 1968.

30 Technical letter 10. Costs of wells and pumps. 9 p. 1968.

31 Technical letter 11. Cost of water treatment in Illinois. 7 p. 1968.

*32 Then and Now: Water resources in Illinois 1818-1968. By Mr. J. Loreena Ivens and Mrs. Patricia A. Motherway. 16 p. 1968.

33 Technical letter 12. Cost of municipal sewage treatment. 12 p. 1969.

WATER RESOURCES CENTER
University of Illinois
2535 Hydrosystems Laboratory
Urbana, Illinois 61801

The University of Illinois Water Resources Center irregularly issues additions to the following series of publications which are available to the public through the Center while the supply lasts. When the supply is depleted, and if the report has a Publication Board Number (PB), it may be obtained from the National Technical Information Service, U. S. Department of Commerce, Springfield, Virginia, 22151.

A. **Research Reports**
    These documents are the final completion or termination reports for the various research projects which have been administered by the Center. These projects include those in Illinois which have been supported in whole or in part by the Office of Water Resources Research, United States Department of the Interior under the Annual Allotment and Matching Grant provisions of Public Law 88-379.

B. **Annual Reports**
    These reports, which are published in September of each year, summarize the activities of the Water Resources Center for the previous fiscal year.

C.   **Research Catalogs**
     The catalogs are compilations of descriptions of current water resources research in the State of Illinois. It is anticipated that in the future the documents will be published during the fall of each year. They provide a current supplement for the State of Illinois to the Water Resources Research Catalog published by the Office of Water Resources Research and the Science Information Exchange.

D.   **Special Reports**
     Special events such as lectures and proceedings of conferences are published in this series.

A. RESEARCH REPORTS

*1   "Occurrence of Nitrate in Well Waters" (June, 1966) (15 p.) by Thurston E. Larson and Laurel Henley. Illinois State Water Survey, Urbana.

*2   "Feasibility Study of Quantitative Radar Measurement of Precipitation on Lake Michigan" (June, 1966) (18+i p.) by Stanley A. Changnon, Jr. and Floyd A. Huff. Illinois State Water Survey, Urbana.

*3   "The Spectrophotometric Determination of Nitrate in Water Using 2-Nitroso-1-Naphthol-4-Sulfonic Acid" (July, 1966) (15 p.) by Albert L. Caskey and Frank N. Abercrombie. Department of Chemistry, Southern Illinois University, Carbondale.

*4   "The Analysis of the Uptake of Water by Plant Root Systems" (August, 1966) (38+ii p.) by Arnold Klute. Department of Agronomy, University of Illinois, Urbana.

*5   "Influence of Turbulence on Surface Reaeration" (September, 1966) (42 p.) by E. R. Holley and K. K. Klintworth. Department of Civil Engineering, University of Illinois, Urbana.

*6   "The Ion-exchange Reactions of Radioactive Ions with Soils and Effects of Organic Compounds" (October, 1966) (150+x p.) by Ben B. Ewing and Bong Taick Kown. Department of Civil Engineering, University of Illinois, Urbana.

*7   "Further Study of Aquifer Performance" (January, 1967) (6 p.) by Walter Rose. Department of Mining, Metallurgy and Petroleum Engineering, University of Illinois, Urbana.

8   "Subsurface Flow in a Southern Illinois Fragipan Soil" (February, 1967) (51+vi p.) by W. R. Boggess and Elon S. Verry, Jr. Department of Forestry, University of Illinois, Urbana.

*9   "Meteorological Drought and Its Social Impact in Illinois" (March, 1967) (31+vi p.) by Alfred W. Booth and Don Voeller. Department of Geography, University of Illinois, Urbana.

10   "Basic Study of Jet Flow Patterns Related to Stream and Reservoir Behavior" (July, 1967) (63+ix p.) by W. Hall, C. Maxwell and Hormoz Pazwash. Department of Civil Engineering, University of Illinois, Urbana.

*11 "Co-oxidation of Organic Molecules by Methane-oxidizing Bacteria Growing at the Expense of Methane" (July, 1967) (5+ii p.) by R. E. Kallio. School of Life Sciences, University of Illinois, Urbana.

12   "An Annotated Bibliography of Observations on Illinois Water Resources 1673-1850" (August, 1967) (78+vii p.) by T. P. Schlunz, R. M. Sutton and G. W. White. Departments of History and Geology, University of Illinois, Urbana.

*13 "Microscopic Determination of Boundary Shear and Sublayer Turbulence Characteristics in an Open Channel" (January, 1968) (77+xiv p.) by H. G. Wenzel and M. J. Mathews. Department of Civil Engineering, University of Illinois, Urbana.

14   "Probabilistic Analysis of Wastewater Treatment and Disposal Systems" (June, 1968) (158+ix p.) by Veerasamy Kothandaraman. Department of Civil Engineering, University of Illinois, Urbana.

*15 "Hydraulic Geometry of Illinois Streams" (July, 1968) (47 + ii p.) by John B. Stall and Yu-Si Fok. Illinois State Water Survey, Urbana.

*16 "Non-Darcy Flow Characteristics of Water as Influenced by Clay Concentration" (June, 1968) (50 + v p.) by Raymond J. Miller, Allen R. Overman, and John H. Peverly. Department of Agronomy, University of Illinois, Urbana.

17   "Statistical Porous Media Hydrodynamics" (July, 1968) (70 + vi p.) by A. E. Scheidegger. Department of Mining, Metallurgy, and Petroleum Engineering, University of Illinois, Urbana.

*18 "Intergovernmental Relationships in the Administration of Water Resources" (September, 1968) (336 + iv p.) by Norman G. P. Krausz. Department of Agricultural Economics, University of Illinois, Urbana.

19   "Development of Drainage Assessment Procedures Based on Physical Features in Illinois" (May, 1969) (27 + vi p.) by Benjamin A. Jones, Jr. and Carroll J. W. Drablos. Department of Agricultural Engineering, University of Illinois, Urbana. PB 188835.

*20 "Impact of Community Water Systems in Small Towns" (June, 1969) (16 + vi p.) by Walter J. Wills and Donald D. Osburn. Department of Agricultural Industries, Southern Illinois University, Carbondale. PB 188841.

*21 "Some Data on Diffusion and Turbulence in Relation to Reaeration" (July, 1969) (53 p.) by E. R. Holley, Jr. Department of Civil Engineering, University of Illinois, Urbana. PB 187838.

22   "Hydraulic Resistance in Alluvial Channels" (July, 1969) (66 p.) by Ben Chie Yen and Ying-Chang Liou. Department of Civil Engineering, University of Illinois, Urbana. PB 189789.

*23 "The Identification and Critical Analysis of Selected Literature Dealing with the Recreational Aspects of Water Resources Use, Planning, and Development" (June, 1969) (293 p.) by Robert B. Ditton. Department of Recreation and Park Administration, University of Illinois, Urbana. PB 189837.

24   "Use of Endocommensal Molluscan Ciliated Protozoa as Indicators of Water Quality and Pollution in Illinois Waters" (July, 1969) (27 p.) by Eugene B. Small and Gregory A. Antipa. Department of Zoology, University of Illinois, Urbana. PB 188496.

25   "Virus Removal by Chemical Coagulation" (November, 1969) (66 p.) by R. S. Engelbrecht and Malay Chaudhuri. Department of Civil Engineering, University of Illinois, Urbana. PB 188911.

*26 "Stochastic Analysis of Hydrologic Streams" (December, 1969) (34 p.) by Ven Te Chow. Department of Civil Engineering, University of Illinois, Urbana. PB 189791.

27   "Studies of the Population Dynamics and Physiological Ecology of Four Species of Fresh-Water Isopods" (January, 1970) (69 p.) by Arthur J. Seidenburg. Department of Zoology, University of Illinois, Urbana. PB 189792.

28 "Boundary Effects on Jet Flow Patterns Related to Water Quality and Pollution Problems" (January 1970) (84 p.) by W. Hall, C. Maxwell and Hormoz Pazwash. Department of Civil Engineering, University of Illinois, Urbana. PB 189787.

29 "An Experimental Study of the Uptake of Water by Soybean Roots" (January 1970) (32 p.) by Arnold Klute. Department of Agronomy, University of Illinois, Urbana. PB 189 788.

30 "The Mechanics of a Drop After Striking a Stagnant Water Layer" (January 1970) (130 p.) by Harry G. Wenzel, Jr. and Raymond Chun Tsung Wang. Department of Civil Engineering, University of Illinois, Urbana. PB 189790.

31 "Microscopic Open Channel Boundary Layer Velocity Measurements Using a Virtual Image Method" (April 1970) (31 p.) by Harry G. Wenzel, Jr. and Kuo C. Chang. Department of Civil Engineering, University of Illinois, Urbana.

32 "Hydraulic Geometry of 12 Selected Stream Systems of the United States" (July 1970) (73 p.) by John B. Stall and Chih Ted Yang. Illinois State Water Survey, Urbana.

33 "Water Quality Criteria for Selected Recreational Uses" (September 1970) (134 p.) by Doyle W. Bishop and Robert Aukerman. Department of Recreation and Park Administration, University of Illinois, Urbana.

B. ANNUAL REPORTS

"Annual report of activities for fiscal year". 1965 – to date.

C. RESEARCH CATALOGS

*1 "Water Resources Research in Illinois" (October, 1965)

2 "Water Resources Research in Illinois" (September, 1967)

D. SPECIAL REPORTS

1 "This Environment – Friend or Foe?" A George A. Miller Centennial Lecture (University of Illinois, October 19, 1967) by Abel Wolman. The Johns Hopkins University, Baltimore.

*2 "Feasibility of Evaluation of Benefits from Improved Great Lakes Water Quality" (May, 1968) (122 + v p.) by Ben B. Ewing *et al.* University of Illinois Water Resources Center, Urbana.

3 "Intergovernmental Relationships in the Administration of Water Resources" (January 1970) (37 p.). Excerpts from Water Research Report No. 18 by Norman G. P. Krausz (September 1968). Water Resources Center, University of Illinois, Urbana.

INDIANA

DEPARTMENT OF NATURAL RESOURCES
Division of Fish and Game
Room 607 State Office Building
Indianapolis, Indiana 46204

Guide to Indiana Lakes. Price: $0.50.

Investigations of Indiana Lakes and Streams. 1928-1931. 3 volumes.

Wetlands, Final Report [by county]. 1962-1964. 13 volumes.

DEPARTMENT OF NATURAL RESOURCES
Division of Water
Room 609 State Office Building
Indianapolis, Indiana 46204

BULLETINS
Preliminary Reports — Basic Data

1   Memorandum Concerning a Pumping Test at Gas City, Indiana. 1945. Price: $1.00.

*2 Water Levels in Indiana. 1946.

*3 Ground-Water Resources of St. Joseph County, Indiana. 1948.

*4 Ground-Water Resources of Boone County, Indiana. 1949.

5   Ground-Water Resources of Noble County, Indiana. 1950. Price: $1.00.

6   Compilation of Monthly & Annual Stream Flow Records of Indiana. 1952. Price: $1.00.

7   Water Level Records of Indiana. 1956. Price: $1.00.

8   Ground-Water Resources of Tippecanoe County, including Basic Data Appendix. 1956. Price: $1.00.

9   Ground-Water Resources of Adams County, Indiana. 1962. Price: $1.00.

10 Ground-Water Resources of Northwestern Indiana, Preliminary Report: Lake County. 1961. Price: $1.00.

11 Ground-Water Resources of West-Central Indiana, Preliminary Report: Greene County. 1961. Price: $1.00.

12 Ground-Water Resources of Northwestern Indiana, Preliminary Report: Porter County. 1962. Price: $1.00.

13 Ground-Water Resources of Northwestern Indiana, Preliminary Report: LaPorte County. 1962. Price: $1.00.

14 Ground-Water Resources of West-Central Indiana, Preliminary Report: Sullivan County. 1962. Price: $1.00.

15 Ground-Water Resources of Northwestern Indiana, Preliminary Report: St. Joseph County. 1962. Price: $1.00.

16 Ground-Water Resources of West-Central Indiana, Preliminary Report: Clay County. 1962. Price: $1.00.

17 Ground-Water Resources of West-Central Indiana, Preliminary Report: Vigo County. 1963. Price: $1.00.

18 Ground-Water Resources of West-Central Indiana, Preliminary Report: Owen County. 1963. Price: $1.00.

19 Ground-Water Resources of Northwestern Indiana, Preliminary Report: Marshall County. 1964. Price: $1.00.

20 Ground-Water Resources of Northwestern Indiana, Preliminary Report: Fulton County. 1964. Price: $1.00.

21 Ground-Water Resources of West-Central Indiana, Preliminary Report: Putnam County. 1964. Price: $1.00.

22 Ground-Water Resources of Northwestern Indiana, Preliminary Report: Starke County. 1964. Price: $1.00.

23 Ground-Water Resources of West-Central Indiana, Preliminary Report: Parke County. 1964. Price: $1.00.

24 Ground-Water Resources of Northwestern Indiana, Preliminary Report: Pulaski County. 1964. Price: $1.00.

25 Ground-Water Resources of Northwestern Indiana, Preliminary Report: Jasper County. 1964. Price: $1.00.

26 Ground-Water Resources of Northwestern Indiana, Preliminary Report: Newton County. 1964. Price: $1.00.

27 Ground-Water Resources of West-Central Indiana, Preliminary Report: Montgomery County. 1964. Price: $1.00.

28 Ground-Water Resources of West-Central Indiana, Preliminary Report: Fountain County. 1964. Price: $1.00.

29 Ground-Water Resources of West-Central Indiana, Preliminary Report: Vermillion County. 1964. Price: $1.00.

30 Ground-Water Levels in Indiana 1955-1962. Price: $1.00.

INTERPRETATIVE STUDIES

31 Geohydrology and Ground-Water Potential of Lake County, Indiana. 1968. Price: $1.00.

32 Geohydrology and Ground-Water Potential of Porter and LaPorte Counties, Indiana. 1968. Price: $1.00.

33 Geohydrology and Ground-Water Potential of St. Joseph County, Indiana. 1969. Price: $1.00.

34 Hydrogeology of the Principal Aquifers in Vigo and Clay Counties, Indiana. (on open file pending publication.)

35   Hydrogeology of the Principal Aquifers in Sullivan and Greene Counties, Indiana. (on open file pending publication.)

36   Ground-Water Resources of Montgomery County, Indiana. (on open file pending publication.)

37   Water Resources of Delaware County, Indiana. 1968. Price: $1.00.

38   Ground Water Resources of Vanderburgh County. (on open file pending publication.)

39   Ground Water Resources of Posey County. (on open file pending publication.)

40   Ground Water Reconnaissance of Harrison County, and Potential of Proposed Industrial Corridor. (on open file pending publication.)

GROUND WATER ATLASES

1   Water Resources of Morgan County. 1964. Price: $0.50.

2   Water Resources of Johnson County. 1966. Price: $0.50.

3   Water Resources of Hendricks County. 1968. Price: $0.50.

4   Water Resources of Tipton County. 1968. Price: $0.50.

5   Water Resources of Grant County. 1968. Price: $0.50.

6   Water Resources of Randolph County. 1969. Price: $0.50.

7   Water Resources of Madison County.

8   Water Resources of Hamilton County. (on open file pending publication.)

9   Water Resources of Henry County. (on open file pending publication.)

MISCELLANEOUS PUBLICATIONS

Ground Water in Indiana. 1965. Free.

Ground Water Resources of the Indianapolis Area, Marion County. 1943. Free.

Ground Water Resources of the Columbus Area, Bartholomew County, Indiana. 1951. 37 p. (Prepared in cooperation with the U. S. Geological Survey.)

Proceedings of Conference of "The Development, Utilization and Conservation of our Ground Water Resources." Free.

Low-Flow Characteristics of Indiana Streams. 1962. Free.

MAPS

Geologic Map of Indiana. (Shows ground water conditions). Price: $0.75.

Hydrographic Lake Maps. 8½" x 11". Price: $0.30. (Write for free list of lakes mapped).

Hydrographic Lake Maps. 17" x 22". Price: $0.60. (Write for free list of lakes mapped).

Reservoir Area Maps. 28" x 22". Price: $0.60.

Reservoir Depth Maps (Geist Cataract, Morse only). 28" x 22". Price: $0.60.

Indiana Lakes and Streams Map. Scale 1:250,000. 47" x 72". Price: $2.00.

Indiana Lakes and Streams Map. Scale 1:500,000. 24" x 36". Price: $0.50.

Canoe Trails (14 sheets to set). Price: $0.30 per set.

DEPARTMENT OF NATURAL RESOURCES
Geological Survey
Indiana University
Bloomington, Indiana 47401

Send orders to the Publications Section, Geological Survey, Indiana University, 611 North Walnut Grove, Bloomington, Indiana 47401. Please make all checks and money orders payable to the Indiana Geological Survey.

Add 10 cents for packaging and mailing for each order under $1.00. Add 10 percent for each order over $1.00 except for orders for maps only over $10.00. Add 5 percent for each order for maps only over $10.00. Maps will be folded unless the customer specifies otherwise.

Out-of-print publications may be consulted in the offices of the Geological Survey.

BULLETINS

4   Glacial sluiceways and lacustrine plains of southern Indiana. W. D. Thornbury. 1950. 21 p., 2 pls., 3 figs. Price: $0.50.

FIELD CONFERENCE GUIDEBOOKS

11   Geomorphology and groundwater hydrology of the Mitchell Plain and Crawford Upland in southern Indiana. H. H. Gray and R. L. Powell. 1965. 26 p., illus. Price: $1.00.

REPORTS OF PROGRESS

13   Natural brines of Indiana and adjoining parts of Illinois and Kentucky. F. H. Walker. 1959. 58 p., 13 figs., 20 tables. Price: $0.75.

19   Engineering geology of dam site and spillway areas for the Monroe Reservoir, southern Indiana. J. D. Winslow, G. R. Gates and W. N. Melhorn. 1960. 10 p., 1 pl., 2 figs., 3 tables. Price: $0.50.

20   Preliminary engineering geology report of dam sites on the East Fork of the Muscatatuck River in Scott, Jennings, and Jefferson Counties, Indiana. J. D. Winslow. 1960. 30 p., 5 pls., 3 figs., 3 tables. Price: $1.00.

ANNUAL REPORTS

*Twenty-fourth annual report of the Indiana Department of Geology and Natural Resources for the year 1899. W. S. Blatchley. 1900. 1078 p., 90 pls., 21 figs., 1 map. (The natural resources of Indiana. p. 3-40.)

*Thirty-first annual report of the Indiana Department of Geology and Natural Resources for the year 1906. W. S. Blatchley. 1907. 772 p., 35 pls., 47 figs., 30 maps. (The natural resources of the State of Indiana. p. 13-72, 3 pls.)

NUMBERED PUBLICATIONS OF THE FORMER INDIANA DEPARTMENT OF CONSERVATION (DIVISION OF GEOLOGY)

*133 Ground water in Indiana. Marshall Harrell. 1935. 504 p., 3 maps.

INDIANA FLOOD CONTROL AND WATER RESOURCES COMMISSION

State Office Building
Indianapolis, Indiana 46204

TECHNICAL MEMORANDA REPORTS

*58-1 Preliminary Water Supply Report for a Proposed Reservoir at Batesville, Indiana. February 15, 1958.

*58-2 Operation of Mansfield Reservoir for Flood Control and Low Flow Regulation. March 1, 1958.

*58-3 Preliminary Engineering Geology Report, Big Pine Creek Dam and Reservoir Site. April 1, 1958.

58-4 Crop Losses on White River Flood Plain; Daviess, Gibson, Knox and Pike Counties, Indiana. Floods of 1957. December 1958.

58-5 Preliminary Engineering Geology of Lafayette Reservoir; Wildcat Creek near Lafayette. December 1958.

*60-1 Preliminary Engineering Geology of Lafayette Reservoir Dam Site; Wildcat Creek near Lafayette. November 1960.

62-1 Preliminary Engineering Geology of Sand Creek Dam Site; Sand Creek near Scipio, Indiana. September 1962.

63-1 Preliminary Hydrology Report, Dry Run Basin. August 1963.

63-2 Preliminary Engineering Geology at Lower Little Blue River Basin. September 1963.

PRELIMINARY EXAMINATION REPORTS

PE-1 Report of Preliminary Examination for Flood Control; Salamonie River at Portland, Indiana. December 1958.

PE-2 Report of Preliminary Examination; Wabash River Flood Problems, Vigo and Sullivan Counties, Indiana. January 1959.

PE-3 Report of Preliminary Examination; Crooked Creek at Madison, Indiana, U. S. 421 Highway Improvements. May 1963.

PE-4 Report of Preliminary Examination; Simon Creek Channel Improvements, I-70 and Wilbur Wright Road. May 1963.

PE-5 Report of Preliminary Examination; Considered Industrial Levee, West Fork of White River near Martinsville. June 1963.

PE-6 Report of Preliminary Examination; Potato Creek Reservoir, Kankakee River Basin, Potato Creek near North Liberty, Indiana. December 1964.

PE-7 Report of Preliminary Examination; Water Supply in the Muscatatuck River Basin, Scott County, Indiana. December 1965.

PE-8 Report of Preliminary Examination; Lake Papakeechie near North Webster, Indiana. March 1965.

PE-9 Report of Preliminary Examination; Williams Dam, East Fork White River at Williams, Indiana. August 1966.

STATUS OF INVESTIGATION REPORTS

SI-1 Progress Report. Investigation of Kankakee and Yellow Rivers, Indiana, for Flood Control and Major Drainage. January 1957.

SI-2 Status of Investigation for Flood Control and Water Resources Development; East Fork of White River, Indiana. December 1958.

SI-3 Status of Investigation for Flood Control and Major Drainage; Kankakee and Yellow Rivers, Indiana. January 1959.

SI-4 Status of Investigation for Flood Control and Water Resources Development; East Fork White River Basin, Indiana. December 1960.

SI-5 Status of Investigation for Flood Control and Water Resources Development; Whitewater River Basin, Indiana. December 1960.

SI-6 Status of Investigation for Flood Control and Water Resources Development; Maumee River Basin, Indiana. December 1960.

SI-7 Status of Investigation for Flood Control and Water Resources Development; Main Stem White River, Indiana. December 1960.

SI-8 Status of Investigation for Flood Control and Water Resources Development; Wabash River Basin, Indiana. December 1960.

SI-9 Status of Investigation for Flood Control and Water Resources Development; Patoka River Basin, Indiana. December 1960.

SI-10 Status of Investigation for Flood Control and Water Resources Development; West Fork White River Basin, Indiana. December 1960.

SI-11 Status of Investigation for Flood Control and Water Resources Development; Kankakee-Yellow Rivers Basin, Indiana. December 1960.

SI-12 Status of Investigation for Flood Control and Major Drainage, Yellow River, Indiana. May 1966.

REPORTS OF INVESTIGATION

1 Report on Muscatatuck State School Water Supply; Jennings County, Indiana. April 7, 1952.

2 Report on City of Greensburg Water Supply; Decatur County, Indiana. Aug. 17, 1953.

*3   Report on Singleton Drainage Ditch. March 1, 1954.

4   Report on City of Jasper Water Supply; Dubois County, Indiana. May 1954.

5   Report on Town of Milan Water Supply; Ripley County, Indiana. Sept. 15, 1954.

6   Report of Investigation; Corydon, Indiana Water Supply. February 1955.

7   Report of Investigation, Eagle Creek at Indianapolis; Channel Improvements for Flood Control. Section B. February 1956.

8   Report of Investigation; Indiana State Farm Water Supply. May 1956.

*9   Report of Investigation, Monroe Reservoir Salt Creek near Harrodsburg, Indiana. December 1956.

10   Report of Investigation, Fairfield Ditch at Fort Wayne, Indiana. September 1960.

11   Feasibility Report – Dam and Reservoir – Clark State Forest Area, Clark County, Indiana. November 1963.

12   Feasibility Report – Little Blue River Basin – Reservoir at Mile 6.30 Little Blue River – Crawford and Perry Counties, Indiana – for Recreation and Allied Purposes. November 1963.

13   Feasibility Report – Little Blue River Basin – Sulphur Springs Reservoir – Crawford and Perry Counties, Indiana – for Recreation and Allied Purposes. November 1963.

14   Economic Projections for Indiana River Basin Areas. April 1965.

15   Water Supply, Adams County, Indiana. April 1967.

*16   Benefits for Recreation – Little Calumet River Report of Investigation, City of Decatur. May 1967.

CIRCULARS

1   Thickness of Glacial Drift. January 1950.

*2   A digest of the Conservancy Act of Indiana (out of print, superseded by Circular No. 8). 1951.

*3   Indiana Flood Control Act (superseded by Circular No. 5). 1954.

4   The Flood Control Revolving Fund. 1959.

5   Indiana Flood Control Act. 1961.

6   Maintenance and Repair of Dams, Levees, Dikes and Floodwalls. 1961.

*7   *Not yet published.*

8   A Digest of the Conservancy Act of Indiana of 1957. 1962.

9   Recommendations for Maintenance and Repair of Earth-fill, Dams and Appurtant Works. 1966.

BULLETINS

1   Indiana's Water Resources. 1951.

SPECIAL AND SUMMARY REPORTS

Crop Losses on White River Flood Plain; Daviess, Gibson, Knox and Pike Counties, Indiana. Floods of 1957 (Summary of Technical Memoranda 58-4). December 1958.

Flood Damage on Eagle Creek; Boone and Marion Counties, Indiana. Floods of 1956, 1957 and 1958. February 1959.

Progress Report on Special River Basin Studies. February 1963.

Small Watershed Program in Indiana under Federal Public Law 566. July 1963.

Brookville Reservoir – East Fork White River. August 1963.

Summary of Corps of Engineers Report on Lafayette and Big Pine Reservoirs; Wabash River Basin, Indiana. January 1964.

Summary of Corps of Engineers Report on Clifty and Patoka Reservoirs; Wabash River Basin, Indiana. May 1964.

Summary of a Report of Preliminary Examination, Potato Creek Reservoir, Kankakee River Basin, Potato Creek near North Liberty, Indiana. December 1964.

1   General Policy on Management and Sale of Water Supplies. Jan. 29, 1965.

2   Recommended Rates and Charges for Water, Monroe Reservoir. Jan. 29, 1965.

Summary Report; Sedimentation Surveys in Indiana. October 1965.

*TM 66-1   Engineering Geology of the Proposed Quick Creek Dam Site, Near Austin, Indiana. August 1966.

*TM 66-2   Considered Maple Creek Reservoir. November 1966.

*TM 67-1   Geologic Investigations for control structure at Dewart Lake, Kosciusko County. October 1967.

*TM 67-2   Engineering Geology of Grouse Ridge Lake Dam – Section 23, T 8 N, R 4 E. Bartholomew County, Indiana.

*Survey Report for Flood Control and Water Resources Development – Patoka River Basin, Indiana. *Not published.*

Appendix A – Hydrology Studies. September 1962.

Appendix B – Ellsworth Reservoir Studies. January 1963.

*Appendix C – *Not published.*

Appendix D – Preliminary Geology of Patoka River Dam Site. May 1964.

ANNUAL PROGRESS REPORTS

*Progress Report. December 1957.

*Progress Report. December 1958.

Progress Report. December 1959.

Progress Report. December 1960.

Progress Report. December 1961.

Progress Report. January 1964.

STREAM POLLUTION CONTROL BOARD
1330 West Michigan Street
Indianapolis, Indiana 46206

Stream Pollution Control Law, Chapter 214, Acts of 1943, as amended. 10 p.

Water Quality Standards – SPC 1R2 and SPC 4 through SPC 10.

Regulations SPC 2, SPC 3, and SPC 11.

Annual Report. *Published in September or October for the previous fiscal year. For early years only file copies are available.*

Indiana Water Quality – Monitor Station Records; Rivers and Streams. *Published every two years. For early years only file copies are available.*

INDIANA WATER RESOURCES STUDY COMMITTEE

This Committee is no longer in existence.

For information regarding the publications listed below, contact the Department of Natural Resources, Division of Water, State Office Building, Indianapolis, Indiana 46204.

*Indiana Water Resources. December 1956. 42 p.

Indiana Water Resources, Technical Appendix. December 1956. 127 p.

The Indiana Conservancy Act of 1957 (amended 1961). 1960.

The Indiana Conservancy Act. 1961.

WATER RESOURCES RESEARCH CENTER
Purdue University
Lilly Hall of Life Science
Lafayette, Indiana 47907

TECHNICAL REPORTS

*1 Mathematical Simulation of the Hydrology of Small Watersheds. L. F. Huggins and E. J. Monke.

*2 Statistical Analysis of Ground Water Use and Replenishment. J. D. Rockaway and R. B. Johnson. August 1966.

3 Analysis of Ground Water Use, Replenishment and Aquifer Characteristics in Bartholomew County, Indiana. W. N. Melhorn. June 1969.

4 Program for Estimating Runoff from Indiana Watersheds –Part I: Linear Systems Analysis in Surface Hydrology. D. Blank and J. W. Delleur. August 1968.

*5 Characterization of the Rate of Water Infiltration into Soils. D. Swartzendruber, R. W. Skaggs and Dan Wiersma. December 1968.

*6 Manpower Requirements for Pollution Control and Water Resources in Indiana and a Related Pollution Control Technology Curriculum. J. P. Lisack and Dan Wiersma. March 1969.

*7 Statistical Analysis of Meandering River Geometry. G. H. Toebes and T. P. Chang. June 1969.

*8 Erodibility of Sand-Clay Mixture as Evaluated by a Water Jet. R. N. Bhasin, C. W. Lovell, Jr. and G. H. Toebes. June 1969.

*9 A Program in Urban Hydrology–Part II: An Evaluation of Rainfall-Runoff for Small Urbanized Watersheds and the Effect of Urbanization on Runoff. P. B. S. Sarma, J. W. Delleur and A. R. Rao. October 1969.

10 *(In preparation.)*

11 An Approximate Method for Determining the Hydraulic Conductivity Function of Unsaturated Soil. R. W. Skaggs, E. J. Monke and L. F. Huggins. June 1970.

12 *(In preparation.)*

13 Electrical Effects and the Movement of Water in Soils. D. Swartzendruber and S. Gairon. June 1970.

WATER RESOURCES RESEARCH CENTER
Indiana University
Geology Building
1005 East Tenth Street
Bloomington, Indiana 47401

REPORTS OF INVESTIGATIONS

Available free of charge as long as supply lasts.

1 Water Supplied by Coal Surface Mines, Pike County, Indiana. By Don M. Corbett. 1965, 67 p.

2 Coal Mining Effect on Busseron Creek Watershed, Sullivan County, Indiana. By Don M. Corbett and Allen F. Agnew. 1968. 187 p.

3 Effects of Heated Discharge upon Aquatic Resources of White River at Petersburg, Indiana. By Max A. Proffitt. 1969. 101 p.

4 Acid Mine-Drainage Problem of the Patoka River Watershed, Southwestern Indiana. By Don M. Corbett. 1969. 173 p.

OTHER

Water Geology and the Future. A conference sponsored by the Water Resources Research Center, Indiana University. 1967. 117 p.

IOWA

IOWA STATE DEPARTMENT OF HEALTH

Environmental Engineering Service
Lucas State Office Building
Des Moines, Iowa 50319

Iowa Water Pollution Control Law, Code of Iowa 1966, as amended. 15 p.

Water Pollution Control: Progress Report of the Iowa Water Pollution Control Commission. 1970. 16 p.

IOWA GEOLOGICAL SURVEY

16 West Jefferson St.
Iowa City, Iowa 52240

When ordering, send money by draft, money order, or check. Make all remittances payable to Iowa Geological Survey. Publications which are not available for sale may be borrowed or copied at borrower's expense with the permission of the State Geologist.

ANNUAL REPORTS

*Volume 3. Annual Report, 1893. 501 p., 37 pls., 34 figs.
   Buried River Channels in Southeastern Iowa: C. H. Gordon. Pages 237 to 255. Separate available. Price: $0.20, handling $0.10.

Volume 6. Lead and Zinc, Artesian Wells, etc. 487 p., 28 pls., 57 figs. Price: $7.30, handling $0.35.
   *Artesian Wells of Iowa: W. H. Norton. Pages 113 to 428. (Superseded by Vol. 21.) No separate available for sale.

*Volume 9. Annual Report, 1898. 572 p., 13 pls., 8 maps, 56 figs.
   *Artesian Wells of the Belle Plaine Area: H. R. Mosnat. Pages 521 to 562.

*Volume 21. Annual Report, 1910 and 1911. 1214 p., 18 pls., 1 map, 7 figs.
   *Underground Water Resources of Iowa: W. H. Norton and others. Pages 29 to 1,214.

   *Introduction: W. H. Norton. Pages 31 to 47.

   *Chap. 1, Topography and Climate: Howard E. Simpson. Pages 48 to 66.

   *Chap. 2, Geology: W. H. Norton and H. E. Simpson. Pages 67 to 104.

*Chap. 3, Geologic Occurrence of Underground Water: W. H. Norton, H. E. Simpson, and W. S. Hendrixson. Pages 105 to 137.

*Chap. 4, Artesian Phenomena: W. H. Norton. Pages 138 to 158.

*Chap. 5, Chemical Composition of Underground Waters: W. S. Hendrixson. Pages 159 to 211.

*Chap. 6, Municipal, Domestic and Industrial Water Supplies: W. S. Hendrixson. Pages 212 to 260.

*Chap. 7, Mineral Waters: W. S. Hendrixson. Pages 261 to 279.

*Chap. 8, Underground Waters of the Northeast District. Pages 279 to 420.

*Chap. 9, Underground Waters of the East Central District. Pages 420 to 612.

*Chap. 10, Underground Waters of the Southeastern District. Pages 613 to 748.

*Chap. 11, Underground Waters of the North-Central District. Pages 749 to 810.

*Chap. 12, Underground Waters of the Central District. Pages 811 to 922.

*Chap. 13, Underground Waters of the South-Central District. Pages 923 to 1,004.

*Chap. 14, Underground Waters of the Northwest District. Pages 1,005 to 1,099.

*Chap. 15, Underground Waters of the Southwest District. Pages 1,100 to 1,214.

Volume 26. Annual Report, 1915. 556 p., 25 pls., and maps, 63 figs. Price: $8.35, handling $0.35.
   River Waters in Iowa: George A. Gabriel. Pages 29 to 48. Separate available, Price: $0.30, handling $0.10.

*Volume 33. Annual Report, 1927. 447 p., 1 pl., 5 figs.
   *Deep Wells of Iowa, A Supplementary Report: W. H. Norton. Pages 9 to 374.

   *Well Water Recessions in Iowa: James H. Lees. Pages 375 to 400.

   *Table Showing Municipal Water Supplies of Iowa Cities and Towns. Pages 401 to 427.

Volume 36. Annual Report, 1930, 1931, 1932 and 1933. 471 p., 39 pls., 34 figs. Price: $7.05, handling $0.30.
   Deep Wells of Iowa, 1928-1932: W. H. Norton. Pages 311 to 364. Additional Deep Wells: James H. Lees. Pages 365 to 419. (Bound together as a separate.) Price: $1.65, handling $1.10.

WATER-SUPPLY BULLETINS

In cooperation with the U. S. Geological Survey, other federal and state agencies and Iowa municipalities.

*1 Summaries of Yearly and Flood Flow Relating to Iowa Streams, 1873-1940: prepared under the direction of Lawrence C. Crawford, 1942. 129 p., 5 pls., 4 figs.

*2 Surface Water Resources of Iowa for the period October 1, 1940, to September 30, 1942: prepared under the direction of Lawrence C. Crawford, 1944. 222 p., 5 pls.

3 Surface Water Resources of Iowa for the period October 1, 1942, to September 30, 1950: prepared under the direction of V. R. Bennion, 1953. 583 p., 5 pls. Price: $8.80, handling $0.25.

4 Geology and Ground-Water Resources of Webster County, Iowa: William E. Hale, 1955. 257 p., 16 pls., 29 figs., 12 tables. Price: $3.15, handling $0.20.

5 Quality of Surface Waters of Iowa, 1886-1954. Prepared under direction of V. R. Bennion, 1955. 351 p., 4 pls., 19 figs., 13 tables. Price: $5.80, handling $0.20.

6 Surface Water Resources of Iowa for the period October 1, 1950, to September 30, 1955. Prepared under the direction of V. R. Bennion, 1956. 405 p., 5 pls., 1 fig., 1 table. Price: $6.20, handling $0.20.

7 Geology of Ground-Water Resources of Clayton County, Iowa: W. L. Steinhilber, O. J. Van Eck, and A. J. Feulner, 1961. 142 p., 9 pls., 25 figs., 8 tables. Price: $2.75, handling $0.20.

8 Surface Water Resources of Iowa from October 1, 1955, to September 30, 1960: Richard E. Myers, 1963. 523 p., 1 pl., 1 table, 1 fig. Price: $7.90, handling $0.20.

9 Geology and Ground-Water Resources of Cerro Gordo County, Iowa: H. G. Hershey, K. D. Wahl, and W. L. Steinhilber, 1970. Approx. 75 p., 1 pl., 24 figs., 10 tables. (In press.)

10 Geology and Ground-Water Resources of Linn County, Iowa: R. E. Hansen, 1970. Approx. 70 p., 6 pls., 25 figs., 8 tables. (In press.)

MISCELLANEOUS PAPERS

A Description of the Region about Camp Dodge, 1918. Describes the surface features, the rocks, climate, water, geologic history and other features of the region. James H. Lees. Topographical map of Camp Dodge quadrangle. 60 p., 22 figs. Price: $0.90, handling $0.10.

Iowa Water Atlas No. 1, 1965. The Water Story in Central Iowa: F. R. Twenter and R. W. Coble. 89 p. Price: $2.00, handling $0.10.

Iowa Water Atlas No. 2, 1967. Availability of Ground Water in Decatur County, Iowa: J. W. Cagle and W. L. Steinhilber. 28 p. Price: $1.35, handling $0.10.

Iowa Water Atlas No. 3, 1969. Availability of Ground Water in Wayne County, Iowa: J. W. Cagle. 33 p. Price: $1.10, handling $0.10.

MAPS

Map Showing Mineral Resources of Iowa, 1947. H. Garland Hershey. Lithographed in 5 colors. Scale: 1:500,000. Shows distribution of cement, coal, peat, gypsum, limestone and dolomite, clay, petroleum and natural gas, sand and gravel, lead and zinc, iron, electric power, surface water and ground water. Price: $0.50, handling $0.10.

*Map Showing Major Drainage Basins of Iowa, 1949. Printed in two colors. Scale: 1:1,000,000 or approximately 16 miles to the inch. Shows boundaries of major drainage basins within the State, superimposed on a base map showing towns, streams, railroads, and land survey divisions.

IOWA STATE HIGHWAY COMMISSION
Ames, Iowa 50010

*Report of the State Highway Commission on the Iowa lakes and lake beds. 1917. 250 p.

*Drainage Areas of Iowa Streams. December 1957. Bulletin No. 7.

*Magnitude and Frequency of Iowa Floods. July 1966. Bulletin No. 28.

IOWA NATURAL RESOURCES COUNCIL
Grimes State Office Building
East 14th and Grand
Des Moines, Iowa 50319

BULLETINS

1 An Inventory of Water Resources and Water Problems — Des Moines River Basin, Iowa.

2 An Inventory of Water Resources and Water Problems — Nishnabotna River Basin, Iowa.

3 An Inventory of Water Resources and Water Problems — Iowa-Cedar River Basin, Iowa.

4 An Inventory of Water Resources and Water Problems — Floyd-Big Sioux River Basins, Iowa.

5 An Inventory of Water Resources and Water Problems — Skunk River Basin, Iowa.

6 An Inventory of Water Resources and Water Problems — Southern Iowa River Basins, Iowa.

7 An Inventory of Water Resources and Water Problems — Northeastern Iowa River Basins, Iowa.

8 An Inventory of Water Resources and Water Problems — Western Iowa River Basins, Iowa.

9 Low-Flow Characteristics of Iowa Streams. 1958.

10 Low-Flow Characteristics of Iowa Streams through 1966. 1970.

Ten Biennial Reports of the Iowa Natural Resources Council.

A Decade of Experience under the Iowa Water Permit System — Published in cooperation with the Agricultural Law Center, University of Iowa.

Miscellaneous Flood Plain Studies — published in cooperation with the U. S. Corps of Engineers.

IOWA STATE WATER RESOURCES RESEARCH INSTITUTE (ISWRRI)

Iowa State University
205 Agronomy Building
Ames, Iowa 50010

Books and project completion reports listed relate to research program activities supported under Office of Water Resources Research (OWRR) annual allotments and matching grants to the Iowa State Water Resources Research Institute (ISWRRI).

Books are available from the publisher.

Some project completion reports as noted in citations are available from the Clearinghouse for Federal Scientific and Technical Information (CFSTI), Springfield, Virginia 22151 at $3.00 per copy in paper or $0.65 in microfiche. When ordering reports from CFSTI the PB number should be given to expedite the orders. Prepayment of all orders is required. Checks or money orders should be made payable to the Clearinghouse.

Information concerning project completion reports which are not marked with an asterisk should be requested from the authors.

Copies of the annual reports for fiscal years 1968, 1969, and 1970 are available from the Iowa State Water Resources Research Institute, 206 Agronomy Building, Iowa State University, Ames, Iowa 50010.

Questions concerning specific projects supported by ISWRRI should be directed to the principal investigators.

ISWRRI maintains one file copy of each book, publication, project completion report, and annual report.

BOOKS

Pierre, W. H., Don Kirkham, John Pesek and Robert Shaw (ed.) Plant environment and efficient water use. Book based on symposium held at Iowa State University, Nov. 30 and Dec. 1, 1965. American Society of Agronomy, Madison, Wisconsin. xii + 295 p. 1965.

Willrich, T. L. and N. William Hines (ed.). Water pollution control and abatement. Book based on an Iowa Water Resources Pollution Control and Abatement Seminar held at Iowa State University, Ames, Iowa, November 9-11, 1965. Iowa State University Press. Ames, Iowa. xiii + 194 p. 1967.

Dougal, Merwin D. (ed.). Flood plain management, Iowa's experience. Papers presented at the conference on Flood Plain Management, Sixth Water Resources Design Conference, Iowa State University. Iowa State University Press. Ames, Iowa. xxi + 270 p. 1969.

PROJECT COMPLETION REPORTS

A-001-IA   Dougal, Merwin D., E. Robert Baumann and John F. Timmons. Physical and economic factors associated with the establishment of stream water quality standards. Iowa State University, Engineering Research Institute, Completion Report, ISU-ERI-Ames 64000, Vol. I. 343 p. 1970. Available from CFSTI as PB 191 167.

A-002-IA   Beer, Craig E. Evaluation of flood damage to corn from controlled depth and frequency of flooding. Iowa State University, Iowa State Water Resources Research Institute, Completion Report. 12 p. 1968.

A-003-IA   Kirkham, Don. Moisture movement to vertical sinks in water unsaturated soil. Iowa State University, Iowa State Water Resources Research Institute, Completion Report. 12 p. 1968.

A-004-IA   Howe, J. W. Recession characteristics of Iowa streams. The University of Iowa, Iowa State Water Resources Research Institute, Completion Report. 32 p. 1968.
(Obtainable from the Department of Publications, The University of Iowa, Iowa City, Iowa — $1.00)

A-005-IA   Haugen, Arnold O. and Arnold J. Sohn. Competitive recreational uses of selected Iowa lakes. Iowa State University, Iowa State Water Resources Research Institute, Completion Report. 173 p. 1968. Available from CFSTI.

A-006-IA   Salisbury, Neil E., James C. Knox and Richard A. Stephenson. The valleys of Iowa — 1: valley width and stream discharge relationships in the major streams. Iowa State University, Iowa State Water Resources Research Institute, Completion Report. 107 p. 1968.
(Obtainable from the Department of Geography, The University of Iowa, Iowa City, Iowa — $3.00).

A-007-IA   Johnson, R. L. and Owen Sletten. Collection, characterization, and study of biodegradability and chemical oxidation of carbon-absorbed materials from effluents from sewage treatment plants. Iowa State University, Engineering Research Institute, Final Report ERI-369. 96 p. 1968.

A-008-IA   Dodd, John D. Pollen and diatoms in sediments of a Post-Pleistocene lake. Iowa State University, Iowa State Water Resources Research Institute, Project Report. 16 p. 1968.

A-009-IA   Landers, R. Q. and D. R. Sanders. Preimpoundment survey of vegetation of Saylorville Dam impoundment area. Iowa State University, Iowa State Water Resources Research Institute. Completion Report. 2 p. 1968.

A-010-IA   Campbell, Charles, N. William Hines and Marshall Harris. Legal aspects of the small watershed program in Iowa. The University of Iowa, College of Law, Monograph No. 6. 45 p. 1965.

A-011-IA   Oulman, Charles S. and Lyle V. A. Sendlein. The movement of radionuclides through soil formations. Iowa State University, Engineering Research Institute, Final Report. 26 p. 1968.

A-012-IA   Sendlein, Lyle V. A., Donald E. Henkel and Keith M. Hussey. Geology of the regolith aquifers of the Nishnabotna Basin. Iowa State University, Iowa State Water Resources Research Institute, Completion Report. 29 p. 1968.

A-013-IA   Willrich, T. L. Properties of tile drainage water. Iowa State University, Iowa State Water Resources Research Institute, Completion Report. 39 p. 1969.
Available from CFSTI as PB 191 064.

A-014-IA   Ruhe, R. V. and W. J. Vreeken. Hydrologic system related to geology and soils, Four Mile Creek Area, Tama County, Iowa. Iowa State University, Iowa State Water Resources Research Institute, Completion Report. 81 p. 1969. Available from CFSTI as PB 190 166.

A-015-IA   Squarer, David. An analysis of relationships between flow conditions and statistical measures of bed configurations in straight and curved alluvial channels. Iowa State University, Iowa State Water Resources Research Institute, Final Report. 173 p. 1968.

A-016-IA   McDonald, D. B., W. L. Paulson and C. A. Merritt. The effect of photosynthesis on the oxygen balance in a mid-western stream. Iowa State University, Iowa State Water Resources Research Institute, Completion Report. 27 p. 1968.

A-017-IA   Huggins, Thomas G. and Roger W. Bachmann. Production of channel catfish (*Ictalurus punctatus*) in tertiary treatment ponds. Iowa State University, Iowa State Water Resources Research Institute, Completion Report. 119 p. 1969. Available from CFSTI as PB 190 165.

A-019-IA   N. William Hines. Model flood plain zoning ordinance. Iowa State University, Iowa State Water Resources Research Institute, Completion Report. 2 p. 1968.

A-022-IA   Dague, Richard R. and Kenneth J. Kline. Management of cattle feedlot wastes. University of Iowa, College of Engineering, Report No. 69-4. 195 p. 1969. Available from CFSTI as PB 190 830.

A-022-IA   Dague, Richard R., Wayne L. Paulson and Kenneth J. Kline. Hydrologic aspects of feedlot waste control. University of Iowa, College of Engineering, Report No. 69-2. 37 p. 1969. Available from CFSTI as PB 191 248.

A-024-IA   DeBoer, D. W. and H. P. Johnson. Development of a mathematical model for the simulation of flatland watershed hydraulics. Iowa State University, Iowa State Water Resources Research Institute, Completion Report. 255 p. 1969. Available from CFSTI as PB 188 793.

B-001-IA   N. William Hines. A decade of experience under the Iowa Water Permit System. The University of Iowa, Agricultural Law Center, Monograph No. 9. 99 p. 1966.

B-002-IA   Kirkham, Don. Groundwater seepage patterns to wells for unconfined flow. Iowa State University, Iowa State Water Resources Research Institute, Completion Report. 9 p. 1969. Available from CFSTI as PB 189 525.

B-005-IA   Hines, N. William and Frank W. Pechacek. Physical, legal and economic aspects of assessment of costs among drainage districts: legal phase. Iowa State University, Iowa State Water Resources Research Institute, Completion Report. 77 p. 1969. Available from CFSTI as PB 189 767.

B-005-IA   Kumar, S. and H. P. Johnson. Effect of channel straightening on the movement of flood waves on Boyer River. Iowa State University, Iowa State Water Resources Research Institute, Completion Report. 107 p. 1969. Available from CFSTI as PB 190 355.

B-006-IA   Landers, Roger Q. and Dana R. Sanders. Structure of forest vegetation bordering the Saylorville Impoundment. Iowa State University, Iowa State Water Resources Research Institute, Completion Report. 29 p. 1967.

B-013-IA   Toksöz, Sadik and M. Y. Khan. Flow of water into tile drains in stratified soils. Iowa State University, Iowa State Water Resources Research Institute, Completion Report. 7 p. 1970.

ANNUAL REPORTS

Kirkham, Don and A. W. Warrick. Annual Report of the Iowa State Water Resources Research Institute for FY 1967. Iowa State University, Iowa State Water Resources Research Institute. 102 p.

Kirkham, Don and Sadik Toksöz. Annual Report of the Iowa State Water Resources Research Institute for FY 1968. Iowa State University, Iowa State Water Resources Research Institute. 108 p.

Kirkham, Don and Sadik Toksöz. Annual Report of the Iowa State Water Resources Research Institute for FY 1969. Iowa State University, Iowa State Water Resources Research Institute. 105 p.

Kirkham, Don and Norris L. Powell. Annual Report of the Iowa State Water Resources Research Institute for FY 1970. Iowa State University, Iowa State Water Resources Research Institute. 174 p.

KANSAS

KANSAS STATE BOARD OF AGRICULTURE
Division of Water Resources
This agency is no longer in existence.

Report. 1926/28 - 1944/46.

Stream flow data. 1924-1947.

KANSAS STATE COMMITTEE TO STUDY AND INVESTIGATE THE LAWS OF THE STATE RELATING TO THE APPROPRIATION OF WATER
State Legislature
Topeka, Kansas 66612
This Committee is no longer in existence.

A Report to the Governor of Kansas by a committee appointed by him to study and to report its findings and suggestions to him, containing the results of the committee's investigations and the suggestions of the committee for legislation to enable progress to be made with development of the state's water resources for beneficial purposes. 1944. 79 p.

KANSAS STATE DEPARTMENT OF HEALTH
Division of Environmental Health
Topeka, Kansas 66612

WATER SUPPLY AND BASIC DATA

1-1 Water Quality in Tuttle Creek and Kanopolis Reservoirs (Interim Report).

1-2 The Relation of the Chemical Quality of the Whitewater River at Towanda to that of the Walnut River at Winfield, Kansas during the 1963 Water Year (Interim Report).

1-3 Results of Four Chemical Quality Surveys in the Walnut River Basin, Kansas (December 1961 to October 1963).

1-4 Chemical Quality of Surface Waters in Kansas — 1962 Water Year.

1-5 Brine in Surface Water of the Little Arkansas River Basin, Kansas.

1-6 Policies Governing the Design of Public Water Supply Systems in Kansas — February 1965.

1-7 Chemical Quality of Public Water Supplies in Kansas. Price: $1.00.

1-8 Chemical Quality of Surface Waters in Kansas — 1963 Water Year.

1-9 Maintenance and Repair of Equipment for Water Supply and Sewerage Systems. Price: $2.00.

1-10 Effect of Irrigation on the Chemical Quality of Low Streamflow Adjacent to Cedar Bluff Irrigation District, Kansas.

1-11 Variations in the Chemical Quality of Ground Water beneath an Irrigated Field — Cedar Bluff Irrigation District, Kansas.

WATER POLLUTION CONTROL

*2-1 Stream Pollution from Feedlot Runoff.

OIL FIELD

3-1 Residual Salt Study of Brine-Affected Soil and Shale — Potwin Area, Butler County, Kansas.

GENERAL ENGINEERING AND SANITATION

4-1 Manual of Recommended Practice for Locating, Constructing and Equipping Water Wells for Rural Homes.

4-2 Manual of Recommended Practice for Locating, Constructing and Operating Septic Tank Systems for Rural Homes.

STATE GEOLOGICAL SURVEY
The University of Kansas
Lawrence, Kansas 66044

BULLETINS

Price: $2.00 per Bulletin; $1.00 for 1 part (except Bulletin 169).

41 1942 Reports of Studies.

Part 1. Ground-Water Supplies Available for National Defense Industries in South-Central Kansas, by Stanley W. Lohman, 20 p.

Part 2. Ground-Water Supplies in Kansas Available for National Defense Industries, by S. W. Lohman, J. C. Frye, H. A. Waite, V. C. Fishel, T. G. McLaughlin, B. F. Latta, G. E. Abernathy, George S. Knapp, and J. B. Spiegel, 48 p.

47   1943 Reports of Studies.

    Part 2. Kansas Oil Field Brines and Their Magnesium Content, by Walter H. Schoewe, 40 p.

76   1948 Reports of Studies.

    *Part 1. Graphic Representation of Oil-Field Brines in Kansas, by Russell M. Jeffords, 12 p.

    Part 2. Contamination of Deep Water Wells in Southeastern Kansas, by Charles C. Williams, 16 p.

    Part 6. Ground-Water Supplies at Hays, Victoria, Walker, Gorham, and Russell, Kansas, with Special Reference to Future Needs, by Bruce F. Latta, 76 p.

80   Geology and Ground-Water Resources of Pawnee and Edwards Counties, Kansas, by Thad G. McLaughlin, 189 p., 1949.

81   Geology and Ground-Water Resources of Norton County and Northwestern Phillips County, Kansas, by John C. Frye and A. R. Leonard, 144 p., 1949.

85   Geology and Ground-Water Resources of Rice County, Kansas, by O. S. Fent, 142 p., 1950.

94   Ground-Water Resources of Pawnee Valley, Kansas, by V. C. Fishel, 144 p., 1952.

95   Geology and Ground-Water Resources of Lincoln County, Kansas, by Delmar W. Berry, 96 p., 1952.

98   Geology and Ground-Water Resources of the North Fork Solomon River in Mitchell, Osborne, Smith, and Phillips Counties, Kansas, by Alvin R. Leonard, 124 p., 1952.

100   Geology and Ground-Water Resources of Cheyenne County, Kansas, by Glenn C. Prescott, Jr., 106 p., 1953.

101   Geology and Ground-Water Resources of Jackson County, Kansas, by Kenneth L. Walters, 91 p., 1953.

105   Geology and Ground-Water Resources of Sherman County, Kansas, by Glenn C. Prescott, Jr., 130 p., 1953.

106   Geology and Ground-Water Resources of Marshall County, Kansas, by Kenneth L. Walters, 116 p., 1954.

108   Geology and Ground-Water Resources of Wichita and Greeley Counties, Kansas, by Glenn C. Prescott, Jr., John R. Branch, and Woodrow W. Wilson, 134 p., 1954.

110   Geology and Ground-Water Resources of Graham County, Kansas, by Glenn C. Prescott, Jr., 98 p., 1955.

115   Geology and Ground-Water Resources of Jewell County, Kansas, by V. C. Fishel and A. R. Leonard, 152 p., 1956.

116   Geology and Ground-Water Resources of Sheridan County, Kansas, by Charles K. Bayne, 94 p., 1956.

117   Geology and Ground-Water Resources of Rawlins County, Kansas, by Kenneth L. Walters, 100 p., 1956.

119   1956 Reports of Studies.

    Part 1. Progress Report on the Ground-Water Hydrology of the Equus Beds Area, Kansas, by G. J. Stramel, 59 p.

120   Geology and Ground-Water Resources of Reno County, Kansas, by Charles K. Bayne, 130 p., 1956.

125   Ground-Water Levels in Observation Wells in Kansas, 1956, by V. C. Fishel and Betty J. Mason, 158 p., 1957.

126   Ground-Water Resources of the Ladder Creek Area in Kansas, by Edward Bradley and Carlton Johnson, with a section on the chemical quality of water by Robert A. Krieger, 192 p., 1957.

127   1957 Reports of Studies.

    Part 2. Evaluation of a Conducting-Paper Analog Field Plotter as an Aid in Solving Ground-Water Problems, by Leslie Mack, 23 p.

    Part 5. The Hydraulic Properties of the Ordovician Rocks at Pittsburg, Kansas, by G. J. Stramel, 25 p.

129   Geology and Ground-Water Resources of Logan County, Kansas, by Carlton R. Johnson, 177 p., 1958.

130   1958 Reports of Studies.

    Part 1. Quaternary Geology and Ground-Water Resources of Kansas River Valley between Bonner Springs and Lawrence, Kansas, by Alvin E. Dufford, 96 p.

131   Ground-Water Levels in Observation Wells in Kansas, 1957, by V. C. Fishel and Betty J. Mason, 152 p., 1958.

132   Geology and Ground-Water Hydrology of the Ingalls Area, Kansas, by G. J. Stramel, Charles W. Lane, and Warren G. Hodson, 154 p.

135   Geology and Ground-Water Resources of Kansas River Valley between Wamego and Topeka Vicinity, by Henry V. Beck, 88 p., 1959.

136   Geology and Ground-Water Resources of Clay County, Kansas, by Kenneth L. Walters and Charles K. Bayne, 106 p., 1959.

139   Geology and Ground-Water Resources of Cloud County, Kansas, by Charles K. Bayne and Kenneth L. Walters, with a section on ceramic materials by Norman Plummer, 144 p., 1959.

140   Geology and Ground-Water Resources of Mitchell County, Kansas, by Warren G. Hodson, 132 p., 1959.

141   Ground-Water Levels in Observation Wells in Kansas, 1958, by V. C. Fishel, E. L. Gulley, and E. L. Reavis, 146 p., 1959.

143   Geology and Ground-Water Resources of Harper County, Kansas, by Charles K. Bayne, 183 p., 1960.

144   Geology and Ground-Water Resources of Kingman County, Kansas, by Charles W. Lane, 173 p., 1960.

145   Geology and Ground-Water Resources of Gove County, Kansas, by Warren G. Hodson and Kenneth D. Wahl, 126 p., 1960.

146   Ground-Water Levels in Observation Wells in Kansas, 1959, by V. C. Fishel and Margaret E. Broeker, 174 p., 1960.

148   Geology and Ground-Water Resources of Douglas County, Kansas, by Howard G. O'Connor, 200 p., 1960.

149   Geology and Ground-Water Resources of Southern Ellis County and Parts of Trego and Rush Counties, Kansas, by Alvin R. Leonard and Delmar W. Berry, 156 p., 1961.

151   Geology and Ground-Water Resources of Sumner County, Kansas, by Kenneth L. Walters, 198 p., 1961.

153   Ground-Water Levels in Observation Wells in Kansas, 1960, by Margaret E. Broeker and V. C. Fishel, 183 p., 1961.

154 Geology and Ground-Water Resources of Ottawa County, Kansas, by Leslie E. Mack, 145 p., 1962.

158 Geology and Ground-Water Resources of Cowley County, Kansas, by Charles K. Bayne, 219 p., 1962.

159 Ground-Water Levels in Observation Wells in Kansas, 1961, by Margaret E. Broeker and V. C. Fishel, 166 p., 1962.

161 Geology and Ground-Water Resources of Wallace County, Kansas, by Warren G. Hodson, 108 p., 3 maps, 1963.

167 Ground-Water Levels in Observation Wells in Kansas, 1962, by Margaret E. Broeker and John D. Winslow, 89 p., 1963.

168 Geohydrology of Grant and Stanton Counties, Kansas, by Stuart W. Fader, Edwin D. Gutentag, David H. Lobmeyer, and Walter R. Meyer, 147 p., folio of 9 pls., 1964.

169 Symposium on Cyclic Sedimentation, edited by Daniel F. Merriam, 636 p., 1964. (Two vol., not sold separately) Price: $4.00.

173 Ground-Water Levels in Observation Wells in Kansas, 1963, by Margaret E. Broeker and John D. Winslow, 94 p., 1964.

174 Geology and Ground-Water Resources in Trego County, Kansas, by Warren G. Hodson, 80 p., 2 pls., 1965.

176 Geohydrology of Sedgwick County, Kansas, by Charles W. Lane and Don E. Miller, 100 p., 4 pls., 1965.

181 Geology and Ground-Water Resources of Miami County, Kansas, by Don E. Miller, 66 p., 3 pls., 1966.

182 Bibliography and Index of Ground Water in Kansas, by Robert S. Roberts and Warren G. Hodson, 41 p., 1966.

183 Geology and Ground-Water Resources of Neosho County, Kansas, by William L. Jungmann, 46 p., 1 pl., 1966.

184 Ground-Water Levels in Observation Wells in Kansas, 1965, by Margaret E. Broeker and John D. Winslow, 92 p., 1966.

186 Geology and Ground-Water Resources of Brown County, Kansas, by Charles K. Bayne and Walter H. Schoewe, 68 p., 2 pls., 1967.

187 1967 Reports of Studies.
Part 2. Progress Report on the Ground-Water Hydrology of the Equus-Beds Area, Kansas—1966, by G. J. Stramel, 27 p.

188 Ground Water in the Republican River Area, Cloud, Jewell, and Republic Counties, Kansas, by Stuart W. Fader, 27 p., 4 pls., 1968.

193 Geology and Ground-Water Resources of Linn County, Kansas, by William J. Seevers, 62 p., 1 pl., 1969.

195 Geology and Ground-Water Resources of Allen County, Kansas, by Don E. Miller.

196 Geology and Ground-Water Resources of Decatur County, Kansas, by Warren G. Hodson.

SPECIAL DISTRIBUTION PUBLICATIONS

Price: $1.00 each. Not part of library distribution or exchange; available on request.

10 Water-Level Changes in Grant and Stanton Counties, 1939-1964, by John D. Winslow, Carl E. Nuzman, and Stuart W. Fader, 11 p., 1964.

18 Water-Level Changes in Grant and Stanton Counties, Kansas, 1939-1965, by Carl E. Nuzman and Walter R Meyer, 11 p., 1965.

29 Electronic Simulation of Ground-Water Hydrology in the Kansas River Valley near Topeka, Kansas, by John D. Winslow and Carl E. Nuzman, 24 p., 1966.

33 Notes on the Shape of the Truncated Cone of Depression in the Vicinity of an Infinite Well Field, by Stuart W. Fader, 11 p., 1967.

37 Water-Level Changes in Grant and Stanton Counties, Kansas, 1938-1968, by J. D. Winslow, H. E. McGovern, and H. L. Mackey, 18 p., 1968.

39 FORTRAN IV Program for Synthesis and Plotting of Water-Quality Data, by Leverett H. Ropes, Charles O. Morgan, and Jesse M. McNellis, 59 p., 1969.

43 Stiff Diagrams of Water-Quality Data Programmed for the Digital Computer, by Charles O. Morgan and Jesse M. McNellis, 26 p., 1969.

VOLUMES

Price: $1.00 each. Discontinued series.

XI Geology, Mineral Resources, and Ground-Water Resources of Chase County, Kansas, by R. C. Moore, J. M. Jewett, H. G. O'Connor, and R. K. Smith, 48 p., 1951.

XII Geology, Mineral Resources, and Ground-Water Resources of Lyon County, Kansas, by Howard G. O'Connor, E. D. Goebel, and Norman Plummer, 59 p., 1953.

XIII Geology, Mineral Resources, and Ground-Water Resources of Osage County, Kansas, by H. G. O'Connor, E. D. Goebel, W. H. Schoewe, and Norman Plummer, 50 p., 1955.

XIV Geology, Mineral Resources, and Ground-Water Resources of Elk County, Kansas, by G. J. Verville, J. M. Jewett, R. O. Kulstad, Norman Plummer, W. H. Schoewe, E. D. Goebel, and C. K. Bayne, 56 p., 1958.

MAPS

Price: $1.00 each.

M-4 General Availability of Ground Water in Kansas, compiled by C. K. Bayne and J. R. Ward. 1967 ed. Scale 1:500,000.

M-5 Saturated Thickness and Specific [Water] Yield of Cenozoic Deposits in Kansas, compiled by Charles K. Bayne and John R. Ward in 1967, 1969. Scale 1:500,000.

STATE SOIL CONSERVATION COMMITTEE
Room 1252W
State Office Building
Topeka, Kansas 66612

Conservation in Kansas. 1970 Annual Report. 15 p.

KANSAS STATE WATER COMMISSION
This Commission is no longer in existence.

Biennial Report. 1917/18 - 1923/24.

Stream flow data. 1895-1924.

KANSAS WATER RESOURCES BOARD
11th Floor, State Office Building
Topeka, Kansas 66612

Contact the Board for further information on these publications.

STATE WATER PLAN STUDIES SERIES, PART A
PRELIMINARY APPRAISAL OF
KANSAS WATER PROBLEMS

Note: A Summary is available for those reports in this series which are out of print.

Section *1 Marais des Cygnes Unit, June 1958.

2 Cimarron Unit, September, 1958.

3 Kansas Unit, June, 1959.

4 Lower Arkansas Unit, January, 1960.

5 Walnut-Verdigris Unit, June, 1960.

6 Upper Republican Unit, June, 1960.

7 Neosho Unit, June, 1961.

*8 Solomon-Saline Unit, June, 1961.

*9 Lower Republican Unit, June, 1961.

10 Missouri Unit, June, 1962.

*11 Upper Arkansas Unit, June, 1962.

*12 Smoky Hill Unit, June, 1962.

TECHNICAL REPORT SERIES

1 Kansas Streamflow Characteristics, Part 1, Flow Duration, June 1959.

2 Kansas Streamflow Characteristics, Part 2, Low-Flow Frequency, June 1960.

*3 Kansas Streamflow Characteristics, Part 3, Flood Frequency, October 1960.

*4 Kansas Streamflow Characteristics, Part 4, Storage Requirements to Sustain Gross Reservoir Outflow, April 1962.

5 Kansas Streamflow Characteristics, Part 5, Storage Requirements to Control High Flow, June 1964.

6A Kansas Streamflow Characteristics, Part 6A, Base Flow Data, June 1965.

6B Kansas Streamflow Characteristics, Part 6B, Base Flow Distribution, October 1966.

7 Kansas Streamflow Characteristics, Part 7, Annual Streamflow Summary Tables, June 1967.

BULLETINS

1 Developing a State Water Plan, October 1956.

2 State-Federal Relationships in Water Resources Development Programs, October 1956.

*3 Report on the Laws of Kansas Pertaining to the Beneficial Use of Water, November 1956.

*4 Development of a Balanced Stream-Gaging Program for Kansas, March 1957.

*5 Report on the Laws of Kansas Pertaining to Ground Water, November 1960.

6 A Program of Fluvial Sediment Investigation in Kansas, July 1961.

7 Fluvial Sediment in the Lower Kansas River Basin, 1957-60; A Progress Report, June 1964.

*8 A General Classification of Source Areas of Fluvial Sediment in Kansas, June 1965.

9 Economic Implications of Irrigation from Ground Water (Southwest Kansas), December 1968.

10 Total Sediment Discharge, May 1969.

11 Future Irrigation Water Demands, December 1969.

*12 Evaluation of the Surface-Water Data Program in Kansas, January 1969.

13 Water for Rural Kansas, 1970.

KANSAS ECONOMIC DEVELOPMENT
PLANNING REPORTS

A Kansas Water Atlas, December 1967.

*Kansas Water Law, September 1967.

*A Study of Kansas Water Quality Control Needs, September 1967.

A Hydrologic Ground-Water Study, September 1967.

*Irrigation in Kansas, September 1967.

Special Water Districts in Kansas, September 1967.

*Industrial, Municipal, and Rural Domestic Water Demands, 1967.

MISCELLANEOUS

Kansas Water News, bimonthly newsletter started in December, 1957.

*The Kansas Law of Water Rights, by Wells A. Hutchins. Published by the Division of Water Resources of the State Board of Agriculture and the Kansas Water Resources Board in cooperation with the Farm Economics Research Division, Agricultural Research Service, U. S. Department of Agriculture, 1957.

A Survey of Programs of State Financial Participation in Water Projects, December 1957.

Planning for Plenty – The Management of Kansas Water, Second Edition, May 1966.

LEGISLATION

State Water Plan Act, Laws of Kansas, 1963, K.S.A. 82a-901-926.

State Water Plan, Laws of Kansas, 1965, K.S.A. 82a-927-946.

Report to the Kansas Legislature on the Kansas Water Storage Act, January 1969.

Report to the 1961 Kansas Legislature Concerning State Water Policy and Program Needs, November 1960.

*A Suggested Water Development Program for Kansas, Kansas Legislative Council, January, 1963.

*A Report to the Kansas Legislature on the State Water Plan, February 1965.

PROGRESS REPORTS

*Progress Report Number 1, Artificial Ground-Water Recharge, 1968.

KANSAS STATE WATER RESOURCES FACT-FINDING AND RESEARCH COMMITTEE

This Committee is no longer in existence.

Water in Kansas – 1955. 1955. 216 p.

Water in Kansas – Supplement. 1955. Various pagings.

KANSAS WATER RESOURCES RESEARCH INSTITUTE

146 D Waters Hall
Manhattan, Kansas 66502

1 Loehr, Raymond C. and Diann T. Schwegler. Evaluation of an Index for Viral Pollution. KWRRI Project Completion Report. Project A-001-KAN. 59 p. 1966.

2 Haynie, Richard M. Energy Dissipation Devices for Flow from Vertical Conduits. KWRRI Project Completion Report. Project A-009-KAN. 44 p., 1966.

3 Green, D. W. and R. L. Cox. Storage of Fresh Water in Underground Reservoirs Containing Saline Water – Phase I. KWRRI Project Completion Report. Project B-003-KAN. 113 p., 1966.

4 Daicoff, Darwin W. Methods of Financing State Participation in Water Resources Development. KWRRI Project Completion Report. Project A-006-KAN. 36 p. 1967.

5 Weinaug, Charles F. and D. W. Green. Numerical Modeling of Ground Water Flow. KWRRI Project Completion Report. Project A-002-KAN. 25 p. 1967.

6 Miner, J. R., R. I. Lipper, L. R. Fina, and J. W. Funk. Cattle Feedlot Runoff – Its Nature and Variation. J. Water Pollution Control Fed. 38:(10) 1582, 1966.

7 Miner, J. R., L. R. Fina, J. W. Funk, R. I. Lipper and G. H. Larson. Stormwater Runoff from Cattle Feedlots. Proc. Nat'l. Symp., Management of Farm Animal Wastes, American Society of Agricultural Engineers, 23, 1966.

8 Lipper, R. I., J. R. Miner, and G. H. Larson. Cattle Feedlot Waste Problems. Proc. Oklahoma Cattle Feeders Seminar, 1967.

9 Haynie, Richard M. Energy Dissipation for Flow from Vertical Conduits.

10 Erickson, L. E., Y. S. Ho and L. T. Fan. Modeling and Optimization of Step Aeration Waste Treatment Systems. 33 p. 1967.

11 Eagleman, Joe R. and Richard K. Moore. The Relationship between Field Strength of Radio Waves and Soil Moisture Content. KWRRI Project Completion Report. Project A-004-KAN. 32 p.

12 Lee, E. Stanley. Reduction in Dimensionality, Dynamic Programming and Quasilinearization, I, General Theory. 32 p. 1967.

13 Erickson, L. E. and L. T. Fan. Optimization of the Hydraulic Regime of Activated Sludge Systems. 24 p. 1967.

14 Erickson, L. E. Optimal Aeration Systems. KWRRI Project Completion Report. Project B-001-KAN. 61 p. 1967.

15 Erickson, L. E., L. T. Fan, and G. K. C. Chen. Modeling and Optimization of Biological Waste Treatment Systems. 31 p. 1968.

16 Kadoum, A. M. Cleanup Procedure for Water, Soil, Animal and Plant Extracts for the Use of Electron-Capture Detector in the Gas Chromatographic Analysis of Organophosphorus Insecticide Residues. 6 p. 1968.

17 Miner, J. R., R. I. Lipper, and L. E. Erickson. Modeling Feedlot Runoff Pollution. 5 p. 1967.

18 Cairns, John, Jr. and Hampton Shirer. Activity Patterns of Fish Exposed to Toxic Materials. KWRRI Project Completion Report. Project A-014-KAN. 9 p. 1968.

19 Smith, R. L. and Alan M. Lumb. Derivation of Basin Hydrographs. KWRRI Project Completion Report. Project A-003-KAN. 21 p. 1968.

20 Nelson, David M. and Wilfred H. Pine. The Value of Water for Irrigation in the Kansas River Valley. KWRRI Project Completion Report. Project A-007-KAN. 28 p. 1969.

21 Kadoum, A. M. Modifications of the Micromethod of Sample Cleanup for Thin-Layer and Gas Chromatographic Separation and Determination of Common Organic Pesticide Residues. 4 p. 1968.

22 Armitage, Kenneth B. and Ernest E. Angino. Trace Element Chemistry of a Small Pond in Relation to Productivity. KWRRI Project Completion Report. Project A-013-KAN. 7 p. 1968.

23 O'Brien, Walter J. Reserved for project completion report on project A-010-KAN entitled Chemical Removal of Nitrate from Potable Water. 86 p. 1968.

24 McKinney, Ross E. Water Quality Changes in Confined Hog Waste Treatment. KWRRI Project Completion Report. Project A-011-KAN. 55 p. 1968.

25 Yu, Y. S. Unsteady Flow Parameters in Hydraulic Design. KWRRI Project Completion Report. Project A-017-KAN. 25 p. 1968.

26 Lee, E. Stanley. Iterative Techniques in Optimization 1. Dynamic Programming and Quasilinearization. 9 p. 1968.

27 Naito, Masaaki, Takeichiro Takamatsu, L. T. Fan, and E. S. Lee. Model Identification of Biochemical Oxidation Process. 14 p. 1968.

28 Naito, Masaaki, Takeichiro Takamatsu, and L. T. Fan. Optimization of the Activated Sludge Process-Optimum Volume Ratio of Aeration and Sedimentation Vessels. 11 p. 1968.

29 Lee, E. Stanley. Dynamic Programming, Quasilinearization and the Dimensionality Difficulty. 30 p. 1968.

30 Harris, John O. Reserved for project completion report on project A-012-KAN entitled Ecological Relationships of Organic Matter and Bacteria in Tuttle Creek Reservoir.

31 Green, D. W. Numerical Modeling of Unsaturated Ground Water Flow. KWRRI Project Completion Report. Project B-011-KAN. 105 p. 1969.

32 Fan, L. T., G. K. C. Chen, L. E. Erickson, and M. Naito. Effects of Axial Dispersion on the Optimal Design of the Activated Sludge Process. 18 p. 1969.

33 Pogge, E. C. Effects of Bank Seepage on Flood Hydrographs. KWRRI Project Completion Report. Project A-018-KAN. 14 p. plus appendices. 1969.

34 Myers, David J. and Clark E. Bricker. The Effects of Iron and Thorium Ions on the Kinetics of Precipitation $BaSO_4$. KWRRI Project Completion Report. Project A-020-KAN. 13 p. 1969.

35 Lee, E. S. and Irving Hwang. Stream Quality Modeling by Quasilinearization. 28 p. 1969.

36 Green, Don W. Storage of Fresh Water in Underground Reservoirs Containing Saline Water. Phase II. KWRRI Project B-008-KAN. Completion Report. 79 p. 1970.

37 Yu, Y. S. Reserved for project completion report on project A-024-KAN entitled Longitudinal Dispersion of the Lower Kansas River Basin. 35 p. 1970.

38 Fan, L. T., G. K. C. Chen, L. E. Erickson. Efficiency and Utility of Collocation Methods in Solving the Performance Equations of Flow Chemical Reactors with Axial Dispersion. 22 p. 1970.

39 Taylor, S. L., L. R. Fina, and J. L. Lambert. A New Water Disinfectant: An Insoluble Quaternary Ammonium Resin-triiodide Combination that Releases Bactericide Upon Demand. 13 p. 1970.

40 Powers, W. L., D. O. Travis, L. S. Murphy, and R. I. Lipper. Effect of Feedlot Lagoon Water on Some Physical and Chemical Properties of Soils. 13 p. 1970.

41 Erickson, L. E., Michael S. K. Chen and Liang-tseng Fan. Consideration of Sensitivity and Parameter Uncertainty in Optimal Process Design. 18 p. 1970.

42 Fan, L. T., P. S. Shah, and L. E. Erickson. Simulation of Biological Processes by Analog and Digital Computers. 73 p. 1970.

43 (Title not available).

44 Knutson, H., A. M. Kadoum, T. L. Hopkins, G. F. Swoyer and T. L. Harvey. Insecticide Residues in a Newly Developed Irrigation Area. 28 p. 1970.

KENTUCKY

KENTUCKY DEPARTMENT OF COMMERCE
Division of Planning
Frankfort, Kentucky 40601

Flood Damage Abatement in Kentucky, prepared by Francis H. Parker, Special Projects Planner. October 1964. 134 p.

KENTUCKY DEPARTMENT OF ECONOMIC DEVELOPMENT
Frankfort, Kentucky 40601

Eastern Kentucky Flood Rehabilitation Study, Interim Report. Frankfort, May 1957. 40 p.

Action Programs for Eastern Kentucky, Final Report of the Eastern Kentucky Flood Rehabilitation Study. Frankfort, 1957. 85 p.

Mineral and Water Resources of Kentucky, by J. H. Johnson and J. M. Stapleton. Frankfort, 1961. 35 p.

KENTUCKY DEPARTMENT OF HEALTH
275 East Main Street
Frankfort, Kentucky 40601

Kentucky Solid Waste Disposal Laws and Regulations. Revised June 1970. 16 p.

Kentucky State Plumbing Law, Regulations and Code – 1970. 74 p.

How to Build a Rural Water Supply. Revised July 1964. 14 p.

Kentucky Law Relating to Cleaning and Servicing of Septic Tanks, Seepage Pits and Cesspools. Revised September 1968. 7 p.

Kentucky Water Treatment Plant, Water Distribution System, Sewage Treatment Plant Operators: Law – Regulation. Revised November 1969. 14 p.

Water Pollution Control Law of the Commonwealth of Kentucky. Reproduced from Baldwin's Kentucky Revised Statutes Annotated, Fourth Edition. 6 p.

DEPARTMENT OF HIGHWAYS
Highway Materials Research Laboratory
Lexington, Kentucky 40506

A Study of Runoff from Small Drainage Areas and the Openings in Attendant Drainage Structures, by Eugene M. West and William H. Sammons. Report No. 1 – April 1952. Report No. 2 – July 1955.

DEPARTMENT OF NATURAL RESOURCES
Division of Flood Control and Water Resources
Frankfort, Kentucky 40601

Water Projects in Kentucky (map). Frankfort, 1964.

Water Crisis in Kentucky? Edited by P. R. Jordan and P. Camplin. 1965. 32 p.

Kentucky Water Resources – 1965. 79 p.

DEPARTMENT OF NATURAL RESOURCES
Division of Soil and Water Resources
Capitol Annex Building
Frankfort, Kentucky 40601

Soil and Water Resources News. Issued April, August and December, annually. Available upon request.

Kentucky's Watersheds Developed Through Teamwork, Local-State-Federal. Available upon request.

KENTUCKY GEOLOGICAL SURVEY
University of Kentucky
307 Mineral Industries Building
Lexington, Kentucky 40506

Please direct requests to the above address. Make all checks and money orders payable to the Kentucky Geological Survey. Remittance must accompany order.

MAPS

Free Kentucky Index Maps

Index to Hydrologic Atlases for Kentucky (Index to statewide, regional, quadrangle, and area water maps).

GROUND WATER

Designation "HA" refers to U. S. Geological Survey Hydrologic Atlas series published cooperatively with Kentucky Geological Survey. See free index map to Kentucky Hydrologic Atlases for locations of regional and quadrangle maps.

Statewide

HA-10   Kentucky, by G. E. Hendrickson, 1958. $0.75.

Fresh-Saline Water Interface Map of Kentucky, by H. T. Hopkins, 1966. $1.00.

Blue Grass Region

Bourbon County, by D. K. Hamilton and E. M. O'Connell, 1948. $0.50.

Fayette County, by D. K. Hamilton, E. M. O'Connell, and L. F. Boland, 1948. $0.50.

Jessamine County, by D. K. Hamilton, L. F. Boland, and E. M. O'Connell, 1948. $0.50.

Scott County, by D. K. Hamilton and E. M. O'Connell, 1948. $0.50.

HA-8   Jefferson County, by L. M. MacCary, 1956. $0.75.

HA-15   Boone, Campbell, Grant, Kenton, and Pendleton Counties, by W. N. Palmquist, Jr., and F. R. Hall, 1960. $1.00.

HA-16   Bracken, Harrison, Mason, Nicholas, and Robertson Counties, by W. N. Palmquist, Jr., and F. R. Hall, 1960. $1.00.

HA-17   Lewis and Rowan Counties, by W. N. Palmquist, Jr., and F. R. Hall, 1960. $1.00.

HA-18   Bath, Fleming, and Montgomery Counties, by F. R. Hall and W. N. Palmquist, Jr., 1960. $1.00.

HA-19   Clark, Estill, Madison, and Powell Counties, by F. R. Hall and W. N. Palmquist, Jr., 1960. $1.00.

HA-20   Boyle, Garrard, Lincoln, and Mercer Counties, by W. N. Palmquist, Jr., and F. R. Hall, 1960. $1.00.

HA-21   Marion, Nelson, and Washington Counties, by F. R. Hall and W. N. Palmquist, Jr., 1960. $1.00.

HA-22   Bullitt, Jefferson, and Oldham Counties, by W. N. Palmquist, Jr., and F. R. Hall, 1960. $1.00.

HA-23   Carroll, Gallatin, Henry, Owen, and Trimble Counties, by F. R. Hall and W. N. Palmquist, Jr., 1960. $1.00.

HA-24   Anderson, Franklin, Shelby, Spencer, and Woodford Counties, by F. R. Hall and W. N. Palmquist, Jr., 1960. $1.00.

HA-25   Bourbon, Fayette, Jessamine, and Scott Counties, by W. N. Palmquist, Jr., and F. R. Hall, 1960. $1.00.

Western Coal Field Region

HA-26   Butler and Ohio Counties, by B. W. Maxwell and R. W. Devaul, 1962. $1.25.

HA-27   Daviess and Hancock Counties, by R. W. Devaul and B. W. Maxwell, 1962. $1.25.

HA-28   Union and Henderson Counties, by B. W. Maxwell and R. W. Devaul, 1962. $1.25.

HA-29   McLean and Muhlenberg Counties, by R. W. Devaul and B. W. Maxwell, 1962. $1.25.

HA-30   Hopkins and Webster Counties, by B. W. Maxwell and R. W. Devaul, 1962. $1.25.

Eastern Coal Field Region

HA-36   Breathitt, Floyd, Harlan, Knott, Letcher, Martin, Magoffin, Perry, and Pike Counties, by W. E. Price, Jr., Chabot Kilburn, and D. S. Mull, 1962. $1.25.

HA-37   Boyd, Carter, Elliott, Greenup, Johnson, Lawrence, Lee, Menifee, Morgan, and Wolfe Counties, by W. E. Price, Jr., Chabot Kilburn, and D. S. Mull, 1962. $1.25.

HA-38   Bell, Clay, Jackson, Knox, Laurel, Leslie, McCreary, Owsley, Rockcastle, and Whitley Counties, by Chabot Kilburn, W. E. Price, Jr., and D. S. Mull, 1962. $1.25.

Mississippian Plateau Region

HA-32   Allen, Barren, Edmonson, Green, Hart, Logan, Metcalfe, Monroe, Simpson, and Warren Counties, by R. F. Brown and T. W. Lambert, 1962. $1.25.

HA-33   Breckinridge, Grayson, Hardin, Larue, and Meade Counties, by R. F. Brown and T. W. Lambert, 1963. $1.25.

HA-34   Caldwell, Christian, Crittenden, Livingston, Lyon, Todd, and Trigg Counties, by T. W. Lambert and R. F. Brown, 1963. $1.25.

HA-35   Adair, Casey, Clinton, Cumberland, Pulaski, Russell, Taylor, and Wayne Counties, by T. W. Lambert and R. F. Brown, 1963. $1.00.

Jackson Purchase Region

Quadrangles listed cover 7½ minutes of latitude and longitude representing an area of approximately 59 square miles. Portions of counties and other states covered are indicated in parentheses.

HA-13   Jackson Purchase Region (Ballard, Calloway, Carlisle, Fulton, Graves, Hickman, McCracken and Marshall Cos.), by L. M. MacCary and T. W. Lambert, 1962. $1.50.

HA-92   Farmington Quadrangle (Graves Co.), by J. H. Morgan, 1964. $0.50.

HA-93   Dexter Quadrangle (Calloway and Marshall Cos.), by R. W. Davis, 1964. $0.75.

HA-112   Lynn Grove Quadrangle (Calloway and Graves Cos.), by R. W. Davis, 1964. $0.50.

HA-113   Kirksey Quadrangle (Calloway, Graves, and Marshall Cos.), by J. H. Morgan, 1964. $0.50.

HA-114   Briensburg Quadrangle (Marshall and Livingston Cos.), by L. M. MacCary, 1964. $0.50.

HA-115   Hardin Quadrangle (Marshall and Calloway Cos.), by L. M. MacCary, 1964. $0.50.

HA-116   Oak Level Quadrangle (Marshall, Graves, and Calloway Cos.), by J. H. Morgan, 1964. $0.50.

HA-117   Elva Quadrangle (Marshall, Graves, and McCracken Cos.), by J. H. Morgan, 1964. $0.50.

HA-118   New Concord Quadrangle (Calloway Co.), by T. W. Lambert, 1964. $0.50.

HA-124   Hazel Quadrangle (Calloway Co. and Tenn.), by L. M. MacCary, 1964. $0.50.

HA-125   Lynnville Quadrangle (Graves Co. and Tenn.), by T. W. Lambert, 1965. $0.50.

HA-155   Little Cypress and Calvert City Quadrangles (Marshall and McCracken Cos.), by J. H. Morgan, 1965. $0.50.

HA-156   Fairdealing Quadrangle (Marshall, Trigg, and Lyon Cos.), by T. W. Lambert, 1965. $0.50.

HA-157   Symsonia Quadrangle (Graves and McCracken Cos.), by R. W. Davis, 1965. $0.50.

HA-158   Hico Quadrangle (Calloway and Marshall Cos.), by J. H. Morgan, 1965. $0.50.

HA-159   Birmingham Point Quadrangle (Marshall, Lyon, and Livingston Cos.), by L. M. MacCary, 1965. $0.50.

HA-160   Rushing Creek Quadrangle (Calloway, Trigg, and Marshall Cos.), by T. W. Lambert, 1965. $0.50.

HA-161   Cuba Quadrangle (Graves Co. and Tenn.), by J. H. Morgan, 1965. $0.50.

HA-162   Water Valley Quadrangle (Graves, Hickman, and Fulton Cos. and Tenn.), by T. W. Lambert, 1965. $0.50.

HA-163   Hickory Quadrangle (Graves Co.), by J. H. Morgan, 1965. $0.50.

HA-164   Mayfield Quadrangle (Graves Co.), by R. W. Davis, 1965. $0.50.

HA-165   Hamlin and Paris Landing Quadrangles (Calloway Co.), by T. W. Lambert, 1966. $0.50.

HA-166   Westplains Quadrangle (Graves Co.), by L. M. MacCary and R. W. Davis, 1966. $0.50.

HA-167   Crutchfield Quadrangle (Fulton and Hickman Cos. and Tenn.), by A. J. Hansen, Jr., 1966. $0.50.

HA-168   Health Quadrangle (McCracken and Ballard Cos.), by T. W. Lambert, 1966. $0.50.

HA-169   Fancy Farm Quadrangle (Graves, Carlisle, and Hickman Cos.), by R. W. Davis, 1966. $0.50.

HA-170   Dublin Quadrangle (Graves and Hickman Cos.), by A. J. Hansen, Jr., 1966. $0.50.

HA-171   Joppa and Metropolis Quadrangles (McCracken Co.), by A. J. Hansen, Jr., 1966. $0.75.

HA-172   Lovelaceville Quadrangle (Carlisle, Graves, McCracken, and Ballard Cos.), by R. W. Davis, 1966. $0.75.

HA-173   La Center Quadrangle (Ballard and McCracken Cos.), by T. W. Lambert, 1966. $0.75.

HA-174   Melber Quadrangle (McCracken and Graves Cos.), by R. W. Davis, 1967. $0.75.

HA-175   Clinton Quadrangle (Hickman Co.), by A. J. Hansen, Jr., 1967. $0.75.

HA-176   Olmsted and Bandana Quadrangles (Ballard and McCracken Cos.), by A. J. Hansen, Jr., 1967. $0.75.

HA-177   Paducah West and Paducah East Quadrangles (McCracken Co. and Ill.), by T. W. Lambert, 1967. $1.00.

HA-178   New Madrid SE, Hubbard Lake, and Bondurant Quadrangles (Fulton Co. and Tenn.), by T. W. Lambert, 1967. $1.00.

HA-179   Milburn Quadrangle (Carlisle and Hickman Cos.), by R. W. Davis, 1967. $0.75.

HA-180   Cayce Quadrangle (Fulton and Hickman Cos. and Tenn.), by A. J. Hansen, Jr., 1967. $0.75.

HA-184   Blandville Quadrangle (Ballard and Carlisle Cos.), by A. J. Hansen, Jr., 1968. $0.75.

HA-185   Wickliffe and Wickliffe NW Quadrangles. (Carlisle and Ballard Cos.), by T. W. Lambert, 1968. $0.75.

HA-186   Cairo and Barlow Quadrangles (Ballard Co.), by A. J. Hansen, Jr., 1968. $0.75.

Ohio River Valley

HA-72   Breckinridge and Hancock Co. alluvial deposits, by J. T. Gallaher, 1963. $0.75.

HA-73   Greenup and Lewis Co. alluvial deposits, by W. E. Price, Jr., 1963. $0.75.

HA-74   Hancock and Daviess Co. alluvial deposits, by J. T. Gallaher, 1963. $1.00.

HA-75   Boyd and Greenup Co. alluvial deposits, by W. E. Price, Jr., 1964. $1.00.

HA-91   Henderson Co. alluvial deposits, by J. T. Gallaher, 1964. $1.00.

HA-94   Lewis, Mason, Bracken, Pendleton, and Campbell Co. alluvial deposits, by W. E. Price, Jr., 1964. $1.00.

HA-95   Hardin and Meade Co. alluvial deposits, by J. T. Gallaher, 1964. $0.75.

HA-96   Daviess and Henderson Co. alluvial deposits, by J. T. Gallaher, 1963. $1.00.

HA-97   Gallatin, Carroll, Trimble, and Oldham Co. alluvial deposits, by W. E. Price, Jr., 1964. $1.00.

HA-98   Campbell, Kenton, Boone, and Gallatin Co. alluvial deposits, by W. E. Price, Jr., 1964. $1.00.

HA-110   Daviess Co. alluvial deposits, by J. T. Gallaher, 1964. $1.00.

HA-111   Southwestern Jefferson Co. alluvial deposits, by W. E. Price, Jr., 1964. $1.00.

HA-129   Henderson, Union, Crittenden, Livingston, Marshall, McCracken, and Ballard Co. alluvial deposits, by J. T. Gallaher, 1964. $1.00.

HA-130   Northern Jefferson Co. alluvial deposits, by W. E. Price, Jr., 1964. $1.00.

FLOOD MAPS

Floods on Levisa Fork in Vicinity of Paintsville, Kentucky, by C. H. Hannum, 1969 (USGS Hydrol. Atlas HA-328). $0.75.

Floods on Licking River in Vicinity of Salyersville, Kentucky, by C. H. Hannum, 1969 (USGS Hydrol. Atlas HA-329). $0.75.

Floods on Triplett Creek in Vicinity of Morehead, Kentucky, by C. H. Hannum, 1969 (USGS Hydrol. Atlas HA-342). $0.75.

BULLETINS

Series IX

B 2 Index of Published Well Records of Kentucky Geological Survey, by D. J. Jones, 1949; reprinted 1960. $1.00.

*B 5 Areas and Principles of Ground-Water Occurrence in the Inner Bluegrass Region, Kentucky, by D. K. Hamilton, 1950.

REPORTS OF INVESTIGATIONS

Series IX

RI 3 Preliminary Report on the Natural Brines of Eastern Kentucky, by Preston McGrain and G. R. Thomas, 1951. $0.50.

RI 7 Miscellaneous Analyses of Kentucky Brines, by Preston McGrain, 1953. $0.50.

Series X

RI 2 Effects of Greensburg Oilfield Brines on the Streams, Wells, and Springs of the Upper Green River Basin, Kentucky, by R. A. Krieger and G. E. Hendrickson, 1960. $1.00.

RI 4 The Effect of Oilfield Brines on the Potable Ground Water in the Upper Big Pitman Creek Basin, Kentucky, by H. T. Hopkins, 1963. $1.00.

RI 5 Water Resources of Eastern Kentucky—Progress Report, by G. A. Kirkpatrick, W. E. Price, Jr., and R. A. Madison, 1963. $2.00.

RI 9 Water Resources of the Middlesboro Area, Kentucky, by D. S. Mull and R. J. Pickering, 1968. $2.00.

INFORMATION CIRCULARS

Series IX

IC 5 Index List of Early Western Kentucky Well Records, by D. J. Jones, 1956. $3.00.

*IC 7 Index List of Well Cuttings Filed at Kentucky Geological Survey, by H. B. Wood and A. J. Walker, 1956.

IC 8 Records of Known Wells in the Jackson Purchase Region, Kentucky, by F. H. Walker, 1956. $1.00.

Series X

IC 3 Supplement to Index List of Well Cuttings Filed at Kentucky Geological Survey, by A. C. Pitts, D. S. Fullerton, and T. J. Crawford, 1960. $1.00.

IC 4 Public and Industrial Water Supplies of Kentucky, by W. K. Kulp and H. T. Hopkins, 1960. $1.00.

IC 6 Water Levels in Observation Wells in Jefferson County, Kentucky, 1935 through 1960, by D. V. Whitesides and E. S. Nichols, 1961. $1.00.

IC 7 Water Levels in Observation Wells in Kentucky Excluding Jefferson County, 1948 through 1960, by D. V. Whitesides and E. S. Nichols, 1961. $1.00.

IC 8 Characteristics of Large Springs in Kentucky, by J. A. Van Couvering, 1962. $1.00.

IC 9 Floods in Kentucky—Magnitude and Frequency, by J. A. McCabe, 1962. $2.00.

IC 10 The Ground-Water Situation in the Louisville Area, Kentucky, 1945-61, by E. A. Bell, 1962. $0.75.

IC 12 A Deep Fresh Water Aquifer in New Cypress Pool, Muhlenberg County, Kentucky, Corroborated by Geophysical Logs, by E. N. Wilson and J. A. Van Couvering, 1965. $0.75.

IC 15 Pumping Test of an Eocene Aquifer near Mayfield, Kentucky, by J. H. Morgan, 1967. $0.50.

IC 17 Catalog of Devonian and Deeper Wells in Western Kentucky, by H. R. Schwalb, 1969. $0.25.

IC 18 Effects of Pumping from the Ohio River Valley Alluvium Between Carrollton and Ghent, Kentucky, by D. V. Whitesides and P. D. Ryder, 1969. $0.50.

THESIS SERIES

Series X

TS 1 Geology and Successful Farm Ponds in the Inner Blue Grass Region of Kentucky, by M. O. Smith, 1966. $2.00.

SPECIAL PUBLICATIONS

Series IX

SP 1 Proceedings of the Southeastern Mineral Symposium 1950: Techniques of Mineral Resources Exploration and Evaluation (1953). $2.00.

    c. Artesian water in the southeastern states, by V. T. Stringfield.

SP 3 Proceedings of the Technical Session, Kentucky Oil and Gas Association Annual Mid-Year Meeting, June 5, 1953 (1953). $1.00.

    a. Water-flood development in western Kentucky, by F. E. Moran.
    b. Resume of water flooding in eastern Kentucky, by R. B. Bossler.
    g. Review of water flooding in limestones in the Tri-State area, by Leon Krause.
    i. Comments on shooting practices in water flood areas, by G. C. Roberts.

SP 6 Proceedings of the Technical Session, Kentucky Oil and Gas Association Annual Mid-Year Meeting, May 21, 1954 (1954). $1.00.

　　f. Selective plugging of water injection wells with Perma-Plugs, by J. N. Breston.
　　g. Legal aspects of waterflooding in Kentucky, by D. E. Perdue.

SP 8 Proceedings of the Technical Session, Kentucky Oil and Gas Association Annual Mid-Year Meeting, May 26-27, 1955 (1955). $1.00.

　　g. The use of radioactive-tracer surveys in water-injection wells, by J. M. Bird and J. C. Dempsey.
　　j. Waterflood developments in West Virginia, by A. J. W. Headlee and Thomas Arkle, Jr.

SP 9 Proceedings of the Technical Session, Kentucky Oil and Gas Association Annual Mid-Year Meeting, May 25, 1956 (1956). $1.00.

　　a. Probabilities of the presence of reservoirs in the Cambrian and Ordovician of the Allegheny synclinorium, by O. L. Haught.
　　c. Waterflood development of the Weir sand of eastern Kentucky, by A. C. Simmons.

SP 11 Proceedings of the Technical Session, Kentucky Oil and Gas Association Annual Meeting, May 24, 1957 (1957). $1.00.

　　d. Panther pool Bethel waterflood, Daviess County, Kentucky, by H. S. Barger.

Series X

SP 1 Proceedings of the Technical Session, Kentucky Oil and Gas Association Annual Meeting, June 5-6, 1958 (1958). $1.00.

　　b. Stream pollution, by Tom Lewis.

SP 3 Proceedings of the Technical Session, Kentucky Oil and Gas Association Annual Meeting, June 3, 1960 (1960). $1.00.

　　a. Recent trends of waterflooding of the Weir oil sands in eastern Kentucky, by W. H. Litton.

SP 10 Proceedings of the Technical Sessions, Kentucky Oil and Gas Association Annual Meeting, June 4-5, 1964 (1965). $2.00.

　　d. Improved secondary recovery by control of water mobility, by W. F. Seifert.
　　f. Some aspects of waterflooding in the Big Sinking field, Lee County, Kentucky, by Wayne Stack.
　　g. Porosity zones in the Knox of northeastern Kentucky, by W. H. McGuire.

SP 16 Water in Kentucky, by R. A. Krieger, R. V. Cushman, and N. O. Thomas, 1969. $1.00.

GUIDEBOOKS FOR GEOLOGY FIELD TRIPS

Selected Features of the Kentucky Fluorspar District and the Barkley Dam Site (Road log for Geological Society of Kentucky 1962 Field Excursion), by J. W. Hook and B. E. Clark, 1962. $1.00.

LEGISLATIVE RESEARCH COMMISSION
Frankfort, Kentucky 40601

Water Rights Law in Kentucky. Research Publication No. 42, Frankfort, 1956.

Flood Insurance and Flood-Plain Zoning. Informational Bulletin 17, Frankfort, 1957. 31 p.

Kentucky Law on Water. Research Report No. 25. Frankfort, 1965. 19 p.

WATER RESOURCES INSTITUTE
University of Kentucky
Lexington, Kentucky 40506

Report No.

*1 Economic Analysis of Alternative Flood Control Measures by Digital Computer, by Thomas M. Rachford.

*2 Analysis of Reservoir Recreation Benefits, by Robert C. Tussey.

*3 The Effect of Landowner Attitude on the Financial and the Economic Costs of Acquiring Land for a Large Public Works Project, by John M. Higgins.

*4 Covariance Analysis of Reservoir Development Effects on Property Tax Base, by Claude M. Vaughn.

*5 Review of the Economic Benefits and Costs Resulting from Dewey Reservoir, by David H. Rosenbaum.

*6 Derivation of Reservoir Operating Rules by Economic Analysis, by Charles O. Dowell.

7 Factors Controlling Porosity and Permeability in the Curdsville Member of the Lexington Limestone, by William C. MacQuown.

8 A Study of the Removal of Pesticides from Water, by James D. Whitehouse.

9 Economic Analysis of Flood Detention Storage by Digital Computer, by James Ray Villines.

10 The Effects of Geographical and Climatic Setting on the Economic Advantages of Alternative Flood Control Measures, by Clyde R. Dempsey.

11 Planning Flood Control Measures by Digital Computer, by James Norris Cline.

12 Application of Marginal Economic Analysis to Reservoir Recreation Planning, by John Ellis Sirles III.

13 Esthetic and Recreational Potential of Small Naturalistic Streams Near Urban Areas, by John A. Dearinger.

14 Evaluation of Runoff Coefficients from Small Natural Drainage Areas, by Carlos Fix Miller.

15 Evaluation of the Legal Institutions of Diversion, Transfer, Storage, and Distribution of Water in Kentucky, by A. Dan Tarlock.

LOUISIANA

DEPARTMENT OF CONSERVATION
Louisiana Geological Survey
Geology Building, Louisiana State University
P. O. Box G, University Station
Baton Rouge, Louisiana 70803

These publications can be purchased only from the Louisiana Geological Survey. Postage is included in the quoted prices. Payment should be made by check or money order payable to the Louisiana Geological Survey.

The Survey maintains a notification list to announce new publications. Names are placed on this notification list upon request. Information concerning free exchange of publications with other agencies may be had upon request.

Many of the publications listed are out of print and no longer available for purchase; however, these reports may be examined in public or university libraries or in the office of the Louisiana Geological Survey.

GEOLOGICAL BULLETINS

*1   Geology of Iberia Parish, by H. V. Howe and C. K. Moresi. 187 p., 18 figs., 1931. (Includes discussions on drainage.)

*3   Geology of Lafayette and St. Martin Parishes, by H. V. Howe and C. K. Moresi. 238 p., 52 figs., 2 pls., 1933. (Includes discussions on Mississippi River meanders and drainage.)

6   Reports on the Geology of Cameron and Vermilion Parishes, by H. V. Howe and others. 242 p., 24 figs., 10 pls., 1935. Price: $1.50. (Includes discussions on Mississippi deltas and gulf coast subsidence.)

8   Lower Mississippi River Delta; reports on the geology of Plaquemines and St. Bernard Parishes, by R. J. Russell and others. 454 p., 35 figs., 17 pls., 1936. Price: $1.50.

9   Geology of Catahoula and Concordia Parishes, by W. D. Chawner. 232 p., 6 figs., 15 pls., 1 map, 1936. Price: $1.50. (Includes a discussion of the alluvial valley of the Mississippi River.)

13   Reports of the Geology of Iberville and Ascension Parishes, by H. V. Howe and others. 223 p., 25 illus., 1938. Price: $1.50. (Includes a discussion of the existing delta of the Mississippi River.)

15   Geology of Caldwell and Winn Parishes, by J. Huner, Jr. 356 p., 60 maps and illus., 1939. Price: $1.50. (Includes a discussion of the alluvial valleys of the Ouachita River and Saline Bayou.)

16   Reports on the Surface Water Supply of Louisiana to September 30, 1938, by R. E. Marsh. 198 p., 1 map and 20 illus., 1939. Price: $1.50.

17   Ground-Water Resources of Rapides Parish, Louisiana, by J. C. Maher. 100 p., 8 maps, 23 illus., 1940. Price: $1.50.

18   Geology of Avoyelles and Rapides Parishes, by H. N. Fisk. 240 p., 12 pls., 50 figs., 1940. Price: $1.50. (Contains detailed discussion of ancient and present channels of the Mississippi and Red Rivers.)

19   The Sand and Gravel Deposits of Louisiana, by T. P. Woodward and A. J. Gueno, Jr. 429 p., 4 pls., 43 figs., 4 tables, 1 large map, 1940. Price: $1.50.

20   Ground-Water Resources of Grant and La Salle Parishes, Louisiana, by J. C. Maher. 95 p., 1 pl., 14 figs., 5 tables, 1941. Price: $1.00.

*24   Ground-Water Conditions in the Monroe Area, Louisiana, by Paul S. Jones and C. N. Holmes. 47 p., 5 pls., including a piezometric map of water in the Sparta sand, 5 tables, one of which includes the drillers logs of 31 wells in the area, 1947. Price: $1.50.

30   Geology and Ground-Water Resources of Southwestern Louisiana, by Paul H. Jones, A. N. Turcan, Jr., and Herbert E. Skibitzke. 285 p., 36 pls., 60 figs., and 15 tables, 1954. (Map pack.) Price: $2.00.

GEOLOGICAL PAMPHLETS

*1   Flouride in the Ground Water of Avoyelles and Rapides Parishes, Louisiana, by J. C. Maher. 23 p., 5 pls., 1939.

2   Preliminary Report on Ground-Water Conditions at Alexandria, Louisiana, by J. C. Maher. 54 p., 6 pls., 1940. Price: $0.50.

GEOLOGY AND AGRICULTURE OF LOUISIANA

The available books in this series are not in good condition.

*1902, Part VI:
A Report on the Geology of Louisiana, by G. D. Harris, A. C. Veatch, and J. A. A. Pacheco. 288 p., 1899. This book contains eight special reports of which the following are water-related:

3   The Geography and Geology of the Sabine River, Veatch.

6   The Subterranean Waters of Louisiana, Harris and Pacheco.

7   The Tides in the Rigolets, R. A. Harris (USC & GS).

*1905, Report of 1905, by G. D. Harris and others. 514 p., 1907. This report contains four bulletins of which three are water-related. These are listed below and are issued separately:

1   A Report on the Underground Waters of Louisiana, by G. D. Harris, and others. 164 p., 1905. Price: $1.00.

3   A Report on the Establishment of Tide Gage Work in Louisiana, by G. D. Harris. 28 p., 1905. Price: $0.50.

*4 Geology and Underground Water Resources of Northern Louisiana, by A. C. Veatch. 209 p., 1905.

WATER RESOURCES PUBLICATIONS

These publications were prepared by the U. S. Geological Survey under a cooperative program with the Louisiana Geological Survey, Dept. of Conservation and the Dept. of Public Works.

WATER RESOURCES BULLETINS

1   Ground Water in Louisiana, by J. R. Rollo. 83 p., 4 pls., 16 figs., 10 tables. 1960. (Map pack). Price: $1.50.

*— Ground-water resources of East Carroll and West Carroll Parishes, Louisiana, by J. L. Poole. 174 p., 15 pls., 30 figs., 13 tables. 1961.

2   Ground Water Conditions in the Baton Rouge Area, 1954-59, with Special Reference to Increased Pumpage, by C. O. Morgan. 78 p., 3 pls., 30 figs., 4 tables. 1962. (Map pack). Price: $1.50.

*— Ground Water for Louisiana's Public Supplies, by J. L. Snider, M. D. Winner Jr., and J. B. Epstein. 267 p., 1 pl., 1 table. 1962.

3   Water Resources of Sabine Parish, Louisiana, by Leland V. Page, Roy Newcome, Jr., and George D. Graeff, Jr. 146 p., 8 pls., 36 figs., 20 tables. 1963. (Map pack). Price: $1.50.

4   Water Resources of Natchitoches Parish, Louisiana, by Roy Newcome, Jr., Leland V. Page, and Raymond Sloss. 12 pls., 39 figs., 12 tables. 1963. (Map pack). Price: $1.50.

*— Ground-water Resources of East Feliciana and West Feliciana Parishes, Louisiana, by C. O. Morgan. 58 p., 2 pls., 16 figs., 10 tables. 1963.

*— Basic Ground-water Data for the Mississippi River Parishes South of Baton Rouge, Louisiana, by G. T. Cardwell, J. R. Rollo, and R. A. Long. 5 p., 2 pls., 15 figs., 5 tables. 1963.

*— The Florida Parishes – An Area of Large, Undeveloped Ground-water Potential in Southeastern Louisiana, by M. D. Winner, Jr. 50 p., 3 pls., 5 figs., 5 tables. 1963.

5   Water Resources of Bossier and Caddo Parishes, Louisiana, by Leland V. Page and Harold G. May. 105 p., 7 pls., 24 figs., 11 tables. 1964. (Map pack.) Price: $1.50.

6   Water Resources of Vernon Parish, Louisiana, by James E. Rogers and Anthony J. Calandro. 104 p., 2 pls., 21 figs., and 10 tables. 1965. Price: $1.50.

7   Ground Water in the Geismar-Gonzales Area, Ascension Parish, Louisiana, by Richard A. Long. 67 p., 2 pls., 11 figs., 2 tables. 1965. Price: $1.50.

8   Water Resources of Rapides Parish, Louisiana, by Roy Newcome, Jr. and Raymond Sloss. 104 p., 6 pls., 18 figs., 11 tables. 1966. Price: $1.50.

9   Ground-Water Resources of the Greater New Orleans Area, Louisiana, by J. R. Rollo, 69 p., 14 pls., 11 figs., 5 tables. 1966. (Map pack.) Price: $1.50.

10 Effects of Ground-Water Withdrawals on Water Levels and Salt-Water Encroachment in Southwestern Louisiana, by A. H. Harder and others. 56 p., 7 pls., 16 figs. 1967. Price: $1.50.

11 Water Resources of Pointe Coupee Parish, Louisiana, by M. D. Winner, Jr., M. J. Forbes, Jr., and W. L. Broussard. 110 p., 11 pls., 25 figs., 5 tables. 1968. (Map pack.) Price: $1.50.

12 Water Resources of the Lake Pontchartrain Area, Louisiana, by G. T. Cardwell, M. J. Forbes, Jr., and M. W. Gaydos. 105 p., 7 pls., 23 figs., 8 tables. 1967. Price: $1.50.

13 Salt-Water Encroachment in Aquifers of the Baton Rouge Area, Louisiana, by J. R. Rollo (U. S. Geological Survey). August 1969. Price: $1.50.

14 Water Resources of Ouachita Parish, Louisiana, by J. E. Rogers, A. J. Calandro and M. W. Gaydos. (In press).

15 Ground-water Resources of Avoyelles Parish, Louisiana, by J. R. Marie. (In press).

WATER RESOURCES PAMPHLETS

1   An Analysis of Contour Maps of Water Levels in Wells in Southwestern Louisiana, 1952 and 1953, by Stuart W. Fader. 7 p., 4 pls., and 1 fig. 1954. Price: $0.50. (Discussion relates to Chicot Reservoir.)

*— Fluoride in the Ground Water of Avoyelles and Rapides Parishes, Louisiana, by J. C. Maher. 23 p., 2 pls., 3 tables. 1939.

2   An Analysis of Contour Maps of Water Levels in Southwestern Louisiana, 1954, by Stuart W. Fader. 11 p., 2 pls., and 5 figs. 1955. Price: $0.50. (Discussion relates to the Chicot Reservoir.)

3   Geology and Ground Water Resources of the Alexandria Area, Rapides Parish, Louisiana, by Mervin L. Klug. 21 p., 4 figs., and 4 tables. 1955. Price: $0.50. (Supplementary report of the data presented in the Louisiana Geological Survey Bulletin No. 17.)

4   An Analysis of 1955 Water-Level Contour Maps with a Discussion of Salt-Water Problems in Southwestern Louisiana, by Stuart W. Fader. 27 p., 3 pls., 9 figs., and 2 tables. 1957. Price: $0.50.

5   Water Levels and Water-Level Contour Maps for Southwestern Louisiana, 1956 and 1957, by Stuart W. Fader. 23 p., 4 pls., 4 figs., and 2 tables. 1958. Price: $0.50.

6   Summary of Ground-Water Conditions in Southwestern Louisiana, 1957 and 1958, by A. N. Turcan, Jr., and S. W. Fader. 29 p., 7 illus., 4 tables. 1959. Price: $0.50.

7   Ground-Water Resources of the Red River Valley Alluvium in Louisiana, by Roy Newcome, Jr. 21 p., 5 pls., 9 figs., 3 tables. 1960. Price: $0.50.

8   Water Levels & Water Level Contour Maps for Southwestern Louisiana, 1958 and 1959, by Alfred H. Harder. 27 p., 3 pls., 7 figs., 2 tables. 1960. Price: $0.50.

9   Ground-Water Conditions Between Baton Rouge and New Orleans, Louisiana, by G. T. Cardwell and J. R. Rollo. 43 p., 3 pls., 6 figs., 4 tables. 1960. Price: $0.50.

— The Geology and Ground-Water Resources of Calcasieu Parish, by A. H. Harder. (U.S.G.S. Water Supply Paper 1488). 102 p., 9 pls., 29 figs., 9 tables. 1960. Price: $1.50.

10 Water Levels and Water-Level Contour Maps for Southwestern Louisiana, 1959 and Spring 1960, with a discussion of Ground-Water Withdrawals, by Alfred H. Harder. 25 p., 3 pls., 5 figs., 2 tables. 1961. (Water-level maps with pertinent statistics.) Price: $0.50.

*— Pumpage of Water in Louisiana, 1960, by J. L. Snider and M. J. Forbes, Jr. 6 p., 1 fig., 1 table. 1961.

11 Water Levels in Southwestern Louisiana, April 1960 to April 1961, with a discussion of Water-Level Trends from 1950 to 1960. 21 p., 6 pls., 2 figs., 2 tables. 1962. Price: $0.50.

12 Ground-water Conditions in Southwestern Louisiana, 1961 and 1962, with a discussion of the Chicot Aquifer in the Coastal Area. 32 p., 3 pls., 3 figs., 3 tables. 1963. Price: $0.50.

13 Gas and Brackish Water in Fresh-Water Aquifers, Lake Charles Area. 35 p., 4 pls., 8 figs., 3 tables. 1963. Price: $0.50.

— Pumpage of Water in Louisiana, 1960, by J. L. Snider and M. J. Forbes, Jr. 6 p., 1 fig., 1 table. 1961. (Water-use and pumpage statistics by parishes.) Price: $0.50.

— Sources of Emergency Water Supply in the Alexandria Area, Louisiana, by Roy Newcome, Jr. 7 p. 1961. (Location and statistics of wells which may be used at a time of emergency or disaster.) Price: $0.50.

— Emergency Ground-Water Supplies in Calcasieu Parish, Louisiana, by George W. Swindel and Arthur L. Hodges, Jr. (Text on reverse of map.) Price: $0.50.

— Emergency Ground-Water Supplies in the Monroe Area, Louisiana, by John L. Snider. 1962. Price: $0.50.

14 Methane in the Fresh-Water Aquifers of Southwestern Louisiana and Theoretical Explosion Hazards, by A. H. Harder, H. M. Whitman, and S. M. Rogers. 22 p., 1 pl., 6 figs., and 1 table. 1965. Price: $0.50.

15 Feasibility of a Scavenger-Well System as a Solution to the Problem of Vertical Salt-Water Encroachment, by Richard A. Long. 27 p., 7 figs., 1 table. 1965. Price: $0.50.

16 Estimating Water Quality from Electrical Logs in Southwestern Louisiana, by Harry M. Whitman. 13 p., 1 pl., 6 figs., 1 table. 1965. Price: $0.50.

17 Salt-Water Encroachment Baton Rouge Area, Louisiana, by R. R. Meyer and J. R. Rollo. 9 p., 4 figs., 1965. Price: $0.50.

18 Progress Report on the Availability of Fresh Water, Lake Pontchartrain Area, Louisiana, by G. T. Cardwell, M. J. Forbes, Jr., and M. W. Gaydos. 24 p., 1 pl., 3 figs. 1966. Price: $0.50.

19 Calculation of Water Quality from Electrical Logs, Theory and Practice, by A. N. Turcan, Jr. 23 p., 7 figs., 3 tables. 1966. Price: $0.50.

20 Pumpage of Water in Louisiana, 1965, by P. P. Bieber and M. J. Forbes, Jr. 8 p., 1 fig., 1 table. 1966. Price: $0.50.

21 Water Resources of the Lettsworth-Innis-Batchelor Area, Pointe Coupee Parish, by A. H. Harder, V. B. Sauer and

W. L. Broussard. 28 p., 1 pl., 6 tables. 1968. Price: $0.50.

22 Water-Level Trends in Southeastern Louisiana, by D. C. Dial. 11 p., 1 pl., 2 figs. 1968. Price: $0.50.

23 Water Resources of Northwestern St. Landry Parish and Vicinity, Louisiana, by R. L. Hosman, W. L. Broussard and A. J. Calandro (U. S. Geological Survey). January 1970. Price: $0.50.

24 Water Resources of the Slagle-Simpson-Flatwoods Area, Louisiana, by C. D. Whiteman, Jr., A. J. Calandro and W. L. Broussard. (In press).

25 Water Resources of the Belmont-Marthaville-Robeline Area, Louisiana, by A. J. Calandro, W. L. Broussard and R. L. Hosman. (In press).

26 Pumpage of Water in Louisiana, 1970, by Don C. Dial (U. S. Geological Survey). July 1970. Price: $0.50.

CONTROL OF WATER POLLUTION

— Protection of Underground Fresh Water Sands in Louisiana, by Leo W. Hough. 6 p., 2 figs. 1963.

— Progress in Control of Pollution of Surface Waters by Oil Field Brine and Waste Oil, by Leo W. Hough. 13 p., 4 figs. 1965.

LOUISIANA DEPARTMENT OF HIGHWAYS
P. O. Box 4245
Capitol Station
Baton Rouge, Louisiana 70804

*Floods in Louisiana – Magnitude and Frequency, by J. S. Cragwall, Jr. 1952. 281 p.

*Floods in Louisiana – Magnitude and Frequency, 2nd edition, by V. B. Sauer. 1964. 402 p., 13 figs.

LOUISIANA STATE DEPARTMENT OF PUBLIC WORKS
Capitol Annex
P. O. Box 44155
Baton Rouge, Louisiana 70804

A Brief Statement on Flood Control, Mississippi River and Tributaries Project in Louisiana. 1958. 10 p.

[Same title]. 1959. Various pagings.

[Same title]. 1960. 13 p. and appendix.

A Brief Written Statement Concerning Bayou Bodcau, Red Chute and Loggy Bayou, Bland and Cypress Bayous, Louisiana; in the Interest of Flood Control, Water Supply and Related Purposes. 1959. 10 p.

The Case for the Red River Lateral Canal, prepared for presentation to the Corps of Engineers. 1945. 52 p.

Chemical Analysis of Surface Waters in Louisiana, October 1943-March 1945, by W. W. Hastings. 1945. 17 p.

Chemical Composition of Surface Waters of Louisiana 1943-1958, by S. F. Kapustka. 1964. 212 p., 1 pl., 11 figs., 123 tables.

Flood Control Plan for West Agurs Industrial Area, Caddo Parish, Louisiana. 1959. 9 p.

*Ground-water Conditions in the Vicinity of Baton Rouge, a Progress Report, by E. M. Cushing and P. H. Jones. 1945. 33 p.

Ground-water Resources of East Carroll and West Carroll Parishes, Louisiana. 1961. 174 p.

Ground-water Resources of Jefferson Davis and Acadia Parishes, Louisiana, by T. B. Stanley, Jr. and J. C. Maher. 1944. 93 p.

Louisiana Rainfall; Intensity, Duration, Frequency Data, and Depth, Area [and] Duration Data. 1952. 142 p.

Louisiana – Resources and Facilities [by parish] :

Avoyelles Parish	1947.	100 p.
Beauregard Parish	1949.	110 p.
Bienville Parish	[1952?].	114 p.
Catahoula Parish	1949.	80 p.
Claiborne Parish	1948.	114 p.
Concordia Parish	1950.	111 p.
Grant Parish	1947.	138 p.
Iberia Parish	1949.	174 p.
Jackson Parish	1947	72 p.
Jefferson Davis Parish	1947.	98 p.
Lafayette Parish	1945.	88 p.
Livingston Parish	[1955?].	77 p.
Richland Parish	[1953?].	121 p.
St. Charles Parish	[1952?].	103 p.
St. Landry Parish	1947.	125 p.
St. Mary Parish	1949.	135 p.
St. Martin Parish	1950.	123 p.
Tensas Parish	1949.	81 p.
Vermilion Parish	1946.	98 p.
Vernon Parish	1949.	93 p.
West Carroll Parish	[1952?].	114 p.

The Purpose and Value of Test Wells and Well-Measurement Data, by A. N. Turcan, Jr. 1959. 12 p.

Quality of Surface Waters Near Monroe, Louisiana, by S. M. Rogers and S. F. Kapustka. 1964. 53 p., 1 pl., 7 figs., 9 tables.

Report. Biennial. 1942-43 to date.

Report and Recommendations for the Destruction of Water Hyacinths and Providing a Fresh Water Supply to the Henderson Area of St. Martin Parish, Louisiana. 1954. 18 p.

Report on the Proposed Conversion of Plaquemine Lock for Surface Water Supply. 1962. 12 p.

Tiger Island Drainage Study. 1958. 12 p., 5 pls.

Water and Related Land Resources; Comprehensive Planning Program. 1968. 94 p.

Water-supply Characteristics of Louisiana Streams, by L. V. Page. 1963. Tech. Report 1. 109 p., 30 figs.

LOUISIANA SOIL AND WATER CONSERVATION COMMITTEE

P. O. Drawer CS
Baton Rouge, Louisiana 70803

Newsletter. January 1947 (Vol. 1, No. 1) to date.

LOUISIANA WILDLIFE AND FISHERIES COMMISSION

400 Royal Street
New Orleans, Louisiana 70130

FISHERIES BULLETINS

1   Fish Populations and Aquatic Conditions in Polluted Waters in Louisiana, by James T. Davis. 1960. 121 p.

3   An Ecological Survey of Factors Affecting Fish Production in Louisiana Waters, by Donald W. Geagan and Thomas D. Allen. 1960. 100 p.

4   Managing Louisiana Fish Ponds, by Max W. Summers. 1963. 64 p.

5   An Ecological Survey of Factors Affecting Fish Production in a Louisiana Backwater Area and River, by Kenneth E. Lantz. 1970. 60 p.

LOUISIANA WATER RESOURCES RESEARCH INSTITUTE

Louisiana State University
Baton Rouge, Louisiana 70803

Note: Orders, with payment accompanying, should be placed only with the Louisiana State University Bookstore, Baton Rouge, Louisiana 70803. The prices do not include postage.

REGULAR SERIES BULLETINS

1   Handbook of Basic Water Law (with special reference to Louisiana), by George W. Hardy III. June 1966. 77 p. Price: $1.50.

2   The Measurement and Comparison of Costs for Alternative Water Replacement Projects, by L. H. Falk and W. J. Stober. October 1966. 33 p. Price: $1.00.

3   Salt-Water Encroachment into Aquifers, Proceedings of the Limited Professional Symposium Held at Louisiana State University, Baton Rouge, May 4-5, 1967. October 1968. 192 p. Price: $5.00.

4   Water-Resources Manpower: Supply and Demand Patterns to 1980, by James E. Lewis. May 1970. 48 p. Price: $2.00.

5   The Present and Future Ground-Water Supply of the Baton Rouge Area, by Raphael G. Kazmann. February 1970. 126 p. Price: $3.00.

6   Subsidence and Ground-Water Offtake in the Baton Rouge Area, by William A. Wintz Jr., Raphael G. Kazmann and Charles G. Smith, Jr. October 1970. 20 p. Price: $4.00.

7   An Economic Reappraisal of the Toledo Bend Multiple-Purpose Water Project, by L. H. Falk and W. J. Stober. October 1970. 36 p. Price: $2.00.

GRADUATE THESIS SERIES BULLETINS

*GT-1 The Flood Control Capabilities of the Atchafalaya Basin Floodway, by Kermit L. Hebert. April 1967. 88 p.

GT-2 Hydrology of Neogene Deposits in the Northern Gulf of Mexico Basin, by Paul H. Jones. April 1969. 105 p. Price: $3.00.

GT-3 Economic Aspects of Ground-Water Basin Control, by Laurence H. Falk. 1970. Price: $2.00.

GT-4 Geohydrology of the Shallow Aquifers of Baton Rouge, Louisiana, by Charles G. Smith, Jr. October 1969. Price: $1.50.

TECHNICAL REPORTS

*TR-1 The Recent Alluvium of Thomas and Duncan Points, by Joseph D. Martinez. June 1967. 24 p.

*TR-2 The Present and Future Ground Water Supply of the Baton Rouge Area, by Raphael G. Kazmann. September 1967.

TR-3 A Summer Limnological Study of Lake Pontchartrain, Louisiana, by D. H. Stern and B. H. Atwell. September 1968. Price: $1.00.

TR-4 Physical, Chemical, Bacterial and Plankton Dynamics of Lake Pontchartrain, Louisiana. September 1969. 60 p. Price: $2.50.

INSTITUTE-SPONSORED PUBLICATIONS

These publications are not available through the Louisiana State University Bookstore.

Persistency of 2, 4-Dichlorophenoxacetic Acid and its Derivatives in Surface Waters When Used to Control Aquatic Vegetation, by William K. Averitt. September 1967. Price: $5.00. (This publication is obtainable from the Dept. of Chemical Engineering, University of Southwestern Louisiana, Lafayette, La. 70501.)

The Use of Municipal Sewage Effluent for Irrigation, by C. W. Wilson and F. E. Beckett. July 1968. Price: $15.00. (This publication may be obtained from the Alumni Foundation, Louisiana Tech University, Box 4001, Ruston, La. 71270.)

A Technique for Irrigating Bottomland Hardwood Trees with Papermill Effluent in North Louisiana, by Ishtiaq Ahmed. May 1970. Price: $10.00. (Master of Science thesis, Louisiana Tech University, Ruston, La. 71270.)

LOUISIANA STATE DEPARTMENT OF HEALTH
Louisiana State Office Building
P. O. Box 60630
New Orleans, Louisiana 70160

Lake Pontchartrain Pollution Evaluation. 1962. 17 p. plus appendices.

Lower Calcasieu Basin Oyster Water Survey. 1962. 11 p. plus appendix.

Barataria Bay and Vicinity Oyster Water Survey. 1964. 8 p., 5 data sheets, 1 map.

East Delta Marshes, Plaquemines Parish Oyster Water Survey. 1964. 8 p., 8 data sheets, 1 map.

Lower Vermilion Bay — Gulf of Mexico Oyster Water Survey. 1964. 5 p., 14 data sheets, 1 map.

West Delta Marshes, Plaquemines Parish Oyster Water Survey. 1964. 6 p., 9 data sheets, 1 map.

Coastal Marshes — Western Terrebonne Parish Oyster Water Survey. 1966. 9 p., 7 data sheets, 2 maps.

Terrebonne Bay and Vicinity Oyster Water Survey. 1966. 12 p., 9 data sheets, 2 maps.

Timbalier Bay and Vicinity Oyster Water Survey. 1966. 9 p., 5 data sheets, 1 map.

Vermilion River Sanitary Survey Report. August 1969. 31 p. plus appendices.

Pearl River — Mississippi Sound Oyster Water Survey. 1968-70. 31 p., appendices, 1 map.

MAINE

ENVIRONMENTAL IMPROVEMENT COMMISSION

State House
Augusta, Maine 04330

Progress Report. 1959/60 to date. (Only the most current issue is available).

(Water and Air) Environmental Improvement Commission Revised Statutes of 1964: Title 38 (as amended). 1970. 93 p.

MAINE FORESTRY DEPARTMENT

Information & Education Division
State Office Building
Augusta, Maine 04330

Laws Relating to Forests, Parks, Lakes and Rivers. Amended in 1965. (Limited printing with single copies available as the supply lasts.)

Aquatic Insects and DDT Forest Spraying in Maine – 1961. Maine Forestry Department–Conservation Foundation, Bulletin No. 19. (Limited printing with single copies available as the supply lasts.)

Pesticides and Stream Insects. Maine Forestry Department–Conservation Foundation Bulletin No. 23.

WATER RESOURCES CENTER

University of Maine
Orono, Maine 04473

REPORTS

A. ANNUAL REPORTS:

    Fiscal Year 1965 – unpublished.

    Fiscal Year 1966 – unpublished.

    *Fiscal Year 1967 (publication no. 2).

    *Fiscal Year 1968 (publication no. 4).

    *Fiscal Year 1969 (annual report no. 5).

    *Fiscal Year 1970 (annual report no. 6).

B. PROJECT COMPLETION REPORTS:

To Investigate the Disposal of Agricultural Product Wastes Through the Soil, by Robert V. Rourke. 1966. (A-002-ME).

Water Conservation in Food Processing Plants, by Matthew E. Highlands. 1966. (A-008-ME).

Removal of Viruses from Water, by Otis J. Sproul. 1966. (A-004-ME).

Chemical Reactor Theory Applied to Modeling the Dynamics of a Control System for Water Quality of a River, by Edward G. Bobalek. 1967. (B-001-ME).

Effect of Nitrification of Organic Wastes on Waters in the Natural Environment, by K. Keshavan. 1967. (A-003-ME).

Basic Water Research on New England Soils, by Robert V. Rourke. 1968. (A-011-ME).

Urban Hydrologic Relationships, by Warren Viessman, Jr. 1968. (A-010-ME). (Publication no. 6).

Water Quality Degradation by Wood Bark Pollutants, by Otis J. Sproul and Clifford A. Sharpe. 1968. (A-009-ME). (Publication no. 5).

Pattern of Precipitation Dispersion as Affected by Different Vegetative Covers in Maine, by Charles E. Schomaker. 1968. (A-005-ME).

Chemical Contaminants Found in Surface and Subsurface Water as Related to Soil and Climatic Conditions, by Eliot Epstein and Ronald Struchtemeyer. 1969. (A-006-ME).

The Influence of Salts Applied to Highways on the Levels of Sodium and Chloride Ions Present in Water and Soil Samples, by Dr. Frederick Hutchinson. 1969. (A-007-ME).

Phase II – Study of a River System as a Chemical Reactor, by Edward G. Bobalek. 1969. (B-003-ME).

Water Quality Degradation by Septic Tank Drainage, by Millard W. Hall. 1970. (A-014-ME).

Water Quality – Benthic Invertebrate Relationships in Estuaries, by David Dean. 1970. (A-011-ME).

Adsorption of Viruses on Mineral Surfaces, by Otis J. Sproul. 1970. (A-013-ME).

C. MISCELLANEOUS:

A Compilation of Current Water-Related Studies in the State of Maine, by Viessman. October 1966. (Publication no. 1).

Current Water-Related Studies in the State of Maine, by Viessman. April 1968. (Publication no. 3).

Water Resources Research Interests in the Colleges and Universities of Maine, by Imhoff. August 1969. (un-numbered).

Proceedings and Analysis Workshop on the Planning Research Interface. November 18-19, 1969. Sponsored by Water Resources Center and Dept. of Agricultural and Resource Economics.

Cultural Eutrophication of Maine Lakes. A survey by an ad hoc committee on problem lakes; information memorandum Water Resources Center. September 1970. (un-numbered).

RELATED PUBLICATIONS

Soil-Water Chemical and Physical Characteristics of Eight Soil Series in Maine, by R. V. Rourke and C. Beek. February 1968. 95 p.

Chemical and Physical Properties of the Charlton, Sutton, Paxton and Woodbridge Soil Series, by R. V. Rourke and C. Beek. February 1969. 81 p.

Seasonal Variation in the Interception of Precipitation by a Spruce and a Birch Stand, by Charles E. Schomaker. 1968. (Pamphlet).

Comparison of Snow Interception by a Hardwood and a Conifer Forest, by C. E. Schomaker. 1968. (Pamphlet).

Proceedings of the Atlantic Section of the Chemical Institute of Canada: Water Quality Aspects of Recreational Land Use, by Millard W. Hall and Otis J. Sproul. August 24-26, 1969. Saint Mary's University, Halifax, Nova Scotia (in press).

MARYLAND

MARYLAND DEPARTMENT OF STATE PLANNING

301 West Preston Street
Baltimore, Maryland 21201

*9 Conservation Problems in Maryland. 1935.

*28 Flow Data and Draft Storage Curves for Major Streams 1929-1937. 1940.

44 Ground Water in the Baltimore Industrial Area. 1945.

65 Development Plan for Patapsco River Valley Park. 1950.

70 A Program for the Monocacy Watershed. 1951.

112 Future Administration of State of Maryland Water Resources Activities. 1961.

112A Appendices. 1961.

132-A Water Supply and Demand Study. Part II, Future Water Supply and Demand, Vol. 1, The Report. 1965.

132-B Vol. 2, A Summary Statement. 1965.

132-C Vol. 3, A Computer Model of Stream Quality. 1966.

*133-A Water Supply and Demand Study. Part I, Basic Data – Vol. 1 – Chesapeake Bay West Drainage Basin. 1965.

*133-B Vol. 2 – Susquehanna River Basin. 1965.

*133-C Vol. 5 – The Eastern Shore. 1966.

133-D Vol. 4 – Youghiogheny River Basin. 1967.

*133-E Vol. 3 – Potomac River. 1967.

133-F Vol. 6 – General Reference Section. 1968.

*137 Maryland State Laws, Policies and Programs Pertaining to Water; and Related Land Resources. 1966.

148 Catalog of Natural Areas in Maryland. 1968.

149 Patuxent River – Maryland's Asset, Maryland's Responsibility. 1968.

*149-A Appendices. 1968.

152 Ground-Water Aquifers and Mineral Commodities of Maryland. 1969.

— Scenic Rivers in Maryland. 1970.

SPECIAL REPORTS PERTAINING TO WATER RESOURCES

Note: The Special Report series was discontinued in 1965. All departmental publications are now issued serially.

*Comprehensive Report on the Upper Chesapeake Bay Drainage Basin. 1936.

*Comprehensive Report on the Potomac River Drainage Basin in Maryland. 1936.

*Resume of Report on Oyster Conservation Problems in Maryland. 1936.

*Progress Report of the Natural Resources Committee. 1937.

*Fish and Game Habitats and Recreational Areas in the State of Maryland. 1939.

A Study and Recommendations for the Recreational Development of the Patapsco River Valley Parkway. 1946.

*Limnological Observations on Lake Roland. 1948.

*Survey Report – Youghiogheny River Watershed. Synopsis. 1951.

Report of the Joint Committee on the Chesapeake and Ohio Canal Parkway. 1952.

Bibliography of Maryland Water Resources Data. 1962.

*Susquehanna River Basin Study. Appendix B, Part 3 – Maryland. Corps of Engineers, Baltimore District. (Produced in cooperation with the Maryland Department of Natural Resources). 1970.

DEPARTMENT OF WATER RESOURCES

State Office Building
Annapolis, Maryland 21401

All titles dated prior to June 1, 1964, are publications of the predecessor agency, the Water Pollution Control Commission.

*Gwynns Falls: An Analysis of a Water Pollution Problem: Special Report, May 2, 1955.

*Water Pollution Survey of the Patapsco River: A Cooperative Report by the Water Pollution Control Commission and the Department of Health of the State of Maryland, March 1, 1957.

Gunpowder Falls: Report on Program to Control Water Pollution From Industrial Sources, August 1, 1958.

1962 Supplement to the Gunpowder Falls Report, August 1, 1958.

Little Patuxent River Survey, December 15, 1958.

Final Data Report for Zekiah Swamp (3/9/61 – 2/28/62) – Survey Report No. 62-5-WcW.

Patapsco River Survey: Data Report, March 1961 – December 1962.

Youghiogheny River Survey: Data Report, November 1960 – January 1963.

St. Mary's River: Water Quality Data, 1962 (Survey 62-17-SM).

St. Mary's River: Water Quality Data Supplement, 1963 (Survey 63-6-SM).

A Report on the Buntings Branch Survey: Survey Report, January, 1964 (63-9-BB).

Proceedings Second Annual Symposium on Industrial Waste Control, Held at Johns Hopkins University, Baltimore, Maryland, May 1, 1961.

Proceedings Fourth Annual Symposium on Industrial Waste Control, Held at Johns Hopkins University, Baltimore, Maryland, May 6, 1963.

Proceedings Fifth Annual Symposium on Industrial Waste Control, Held at Frostburg State College, Frostburg, Maryland, May 7 and 8, 1964.

Proceedings Sixth Annual Symposium on Industrial Waste Control, Held at the University of Maryland, College Park, Maryland, May 10, 1966.

Problems Posed by Sediment Derived From Construction Activities in Maryland, 1964, January.

Interim Report No. I On the Western Maryland pH Survey, June 10, 1964.

Physical, Chemical and Bacteriological Water Quality in Gunpowder Falls and Little Gunpowder Falls, August 1962, August 1963.

Coliform and E. Coli Bacteria Counts at a Major Chesapeake Bay Boating-Bathing Site During the Independence Day Holiday Period, 1964.

Report to the Director on Severn Run Investigations, April 29, 1965.

Western Maryland Mine Drainage Survey, 1962-1965 (three volumes).

A Report of the Effects of Cannery Waste on Marshall Creek, July 14, to October 19, 1965.

Water Resources Law.

Water Resources Regulations and Rules of Procedure.

Report Number Two — On Coliform and E. Coli Bacteria Counts at a Major Chesapeake Bay Boating-Bathing Site During the Independence Day Holiday Period, 1965.

The Patuxent River — Report Number 1: Physical, Chemical and Bacteriological Water Quality, January 1961—February 1963.

Physical, Chemical and Bacteriological Water Quality in the Patapsco River: Summer Surveys, 1963, 1964, 1965.

Maryland Water Law: Water Laws and Legal Principles Affecting the Use of Water in Maryland, by Paul M. Galbreath (Published by the Water Resources Study Committee, University of Maryland, College Park, Maryland, under contract with the Maryland Department of Water Resources). 1965.

Maryland's Role in Water Resources Development, by Lyle E. Craine, School of Natural Resources, The University of Michigan (Published by the Water Resources Study Committee, University of Maryland, College Park, Maryland under contract with the Maryland Department of Water Resources). 1966.

Selected Opinions of the Attorney General of Maryland Pertaining to Water Resources Management, Compiled by Paul M. Galbreath (Published by the Water Resources Study Committee, University of Maryland, College Park, Maryland, under contract

with the Maryland Department of Water Resources). December 1966.

Water Resources Management in Maryland: Appendices, (Published by the Water Resources Study Committee, University of Maryland, College Park, Maryland, under contract with the Maryland Department of Water Resources). December 1966.

Physical and Chemical Water Quality in Back River, Baltimore County, 1963-1966.

Physical, Chemical, and Bacteriological Water Quality in Gunpowder Falls and Little Gunpowder Falls, 1965 Summer Survey.

Physical, Chemical and Bacteriological Water Quality in the Choptank River, March 1965 — March 1966.

Little Elk Creek Survey, 1966.

Water Resources Management in Maryland (Published by the Water Resources Study Committee, University of Maryland, College Park, Maryland, under contract with the Maryland Department of Water Resources), August 1967.

The Patuxent River Report No. 4: Physical, Chemical and Bacteriological Water Quality, Summer Surveys 1964-1965-1966.

Physical and Chemical Water Quality from the Effects of Mine Drainage in Western Maryland, 1966.

Proceedings Seventh Annual Symposium on Industrial Waste Control, Held at Johns Hopkins University, Baltimore, Maryland, May 9, 1967.

Water Resources Regulation 4.8: General Water Quality Criteria and Specific Water Quality Standards for all Maryland Waters, July 1967.

Water Resources Law: 1968 Fiscal Year.

Water Resources Regulation 2.3: Well Drillers and Well Construction, March 1968.

The Monocacy River, Physical, Chemical and Bacteriological Water Quality, Report Number One, March — December, 1966.

Water Resources Law: 1969 Fiscal Year.

Water Resources Rules of Procedure, Section 1 (General); December 1968.

Water Resources Regulations and Rules of Procedure, Section 3, December 1968.

Water Quality Status Report, February, 1969.

Statewide Water Quality Surveillance Network, 1968 Survey Results, March, 1969.

Water Resources Law: 1970 Fiscal Year, July, 1969.

Water Resources Regulation 4.8: General Water Quality Criteria and Specific Water Quality Standards for all Maryland Waters, Issued April, 1969.

MARYLAND GEOLOGICAL SURVEY
214 Latrobe Hall
The Johns Hopkins University
Baltimore, Maryland 21218

BULLETINS

1 Summary of Records of Surface Waters of Maryland and the Potomac River Basin. 1892-1943, 296 p., 1944. Price: $0.50 (paper).

4 Geology and Ground-Water Resources of the Baltimore Area. Bennett, R. R., and Meyer, R. R., 573 p., 17 tables, 30 figs., 26 pls., 1952. Price: $6.00 (paper).

5 Water Resources of Anne Arundel County. 149 p., 5 tables, 10 figs., 7 pls., 1949. Price: $1.00 (paper).
   Bennion, V. R.: The Surface-Water Resources.
   Brookhart, J. W.: The Ground-Water Resources.

*6 Shore Erosion in Tidewater Maryland. 141 p., 21 tables, 10 figs., 35 pls., 1949.
   Singewald, J. T., Jr.: The Shore Erosion Problem.
   Slaughter, T. H.: The Shore Erosion Measurements.
   Slaughter, T. H.: Navigation Restoration Expenditures.

   Reprint from Bulletin 6, Shore Erosion in Tidewater Maryland. 30 p., 6 tables, 4 figs., 7 pls., 1949. Price: $0.25 (paper).
   The Shore Erosion Problem.
   Summary of Shore Erosion in Tidewater Maryland.
   Navigation Restoration Expenditures.

8 Water Resources of Calvert County. 100 p., 5 tables, 5 figs., 3 pls., 1951. Price: $0.75 (paper).
   Bennion, V. K., and Dougherty, D. F.: The Surface-Water Resources.
   Overbeck, R. M.: The Ground-Water Resources.

*10 Geology and Water Resources of Prince George's County. 270 p., 9 tables, 9 figs., 6 pls., 1952.
   Cooke, C. Wythe.: Sedimentary Deposits.
   Martin, R. O. R.: Surface-Water Resources.
   Meyer, Gerald.: Ground-Water Resources.

11 Water Resources of St. Mary's County. 195 p., 11 tables, 5 figs., 7 pls., 1953. Price: $1.00 (paper); $2.00 (cloth).
   Martin, R. O. R.: Surface-Water Resources.
   Ferguson, H. F.: Ground-Water Resources.

12 The Sediments of Chesapeake Bay, Ryan, J. Donald. 120 p., 6 tables, 7 figs., 18 pls., 1953. Price: $2.00 (cloth).

13 Geology and Water Resources of Garrett County. 349 p., 26 tables, 24 figs., 11 pls., 1954. Price: $3.00 (cloth).
   Amsden, T. W.: Geology of Garrett County.
   Overbeck, R. M.: Ground-Water Resources.
   Martin, R. O. R.: Surface-Water Resources.

14 Water Resources of Howard and Montgomery Counties. 260 p., 22 tables, 18 figs., 8 pls., 1954. Price: $2.00 (paper); $3.00 (cloth).
   Dingman, R. J. and Meyer, Gerald.: Ground-water Resources.
   Martin, R. O. R.: Surface-Water Resources.

15 Ground-Water Resources of the Southern Maryland Coastal Plain. Otton, E. G. 347 p., 35 tables, 25 figs., 15 pls., 1955. Price: $5.00 (cloth).

16 Water Resources of Somerset, Wicomico and Worcester Counties, 535 p., 48 tables, 53 figs., 17 pls., 1955. Price: $5.00 (cloth).
   Rasmussen, Wm. C. and Slaughter, T. H.: Ground-Water Resources.
   Bennett, R. R. and Meyer, R. R.: Salisbury Area.
   Hulme, A. E.: Surface-Water Resources.

17 Water Resources of Baltimore and Hartford Counties. 233 p., 24 tables, 26 figs., 11 pls., 1956. Price: $2.00 (paper); $3.00 (cloth).
   Dingman, R. J. and Ferguson, H. F.: Ground-Water Resources of Piedmont part.
   Martin, R. O. R.: Surface-Water Resources.

18 Water Resources of Caroline, Dorchester and Talbot Counties. 465 p., 56 tables, 16 figs., 17 pls., 1956. Price: $5.00 (cloth).
   Rasmussen, Wm. C. and Slaughter, T. H.: Ground-Water Resources.
   Hulme, A. E.: Surface-Water Resources.
   Murphy, J. J.: Salinity Studies in Estuaries of the Eastern Shore.

19 Geography and Geology of Maryland. Vokes, Harold E. 243 p., 12 tables, 32 figs., 28 pls., 1956 (Revised edition 1968). Price: $2.50 (cloth).

21 Water Resources of Cecil, Kent and Queen Anne's Counties. 478 p., 58 tables, 18 figs., 13 pls., 1958. Price: $5.00 (cloth).
   Overbeck, R. M. and Slaughter, T. H.: Ground-Water Resources.
   Hulme, A. E.: Surface-Water Resources.

22 Water Resources of Carroll and Frederick Counties. 355 p., 37 tables, 35 figs., 5 pls., 1958. Price: $3.00 (cloth).
   Meyer, Gerald: Ground-Water Resources.
   Beall, R. M.: Surface-Water Resources.

24 Water Resources of Allegany and Washington Counties. 408 p., 49 tables, 25 figs., 9 pls., 1961. Price: $4.00 (cloth).
   Slaughter, T. H.: Ground-Water Resources.
   Darling, John M.: Surface-Water Resources.

25 Maryland Streamflow Characteristics, 136 p., 6 tables, 14 figs., 1962. Price: $3.00 (cloth).
   Darling, John M.: Flood Frequency, Low Flow Frequency and Flow Duration.

26 Ground-Water Supplies for Industrial and Urban Development in Anne Arundel County. 90 p., 28 tables, 13 figs., 22 pls., 1962. Price: $4.00 (cloth).
   Mack, F. K.: Ground-Water Supplies.
   Richardson, C. A.: Chemical Character.

29 Ground-Water in Prince George's County. 101 p., 15 tables, 40 figs., 1966. Price: $2.00 (paper). Mack, F. K.

30 Availability of Ground Water in Charles County. 100 p., 14 tables, 31 figs., 1968. Price: $3.00 (paper); $4.00 (cloth).
   Slaughter, T. H. and Otton, E. G.
   Laughlin, C. P.: Chemical Character of the Water.

REPORTS OF INVESTIGATIONS

R.I. 1 Chemical Quality of Water and Trace Elements in the Patuxent River Basin. 52 p., 13 figs., 11 tables. Price: $1.00 (paper). Heidel, S. G. and Frenier, W. W.

R.I. 3 Water Resources of the Salisbury Area, Maryland, 1968: Boggess, D. H., Gardner, R. A., Heidel, S. G. Price: $3.00 (paper).

R.I. 5 Chemical Quality Reconnaissance of Water of Maryland Streams. 61 p., 33 figs., 1966. Price: $2.00 (paper). Thomas, Jolly D.

R.I. 8 Piedmont and Coastal Plain Geology along the Susquehanna Aqueduct: Baltimore to Aberdeen, Maryland. Price: $2.00 (paper). Cleaves, E. T.

R.I. 9 Chemical and Physical Character of Municipal Water Supplies in Maryland. 52 p., 1 fig., 70 tables, 1969. Price: $1.00 (paper). Thomas, J. D. and Heidel, S. G.

R.I. 10 Ground Water Occurrence in the Maryland Piedmont. 56 p., 27 figs., 1 pl., 9 tables. Price: $2.50 (paper). Nutter, L. J. and Otton, E. G.

R.I. 13 Extent of Brackish Water in the Tidal Rivers of Maryland. 45 p., 18 figs., 12 tables. Price: $1.50 (paper). Webb., W. E. and Heidel, S. G.

WATER RESOURCES: BASIC DATA REPORTS

B.D.R. 1 Records of Wells and Springs in Baltimore County, Md. 406 p., 1966. Price: $6.00 (paper). Laughlin, C. P.

B.D.R. 2 Records of Wells and Springs, Chemical Analyses, and Selected Well Logs in Charles County, Md. 93 p., 1966. Price: $4.00 (paper). Slaughter, T. H. and Laughlin, C. P.

B.D.R. 3 Hydrogeologic Data from the Janes Island State Park Test Well (1,514 feet), Somerset County, Maryland. 24 p., 11 figs., 13 tables, 1967. Price: $2.50 (paper). Hansen, H. J.

B.D.R. 4 Southern Maryland — Records of selected wells, water levels, and chemical analyses of water and U. S. Geol. Survey Hydrologic Atlas HA-365. Reports by Weigle, J. M., Webb, W. E. and Gardner, R. A. Price: $5.25 (paper).

INFORMATION CIRCULARS

*I.C. 4 The Electric Log: Geophysics' Contribution to Ground Water Prospecting and Evaluation. Hansen, H. J.

I.C. 9 Traveltime and Concentration Attenuation of a Soluable Dye in the Monocacy River, Md. Price: $0.75 (paper). Taylor, K. R.

VOLUMES

*Volume X 563 p., 96 figs., 1918.

Part 1 Clark, W. B. The Geography of Maryland. 127 p.

Part 2 Clark, W. B., Mathews, E. B., and Berry, E. W. The Surface and Underground Water Resources of Maryland, including Delaware and the District of Columbia. 372 p. Price: $0.50 (paper); $1.00 (cloth).

*Volume XII 336 p., 16 pls., 9 figs., 1928. Price: $1.00 (paper).

Appendix Report on the Location of the Boundary Line along the Potomac River between Virginia and

Maryland, in accordance with the Award of 1877, by Mathews, E. B., and Nelson, W. A. 48 p. Price: $0.25 (cloth).

EDUCATIONAL SERIES NO. 2

Water in Maryland: A Review of the free State's liquid assets. (in press) Walker, P. N.

SPECIAL PUBLICATIONS

Ground Water Aquifers and Mineral Commodities of Maryland. 36 p., 16 maps (1 inch equals 15 miles). Price: $0.50 (paper).

MISCELLANEOUS

Reprints:

An Ancient Buried River Channel is Discovered. Free. Hansen, H. J.

*Shore Erosion Control in Tidewater Maryland. Slaughter, T. H.

Zoning Plan for Managing a Coastal Plain Aquifer. (technical) Free. Hansen, H. J.

GOVERNOR'S SPECIAL COMMITTEE TO STUDY SHORE EROSION.

A Shore Erosion Policy for Maryland. Annapolis, Maryland, December 1961. 63 p.

SPECIAL COMMISSION TO STUDY THE WATER RESOURCES PROBLEM IN MARYLAND.

Water in Maryland; a Preliminary Report on the Water Resources Problem in Maryland. Prepared at the Request of the General Assembly of Maryland. January 1956. 50 p.

WATER RESOURCES RESEARCH CENTER
Shriver Laboratory
University of Maryland
College Park, Maryland 20742

Annual Report — Program Activities. 1964-65 to date.

Maryland Water Law. Water Laws and Legal Principles Affecting the Use of Water in Maryland. By Paul M. Galbreath. 1965. 87 p.

Maryland's Role in Water Resources Development — A Study. Prepared for the Water Resources Study Committee, University of Maryland, by Lyle E. Craine, School of Natural Resources, the University of Michigan. 1966. 85 p.

Water Resources and Steam Generation of Electricity. Seminar Proceedings. Joint Sponsors: Water Resources Research Center, University of Maryland, and Potomac Electric Power Company, Washington, D. C. November 21, 1966. 76 p. 23 figs.

Water Resources Management in Maryland — A Study. Prepared for the Maryland Department of Water Resources by the Water Resources Study Committee, University of Maryland. August 1967. 87 p.

MASSACHUSETTS

MASSACHUSETTS DEPARTMENT OF NATURAL RESOURCES

Division of Marine Fisheries
100 Cambridge Street
Boston, Massachusetts 02202

Note: Copies of out of print publications are on file at the State Library, State House, Boston, Massachusetts.

EDUCATIONAL SERIES

*Hutton, R. F. and F. C. Wilbour, Jr., 1964. The Massachusetts marine fisheries advisory commission. 19 p.

*Hutton, R. F. 1964. Coastal alterations. 8 p.

*Marine Fisheries Advisory Commission 1961. Final report on the studies of Massachusetts marine fisheries problems. 14 p.

LEGISLATIVE STUDIES

*Fiske, J. D. 1963. Report of the Department of Natural Resources relative to the coastal wetlands in the Commonwealth and certain shellfish grants (under chapter 75 of the resolves of 1962). Senate Document No. 635, 22 p.

*Fiske, J. D. 1964. Report of the Department of Natural Resources relative to the coastal wetlands in the Commonwealth (under chapter 15 of the resolves of 1963). Senate Document No. 855, 77 p.

PROFESSIONAL MONOGRAPH SERIES

Jerome, W. C., A. P. Chesmore, C. O. Anderson, Jr., and F. Grice. 1965. A study of the marine resources of the Merrimack River estuary. Monograph No. 1, 90 p.

Jerome, W. C., A. P. Chesmore, and C. O. Anderson, Jr. 1966. A study of the marine resources of Quincy Bay. Monograph No. 2, 62 p.

Fiske, J. D., C. E. Watson, and P. G. Coates. 1966. A study of the marine resources of the North River. Monograph No. 3, 53 p.

*Jerome, W. C., A. P. Chesmore, and C. O. Anderson, Jr., 1967. A study of the marine resources of Beverly-Salem Harbor. Monograph No. 4, 74 p.

*Fiske, J. D., C. E. Watson, and P. G. Coates. 1967. A study of the marine resources of Pleasant Bay. Monograph No. 5, 56 p.

Jerome, W. C., A. P. Chesmore, and C. O. Anderson, Jr. 1968. A study of the marine resources of the Parker River—Plum Island Sound estuary. Monograph No. 6, 79 p.

Fiske, J. D., J. R. Curley, and R. P. Lawton. 1968. A study of the marine resources of the Westport River. Monograph No. 7, 52 p.

SCIENTIFIC CONTRIBUTIONS

*Alperin, I. M. 1967. Marine fisheries and geophysical exploration, a review. 42 p. mimeo.

Chesmore, A. P. and A. E. Peterson, Jr. 1970 Massachusetts estuarine and protection programs. 16 p. mimeo.

Collins, G. B. 1950. The Bournedale fishway at Cape Cod Canal. 8 p.

MASSACHUSETTS DEPARTMENT OF PUBLIC HEALTH

Division of Environmental Health
Room 320
600 Washington Street
Boston, Massachusetts 02111

Report of Routine Chemical and Physical Analyses of Public Water Supplies in Massachusetts, 1969. Part I – Ground Water Analyses; Part II – Surface Water Analyses. 87 p.

MASSACHUSETTS STATE LEGISLATIVE RESEARCH COUNCIL

Boston
Massachusetts

Note: For information regarding availability of copies, please write to Documents Room, State House, Boston, Massachusetts.

Report relative to water shortage and industrial water use and reuse. April 1966. 163R (Senate No. 930).

MASSACHUSETTS STATE METROPOLITAN DISTRICT WATER SUPPLY COMMISSION

20 Somerset Street
Boston, Massachusetts 02108

Annual Report. 1926-1947. (Massachusetts Public Document No. 147). No longer issued.

Special report relative to improvements in distribution and to adequate prevention of pollution of sources of water supply of the Metropolitan Water District. 1938. 213 p. (House no. 262).

THE MASSACHUSETTS WATER RESOURCES COMMISSION

100 Cambridge Street
Boston, Massachusetts 02202

SPECIAL LEGISLATIVE REPORTS OF THE COMMISSION

*House No. 3123   Report Relative to the Water Resources and Sewerage Disposal Facilities of Plum Island within the Town of Newbury and the City of Newburyport. June, 1958.

House No. 2791   Report Relative to Methods of Providing an Adequate Water Supply to the Cities and Towns of the Commonwealth During a Period of Drought or other Emergency. December, 1958.

*House No. 3120   Report Relative to Flood Control Works in the Watershed of the Concord, Sudbury and Assabet Valley. January, 1961.

*House No. 2977   Report Relative to the Water Resources in the Watershed of the Concord, Sudbury and Assabet River Valleys. January, 1961.

*House No. 3444   Report Relative to State Aid to Cities and Towns for Municipal Sewage Treatment. December, 1961.

*House No. 3654   Report Relative to the Water Resources in the Watershed of the Concord, Sudbury and Assabet River Valleys. December, 1964.

Senate No. 937   Report Relative to the Water Resources of the Westfield River Valley. January, 1965.

House No. 3774   Report Relative to the Water Resources in the Counties of Plymouth and Bristol and in Certain Towns in the County of Norfolk. January, 1965.

House No. 4049   Report Relative to the Water Resources of Bristol and Plymouth Counties. January, 1965.

*House No. 4100   Report Relative to the Public Water Supply Resources of the Ipswich River. January, 1965.

House No. 3866   Report Relative to Authorizing the Department of Public Works to Improve the Braintree Great Pond in the Towns of Braintree and Randolph. February, 1965.

House No. 5170   Special Report of the Water Resources Commission Relative to the Water Supply of Berkshire County. January, 1967.

House No. 4015   Special Report of the Division of Water Resources in the Department of Natural Resources Authorized to Make an Investigation and Study Relative to Authorizing the Formation of Water and Sewer Districts. December, 1967.

Senate No. 1177   Report of the Water Resources Commission on an Investigation and Study Relative to Water Resources in the Towns of Braintree, Randolph, and the Surrounding Area. April, 1967.

Senate No. 374   Report of the Water Resources Commission Relative to a Study of the Water Supply of the Berkshire County Region. December, 1965.

House No. 1300   Report of the Special Commission Directed to Study the Use of Certain Lands and Waters in the Commonwealth for Recreational Purposes. December, 1934. Reprinted 1969.

OTHER SPECIAL LEGISLATIVE REPORTS OBTAINABLE FROM THE COMMISSION

Senate No. 600   Report by a Special Commission Relative to the Development and Use by Cities and Towns of Water Systems and Sources of Water Supply. March, 1949.

Senate No. 665   Report of the Department of Public Health Relative to the Preservation of the Purity of Certain Water Supplies Within the Commonwealth. December, 1956.

Senate No. 695   Report by the Legislative Research Council Relative to Rights to Surface and Sub-Surface Water in Massachusetts. February, 1957.

House No. 2627   Report by the Legislative Research Council Relative to State Licensing and Control of the Use of Tidelands. January, 1959.

*Senate No. 745   Report of the Special Commission Relative to Authorizing the City of Brockton to Extend its Source of Water Supply. March, 1964. (Appendix A of this report amended by Senate No. 814 – April, 1964).

House No. 3733   Report of the Department of Public Health Relative to the Preparation of Plans and Maps for the Disposal of Sewage in the Merrimack River Valley. June, 1964.

House No. 3567   The Advisability of Preserving the Wetlands, so-called, of the Neponset River Valley for Certain Purposes. January, 1964.

House No. 5143   Special Commission Established to make an Investigation and Study Relative to Improving the Recreational Facilities and Expanding the Recreation, Travel, Vacation and Tourist Industry of the Commonwealth. June, 1967.

Senate No. 691   Legislative Research Council on Historic Preservation Program for Cities and Towns. January, 1966.

COMMISSION REPORTS

A Summary of Massachusetts State Laws, Policies and Programs Pertaining to Water and Related Land Resources, 1969.

Appendix J — Comprehensive Water and Related Land Resources Investigation, Connecticut River Basin. 1969.

Division of Water Resources, Annual Report.

Compilation and Summarization of the Massachusetts General Laws, Special Laws, Pertinent Court Decisions, etc. Relating to Water and Water Rights. 1970.

COMMISSION BULLETINS

1 Report on Ground Water in the Mattaposett River Valley. May, 1960.

2 Coastal Flooding in Barnstable County, Cape Cod, Massachusetts. March, 1963.

3 Water Resources in Barnstable County, Cape Cod, Massachusetts. July, 1963.

COMMISSION INFORMATION CIRCULARS

1 Preventing Water Shortages. April, 1965.

2 Legislative Information Release. April, 1967.

SPECIAL REPORTS PREPARED FOR THE COMMISSION

Division of Water Resources, Massachusetts Water Resources Commission, Report on Water Resources Management. 1968.

Hydrology Studies in Massachusetts. 1964.

Yield of Streams in Massachusetts. March, 1967.

Preliminary Report on Development of Mathematical Model for Ipswich River. May, 1968.

BASIC DATA REPORTS — MASSACHUSETTS GROUND WATER SERIES

These reports are prepared cooperatively with the U. S. Geological Survey and include records of wells and test holes, chemical analyses of water, etc.

1 Wilmington-Reading Area. 1961.

2 Lower Ipswich River Drainage Basin. 1962.

3 Lowell Area. 1962.

4 Parker and Rowley River Basins. 1962.

5 Brockton-Pembroke Area. 1962.

6 Western Massachusetts Area. 1962.

7 Southeastern Massachusetts. 1963.

8 Assabet River Basin. 1964.

9 Housatonic River Basin. 1966.

10 Northern Part Ten Mile & Taunton River Basins. 1967.

11 Millers River Basin. 1967.

12 Taunton River Basin. 1970.

GROUND WATER FAVORABILITY MAPS
(Generalized surficial geology)

This work is done cooperatively with the U. S. Geological Survey.

Brockton-Pembroke Area. 1961.

Ware-Quaboag-Quinebaug-Fresh Rivers. 1962.

Water Problems in the Springfield-Holyoke Area. 1962. (Water-Supply Paper 1670).

Geology and Ground-Water Conditions in the Wilmington-Reading Area. 1964. (Water-Supply Paper 1694).

Synopsis of Water Resources of the Ipswich River Basin. 1964. (Hydrologic Investigations Atlas HA-196).

Westfield River Basin. 1965.

Housatonic River Basin. 1966.

Connecticut River Basin — New England States. 1967. (Hydrologic Investigations Atlas HA-249).

Water Resources of the Parker & Rowley River Basins. 1967. (Hydrologic Investigations Atlas HA-247).

Flood Information for Flood-Plain Planning, by Conrad D. Bue. 1967.

Northern Part Ten Mile & Taunton River Basins. 1968. (Hydrologic Investigations Atlas HA-300).

Hydrology and Water Resources of the Housatonic River Basin. 1968. (Hydrologic Investigations Atlas HA-281).

Water Resources of the Assabet River Basin, Central Massachusetts. 1969.

Water Resources of the Millers River Basin, North-Central Massachusetts and Southwestern New Hampshire. 1969.

U. S. SOIL CONSERVATION SERVICE PUBLICATIONS

This work is done cooperatively with the Mass. Water Resources Commission.

Plan of Work, Massachusetts Water Resources Study. 1969.

Water Facts (PA-337). 1964.

Teaching Soil and Water Conservation — A Classroom and Field Guide (PA-341). 1957.

An Outline for Teaching Conservation in Elementary Schools. (PA-201). 1958.

A Study of Potential Reservoir Sites in Massachusetts — Hudson River Basin. January 1958.

A Study of Potential Reservoir Sites, Housatonic Study Area. 1969.

MISCELLANEOUS PUBLICATIONS

Special Report by the Water Resources Commission on the Current Water Shortage in Massachusetts with Recommendations for Insuring Adequate Supplies During Drought Periods and for Future Use. July 15, 1965. Prepared for Governor John A. Volpe.

Compilation and Evaluation of Geophysical Data, Cape Cod, Massachusetts – Study dated June 1962. Prepared for the Commission by Weston Geophysical Research, Inc.

Report on Seismic Survey in Adams, Cheshire, Clarksburg, North Adams and Williamstown, Massachusetts. Weston Geophysical Engr. Inc: 1965.

Compilation of Geophysical Studies Conducted by Weston Geophysical Engineers, Inc. throughout Massachusetts. Part I and Part II.

Massachusetts Guidelines for the Federal Land and Water Conservation Fund. 1968. 11 p.

THE MASSACHUSETTS WATER RESOURCES COMMISSION
Division of Water Pollution Control
100 Cambridge Street
Boston, Massachusetts 02202

Water Quality Standards. Adopted by the Massachusetts Division of Water Pollution Control on March 3, 1967. 12 p.

WATER RESOURCES RESEARCH CENTER
University of Massachusetts
Room 115, Holdsworth Hall
Amherst, Massachusetts 01002

Excerpts from the 1967 Annual Report of the Center, Publication No. 2, 1967.

Proceedings of the Water Resources Research Symposium, Publication No. 3, 1967.

Shanley, Robert A., Community Leader Attitudes on Water Pollution Abatement in Selected Massachusetts Communities on the Connecticut River, Publication No. 4, 1968.

Higgins, George R., Yield of Streams in Massachusetts, 1967.

*Higgins, George R., Hydrological Studies in Massachusetts, Publication No. 6, 1968.

Motts, Ward S. and Marvin Saines, The Occurrence and Characteristics of Ground-Water Contamination in Massachusetts, Publication No. 7, 1969.

Excerpts from the 1968 Annual Report of the Center, Publication No. 8, 1969.

Erickson, Paul A. and John T. Reynolds, Vertical and Horizontal Distribution of Phytoplankton in Quabbin Reservoir, Publication No. 9, 1969.

McCann, John A., An Inventory of the Ponds, Lakes and Reservoirs of Massachusetts ... Barnstable County, Publication No. 10-A, 1969. ($1.50 prepayment required.)

CONFERENCE PROCEEDINGS

Proceedings: Municipal Watershed Management Symposium, Publication 446, 1965.

Proceedings: Water Rights Law Conference, 1966.

Proceedings: Water Resources Planning Conference, 1968.

MICHIGAN

MICHIGAN DEPARTMENT OF AGRICULTURE

Lewis Cass Building
Lansing, Michigan 48913

Michigan Watershed Projects under Public Law 566 – Questions and Answers, by Robert S. Fellows, Russell G. Hill and Eckhart Dersch. 1971.

DEPARTMENT OF NATURAL RESOURCES

Stevens T. Mason Building
Lansing, Michigan 48926

Michigan Harbors Guide. 1969. Michigan Waterways Commission, Dept. of Natural Resources.

Michigan Recreational Harbor Facilities. 1971. Waterways Division, Dept. of Natural Resources.

Michigan Water Access Sites.

Approximate Temperature Preference of Certain Michigan Fish, by Stanley Lievense. Fish Division, Dept. of Natural Resources.

OTHER

Drought Flow Characteristics of Michigan Streams, by Clarence J. Velz and John J. Gannon. June 1960. Prepared for Michigan Water Resources Commission (part of the Dept. of Natural Resources) by the Dept. of Environmental Health.

DEPARTMENT OF NATURAL RESOURCES

Geological Survey Division
Stevens T. Mason Building
Lansing, Michigan 48926

PUBLICATION SERIES
Discontinued 1958

48   I, The glacial geology and ground-water resources of Van Buren County, Michigan, (1954), 95 p., paper. Price: $1.00.

II, A Survey of the ground-water resources in Oakland County, Michigan, (1954), 247 p., paperbound. Price: $1.00.

Parts I and II above, hardbound. Price: $2.00.

BULLETIN SERIES
Supersedes Publication Series

3   The AuSable river; today and tomorrow, (1966), 80 p. Price: $0.50.

4   The glacial lakes around Michigan, (1967), 23 p. Price: $0.25.

PROGRESS REPORT SERIES
Discontinued 1962

17   Reconnaissance of the ground-water resources of Chippewa County, Michigan, (1958), 56 p. Price: $0.50.

19   Reconnaissance of the ground-water resources of Mackinac County, Michigan, (1958), 82 p. Price: $0.50.

20   Summary of ground-water investigations in the Holland area, Michigan, (1958), 87 p. Price: $0.50.

21   Reconnaissance of the ground-water resources of Luce County, Michigan, (1959), 76 p. Price: $0.50.

22   Reconnaissance of the ground-water resources of Schoolcraft County, Michigan, (1959), 84 p. Price: $0.50.

23   Ground-water hydrology and glacial geology of the Kalamazoo area, Michigan, (1960), 122 p. Price: $0.50.

24   Reconnaissance of the ground-water resources of Delta County, Michigan, (1960), 93 p. Price: $0.50.

25   Summary of ground-water conditions in the Elsie area, Michigan, (1962), 35 p. Price: $0.50.

REPORT OF INVESTIGATION SERIES
Supersedes Progress Report Series

3   Geology for land and ground-water development in Wayne County, Michigan, (1969), 31 p., 6 pls. Price: $2.00.

WATER INVESTIGATION SERIES
Established in 1963

*1   Reconnaissance of the ground-water resources of Alger County, Michigan, (1963), 55 p. Price: $0.50.

2   Ground water in Menominee County, (1963), 55 p. Price: $0.50.

*3   Water resources of Van Buren County, Michigan, (1964), 144 p. Price: $0.50.

4   Ground-water resources of the Battle Creek area, Michigan, (1966), 52 p. Price: $0.50.

5   Ground-water resources of Dickinson County, Michigan, (1966), 49 p. Price: $0.50.

7   Ground-water resources of Iron County, Michigan,
     (1967), 59 p. Price: $0.50.

8   Ground water in Gogebic County, Michigan, (1968), 32
     p., 2 pls. Price: $0.50.

9   Ground water in Ontonagon County, Michigan, (1969),
     29 p., 1 pl. Price: $0.50.

10   Ground water and geology of Keweenaw Peninsula
     (1970), 47 p., 2 pls. Price: $2.00.

PAMPHLET SERIES
Established in 1966

2   A few pointers on ground-water supplies, (1952), 32 p.
     Price: first copy free; second copy $0.10.

WELL LOGS

Copies of records for most oil and gas wells, and many water
wells. Price: $0.20 each.

DEPARTMENT OF NATURAL RESOURCES
**Water Resources Commission
Bureau of Water Management
Stevens T. Mason Building
Lansing, Michigan 48926**

*Note: File copies are maintained for reports which are out
of print. These are available for study at the Commission office.*

GENERAL INFORMATION

Water Pollution Control in Michigan.

Water Pollution Problems and Control Programs in Michigan's
Portion of the Great Lakes.

Pollution Problems Ahead, Waste Treatment Primer.

Phosphorus and Pollution – Detergents.

Enforcement Procedures of the Michigan Water Resources Commission.

Water Resources Commission – Bureau of Water Management
Organization.

1968-1970 Biennial Report, Water Resources Commission –
Bureau of Water Management.

Hydrologic Cycle Chart.

Water Pollution Control Programs in the Detroit Metropolitan
Area.

The Mercury Pollution Problem in Michigan and the Lower
Great Lakes Area, September 1970.

How Your Michigan Water Resources Commission Protects
Michigan's Lakes and Streams.

Michigan Water Resource Needs – Michigan State University
Study.

Excerpts from a summary statement: Eutrophication Conditions
and Needs in Lake Michigan, by A. F. Bartsch, Director, Pacific
Northwest Water Laboratory.

Physiography of the Great Lakes. 1961.

Stream Life and the Pollution Environment. 1959. (technical
paper reprint)

Water Pollution Control, Lake Michigan. 1969.

SPEECHES

Local Government Responsibility in Water Pollution Control –
Billings.

Facing Our Water Pollution Problems – Purdy.

LAWS

Act 245 of 1929 as amended (Water Pollution Control Act).

Summary of Act 245.

Act 167 of 1970 (Watercraft Pollution Control).

Summary of Act 167:
        Rules.
        Michigan Pumpout Stations.

Act 136 of 1969 (Industrial Waste Haulers Licensing).

Act 200 of 1970 (amendment to 245, Truth in Pollution Act).

Summary of Act 200.

Act 127 of 1970 (right of individuals to sue polluters).

Summary of Act 127.

Act 291 of 1965 as amended (Inland Lakes and Streams Act).
(See other related laws listed under Hydrological Survey.)

Act 245 of 1970 (Shorelands Protection and Management Act).

EDUCATIONAL MATERIAL

Water – Projects for Classroom, Laboratory or Field Trip.

Freddie, the Tortured Trout (for elementary school children).

Water Stories – reprints (for elementary school children):
        Bright Eyes the Lake.
        Tinkle the Brook.
        Slinky the Groundwater.

WATER QUALITY CONTROL –
COMPREHENSIVE STUDIES

Annual Waste Water Control Status Report (Industrial and
Commercial).

ENFORCEMENT CONFERENCES

Report on Water Pollution Control in the Michigan Portion of
the Lake Superior Basin and its Tributaries. May 1, 1969.

For the Reconvened Conference, Second Session, on Pollution
of the Interstate Waters of Lake Superior and its Tributary
Basin. April 1970.

For the Reconvened Conference, Third Session, on Pollution of the Interstate Waters of Lake Superior and its Tributary Basin. August 1970.

*Report on Water Pollution Control in the Michigan Portion of the Lake Michigan Basin and its Tributaries. January 31, 1968.

Interim Dates for Compliance with Recommendations of the Reconvened Session of the Lake Michigan Enforcement Conference.

Pollution of Lake Michigan and its Tributary Basins – Second Session. February 1969.

Pollution of Lake Michigan and its Tributary Basins – Third Session. March 31, 1970.

For the Reconvened Fourth Session on Pollution of the Interstate and Ohio Intrastate Waters of Lake Erie and its Tributaries (Indiana, Michigan, New York, Ohio, and Pennsylvania). May 1968.

For the Reconvened Fifth Session on Pollution of the Interstate and Ohio Intrastate Waters of Lake Erie and its Tributaries (Indiana, Michigan, New York, Ohio and Pennsylvania). June 1969.

For the Reconvened Sixth Session on Pollution of the Interstate and Ohio Intrastate Waters of Lake Erie and its Tributaries (Indiana, Michigan, New York, Ohio and Pennsylvania). May 1970.

RIVER REPORTS
See also River Basin Report Series

Black River at Croswell, Michigan, A Water Quality Study During Fall and Winter Months. November 1969.

Cass River, Oxygen Relationships, Downstream from Caro, Michigan. January 1971.

Cass River, Oxygen Relationships, Frankenmuth to Bridgeport. 1960 Survey.

*Clinton River, Self Purification Capacities – 1958 Survey. Pontiac to Rochester.

Ecorse River – Water Quality Study. May–June, 1969.

Escanaba River, Lower, Oxygen Relationships. Aug., 1967 Study.

Escanaba River, Lower, Oxygen Relationships, Spring-Fall & Winter Conditions.

Flint River, Water Quality Study. Sept., 1970.

*Flint River, Report on Oxygen Relationships, 1959 Survey, Flint to Montrose. April, 1960.

Flint River Tributaries, Water Quality Study, Flint, Michigan. April, 1970.

*Grand River, below Jackson, Report on Oxygen Relationships. 1962 Survey.

Grand River, Jackson, Mich., Review of Oxygen Relationships. April, 1965.

Menominee River Basin, Report on Water Pollution Control in the Mich. Portion. Nov. 1963.

Pine River Water Quality Study, 1967-1970.

Paw Paw River, Water Resource Conditions and Uses. 1955.

*Portage Creek – Escanaba – Water Quality Evaluation of the Lower Portion, 1968.

River Rouge Basin, Middle, Water Quality Relationships. 1964.

River Rouge Basin, Middle, Water Quality Evaluation. 1967.

Rogue River, Report on Oxygen Relationships. 1964.

Saginaw River, Water Quality Study. July & October 1965.

Shiawassee River, Oxygen Relationships. 1968.

*Report On Waste Assimilation Capacity, Tittabawassee River below Midland, Michigan. Nov., 1968.

*Report On Self Purification Capacities, Kalamazoo River, 1956 Survey, Comstock to Trowbridge. March, 1958.

*The Significance of Nitrification in Stream Analysis, Effects on the Oxygen Balance.

*Review of Oxygen Relationships in the Grand River, Jackson, Michigan. April, 1965.

Water Quality Study, South Branch of Tobacco River. June 1965.

*Water Quality of the Huron as Influenced by Existing Conditions and by the Proposed Impoundment in the Island Lake Recreation Area. June, 1968.

*Water Quality of the Upper Thread Creek Basin. August, 1968.

Water Quality of the Flint River Upstream from Flint as Influenced by Existing Conditions and by the Proposed Impoundment that Will Form Charles Stewart Mott Lake. 1970.

MONITORING REPORTS

Water Temperatures of Michigan's Lower Peninsula Great Lakes Beaches. 1965-1968.

Report on Bacteriological Quality of Michigan Surface Waters Along the Lower Peninsula Coastline. 1965 & 1966.

Report on Bacteriological Quality of Michigan Surface Waters Along the Great Lakes Coastline. 1967.

Report on Bacteriological Quality of Michigan Surface Waters Along the Great Lakes Coastline. 1968.

Interstate Water Quality Monitoring Program. 1967.

Water Quality Monitoring Program, Water Quality Records, 1963.

Water Quality Monitoring Program, Water Quality Records, 1964.

Water Quality Monitoring Program, Water Quality Records, 1965.

Water Quality Monitoring Program, Water Quality Records, 1966.

Water Quality Monitoring Program, Water Quality Records, 1967.

LAKE ERIE – DETROIT RIVER REPORTS

Industrial Waste Effluent Surveillance Program – Detroit River-Lake Erie Area. 1966-1967-1968 Data.

Industrial Waste Effluent Surveillance Program. Detroit River-Lake Erie Area. 1969 Data.

Water Quality Surveillance Program, Detroit River-Lake Erie. 1966-1967-1968.

Water Quality Surveillance Program, Detroit River-Lake Erie. 1966-1969 Data.

OTHER STUDIES

State of Michigan Intrastate Water Quality Monitoring Program – 1970 Water Quality of Waters Protected for Use as Domestic Water Supply Sources. March 1971.

Report to the International Joint Commission Advisory Board on Control of Pollution of Boundary Waters, Lake Superior-Huron-Erie Section Connecting Channels – Status of Compliance with IJC Objectives Based on Evaluation of 1970 Water Quality. February 1971.

A Survey of Background Water Quality in Michigan Streams. 1970.

*Great Lakes Algae Monitoring Program. 1970.

*Water Resource Uses Present and Prospective for the St. Joseph River Basin in Michigan and Water Quality Standards and Plan of Implementation. 1967.

*Water Resource Uses Present and Prospective for Lake Michigan and Water Quality Standards and Plan of Implementation. 1967.

*Water Resource Uses Present and Prospective for the St. Clair River-Lake St. Clair, Detroit River-Lake Erie, Maumee River Basin and Water Quality Standards and Plan of Implementation. 1967.

*Water Resource Uses Present and Prospective for the Menominee and Montreal River Basins in Michigan and the Other Michigan-Wisconsin Interstate Boundary Waters and Water Quality Standards and Plan of Implementation. 1967.

WATER QUALITY CONTROL – WATER QUALITY APPRAISAL

Water Quality of Selected Lakes and Streams in the Grand Traverse Bay Region. March 1971.

*Biological Investigation of Lake Muskegon Vicinity of the Westran Corporation Lake Fill, Muskegon, Michigan. February 17, 1970.

*Biological Evaluation of Ox Creek, Benton Harbor, Mich. June 3, 1969.

*Evaluation of the Nutrient Contribution of Gun Lake from the State Park Sewage Lagoon and Recreational Boat Canal.

The Cause and Control of Swimmers' Itch in Michigan.

Michigan's Major Steam Electric Generating Plant Data. Feb., 1970.

*A Secondary Fish Taint Test of Muskegon Lake with Special Tests on the Fish and Water Near Continental Motors Corporation. May, 1969.

*A Biological Evaluation of Six Chemicals Used to Disperse Oil Spills.

Taint Test of Chinook Salmon from Manistee Lake, Manistee County, Mich. Oct. 21, 1969.

The Toxic Effects of the Grandville Wastewater Treatment Plant Effluent to the Fathead Minnow, *Pimephales Promelas.* Nov. 17-21, 1969.

Fish Toxicity Studies at the Lansing Wastewater Treatment Plant on the Grand River, Jan. 9-22, 1970.

The Toxic Effects of the Lansing Wastewater Treatment Plant Effluent to the Fathead Minnow, *Pimephales Promelas,* Jan. 19-20, 1970.

The Toxicity of the Wyoming Wastewater Treatment Plant Effluent to the Fathead Minnow and the White Suckers, July 28-Aug. 1, 1970.

The Toxicity of the Wyoming Wastewater Treatment Plant Effluent to the Fathead Minnow, Dec. 8-12, 1969.

*Evaluation of the Algal Nutrient Contribution to the Barton and Kimble Lakes From the Village of Vicksburg, April 15, 1970.

Gross Beta Radiation in Lake Michigan Aquatic Biota, Vicinity of Big Rock Point Nuclear Reactor, 1960-1969.

*Evaluation of Aquatic Plant Nutrient Contributions from Point Waste Sources to the Pentwater River and Hart Lake, Feb. 27, 1970.

*Evaluation of the Algal Nutrient Contribution to Fremont Lake from the Village of Fremont, February 16, 1970.

*Evaluation of the Phosphorous Nutrient Contribution to the Thornapple River by the Village of Nashville, Dec. 17, 1969.

*Evaluation of a Proposal to Discharge Sewage Stabilization Lagoon Wastes to the St. Joseph River from the Village of Colon, Dec. 17, 1969.

Biological Studies on the Lower Manistique River and Inshore Waters of Lake Michigan, Manistique, Mich., Aug. 14 and 24, 1968 and Sept. 18, 1969.

Causes and Control of Eutrophication. 1970.

Biological Survey of the Ontonagon River and Lake Superior, in the Vicinity of Ontonagon, Mich., Aug. 15, 1968.

Biological Surveys of the Black River, Vicinity of Michigan Sugar Company, Croswell, Sanilac County, Mich., Sept. 4 and Nov. 7-8, 1968.

*Biological Monitoring of the Kalamazoo River at Saugatuck, Mich. Aug. 4, 1969.

*Wastewater and Biological Survey Grand Traverse Street Storm Drain Discharge to Thread Creek, City of Flint, Sept. 19, 1969.

*Effects of the Earl Johnson Cattle Feedlot on the Water Quality of a Drainage Stream Tributary to the Flint River, Genesee, Mich., April 10 and 19, 1969.

Discussion of "Water Quality Standards for Temperature" Talk by Robert S. Burd, Federal Water Pollution Control Administration, Aug., 1968.

Are We in Hot Water with Thermal Discharges? Fetterolf. June, 1970.

Statement of Carlos M. Fetterolf, Jr., Supervisor, Water Quality Appraisal Section, Bureau of Water Management, for the Michigan Department of Natural Resources, at the Hearing before the Subcommittee on Energy, Natural Resources and the Environment of the Committee on Commerce, U. S. Senate, to Consider the Environmental Effects of Energy Generation on Lake Michigan, March 30, 1970.

Biological Surveys of Thunder Bay and Thunder Bay River, Alpena, Mich., 1957 and 1965.

Possible Effects of the Alewife Die-off on Lake Michigan Water Quality, 1967.

Biological Surveys of the Harbor Vicinity, Lake Huron, Harbor Beach, June 6, 1958 and Aug. 5, 1965.

A Biological Survey of South Bay, Lake Superior and Observations on The Anna River, Munising, Alger County, Mich., Aug. 6, 1968.

Water Quality Survey of Lake Superior in the Marquette Vicinity, Aug. 8-11, 1968.

Biological Survey of the Iron and Brule Rivers, Iron River, Mich. to Florence, Wisc., Aug. 13-14, 1968.

Investigation of Nuisance Algae Conditions in the Huron River Lakes, Livingston County, Mich., Aug. 29, 1968.

White Lake Nutrient Survey, Muskegon County. 1967.

Limnological Data From Ten Lakes (Chemung, Crooked, Fenton, Lobdell, Ore, Ponemah, Potter, Silver, Squaw, Woodland), Genesee and Livingston Counties, Michigan. September 1965.

WATER DEVELOPMENT SERVICES

Implications of Land and Water Use Development in Michigan for Future Water Resource Policy. 1966.

General Availability and Quality of Groundwater in the Bedrock Deposits in Michigan.

General Availability of Groundwater in the Glacial Deposits in Michigan.

Water Holding Capacities and Infiltration Rates of Michigan Soils.

*The Planning Process as it Relates to the Water Resources of Michigan. 1966.

Water Resources Commission; Programs, Functions and Authority.

Great Lakes Shoreland Management and Erosion Damage Control for Michigan. 1970.

*Recommended Program for Great Lakes Shoreland Management and Erosion Damage Control. 1969.

Low Cost Shore Protection for the Great Lakes, published by the University of Michigan Lake Hydraulics Laboratory in Cooperation with Michigan Water Resources Commission.

*Status Report – Great Lakes Shore Erosion in Michigan. 1969.

Michigan Water and Related Resource Data. 1969.

Michigan's Water Resource Needs. 1969.

*Governor's Conference on Thermal Pollution. 1969.

The Water Resources of the Lower Lake Huron Drainage Basin, An Overview of Regional Water Uses. 1968.

The Water Resources of the Lower Lake Michigan Drainage Basin, An Overview of Regional Water Uses. 1968.

The Water Resources of the Upper Peninsula Drainage Area, An Overview of Regional Water Uses. 1968.

The Water Resources of the Northern Lake Michigan and Lake Huron Drainage Area, Lower Peninsula, An Overview of Regional Water Uses. 1968.

*The Water Resources of Southeastern Michigan, An Overview of Region Water Uses. 1968.

*Water Resource Uses Present and Prospective for Lake Huron and Water Quality Standards and Plan of Implementation. 1967.

*Water Resource Uses Present and Prospective for Lake Superior and the St. Marys River and Water Quality Standards and Plan of Implementation. 1967.

*Movement and Transformation of Various Phosphorus Compounds in Soils. 1967-1969.

*The Nutrient Content of Drainage Water from Agricultural Land in Michigan. 1967-1970.

*Irrigation in Michigan. 1970.

State of Michigan Clean Water Bond Grants.

WATER QUALITY STANDARDS

*Summary of Water Quality Standards for Designated Use Areas in Michigan Interstate Waters. 1968. (charts available).

*Use Designation Areas for Michigan's Intrastate Water Quality Standards. 1969. (charts available).

HYDROLOGICAL SURVEY

*Flood Conditions in the Kalamazoo Area. 1957.

Statistical Summaries of Michigan Streamflow Data. 1970. (Compiled in cooperation with U. S. Geological Survey.)

*Compilation Data for Michigan Lakes. (Compiled in cooperation with U. S. Geological Survey.)

Uniform Technique for Determining Flood Flow Frequencies. 1967.

Hydrologic Studies of Small Watershed in Agricultural Areas of Southern Michigan, Deer-Sloan Basin: *Report No. 1 – 1958; *Report No. 2 – 1960; and Report No. 3 – 1968.

Rules of the Inland Lakes and Streams Act.

Rules of Great Lakes Submerged Lands Act.

Illustrations of Applications of Great Lakes Submerged Lands Act.

Great Lakes Shoreline Problems – An Appraisal. 1957.

Flood of August, 1942, in the Ontonagon River Basin, Michigan. 1969.

RIVER BASIN REPORT SERIES

Water Resource Conditions and Use in the:

Clinton River Basin. 1953.

Flint River Basin. 1956.

Huron River Basin. 1957.

Upper Grand River Basin. 1961.

Shiawassee River Basin. 1963.

Michigan Portion of the Maumee River Basin. 1964.

Paw Paw River Basin. 1964 (Rev.).

River Raisin Basin. 1965.

AuSable River Basin. 1966.

*River Raisin Basin. 1969 Special Report.

Lower Grand River Basin. 1968.

*Tittabawassee River Basin. 1960.

FLOOD PLAIN INFORMATION REPORTS

These studies are cooperative efforts with the U. S. Army Corps of Engineers.

*Upper River Rouge at Farmington – Main Report.

Red Cedar from Michigan State University Dam in the City of East Lansing to the Straight Dam in the City of Williamston, Ingham County – Summary.

Grand, Red Cedar, Sycamore Creek – Lansing and Vicinity.

Lookinglass River, Clinton County, Michigan. 1969.

Grand River, Ingham – Jackson County Line to the Dimondale Dam.

*Clinton River, Michigan, Middle Branch in Macomb County – both Main Report and Summary; Clinton River, Michigan, North Branch in Macomb County – Summary.

LAWS

Act 288, 1967. Plat Act.

Act 167, 1968. Flood Plain Control.

Act 184, 1963. Dam Control.

Act 291, 1965. Inland Lakes and Streams Act.

Act 247, 1955. Great Lakes Submerged Lands.

Act 146, 1961. Inland Lakes Levels.

Act 200, 1957. Intermunicipality Committee Act.

Act 20, 1964. Surplus Waters Management.

Act 253, 1964. Local River Management Act.

Act 345, 1966. Inland Lake Improvement Act.

Act 143, 1959. Low Grade Iron Ore Mining.

Act 205, 1967. Irrigation District Act.

MICHIGAN STATE OFFICE OF PLANNING COORDINATION

Bureau of Policies and Programs
Second Floor, Lewis Cass Building
Lansing, Michigan 48913

WORKING PAPERS

*WP-6 Program Design for Comprehensive Water and Related Land Resources Planning in Michigan.

*WP-7 Project for Improved and Expanded Data Related to Environmental Problems in Michigan.

OTHER PUBLICATIONS

*A Summary of Water and Related Land Resources in Michigan – 1966.

*Implications of Land and Water Use Development in Michigan for Future Public Water Resource Policy.

Industrial Uses of Water.

*Lake Inventory Study.

Map of Availability of Groundwater in Glacial Deposits in Michigan.

*Map of Water-Holding Capacity and Infiltration Rates of Soils in Michigan.

*Michigan Water Resources, Public Education Program.

*The Planning Process as it Relates to the Water Resources of Michigan.

*Water Resources Planning Methodologies and Techniques Investigation.

*Water Conservation Conference, Lansing, Michigan, 1944. 118 p.

INSTITUTE OF WATER RESEARCH

Michigan State University
334 Natural Resources Building
East Lansing, Michigan 48823

TECHNICAL REPORTS

1 Red Cedar River Series: An Evaluation of Artificial Substrates for Measuring Periphyton Production, by John C. Peters, Robert C. Ball and Niles R. Kevern.

2 Red Cedar River Series: Primary Production, Energetics, and Nutrient Utilization in a Warm-Water Stream, by Alfred R. Grzenda, Robert C. Ball and Niles R. Kevern.

3 Red Cedar River Series: The Biology and Chemistry of a Warm-Water Stream, by Morris L. Brehmer, Robert C. Ball, and Niles R. Kevern.

4 Red Cedar River Series: Nutrients and Primary Production in a Warm-Water Stream, by Morris L. Brehmer, Robert C. Ball and Niles R. Kevern.

5 Water-Quality on the Kalamazoo River, by Allen W. Knight and George H. Lauff.

6 Red Cedar River Series: The Nutrient Composition, Dynamics, and Ecological Significance of Drift Material in the Red Cedar River, by Niles R. Kevern and Robert C. Ball.

7 The Stream Ecosystem. An American Association for the Advancement of Science Symposium.

OTHER PUBLICATIONS

The Red Cedar River Report I: Chemistry and Hydrology, by Robert C. Ball, Kenneth J. Linton and Niles R. Kevern. (Michigan State University Museum Publication, Biological Series Vol. 4, No. 2).

The Red Cedar River Report II: Bioecology, by Robert C. Ball, Niles R. Kevern and Kenneth J. Linton. (Michigan State University Museum Publication, Biological Series Vol. 4, No. 4).

MINNESOTA

STATE DEPARTMENT OF HEALTH
717 Delaware Street S.E.
Minneapolis, Minnesota 55440

Report of the investigation of the pollution of the Mississippi River, Minneapolis to LaCrosse, inclusive. 1928. (Minn. State Board of Health.)

Minnesota Water Supply and Pollution Problems. 1960.

Long-range water pollution control plan and program. 1963. (Minn. Water Pollution Control Commission.)

Water Quality Sampling Program. 1963.

Public water supply data. 1971. 170 p. (Not yet available).

DEPARTMENT OF IRON RANGE RESOURCES AND REHABILITATION
206 Mea Office Building
55 Sherburne Avenue
St. Paul, Minnesota 55103

The publications listed below are available from this Dept. only in limited supply. Copies may be borrowed for a short period of time. Those prepared in cooperation with the U.S. Geological Survey may also be obtained from that agency.

GOVERNOR'S CONFERENCE REPORTS

*Outlook on Minnesota's Resources – 1956

*The Future of Minnesota Resources – 1958

*The Focus of N. E. Minnesota Resources Developments – 1960

RESOURCE DEVELOPMENT

*Carey Lake Area Recreation Development – 1964

*St. Louis County Resource and Conservation Needs – 1963

*Resource Development Opportunities in Minnesota's Mid-Vacation Land – 1959

*Ely and Its Resources – 1959

*Report of the Eveleth Rural Survey – 1960

WATER

These publications were prepared by the U.S. Geological Survey in cooperation with the Dept. of Iron Range Resources and Rehabilitation.

*Municipal Water Supplies on the Mesabi and Vermilion Iron Ranges in Northeastern Minnesota – 1960

*Reconnaisance of the Geology and Ground-Water Resources in the Aurora Area, Minn. – 1960

*Ground Water Exploration and Test Pumping in the Halma-Lake Bronson Area, Kittson County, Minnesota –1960

*Geology and Water Resources of the Hibbing Area, North-Eastern Minnesota – 1968

*Ground and Surface Water in the Mesabi and Vermilion Iron Range Area, Northeastern Minnesota – 1965

*Water Resources in the Vicinity of Municipalities on the Western Mesabi Iron Range, Northeastern Minnesota – 1965

*Water Resources in the Vicinity of Municipalities on the West-Central Mesabi Iron Range, Northeastern Minnesota – 1965

*Water Resources in the Vicinity of Municipalities on the Central Mesabi Iron Range, Northeastern Minnesota – 1965

*Water Resources in the Vicinity of Municipalities on the East-Central Mesabi Iron Range, Northeastern Minnesota – 1965

*Water Resources in the Vicinity of Municipalities on the Eastern Mesabi Iron Range and Vermilion Iron Range, North-eastern Minnesota – 1965

*Reconnaisance of the Geology and Ground Water Resources in the Aurora Area, St. Louis County, Minnesota – 1966

*Exploratory Drilling for Ground Water in the Mountain Iron-Virginia Area, St. Louis County, Minnesota – 1961

*Bedrock Topography of the Eastern and Central Mesabi Range, Northeastern Minnesota – 1964

*Water and the Minnesota Iron Range – 1963

*Evaporation from Lakes and Reservoirs – 1942

DEPARTMENT OF NATURAL RESOURCES

Division of Game & Fish
Centennial Building
658 Cedar Street
St. Paul, Minnesota 55101

A biological survey of the Upper Mississippi River System, by J. B. Moyle. 1940. Fish. Res. Unit, Inves. Rept. No. 10.

Report of the investigation of biological conditions of Lakes Kabetoga, Namakan, and Crane as influenced by fluctuating water levels, by R. W. Sharp. 1941. Fish. Res. Unit, Inves. Rept. No. 30.

An investigation of Lake of the Woods, Minnesota with particular reference to the commercial fisheries, by K. D. Carlander. 1942. Fish. Res. Unit, Inves. Rept. No. 42.

Fisheries investigation and management report for Lake Vermilion, St. Louis County, by L. E. Hiner and K. D. Carlander, 1943. Fish. Res. Unit, Invest. Rept. No. 54.

Report on the effects of tube root (Rotenone) on the fish and fish-food organisms of Deer Lake, St. Louis County, by J. Dobie and J. B. Moyle. 1945. Fish. Res. Unit, Inves. Rept. No. 64.

A biological survey and fishery management plan for the streams of the St. Louis River basin, by J. B. Moyle and W. A. Kenyon. 1947. Fish. Res. Unit, Inves. Rept. No. 69.

Physical and chemical properties of taconite tailings and the effect of their disposition on the fishes of Lake Superior, by J. B. Moyle. 1947. Fish. Res. Unit, Inves. Rept. No. 75.

A reconnaissance of the Blue Earth River to determine present status of smallmouth bass and to evaluate present environmental conditions, by J. H. Kuehn. 1948. Fish. Res. Unit, Inves. Rept. No. 81.

A biological survey and fishing management plan for the streams of the Root River basin, by R. E. Johnson, J. B. Moyle and W. A. Kenyon. 1949. Fish. Res. Unit, Inves. Rept. No. 87.

1950 Nemadji River survey, by J. H. Kuehn. 1951. Fish. Res. Unit, Inves. Rept. No. 110.

A study of the suitability of abandoned granite quarries near St. Cloud, Minnesota for put and take fishing of brown and rainbow trout, by D. W. Kelley. 1951. Fish. Res. Unit, Inves. Rept. No. 141.

Report on: designated minnow lakes, by J. Dobie. 1952. Fish. Res. Unit, Inves. Rept. No. 133.

Walleye ponds 1954, by J. Dobie. 1955. Fish. Res. Unit, Inves. Rept. No. 154.

Fisheries Survey of North Branch of Zumbro River, Rice, Goodhue, and Wabasha Counties, by J. B. Moyle. 1955. Fish. Res. Unit, Inves. Rept. No. 165.

Methods used for investigating productivity of fish-rearing ponds in Minnesota, by J. Dobie and J. B. Moyle. 1956. Fish. Res. Unit, Spec. Publ. No. 2.

Preliminary investigations of Rainy Lake, 1959, by T. J. H. Bonde, C. A. Elsey and B. Caldwell. 1961. Fish. Res. Unit, Inves. Rept. No. 234.

Biological survey of Shakopee Creek Watershed, Kandiyohi, Swift, Chippewa Counties, by G. W. Larson. 1964. Special Publ. 19.

Dynamics of Minnesota fish-rearing ponds, by J. Dobie. 1965. Fish. Res. Unit, Spec. Publ. No. 34.

Influence of beaver on some trout streams along the Minnesota North Shore of Lake Superior, by J. G. Hale. 1966. Fish. Res. Unit, Minn. Fish. Inv. No. 4.

Watershed Reports. Biennial Reports of Sec. of Research and Planning.

DEPARTMENT OF NATURAL RESOURCES

Division of Waters
355 Centennial Building
658 Cedar Street
St. Paul, Minnesota 55101

Where price is listed, the publication is available from Documents Section, 140 Centennial Building, St. Paul, Minnesota 55101. Other available publications can be obtained from Division of Waters at no charge.

BULLETINS

1   Magnitude and frequency of floods in Minnesota, by C. H. Prior, 128 p., 1949. Superseded by Bulletin 12.

2   Proceedings of Minnesota conference on underground waters, 1950, 65 p.

*3   Water use problems and wildlife values, by Chester S. Wilson, 1950.

4   Some legal aspects of public and private waters in Minnesota, by V. J. Michaelson, 1951, 19 p.

*5   Surface water supplies of the Mesabi iron range, 1951, 117 p.

*6   Geology and ground water resources of the Cloquet area, Carlton County, Minnesota, by P. D. Akin and J. R. Jones, 1952, 63 p.

*7   An estimate of total water use in Minnesota for 1950 and 1975, by S. A. Frellsen, 1952, 15 p.

*8   Basic geologic and ground water data for Clay County, Minnesota, by J. W. Bingham, 1960, 138 p.

9   Graphs of ground water levels in Minnesota through 1956, by G. C. Straka and Robert Schneider, 1957, 42 p. Price: $1.15.

10   Hydrologic atlas of Minnesota, 1959, 182 p. Price: $1.15.

*11 Water resources of the Minneapolis-St. Paul metropolitan area, 1961, 52 p. Price: $1.90.

12   Floods in Minnesota, magnitude and frequency, by C. H. Prior and J. H. Hess, 1961, 142 p. (Supersedes Bulletin 1). Price: $1.15.

*13 The Minnesota River, report to the Upper Mississippi Reservoir and Minnesota River Valley Devel. Interim Commission, 1960, 34 p.

*14 Ground water in alluvial channel deposits, Nobles County, Minnesota, by Ralph F. Norvitch, 1960, 23 p.

*15 The problem of water supply for Twin and Crystal Lakes in Robbinsdale, Hennepin County, Minnesota, 1961.

16 Water resources of Minnesota, a study guide, 1962, 28 p. Price: $1.15.

17 Water use for irrigation in Minnesota, 1962, 19 p. Price: $1.15.

18 Graphs of ground water levels in Minnesota 1957-61, by G. C. Straka and W. A. Miller, 1963, 58 p. Price: $1.15.

19 Basic geology and ground-water data for Kittson and parts of Marshall and Roseau Counties, Minnesota. G. R. Schiner.

20 Power development in Minnesota, by G. H. Hollenstein, 1962, 35 p. Price: $1.15.

21 Quality of waters, Minnesota, a compilation, 1955-62, by M. L. Maderak, 1963, 104 p. Price: $1.15.

22 The St. Louis River watershed unit, 1964, 53 p. Price: $1.15.

23 Chemical quality of ground water in the Minneapolis-St. Paul area, Minnesota, by M. L. Maderak, 1965, 44 p. Price: $1.15.

24 The Lake Superior watershed unit, 1966, 61 p. Price: $1.15.

25 Inventory of Minnesota Lakes, 1968, 498 p. Price: $4.50.

TECHNICAL PAPERS

1 Correlation of ground water levels and air temperature in the winter and spring in Minnesota, by Robert Schneider, 1958, 17 p. Price: $1.15.

2 Geohydrology of the Jordan aquifer in the Minneapolis-St. Paul area, Minnesota, by B. A. Liesch, 1961, 24 p.

PUBLICATIONS DONE COOPERATIVELY WITH OTHER CITY, STATE AND/OR FEDERAL AGENCIES

Geology and ground-water resources of parts of Cass and Clay Counties, North Dakota and Minn, by P. E. Dennis, P. D. Akin, and F. G. Worts. 1949. North Dakota Water Conserv. Comm. and North Dakota Geol. Survey, North Dakota Ground-Water Studies 10. Minn. Ground-Water Studies 1.

*Water resources of the Minneapolis-St. Paul area, Minnesota, by C. H. Prior, R. Schneider and W. H. Durum. 1953. Done cooperatively with the U.S. Geological Survey and the St. Paul District, Corps of Engrs., U.S. Army. U.S. Geol. Survey Circ. 274.

Occurrence of ground waters of low hardness and of high chloride content in Lyon County, Minn., by H. G. Rodis and R. Schneider. 1960. Done cooperatively with the U.S. Geological Survey. U.S. Geol. Survey Circ. 423.

Availability of ground water in Lyon County, Minn., by H. G. Rodis. 1961. Done cooperatively with U.S. Geological Survey and Marshall Municipal Utilities, Marshall, Minnesota, U.S. Geol. Survey Circ. 444.

Hydrology of melt-water channels in southwestern Minnesota, by G. L. Thompson. 1962. Done cooperatively with the U.S. Geological Survey and the Marshall Municipal Utilities, Marshall, Minnesota. U.S.G.S. Water-Supply Paper 1809-K.

Aquifers in buried shore and glaciofluvial deposits along the Gladstone Beach of Glacial Lake Agassiz near Stephen, Minnesota, by R. W. Maclay and G. R. Schiner. 1962. Done cooperatively with the U.S. Geological Survey and the village of Stephen, Minnesota, U.S.G.S. Prof. Paper 450-D.

Geology and occurrence of ground water in Lyon County, Minnesota, by H. G. Rodis. 1963. Done cooperatively with the U.S. Geological Survey and the Marshall Utilities, Marshall, Minnesota. U.S.G.S. Water-Supply Paper 1619-N.

Geology and ground-water resources of Nobles County, and part of Jackson County, Minnesota, by R. F. Norvitch. 1964. Done cooperatively with U.S. Geological Survey and the city of Worthington, Minnesota. U.S.G.S. Water-Supply Paper 1749.

Geology and ground-water conditions of the Redwood Falls area, Redwood County, Minnesota, by G. R. Schiner and R. Schneider. 1964. Done cooperatively with U.S. Geological Survey and the city of Redwood Falls, Minnesota. U.S.G.S. Water-Supply Paper 1669-R.

Water resources of the Two Rivers watershed, northwestern Minnesota, by R. W. Maclay, T. C. Winter and G. M. Pike. 1964-65. Done cooperatively with the U.S. Geological Survey. U.S.G.S. HA-237.

Water resources of the Middle River watershed, northwestern Minnesota, by R. W. Maclay, T. C. Winter and G. M. Pike. 1965. Done cooperatively with the U.S. Geological Survey. U.S.G.S. HA-201.

Water resources of the Roseau River watershed, northwestern Minn., by T. C. Winter, R. W. Maclay and G. M. Pike. 1965-66. Done cooperatively with U.S. Geological Survey. U.S.G.S. HA-241.

Water resources of the Pomme de Terre Watershed, Minnesota, by R. D. Cotter and L. E. Bidwell. 1966. Done cooperatively with the U.S. Geological Survey. U.S.G.S. HA-220.

Water resources of the Big Stone Lake watershed, Minnesota, by R.D. Cotter and others. 1966. Done cooperatively with the U.S. Geological Survey. U.S.G.S. HA-213.

Water resources of the Mississippi Headwaters watershed, Minnesota, by E. L. Oakes. Done cooperatively with the U.S. Geological Survey.

OTHER PUBLICATIONS

A biological reconnaissance of streams tributary to Lake Superior, Baptism River to Devil Track River, by T. Surber. 1922. Manuscript Report.

*Gazetteer of meandered lakes of Minnesota. 1928.

The reaction of swamp forests to drainage in northern Minnesota, by J. L. Averell and P. C. McGrew. 1929. (The former Minn. Dept. of Drainage and Waters.)

Primary benchmarks in Minnesota. 1942. Non-Serial Publication.

Evaporation from lakes and reservoirs, a study based on 50 years' weather bureau records, by A. F. Meyer. 1942. Minn. Resources Commission but available in limited edition from Minn. Dept. of Nat. Res.

A biological survey and fishery management plan for the streams of the Lake Superior north shore watershed, by L. L. Smith Jr. and J. B. Moyle. 1944. Tech. Bull. No. 1.

The aquatic and marsh vegetation of Minnesota and its value to waterfowl, by J. B. Moyle and N. Hotchkiss. 1945. Tech. Bull. No. 3.

Objectives of water management and related papers. 1954. Presented at 8th Midwestern States Flood Control Conference, Itasca State Park, Minnesota, June 23-25, 1953.

Some aspects of the chemistry of Minnesota surface waters as related to game and fish management, by J. B. Moyle. 1954. Inves. Rept. No. 151.

Annual Summaries of Aquatic Nuisance Control in Minnesota, 1956-63.

Reports on test plot and toxicity tests to show how this work is conducted by the Division of Game and Fish. About 40 herbicides have been tested. Reports included are: (a) Summary of Aquatic Herbicide Field Tests in Minnesota in 1960; (b) Results of Aerial Application of Amitrol to Cattails, 1957; (c) Report on Results of Tests of Experimental Aquatic Herbicides to Determine Phytotoxicity, August 1957; (d) List of Chemicals with Toxicity Test Results, 1947 and 1958, and a sample copy of a toxicity test report on kuron, June 1958; and (e) Report on Survey of Aquatic Vegetation in Forest Lake, Washington County, August 1957. 1960.

Water resources of Minnesota. 1962. Code 1-9.

Minnesota Lakes, an Index and Guide. 1964.

Minnesota Outdoor Recreation Preliminary Plan. 1965.

Guidelines to governmental subdivision for receiving Land and Water Conservation Funds. 1966.

Informational Leaflets for distribution to the public on (1) Control of Aquatic Vegetation; (2) Control of Algae; and (3) Control of Swimmer's Itch and Leeches.

Project 70-A Plan and a Program for Resource Management.

VARIOUS PUBLICATIONS FROM THE SECTION OF RESEARCH & PLANNING

Preliminary report on possible influences of pollution on walleye pike reproduction in the Pine River, Cass and Crow Wing Counties, by B. R. Jones. 1956. Inves. Rept. No. 175.

Summary of Aquatic Nuisances Control in the United States in 1956. 1956.

Some aspects of the chemistry of waters and submerged soils, by J. B. Moyle. 1961. Spec. Publ. No. 7.

Limnological Studies of Hose and Echo Lakes in Superior National Forest, Lake County, Minnesota, by R. C. Micklus. 1961. Inves. Rept. No. 237.

A biological reconnaissance of the upper St. Croix River, by J. H. Kuehn, W. Neimuth, and A. R. Peterson. 1961. Inves. Rept. No. 239.

Aquatic Nuisances and Their Control in Minnesota. 1964. Information Leaflet No. 56.

A biological reconnaissance of the Snake River, by D. C. Reedstrom. 1964. Inves. Rept. No. 275.

A second Rainy Lake Report, 1957-1963, by T. J. H. Bonde, C. A. Elsey and B. Caldwell. 1965. Invest. Rept. No. 284.

MINNESOTA GEOLOGICAL SURVEY
University of Minnesota
Minneapolis, Minnesota 55455

Bulletins are available only from the University of Minnesota Press. Orders should be addressed to same, Minneapolis, Minne-

sota 55455. All other publication orders should be addressed to the Minnesota Geological Survey, with checks made payable to University of Minnesota. Those publications which are not available for sale can be consulted at most technical libraries or at the Winchell Library of Geology, Pillsbury Hall, University of Minnesota.

BULLETINS

*22 1932. The geology and water resources of northwestern Minnesota, by Ira S. Allison. 245 p., 36 figs., 36 tbls.

*26 1935. The history of the upper Mississippi River in late Wisconsin and postglacial time, by W. S. Cooper. 116 p., 4 pls., 46 figs.

*31 1944. The geology and underground waters of southern Minnesota, by G. A. Thiel. 506 p., 91 figs., 134 tbls.

*32 1947. The geology and underground waters of northeastern Minnesota, by G. A. Thiel. 247 p., 45 figs., 52 tbls.

*35 1952. The lakes of Minnesota, by J. H. Zumberge. 128 p., 2 pls., 48 figs.

37 1963. Minnesota's rocks and waters: a geological story, by G. M. Schwartz and G. A. Thiel. 366 p., 161 figs. (Revised edition). $4.00.

REPORT OF INVESTIGATIONS

RI-6 1967. Ground-water contribution to streamflow and its relation to basin characteristics in Minnesota, by E. A. Ackroyd. W. C. Walton and D. L. Hills. 36 p., 13 figs. 6 tbls. Price: $0.50.

MISCELLANEOUS REPORTS

Our land and mineral resources — a long-range plan for geologic research in Minnesota, (Published by the Minnesota Geological Survey, 1965). 37 p., 13 figs. Free.

Ground-water map of Minnesota, by G. A. Thiel and N. Prokopovich. 1954.

Geologic units and aquifers of the Minneapolis-St. Paul area, Minnesota, by J. E. Stone. 1966. Misc. Sheet.

Geologic, hydrologic, and engineering data: New Brighton quadrangle, Minnesota, by J. E. Stone. 1966. IC-3.

GOVERNOR'S ADVISORY COMMITTEE ON WATERS
This Committee is no longer in existence.

*Report. 1951. 43 p.

MINNESOTA

STATE LEGISLATURE INTERIM COMMISSION ON WATER CONSERVATION DRAINAGE AND FLOOD CONTROL

This Commission is no longer in existence.

*Report. 1955. 51 p.

STATE LEGISLATURE INTERIM COMMISSION TO STUDY THE PROBLEM OF WATER POLLUTION

This Commission is no longer in existence.

*Report submitted to the 1959 Legislature of the State of Minnesota. 1958. 40 p.

STATE LEGISLATURE UPPER MISSISSIPPI RESERVOIR AND MINNESOTA RIVER VALLEY DEVELOPMENT INTERIM COMMISSION

This Commission is no longer in existence.

*Report. 1959; 1961; 1965 and 1967. (4 volumes).

MINNESOTA OUTDOOR RECREATION RESOURCES COMMISSION

Room 324 State Capitol
St. Paul, Minnesota 55101

Private Enterprises in Outdoor Recreation. 1964. Study Rept. No. 4.

Minnesota River Valley. 1964. Study Rept. No. 7.

An accelerated program for hydrologic studies in Minnesota. 1964. Rept. No. 8.

Control of Aquatic Nuisance Organisms. 1964. Rept. No. 9.

An accelerated water resource program for the Red River Basin. 1964. Rept. No. 10.

Camping. 1964. Study Rept. No. 10.

Wildlife Lands (Wetlands). 1964. Rept. No. 11.

The St. Croix River. 1964. Study Rept. No. 11.

The Great River Road in Minnesota. 1964. Study Rept. No. 12.

Parks and Recreation. 1964. Rept. No. 12.

Planning in Minnesota. 1964. Rept. No. 13.

Water Resources. 1964. Rept. No. 14.

Legislative and Appropriation Recommendations. 1964. Rept. No. 16.

The Minnesota River Valley. 1965. Staff Study Rept. No. 7.

Recreational use of rivers and streams in Minnesota. 1965. Staff Rept. No. 9.

Recreational use of the St. Croix River. 1965. Staff Study Rept. No. 11.

MINNESOTA STATE PLANNING AGENCY

802 Capitol Square Building
550 Cedar Street
St. Paul, Minnesota 55101

TECHNICAL REPORTS

N1   Summary of Background Information for Framework Statewide Water and Related Land Resources Planning in Minnesota. 1969. 29 p.

N2   Physical Facilities Inventory. 1969. 61 p.

5   Economic Significance and Outlook, Minnesota Waterborne Transportation. 1969. 34 p.

6   Marketing Farm Crops, Minnesota Waterborne Transportation. 1969. 56 p.

7   Iron Ore and Concentrates, Minnesota Waterborne Transportation. 1969. 22 p.

PUBLICATIONS OF THE WATER RESOURCES COORDINATING COMMITTEE

*Papers Presented During Conference on Water and Related Land Resources Planning in Minnesota. 1967. 122 p. (Bulletin No. 1).

*Water and Related Land Resources Planning in Minnesota. 1967. 28 p.

*Background Information for Framework Statewide Water and Related Land Resources Planning in Minnesota. 1969. (Technical Bulletin No. N2).

Minnesota Water and Related Land Resources; First Assessment. 1970. 395 p.

Summary of Minnesota Water and Related Land Resources; First Assessment. 1970. 30 p.

Alternate Programs and Projects for Managing Minnesota's Water and Related Land Resources through the Year 2020. January 1971.

Summary – Alternate Programs and Projects for Managing Minnesota's Water and Related Land Resources through the Year 2020. January 1971.

STATE POLLUTION CONTROL AGENCY

717 Delaware Street S.E.
Minneapolis, Minnesota 55440

For copies of the following publications, please write to: Documents Section, 140 Centennial Building, Capitol Complex, St. Paul, Minnesota 55101.

Minnesota Statutes 115-116, Pollution Control Act. Passed 1967, amended 1969. Cat. No. 2-21. Price: $1.18.

Water Pollution Control Regulations 1-23. Cat. No. 3-40-73. Price: $4.25.

Solid Waste Control Regulations 1-11. Cat. No. 3-79. Price: $1.29.

UPPER MISSISSIPPI AND ST. CROIX RIVER IMPROVEMENT COMMISSION
This Commission is no longer in existence.

*Upper Mississippi River Bulletin. 1932-1944. Vol. 1-14. Published irregularly.

MINNESOTA WATER RESOURCES BOARD
Room 206
555 Wabasha Avenue
St. Paul, Minnesota 55102

Report on Water Law Study and Recommendations. 1963.

A Copy of the Minnesota Watershed Act as amended by Laws of 1965. 1965.

WATER RESOURCES RESEARCH CENTER
University of Minnesota
107 Hubbard Building
2675 University Avenue
St. Paul, Minnesota 55114

BULLETINS

1   Federal, State, & Local Agencies Concerned with Water Resources Research in Minnesota. Dec. 1965. Report of Task Group of Consulting Council.

2   Effects of Induced Streambed Infiltration on Water Levels in Wells During Aquifer Tests. June 1966. By W. C. Walton & E. A. Ackroyd.

3   The Continuous Plankton Recorder — A Review of Literature. June 1966. By T. A. Olson, T. O. Odlaug & W. R. Swain.

4   Lists of References and Selected Books Bearing on Water Resources in Minn. Dec. 1966. Prepared by W. C. Walton.

5   Water Resources Research and Educational Needs in Minnesota. March 1967. A Report of a Task Group of the Consulting Council.

6   Recharge from Induced Streambed Infiltration Under Varying Groundwater level and Streamstage Conditions. June 1967. By W. C. Walton, D. L. Hills, & G. M. Grundeen.

7   Preliminary Studies of Zooplankton Distribution with the Continuous Plankton Recorder. Dec. 1968. By W. R. Swain, T. A. Olson, and T. O. Odlaug.

8   Review & Analysis of Rainfall & Runoff Data for Selected Watersheds in Minn. Nov. 1968. By C. E. Bowers & A. F. Pabst.

9   Codified & Uncodified State Laws & Municipal Ordinances Bearing on Water & Related Land Resources in Minn. Dec. 1968. By W. C. Walton, R. A. Haik, & D. L. Hills.

10   Freezing in Forest Soils as Influenced by Soil Properties, Litter, & Snow, Jan. 1969. By D. B. Thorud and D. A. Anderson.

11   Aspects of Water Resources Laws in Minn. June 1969. By R. A. Haik, W. C. Walton, and D. L. Hills.

12   Inventory of Water Resources Research Conducted in Minn., 1963-65. June 1969. A Report of a Task Group of the Center's Consulting Council.

13   Water Pollution by Nutrients — Sources, Effects & Control. June 1969. Papers presented at 1969 Annual Meeting of Minn. Chap. Soil Conservation Soc. of Amer.

14   The Ecology of Periphyton in Western Lake Superior — Part I, Taxonomy & Distribution. Aug. 1969. By J. L. Fox, T. O. Odlaug, and T. A. Olson.

15   Graduate Education in Water Resources at the U. of Minn. — 1969. A Report of the Subcommittee of the Center's Advisory Committee.

16   Fifth Annual Report of Water Resources Research Center. Oct. 1969.

17   Water Quality Studies on the Great Lakes Based on Carbon-14 Measurements of Primary Productivity. Nov. 1969, By W. G. Parkos, T. A. Olson, T. O. Odlaug.

18   The Photosynthetic Pigments of Lake Superior Periphyton & their Relation to Primary Productivity. Jan. 1970. By L. W. Stokes, T. A. Olson & T. O. Odlaug.

19   Information Concerning Water Resources Research Center Projects. 1965-70.

20   The Potential Productivity of Fresh Water Environments as Determined by an Algal Bioassay Technique. June 1970. By J. M. Johnson, T. O. Odlaug, T. A. Olson & O. R. Ruschmeyer.

21   Proceedings of Conference on Ongoing Water Resources Research in Minn. March 1970. June 1970.

22   Proceedings of Conference on Save the Lakes Symposium. June 1970.

23   Integrating Water Quality Management Into Total Water Resources Management by Ulric P. Gibson, Conrad P. Straub, & Richard G. Bond. Aug. 1970.

24   Sixth Annual Report of Water Resources Research Center. Oct. 1970.

25   The Marginal Costs of Alternative Levels of Water Quality in the Mississippi River. Sept. 1970. By R. C. Lewis.

26   The Ecology of the Second Trophic Level in Lakes Superior, Michigan, and Huron. Oct. 1970. By W. R. Swain, T. A. Olson and T. O. Odlaug.

INFORMATION CIRCULARS

1 Water Resources Research Act of 1964

2 Office of Water Resources Research Established

3 Federal Legislation & Groundwater Development

4 Statements Concerning Education in Hydrology

5 Lists of Water Resources Oriented Courses in Various Departments of the University of Minnesota

6 Water Resources Courses Offered at Other Universities

7 The International Hydrological Decade

8 Approved Rules & Regulations Pursuant to the Water Resources Research Act of 1964

9 Trends in Water Resources Education

10 Comments on Water Resources Research Act of 1964

11 List of Selected Publications Bearing on Water Resources

12 Inventory of Faculty Research Bearing on Water Resources, 1963-1964

13 Meeting of AGU Committee on Status & Needs in Hydrology

14 14 Institutes Named to Receive Initial Allotments from Office of Water Resources Research

15 Need for Cooperative Effort and Coordination

16 Status and Needs in Ground-Water Hydrology

17 Research Needs in Surface-Water Hydrology

18 Statements Concerning the Ground-Water Resources of Minnesota

19 Statement of Water Problems in Minnesota Prepared for Senate Select Committee on National Water Resources

20 Folklore in Water Quality Parameters

21 Water Rights Development in Western States

22 A Lawyer Looks at Pollution

23 Summary Report of Senate Select Committee on National Water Resources

24 Status of Water Resources Use, Control & Planning in United States

25 Water Resources Research Institutes

26 Will there be Enough Water?

27 Effects of Competition on Efficiency of Water Use

28 Federal Organizations Which Offer Assistance in Planning, Development, Administration, and Use of Water

29 Men, Models, Methods, and Machines in Hydrologic Analysis

30 Abstracted Material on Remote Sensing of Interest to Hydrologists

31 Regulation of Water Levels in the Great Lakes

32 Effects of Population Changes on Environmental Health Problems and Programs

33 Status of International Hydrological Decade

34 Prospects for Future Water Supply in the United States

35 Economics of Ground-Water Recharge

36 Status and Needs Committee looks at Data & Instrumentation

37 Research Guidelines to Sound Watershed Development

38 Water as a Recreation & Wildlife Resources

39 Role of Land-Grant Institutions in the Development of Water Policy

40 Research Under P. L. 88-379 in Quality Aspects of Water

41 Establishing a Water Quality Management System

42 Remarks of the Honorable Walter Rogers Before the 1st Annual Conference of the Water Resources Research Institute Directors

43 Our State-Federal Water Resources Research Program

44 Water Resources Planning Act of 1965

45 Flood Damage Prevention

46 Guidelines for Research on Hydrology of Small Watersheds

47 Guide for the Development of Flood Plain Regulations

48 Guidelines for Investigations into the Quality Aspects of Water Resources Research

49 Engineering Foundation Research Conference Urban Hydrology Research

50 National Water Policies and Problems

51 Water Law: Government Discretion or Property Rights?

52 Address of R. R. Renne, Director, OWRR, Dept. of Interior, at Annual Dinner Meeting of Denver Fed. Center Professional Engineer's Group, Denver, Colo. 5-19-1966 — Our Water Problems: The Situation & Solution.

53 An Economic Approach to Coping with Flood Damage

54 References of Socio-Economic Aspects of Water Resources

55 Politics & Organization in Water Resources Administration: A Comparative Study of Decisions

56 Water Resources Commentary

57 Field Level Planning of Water Resource System

58 Institutional Environment & Water Planning

59 Water

60 Water Resources

61 Address of R. R. Renne, Director, OWRR, U.S. Dept. of Interior, At the 14th Annual Farm Business Training Conf. on Resources & Community Development, Oklahoma State Univ., Stillwater, Okla., 6-22-1966

62 Report on Areas on Defense & Space Tech. Applicable to Water Resources Research

63 A 10-yr. Program of Federal Water Resources Research

64 "Familiarity Breeds Contempt."

65 Recommendations for Watershed Research Programs

66 Limnology of Minnesota and the Dakotas

67 Sanitational Limnology

MISSISSIPPI

MISSISSIPPI AIR AND WATER POLLUTION CONTROL COMMISSION

P. O. Box 827
Jackson, Mississippi 39205

Water Quality Criteria for Interstate and Coastal Waters. Regulation 1-67A (amended March 1968). 11 p.

State of Mississippi Air and Water Pollution Control Act. 1968. 14 p.

Regulation 2-68 – Permits for Operating Disposal Systems. Adopted July 18, 1968. 2 p.

MISSISSIPPI BOARD OF WATER COMMISSIONERS

416 North State Street
Jackson, Mississippi 39201

The publications listed below were prepared by or in cooperation with the U. S. Geological Survey. Those available may be obtained by writing to the above address.

BULLETINS

56-1 Records of wells in the alluvium in northwestern Mississippi, by E. J. Harvey. 1956.

*58-1 Ground-water resources of the Jackson area, Mississippi, by E. J. Harvey and J. W. Lang. 1958.

*58-2 Summary of the water resources of the Hattiesburg, Laurel, and Pascagoula areas, Mississippi, by J. W. Lang and W. H. Robinson. 1958.

59-1 Temperature observations of Mississippi streams, by H. G. Golden. 1959.

*60-1 Minimum flows at stream-gaging stations in Mississippi, by W. H. Robinson and John Skelton. 1960.

*60-2 Low-flow characteristics, Sunflower River basin, Mississippi, by H. G. Golden. 1960.

61-2 Ground-water resources of Hinds, Madison, and Rankin Counties, Mississippi, by E. J. Harvey, J. A. Callahan, and B. E. Wasson. 1961.

*62-1 Low-flow measurements at selected sites on Mississippi streams, by John Skelton. 1962.

*62-2 Low-flow characteristics, Tombigbee River basin, Mississippi, by H. G. Golden. 1962.

63-1 Well records, logs, and water analyses, George and Jackson Counties, Mississippi, by E. J. Harvey and T. N. Shows. 1963.

*63-2 Memorandum on the water supply at Kosciusko, Mississippi, by B. E. Wasson and E. J. Harvey. 1963.

*63-5 Ground-water resources in Yazoo County, Mississippi, by J. A. Callahan. 1963.

63-6 Interim report on the hydrology of the Cockfield Formation in the vicinity of Jackson, Mississippi, by E. J. Harvey and P. E. Grantham. 1963.

63-10 Cretaceous aquifers of northeastern Mississippi, by E. H. Boswell. 1963.

*63-12 Water levels and artesian pressures in observation wells in Mississippi, by B. E. Ellison and E. H. Boswell. 1963.

*64-1 Ground-water resources of Hinds, Madison, and Rankin Counties, Mississippi, by E. J. Harvey, J. A. Callahan, and B. E. Wasson. 1964.

64-2 Water for industry in the Corinth area, Mississippi, by Roy Newcome, Jr., and J. A. Callahan. 1964.

64-4 Floods of 1961 in Mississippi, by K. V. Wilson. 1964.

*64-5 Status of salt-water encroachment in aquifers along the Mississippi Gulf Coast – 1964, by J. W. Land and Roy Newcome, Jr. 1964.

64-6 Floods of 1962 in Mississippi, by B. L. Neely, Jr. 1964.

65-1 Chemical composition of Mississippi surface waters, 1945-62, by M. W. Gaydos. 1965.

*65-2 Source and development of public and industrial water supplies in northwestern Mississippi, by B. E. Wasson. 1965.

66-1 Proposed reservoir for Old Fort Bayou at Ocean Springs, Mississippi – a preliminary study, by C. P. Humphreys, Jr. and W. L. Broussard. 1966.

67-1 Low flow in selected subbasins of the Big Black River basin, by F. H. Thomson and C. P. Humphreys, Jr. 1967.

67-2 Floods of 1963 in Mississippi, by B. L. Neely, Jr. 1967.

67-3 Water use and development in Jackson County, Mississippi – 1964-67, by D. E. Shattles, J. A. Callahan, and W. L. Broussard. 1967.

68-1 Floods of 1964 in Mississippi, by K. V. Wilson and B. E. Ellison. 1968.

68-2 Floods of 1965 in Mississippi, by K. V. Wilson and B. E. Ellison. 1968.

OTHER

Configuration of the base of the fresh-ground-water section in Mississippi, by Roy Newcome, Jr. 1965. Water Resources Map 65-1.

Water in Mississippi, by B. E. Ellison and F. M. Hester. 1969. Educational Bulletin.

MISSISSIPPI GAME & FISH COMMISSION
Box 451
Jackson, Mississippi 39205

Pollution Studies on Coastal Streams of Mississippi. Completion Report, 1964-65. By Billy J. Grantham, David Robinson and Dan Cotton.

Pollution Studies on the Pearl River. Completion Report, 1960. By Billy Joe Grantham.

Pollution Studies on the Pascagoula River. Completion Report, 1964. By Billy Joe Grantham.

Pollution Studies on the Leaf River. Completion Report, 1962. By Billy Joe Grantham.

Pollution Studies on Tombigbee River in Mississippi. Completion Report, 1969. By W. D. Cotton, David Robinson and B. J. Grantham.

Pollution Studies on the Chickasaway River. Completion Report, 1967. By W. D. Cotton, David Robinson and B. J. Grantham.

Benthic Sampling According to Specifications Cont. No. PH 86-65-48. 1966. By Billy Joe Grantham.

Flood Control Reservoirs Fisheries Investigation. Annual Report, 1967. By C. A. Schultz.

Fisheries Investigations of Flood Control Reservoirs. 1966. By C. A. Schultz.

Comparative Study of Two Oxbow Lakes. Completion Report, 1969. By Rex Bingham.

Pesticide and Chemical Studies of Two Oxbow Lakes. 1967. By Rex Bingham.

Bottom Fauna and Plankton of Two Oxbow Lakes. 1967. By Rex Bingham.

Survey of Insecticide Levels and Chemical Quality of Twenty Randomly Selected Delta Lakes. Completion Report, 1969. By Dan Cotton and Jack Herring.

Pesticide Residues of 20 Mississippi Delta Lakes. 1970. By Dan Cotton and Jack Herring.

Fisheries Investigation of Flood Control Reservoirs: by Bobby Towery.

1 Evaluation of Auto-body Fish Shelters. 1965.

2 Catch of Game Fish in Commercial Gear. 1965.

3 Experimental Stocking of White Bass. 1965.

4 Age and Size at Maturity of White Crappie. 1962.

5 Age and Size at Maturity of Largemouth Bass. 1963.

6 Creel Census. 1962, 1963, 1964 and 1965.

7 Age and Growth Studies. 1962, 1963, 1964 and 1965.

8 Chemical, Biological and Physical Data. 1958.

9 Tagging and Distribution Studies. 1958.

10 Life History Studies. 1960 and 1964.

11 Food Habit Studies. 1963.

12 Population Studies. 1962, 1963, 1964 and 1965.

13 Quarterly Report for Investigation Project. 1959, 1960, and 1961.

State-wide Lake and Stream Survey. 1960, 1961, 1962, 1963, and 1964. By E. W. Coleman.

Coastal Stream Investigations. By Barry Freeman.

Two Years of Creel Census on Three North Mississippi Flood Control Reservoirs. 1960. By Harry Barkley.

Fisheries Investigation on Flood Control Reservoirs. By Harry Barkley. 1962. (Creel Census).

Pearl River Reservoir Fisheries Investigations: by Harry Barkley.

1 Age and Growth Studies. 1964.

2 Tagging and Distribution Studies. 1964.

3 Population Studies. 1964.

4 Chemical, Physical and Biological Data. 1964.

5 Annual Progress Report. 1964.

Ross R. Barnett Fisheries Investigation: by Harry Barkley.

1 Chemical & Physical Data. 1965, 1966, 1967, and 1968.

2 Tagging and Distribution Studies. 1965, 1966, 1967, and 1968.

3 Fish Population Studies. 1965, 1966, 1967 and 1968.

4 Age & Growth Studies. 1964, 1965, 1966, 1967, and 1968.

5 Creel Census. 1966, 1967, and 1968.

6 Annual Progress Report. 1965 and 1969.

7 Completion Report. 1971.

MISSISSIPPI GEOLOGICAL, ECONOMIC AND TOPOGRAPHICAL SURVEY
P. O. Box 4915
Jackson, Mississippi 39216

Send requests for publications to the above address. Payment must accompany order.

BULLETINS

*12   Mississippi, Its Geology, Geography, Soils and Mineral Resources: E. N. Lowe, 335 p., 1915.

*14   Mississippi, Its Geology, Geography, Soil and Mineral Resources: A revision with additions of Bulletin No. 12; E. N. Lowe, 346 p., 1919.

24 Being a Series of Papers Presented by the State Geological Survey at a Meeting of the Institute on Mississippi Affairs: E. N. Lowe, 33 mimeographed pages, 1933. Price: $0.25.

55 Geology and Ground-Water Supply at Camp McCain: Glen Francis Brown and Robert Wynn Adams, 116 p. 1943. Price: $1.00.

56 Geology and Ground-Water Supply at Camp Van Dorn: Glen Francis Brown and William Franklin Guyton, 68 p. 1943. Price: $0.50.

58 Geology and Ground-Water Resources of the Camp Shelby Area: Glen Francis Brown, 72 p., 1944. Price: $0.50.

60 Geology and Ground-Water Resources of the Coastal Area in Mississippi: Glen Francis Brown and others, 232 p., 1944. Price: $1.00.

65 Geology and Artesian Water of the Alluvial Plain in Northwestern Mississippi: Glen Francis Brown, 424 p., 1947. Price: $2.00.

66 North Mississippi Floods of February 1948: Irving E. Anderson and staff, 55 p., 1948. Price: $0.50.

67 Carroll County Geology: Franklin Earl Vestal, 114 p., 1950. Price: $1.00.

68 Surface Waters of Mississippi: Irving E. Anderson, 338 p., 1950. Price: $1.00.

70 Rate of Depletion of Water-Bearing Sands: Frederic Hartwell Kellogg, 15 p., 1950. Price: $0.25.

72 Ground Water Investigations along Bogue Phalia, between Symonds and Malvina, Bolivar County: Tracy Wallace Lusk, 19 p., 1951. Price: $0.25.

77 Water Levels and Artesian Pressures in Observation Wells in Mississippi, 1938-1952; Tracy W. Lusk, 65 p., 1953. Price: $0.50.

80 Benton County Geology: Tracy Wallace Lusk, 104 p., 1956. Price: $1.00.

81 Panola County Geology: Franklin Earl Vestal, 157 p., 1956. Price: $1.00.

82 Sediments of Mississippi Sound and Inshore Waters: Richard Randall Priddy and others, 54 p., 1955. Price: $0.50.

83 Fresh Water Strata of Mississippi as Revealed by Electrical Log Studies: Richard Randall Priddy, 71 p., 1955. Price: $0.50.

87 Prentiss County Geology: William Scott Parks. Ground-Water Resources: E. B. Ellison and E. H. Boswell. 154 p., 1960. Price: $1.00.

88 Madison County Geology: Richard Randall Priddy. 123 p., 1960. Price: $1.00.

90 Public and Industrial Water Supplies in a Part of Northern Mississippi: Joe W. Lang and Ernest H. Boswell. 104 p., 1960. Price: $1.00.

92 Calhoun County Geology and Ground-Water Resources: William Scott Parks. 113 p., 1961. Price: $1.00.

95 Jasper County Mineral Resources: David A. DeVries, et al. 101 p., 21 figs., 8 pls., 2 tables, 1963. Price: $1.00.

99 Attala County Mineral Resources: William S. Parks, et al. 192 p., 32 figs., 6 pls., 12 tables, 1963. Price: $2.00

105 Hinds County Mineral Resources: William H. Moore, et al. 244 p., 50 figs., 15 pls., 16 tables, frontispiece. 1965. Price: $3.00.

110 Copiah County Geology and Mineral Resources: Alvin R. Bicker, Jr., et al. 172 p., 52 figs., pls., and tables with a surface geologic map in color. 1969. Price: $2.00.

112 Water Resources of Mississippi: Thad N. Shows. 162 p., 31 tables, 11 figs., 8 in color. 1970. Price: $2.00.

MISSISSIPPI RESEARCH AND DEVELOPMENT CENTER
P. O. Drawer 2470
Jackson, Mississippi 39205

*An Evaluation of the Water-Related Economic Resource Development of Appalachia-in-Mississippi. December 1967. 243 p. (Library copy only.)

*Mississippi Supplement: Appalachian Water Resource Plan. August 1968. 125 p. (Library copy only.)

The following are cooperative studies sponsored jointly by the Miss. Research & Devel. Center and the U. S. Geological Survey, Water Resources Division:

Available Water for Industry in Adams, Claiborne, Jefferson, and Warren Counties, Mississippi. 1964. 45 p.

Water for Industrial Development in Clay, Lowndes, Monroe, and Oktibbeha Counties, Mississippi. 1965. 39 p.

Water for Industrial Development in Forrest, Greene, Jones, Perry, and Wayne Counties, Mississippi. 1966. 72 p.

Water for Industrial Development in Covington, Jefferson Davis, Lamar, Lawrence, Marion, and Walthall Counties, Mississippi. 1968. 114 p.

Water for Industrial Development in Amite, Franklin, Lincoln, Pike, and Wilkinson Counties, Mississippi. 1970. 61 p.

Water for Industrial Development in Clarke, Jasper, Lauderdale, Newton, Scott, and Smith Counties, Mississippi. 1970. 62 p.

MISSISSIPPI WATER RESOURCES POLICY COMMISSION
This Commission is no longer in existence.

*Water for the Future in Mississippi; A Report to the 1956 Mississippi Legislature. 1955. 55 p.

*Water for the Future in Mississippi; A Proposal for Implementing the Water Policy of Mississippi. A supplement. 1956. 17 p.

WATER RESOURCES RESEARCH INSTITUTE
Mississippi State University
State College, Mississippi 39762

COMPLETION REPORTS ON OWRR PROJECTS

1966

A-001-MISS Precipitation Probabilities in Mississippi. McWhorter, Matthes and Brooks.

A-002-MISS The Significance of Water Resources as an Attraction to Industry in the Town Creek Watershed. Peden and Wilcox.

A-004-MISS Decontamination of Radioactively Contaminated Water by Slurrying with Yazoo and Zilpha Clays. William A. Goldsmith.

A-005-MISS Ground Water Regulation in the Coastal Flatwoods of Mississippi. W. Frank Miller.

A-006-MISS Law of Water Resources in the State of Mississippi. P. H. Williams.

A-008-MISS Local Action and Acceptance of Watershed Development. Kenneth P. Wilkinson.

1967

A-003-MISS Factors Affecting the Removal of Iron and Manganese from Ground Water. Robinson, Breland and Dixon.

A-007-MISS The Effect of Elevated Temperatures on the Treatment of Normal Domestic Sewage. Brown, Tischer, Ladner and Bostwick.

A-009-MISS An Inventory and Study of Beaver Impounded Water in Mississippi. Arner, Baker, Wesley and Herring.

A-011-MISS The Availability of Water for Industrial Uses in Small Communities in Mississippi. Pedan and Oliphant.

A-012-MISS Removal of Radioisotopes from Water by Slurrying with Yazoo and Zilpha Clays. Sumrall and Middlebrooks.

A-014-MISS The Law of Water Pollution Control. Williams, McDougal and Champion.

A-015-MISS Sociological Factors in Watershed Development. Wilkinson and Cole.

1968

A-010-MISS Rainfall Intensity, Frequency, and Duration of Station and Area Storms with Varying Antecedent Precipitation Amounts. McWhorter and Brooks.

A-016-MISS An Analysis of Alternative Methods of Financing Types of Water Resource Facilities in Mississippi. Peden, Pulley and Roberts.

A-017-MISS The Risk of Damage to Water Resource Projects by Unusual Physical Occurrences. Williams and Daniel.

A-018-MISS The Microbiology of Ground Water Recharge. Brown, Tischer and Broome.

A-019-MISS Social Science of Water Resources Problems: Review of Literature and Annotated Bibliography. Wilkinson and Singh.

A-020-MISS A Quantitative Study of Invertebrates Found in Certain Wetland Plant Communities in Mississippi. Arner, Wesley and Anding.

A-021-MISS Application of Moments to Mapping the Vertical Variability of the Aquifer Systems in Mississippi. Donald M. Keady.

A-022-MISS The Infiltration of Irrigation Water Into the Soil. Fox, Allen, Chang and Alcantara.

A-023-MISS The Meandering of Natural Streams in Alluvial Materials. Shindala and Priest.

1969

A-013-MISS Forest Site Amelioration in the Coastal Flatwoods of Mississippi. W. Frank Miller.

A-024-MISS A Non-dimensional Approach to the Flow of Water in Flumes and Canals. Verma and McWhorter.

A-025-MISS A Long Run Financial Planning Model for Small Water Service Utilities in Mississippi. Armenakis and Peden.

A-026-MISS The Impact of Reservoirs on Land Values: A Case Study. Williams and Daniel.

A-027-MISS The Decomposition of Petroleum Products in our Natural Waters. Brown and Tischer.

A-028-MISS Generalized Participation of Voluntary Leaders in Local Watershed Projects. Wilkinson and Singh.

A-029-MISS An Ecological and Recreational Use Survey of a Small Mississippi River just before Channelization. Arner, Anding, Lunceford and Summerour.

A-030-MISS Changes in Natural Channels Downstream from Man-Made Reservoirs. Shindala and Priest.

This report is a composite of the four publications shown below. Not available for distribution by the Institute.

Some Effects of Man-Made Controls in the Upper Reaches of a Small Drainage Basin. Shindala and Priest. *Water Resources Bulletin,* American Water Resources Assn., Vol. 5, No. 2, June 1969. p. 3.

Channel Degradation Downstream from Large Dams. Priest and Shindala, *Water Power,* Vol. 21, No. 11, London, November 1969, p. 436.

Time Required for Ultimate Channel Degradation Downstream from Large Dams. Priest and Shindala, *Water Power,* Vol. 21, No. 12, London, December 1969, p. 472.

Distance Downstream from a Large Dam to the Limit of Ultimate Channel Degradation. Priest and Shindala, 13th Congress of the IAHR, Vol. No. 5-1, Kyoto, Japan, September 1969, p. 241.

A-031-MISS Water Politics in Mississippi: A Comparative Analysis of Two Water Resource Development Organizations. McLeskey and Jones.

1970

A-032-MISS Inland Port Facilities and Economic Growth. Armenakis, Moore, and Peden.

A-033-MISS The Importance of Water Related Activities at State Parks in Mississippi. Williams and Daniel.

A-034-MISS The Effect of Salinity on the Oxidation of Hydrocarbons in Estuarine Environments. Brown, Phillips, and Tennyson.

A-035-MISS Community Leadership and Watershed Development. Wilkinson and Singh.

A-036-MISS A Study of the Aquatic Ecosystems of Two National Waterfowl Refuges in Mississippi. Arner, Norwood, and Teels.

A-037-MISS Thermal Gradients in Rivers and Reservoirs Due to Heated Plant Effluents. Shindala and Priest.

A-038-MISS A Study of the Hydrochemical Facies of the Wilcox Aquifers in Mississippi. Keady.

A-039-MISS A System Approach for the Study and Control of Factors Affecting Water Pollution. Abouel-Nour.

A-040-MISS Forage Crop Irrigation with Oxidation Pond Effluent. Allen and McWhorter.

B-002-MISS The Effect of Temperature on Water Flow in Soils. Jensen, Haridasan, and Rahi.

COMPLETION REPORTS ON STATE-SUPPORTED PROJECTS
1967

Checking the Correctness of Water Analyses with Freezing Point Depressions. Hobson and Middlebrooks.

1968

The Relation of Water Resources to the Industrial and Recreational Potential of the Mississippi Gulf Coast. Armenakis, Pearson, and Neely.

A Study of the Hydrochemical Facies of the Cretaceous Aquifers of Northeastern Mississippi. Donald M. Keady.

The Prediction of General Paths of Hurricanes. (Thesis). Edward H. Bowker.

PROCEEDINGS

Mississippi Water Resources Conference. From 1966 through 1970.

BULLETINS
1966

The Management of Beaver and Beaver Ponds in the Southeastern United States. Arner, Baker, and Wesley.

1969

Jurisdictional Problems: A Barrier to the Implementation and Coordination of Water Policy. Joel Blass.

MISSOURI

DEPARTMENT OF BUSINESS AND ADMINISTRATION

Water Resources Board
P. O. Box 271
Jefferson City, Missouri 65101

Missouri Water Plan: State Laws, Policy and Programs pertaining to Water and Related Land Resources. July 1969. 78 p. Pub. WRB 2.

Water Resource Management for an Expanding Missouri — A Prospectus for a State Water Plan. 1965. 18 p.

The Water Resources of Missouri. 12 p.

MISSOURI GEOLOGICAL SURVEY AND WATER RESOURCES

P. O. Box 250
Rolla, Missouri 65401

Remittance for publications may be by money order or check. For borrowing privileges of out-of-print publications, please contact the Survey.

VOLUMES: (2nd Series)

*20   Water Resources of Missouri 1857-1926, by H. C. Beckman, 424 p., 12 pls., base map of Missouri showing drainage basin areas, 1927. (Also contains chemical analyses of surface waters.)

26   Surface Waters of Missouri (stream-flow records) 1927-1939, by H. C. Beckman, 900 p., 1940. Price: $2.00. (Prepared in cooperation with the Water Resources Division of the U. S. Geological Survey.)

*29   The Large Springs of Missouri, by H. C. Beckman and N. S. Hinchey, 141 p., 18 pls., 3 figs., 1944.

34   Surface Waters of Missouri (stream-flow records) 1940-1949, by Harry C. Bolon, 934 p., 5 pls., including a drainage map of Missouri, 1952. Price: $2.00. (Prepared in cooperation with the Water Resources Division of the U. S. Geological Survey.)

43   Mineral and Water Resources of Missouri, by the staffs of the Missouri Geological Survey and U. S. Geological Survey, 399 p., 81 figs., 45 tables, 1967. Price: $1.00.

REPORTS OF INVESTIGATIONS

10   Insoluble Residues of some Paleozoic Formations of Missouri, Their Preparation, Characteristics and Application, by John G. Grohskopf and Earl McCracken, 39 p., 11 pls., 1949. Price: $0.25. (Discusses the economic application of residues in groundwater.)

ENGINEERING GEOLOGY SERIES

2   How to Plan a Lagoon for Disposal of Sewage and Waste, brochure, June 1969. Free.

WATER RESOURCES REPORTS

1   Water Possibilities from the Glacial Drift of Grundy County, by Fuller and Russell (multilithed), 7 p., 3 pls., 1956. Price: $0.25.

2   Water Possibilities from the Glacial Drift of Mercer County, by McMillen and Russell (multilithed), 11 p., 4 pls., 1956. Price: $0.25.

3   Water Possibilities from the Glacial Drift of Harrison County, by Fuller, McMillen and Russell, 14 p., 4 pls., 1956. Price: $0.25.

4   Water Possibilities from the Glacial Drift of Putnam County, by Fuller and McMillen (multilithed), 8 p., 3 pls., 1956. Price: $0.25.

5   Water Possibilities from the Glacial Drift of Worth County, by Fuller, McMillen, Pick, Russell, and Wells, 6 p., 3 pls., 1956. Price: $0.25.

6   Water Possibilities from the Glacial Drift of Livingston County, by Fuller, McMillen, Pick, Russell, and Wells, 14 p., 3 pls., 1956. Price: $0.25.

7   Water Possibilities from the Glacial Drift of Gentry County, by Fuller, McMillen, Pick, Russell, and Wells, 10 p., 4 pls., 1956. Price: $0.25.

8   Water Possibilities from the Glacial Drift of DeKalb County, by Fuller, McMillen, Pick, and Russell, 12 p., 3 pls., 1957. Price: $0.25.

9   Water Possibilities from the Glacial Drift of Daviess County, by Fuller, McMillen, Pick, and Russell. 13 p., 3 pls., 1957. Price: $0.25.

10   Water Possibilities from the Glacial Drift of Sullivan County, by Fuller, McMillen, Pick, and Russell, 7 p., 3 pls., 1957. Price: $0.25.

11   Water Possibilities from the Glacial Drift of Linn County, by Fuller, Martin, Pick, Russell, and Wells, 10 p., 3 pls., 1957. Price: $0.25.

12 Water Possibilities from the Glacial Drift of Charlton County, by Fuller, Martin, Pick, Russell, and Wells, 14 p., 3 pls., 1957. Price: $0.25.

13 Water Possibilities from the Glacial Drift of Carroll County, by Fuller, Martin, Pick, Russell, and Wells, 20 p., 3 pls., 1957. Price: $0.25.

14 Water Possibilities from the Glacial Drift of Buchanan County, by Fuller, Pick, Russell, and Wells, 10 p., 3 pls., 1957. Price: $0.25.

15 Water Possibilities from the Glacial Drift of Andrew County, by Fuller, McMillen, Pick, Russell, and Wells, 10 p., 3 pls., 1957. Price: $0.25.

16 Preliminary Report on the Groundwater Resources of Nodaway County, Missouri, by Heim, Martin, and Howe, 24 p., 2 pls., 1959. Price: $0.25.

17 Preliminary Report, Groundwater Resources of Holt County, by Heim, Martin, and Howe, 21 p., 2 pls., 2 figs., 1960. Price: $0.25.

18 Preliminary Report, Groundwater Resources of Atchison County, by Heim, Martin, and Howe, 20 p., 2 pls., 2 figs., 1960. Price: $0.25.

19 Floods of June 17-18, 1964 in Jefferson, Ste. Genevieve and St. Francois Counties, Missouri, by M. S. Petersen, 20 p., 9 figs., 2 tbls., October 1965. Price: $0.50.

20 Low Flow Characteristics of Missouri Streams, by John Skelton, 95 p., 1 pl., 7 figs., 3 appendices, July 1966. Price: $1.00.

21 Floods of July 18-23, 1965 in Northwestern Missouri, by James E. Bowie and E. Eugene Gann, 103 p., 4 pls., 16 figs., 4 tbls., 1967. Price: $1.00.

22 Storage Requirements to Augment Low Flows of Missouri Streams, by John Skelton, with a section on seepage losses by James H. Williams, 78 p., 1 pl., 6 figs., 1 table, 1968. Price: $1.00.

23 Magnitude and Frequency of Missouri Floods, by E. H. Sandhaus and John Skelton, 276 p., 1 pl., 2 figs., 2 tbls., 1968. Price: $2.00.

24 Water Resources of the Joplin Area, Missouri, by G. L. Feder, et al., x + 98 p., 1 pl., 28 figs., 11 tbls., 1969. Price: $1.00.

MISCELLANEOUS PUBLICATIONS

*2 Chemical Analyses of River and Spring Waters, by H. W. Mundt and W. D. Turner, 15 p., 1929. (Later incorporated as Chapter 5, p. 393-407, in Volume 20, 2nd Series, 1927.)

*10 The Truth About Ground Water, by Garrett A. Muilenburg (multilithed), 6 p., 1956. (Presented at the 18th Annual Convention, Conservation Federation of Missouri, Boonville, April 22, 1956.)

*12 A Brief Discussion of Some of the Determinations Made in a Chemical Water Analysis, by W. B. Russell (multilithed), 8 p., 1957.

16 Water Wells in the Glacial Drift of North Missouri, by W. B. Russell (multilithed), 6 p., 1957. No charge.

BIENNIAL REPORTS

Biennial Report of the State Geologist to the 55th General Assembly, by H. A. Buehler, 112 p., 6 pls., 3 appendices, 1929. Price: $0.50.

*Appendix 2. Automatic Water Sampler, by H. W. Mundt, p. 100-101, pl. 4.

*Biennial Report of the State Geologist to the 58th General Assembly, by H. A. Buehler, 56 p., 1 pl., 1 fig., 7 appendices (separately paged), 1935.

*Appendix 5. Underground Waters in St. Louis County and City of St. Louis, Missouri, by Charles D. Gleason, 24 p., 5 pls., 1 fig.

Appendix 7. Pre-Glacial Drainage Pattern of Northwest Missouri, by F. C. Greene and R. M. Trowbridge, 7 p., 1 pl. Price: $0.10.

REPRINTS

*2 Ground Water Supplies in Missouri, Article 1, by John G. Grohskopf, 5 p., 1945. (Reprinted from Journal of the Missouri Water and Sewerage Conference, Vol. 16, No. 4, p. 54-58, October 1945.)

3 Ground Water Supplies in Missouri, Article 2, by John G. Grohskopf, 12 p., 4 figs., 3 tables, 1946. (Reprinted from Journal of the Missouri Water and Sewerage Conference, Vol. 17, No. 2, p. 46-57, April 1946.)

MAPS

Topographic Maps

Gasconade River Topographic Maps (Arlington to Rich Fountain), topography by F. W. Hughes and F. L. Whaley. Scale: 4 inches equals 1 mile. Contour interval 10 feet. 1923. Five sheets (4 plans, 1 profile). (Shows topography of the Gasconade River flood plain from Arlington to Rich Fountain, Missouri.)

Water Resources Maps

Reservoirs and Stream Gauging Station Map. Scale: 1 inch equals 18 miles. 1940. One sheet. Price: $0.10. (Compiled in cooperation with the U. S. Geological Survey.)

*Water Resources Map. Scale: 1 inch equals 12 miles. (No date.) One sheet.

Groundwater Maps of Missouri (packet), includes four maps listed below. Price: $1.00. (Or sold individually.)

1 Water Well Yield Map of Missouri, with well data, by Charles E. Robertson. Scale: 1 inch equals 12 miles. One sheet and one booklet. 1962. Price: $0.25.

2 Groundwater Quality Map of Deep Aquifers in Missouri, by Dale L. Fuller. Scale: 1 inch equals 12 miles. One sheet. 1962. Price: $0.25.

3 Groundwater Areas in Missouri, by Robert D. Knight. Scale: 1 inch equals 12 miles. One sheet. 1962. Price: $0.25.

4 Map of Bedrock Topography of Northwestern Missouri, by George E. Heim and Wallace B. Howe. Scale: 1 inch equals 5 miles. One sheet. 1962. Price: $0.25.

Lake and Reservoir Map of Missouri. Scale: 1 inch equals 8 miles. 1966. One sheet. Price: $0.75. Compiled by Dale L. Fuller in cooperation with Missouri Dept. of Conservation and other governmental agencies.

PUBLICATIONS OF FORMER SURVEYS

*19   Volume III, A Report on the Mineral Waters of Missouri, by Paul Schweitzer, including notes of A. E. Woodward, 256 p., 33 pls., 11 figs., 1 map, 8 vo. cloth. Jefferson City, December 1892.

WATER RESOURCES RESEARCH CENTER
University of Missouri
424 Clark Hall
Columbia, Missouri 65201

Barnekow, Russell G. Jr., Biochemical Capabilities of Surface Filming Benthic Bacteria in Fresh Water Systems. Water Resources Research Center Publication No. 3, University of Missouri, 1967. (A-005-Mo.)

Campbell, R. S., Arthur Witt, Jr. and J. R. Whitley, Possibilities for Beneficial Uses of Heated Water Discharges Into Cooling Reservoirs. Office of Water Resources Research, USDI, Report on 5th Annual Water Resources Research Conference, Washington, D. C., pp. 57-64, 2-3-70. 1970. (A-020-Mo.)

Decker, W. L., Irrigation in Missouri: Missouri's Demand for Irrigation Water to Climatic Setting. Minutes of the 156th Meeting of the Missouri Basin Inter-Agency Committee, Jefferson City, Missouri, March 19-20, 1969. pp. F-1 - F-12. 1969. (B-005-Mo.)

Harbaugh, T. E. and J. E. Thompson, Spillway Design Floods for Small Dams in Rural Missouri. Hydrologic Series Bulletin 6-70, Civil Engineering Studies, University of Missouri-Rolla, Rolla, Missouri. 1970. (A-025-Mo.)

Harbaugh, T. E., Computer Aided Laboratory Investigations of Watershed Hydraulics. ASCE Hydraulics Div. Conf., MIT, August, 1969. (B-019-Mo.)

Harbaugh, T. E., Hydroplanning: The Effect of Grooving on Surface Drainage of Concrete Pavements. Highway Research Board, Committee D-B4. January, 1968. 16 p. (B-019-Mo.)

Harbaugh, T. E. and V. T. Chow, A Study of the Roughness of Conceptual River Systems on Watersheds. Proceedings International Association of Hydraulic Research Conference, Fort Collins, Colorado, Vol. 1, pp. 9-18. 1967. (B-019-Mo.)

Harbaugh, T. E., A Study of the Roughness of Conceptual River Systems on Watersheds. Contribution to the International Hydrological Decade, Proceedings, 12th Congress of the International Association of Hydraulic Research. University of Missouri. 1967. (B-007-Mo.)

Harbaugh, T. E., Numerical Techniques for Spatially Varied Unsteady Flow. Report No. 3. Water Resources Research Center, University of Missouri. 40 p. 1967. (B-007-Mo.)

Harbaugh, T. E., Watershed Hydraulics in the Laboratory. Proc. Third Annual American Water Resources Conference, San Francisco, California, November 1967, pp. 500-513. (B-007-Mo. and B-019-Mo.)

Huang, J. C. and C. S. Liao, Absorption of Pesticides on Clay Minerals. Presented at Missouri Academy of Science Meeting, St. Louis, May 2-3, 1969. (A-016-Mo.)

Keller, W. D. and George E. Smith, Ground-water Contamination by Dissolved Nitrate. Geological Society of America, Special Paper 90, pp. 47-59. 1967.

King, D. L. and R. D. Verma, The Role of Particulate Substrates in Biotic Degradation of Organic Materials, Engineering Extension Series No. 132 Engineering Bulletin of Purdue-Proceedings of 23rd Industrial Waste Conference on May 7-9, 1968, pp. 75-86. (A-007-Mo.)

Lauer, T. E., Reflections on Riparianism. Missouri Law Review, Vol. 35, No. 1, pp. 1-26, Winter of 1970. (A-008-Mo.)

Levi, Donald L., Highest and Best Use: An Economic Goal for Water Law. Missouri Law Review-Spring., 1969. (A-008-Mo.)

Levi, Donald R. and Roy G. McNabb, Water Legislation for Missouri. Business and Government Review. Publication of School of Business and Public Administration, University of Missouri-Columbia, Nov.-Dec., pp. 23-32. 1967. (A-008-Mo.)

McNabb, C. G. and M. G. Blase, Public Water for Rural Areas and Small Towns. MP 105, 1969, Extension Division, University of Missouri-Columbia. (A-018-Mo.)

Manahan, S. E., Ion Selective Electrodes for Nitrate Analysis. Trace Substances in Environmental Health-III, pp. 353-357, 1969, University of Missouri Press, Proceedings of University of Missouri's 3rd Annual Conference on Trace Substances in Environmental Health. (B-023-Mo.)

Powell, G. M. and R. P. Beasley, Effect of Erosion on Water Infiltration Rates. Missouri Agricultural Experiment Station Research Bulletin No. 922. University of Missouri. 1967. (A-003-Mo.)

Scrivner, C. L., Soils and Their Relationships to Potentials for Supplemental Irrigation in Missouri. Published in the Minutes of the 156th Meeting of the Missouri Basin Inter-Agency Committee, Jefferson City, Missouri, March 19-20, 1969, pp. F-13-F-24. (B-022-Mo.)

Smith, G. E., Contribution of Fertilizer to Water Pollution. 2nd Compendium of Animal Waste Management, USDI, FWPCA, Missouri Basin Region, Kansas City, Missouri, pp. 107-122, June 1969.

Smith, G. E., The Quality of Our Environment—Effects of Water Pollution. Proceedings 83rd Annual Convention, Experiment Station Section, The National Association of State Universities and Land Grant Colleges, 8 p., November 12, 1969.

Smith, G. E., Nitrate Pollution of Water Supplies. Proceedings University of Missouri's 3rd Annual Conference on Trace Substances in Environmental Health-III, pp. 273-287, June 25, 1969.

Smith, G. E., Management of Animal Feedlot Wastes-Land Spreading as a Disposal Process. 2nd Compendium of Animal Waste Management, USDI, FWPCA, Missouri Basin Region, Kansas City, Missouri, pp. 73-80, June 1969.

Smith, G. E., Control of Waterborne Pollutants. Proc. of Seminar. Modifying the Soil and Water Environment for Approaching the Agricultural Potential of the Great Plains, Manhattan, Kansas, March 16, 1969.

Smith, G. E., Nitrate Pollution of Water Supplies. Proc. 3rd Annual Conference on Trace Substances in Environmental Health. University of Missouri-Columbia, May 25, 1969.

Smith, G. E., The Contribution of Agriculture to Water Pollution. Proc. National Institute of Farm and Land Brokers, Chicago, May, 1969.

Smith, G. E., Water Pollution—A Problem. Proc. 19th Annual Fertilizer and Soil Management Short Course, S. D. Fertilizer Assn., January 23, 1969, pp. 44-53.

Smith, George E., Nitrates in Water—Facts and Fancy. Proc. 16th Annual California Fertilizer Conference, 1968, pp. 34-45.

Smith, George E., Contribution of Fertilizers to Water Pollution. Proc. Water Pollution Joint Seminar. Mo. Agr. Exp. Station and State Water Pollution Board. April 9, 1968, pp. 13-28.

Smith, George E., Pollution Problems—How Much is Agriculture to Blame? Agricultural Nitrogen News. Vol. XVIII (2), 1968, pp. 32-40.

Smith, G. E., Nitrogen Potential and Usage Pattern Trends-Fantasy vs Facts. Proc. 18th Annual Convention Agricultural Nitrogen Institute, November 19, 1968, pp. 96-101.

Smith, George E., Are Fertilizers Creating Pollution Problems? Soil and American Future. Proc. 22nd annual meeting Soil Conservation Society of America, 1967, pp. 108-114.

Smith, George E., Nitrates in Livestock Production. Fertilizer Solutions. Vol. II (4), 1967, pp. 24-27.

Smith, George E., Contamination of Water by Nitrates. Fertilizer Solutions. Vol. II (3), 1967, pp. 8-17.

Smith, George E., Fertilizer Nutrients as Contaminants in Water Supplies. Agriculture and the Quality of Our Environment. AAAS Publication 85, 1967, pp. 173-186.

Wixson, B. G., Water Quality Protection in Streams in Mining Districts. Proc. International Conference Water Quality Research in Developing Countries, Jersusalem, Israel, June, 1969. (A-021-Mo.)

Wixson, B. G. and E. Bolter, Missouri Stream Studies Relating to the "New Lead Belt," Proceedings, Mining Environmental Conference, University of Missouri-Rolla, 1969. (B-017 and A-021-Mo.)

Wixson, B. G., E. Bolter, N. H. Tibbs, and A. R. Handler, Pollution from Mines in the "New Lead Belt" of Southeastern Missouri. Proc. 24th Annual Purdue Industrial Waste Conference, May, 1969. (B-017-Mo. and A-021-Mo.)

Wixson, B. G. and A. R. Handler, Some Effects of Lead-Zinc Mining Wastewaters on Bluegill Sunfish *Lepomis Macrochirus*. Proc. Missouri Academy Science Meeting, St. Louis, May, 1969. (A-021-Mo.)

Woodruff, C. M., Irrigating Corn on Claypan Soils of Missouri. Science and Technology Guide No. 4137. University of Missouri Extension Division. 1968. 4 p. (A-003-Mo.)

MONTANA

MONTANA STATE BOARD OF HEALTH
State Capitol Building
Helena, Montana 59601

Pollution of the Yellowstone River as Related to Taste and Odor Problems in Municipal Water Supplied in Montana and North Dakota: A cooperative field investigation undertaken jointly by State Board of Health, Helena, Montana; State Department of Health, Bismarck, N. D.; and Department of Health, Education and Welfare, U. S. Public Health Service, Water Supply and Water Pollution Control Activities, Region VI, Nov. 7-13, 1955, Helena, Montana. 1956.

Progress Report on Reduction of Wastes Reaching the Yellowstone River Drainage in Montana. Helena, Montana. 1965.

Proposed Standards and Classifications of Water and Purity for the Yellowstone River and its Tributaries in Montana. Helena, Montana.

Report of a Stream Survey of the St. Mary and Belly River Drainages of Montana. Helena, Montana. 1965.

Sewage Disposal Policy. Helena, Montana. 1952.

Three Forks Area Water Quality Study Progress Report No. 1, Oct. 1959 – September 1960.

Water Pollution in the Missouri River Drainage in Montana. Helena, Montana. 1960.

Water Pollution in the Yellowstone Drainage in Montana; Report to Montana Water Pollution Council. Helena, Montana. 1963.

Clark Fork River–Columbia Drainage Area. Division of Environmental Sanitation, Helena, Montana. 1959.

An Extensive Chemical, Physical, Bacteriological and Biological Survey of the Columbia River Drainage in Montana. Division of Environmental Sanitation, Helena, Montana. 1959.

Flathead River Drainage Area. Division of Environmental Sanitation, Helena, Montana.

Kootenai Drainage Area. Division of Environmental Sanitation, Helena, Montana. 1959.

Minimum Suggested Criteria for Raw Sewage Stabilization Ponds or Sewage Lagoons. Helena, Montana.

Sewage Disposal for Residences, Tourist Camps, and Rural Schools: Circular No. 5. Division of Environmental Sanitation, Helena, Montana. 1965.

Yellowstone River and Tributaries. Division of Environmental Sanitation, Helena, Montana. 1958.

Three Forks Area Water Quality Study: Progress Report, Number 1. Study conducted by State Board of Health and State Fish and Game Department. Helena, Montana. 1960.

Three Forks Area Water Quality Study: Progress Report, Number 2. Study conducted by State Board of Health and the Montana State Fish and Game Department. Helena, Montana. 1961.

A Montana Strategy for a Livable Environment: Conference Proceedings. May 21-23, 1968. Helena, Montana. 112 p.

MONTANA BUREAU OF MINES AND GEOLOGY
Montana College of Mineral Science and Technology
Room 203-B, Main Hall
Butte, Montana 59701

Memoirs, Bulletins, Special Publications, and those publications under the discontinued series that are still available can be obtained by writing or calling personally at the above address. A small charge is required for commercially printed publications. Those which are free are so indicated.

No charge is made for postage on book publications sent within the United States. Canada and foreign countries should include postage with their orders.

At the end of this listing are the costs for reproduction of out-of-print reports.

BOOK PUBLICATIONS — MEMOIRS

*M2 Ground water in eastern and central Montana. E. S. Perry. 1931. 59 p., 10 pls., 1 table.

*M7 Ground-water resources of Judith Basin, Montana. E. S. Perry. 1932. 30 p., 3 pls., 2 tables.

*M11 Geology and artesian water resources along Missouri and Milk Rivers in northeastern Montana. E. S. Perry. 1934. 35 p., 1 pl., 15 figs., 5 tables.

*M12 Physiography and ground-water supply in the Big Hole Basin, Montana. E. S. Perry. 1934. 18 p., 3 pls., 2 figs.

*M14 Geology and ground-water resources of southeastern Montana. E. S. Perry. 1935. 67 p., 3 pls., 27 figs.

M40 Ground-water resources along Cedar Creek anticline in eastern Montana. O. James Taylor. 1965. 99 p., 5 pls., 17 figs., 3 tables. Price: $1.00.

BULLETINS

*B9 Preliminary report on the geology and water resources of the Bitterroot Valley, Montana, by Frank Stermitz, R. G.

McMurtrey, and R. L. Konizeski; with a section on Chemical quality of water, by H. A. Swenson. 1959. 45 p., 2 pls., 12 figs., 6 tables.

B19 Geology and ground-water resources of northeastern Blaine County, Montana. E. A. Zimmerman. 1960. 19 p., 1 pl., 5 figs., 2 tables. (Free).

B21 Preliminary report on the geology and ground-water resources of the northern part of the Deer Lodge Valley, Montana. R. L. Konizeski, R. G. McMurtrey, and Alex Brietkrietz. 1961. 24 p., 1 pl., 7 figs., 2 tables. (Free).

B31 Preliminary report on the geology and ground-water resources of the southern part of the Deer Lodge Valley, Montana. R. L. Konizeski, R. G. McMurtrey, and Alex Brietkrietz. 1962. 24 p., 2 pls., 8 figs., 2 tables. (Free).

B32 Preliminary report on the geology and ground-water resources of southern Judith Basin, Montana. E. A. Zimmerman. 1962. 23 p., 1 pl., 4 figs., 2 tables. (Free).

B37 Basic water data report no. 1, Missoula Valley, Montana. Alex Brietkrietz. 1964. 43 p., 1 pl., 2 figs., 3 tables. (Free).

B47 Geology and ground-water resources of the Missoula Basin, Montana. R. G. McMurtrey, R. L. Konizeski, and Alex Brietkrietz. 1965. 35 p., 3 pls., 13 figs., 3 tables. Price: $1.00.

B48 Geochemical reconnaissance stream-sediment sampling in Flathead and Lincoln Counties, Montana. U. M. Sahinen, W. M. Johns, and D. C. Lawson. 1965. 16 p., 3 pls., (Free).

B50-A Geology and ground-water resources of western and southern parts of Judith Basin, Montana. E. A. Zimmerman. 1966. 33 p., 4 pls., 10 figs., 6 tables. Price: $1.25 (includes 50-B).

B50-B Basic water data report no. 2, western and southern parts of Judith Basin, Montana. E. A. Zimmerman. 1966. 40 p., 4 tables. (Free with 50-A.)

B52 Geology and ground-water resources of the Cascade-Ulm area, Montana. R. D. Fox. 1966. 64 p., 1 pl., 2 figs., 5 tables. (Free).

B53 Basic water data report no. 3, Kalispell Valley, Montana. Alex Brietkrietz. 1966. 25 p., 1 pl., 2 figs., 4 tables. (Free).

B57 Water levels and artesian pressures in observation wells in Montana. R. G. McMurtrey and T. E. Reed. 1967. 28 p., 6 figs., 2 tables. (Free).

B60 Water resources of the Cut Bank area, Glacier and Toole Counties, Montana. E. A. Zimmerman. 1967. 37 p., 3 pls., 9 figs., 6 tables. Price: $1.00.

B65 Water levels and artesian pressures in observation wells in Montana through 1967. R. G. McMurtrey and T. E. Reed. 1968. 40 p., 9 figs., 2 tables. Price: $0.15.

B66 Ground-water resources of the northern Powder River valley, southeastern Montana. O. James Taylor. 1968. 34 p., 1 pl., 17 figs., 9 tables. Price: $1.00.

B68 Geology and ground-water resources of the Kalispell Valley, northwestern Montana. R. L. Konizeski, Alex Brietkrietz, and R. G. McMurtrey. 1968. 42 p., 5 pls., 34 figs., 6 tables. Price: $1.00.

B71 Water levels and artesian pressures in observation wells in Montana through 1968. T. E. Reed and R. G. McMurtrey. 1969. 30 p., 9 figs., 2 tables. Price: $0.15.

B75 Hydrogeology of the upper Silver Bow Creek drainage area, Montana. M. K. Botz, 1969, 32 p., 2 pls., 6 figs., 10 tables. Price: $0.35.

B76 Water levels and artesian pressures in observation wells in Montana, 1966-69, T. E. Reed and R. G. McMurtrey, 1970, 36 p., 9 figs., 2 tables. Price: $0.15.

INFORMATION CIRCULARS

Series discontinued. Publications of this type now issued as Bulletins.

*IC15 Preliminary report on the geology and ground-water resources of parts of Musselshell and Golden Valley Counties, Montana. E. A. Zimmerman. 1956. 13 p., 1 pl., 2 figs., 2 tables.

*IC16 Progress report on the geology and ground water resources of the eastern part of the Bitterroot Valley, Montana. R. G. McMurtrey and R. L. Konizeski. 1956. 28 p., 2 pls., 5 figs., 4 tables. (Free).

*IC17 Biennial report of the Montana Bureau of Mines and Geology, a department of the Montana School of Mines, to the State Board of Education for the reporting period July 1, 1954 to June 30, 1956. 40 p.

*IC25 Biennial report of the Montana Bureau of Mines and Geology, a department of the Montana School of Mines, to the State Board of Education for the reporting period July 1, 1956 to June 30, 1958. 57 p.

*IC26 A summary report of the ground-water situation in Montana, by S. L. Groff, with a chapter on Montana and the law on ground water, by Albert Stone. 1958. 45 p., 7 pls., 1 table.

MISCELLANEOUS CONTRIBUTIONS AND SPECIAL PUBLICATIONS

*MC1 Artesian wells as a source of water for the Winnett irrigation project, Montana. E. S. Perry. 1932. 5 p., 3 pls.

*MC2 Possibilities of ground-water supply for certain towns and cities of Montana. E. S. Perry. 1932. 49 p., 2 pls., 70 figs.

*MC3 Shallow wells near Terry, Montana, as a source of irrigation water. E. S. Perry. 1932. 7 p.

*MC4 Artesian wells as a source of water for municipal supply at Fort Benton, Montana. E. S. Perry. 1932. 7 p., 1 pl.

*MC5 Shallow wells as a source of irrigation water in Frenchtown and Camas Prairie Valleys, Montana. E. S. Perry. 1933. 8 p., 2 pls.

SP19 Biennial report of the Montana Bureau of Mines and Geology, a department of the Montana School of Mines, to the Legislative Assembly, for the reporting period July 1, 1958 to June 30, 1960. 15 p., 1 pl. (Free).

SP24 (Ground-water report 1) Reconnaissance ground-water studies, Wheatland, eastern Meagher, and northern Sweet Grass Counties, Montana. S. L. Groff. 1962. 31 p., 1 pl., 1 fig., 3 tables. (Free).

SP26 (Ground-water report 2) Reconnaissance ground-water studies, northern Park County, Montana. S. L. Groff. 1962. 14 p., 1 pl., 5 tables. (Free).

SP27 Biennial report of the Montana Bureau of Mines and Geology, a department of the Montana School of Mines, to the Legislative Assembly for the reporting period July 1, 1960 to June 30, 1962. 16 p., 1 pl. (Free).

SP28   Mineral and water resources of Montana. U. S. Geological Survey and Montana Bureau of Mines and Geology for U. S. Committee on Interior and Insular Affairs at request of Senator Lee Metcalf. 1963. 17 contributors, 166 p., 51 figs., 10 tables. Price: $1.00.

*SP32   Biennial report of the Montana Bureau of Mines and Geology, a department of the Montana School of Mines, to the Legislative Assembly for the reporting period July 1, 1962 to June 30, 1964. 30 p., 6 figs., 2 tables.

SP35   Reconnaissance ground-water and geologic studies of western Meagher County, Montana. S. L. Groff. 1965. 23 p., 1 pl., 1 fig., 3 tables. (Free).

SP37   Index and bibliography of ground-water studies in Montana. Compiled by M. K. Botz and E. W. Bond. 1966. 1 sheet. Price: $0.25.

SP40   Biennial report of the Montana Bureau of Mines and Geology, a department of Montana College of Mineral Science and Technology, for the reporting period July 1, 1964 to June 30, 1966. 28 p., 6 figs., 2 tables. (Free).

SP45   Biennial report of the Montana Bureau of Mines and Geology, a department of Montana College of Mineral Science and Technology, for the reporting period July 1, 1966 to June 30, 1968. 33 p., 6 figs., 2 tables. (Free).

SP49   Development of a statewide system for computer processing of hydrogeological data, M. K. Botz, 1970, 15 p., 3 apps., 3 figs. (Free).

SP50   Current geological and geophysical studies in Montana, compiled by R. B. Berg, 1970, 24 p. (Free).

REPRODUCTION COSTS OF OUT-OF-PRINT REPORTS

Copies of reports now out of print can be reproduced at the following prices, including maps and plates (or at 10 cents a page):

Memoirs		Bulletins		Information Circulars	
M2	$7.70	B9	$4.80	IC15	$2.20
M7	4.00			IC16	no price listed
M11	4.10			IC17	4.30
M12	2.60			IC25	5.70
M14	7.90			IC26	5.30

Miscellaneous Contributions		Special Publications	
MC1	$0.90	SP32	$3.50
MC2	5.30		
MC3	1.00		
MC4	0.90		
MC5	1.20		

MONTANA COMMISSION ON CONSERVATION

Helena, Montana

This agency is no longer in existence.

Report of the Commission on Conservation, January 14, 1911. Helena, Montana. 1911.

MONTANA CONSERVATION COUNCIL

Anaconda, Montana 59711

The Conservation of Montana's Natural Resources. Missoula, Montana. 1954.

Montana Conservationist: Official Newsletter. Anaconda, Montana. 1951.

Natural Resources, A Tour in Western Montana by the 1954 Caravan Committee. 1954.

Montana Conservation Needs Committee. Montana Soil and Water Conservation Needs Inventory. 1962.

MONTANA DEPARTMENT OF AGRICULTURE AND PUBLICITY

Helena, Montana 59601

This agency is no longer in existence.

Montana Precipitation Charts. Helena, Montana. 1919.

The Resources and Opportunities of Montana. Independent Publishing Company, State Printers, Helena, Montana. 1914 also 1915-1920.

MONTANA STATE ENGINEER

Mitchell Building
Helena, Montana 59601

Irrigation Districts Yellowstone County, Montana. Billings Commercial Club, Billings, Montana. 1943.

Water Resources Survey, Big Horn County. Helena, Montana. 1947.

Water Resources Survey, Blaine County. Helena, Montana. 1967.

Water Resources Survey, Broadwater County. Helena, Montana. 1956.

Water Resources Survey, Carbon County. Helena, Montana. 1966.

Water Resources Survey, Carter, Fallon and Wibaux Counties. Helena, Montana. 1960.

Water Resources Survey, Cascade County. Helena, Montana. 1961.

Water Resources Survey, Choteau County. Helena, Montana. 1964.

Water Resources Survey, Custer County. Helena, Montana. 1948.

Water Resources Survey, Deer Lodge County. Helena, Montana. 1955.

Water Resources Survey, Flathead and Lincoln Counties. Helena, Montana. 1965.

Water Resources Survey, Gallagin County. Helena, Montana. 1953.

Water Resources Survey, Golden Valley County. Helena, Montana. 1949.

Water Resources Survey, Granite County. Helena, Montana. 1959.

Water Resources Survey, Hill County. Helena, Montana. 1967.

Water Resources Survey, Jefferson County. Helena, Montana. 1956.

Water Resources Survey, Judith Basin County. Helena, Montana. 1963.

Montana Law Affecting Water Rights and Appropriations. Helena, Montana.

Water Resources Survey, Lake County. Helena, Montana. 1963.

Water Resources Survey, Lewis & Clark County. Helena, Montana. 1957.

Water Resources Survey, Madison County. Helena, Montana. 1965.

Water Resources Survey, Meagher County. Helena, Montana. 1950.

Water Resources Survey, Missoula County. Helena, Montana. 1960.

Water Resources Survey, Musselshell County. Helena, Montana. 1949.

Water Resources Survey, Park County. Helena, Montana. 1951.

Water Resources Survey, Phillips County. Helena, Montana. 1968.

Water Resources Survey, Pondera County. Helena, Montana. 1964.

Water Resources Survey, Powder River County. Helena, Montana. 1961.

Water Resources Survey, Powell County. Helena, Montana. 1959.

Water Resources Survey, Ravalli County. Helena, Montana. 1958.

Water Resources Survey, Rosebud County. Helena, Montana. 1948.

Water Resources Survey, Silver Bow County. Helena, Montana. 1955.

Water Resources Survey, Stillwater County. Helena, Montana. 1946.

Water Resources Survey, Sweet Grass County. Helena, Montana. 1950.

Water Resources Survey, Teton County. Helena, Montana. 1962.

Water Resources Survey, Treasure County. Helena, Montana. 1951.

Water Resources Survey, Wheatland County. Helena, Montana. 1949.

Water Resources Survey, Yellowstone County. Helena, Montana.

Maps Showing the Irrigated Areas in Yellowstone County by Source of Supply. Billings Commercial Club, Billings, Montana. 1943.

Water Resources Survey: Irrigation Summary For – The Clark Fork River, Big Horn River, Tongue River and completed portion of the Powder River in Montana. Helena, Montana.

MONTANA FISH AND GAME COMMISSION
Helena, Montana 59601

Water Facilities and Wildlife Habitat Development. Wildlife Restoration Project 8-D, Wildlife Restoration Division, Helena, Montana. 1947.

State of Montana Statewide Outdoor Recreation Plan. Helena, Montana. 1965.

MONTANA IRRIGATION COMMISSION
Helena, Montana 59601

This agency is no longer in existence.

Report to Hon. Jos. K. Toole, Governor of Montana, by the Irrigation Code Commission. Helena, Montana. 1906.

Water Makes Wealth in Montana – How to Create an Irrigation District. Helena, Montana. 1919.

MONTANA STATE DEPARTMENT OF PLANNING AND ECONOMIC DEVELOPMENT
Capitol Station
Helena, Montana 59601

Montana Progress Report, State Planning Consultant to the National Resources Committee, June 16, 1936. Helena, Montana.

A Recommended Six-Year State Construction Program and a Program of Public Works for all State Institutions Including Water Conservation Projects and State Highways. Helena, Montana. 1941.

Comprehensive area-wide water and sewer plan 1970. 17 vol. Limited supply, apply to agency for particulars on obtaining copies.

MONTANA STATE SOIL CONSERVATION COMMITTEE
Helena, Montana 59601

Better Use of Montana's Land and Water: Progress Report. 1940-1956.

Better Use of Montana's Land and Water. 1957.

The State Soil and Water Conservation Districts Law, 1961. McKee Printing Company, Butte, Montana.

MONTANA WATER POLLUTION CONTROL COUNCIL

Montana State Board of Health
Helena, Montana

Public Hearing on a Proposed Revision of Water Quality Standards and Water Use Classifications for Montana. Helena, Montana. 1968.

MONTANA WATER RESOURCES BOARD

(formerly Montana Water Conservation Board)
Sam W. Mitchell Building
Helena, Montana 59601

1   Directory of State of Montana, Federal Agencies, and Private Groups Active in the General Field of Water Resources.

2   Water Resources Programs conducted by Government Agencies in Montana.

3   Montana Register of Dams, A compilation of storage reservoirs having a capacity of 50 acre feet or more.

4   Water Resources and Planning, An explanation of the State Water Plan, its authorization, scope and objectives.

5   Montana Water Laws: A Resumé.

6   Catalog of Stream Gaging Stations, A schematic approach to historical collection of stream discharge records.

9   Summary of Potential Projects in Montana, A compilation of anticipated future developments for water storage and control projects by drainage basin.

10   Bibliography of Montana Water Resources and Related Publications.

11   An Atlas of Water Resources in Montana by Hydrologic Basin, A 15 map atlas of Montana's drainage basins and resources. (to be published)

12   Montana's State Water Plan, A Progress Report, A progress report to Montana's 42nd Legislature. (to be published)

16   A Groundwater Report of Montana, a report by Miller Hanson of the Montana Bureau of Mines and Geology on Montana's Groundwater resources.

Water Laws of Montana 1965.

Water Laws of Montana Cumulative Supplement 1969.

Floods in Missoula, Montana. 1967.

Newsletter – issued quarterly.

MONTANA STATE WATER CONSERVATION BOARD

OTHER PUBLICATIONS (Predecessor Agencies)

Annual Reports 1934-1964.

Development Plan – Willow Creek Storage Project: Helena, Montana. 1966.

First Biennial Report, July 1, 1964-June 30, 1966: Helena, Montana.

Fish Creek Structure: Helena, Montana. 1965.

Preliminary Report – Burnt Fork Project: Helena, Montana. 1961.

Preliminary Report – Rock Creek Storage Project: Helena, Montana.

Preliminary Report – Willow Creek Storage Project: Helena, Montana. 1965.

Program Presented to Public Works Administration up to October 1, 1938: Helena, Montana. 1938.

Report on Blodgett Creek Project: Helena, Montana. 1963.

Report on Extraordinary Session, Twenty-Third Legislative Assembly, 1933: Helena, Montana. 1935.

Water Needs of Montana: Helena, Montana. 1962.

Report on the Comprehensive Development of the Yellowstone Drainage Basin: Helena, Montana. 1937.

Discussion of Chapter 35 of the Laws of the Extraordinary Session Twenty-Third Assembly of Montana, In Relation to State Water Conservation–Application for Loans from the Federal Government, In Particular For Application For a Loan For the Rock Creek Project in Carbon County, Montana.

MONTANA UNIVERSITY JOINT WATER RESOURCES RESEARCH CENTER

Montana State University
Bozeman, Montana 59715

REPORTS

2   Bridger Instrumentation Modification, Duain Bowles, Montana State University.

4   Bridger Hydrometeorological Research Area and Facilities, Robert J. Rickabaugh, Montana State University.

5   Bridger Telemetry Communications System, Robert E. Leo, Montana State University.

6   Bridger Hydrometeorological Data Acquisition System, Lee Cannon, Montana State University.

7   Instrumentation and Operation of Meteorological and Stream Gaging Stations on Maynard Creek, Theodore T. Williams, Montana State University.

8   Natural Resources Administration in the Fifty States, Richard G. Sheridan, Montana State University.

9   Water, Water Everywhere, But . . . . ?, Richard G. Sheridan, Montana State University.

10   Simulation Via Time-Partitioned Linear Programming: A Ground and Surface Water Model for the Gallatin Valley of Montana, Donald W. Boyd, Montana State University.

12   Community Water Problems as a Factor in Municipal Incorporation in Montana, Michael Courtney Nash, University of Montana.

13   An Experiment in Finite-Difference Watershed Modeling, Darrel E. Dunn, Montana State University.

Unnumbered   Annual Report, 1966 to date.

NEBRASKA

CONSERVATION AND SURVEY DIVISION

University of Nebraska
113 Nebraska Hall
Lincoln, Nebraska 68508

WATER SURVEY PAPERS

1   Terminology Relating to the Occurrence, Behavior and Use of Water in Nebraska: G. E. Condra (1944). Free.

2   Groundwater Survey of Area North of O'Neill, Holt County, Nebraska: E. C. Reed (1944). Free.

3   Ground-Water Levels in the Lower Platte River Valley, Nebraska: H. A. Waite (1948). Price: $0.20.

*4   Water Levels in Observation Wells in Nebraska, 1957: C. F. Keech (1959).

*5   Water Levels in Observation Wells in Nebraska, 1958: C. F. Keech (1960).

6   Water Levels in Observation Wells in Nebraska, 1959: C. F. Keech (1960). Price: $0.50.

7   Wells in Hamilton County, Nebraska: C. F. Keech (1960). Price: $0.25.

8   Wells in Fillmore County, Nebraska: C. F. Keech (1960). Price: $0.25.

9   Water Levels in Observation Wells in Nebraska, 1960: C. F. Keech (1961). Price: $0.50.

10   Basic-Data Report, Lower Cedar River Drainage Basin, Nebraska: J. B. Hyland (1961). Price: $0.50.

11   The Program of Ground-Water Investigations in Nebraska: C. F. Keech (1962). Price: $0.50.

12   Water Levels in Observation Wells in Nebraska, 1961: C. F. Keech and J. B. Hyland (1962). Price: $0.50.

13   Water Levels in Observation Wells in Nebraska, 1962: Philip A. Emery and Mildred Malhoit (1963). Price: $0.50.

14   Water Levels in Observation Wells in Nebraska, 1963: Philip A. Emery and Mildred Malhoit (1964). Price: $0.50.

15   Basic-Data Report, Saline County, Nebraska: Philip A. Emery (1964). Price: $0.50.

16   Basic-Data Report, York County, Nebraska: C. F. Keech (1964). Price: $0.50.

17   Water Levels in Observation Wells in Nebraska, 1964: Philip A. Emery and Mildred M. Malhoit (1965). Price: $0.50.

18   Water Levels in Observation Wells in Nebraska, 1965: by Philip A. Emery and Mildred M. Malhoit (1966). Price: $0.50.

*19 Availability and Use of Water in Nebraska: F. Butler Shaffer (1966).

*20 Water Levels in Observation Wells in Nebraska, 1966: C. F. Keech (1967).

21   The Nitrate Hazard In Well Water, with special reference to Holt County, Nebraska: by Richard A. Engberg (1967). Price: $0.25.

22   Groundwater Data Polk County, Nebraska: F. A. Smith and E. C. Weakly (1968). Price: $0.50.

23   Water Levels in Observation Wells in Nebraska, 1967: C. F. Keech (1968). Price: $0.50.

24   Water Levels in Observation Wells in Nebraska, 1968: C. F. Keech and G. R. Svoboda (1969). Price: $0.50.

25   Use of Groundwater For Irrigation, Seward County, Nebraska: J. M. Jess (1970). Price: $0.50.

26   Groundwater Levels in Nebraska, 1969: C. F. Keech (1970). Price: $0.50.

HYDROLOGIC ATLASES

Ground Water Atlas of Nebraska (1966). Price: $0.50.

HA-4   Configuration of the Water Table in Nebraska. Price: $0.25.

HA-6   Reconnaissance of the Geology and Ground Water Resources of Southern Sioux County, Nebraska, by Edward Bradley, with a section on the chemical quality of the ground water by F. H. Rainwater (1956). Price: $0.50.

HA-12   Ground-water Reconnaissance of the North Loup Division of the Lower Platte River Basin, Nebraska: C. F. Keech and M. P. Carlson (1959). Price: $1.00.

HA-131 Availability of Ground Water in Hall County, Nebraska: C. F. Keech and V. H. Dreeszen (1946). Price: $0.50.

HA-188 Flood of August 1966 in the Lower Loup River Basin, Nebraska, by F. Butler Shaffer & Kenneth J. Braun. Price: $1.25.

HA-216 Geohydrology of Saline County, Nebraska: Philip A. Emery (1966). Price: $0.50.

HA-217 General Availability of Ground Water and Depth to Water Level in the Missouri River Basin, by G. A. LaRocque, Jr. Price: $0.75.

HA-258 Floods in Seward Quadrangle Southeastern Nebraska by F. Butler Shaffer & Kenneth J. Braun. Price: $0.75.

HA-266 Availability of Water in Eastern Saunders County, Nebraska: V. L. Souders (1967). Price: $0.75.

HA-287 Availability of Ground Water in Adams County, Nebraska: C. F. Keech and V. H. Dreeszen (1968). Price: $0.50.

HA-316 Water Resources of Antelope County, Nebraska: V. L. Souders and F. B. Shaffer (1969). Price: $1.50.

GROUNDWATER MAPS

Underground Water Areas Map, Colored (1969). 1:2,100,000. Free.

Nebraska's Water Supply — in diagrammatic form. Page-size. Free.

Irrigation Map of Nebraska (1958). 1:900,000. Price: $0.25.

Irrigation Well Concentration Map of Nebraska (1967). 1 inch = approx. 25 miles. Price: $0.25.

Groundwater Potential Map of Nebraska (1960). 1:500,000. Price: $1.30.

Groundwater Map of Nebraska (1960). 1:1,000,000. Price: $0.50.

Groundwater Quality Map of Nebraska (1962). 1:1,000,000. Price: $0.50.

Groundwater Storage Map of Nebraska (1962). 1:1,000,000. Price: $0.50.

Groundwater Map of Nebraska. 1 inch = 40 miles. Free.

Groundwater Map of Nebraska Showing Contour of Water Table and Depth to Static Water Level. 1:1,000,000. Price: $0.50.

Configuration, Top of Bedrock (1964). 1:1,000,000. Price: $0.50.

Drainage Map of Nebraska. 1 inch = 25 miles. Free.

Nebraska Water Plain Drainage Areas. 1:500,000. Price: $1.50.

Nebraska Water Plain Drainage Areas. 1:1,000,000. Price: $0.50.

Test Hole Location Map. 1:500,000. Price: $1.30.

PRELIMINARY COUNTY GROUNDWATER STUDIES

Adams — 1948. 1 inch = 2 miles. Price: $1.50.

Boone — 1947. 1 inch = 2 miles. Price: $1.50.

Butler — 1955. 1 inch = 2 miles. Price: $1.50.

Clay — 1952. 1 inch = 2 miles. Price: $1.50.

Deuel and S. Garden Counties — 1966. (printed). 1 inch = 2 miles. Price: $0.25.

Fillmore — 1953. 1 inch = 2 miles. Price: $1.50.

Franklin — 1957. 1 inch = 2 miles. Price: $1.50.

Gage — 1956. 1 inch = 2 miles. Price: $1.50.

Hall — 1961. 1 inch = 2 miles. Price: $1.50.

Hamilton — 1957. 1 inch = 2 miles. Price: $1.50.

Jefferson — 1946. 1 inch = 4 miles. Price: $1.00.

Kearney — 1948. 1 inch = 2 miles. Price: $1.50.

Madison — 1957. 1 inch = 2 miles. Price: $1.50.

Keya Paha — Cherry — 1957. 1 inch = 10 miles. Price: $2.00.

Nuckolls — 1948. 1 inch = 10 miles. Price: $1.50.

Polk — 1955. 1 inch = 10 miles. Price: $1.50.

Phelps — 1953. 1 inch = 10 miles. Price: $1.50.

Platte — 1959. 1 inch = 10 miles. Price: $1.50.

Saline — 1946. 1 inch = 4 miles. Price: $1.00.

Seward — 1946. 1 inch = 4 miles. Price: $1.00.

Thayer — 1947. 1 inch = 4 miles. Price: $1.00.

Webster — 1953. 1 inch = 2 miles. Price: $1.50.

York — 1957. 1 inch = 4 miles. Price: $1.00.

Mid-State Area — 1964 (set of five). 1/4 inch = 1 mile. Price: $1.25.

LOGS OF TEST HOLES

Logs of test holes drilled as a part of groundwater resources studies in Nebraska are available for the following counties at a cost of $0.50 for each test hole report:

Adams
Antelope, Boone, Knox, Pierce
Boone, Greeley, Wheeler
Boone and Southern Antelope
Box Butte, Dawes, Morrill
Brown
Buffalo
Buffalo Supplement
Burt and Cuming
*Butler and Colfax
Butler Supplement
Cass (Test Hole Report 8)
Cass, Douglas, Otoe, Sarpy
Cedar and Dixon
Cheyenne
Clay
Dawson and Custer
Deuel and Garden
Dodge
Fillmore
Franklin
Frenchman Creek Basin
Frontier
*Gage and Pawnee
Gosper
Greeley, Howard, Wheeler
Hall (Test Hole Report 7)

Hamilton (Test Hole Report 3)

Harlan

Howard

*Jefferson

Johnson and Pawnee Supplement

Kearney

Keith and Arthur

Keya Paha and NE Cherry

Kimball

Knox

Lancaster (Test Hole Report 4)

Lincoln and McPherson

Madison and Pierce

Madison Supplement

Merrick and Nance

Nance Supplement

Nuckolls

Phelps

Platte

Platte Supplement

Polk

Richardson

Saline (Test Hole Report 6)

*Saunders

Scotts Bluff

*Seward

Seward Supplement

Sherman (Test Hole Report 1)

Stanton

Thayer

Valley and Garfield

Valley (Test Hole Report 2)

Wayne and Thurston

Webster

York (Test Hole Report 5)

MISCELLANEOUS PUBLICATIONS

Laws, Rules and Regulations Pertaining to Ground Water in Nebraska. Compiled by the Conservation and Survey Division (1966). Price: $0.50.

Minimum Standards for a Sanitary Domestic Well in Nebraska. Standards developed by a joint committee from the Univ. of Nebraska, the Nebraska Well Drillers Association, and the state and local health department. Price: $0.15.

Nebraska Minimum Standards for Artificially Gravel Packed Irrigation Wells. Standards developed by a joint committee from the University of Nebraska and the Nebraska Well Drillers Association. Univ. of Nebraska Extension Service No. E. C. 57-702 (1957). Free.

Nebraska Soil and Water Conservation Needs Inventory, Nebr. Committee on Soil and Water Conservation Needs (1962). Price: $0.75.

Nebraska's Water Story. Prepared by the Division of Nebraska Resources (1962, 1967). Free.

Nebraska's Water Supply: Conservation and Survey Division, University of Nebraska (Prepared in part from data furnished by the U. S. Geological Survey 1969). Free.

CONSERVATION AND SURVEY DIVISION

Nebraska Geological Survey
University of Nebraska
113 Nebraska Hall
Lincoln, Nebraska 68508

PAPERS

7   Groundwater Level Survey in Nebraska. H. A. Waite (1935). Price: $0.20.

*10   Water Bearing Formations of Nebraska. G. E. Condra and E. C. Reed (1936).

GUIDEBOOKS

Re-Exploring the Missouri. Thompson Mylan Stout, prepared for the Second Field Conference, Nebraska Geological Society, on Friday, May 22, 1970, An Excursion Aboard Corps of Engineers Inspection Boat, "The Sergeant Floyd," from Omaha to Rulo, Nebraska. Free.

NEBRASKA STATE DEPARTMENT OF AGRICULTURE

Lincoln, Nebraska

*Nebraska Irrigation Statistics, 1945-1953. (No longer published).

NEBRASKA STATE DEPARTMENT OF HEALTH

State House Station, Box 94757
Lincoln, Nebraska 68509

Rules and Regulations Concerning Water Supply Systems. 1954. 7 p.

Chemical Analyses of Nebraska Municipal Water Supplies. July 1969. 57 p.

Training Course Manual for Operators of Waste Water Treatment Systems, compiled by Owen Sletten. September 1969. 147 p.

The Nebraska Swimming Pool Act and Rules and Regulations Adopted Thereunder. 1970. 10 p.

Criteria for Swimming Pool Design. 1970. 22 p.

Rules and Regulations Concerning State Certification to Applicants for Federal Licenses or Permits to Conduct Activities on Navigable Waters of the United States Flowing Through or Bordering the State of Nebraska. 1970. 4 p.

Methods for Operators of Wastewater Treatment Plants for Determination of BOD Parameters, by Owen Sletten. 1971. 18 p.

Water Quality Standards Applicable to Nebraska Waters. Adopted by Water Pollution Control Council. March 1971. 50 p.

Guidelines – Water Pollution Control Project Grants. Nebraska Water Pollution Control Council. 5 p.

DEPARTMENT OF WATER RESOURCES
P. O. Box 94607
Lincoln, Nebraska 68509

Report – Annual. 1895/96 – to date.

First report covers period April 24, 1895 – November 30, 1896. 1902/04 (5th) never published. Report of the Dept. of Roads and Irrigation (1934/36 – 1954/56) consists of:
1. *its Bureau of Roads and Bridges, later Bureau of Highways, etc. report in Part 1, superseded in 1957 by Report of the Dept. of Roads.*
2. *its Bureau of Irrigation, Water Power and Drainage report in Part 2.*

Successively issued by:
  State Board of Irrigation
  State Board of Irrigation, Highways and Drainage
  Dept. of Public Works
  Dept. of Roads and Irrigation
  Dept. of Water Resources

Special Survey Report of the Department of Public Works, Bureau of Irrigation, Water Power and Drainage. 1931. 397 p.

Hydrographic Report. 1955 – to date.

NEBRASKA STATE OFFICE OF
PLANNING AND PROGRAMMING
Lincoln, Nebraska

Water Resources of Nebraska. Preliminary report by Nebraska State Planning Board. 1936. 695 p.

Maps and Charts. (1940 ?). 66 pls. Includes drainage basins; precipitation; irrigated lands; and water-power production.

Water Resources of Nebraska. Revised 1941. General section. 1941. 99 p.

SOIL AND WATER CONSERVATION
COMMISSION
P. O. Box 94725
State Capitol
Lincoln, Nebraska 68509

Many of the publications listed below are not available for general distribution. Please contact the Commission for further information.

Rules and Regulations, January 1968. Pub. No. 1. (Limited supply).

Nebraska's State Water Plan – Progress Report. January 1969. Pub. No. 2.

*Appendix to Progress Report. January 1969.

Big Blue River Basin Comprehensive Report. September 1968. Pub. No. 201.

Big Blue River Basin Comprehensive Report Appendix. September 1968. Pub. No. 201A.

Status Summary of Potential Projects. March 1969. Pub. No. 301.

Flood Prevention and Damage Reduction. July 1968. Pub. No. 401.

Modernization of Resource District Legislation. March 1969. Pub. No. 402.

Flood Warning and Community Action. August 1969. Pub. No. 403.

Nebraska's Flood Plain Regulation Program. July 1968. Pub. No. 501.

FRAMEWORK STUDY – STATE WATER PLAN

Main Report. Pub. No. 101.

Appendix A. Land Inventory. June 1969. Preliminary Publication. Pub. No. 101A.

Appendix B. Inventory of Water Resources. May 1970. Preliminary Publication. Pub. No. 101B.

Appendix C. Problems and Needs. September 1970. Preliminary Publication. Pub. No. 101C.

Appendix D. Survey of Nebraska Water Law. June 1970. Preliminary Publication. Pub. No. 101D.

WATER RESOURCES RESEARCH
INSTITUTE
The University of Nebraska, East Campus
212 Agricultural Engineering
Lincoln, Nebraska 68503

N.W.R.R.I. PUBLICATIONS

Water Resources Research in Nebraska, Publication No. 1, University of Nebraska, July 1969.

Water Resources Publications Related to the State of Nebraska, Publication No. 2, University of Nebraska, October 1969.

A Status Report, Warren Viessman, Jr., University of Nebraska, March 1970.

A Proposal for an Intra-University Graduate Program with Emphasis on Water Resources Planning & Management, University of Nebraska, May 1970.

PROJECT COMPLETION REPORTS

Research in Evapotranspiration, Norman J. Rosenberg, University of Nebraska, Project Completion Report, Project A-001-NEB, July 1969.

Input-Output Analysis of Water Use for Nebraska Industries, A. W. Epp, Maurice Baker, Project Completion Report, Project A-004-NEB, University of Nebraska, August 1970.

Engineering Phases of Land Treatment Related to Increasing Water-Use Efficiency and Storage Efficiency of Rainfall, Dr. Howard D. Wittmuss, Project Completion Report, A-003-NEB, July 1969.

Internal Water Status of Plants, Jerry D. Eastin, Charles Y. Sullivan, E. J. Kinbacher, Project Completion Report, A-005-NEB, July 1969.

Mechanics of Bank Seepage in Natural Streams During Flood Flows, Dr. Turgut Sarpkaya, Project Completion Report, January 26, 1968.

Brackish Water Purification by Biological Fuel Cell Powered Electrodialysis, Dr. Wm. A. Scheller, Dr. Carl E. Georgi, Project Completion Report, A-007-NEB, September 1, 1969.

A Legal-Economic Analysis of Administrative and Market Procedures Used in the Transfer of Water Rights, Loyd K. Fischer, Maurice Baker, Project Completion Report, A-008-NEB, July 19, 1969.

Eminent Domain and Water Law, Richard S. Harnsberger, Project Completion Report, A-009-NEB, February 1969.

Surface Properties of Teflon Film in Saline Water Processes, Luh C. Tao, Project Completion Report, A-010-NEB, January 24, 1969.

Utilization of the Storage Potential of River Valley Aquifers, Ralph R. Marlette, Leon S. Directo, Project Completion Report, A-011-NEB, 1970.

Partial Technical Completion: Conjunctive Use of Ground & Surface Waters, Richard S. Harnsberger, Project Completion Report, A-013-NEB, 1970.

ANNUAL REPORTS

*Annual Report of Activities for Fiscal Year 1969, Water Resources Research Institute, University of Nebraska, Annual Report No. 5, June 1969.

Annual Report of Activities for Fiscal Year 1970, Water Resources Research Institute, University of Nebraska, Annual Report No. 6, June 1970.

MISCELLANEOUS PUBLICATIONS

Evapotranspiration, Norman J. Rosenberg, Hoyt E. Hart, Kirk W. Brown, University of Nebraska, November 1968.

Effects of Polyfluorocarbon Coatings on Scaling in Evaporators with Continuous Feed $CaSO_4$ Solutions, Dennis D. Kos & Luh C. Tao, University of Nebraska, Reprinted from I&EC Product Research & Development, 1969.

Research Relates Weather to Nebraska Water Use, Norman J. Rosenberg, University of Nebraska.

Computer Program for Plotting Time Dependent Data with Instruction and Examples, K. W. Brown & Norman J. Rosenberg, University of Nebraska, July 1969.

Evapotranspiration, Norman J. Rosenberg, University of Nebraska, 1966-1967, Project A-001-NEB.

NEVADA

NEVADA BUREAU OF MINES
University of Nevada
Reno, Nevada 89507

BULLETINS

65 Mineral and water resources of Nevada. Prepared by the United States Geological Survey and the Nevada Bureau of Mines as a United States Senate Document. 314 p., maps, tables. 1964. Price: $1.00.

MAPS

Note: These are available folded or rolled. Rolled maps are mailed with protective support to prevent damage, and require an additional $0.50 per order.

25 Hot springs, sinter deposits, and volcanic cinder cones in Nevada, by R. C. Horton. 1964. Scale, 1:1,000,000. Price: $0.75.

NEVADA COLORADO RIVER COMMISSION
P. O. Box 1748
410 South Third Street
Carson City, Nevada 89101

Report of Colorado River Commission of Nevada. Includes a study of proposed uses of power and water from Boulder Dam. January 1, 1927 to September 1935. 1935. 179 p.

Report. 1935-1944/46. Compiled from Report of State Engineer and issued with title "Compiled Reports".

Report. 1965 to date. (Became annual in 1965).

DEPARTMENT OF CONSERVATION AND NATURAL RESOURCES
Nye Building
Carson City, Nevada 89701

Annual Report of Department of Conservation and Natural Resources. 1957 to present. *These reports contain the annual reports of the Division of Water Resources; Division of Forestry; Division of State Lands; Division of Oil and Gas Conservation; and since 1963, the Division of State Parks.*

Proceedings of Annual Water Conference, 1946 to date, excluding 1953.

Nevada Soil and Water Conservation Needs Inventory. 1970. 76 p. Prepared by the Nevada Conservation Needs Committee.

Humboldt River Research Project. *A cooperative program under the direction of the Nevada State Department of Conservation and Natural Resources but involving several other state and federal agencies.*

Progress Reports

First — January 1960.

Second — January 1961.

Third — February 1962.

Fourth — January 1963.

Fifth — February 1964.

Sixth — February 1965.

Seventh — May 1966.

Eighth — April 1967.

Humboldt River Basin Cooperative Survey. *A cooperative program under the direction of the Nevada State Department of Conservation and Natural Resources but involving several other state and federal agencies.*

Reports

1   Little Humboldt Sub-Basin. March 1962.

2   Pine Valley Sub-Basin. June 1962.

3   Ruby Mountains Sub-Basin. May 1963

4   Mary's River Sub-Basin. June 1963.

5   North Fork Sub-Basin. August 1963.

6   Maggie Creek Sub-Basin. October 1963.

7   Elko Reach. April 1964.

8   Reese River Sub-Basin. June 1964.

9   Battle Mountain Sub-Basin. October 1964.

10 Sonoma Sub-Basin. May 1965.

11 Lovelock Sub-Basin. November 1965.

12 Basinwide report. November 1966.

Special Report

Chronology of Flood Years and High Water Years. June 1962.

DEPARTMENT OF CONSERVATION AND NATURAL RESOURCES
Division of Forestry
Nye Building
Carson City, Nevada 89701

Gray Creek Flood Report, by William C. Wood. 1965.

DEPARTMENT OF CONSERVATION AND NATURAL RESOURCES
Division of State Parks
Nye Building
Carson City, Nevada 89701

Part I and Part II, Recreation in Nevada, by M. J. Serven and Associates. 1965 and 1966.

Interpreting the State Outdoor Recreation Master Plan, by Dean L. Kastens. 1965.

Information Report – Proposed Lake Tahoe Park. 1963.

A Park for Lake Tahoe. 1963.

DEPARTMENT OF CONSERVATION AND NATURAL RESOURCES
Division of Water Resources
201 South Fall Street
Carson City, Nevada 89701

STATE WATER PLAN

Special Planning Report Summary: Water Supply for the Future in Southern Nevada. 1971. 16 p.

Guidelines for Nevada Water Planning – Report No. 1. 1971. 9 p.

Estimated Water Use in Nevada – Report No. 2. 1971. 32 p.

GROUND-WATER RESOURCES – RECONNAISSANCE SERIES

Prepared in cooperation with the U. S. Geological Survey.

1 Newark Valley, by T. E. Eakin, 1960.
2 Pine Valley, by T. E. Eakin, 1961.
3 Long Valley (White Pine County), by T. E. Eakin, 1961.
4 Pine Forest Valley, by W. C. Sinclair, 1962.
5 Imlay area, by T. E. Eakin, 1962.
6 Diamond Valley, by T. E. Eakin, 1962.
7 Desert Valley, by W. C. Sinclair, 1962.
8 Independence Valley, by T. E. Eakin, 1962.

9 Gabbs Valley, by T. E. Eakin, 1962.
10 Sarcobatus Flat and Oasis Valley, by G. T. Malmberg and T. E. Eakin, 1962.
11 Hualapai Flat, by W. C. Sinclair, 1962.
12 Ralston and Stonecabin Valley, by T. E. Eakin, 1962.
13 Cave Valley, by T. E. Eakin, 1962.
14 Amargosa Desert, by G. E. Walker and T. E. Eakin, 1963.
15 Long Valley-Massacre Lake region, by W. C. Sinclair, 1963.
16 Dry Lake and Delamar Valley, by T. E. Eakin, 1963.
17 Duck Lake Valley, by W. C. Sinclair, 1963.
18 Garden and Coal Valleys, by T. E. Eakin, 1963.
19 Antelope and Middle Reese River Valleys, by E. G. Crosthwaite, 1963.
20 Black Rock Desert area, by W. C. Sinclair, 1963.
21 Pahranagat and Pahroc Valleys, by T. E. Eakin, 1963.
22 Pueblo Valley – Continental Lake region, by W. C. Sinclair, 1963.
23 Dixie – Fairview Valley area, by Philip Cohen and D. E. Everett, 1963.
24 Lake Valley, by F. E. Rush and T. E. Eakin, 1963.
25 Coyote Spring and Kane Spring Valleys and Muddy River Springs area, by T. E. Eakin, 1964.
26 Edwards Creek Valley, by D. E. Everett, 1964.
27 Meadow Valley area, by F. E. Rush, 1964.
28 Smith Creek and Ione Valleys, by D. E. Everett and F. E. Rush, 1964.
29 Grass Valley, Pershing County, by Philip Cohen, 1964.
30 Monitor, Antelope and Kobeh Valleys, Nevada, by F. Eugene Rush and D. E. Everett, 1964.
31 Upper Reese River Valley, Lander and Nye Counties, Nevada, by T. E. Eakin, D. O. Moore, and D. E. Everett, 1965.
32 Lovelock Valley, Pershing County, Nevada, by D. E. Everett, and F. E. Rush, 1965.
33 Spring Valley, White Pine and Lincoln Counties, Nevada, by F. E. Rush and Kazmi, S. A. T., 1965.
34 Snake Valley area, Utah and Nevada, by J. W. Hood and F. E. Rush, 1965.
35 Huntington Valley area, Elko and White Pine Counties, Nevada, by F. E. Rush, and D. E. Everett, 1966.
36 Eldorado-Piute Valley area, Nevada, and California, by F. E. Rush and C. J. Huxel, Jr., 1966.
37 Grass and Carico Lake Valleys, Lander and Eureka Counties, Nevada, by D. E. Everett and F. E. Rush, 1966.
38 Water-Resources Appraisal of Little Fish Lake, Hot Creek, and Little Smoky Valleys, Nevada, by F. Eugene Rush and Duane E. Everett, 1966.
39 Hydrologic Appraisal of Eagle Valley, Ormsby County, Nevada, by G. F. Worts, Jr. and G. T. Malmberg (1966).

40 A brief appraisal of the water resources of the Walker Lake Area, Mineral, Lyon and Churchill Counties, Nevada, by D. E. Everett, and F. Eugene Rush (1967).

41 Water Resources Appraisal of Washoe Valley, Washoe County, Nevada, by F. Eugene Rush (1967).

42 Steptoe Valley — White Pine County, Nevada, by T. E. Eakin, 1967.

43 Warm Springs — Lemmon Valley Area — Washoe County, Nevada, by F. E. Rush and P. A. Glancy, 1967.

44 Smoke Creek — San Emidio Desert Area, Washoe County, Nevada, by P. A. Glancy and F. E. Rush, 1968.

45 Clayton Valley — Stonewall Flat Area, Nye County, Nevada, by F. E. Rush, 1968.

46 Mesquite — Ivanpah Valleys, Nye County, Nevada, by P. A. Glancy, 1968.

47 Thousand Springs Valley, Elko County, Nevada, by F. E. Rush, 1968.

48 Snake River tributaries, Elko and Humboldt Counties, Nevada, by D. O. Moore and T. E. Eakin, 1968.

49 Water Resources Appraisal of Butte Valley.

50 Water Resources Appraisal of the Lower Moapa-Lake Mead Area.

51 Water Resources Appraisal of the Lower Virgin River Valley Area.

Nevada Test Site and Vicinity, Nye County, Nevada, by T. E. Eakin, 1968.

WATER RESOURCES BULLETINS

2 Ground Water in Lovelock Valley, Nevada, by T. W. Robinson and J. C. Fredericks, USGS (1946).

3 Water levels and artesian pressure in wells in Las Vegas Valley and in other valleys, Nevada, 1913-45, by T. W. Robinson, G. B. Maxey, J. C. Fredericks, and C. H. Jameson, USGS (1947).

4 Well data in Las Vegas and Indian Springs Valleys, Nevada, by G. B. Maxey and C. H. Jameson, USGS, (1946).

5 Geology and water resources of Las Vegas, Pahrump, and Indian Springs Valley, Clark and Nye Counties, Nevada, by G. B. Maxey and C. H. Jameson, USGS, 1948.

6 Ground Water in Las Vegas, Pahrump, and Indian Spring Valley, Nevada (a summary), by G. B. Maxey and T. W. Robinson, USGS, 1947.

7 Geology and ground water in the Meadow Valley Wash drainage area, above the vicinity of Caliente, Nevada, by D. A. Phoenix, USGS, 1948.

8 Ground Water in White River Valley, White Pine, Nye, and Lincoln Counties, Nevada, by G. B. Maxey and T. E. Eakin, USGS, 1949.

10 Ground Water in Paradise Valley, Humboldt County, Nevada, by O. J. Loeltz, D. A. Phoenix, and T. W. Robinson, USGS, 1949.

11 Preliminary report on ground water in the Fish Lake Valley, Nevada and California, by T. E. Eakins, USGS, 1950.

12 Contributions to the hydrology of Eastern Nevada including Goshute-Antelope Valley, Elko County, Ground Water in the vicinity of Elko, Nevada, Ground Water in Clover and Independence Valleys, Elko County, and Ground Water in Railroad, Hot Creek, Reveille, Kawich and Penoyer Valleys, Nye, Lincoln and White Pine Counties, by T. E. Eakin, G. B. Maxey, T. W. Robinson, J. C. Fredericks, and O. J. Loeltz, USGS, 1951.

13 Geology and ground-water resources of Buena Vista Valley, Pershing County, Nevada, by O. J. Loeltz, and D. A. Phoenix, USGS, 1955.

14 Geology and ground-water resources of Quinn River Valley, Humboldt County, Nevada, by F. N. Visher, USGS, 1957.

15 Ground-Water Reconnaissance of Winnemucca Lake Valley, Pershing and Washoe Counties, Nevada, by C. P. Zones. Also published as USGS Water Supply Paper No. 1539-C, 1961.

and

Ground-Water Potentialities in the Crescent Valley, Eureka and Lander Counties, Nevada, by C. P. Zones. Also published as USGS Water Supply Paper No. 1581, 1961.

16 Ground-Water in the Alluvium of Kings River Valley, Humboldt County, Nevada, by C. P. Zones, 1963. Also published as USGS Water Supply Paper No. 1619-L, 1963.

17 Ground-Water Conditions in the Fernley-Wadsworth area, Churchill, Lyon, Storey, and Washoe Counties, Nevada, by W. C. Sinclair, and O. J. Loeltz, 1963. Also published as USGS Water Supply Paper 1619-AA, 1963.

18 A Summary of the Hydrology of the Las Vegas Ground-Water basin, Nevada, with special reference to the available supply, by G. T. Malmberg, USGS, 1961.

19 Preliminary Results of Hydrogeochemical Studies in the Humboldt River Valley near Winnemucca, Nevada, by Philip Cohen, USGS, 1962.

20 A Summary of the Specific Yield and Particle Size Relations of Quaternary Alluvium, Humboldt River Valley, Nevada, by Philip Cohen. Also published as USGS Water Supply Paper No. 1669-M, 1963.

21 Hydrology of the Lower Humboldt River Basin, Nevada, by J. D. Bredehoeft, DRI Tech. Rpt. No. 3, 1963.

22 Preliminary Results of Hydrogeologic Investigations in the Valley of the Humboldt River near Winnemucca, Nevada, by Philip Cohen. Also published as USGS Water Supply Paper No. 1754, 1964.

23 Ground-Water Conditions in the Vicinity of Lake Mead Base, Las Vegas, Nevada, by O. J. Loeltz, USGS, 1963.

24 An Evaluation of the Water Resources of the Humboldt River Valley near Winnemucca, Nevada, by Philip Cohen, USGS, 1963.

25 Extension of the East Range Fault by Gravity Exploration by K. Cartwright, J. N. Swinderman, and J. I. Gimlett, p. 39-46 (A64). Also Seismic Studies of Three Areas in Northern Nevada by C. D. McGinnis and W. W. Dudley, p. 25-37, 1964. Also Seismic Refraction and Earth Resistivity Investigation of Hydrogeologic Problems in the Humboldt River Basin, Nevada, by W. W. Dudley, Jr., and L. D. McGinnis, DRI Tech. Rpt. No. 1, 1964.

27   Water in Humboldt River Valley near Winnemucca, Nevada, by Philip Cohen, USGS, 1964.

28   Evaluation of Hydrogeology and Hydrogeochemistry of Truckee Meadows Area, Washoe County, Nevada, by Philip Cohen and O. J. Loeltz. Also published as USGS Water Supply Paper No. 1779-S, 1964.

29   Ground-Water in Las Vegas Valley, by P. A. Domenico, D. A. Stephenson, and G. B. Maxey, DRI Tech. Rpt. No. 7, 1964.

30   Interim Inventory of Surface Water Resources of Nevada by R. D. Lamke and D. O. Moore, USGS, 1965.

31   The Effects of Pumping on the Hydrology of Kings River Valley, Humboldt County, Nevada, 1957-64 by G. T. Malmberg,and G. F. Worts, Jr. (1966).

32   Hydrologic Reconnaissance of the Humboldt River Basin, Nevada, by Thomas E. Eakin and Robert D. Lamke, (1966).

33   A Regional Interbasin Groundwater System in the White River area, Southeastern Nevada, by Thomas E. Eakin, Water Resources Research Vol. 2, No. 2 (1966).

34   Effects of Irrigation Development on the Water Supply of Quinn River Valley Area, Nevada and Oregon, 1950-64, (1966), by C. J. Huxel Jr., J. E. Parks, and D. E. Everett, (1966).

35   Ground Water in Diamond Valley, Eureka County, Nevada, by J. R. Harrill, 1968.

36   Estimating Mean Runoff in Ungaged Semi-Arid Areas.

37   Hydrologic Response of Irrigation Pumping in Hualapai Flat.

38   Ground Water in Mason Valley, Lyon County, Nevada, by C. J. Husel, 1968.

40   A Proposed Streamflow Data Program for Nevada.

      Runoff to Truckee Meadows, by R. D. Lamke, 1968.

      Ground Water in Hualapai Flat, Washoe County, Nevada, by J. R. Harrill, 1968.

INFORMATION SERIES REPORTS

1   The Ground-Water Situation in Nevada, by O. J. Loeltz and G. T. Malmberg. 1961.

2   A Preliminary Evaluation of the Ground-Water Hydrology of the Valley of the Humboldt River, near Winnemucca, Nevada, (and) Specific Yield of Sediments of the Humboldt River Valley, Humboldt County, Nevada, by Philip Cohen, 1962.

3   Contributions to the Hydrology of Northern Nevada, by Philip Cohen, 1962.

4   A Proposed Ten-Year Cooperative Water Resources Program between the State of Nevada and U. S. Geological Survey, by Hugh A. Shamberger, 1962.

5   Land Subsidence in Las Vegas Valley, Nevada, 1935-63, by G. T. Malmberg, 1964.

6   Geographical Features of the Hydrographic Areas of Nevada, by F. E. Rush, 1968.

7   Water Use in Nevada, by J. R. Harrill and G. F. Worts, Jr., 1968.

OTHER

Included here are various reports prepared by the Nevada State Engineer. That office was succeeded by the Dept. of Conservation and Natural Resources.

Hydrographic Areas of Nevada (map), by F. E. Rush and others, 1968.

Report of Field Investigation of Water Filings and Diversions in the Lake Tahoe Basin, Nevada, by William J. Newman. December 1966.

Biennial Reports of State Engineer – 1903-1958. Subsequent reports of the Division of Water Resources contained in Annual Report of the State of Nevada Department of Conservation and Natural Resources.

Progress report on the ground water resources of the Las Vegas artesian basin, Nevada, by George B. Maxey and C. H. Jameson. 1945. 36 p.

Ground water in Spanish Spring and Sun Valleys, Washoe County, Nevada, by Thomas W. Robinson and David A. Phoenix. 1948. 25 p.

Nevada and California State Engineers Joint Report on the Use of Water in the Lake Tahoe Watershed. 1949.

Ground-water conditions in Whisky Flat, Mineral County, Nevada, by T. E. Eakin and T. W. Robinson. 1950. 5 p.

Ground water for Indian Service Hospital at Schurz, Nevada, by Thomas W. Robinson. 1950. 9 p.

Ground water in the vicinity of Verdi, Washoe County, Nevada, by T. W. Robinson and others. 1951. 28 p.

Nevada water law. 1953. 75 p.

Nevada law of water rights, by Wells A. Hutchins. 1955. 66 p.

STATE DEPARTMENT OF HIGHWAYS
Highway Building
1263 South Stewart Street
Carson City, Nevada 89701

Annual Meteorological Summaries for Carson City, Nevada, 1950-1961. 1962.

STATE FISH AND GAME COMMISSION
1100 Valley Road
P. O. Box 10678
Reno, Nevada 89510

Reservoirs and their Significance to the Sport Fisheries of Nevada. 1966.

Economics of an Arid Southwest Impoundment. Dale Lockard. 1965.

Lake Tahoe Basin Report. Tahoe Area Council. 1963.

Fishes and Fisheries of Nevada. Dr. Ira LaRivers. 1962.

Lake Topaz Report. Ray Corlett. 1958.

Lake Tahoe Report. Ray Corlett. 1958.

Pyramid Lake Report. Virgil K. Johnson. 1958.

Fisheries Management Report — Tahoe and Topaz Lakes. July 1, 1954 to June 30, 1958.

Walker Lake Report. Robert C. Allan. 1958.

Stream and Lake Survey Report. T. C. Frantz and Donald King. 1958.

Lahontan Reservoir Report. Robert C. Sumner. 1957.

Indian Lakes Report. Robert C. Sumner and V. K. Johnson. 1957.

Ryepatch Reservoir Report. Robert C. Sumner and V. K. Johnson. 1957.

Stillwater Marsh Report. R. C. Sumner and V. K. Johnson. 1957.

Washoe Lake Report. Robert C. Sumner and V. K. Johnson. 1957.

Lake Mead and Mohave Survey Report. A. R. Jonez and Robert C. Sumner. 1954.

Death of a Lake. Thomas J. Trelease. 1952.

A Contribution to the Limnology of Arid Regions. 1937.

DEPARTMENT OF HEALTH, WELFARE AND REHABILITATION
Division of Health
Bureau of Environmental Health
Carson City, Nevada 89701

LAWS AND REGULATIONS

(Only those having some connection with water are cited here.)

Chemical Analysis of Municipal Water Supplies of Nevada.

Law Relating to Protection of Lake Tahoe Watershed and Regulations Governing the Lake Tahoe Watershed.

Water Supply Regulations, 1952.

*Water Pollution Control Regulations.

OTHER

Report on Water Pollution Control, Lake Tahoe Watershed, by Nevada Division of Public Engineering. 1953.

CENTER FOR WATER RESOURCES RESEARCH
Desert Research Institute
University of Nevada System
Reno, Nevada 89507

TECHNICAL REPORT SERIES (H-W)

1 Domenico, P. A., D. F. Schulke & G. B. Maxey, Physical and Economical Aspects of Conjunctive Use of Irrigation Water in Smith Valley, Lyon County, Nevada. (July 1966).

*2 Orcutt, R. G. & G. F. Cochran, A Reconnaissance of the Technology for Recharging Reclaimed Waste Water into the Las Vegas Valley Ground-Water Basin. (July 1967).

3 Domenico, P. A., Valuation of a Ground-Water Supply for Management and Development. (July 1967).

4 Mifflin, M. D., Delineation of Ground-Water Flow Systems in Nevada. (July 1968).

*5 Orcutt, R. G., An Engineering-Economic Analysis of Systems Utilizing Aquifer Storage for the Irrigation of Parks and Gold Courses with Reclaimed Wastewater. (October 1967).

6 Sharp, John V. A. & Richard L. Bateman, Jerome A. Westphal, Digital Simulation Model of Inorganic Water Quality of Tahoe-Truckee System, Nevada — California. (April 1970).

TECHNICAL REPORTS (DRI)

*1 Dudley, W. W. and L. D. McGinnis, Seismic-Refraction and Earth Resistivity Investigation of Hydrogeological Problems in the Humboldt River Basin, Nevada. (1962). Reprinted in DRI Technical Report No. 2.

2 Desert Research Institute, Geophysical Studies in Nevada Relating to Hydrology. (January 1964).

3 Bredehoeft, John D., Hydrogeology of the Lower Humboldt River Basin, Nevada. (June 1963).

*4 Farvolden, R., Hydrology of Lower Humboldt River Basin, Nevada. (1965).

5 Hawley, John W. & William E. Wilson III, Quaternary Geology of the Winnemucca Area, Nevada. (November 1965).

6 Domenico, P. A., D. A. Stephenson, & G. B. Maxey, Ground Water in Las Vegas Valley. (April 1964). Prepared in cooperation with the Dept. of Conservation and Natural Resources, State of Nevada.

PROJECT REPORT SERIES

1 Kashef, A. I., Evaluation of Drainage Problems in Waterlogged Areas and Bolsons in Nevada. (September 1965).

2 Rogers, L. F. and W. V. Neely, Costs and Returns from Crops and Livestock in the Upland Desert Valleys of Nevada. (August 1966).

2A Bourns, C. T., Irrigated Lands of Nevada. (October 1966).

*3 Myles, G. A., Water Based Recreation — Tahoe. (November 1966).

*3A Myles, G. A., Water Based Recreation — Mead and Mohave. (December 1966).

*3B Myles, G. A., Water Based Recreation — Western Desert and Northern Lakes. (March 1967).

*3C Myles, G. A., Water Based Recreation — Statistical Appendix. (February 1968).

3D   Myles, G. A., Participation in Water Based Recreation by Tourists. (September 1969).

*3E   Myles, G. A., Effect of Quality Factors on Water Based Recreation in Western Nevada. (September 1969).

4   Fordham, J., and C. K. Stidd, Location of Hydrologic Gages in Nevada and the Adjacent Sierra. (March 1967).

5   Crouse, L. and G. B. Maxey, A Storage and Retrieval System for the Nevada Water Resources Data Center. (February 1967).

6   Schulke, D. F., P. A. Domenico and G. B. Maxey, Aspects of Surface Water Resources, Humboldt River Basin, Nevada. (August 1967).

7   Schulke, D. F., P. A. Domenico and G. B. Maxey, Analog Computer for Hydrologic Research. (November 1966).

*8   Weyler, P. A., Use of Atomic Absorption Spectrometry to Study the Distribution of Trace Elements in Various Hydrological and Geological Environments. (October 1966).

*9   Anderson, David V., Theoretical Framework for Ascertaining Porewater Pressure in Confining Layers in the Vicinity of a Pumping Well. (July 1968).

10   Center for Water Resources Research, Humboldt River Studies. (July 1969).

*11   Center for Water Resources Research, Infiltration Studies on Non-wettable Soils. (July 1968).

*12   Timko, S. T. and C. M. Skau, A Low Intensity Rain Simulator for Long Duration Rain-on-Snow Events. (October 1968).

13   Morris, R. J., and Michael Natalino, The Chemical Nature of the Organic Matrix Believed to Limit Water Penetration in Granitic Soils. (July 1969).

PROJECT REPORT SERIES

*Preliminary First Report: Roelofs, Robert; Values, Ethics and Policy in Relation to Resource Development and Conservation: A Selected Bibliography. (April 1968).

Fiero, Jr., G. W. & J. R. Illian, Interim Report, Regional Hydrology – Hot Creek Valley Flow System – Nye County, Nevada. (1969). Review copy only.

*Shamberger, Hugh A., Directory of Federal and State Agencies Operating in the Field of Water and Related Land Resources. Dept. of Conservation and Natural Resources, Inventory Series No. 1, July 1967.

Shamberger, Hugh A., Inventory of Printed Information and Data Pertaining to Water and Related Land Resources in Nevada. Dept. of Conservation and Natural Resources, Inventory Series No. 2, October 1967.

Shamberger, Hugh A., Outline of Activities of Agencies and Organizations Concerned with Problems of Water and Related Land Resources in Nevada. Dept. of Conservation and Natural Resources, Inventory Series No. 3, 1968.

PREPRINTS

DRI 45   Stidd, C. K., Local Moisture and Precipitation; August 1967.

*DRI 66   Stidd, C. K., Synthetic Rainfall Data; April 1969.

DRI 68   Sharp, J. V. A., Time-Dependent Behavior of Water Chemistry in Hydrologic Systems; May 1969.

DRI 71   Sharp, J. V. A., Analysis of Time-Variant Behavior of Water Chemistry, Paper H-23, 51st Annual Meeting, American Geophysical Union, Washington, D. C., (April 21, 1970).

NEW HAMPSHIRE

DEPARTMENT OF RESOURCES AND ECONOMIC DEVELOPMENT

Division of Economic Development
P. O. Box 856
State House Annex
Concord, New Hampshire 03301

Note: When ordering any of the publications listed below, please make checks payable to the State of New Hampshire.

MINERAL RESOURCE REPORTS

New Hampshire Mineral Resources Survey: (only those sections dealing with water are listed here).

Part XI   Artesian Wells in New Hampshire. Richard P. Goldthwait. Studies by J. W. Goldthwait, D. H. Chapman, L. Goldthwait. 1949. 24 p., illus.

Part XVIII   Suburban and Rural Water Supplies in Southeastern New Hampshire. T. R. Meyers and Edward Bradley. 1960. 31 p., Price: $0.75.

Part XX   Drilled Water Wells in New Hampshire. Glenn W. Stewart. 1968. 58 p., Price: $0.50.

MISCELLANEOUS

Navigation Charts: Single copies only may be procured from the Division of Economic Development. Write to the Division for information regarding quantity supplies. Scale 1 inch equals 2,000 feet. Price: $0.50 each.

Newfound Lake	13" x 18" border size
Ossipee Lake	19" x 21 3/4" border size
Squam Lake	21 3/4" x 24" border size
Lake Sunapee	16 1/2" x 27" border size
Winnisquam Lake	16 1/2" x 27" border size
Lake Winnipesaukee	25" x 21" border size

New Hampshire Water. December 1953. Maps, charts. Price: $2.00.

STATE PLANNING PROJECT
Concord
New Hampshire 03301

Note: This agency is no longer in existence.

REPORTS
Only those dealing with water are cited here

1   Baker River Watershed Development Potential. 1964. 51 p.

4   New Hampshire Water Bodies and Public Access Points. Part I. 1964. 100 p.

10   The Water Resources of New Hampshire. 1965. 216 p.

12   New Hampshire Public Water Bodies and Public Access Points — Part II. 1965. 123 p.

13   The New Hampshire Outdoor Recreation Plan. 1966. 231 p.

NEW HAMPSHIRE WATER RESOURCES BOARD

State House Annex
Concord, New Hampshire 03301

The following studies have been prepared in cooperation with the United States Geological Survey:

New Hampshire Basic-Data Report No. I, Ground Water Series, Southeastern Area. Edward Bradley and Richard G. Petersen. 1962. 53 p., Maps.

Ground-Water Favorability Map of the Nashua-Merrimack Area, New Hampshire. James M. Weigle. 1963.

Ground-Water Favorability Map of the Salem-Plaistow Area, New Hampshire. James M. Weigle. 1964.

New Hampshire Basic-Data Report No. II, Ground Water Series, Lower Merrimack River Valley. James P. Weigle and Richard Kranes. 1966. 44 p., Map.

WATER SUPPLY AND POLLUTION CONTROL COMMISSION

Prescott Park
105 Loudon Road
Concord, New Hampshire 03301

All of the following reports are concerned with water resources. The transcript of the Public Hearing is available for many of them. For more information, please contact the Commission.

Ammonoosuc River. August 1949.

Nubanusit Brook and Skatutakee Lake. Nov. 1949.

Bacterial Reductions in the Chlorination of Sewage Report No. 1. March 1950. (Revised and Reprinted) March 1959.

Laconia Study. May 1950.

Report for Hearing on:
    Clark Brook
    Oliverian Brook
    Indian Pond Brook
    Jacobs Brook
    Clay Brook
    Grant Brook. May 1950.

Report for Hearing on:
    Bloods Brook
    Mink Brook
    Hewes Brook
    Camp Brook
    Boston Lot Reservoir. July 1950.

Eastman Brook. July 1950.

Meredith Sewage Treatment Requirements. July 1950.

Sugar River. Jan. 1951.

Mascoma River. April 1952.

Piscataquog River. May 1952.

Saco River. May 1952.

Little Sugar River. June 1952.

Ashuelot River (upper portion). June 1952.

Cold River. June 1952.

Partridge Brook. Dec. 1953.

Pennichuck Brook. Jan. 1954.

Salmon Brook. Feb. 1954.

Beaver Brook. Mar. 1954.

Pemigewasset River Tributaries (Horner Brook to Willow Brook). Oct. 1954.

Baker River (Lower Portion). Oct. 1954.

Copper Sulfate Control of *Vaucheria Sp.*, Bay Point Beach, Lake Sunapee, New Hampshire, Frost, Terrence P., May 15, 1955.

Aftergrowth of Coliform Organisms in Dilute Chlorinated Sewage, Frost, Terrence P., May 21, 1955.

Bacterial Reductions in the Chlorination of Sewage Report No. 2. Feb. 1955. (Revised & Reprinted) Feb. 1968.

Results of Acceptance Tests on Automatic Chlorinating Facilities at the Laconia Sewage Treatment Plant. Feb. 1956.

Great Brook (Re-Study). May 1956.

Ossipee River Watershed. Oct. 1956.

Brezner Tanning Corp. (wastes from side division). Feb. 1957.

Connecticut River and Tributaries (Canadian Border to Upper Ammonoosuc River). Oct. 1958.

Spicket River. Oct. 1958.

Why Control Water Pollution? (philosophy). Nov. 1958.

Pemigewasset River Watershed. Nov. 1958.

Piscetaqua River Watershed (progress report). Feb. 1959.

Bacterial Reductions in the Chlorination of Sewage Report No. 2. Feb. 1955. (Revised & Reprinted) Feb. 1968.

Lake Sunapee Classification Enforcement Program. Mar. 1959.

Treatment of Overflows from Combined Sewerage Systems By Use of Storm Water Storage and Chlorination. Mar. 1959.

Public Water Supplies. April 1959.

Water Pollution Control Activities. Feb. 1960.

Observations and Experiences in the Control of Algae, Terrence P. Frost for N. H. Water Works Association. April 1960.

Bacterial Reductions in the Chlorination of Sewage Report No. 3. Mar. 1960.

Piscataqua River Watershed Vol. I & Vol. II. Sept. 1960.

Progress Report to the N. H. Water Pollution Control Board On Fertilization of Lake Winnisquam. Report by Metcalf & Eddy, Consulting Engineers, Boston, Massachusetts, and was financed by special appropriation by Governor and Council. Jan. 1961.

Millers River Watershed. Jan. 1961.

Massabasic Lake Watershed. April 1961.

Water-Borne Typhoid Epidemic at Keene, N. H., Healy, W. A. and Grossman, R. P. Journal of New England Water Works Assoc. (printing only paid for by NEWWA.) 1961.

Water Pollution Control During Construction, Gravel Washing and Logging Activities. Oct. 1961. (Revised & Reprinted) Aug. 1968.

Little River and Powwow River Watersheds. March 1963.

Nashua River Watershed. Oct. 1964.

Household Detergents in New Hampshire, Vosa, W. C., P. E. 1964.

Androscoggin River Tributaries. Oct. 1964.

Report to the 1965 Legislature From the Interim Committee on Improved Pesticide Controls. (financed by N. H. Water Pollution Comm.) Dec. 1964.

Coastal Watershed. July 1965.

Guide to Stream Classifications. 1947-1965. (with supplement listings) 1967-1969 classifications.

Portions of Androscoggin River, Connecticut River & Merrimack River Watershed. July 1966.

Pemigewasset River. Oct. 1966.

Report on Water Quality Standards Initiated by FWPCA, compiled and submitted by NHWSPCC staff. Printed and published by FWPCA. June 1967.

Aquatic Nuisance Control Program Status Report, by Robert Normandin, Ph.D. (financed by special Legislative appropriation). Nov. 1967.

Comprehensive Report on Water Supplies and Sewerage (Cheshire and Hillsborough Counties) (Towns Under 5500 Population), prepared by Brown & Long, Engineers, Hanover, N. H. Dec. 1967.

The Galloping Ghost of Eutrophy, Frost, T. P. for "Appalachia" Vol. XXXVII, No. 1. Reprinted by N. H. Water Supply & Pollution Control Commission. June 1968.

Briefing on Lake Winnisquam Algae Problem by T. P. Frost, initiated by Governor & Council Special Committee. Feb. 1968.

Protect Yourself and Your State Before It's Too Late — 1967-1968 (brochure for prospective buyers & builders). July 1968.

Weekly Variation of Algae in Sewage Stabilization Pond System at Exeter, N. H., Frost, T. P. Jan. 1969.

Laws Relating to the Water Supply and Pollution Control Commission. Jan. 1969.

Regulations Governing the Sanitation of Juvenile Recreational Camps. June 1969.

The Industrial Pollution Problem in New Hampshire, by R. A. Nylander, P. E., NHWSPCC staff for Citizens Task Force. July 1969.

Oil Pollution Control in Portsmouth Harbor, by R. A. Nylander, P. E., NHWSPCC staff for Citizens Task Force. July 1969.

Land Developments and Waste Disposal Shoreline Law, Chapter 149-E RSA, by R. A. Eckloff, P. E., NHWSPCC staff for Citizens Task Force. July 1969.

Treatment Plants in Operation-Treatment Plants Under Construction-Interstate and Intrastate Construction, by C. W. Metcalf, NHWSPCC staff for Citizens Task Force. July 1969.

Planning and Construction of Municipal and Industrial Waste Treatment Facilities in New Hampshire, by C. W. Metcalf, NHWSPCC staff for Citizens Task Force. July 1969.

Thermal Considerations In Relation to Water Quality — Testimony given to Citizens Task Force sub-committee on Industrial and Domestic Wastes, by T. P. Frost, Chief Aquatic Biologist, NHWSPCC staff. July 1969.

Detergent Problems and Some Solutions, Testimony given to Citizens Task Force sub-committee on Industrial and Domestic Wastes by T. P. Frost, Chief Aquatic Biologist, NHWSPCC staff. July 1969.

Deterioration of Lakes From Excessive Fertilization, Testimony given to Citizens Task Force sub-committee on Industrial and Domestic Wastes by T. P. Frost, Chief Aquatic Biologist, NHWSPCC staff. July 1969.

Dredging, Filling, Excavating, Mining and Construction In Surface Waters of the State, Testimony given to Citizens Task Force sub-committee on Industrial and Domestic Wastes by T. P. Frost, Chief Aquatic Biologist, NHWSPCC staff. July 1969.

Comments on Pesticides Control, Testimony given to Citizens Task Force sub-committee on Industrial and Domestic Wastes by T. P. Frost, Chief Aquatic Biologist, NHWSPCC staff. July 1969.

Estimated Aid and Construction Costs for Pollution Abatement Facilities — 1969-1976, by C. W. Metcalf, NHWSPCC staff for Citizens Task Force. Aug. 1969.

Destratification of Kezar Lake — Report. In preparation.

WATER RESOURCES RESEARCH CENTER
University of New Hampshire
Durham, New Hampshire 03824

Water Resources Research Center, University of New Hampshire. 1966. Proceedings of Water Rights Law Conference. Boston, Massachusetts. Sponsored jointly by the New England Council of Water Center Directors.

Bourcier, Donald V., and Robert H. Forste. 1967. Economic Analysis of Public Water Supply in the Piscataqua River Watershed — I: An Average Cost Approach. Bulletin No. 1, UNH-WRRC-B1.

Drooker, Penelope B. 1968. Application of the Stanford Watershed Model to a Small New England Watershed. Thesis — Master of Science, Graduate School, Department of Soil and Water Science, University of New Hampshire, Durham, New Hampshire.

Forste, Robert H., and Robert L. Christensen. 1968. Economic Analysis of Public Water Supply in the Piscataqua River Watershed — II: Economic Analysis in Public Water Supply Systems. Bulletin No. 2, UNH-WRRC-B2.

Hoeh, Roger S. 1968. A Study of the Feasibility of Social Science Research Designed to Identify and Analyze Social Responses to Precipitation Management Operations in New England. Department of Political Science, University of New Hampshire, Durham, New Hampshire.

Water Resources Research Center, University of New Hampshire. 1968. Proceedings of Water Resources Planning Conference, Boston, Massachusetts, May 16-17, 1968. Sponsored jointly by the New England Council of Water Center Directors.

Gruendling, Gerhard K., and Arthur C. Mathieson. 1969. Phytoplankton Populations in Relation to Trophic Levels of Lakes in New Hampshire, U. S. A. Research Report No. 1, UNH-WRRC-RR1.

Norton, Kenneth W., and Robert H. Forste. 1969. Minimal Cost Estimation for Lakefront Sewage Systems. Technical Working Paper No. 1. UNH-WRRC-TWP1.

Water Resources Research Center, University of New Hampshire. 1970. Sixth Annual Report. UNH-WRRC-BAR.

Forste, Robert H., and Alexander J. Kalinski. 1970. A Survey of New Hampshire Water Law. Bulletin No. 3, UNH-WRRC-B3.

Sawyer, Philip J. 1970. The Effects of Copper Sulfate on Certain Algae and Zooplankters in Winnisquam Lake, New Hampshire. Research Report No. 2, UNH-WRRC-RR2.

NEW JERSEY

NEW JERSEY DEPARTMENT OF COMMUNITY AFFAIRS
P. O. Box 2768
Trenton, New Jersey 08625

Note: Orders should include the number of copies desired, the catalog code number, unit price, and total amount. Make checks or money orders payable to "Treasurer, State of New Jersey." Send order with check or money order to the Office of Public Information (address as given above).

SRP SERIES

9 Fishery and Wildlife Resources in New Jersey. 1964. 32 p. Price: $1.00.

13 New Jersey's Delaware Bay Shore. 1964. 39 p. Price: $1.50.

15 New Jersey's Shore. 1966. 95 p. Price: $2.00.

MAPS

B4A-33 Major and Secondary Drainage Basins of New Jersey. 1963. (27" x 47", four miles to inch.) Price: $1.00.

B4A-34 Major and Secondary Drainage Basins of New Jersey Showing Major Stream Beds. 1963. (27" x 47", four miles to inch.) Price: $1.00.

B4A-45 Public and Privately Owned Potable Watershed Properties in New Jersey. 1964. (27" x 47", four miles to inch.) Price: $1.00.

B8A-28 Public and Privately Owned Potable Watershed Properties in New Jersey. 1964. (14" x 24", eight miles to inch.) Price: $0.50.

DEPARTMENT OF ENVIRONMENTAL PROTECTION
Bureau of Geology and Topography
P. O. Box 1889
Trenton, New Jersey 08625

Note: When ordering publications, please make check payable to: "Treasurer, State of New Jersey (EP-GT)".

REPORTS OF THE STATE GEOLOGIST
(issued between 1890 and 1927)

Vol. III Water Supply. 1894. xvi plus 448 p. Price: $1.00.

BULLETINS

*2 Report on the approximate cost of a canal between Bay Head and the Shrewsbury River, by H. B. Kummel. 1911.

*— Report on Shark River Inlet, by C. C. Vermeule. 1912.

*— Second Report on Shark River Inlet, by C. C. Vermeule. 1913.

*30 Ground-Water Supplies of the Atlantic City Region, by D. G. Thompson. 1928.

*33 Surface Water Supply of New Jersey to September 30, 1928, by O. W. Hartwell. 1929.

*35 Ground Water Supplies in the Vicinity of Asbury Park, by D. G. Thompson. 1930.

*38 Ground-Water Supplies of the Passaic River Valley Near Chatham, New Jersey, by D. G. Thompson. 1932.

*39 Ground-Water Supplies of the Camden Area, New Jersey, by D. G. Thompson. 1932.

GEOLOGIC REPORT SERIES

2 Thirty-One Selected Deep Wells—Logs and Map, by Meredith E. Johnson. Price: $10.00.

3 Deep Wells of the New Jersey Coastal Plain, by Haig Kasabach and Ronald Scudder. Price: $10.00.

7 Geology of Ground Water Resources of Mercer County, New Jersey, by Kemble Widmer. 115 p., map. Price: $3.00.

8 Geology as a Guide to Regional Estimates of The Water Resource, by Kemble Widmer. 15 p. Price: $1.00.

10 Water Resources Resume, by Kemble Widmer. State Atlas Sheet No. 23, parts of Bergen, Morris and Passaic Counties. 34 p., map. Price: $2.00.

REPORTS
(last issued in 1917)

*3 Report on Water-Supply, Water-Power, the Flow of Streams and Attendant Phenomena, by C. C. Vermeule. 1894.

*4 Physical Geography of New Jersey, by R. D. Salisbury and C. C. Vermeule. 1898.

PUBLICATIONS

The Geology and Geography of New Jersey, by Kemble Widmer. The New Jersey Historical Series, Vol. 19. Price: $3.95.

MISCELLANEOUS PUBLICATIONS

*Cruising New Jersey Tidewater, by Fred Van Deventer. A Boating and Touring Guide. Price: $4.95.

The Macmillan Marine Atlas, New Jersey and Delaware Waters including the Atlantic Intracoastal Waterway. 1968/1969 Edition. Price: $7.95.

Geologic, Hydrologic and Well-Drilling Characteristics of the Rocks of Northern and Central New Jersey. Price: $0.50.

The Origin of Roaring Brook. Price: $0.50.

MISCELLANEOUS MAPS

Stream Maps. Streams, ponds and lakes only — by individual counties. (Burlington County is in two portions, upper and lower.) Price: $1.00 each.

Ground Water Protected Areas of New Jersey. Price: $2.00.

DEPARTMENT OF ENVIRONMENTAL PROTECTION

Division of Water Policy and Supply
P. O. Box 1390
Trenton, New Jersey 08625

Note: Where available, publications are free upon request for as long as the supply lasts.

WATER RESOURCES CIRCULARS

3   Flood Damage Alleviation in New Jersey.

*4   Factual Data for Public Supply Wells and Selected Irrigation Wells in Monmouth County, 1961.

*5   Earthquake Fluctuations in Wells in New Jersey, 1961.

7   Records of Wells and Ground Water Quality in Burlington County, New Jersey.

8   Factual Report Summarizing Records of Wells, Well Logs, and Summary of Stratigraphy of Cape May County, New Jersey.

9   Public Water Supplies in Gloucester County, New Jersey.

11   Present and Prospective Use of Water by the Manufacturing Industries of New Jersey.

12   Data from the Test Drilling Program at Island Beach State Park, New Jersey.

*13 Floods in New Jersey, Magnitude & Frequency.

14   Flood Depth — Frequency in New Jersey.

*15 Flow Probability of New Jersey Streams.

*16 Results of the Drought-Disaster Test-Drilling Program near Morristown, New Jersey.

17   Results of the Second Phase of the Drought-Disaster Test-Drilling near Morristown, New Jersey.

18   Summary of Ground Water Resources of Atlantic County, New Jersey.

19   Iron in Ground Waters of the Magothy and Raritan Formations in Camden and Burlington Counties.

20   Water Resources of the Sayreville Area, Middlesex County, New Jersey.

21   Preliminary Report on Available Water Supply Sources, Water Demand Projections and Proposed New Water Resources Development for Northeastern New Jersey.

SPECIAL REPORTS

5   Surface Water Supply of New Jersey, Stream Flow Records October 1, 1928 — September 30, 1934.

6   Supplementary Report on the Ground Water Supplies of the Atlantic City Region.

9   Surface Water Supply of New Jersey, Stream Flow Records October 1, 1934 — September 30, 1940.

10   Preliminary Report on the Geology and Ground Water Supply of Newark, New Jersey.

12   Surface Water Supply of New Jersey, Stream Flow Records October 1940 — September 1945.

13   Ground Water Resources in the Tri-State Region Adjacent to the Lower Delaware River.

14   Surface Water Supply of New Jersey, Stream Flow Records October 1945 — September 1950.

16   Surface Water Supply of New Jersey, Stream-Flow Records October 1950 — September 1955.

17   Salt Water Encroachment into Aquifers of the Raritan Formation in the Sayreville Area, Middlesex County.

18   Ground Water Resources of Cape May County, New Jersey — Salt Water Invasion of Principal Aquifers.

19   Geology and Ground Water Resources of Mercer County.

20   Surface Water Records 1955-1960.

22   Chloride Concentrations of Water from Wells in the Atlantic Coastal Plain of New Jersey, 1923-1961.

23   Geology and Ground Water Resources of Monmouth County, New Jersey.

24   Geology and Ground Water Resources of Hunterdon County, New Jersey.

25   Availability of Ground Water in Morris County, New Jersey.

26   Geology and Ground Water Resources of Burlington County, New Jersey.

27   Geology and Ground Water Resources of the Rahway Area, New Jersey.

28   Ground Water Resources of Essex County, New Jersey.

29   Geology and Ground Water Resources of Ocean County, New Jersey.

30   Water Resources and Geology of Gloucester County, New Jersey.

31   Surface Water Supply of New Jersey, 1960-1965.

33   Geology and Ground Water Resources of Salem County, New Jersey.

OTHER

*Report on Water Resources of the State and Their Development, by Allen Hazen, et al. 1922. 76 p.

NEW JERSEY STATE WATER POLICY COMMISSION

This Commission is no longer in existence.

*Annual Report. 1930-1936.

*New Jersey Ship Canal Effect Upon Potable Waters. Report to the Senate of the State. 1943. 26 p.

*Report on the Development of Adequate Water Supplies for North and South Jersey. 1945. 22 p.

WATER RESOURCES RESEARCH INSTITUTE

Rutgers University
College of Agriculture Campus
New Brunswick, New Jersey 08903

Note: Some of the publications listed below are available from the author or the publisher. This has been indicated where applicable.

1968

Brush, L. M. Jr., McMichael, F. C., and Kuo, C. Y., Artificial Mixing of Density Stratified Fluids: A Laboratory Investigation. Final Report of Research Project B-005-N.J. WRRI & L. F. Moody Hydrodynamics Lab. Report No. MH-R-2, 1968. 80 p. (Related to project B-024-N.J.)

Hanks, E. M., New Jersey Water Law: Part I. Rutgers Law Review, 22:621-715, 1968. Reprinted WRRI. Project Completion Report available only.

Havens, A. V., Snow, W. B., Horowitz, I. L., and Liu, C. S., Drought Frequency Intensity and Duration: Its Correlation to Stream Flow and Its Impact Upon Synthetic Hydrology. N.J. WRRI. April 1968. (Available from author.)

Hsu, Pa Ho, Removal of Phosphate from Water by Aluminum and Iron. October 1968. (Completion Report B-008-N.J.) WRRI.

Hsu, Pa Ho, Precipitation of Hydroxy-Aluminum Polymers by Sulfate. Paper presented at Division II, Soil Science Society of America, New Orleans, Louisiana. November 12, 1968. (Available from author.)

Tarassov, V. J. and Perlis, H. J., The Optimization of Multivariable Systems and Distributed Parameters. Paper presented at the Sixth Annual Allerton Conference on Circuit and System Theory, Monticello, Illinois. October 1968. (Available from author.)

Tarassov, V. J. and Perlis, H. J., The Sub-Optimal Control of Multivariable Distributed Parameter Systems. Paper presented at the Second Annual Asilomar Conference on Systems and Circuit Theory, Naval Postgraduate School, Monterey, California. October 1968. (Available from author.)

Whipple, W. Jr., Economic Basis for Water Resources Analysis. June 1968. Price: $2.00. WRRI.

Whipple, W. Jr., Flood Control Policy and Flood Management, (Interstate Conference on Water Problems.) New Orleans, Louisiana. 1968.

Whipple, W. Jr., Metropolitan Area Water Resource Problems. Proceedings, Fourth Annual Meeting of the American Water Resources Association, New York. November 18-21, 1968.

1969

Beyer, J., Water Quality and Value of Homesites on the Rockaway River, New Jersey. December 1969. (Completion Report A-024-N.J.). WRRI.

Brush, L. M. Jr., McMichael, F. C., and Kuo, C. Y., Artificial Mixing of Density Stratified Fluids: A Laboratory Investigation. Report No. MH-R-2, L. F. Moody Hydrodynamics Laboratory, Princeton, New Jersey. 1969.

Granstrom, M. L., Dutta, M., and DeRooy, J., Water Resources and The Chemical Industry in New Jersey — An Econometric and Engineering Analysis. October 1969. 311 p. (Completion Report B-002-N.J.). WRRI. (Available from author.)

Perlis, H. J. and Davidson, B., Engineering Application of Multivariable Distributed Parameter Control Theory. September 1969. 7 p. (Completion Report A-017-N.J.). WRRI.

Peskin, R. L. and Krasnoff, E. L., Laws of Dispersion. 1969. (Completion Report, Project A-005-N.J.). WRRI. (Available from author.)

Tarassov, V. J. and Perlis, H. J., Digital Generation of Space Dependent Sub-Optimal Control for a Distributed Parameter System. Paper presented at the First Annual Houston Conference on Systems and Circuit Theory, Houston, Texas. May 1969. (Available from author.)

Whipple, W. Jr., Preliminary Mass Balance of BOD on Three New Jersey Rivers. October 1969. 94 p. (Part I Completion Report, Project B-002-N.J.) WRRI. (Out of print but available from Clearinghouse for $3.00.)

1970

Ahlert, R. C., The Influence of Thermal Mixing on Oxygen Dynamics of Streams. Presented at 5th International Conference of Water Pollution Control, San Francisco. July 1970. (Available from author.)

Bourodimos, E. L. and Michna, L., Flow Concentration Groins for Reaeration in Passaic River — A Hydraulic Model Study, Water Resources Research Institute, Rutgers, New Brunswick, N. J. September 1970. 99 p.

Brush, L. M., Artificial Mixing of Stratified Fluids Formed by Salt and Heat in a Laboratory Reservoir, Water Resources Research Institute, Rutgers, New Brunswick, N. J. (Phase II.) September 1970. 37 p.

Davidson, B., and Hunter, J. V., Process Control Model for Oxygen Regeneration of Polluted Rivers. March 1970. 6 p. (Completion Report B-011-N.J.). WRRI.

Dorfman, D., and Westman, J., Responses of Some Anadromous Fishes to Varied Oxygen Concentrations and Increased Temperatures. June 1970. Part II, Final Completion Report, Project B-012-N.J.

Hsu, Pa Ho, Removal of Phosphate from Waste Water by Aluminum and Iron, Water Resources Research Institute, Rutgers, New Brunswick, N. J. December 1970. 5 p. Technical Completion Report.

Hunter, J. V., Allen, H. L., and Shelton, T. B., Benthal Decomposition of Absorbed Oil Pollutants. May 1970. (Completion Report, Project M-6).

Kown, Bong T., The Organic Gradient in a Concentration Column, Water Resources Research Institute, Rutgers, New Brunswick, N. J. October 1970. 19 p.

Lesser, A., Spinner, H., and Tirabassi, A., An Engineering Economic Study of the Industrial Growth Potential of the Upper Passaic River Basins. Stevens Institute of Technology. 1970. 51 p.

Marcus, M., and Whipple, W. Jr., Predicting Future Growth of Organic Pollution in Metropolitan Area Rivers. February 1970. 29 p. (Part III Completion Report, Project B-002-N.J.). WRRI.

Nathan, K., Nieswand, H., and Esser, A. J., Hydrology of a Small Rural Watershed Under Suburban Development — Phase I. 1970. 86 p., illustrated. (Related to Project A-009-N.J.). WRRI.

Nieswand, G. H., and Granstrom, M. L., A Chance Constrained Linear Programming Approach to the Conjunctive Use of Surface and Ground Waters for the Mullica River Basin, New Jersey. A paper presented at the 51st annual meeting of the American Geophysical Union in Washington, D.C., April 20-24, 1970. (Related to Project B-014-N.J.). (Available from author.)

Tokarski, R. P., The Effect of Land Utilization on Water Quality Variations, Water Resources Research Institute, Rutgers, New Brunswick, N. J. October 1970. 64 p.

Whipple, W. Jr., Engelbert, E. A., and Tock, W. L., Editors, Evaluation Processes in Water Resources Planning, Proceedings Series No. 10, American Water Resources Association, Urbana, Illinois. July 1970. (See author re availability.)

Wilson, T. E., and Wang, M. H., Removal of Lignin by Foam Separation Processes, Water Resources Research Institute, Rutgers, New Brunswick, N. J. November 1970. 16 p.

Yuan, W. L., and Hsu, Pa Ho, Effects of Foreign Components on the Precipitation of Phosphate by Aluminum. Presented before the Fifth International Conference on Water Pollution Control, San Francisco, California. July 29, 1970. (Related to Project A-021-N.J.). (Available from author.)

OTHER PUBLICATIONS

Annual Report, 1968/69 to date.

NEW MEXICO

STATE BUREAU OF MINES AND MINERAL RESOURCES

New Mexico Institute of Mining and Technology
Campus Station
Socorro, New Mexico 87801

BULLETINS

87 Mineral and Water Resources of New Mexico. 1965. Compiled in cooperation with U. S. Geological Survey, State Engineer of New Mexico, New Mexico Oil Conservation Commission, and U. S. Bureau of Mines. Price: $2.00.

MEMOIRS

4 High Mountain Stream: Effects of Geology on Channel Characteristics and Bed Material, by John P. Miller. 1958. Price: $3.50.

GROUND-WATER REPORTS

Prepared in cooperation with the U. S. Geological Survey and the State Engineer of New Mexico.

1 Geology and Ground-Water Resources of the Eastern Part of Colfax County, New Mexico, by Roy L. Griggs. 1948. Price: $3.00.

2 Geology and Ground-Water Resources of San Miguel County, New Mexico, by R. L. Griggs and G. E. Hendrickson. 1951. Price: $2.00.

3 Geology and Ground-Water Resources of Eddy County, New Mexico, by G. E. Hendrickson and R. S. Jones. 1952. Price: $2.50.

4 Geology and Ground-Water Resources of Northeastern Socorro County, New Mexico, by Zane Spiegel. 1955. Price: $2.00.

5 Geology and Ground-Water Resources of Torrance County, New Mexico, by R. E. Smith. 1957. Price: $3.50.

6 Geology and Ground-Water Conditions in Southern Lea County, New Mexico, by Alexander Nicholson, Jr. and Alfred Clebsch, Jr. 1961. Price: $3.00.

7 Geology and Ground-Water Conditions in Eastern Valencia County, New Mexico, by Frank B. Titus, Jr. 1963. Price: $3.00.

8 General Occurrence and Quality of Ground Water in Union County, New Mexico, by James B. Cooper and Leon V. Davis. 1967. Price: $3.00.

9 Geology and Ground-Water Resources of Quay County, New Mexico, by Charles F. Berkstresser, Jr. and Walter A. Mourant. 1966. Price: $3.00.

10 Hydrologic Reconnaissance of De Baca County, New Mexico, by Walter A. Mourant and John A. Shomaker.

MISCELLANEOUS REPORTS

New Mexico's Underground Resources, revised by George B. Griswold. 1958. No charge.

CIRCULARS

26 Water Well Records and Well Water Quality in Southwestern San Agustin Plains, Catron County, New Mexico, by F. X. Bushman and C. P. Valentine. 1954. Price: $0.25.

37 Ground-Water Data for Dwyer Quadrangle, Grant and Luna Counties, New Mexico, by F. X. Bushman. 1955. Price: $0.20.

46 Guides for Development of Irrigation Wells Near Clayton, Union County, New Mexico, by Brewster Baldwin and F. X. Bushman. 1957. Price: $0.50.

80 A Preliminary Report on New Mexico's Geothermal Energy Resources, by W. K. Summers. 1965. Price: $0.75.

83 Chemical Characteristics of New Mexico's Thermal Waters — A Critique, by W. K. Summers. 1965. Price: $1.00.

85 Mercury Content of Stream Sediments — A Geochemical Survey of the Magdalena Mining District, New Mexico, by Fazlollah Missaghi. 1966. Price: $1.00.

93 Structure, Stratigraphy, and Hydrogeology of the Northern Roswell Artesian Basin, Chaves County, New Mexico, by Kay C. Havenor. 1968. Price: $2.00.

95 Water Law Atlas, by Thomas A. Garrity, Jr. and Elmer T. Nitzschke, Jr. 1968. Price: $0.50.

98 Geothermics — New Mexico's Untapped Resource, by W. Kelly Summers. 1968. Price: $0.25.

GUIDEBOOKS

9 Albuquerque — Its Mountains, Valley, Water, and Volcanoes, by Vincent C. Kelley. 1968. Price: $1.50.

RESOURCES AND LAND STATUS MAPS

New Mexico Energy Resources Map (revised). 1969. Price: $0.50.

OTHER

Preliminary Quantitative Study of the Roswell Ground-Water Reservoir, New Mexico, by Mahdi S. Hantush. 1957. Price: $1.50.

PUBLICATIONS OF THE NEW MEXICO GEOLOGICAL SOCIETY

Special Publication 3. The San Andres Limestone, A Reservoir for Oil and Water in New Mexico, by W. K. Summers and F. E. Kottlowski. 1969. Price: $3.25.

NEW MEXICO DEPARTMENT OF GAME AND FISH
State Capitol
Santa Fe, New Mexico 87501

Fishing Waters: Trout Waters and Warm Waters. A large color-keyed map to the streams and lakes of the state.

New Mexico Wildlife Magazine. Issued six times a year. Price: $1.00 a year.

STATE ENGINEER OFFICE
State Capitol
Santa Fe, New Mexico 87501

The publications listed below are those issued by this office since 1954. Prior to that time, reports of hydrological investigations were published in biennial reports of the State Engineer.

TECHNICAL REPORTS

1 Reconnaissance of ground-water conditions in Curry County, New Mexico, by James W. Howard. 1954.

2 Possible flow of water between Rito Resumidera and Poleo Canyon Spring, Rio Arriba County, New Mexico, by Theodore J. Hollander. 1954.

*3 Ground-water conditions in the vicinity of Rattlesnake Springs, Eddy County, New Mexico, by W. E. Hale. 1955.

*4 The New Mexico law of water rights, by Wells A. Hutchins. 1955.

*5 Climatological summary, New Mexico – temperature 1850-1954; frost 1850-1954; evaporation 1912-1954, by the N. M. State Engineer. 1956.

*6 Climatological summary, New Mexico – precipitation 1849-1954, by N. M. State Engineer. 1956.

7 Hydrologic summary, New Mexico – streamflow and reservoir content, 1888-1954, by N. M. State Engineer. 1959.

8 Reconnaissance of ground-water conditions in the Crow Flats area, Otero County, New Mexico, by L. J. Bjorklund. 1957.

9 Geology of the Roswell artesian basin, New Mexico, and its relation to the Hondo Reservoir, by Robert T. Bean. 1949. [1957].

Effect on artesian aquifer of storage of flood water in Hondo Reservoir, by Charles V. Theis. 1957. [1957].

10 Ground-water conditions in the nonthermal artesian-water basin south of Hot Springs, Sierra County, New Mexico, by C. Richard Murray. 1949. [1959].

11 Ground water in Animas Valley, Hidalgo County, New Mexico, by H. O. Reeder. 1957.

12 Ground-water conditions and geology of Sunshine Valley and western Taos County, New Mexico, by I. J. Winograd. 1959.

13 Annual water-level measurements in observation wells, 1951-1955, and atlas of maps showing changes in water levels for various periods from beginning of record through 1954, New Mexico, by H. O. Reeder and others. 1959. (Issued in one volume, also as four separates: Part A – High Plains; Part B – Pecos River Valley; Part C – South-Central Closed Basins & Rio Grande Valley; Part D – Southwestern New Mexico.)

14 Ground water in the Causey-Lingo area, Roosevelt County, New Mexico, by James B. Cooper. 1960.

15 Reconnaissance of ground water in Playas Valley, Hidalgo County, New Mexico, by Gene C. Doty. 1960.

16 Changes in water levels in 1955 and annual water-level measurements in January and February 1956 in observation wells in New Mexico, by H. O. Reeder and others. 1960.

*17 The occurrence of saline ground water near Roswell, Chaves County, New Mexico, by J. W. Hood and others. 1960.

18 Availability of ground water at proposed well sites in Gila National Forest, Sierra and Catron Counties, New Mexico, by F. D. Trauger. 1960.

19 Ground-water levels in New Mexico, 1956, by H. O. Reeder and others. 1960.

20 Geology and ground-water resources of the Grants-Bluewater area, Valencia County, New Mexico, by Ellis D. Gordon. 1961.

*21 Availability of ground water in the Albuquerque area, Bernalillo and Sandoval Counties, New Mexico, by Louis J. Bjorklund and Bruce W. Maxwell. 1961.

*22 Ground-water levels in New Mexico, 1957, by H. O. Reeder and others. 1961.

*23 Ground-water levels in New Mexico, 1958, by H. O. Reeder and others. 1962.

*24 Ground-water levels in New Mexico, 1959, by H. O. Reeder and others. 1962.

25 Ground-water conditions in the Rio Grande Valley between Truth or Consequences and Las Palomas, Sierra County, New Mexico, by E. R. Cox and H. O. Reeder. 1962.

26 Ground water in Central Hachita Valley northeast of the Big Hatchet Mountains, Hidalgo County, New Mexico, by Fred D. Trauger and E. H. Herrick. 1962.

27 Ground-water levels in New Mexico, 1960, by W. C. Ballance and others. 1962.

28 Water resources and geology of the Rio Hondo drainage basin, Chaves, Lincoln, and Otero Counties, New Mexico, by W. A. Mourant. 1963.

29A Municipal water supplies and uses, southeastern New Mexico, by G. A. Dinwiddie. 1963.

29B Municipal water supplies and uses, northeastern New Mexico, by G. A. Dinwiddie. 1964.

29C Municipal water supplies and uses, northwestern New Mexico, by G. A. Dinwiddie, W. A. Mourant, and J. A. Basler. 1966.

29D Municipal water supplies and uses, southwestern New Mexico, by G. A. Dinwiddie, W. A. Mourant and J. A. Basler. 1966.

30 Geology and ground water in the vicinity of Tucumcari, Quay County, New Mexico, by F. D. Trauger and F. X. Bushman. 1964.

31 Characteristics of the water supply in New Mexico, by W. E. Hale, L. J. Reiland and J. P. Beverage. 1965.

32 Consumptive use and water requirements in New Mexico, by Harry F. Blaney and Eldon G. Hanson. 1965.

33 Quantitative analysis of water resources in the Albuquerque area, New Mexico, by H. O. Reeder, L. J. Bjorklund and G. A. Dinwiddie. 1967.

34 Ground-water levels in New Mexico, 1965 and changes in water levels, 1961-65, by F. E. Busch and J. D. Hudson. 1967.

35 Geology and ground-water resources in southeastern McKinley County, New Mexico, by J. B. Cooper and E. C. John. 1968.

36 Water resources of the Silver City area, Grant County, New Mexico, by F. C. Koopman, F. D. Trauger and J. A. Basler. 1969.

BASIC DATA REPORTS

Note: Data of water-level fluctuation in New Mexico for the period 1950-60, together with interpretive maps and text, were published in the technical report series. Data for the period 1961-64, restricted to tabulations and maps of annual fluctuations in water levels in areas of intensive use, were published as unnumbered "basic data" reports. Data for 1965, accompanied by interpretive text and summary maps of changes in water levels for the 5-year period, 1961-65, were published as Technical Report 34. Basic data of water levels will continue to be published on an annual basis in the future, as will periodic interpretive summaries of ground-water occurrence and use.

*Ground-water levels in New Mexico, 1961, by W. C. Ballance. 1962.

*Ground-water levels in New Mexico, 1962, by W. C. Ballance. 1963.

*Ground-water levels in New Mexico, 1963, by W. C. Ballance. 1964.

Ground-water levels in New Mexico, 1964, by F. E. Busch. 1966.

Ground-water levels in New Mexico, 1966, by F. E. Busch and J. D. Hudson. 1968.

Ground-water levels in New Mexico, 1967, by F. E. Busch and J. D. Hudson. 1969.

Ground-water levels in New Mexico, 1968, by F. E. Busch and J. D. Hudson. 1970.

SPECIAL REPORTS

Hydraulics of certain stream-connected aquifer systems, by Zane Spiegel. 1962.

Flow characteristics of New Mexico streams; flow-duration, high-flow, and low-flow tables for selected stations through water year 1959, by L. J. Reiland and G. L. Haynes, Jr. 1963.

BIENNIAL REPORTS

*First through Thirteenth Biennial Reports. 1912/1914 to 1936/1938.

Fourteenth through Seventeenth Biennial Reports. 1938/1940 to 1944/1946.

Eighteenth through Twentieth Biennial Reports. 1946/48 to 1950/1952. (These were not published owing to dislocations in office operations during the wartime and early post-war years.)

Twenty-first through Twenty-ninth Biennial Reports. 1952/1954 to 1968/1970.

STATE PLANNING OFFICE
State Capitol
Santa Fe, New Mexico 87501

Agricultural Land and Water in New Mexico, by Donald C. Henderson and H. R. Stucky. 1966. 62 p. No charge but limited copies.

*Water Resources of New Mexico: Occurrence, Development and Use. 1967. 321 p.

New Mexico Water Resources Law: A Survey of Legislation and Decision, by Robert Emmet Clark. This publication was prepared under the N. M. State Resources Development Plan but published by the Division of Government Research, University of New Mexico.

STATE SOIL & WATER CONSERVATION COMMITTEE OF NEW MEXICO
Room 219
State Land Office Building
Santa Fe, New Mexico 87501

N. M. State Soil and Water Conservation Committee Annual Report, June 30, 1967. 36 p.

Proceedings, 1st State-Wide Land Use Planning Symposium, October 16-17, 1969. 68 p. Price: $2.00.

Proceedings, 2nd State-Wide Land Use Planning Symposium, October 13-14, 1970. 107 p. Price: $2.00.

New Mexico Soil & Water Conservation Needs Inventory:
    Statistical Report. 289 p.
    General Report. 48 p.
This publication was the combined effort of many State and Federal agencies. Copies are available from the Soil Conservation Service, P. O. Box 2007, Albuquerque, New Mexico.

NEW MEXICO WATER RESOURCES RESEARCH INSTITUTE

New Mexico State University
Box 3167
Las Cruces, New Mexico 88001

*Anderson, J. U., P. S. Derr, and O. F. Bailey, The Use of a Rainfall Simulator to Study Soil Water Relationships in Semi-arid Rangeland, Abstract published in the Proceedings of the International Arid Lands Conference, June 1969.

*Barnes, Carl, E., Irrigation Water Requirements for Crop Production Roswell Artesian Basin (An Agronomic Analysis and Basic Data), Water Resources Research Institute in cooperation with Agricultural Experiment Station, New Mexico State University, WRRI Report 4 Part I, June 1969, 121 p.

*Carroon, Evan, and E. G. Hanson, Irrigation Water Requirements for Crop Production Roswell Artesian Basin, Water Resources Research Institute in cooperation with the Agricultural Experiment Station, New Mexico State University, WRRI 4 Part 3, June 1969, 56 p.

Clark, Ira G., Administration of Water Resources in New Mexico, Water Resources Research Institute in cooperation with the Department of History, New Mexico State University, WRRI Report No. 3, June 1968, 32 p.

Coppedge, R. O., and J. R. Gray, Recreational Use and Value of Water at Elephant Butte and Navajo Reservoirs, Agricultural Experiment Station in cooperation with Water Resources Research Institute, New Mexico State University, Bulletin No. 535, October 1968, 24 p.

*Coppedge, R. O. Recreational Values of Water in a New Mexico Reservoir, paper submitted for consideration in the Contributed Papers Section, Western Farm Economics Association Annual Proceedings, Las Cruces, New Mexico, July 19-21, 1967.

*d'Arge, Ralph, Quantitative Water Resources Basin Planning – An Analysis of the Pecos River Basin, New Mexico, Department of Economics, University of New Mexico in cooperation with the Water Resources Research Institute, Technical Research Report (unnumbered) June 1968, 147 p.

*Garner, William and R. N. Gennaro, Gas Chromatographic Differentiation of Closely Related Species of Micro-organisms, presented to the Meeting of the American Chemical Society, September 1965, Atlantic City, New Jersey. The paper received special recognition by review in Chemical and Engineering News of September 27, 1965.

*Hanson, E. G., and B. C. Williams, Influence of Subsurface Irrigation on Cotton Yields and Water Use, (paper presented at the 1968 Winter Meeting of the American Society of Agricultural Engineers, Chicago, Illinois, December 10-13, 1968).

*Hanson, E. G., and B. C. Williams, Subsurface Irrigation of Cotton, (paper presented at the Automation of Irrigation and Drainage Systems, ASCE National Irrigation and Drainage Specialty Conference, November 1968).

*Hanson, E. G., The Future of Subsurface Irrigation: A Method of Saving Water, (paper published in the proceedings of the Fourteenth Annual New Mexico Water Conference, March 27-28, 1969, New Mexico State University).

Hernandez, John W., A Compilation of Water Resources Research and Graduate Training Activities at New Mexico State University, Water Resources Research Institute in cooperation with Engineering Experiment Station, New Mexico State University, WRRI Publication No. 1, 1966, 72 p.

Hernandez, John W. and Thomas J. Eaton, A Bibliography Pertaining to the Pecos River Basin in New Mexico, Water Resources Research Institute in cooperation with Engineering Experiment Station, New Mexico State University, WRRI Publication No. 2, 1966, 50 p.

*Hughes, William C., Economic Feasibility of Increasing Pecos Basin Water Supplies through Reduction of Evaporation and Evapo-Transpiration, Water Resources Research Institute in cooperation with Department of Economics, University of New Mexico, Technical Research Report, September 1968, 80 p.

Ingram, Helen M., Patterns of Politics in Water Resources Development: A Case Study of New Mexico's Role in the Colorado River Basin Bill, Division of Government Research, University of New Mexico, Publication No. 79, December 1969, 96 p.

*King, W. E., J. W. Hawley, A. M. Taylor, and R. P. Wilson, Hydrogeology of the Rio Grande Valley and Adjacent Intermontane Areas of Southern New Mexico, Water Resources Research Institute in cooperation with Earth Science Department, New Mexico State University, WRRI Report No. 6, June 1969, 141 p.

*Lansford, R. R. and Bobby J. Creel, Irrigation Water Requirements for Crop Production Roswell Artesian Basin, (An Economic Analysis and Basic Data), Water Resources Research Institute in cooperation with Agricultural Experiment Station, New Mexico State University, WRRI Report 4, Part II, June 1969, 275 p.

*Lansford, Robert R., Carl E. Barnes, Bobby J. Creel, Eldon G. Hanson, Harold E. Dregne, Evan Carroon, and H. R. Stucky, Irrigation Water Requirements for Crop Production Roswell Artesian Basin, (Project Analysis and Summary), Water Resources Research Institute in cooperation with the Agricultural Experiment Station, New Mexico State University, WRRI Report 4, Part IV, June 1969, 116 p.

Lansford, Robert R., Carl E. Barnes, Bobby J. Creel, Eldon G. Hanson, Harold E. Dregne, Evan Carroon and H. R. Stucky, Irrigation Water Requirements for Crop Production Roswell Artesian Basin, New Mexico, Water Resources Research Institute in cooperation with the Agricultural Experiment Station, New Mexico State University, WRRI Report 5, November 1969, 59 p.

Maker, H. J., C. W. Keetch, and J. U. Anderson, Soil Associations and Land Classification for Irrigation, San Juan County, Agricultural Experiment Station in cooperation with Water Resources Research Institute and Soil Conservation Service, New Mexico State University, Research Report 161, September 1969, 40 p.

*Myers, William R. and B. C. Williams, Three Regimes of Flow from an Orifice in a Sub-Surface Irrigation, (Paper presented at the Irrigation and Drainage Division Specialty Conference, Phoenix, Arizona, November 15, 1968).

Spiegel, Zane, Fundamental Concepts of Geohydrology Applied to the Pecos Valley and Related Aquifer Systems, prepared for New Mexico Water Resources Research Institute Project No. B-006-NMEX—3109-102, State Engineer Office, August 1967, 47 p.

Stucky, H. R., (Editor), Eleventh Annual New Mexico Water Conference, Water Resources Research Institute, New Mexico State University, 1967, 167 p.

Stucky, H. R., (Editor), Twelfth Annual New Mexico Water Conference, Water Resources Research Institute, New Mexico State University, 1967, 116 p.

Stucky, H. R., (Editor), Thirteenth Annual New Mexico Water Conference, Water Resources Research Institute, New Mexico State University, 1968, 167 p.

Stucky, H. R., (Editor), Fourteenth Annual New Mexico Water Conference, Water Resources Research Institute, New Mexico State University, 1969, 111 p.

Summers, W. K., Distribution and Occurrence of New Mexico's Thermal Waters — A Statistical Summary, (paper presented at the New Mexico Geological Society Meeting in Roswell, Spring 1966).

Summers, W. K., The Hydrologic Significance of the Animas Valley Hot Spot, Hidalgo County, New Mexico, (paper given at the 1966 annual meeting of the New Mexico Academy of Science, Portales, New Mexico).

Summers, W. K. and L. A. Brandvold, Physical and Chemical Variations in the Discharge of a Flowing Well, (paper presented for circulation and discussion, New Mexico Institute of Mining and Technology, 1967).

NEW YORK

HUDSON RIVER VALLEY COMMISSION
105 White Plains Road
Tarrytown, New York 10591

Annual report, 1967. [1969]. 39 p.

Annual report, 1968. [1969]. 40 p.

Historic resources of the Hudson; a preliminary inventory, January 1969. [1969]. 96 p.

Newsletter. 1968 – to date. (Irregular.)

Power lines and scenic values in the Hudson River valley, December 1968. [1969]. 23 p.

JOINT LEGISLATIVE COMMITTEE TO INVESTIGATE AND STUDY THE CONSERVATION, DEVELOPMENT AND EQUITABLE USE OF THE WATER RESOURCES OF THE STATE
State Capitol
Albany, New York 12224

Created in 1967. Superseded the Temporary State Commission on Water Resources Planning.

*First Report ... , 1968. 207 p. (Legis. Doc. 1968 no. 18.)

NEW YORK CONTROLLER'S OFFICE
State Capitol
Albany, New York 12224

*Controller's committee on problems affecting the distribution of water. 1953. 14 p.

NEW YORK STATE DEPARTMENT OF ENVIRONMENTAL CONSERVATION
50 Wolf Road
Albany, New York 12201

Many of the documents listed below were prepared for departmental use only, and do not constitute reference material which is readily obtainable. Furthermore, limitations of staff and funds do not allow wide distribution of these publications. Please direct inquiries to the attention of Mr. John Finck, Bureau of Water Resources Planning, Room 418, at the above address.

PUBLISHED PAPERS

A. General Statewide Reports

*1   Flood Plain Management – A Challenge for the State. 1967.

2   The Coordinated Programs for the Water Resources of New York State. 1966.

3   Developing and Managing the Water Resources of New York State. 1967.

4   Flood Plain Management – A Plan for Action. 1967. 15 p.

5   The ABC's of the Erie-Niagara Comprehensive Water Resources Plan – Prepared by the Erie-Niagara Basin Regional Water Resources Planning Board and the Water Resources Commission. 1970.

6   Water for the Future of Long Island, New York – Prepared by the U.S. Geological Survey in Cooperation with the New York State Department of Environmental Conservation, Division of Water Resources. 1970.

B. Regional Water Resources Studies

*1   Program for Cooperative Study for Comprehensive Water Resources Development.
   a. Erie-Niagara Basin Board – 1964.
   b. Cayuga Basin Board – 1965.
   c. Wa-Ont-Ya Board – 1966.
   d. Eastern Oswego Board – 1967.
   e. Eastern Susquehanna Board – 1968.
   f. Black River Basin Board – 1970.
   g. St. Lawrence Basin Board – 1969.
   h. Upper Delaware Basin Board – 1970.

*2   Water Resources of Lake Champlain – Upper Hudson Region – 1969.

*3   Long Island Fresh Water Resources Study – 1967.

*4   Newsletter No. 1 – Black River Basin Regional Water Resources Planning Board.

*5   Newsletter No. 1 – St. Lawrence-Franklin Regional Water Resources Planning Board.

*6   Newsletter No. 1 – Upper Delaware River Regional Water Resources Planning Board.

*7   Comprehensive Water Resources Plan, Main Report – Prepared by Erie-Niagara Basin Regional Water Resources Planning Board and the Water Resources Commission.

*8   Newsletters 1 to 11 – Erie-Niagara Basin Regional Water
      Resources Planning Board.

C. Bulletins Published by the New York Water Resources Commission and Prepared in Cooperation with the U. S. Geological Survey

*GW-1   Withdrawal of ground water on Long Island, N. Y.
         D. G. Thompson and R. M. Leggette (1936).

*GW-2   Engineering report on the water supplies of Long Island. Russell Suter (1937).

*GW-3   Record of wells in Kings County, N. Y. R. M. Leggette and others (1937).

*GW-4   Record of wells in Suffolk County, N. Y. R. M. Leggette and others (1938).

*GW-5   Record of wells in Nassau County, N. Y. R. M. Leggette and others (1938).

*GW-6   Record of wells in Queens County, N. Y. R. M. Leggette and others (1938).

*GW-7   Report on the geology and hydrology of Kings and Queens Counties, Long Island. Homer Sanford (1938).

GW-8   Record of wells in Kings County, N. Y. Supplement 1. R. M. Leggette and M. L. Brashears, Jr. (1944).

GW-9   Record of wells in Suffolk County, N. Y. Supplement 1. C. M. Roberts and M. L. Brashears, Jr. (1945).

GW-10   Record of wells in Nassau County, N. Y. Supplement 1. C. M. Roberts and M. L. Brashears, Jr. (1946).

*GW-11   Record of wells in Queens County, N. Y. Supplement 1. C. M. Roberts and M. C. Jaster (1947).

*GW-12   The water table in the western and central parts of Long Island, N. Y. C. E. Jacob (1945).

*GW-13   The configuration of the rock floor in western Long Island. Wallace de Laguna and M. L. Brashears, Jr. (1948).

*GW-14   Correlation of ground-water levels and precipitation on Long Island, N. Y. C. E. Jacob (1945).

*GW-15   Progress report on ground-water resources of the southwestern part of Broome County, N. Y. R. H. Brown and J. G. Ferris (1946).

*GW-16   Progress report on ground-water conditions in the Cortland Quadrangle, N. Y. E. S. Asselstine (1946).

*GW-17   Geologic correlation of logs of wells in Kings County, N. Y. Wallace de Laguna (1948).

*GW-18   Mapping of geologic formations and aquifers of Long Island, N. Y. Russell Suter, Wallace de Luguna, and N. M. Perlmutter (1949).

*GW-19   Geologic atlas of Long Island. (Consists of large-scale reproductions of maps of GW-18). (1950).

*GW-20   The ground-water resources of Albany County, N. Y. Theodore Arnow (1949).

GW-20A   Buried preglacial ground-water channels in the Albany-Schenectady area in New York. E. S. Simpson (1949).

GW-21   The ground-water resources of Rensselaer County, N. Y. R. V. Cushman (1950).

GW-22   The ground-water resources of Schoharie County, N. Y. J. M. Berden (1950).

GW-23   The ground-water resources of Montgomery County, N. Y. R. M. Jeffords (1950).

GW-24   The ground-water resources of Fulton County, N. Y. Theodore Arnow (1951).

GW-25   The ground-water resources of Columbia County, N. Y. Theodore Arnow (1951).

GW-26   The ground-water resources of Seneca County, N. Y. A. J. Mozola (1951).

*GW-27   The water table in Long Island, N. Y. in January 1951. N. J. Lusczynski and A. H. Johnson (1951).

*GW-28   Withdrawal of ground water on Long Island, N. Y. Supplement 1. A. H. Johnson and others (1952).

GW-29   The ground-water resources of Wayne County, N. Y. R. E. Griswold (1951).

GW-30   The ground-water resources of Schenectady County, N. Y. E. S. Simpson (1952).

*GW-31   Records of wells in Suffolk County, N. Y., Supplement 2. Staff, Long Island Office, Water Power and Control Commission.

*GW-32   Ground water in Bronx, New York, and Richmond Counties with summary data on Kings and Queens Counties, New York City, N. Y. N. M. Perlmutter and Theodore Arnow (1953).

GW-33   The ground-water resources of Washington County, N. Y. R. V. Cushman (1953).

*GW-34   The ground-water resources of Greene County, N. Y. J. M. Berdan (1954).

GW-35   The ground-water resources of Westchester County, N. Y., Part 1 records of wells and test holes. E. S. Asselstine and I. G. Grossman (1955).

GW-36   Saline waters in New York State. N. J. Lusczynski, J. J. Geraghty, E. S. Asselstine, and I. G. Grossman (1956).

GW-37   The ground-water resources of Putnam County, N. Y. I. G. Grossman (1957).

GW-38   Chloride concentration and temperature of water from wells in Suffolk County, Long Island, N. Y. 1928-53 (1958).

*GW-39   Record of wells in Nassau County, N. Y., Supplement 2. Staff, Long Island Office, Water Power and Control Commission (1958).

GW-40   The ground-water resources of Chemung County, N. Y. W. S. Wetterhall (1959).

GW-41   Ground-water levels and related hydrologic data from selected observation wells in Nassau County, Long Island, N. Y. John Isbister (1959).

GW-42   Geology and ground-water resources of Rockland County, N. Y. N. M. Perlmutter (1959).

GW-43   Ground-water resources of Dutchess County, N. Y. E. T. Simmons, I. G. Grossman, and R. C. Heath (1961).

GW-44   Ground-water levels and their relationship to ground-water problems in Suffolk County, Long Island, N.Y. J. F. Hoffman and E. R. Lubke (1961).

*GW-45   Hydrology of the shallow ground-water reservoir of the town of Southold, Suffolk County, N. Y. J. F. Hoffman (1961).

*GW-46   The ground-water resources of Sullivan County, N. Y. Julian Soren (1961).

GW-47   Ground-water resources of the Massena-Waddington area, St. Lawrence County, N. Y. (1962).

GW-48   The ground-water resources of Ontario County, N. Y. F. K. Mack and R. E. Digman (1962).

*GW-49   Ground-water studies in Saratoga County, N. Y. R. C. Heath, F. K. Mack, and J. A. Tannenbaum (1963).

GW-50   The ground-water resources of Delaware County, N. Y. Julian Soren (1963).

GW-51   Ground water in New York. R. C. Heath (1964).

GW-52   Water resources of the Lake Erie-Niagara area, N. Y. – a preliminary appraisal. A. M. LaSala, Jr., W. E. Harding, and R. J. Archer (1964).

GW-53   Ground water in the Niagara Falls area, N. Y. R. H. Johnston (1964).

*54   Maximum known discharges of New York streams. F. L. Robison (1965).

55   Chloride concentration and temperature of the waters of Nassau County, Long Island, N. Y. F. A. DeLuca, J. F. Hoffman, and E. R. Lubke (1965).

56   Summary of water-resources records at principal measurement sites in the Genesee River Basin, through 1963. B. K. Gilbert and J. C. Kammerer (1965).

57   Ground-water resources of Eastern Schenectady County, N. Y. J. D. Winslow, H. G. Stewart, Jr., R. H. Johnston, and L. J. Crain (1965).

58   Ground-water resources of the Jamestown area, N. Y. L. J. Crain (1966).

59   Surface-water regimen of the upper Flint Creek Basin, N. Y. D. E. Vaupel (1967).

60   Duration curves and low-flow frequency curves of streamflow in the Susquehanna River Basin, N. Y. O. P. Hunt (1967).

*61   The Hudson River estuary – a preliminary investigation of flow and water-quality characteristics. G. L. Giese and J. W. Barr (1967).

62   An atlas of Long Island's water resources.

63   Streams in Dutchess County, N. Y. G. R. Ayer and F. H. Pauszek (1968).

64   Water resources of the central New York region. William G. Weist, Jr., and G. L. Giese (1970).

65   Ground-water basic data Orange and Ulster Counties New York. Michael H. Frimpter (1970).

66   Bibliography of the ground-water resources of New York through 1967. R. D. MacNish, R. C. Heath, L. E. Johnson, R. A. Wilkens, R. D. Duryea (1969).

67   Maximum known stages and discharges of New York streams through 1967. Bernard Dunn (1970).

68   Characteristics of New York lakes – Part 1. Gazetteer of lakes, ponds, and reservoirs. P. E. Greeson and F. L. Robison (1970).

68A   Characteristics of New York lakes – Part 1A. Gazetteer of lakes, ponds, and reservoirs (by counties). P. E. Greeson and G. E. Williams (1970).

68B   Characteristics of New York lakes – Part 1B. Gazetteer of lakes, ponds, and reservoirs (by drainage basins). P. E. Greeson and G. E. Williams (1970).

D. Additional Bulletins Published in Cooperation with the United States Geological Survey

*1   A Preliminary Analysis of Low Flows at Selected Sites in the Southern Part of the Town of Bethlehem, N. Y., 1968 – (RI-1).

*2   Ground-Water Resources in the Vicinity of the Crown Point Fish Hatchery, Essex County, N. Y., 1968 – (RI-2).

*3   Floods in New York, 1967 – (RI-3).

*4   Instructions for Data Storage – Characteristics of New York Lakes – Part I – Gazetteer of Lakes, Ponds, and Reservoirs, 1969 – (RI-4).

*5   Ground Water Pollution from Natural Gas and Oil Production in New York, Report of Investigation 5, 1969 – (RI-5).

*6   Time-of-Travel Study, Mohawk River, Rome, New York to Cohoes, New York, 1969 – (RI-6).

*7   Water Availability in Urban Areas of the Susquehanna River Basin, A Preliminary Appraisal, 1969 – (RI-7).

*8   The Limnology of Oneida Lake, An Interim Report, 1969 – (RI-8).

*9   Flood in New York, 1968 – (RI-9).

*10   Time-of-Travel Study, Upper Hudson River, Fort Edward, New York to Troy Lock and Dam, Troy, New York, 1970 – (RI-10).

*11   Time-of-Travel Studies in the Fall Creek Basin, Tompkins County, 1970 – (RI-11).

*12   Surface Water, ENB 2 – Prepared by the U. S. Geological Survey for the Erie-Niagara Basin Regional Water Resources Planning Board.

*13   Ground Water Resources, ENB 3 – Prepared for the Erie-Niagara Board by USGS.

*14   Chemical Quality of Streams, ENB 4 – Prepared for the Erie-Niagara by USGS.

*15   Sediment in Streams, ENB 5 – Prepared for the Erie-Niagara Board by USGS.

*16   Eastern Oswego Ground Water – ORB 2 Prepared for the Eastern Oswego Basin Regional Water Resources Planning Board.

UNPUBLISHED PAPERS

1 **General Statewide Reports**

a. Reports completed:

*Project Aqua-Map: Development of Aerial Photography as an Aid to Water Quality Management – September 1967.

*Project Aqua-Map, Phase II: Development of Aerial Photography as an Aid to Water Quality Management – January 1969.

*New York State Supplement to the Susquehanna Coordinating Committee Report (Appendix B).

*The Economics and Use of Large Scale Electrodialysis Plants on Selected Tidal Estuarial Waters – Prepared by consultants for the Division of Water Resources.

b. Staff memorandum or working paper:

*Summary of New York State's Programs in Algae and Weed Control Research – April 1968.

*The Use of Systems Analysis in the Development of Water Resources Management Plans for New York State – Prepared by DWR.

2 Regional Water Resources Studies

a. Reports completed:

*Reconnaissance of Water Resources Potentials – 1966.

(1) Hudson-Mohawk–Long Island Area.

(2) Black, St. Lawrence, Lake Champlain, Delaware Areas.

(3) Central New York Area.

(4) Western New York Area.

*Water Quality Management Study, Oswego River Basin – April 1969.

*Multipurpose Water Resources Study, Chemung Basin, Susquehanna Basin – May 1969.

*Multipurpose Water Resources Study – Eastern Susquehanna, Susquehanna Basin – April 1969.

*Interim Report on Charlotte Creek Basin, Susquehanna Basin – September 1968.

*New York State Supplement to Genesee Coordinating Committee Report, Genesee Basin – 1969.

*Water Oriented Recreation Study – Oswego River Basin – 1970.

*Black River Basin Water Resources Potentials, Needs and Opportunities, Phase I Study – 1969.

*St. Lawrence River Basin Water Resources Potentials, Needs and Opportunities, Phase I Study – 1969.

b. Staff memorandum or working paper

*Inventory of Available Data and Reports – Erie-Niagara Basin – 1964.

*Survey of Reference Material, Phase I of Task 1, Oswego Basin Study – 1967.

*New York State Supplement to the Report of the Water Coordinating Committee of Appalachia Study – 1968.

*Preliminary Inventory of Reservoir Sites – Erie-Niagara Basin – 1965.

*General Soil Areas – Erie-Niagara Basin – 1965.

*Fish and Wildlife Studies – Erie-Niagara Basin – 1965.

*Upland Channel Improvement Project, Erie-Niagara Basin – 1965.

*Water Resources Council, 1967 National Assessment, North Atlantic Region within New York State.

*Water Resources Council, 1967 National Assessment, Great Lakes Region within New York State.

*Oswego River Basin Comprehensive Study, Phase I Report, Lake Level Regulation.

*Preliminary Agricultural Land Use Survey in Erie County, Erie-Niagara Basin – 1965.

*Appraisal for Flood Plain Management, Erie-Niagara Basin – April 1968.

*Appraisal of the Potential for Irrigated Agriculture by Project Type Development – Erie-Niagara Basin – April 1968.

*Investigations of Dams and Reservoirs having Potential for Multiple Purpose Use – Erie-Niagara Basin – February 1968.

*Appraisal of Water Oriented Recreation Development – Erie-Niagara Basin – May 1968.

*Erie-Niagara Basin Comprehensive Water Resources Plan – Plan Formulation – June 1968.

*Preliminary Upstream Reservoir Studies, Western New York River Basin Study, Erie-Niagara Basin – 1968.

*Rights in the Case of the Waters within the Oswego River Basin – 1967.

*Plan Prospectus, Erie-Niagara Basin – 1969.

*First Screening of Reservoir Sites, Oswego River Basin – 1969.

*Storage-yield Curves for Potential Reservoir Sites, Oswego River Basin – 1969.

*Task 15, Phase I – Lake Level Regulation, Oswego River Basin – 1968.

*Hydrology Report (Draft), Chapters 1-4, Low Flow, Peak Flow, Monthly Flows and Flood Analyses, Oswego River Basin – 1969.

*New York State Supplement to Water Development Coordinating Committee Report – Appalachian Region – 1969.

*Tentative Development Prospectus – Oswego River Basin – 1970.

*Hydrology and Hydraulics, Planning Memorandum – Oswego River Basin – 1970.

*Electric Power, Planning Memorandum – Oswego River Basin – 1969.

*Shoreline Development, Planning Memorandum – Oswego River Basin – 1970.

*Project Analysis Study of Limestone Creek, Draft Report – 1970.

*Commercial and Recreational Navigation in the St. Lawrence Basin, New York – 1970.

*Potential Fishing Reservoirs of the Susquehanna River Basin in New York – Prepared by the Divisions of Water Resources and Fish and Wildlife – 1969.

*Hydraulics and Hydrology, Planning Memorandum, Upper Susquehanna River Basin, New York – 1970.

3 Statewide and Regional Economic Studies

a. Reports completed:

*Economic Base Study – Black River Basin – Prepared by Consultants for the DWR.

*Potential Economic Impact of the Salmon River Project – Prepared by Consultants for the DWR.

b. Staff memorandum or working paper:

*A Study of the Agricultural Economy and Agricultural Water Use in the Five County Lake Champlain-Lake George Region in New York State – October 1967.

*Oswego River Basin, Economic Base Study, Phase II, Technical and Statistical Appendix, Volume II.

*Economic Base Study, Phase I, Erie-Niagara Basin, Delineation of Areas and Subareas – 1963.

*Economic Base Study Methodology – Erie-Niagara Basin – 1964.

*Population and Employment Projections 1970-2020, Genesee River Basin Economic Base Study, Phase II – 1965.

*Delineation of Economic Areas and Subareas, Genesee River Basin, Phase I – 1963.

*Water Resources and the Lag in Economic Development in New York's Southern Tier Counties – 1965.

*Economic Potentials of Davenport Center Dam and Reservoir as Site for Pulp and Paper Mill – 1967.

*Preliminary Population Projects for Cities, Towns and Villages in the Erie-Niagara Basin – 1965.

*Lake George-Lake Champlain Agricultural Water Use – 1968.

*Economic Base Study – Phase II, Oswego River Basin, Summary, Vol. I – 1969.

*Economic Impact of Davenport Center Reservoir, Susquehanna Basin – 1969.

*Economic Impact of Davenport Center Dam and Reservoir – 1968.

*Agricultural Economics of Oswego River Basin – 1967.

*Economic Base Study – St. Lawrence River Basin – 1970.

*Economic Base Study, Upper Susquehanna River, New York – 1970.

REPORTS BY OTHER AGENCIES ON FEDERAL-STATE WATER RESOURCES STUDY

In cooperation with the Department of Environmental Conservation (formerly called the Department of Water Resources)

1 Regional Reports Published

a. *Allegheny – Ohio*

*Ohio River Basin Comprehensive Survey – Main Report and Appendices – Prepared by U. S. Army Engineer Division, Ohio River, Cincinnati, Ohio 1966.

b. *Appalachia*

*Development of Water Resources in Appalachia, Main Report and Appendices – Prepared by the Office of Appalachian Studies, Corps of Engineers with contributions by DWR staff.

*New York State Water Resources Development and the Appalachian Program – 1965.

c. *Erie-Niagara*

*Ellicott Creek, New York, Survey Report for Flood Control and Allied Purposes – Prepared by Corps of Engineers, Buffalo District with contributions by DWR staff and consultants – 1970.

d. *Genesee*

*Genesee River Basin Comprehensive Water and Related Land Resources Study – Main Report and Appendices – Prepared by the Genesee River Basin Coordinating Committee with contributions by DWR staff and consultants.

e. *Hudson*

*The Hudson River as a Resource – A Report for the Hudson River Valley Commission – 1966.

f. *Long Island*

*Report on the Great South Bay, New York in June and July 1967-1968.

g. *Oswego*

*Preliminary Data Compendium-Oswego River Basin – Prepared by USDA, Soil Conservation Service for the Division of Water Resources – 1969.

h. *Susquehanna*

*Susquehanna River Basin Study, Main Report, Supplements and Appendices – Prepared by the Susquehanna Coordinating Committee.

*Susquehanna River Basin Compact – Published by the Interstate Advisory Committee on the Susquehanna River Basin – 1967.

2 General Reports Published

a. *New England River Basins Commission*

*Laws and Procedures of Power Plant Siting in New England – Power and the Environment – Report No. 1 – Prepared by the New England River Basins Commission – (NERBC) – 1970.

*Safety Control of Private Dams – Technical Report No. 1, New England River Basins Commission – 1969.

*Water and Related Land Resources – Priority Programs – Fiscal Years 1972-1976 – New England River Basins Commission 1970.

*Wise Use of Flood Plains – Interim Report – New England River Basins Commission 1969.

b. *Flood Plain Information Reports*

*Flood Plain Information Report – Buffalo Creek – 1966.

*Flood Plain Information Report – Canandaigua Lake – 1967.

*Flood Plain Information Report – Cattaraugus Creek – 1968.

*Flood Plain Information Report – Cayuga Lake – 1967.

*Flood Plain Information Report – Ellicott Creek – 1968.

*Flood Plain Information Report – Mamaroneck and Sheldrake Rivers – 1967.

*Flood Plain Information Report – Seneca Lake – 1967.

*Flood Plain Information Report – Smokes Creek – 1965.

*Flood Plain Information Report Appendix – Smokes Creek – 1965.

*Flood Plain Information Report – Tonawando Creek – 1967.

3 Reports Not Published

*Engineering Feasibility Study of Regional Alternatives in Water Supply Planning for Northern New Jersey-New York City-Western Connecticut Metropolitan Area – Prepared by Consultants for the Northeastern United States Water Supply Study (NEWS) being performed by the Corps of Engineers, North Atlantic Division.

*North Atlantic Regional Water Resources Study (NAR) – Main Report and Appendices – Being prepared by the Corps of Engineers – North Atlantic Division – under the direction of the Coordinating Committee of the North Atlantic Regional Water Resources Study.

PUBLICATIONS OF PREDECESSOR AGENCIES

WATER SUPPLY COMMISSION

*Annual report. 1st, 1906 – 6th, 1911.

*Final order for the regulation of the flow of the Hudson River, etc. 1911. 28 p. (Assembly Document 53.)

*New York's water supply and its conservation, distribution and uses ... 1910. 36 p.

*Studies of water storage for flood prevention and power development in New York state under public ownership and control ... 1908. 252 p.

*Water power for the farm and country home ... 1911. 45 p.

NEW YORK CONSERVATION COMMISSION

*Annual report. 1911 – 1964. (After 1948 the annual reports are included in the State Legislature's "New York Legislative Documents".)

*Power available at Crescent and Vischer Ferry from surplus canal waters. 1914. 8 p.

*Power possibilities of the Seranac River. No date. 18 p.

*Power possibilities on the Oswegatchie River. 1914. 66 p.

*Power possibilities on the Raquette River. 1916. 112 p.

*Report of the Conservation Commission to the Charlton Union Water District. 1914. 41 p.

*Report on investigation of the pollution of streams. 1923. 50 p.

*Report ... on the subject of high and low water in Lake George under provisions of Chapter 255, Laws 1912. 1913. 6 p.

*Rules and regulations governing water supply applications. 1912. 16 p.

*State development of water power. 1912. 23 p.

*State hydro-electric development ... 1913. 11 p.

*Stream pollution in New York state. 1919. 78 p.

*Stream pollution studies ... and studies in oyster culture. 1922. 34 p.

WATER RESOURCES COMMISSION

A number of the publications of this agency have been incorporated into the listing of the currently existing agency – the Department of Environmental Conservation.

*Annual report, 1965 – to date.

*Criteria governing thermal discharges (heated liquids.) [1969]. 6 p.

*Rules and regulations applicable to thermal discharges. [1969]. 15 p.

NEW YORK STATE DEPARTMENT OF HEALTH
84 Holland Avenue
Albany, New York 12208

DRAINAGE BASIN SERIES

Recommended classifications and assignments of standards of quality and purity for designated waters of New York State:

Allegheny River Drainage Basin Series; [Report 1-3]. 1951.

Black River Drainage Basin; report ... 1953. 197 p.

Chemung River Drainage Basin Series; report ... (No. 1, 1955; No. 2, 1961).

The Delaware River Drainage Basin; report ... 1960. 305 p.

Genesee River Drainage Basin Survey Series; report ... (No. 1, 1956; No. 2, 1962).

Lake Champlain Drainage Basin; report ... 1954. 195 p.

Lake Erie, Niagara River Drainage Basin Series; report ... (No. 1, 1951 through No. 6, 1963).

Housatonic River Drainage Basin Survey Report ... 1963. 71 p.

Lake Ontario Drainage Basin Survey Series; report ... (No. 1, 1956 through No. 4, 1958).

Lower Hudson River Series; report ... (No. 1, 1952 through No. 11, 1963).

Mohawk River Drainage Basin Series; report ... (No. 1, 1952 through No. 5, 1960).

Nassau County, Surface Waters of ... 1963. 113 p.

New York City Waters Survey Series; report ... (No. 1, 1960 through No. 7, 1965).

Oswego River Drainage Basin Survey Series; report ... (No. 1, 1951 through No. 5, 1957).

Suffolk County Survey Series; report ... (No. 1, 1951 through No. 6, 1963).

Susquehanna River Drainage Basin; report ... 1954. 325 p.

Upper Hudson River Drainage Basin Survey Series; report ... (No. 1, 1955; No. 2, 1963).

RESEARCH REPORTS

1 Statistical Analysis of Drought Flows of Rivers of New York State, prepared by Donald J. O'Connor, Civil Engineering Department, Manhattan College, New York City [1959]. 61 p.

2 Efficiency of Various Methods of Treatment, Milk Plant Wastes, New York State, prepared under direction of William T. Ingram, Research Division, New York University College of Engineering. [1959]. 138 p.

3 Experimental Treatment Plant at Dutch Hollow Foods, Inc., Honeoye Falls, New York, prepared under direction of William T. Ingram, Research Division, New York University College of Engineering. [1959]. 66 p.

4 Treatment of Long Island Duck Farm Wastes, prepared by Charles D. Gates, Head, Department of Sanitary Engineering, School of Civil Engineering, Cornell University, Ithaca, New York. [1959]. 76 p.

5 Removal of Synthetic Detergents from Laundry and Laundramat Wastes, prepared by W. Wesley Eckenfelder, Jr. and Edwin Barnhart in cooperation with Arthur B. Kemper. [1960]. 47 p.

6 Effect of Synthetic Detergents on the Ground Waters of Long Island, New York. [1960]. 18 p. + appendices.

7 Treatment of Organic Wastes in Aerated Lagoons. [1961]. 33 p. + appendix.

8 Chemical and Microbiological Aspects of Oneida Lake, New York, prepared by R. C. Mt. Pleasant [and others], Civil Engineering Department, Syracuse University. [1962]. 95 p.

9 Evaluation of Marine Toilet Chlorinator Units, prepared by Patrick R. Dugan [and others], Syracuse University Research Corporation. [1962]. 57 p.

10 Pt. 1 Evaluation of the Extent and Nature of Pesticide and Detergent Involvement in Surface Waters of a Selected Watershed, August 1963, prepared by Syracuse University Research Corporation. [1964]. 74 p.

10 Pt. 2 Bibliography of Organic Pesticide Publications Having Relevance to Public Health and Water Pollution Problems, prepared by Syracuse University Research Corporation. [1964]. 122 p.

11 Pt. 1 Removal of Algal Nutrients from Domestic Wastewater, by M. C. Rand [and] N. L. Nemerow; Part I: Literature Survey. [1964]. 76 p.

11 Pt. 2 Removal of Algal Nutrients from Domestic Wastewater, by M. C. Rand [and] N. L. Nemerow; Part II: Laboratory Studies. [1965]. 114 p.

12 Pt. 1 Studies on Chicken Manure Disposal, by E. Alan Cassell and Arthur Anthonisen; Part I: Laboratory Studies. [1966]. 128 p.

13 Rapid Screening for the Detection of Organophosphate Pesticides for Water Quality Surveillance, prepared by Syracuse University Research Corporation. [1966]. 29 p.

14 Characteristics of and Methodology for Measuring Water Filtration Plant Wastes, prepared by Cornell University. [1966]. 51 p.

15 Waste Alum Sludge Characteristics and Treatment, prepared by O'Brien and Gere, Consulting Engineers, December 1966. [1967]. 99 p. + appendices.

16 A Study of Fat and Oil Pollution of New York State Waters, prepared by Syracuse University Research Corporation. [1967]. 90 p.

OTHER

Fluoridation of Public Water Systems; Requirements and Procedures, September 1968. Bureau of Water and Wastewater Utilities Management. [1968]. 27 p.

Fluoridation of Public Waters in New York State; Status, Design, Consideration, Safety, Costs; report, August 1968. Bureau of Water and Wastewater Utilities Management. [1968]. 63 p.

Industrial Wastewater Discharges; Flow Measurement, Sampling, Analysis. Compiled and edited by the Industrial Works Section, Bureau of Water and Wastewater Utilities Management, Division of Pure Waters. 1969. 60 p.

Information Kit; Pure Waters Program. 1965. 1 folder.

Manual of Instruction for Water Treatment Plant Operators. 1957. 168 p.

Municipal Sewerage Service Contracts for Public Officials, Municipal Attorneys, Utility Managers, City Engineers, Consulting Engineers; September 1968. Bureau of Water and Wastewater Utilities Management. [1968]. 36 p.

New York's Pure Waters Progress '69. 1969. 21 p.

Periodic Report of the Water Quality Surveillance Network, 1960 through 1964. Bureau of Water Resource Services. [1966]. 34 p.

Proceedings, Fifth Annual Environmental Health Research Symposium; Thermal Discharges. 1968. 113 p.

Proceedings, Second Water Quality Research Symposium, Albany, New York ... Advanced Waste Treatment. 1965. 119 p.

Legal Requirements and Administrative Procedures for Approval of County Sewer Districts by State Comptroller, September 1968. Bureau of Water and Wastewater Utilities Management. 34 p.

Recommended Standards for Sewage Works, [prepared by] Great Lakes-Upper Mississippi River, Board of State Sanitary Engineers, 1968 edition. Division of Environmental Health Services, Division of Pure Waters. [1969]. 97 p.

Rural Water Supply. 66 p.

Tests for Free Chlorine Residual in the Control of Water Treatment. 1969. 18 p. (Bulletin 33).

Waterworks News of New York State. 1945 to date. Quarterly.

NEW YORK FLOOD CONTROL COMMISSION

This Commission is no longer in existence.

*Report. 1st (1936) – 25th (1960).

NEW YORK STATE MUSEUM & SCIENCE SERVICE

The State Education Department
Albany, New York 12224

Although many of the documents listed below are no longer available for purchase, they may be consulted at a number of the larger public and institutional libraries, and at most New York State Libraries. Orders for the publications still in print must be accompanied by remittance. Check or money order should be made payable to the New York State Education Department, but mailed to the above address.

BULLETINS

*84   Ancient Water Levels of the Champlain and Hudson Valleys, by J. B. Woodworth. 203 p., 28 pls., 24 figs., maps. 1905.

*85   Hydrology of the State of New York, by G. W. Rafter. 902 p., 45 pls., 74 figs., 5 maps. 1905.

*106   Glacial Waters in the Lake Erie Basin, by H. L. Fairchild. 86 p., 23 pls., 4 figs. 1907.

*127   Glacial Waters in Central New York, by H. L. Fairchild. 66 p., 42 pls. 1909.

*159   The Mineral Springs of Saratoga, by J. F. Kemp. 79 p., 8 figs., map. 1912.

*160   The Glacial Waters in the Black and Mohawk Valleys, by H. L. Fairchild. 47 p., 25 pls. including 17 maps, 1 fig. 1912.

*256   The Susquehanna River in New York and Evolution of Western New York Drainage, by H. L. Fairchild. 99 p., 39 pls., including maps, 10 figs. 1925.

280   Glacial Geology and Geographic Conditions of the Lower Mohawk Valley; a Survey of the Amsterdam, Fonda, Gloversville and Broadalbin Quadrangles, by A. P. Brigham. 133 p., 72 figs., map. 1929. Price: $1.50.

CIRCULARS

11   Ground Water Supplies of Alleghany State Park, 1932, by F. T. Thwaites. 62 p., 17 figs. 1935. Price: $.20.

SPECIAL PUBLICATIONS

*Glacial Geology of the St. Lawrence Seaway and Power Projects, by Paul MacClintock. 26 p., 13 figs. 1958.

NEW YORK STATE OFFICE FOR LOCAL GOVERNMENT

State Capitol
Albany, New York 12224

*Study of needs for sewage works; a new ten-year program for aiding municipalities. 1962. 84 p. (Office Report No. 1)

OFFICE OF PLANNING COORDINATION

Broadway Arcade Building
488 Broadway
Albany, New York 12207

Water resources of the Champlain-Upper Hudson basins in New York State. 1970. 153 p.

TEMPORARY STATE COMMISSION ON PROTECTION AND PRESERVATION OF THE ATLANTIC SHORE FRONT

Created in 1962; discontinued in 1963.

Final report, July 27, 1962. [1963]. 36 p.

Supplement, July 27, 1962. [1963]. 11 p.

TEMPORARY STATE COMMISSION ON WATER RESOURCES PLANNING

Created in 1959; discontinued in 1967. Superseded by Joint Legislative Committee to Investigate and Study the Conservation, Development and Equitable Use of the Water Resources of the State.

*State-wide conference and workshops on water resources planning and development in New York State, Syracuse, New York, December 10-11, 1959. [1961]. 104 p.

*Conference held by . . . , Rochester, New York, December 16, 1960. [1961]. 57 p.

*Progress report . . . , 1960. 260 p. (Legis. Doc. 1960 no. 24. Cover title: Dynamic planning: first step in water resources development for New York State.)

*Minutes of a meeting held December 14, 1961, Tarrytown, New York. [1962]. Various pagings; July 1-2, 1963, Garden City, New York. [1964]. 46 p.; December 10, 1964. [1965]. 170 p.

*New York State soil and water conservation needs inventory. 1962. 83 p.

*Progress report . . . , 1962. 187 p. (Legis. Doc. 1962 no. 32. Cover title: Legislative guidelines—twelve ways to meet the water resources needs of the Empire State.)

*Minutes of a public hearing on September 10, 1963 at Rochester, New York; December 9, 1963 at Albany, New York; December 10, 1964 at Albany, New York.

*Progress report . . . , 1963. 210 p. (Legis. Doc. 1963 no. 40.)

*Progress report . . . , 1964. 221 p. (Legis. Doc. 1964 no. 15. Cover title: 'Drought insurance' through water resources planning and development in New York State.)

*Six-year progress report, 1965. 262 p. (Legis. Doc. 1965 no. 27.)

*A short-term report . . . , 1966. 245 p. (Legis. Doc. 1966 no. 9. Cover title: The people's mandate—keep water pure and plentiful in New York State.)

*Progress report . . . , 1967. 278 p. (Legis. Doc. 1967 no. 45. Cover title: P + D = 2 Q: Formula for water resources management in New York State.)

WATER RESOURCES AND MARINE SCIENCES CENTER

Cornell University
468 Hollister Hall
Ithaca, New York 14850

The following is a list of publications and technical reports issued under sponsorship of the Water Resources and Marine Sciences Center. Xerox copies of out-of-print publications are available at the cost of $.10 per page. When ordering, please indicate publications requested by the I.D. Number.

*1 Pore-water pressures developed in homogeneous earth embankment during rapid drawdown, by James A. Liggett and Melvin I. Esrig. 66 p.

*2 Profile of a watershed: Flint Creek, by William H. Farnham. 44 p.

*3 A reprint series in systems analysis, by Walter R. Lynn. 100 p.

*4 Synthesis of hydrographs and water surface profiles for unsteady open channel flow with lateral inflows, by Robert M. Ragan. 140 p.

*5 New York State barge canal system, by Ronald L. Shelton. 66 p.

*6 A probabilistic analysis of wastewater treatment systems, by Daniel P. Loucks. 148 p.

7 Small river basin development in Eastern North America, by Timothy O'Riordan. 125 p.

8 The optimal allocation of stream dissolved oxygen resources, by Jon C. Liebman. 235 p.

*9 Pollution control as a bargaining process: an essay on regulatory decision-making, by Matthew Holden, Jr. 53 p.

10 A study of selected aspects of the powers of New York State over the waters of the State, by Armand L. Adams. 102 p.

*11 Canadian-United States water resources problems and policies. (Term papers of civil engineering course 2515 – Fall 1965). 246 p.

12 A framework for the multiple use of municipal water supply areas, by Emmanuel Theodorus Van Nierop. 153 p.

13 Markov chain storage models for statistical hydrology, by William H. Kirby. 155 p.

*14 Eutrophication of water resources of New York State – a study of phytoplankton and nutrients in Lakes Cayuga and Seneca, by John P. Barlow and D. Heyward Hamilton, Jr. 24 p.

*15 Policy models for operating water resource systems, by Daniel P. Loucks. 26 p.

16 Assessment of the adequacy of water supplies – water quality aspects. (A report to the water resources council.) By Leonard B. Dworsky and William B. Strandberg. 122 p.

17 Industrial wastewater quality in relation to industrial productivity. (A report to the water resources council.) By Louis F. Warrick. 36 p.

18 Atlas of industrial water use. (A report to the water resources council.) By Barry R. Lawson. 47 p. Price: $3.00.

*19 Computer graphics and water quality analysis: The Hudson River. (A report to the water resources council.) By Carl Steinitz, Stephen S. Fuller and Ronald L. Shelton. 10 p.

*20 The allocation of regional water supplies – a case study of the Northeastern United States, by William B. Strandberg. 226 p.

21 A reprint series in hydrology, by Wilfried Brutsaert *et al.* (1967).

22 Economic analysis of large water systems, by Nephi A. Christensen. 100 p. Price: $4.00.

*23 Agenda for the National Water Commission. (Term papers of civil engineering course 2515 – Fall 1968.) 300 p.

24 A reprint series in shallow water hydraulics, by James A. Liggett.

25 A selected annotated bibliography on the analysis of water resource systems, by Marshall Gysi and Daniel P. Loucks. 184 p. Price: $3.00.

26 A reprint series in hydrology, by Wilfried Brutsaert *et al.* (1969). Price: $2.00.

*27 Ecology of Cayuga Lake and the proposed Bell Station (nuclear powered). Ray T. Oglesby and David J. Allee, editors. 205 p.

28 Summary report containing summary and conclusions with explanatory notes. Price: $2.00. 11 p.

29 Service to New York State: a summary report 1965-69 by Leonard Dworsky. Price: $2.00.

30 Annotated bibliography of limnological and related literature dealing with the Finger Lakes region, by D. Child and R. Oglesby.

31 Not for distribution.

32 Water uses and water development in Fall Creek – possible conflicts, by L. Hamilton.

33 Prediction of changes in the thermal cycle of a stratified lake used to cool a 1000 mw power plant, by F. Moore and J. Mackenzie.

34 Land use data for the Finger Lakes region of New York State, by D. Child, R. Oglesby and L. Raymond.

35 Problems of executive reorganization: the Federal Environmental Protection Agency, by J. Wall and L. Dworsky. Price: $3.00.

36 A selected annotated bibliography on the analysis of water resource systems, by C. Kriss and D. Loucks. Price: $3.50.

*37 Management models for water resource systems, by Daniel P. Loucks. 130 p.

*38 Investigation of two-phase (liquid-solid) problems, by Walter H. Graf and Ertan R. Acaroglu. 26 p.

*39 Industrial water use – Northeastern United States, by Barry R. Lawson. 56 p.

40 A preliminary investigation of discharge characteristics of drainage basins derived from airphoto analysis and climatic data, by Donald J. Belcher and S. Majtenyi. 149 p.

41 Steady and unsteady effects on discharge in a river connecting two reservoirs, by James A. Liggett and Walter H. Graf. 10 p. Price: $0.75.

42 Difference solutions of the shallow-water equation, by James A. Liggett and David A. Woolhiser. 34 p. Price: $2.00.

*43 The hydrodynamic and energy budget aspects of pan evaporation, by Wilfried Brutsaert and Shaw Lei Yu. 31 p.

44 Water and related land resources law and political institutions, by William H. Farnham. 55 p. Price: $3.00.

*45 The hydraulics of channels, connecting two reservoirs, with special attention to the problem in the Great Lakes, by Walter H. Graf and Kuo-Hsiung Yu. 87 p.

*46 Stochastic models for hydrology, by Narahari U. Prabhu. 23 p.

*47 Effect of chemical structure on the biodegradability of organic molecules, by Martin Alexander. 36 p.

48 Hydrologic analysis for Lake Ontario: stochastic aspects of evaporation, by Wilfried Brutsaert and Shaw Lei Yu. 34 p. Price: $2.00.

49 Phosphate fixation in organic lake sediments, by Carl Schofield. 30 p. Price: $2.00.

*50 The irrigation demand phase of the water supply and demand project, by Gilbert S. Levine. 44 p.

51 Oxidation reactions of nitrogen in water receiving secondary treatment plant effluents, by Charles D. Gates. 18 p. Price: $1.50.

52 Stochastic methods for analyzing river basin systems, by Daniel P. Loucks. 305 p. Price: $5.00.

53 Industrial water use and projections (Corps of Engineers), by Norman W. Rollins, David J. Allee and Barry Lawson. Price: $2.00.

54 The impact of reservoir recreation on the Whitney Point microregion of New York State, by Robert C. Hinman. 73 p. Price: $1.50.

55 The value of reservoir recreation, by Jeffrey M. Romm. 102 p. Price: $2.00.

*56 The uses of a reservoir for recreation, by Charles S. Hunt and David J. Allee.

57 Eutrophication of water resources of New York State: observations on nutrient limitation on summer phytoplankton in Cayuga Lake, by John P. Barlow, *et al*. Price: $2.00.

58 Water supply-demand, by Louis M. Falkson, *et al*. Price: $1.50.

59 A kinetic approach to biological wastewater treatment design and operation, by Alonzo Wm. Lawrence. 56 p. Price: $2.50.

60 Federal evaluation of resource investments: a case study, by Robert J. Kalter *et al*. 89 p. Price: $2.00.

61 The long run effects of water pricing policies, by M. Gysi. Price: $3.50.

62 Reservoir regulation: some techniques and results, by M. Gablinger. Price: $3.00.

63 Planning analysis for the non-market values of water resources with particular emphasis on recreation, by R. Kalter.

64 A case study of water resources development – an analysis of a proposed project on the Missouri River, by L. Hamilton and C. Stern.

65 Mineralization of organic phosphorous in oligotrophic lake sediments, by C. Schofield.

66 A three-dimensional approach to the exchange of heat and water vapor between a large water body and the atmosphere, by W. Brutsaert and G. Yeh. Price: $2.00.

NORTH CAROLINA

NORTH CAROLINA STATE BOARD OF HEALTH
P. O. Box 2091
Raleigh, North Carolina 27602

Protection of Private Water Supplies. No charge.

Operation of Water Filtration Plants of the Mechanical Gravity Type. Limited supply. Price: $1.00.

Reference Manual Water and Sewerage Systems. Price: $1.00.

Rules and Regulations Providing for the Protection of Public Water Supplies. No charge.

DEPARTMENT OF ADMINISTRATION
State Planning Division
116 West Jones Street
P. O. Box 1351
Raleigh, North Carolina 27602

Note: The volumes listed below are available from this agency only on loan from the Planning Library.

Water Resource Needs for Selected Development Corridors in Appalachian North Carolina. Prepared by Rummel, Klepper & Kahl. Nine volumes, as follows:

*Vol. I	Introduction, Methodology, etc.	
*	II	Murphy-Andrews
*	III	Asheville-Hendersonville
*	IV	Rutherfordton-Spindale-Forest City
*	V	Spruce Pine
*	VI	Boone
*	VII	Morganton-Hickory-Lenoir
*	VIII	Wilkesboro-Elkin-Jonesville
*	IX	Winston-Salem-Kernersville

DEPARTMENT OF CONSERVATION AND DEVELOPMENT
Division of Commercial & Sports Fisheries
P. O. Box 769
Morehead City, North Carolina 28557

MISCELLANEOUS PUBLICATIONS

State's Role in Management of Sea Resources, by David A. Adams, Division of Commercial & Sports Fisheries. July 1967.

A Comprehensive Program for the State of North Carolina. Prepared by the Estuarine Study Committee. May 1968.

1967 Proceedings – The State's Role in Management of Sea Resources, by Davis A. Adams, N. C. Dept. of Conservation & Development. June 1968

Waves of Development Threaten the Tidewater, by Chester Davis.

Possible State Programs for Estuarine Management.

North Carolina's Estuarine Systems.

DEPARTMENT OF CONSERVATION AND DEVELOPMENT
Division of Community Planning
Raleigh, North Carolina 27603

A Geographical Study of Wilkes County, North Carolina. 1961. 33 p.

White Lake Development Study. February 1963. 25 p.

Development Plan – Lake Gaston. January 1964. 75 p.

DEPARTMENT OF CONSERVATION AND DEVELOPMENT
Division of Mineral Resources
Education Building
P. O. Box 27687
Raleigh, North Carolina 27611

Note: Mail orders for all available publications require prepayment by money order or check payable to the Department of Conservation and Development, Division of Mineral Resources. Some of the Bulletins may be obtained from the Department of Water and Air Resources. This has been indicated where applicable.

BULLETINS

*8   Papers on the Water-power in North Carolina, a Preliminary Report, by G. F. Swain, J. A. Holmes, and E. W. Myers. 1899. 362 p.

*17 Terracing of Farm Lands, by W. W. Ashe. 1908. 38 p.

18 Bibliography of North Carolina Geology, Mineralogy and Geography, by Francis Baker Laney and Katherine Hill Wood. 1909. Price: $1.00.

*20 Waterpowers of North Carolina (a supplement to Bulletin No. 8), prepared by the Hydrographic Division of the U.S. Geological Survey. 1911. 383 p.

*34 Discharge Records of North Carolina, 1889-1923, by T. Saville and G. W. Smith. 1926. 405 p.

*39 Discharge Records of North Carolina Streams, 1889-1936, by T. S. Johnson and C. L. Mann. 1938. 220 p.

*46 Progress Report on Groundwater in North Carolina, by M. J. Mundorff. 1945.

47 Progress Report on Groundwater in North Carolina, by M. J. Mundorff. 1945. (May be obtained from the Dept. of Water & Air Resources.)

51 Ground Water in the Halifax Area, North Carolina, by M. J. Mundorff. 1946. (May be obtained from the Dept. of Water & Air Resources.)

55 Geology and Ground Water in the Greensboro Area, North Carolina, by M. J. Mundorff. 1948. (May be obtained from the Dept. of Water & Air Resources.)

59 Flood-Plain Deposits of North Carolina Piedmont and Mountain Streams as a Possible Source of Ground-Water Supply, by M. J. Mundorff. 1950. (May be obtained from the Dept. of Water & Air Resources.)

63 Geology and Ground Water in the Charlotte Area, North Carolina, by H. E. LeGrand and M. J. Mundorff. 1952. (May be obtained from the Dept. of Water & Air Resources.)

68 Geology and Ground-Water in the Statesville Area, North Carolina, by Harry E. LeGrand. 1954. (May be obtained from the Dept. of Water & Air Resources.)

*69 Ground-Water Resources in North Carolina, by H. E. LeGrand. 1956.

72 Well Logs from the Coastal Plain of North Carolina, by Philip Monroe Brown. 1958. Price: $1.25.

73 Geology and Ground-Water Resources in the Greenville Area, North Carolina, by Philip Monroe Brown. 1959. (May be obtained from the Dept. of Water & Air Resources.)

79 Description of the Pungo River Formation in Beaufort County, North Carolina, by Joel O. Kimrey. 1965. Price: $2.00.

ECONOMIC PAPERS

*17 Proceedings of Drainage Convention Held at New Bern, North Carolina, Sept. 9, 1908, by J. H. Pratt. 1908.

*18 Proceedings of Second Annual Drainage Convention Held at New Bern, North Carolina, Nov. 11-12, 1909; and North Carolina Drainage Law, by J. H. Pratt. 1909.

*21 Proceedings of Third Annual Drainage Convention Held at Wilmington, North Carolina, Nov. 22-23, 1910; and North Carolina Drainage Law (codified), by J. H. Pratt. 1911.

*26 Proceedings of Fourth Annual Drainage Convention Held at Elizabeth City, North Carolina, Nov. 15-16, 1911, by J. H. Pratt. 1912.

*28 Culverts and Small Bridges for County Roads in North Carolina, by C. R. Thomas and T. F. Hickerson. 1912.

*31 Proceedings of Fifth Annual Drainage Convention Held at Raleigh, North Carolina, Nov. 26-27, 1912, by J. H. Pratt. 1913.

*38 Forms Covering the Organization of Drainage Districts Under the North Carolina Drainage Law, Chapter 442, Public Laws of 1909, and Amendments and Forms for Minutes of Board of Drainage Commissioner, covering the Organization of the Board up to and Including the Issuing of the Drainage Bonds, by G. R. Boyd. 1914.

*41 Proceedings of the Seventh Annual Drainage Convention of the North Carolina Drainage Association Held at Wilson, North Carolina, Nov. 18-19, 1914, by J. H. Pratt and H. M. Berry. 1915.

*45 Proceedings of Eighth Annual Drainage Convention of the North Carolina Drainage Association Held at Belhaven, North Carolina, Nov. 29, 30 and Dec. 1, 1915, by J. H. Pratt and H. M. Berry. 1917.

*47 Proceedings of the Ninth Drainage Convention of the North Carolina Drainage Association Held at Greensboro, North Carolina, Nov. 22-23, 1916, by J. H. Pratt and H. M. Berry. 1917.

*50 Proceedings of the Tenth Annual Drainage Convention Held at Washington, North Carolina, March 31 and April 1, 1920. 1920.

*52 Proceedings of the Eleventh Annual Drainage Convention Held at Elizabeth City, North Carolina, April 12-13, 1921. 1921.

*53 Water Power Survey of Surry and Wilkes Counties, by T. Saville. 1922. 41 p.

*54 Water-Power Investigation of Deep River, by T. Saville. 1924. 43 p.

*61 Preliminary Report on the Chemical Quality of the Surface Waters of North Carolina with Relation to Industrial Use, by C. E. Ray, Jr. and E. E. Randolph. 1928. 76 p.

INFORMATION CIRCULARS

*3 Selected Well Logs in the Coastal Plain of North Carolina, by M. J. Mundorff. 1944.

*6 A Possible New Source of Ground-Water Supply in the Elizabeth City Area, North Carolina, by M. J. Mundorff. 1947.

GEOLOGY AND PALEONTOLOGY

*Vol. III The Coastal Plain Deposits of North Carolina, by William Bullock Clark and others. 1912. (In 2 parts.)

*Part II The Water Resources of the Coastal Plain of North Carolina, by L. W. Stephenson and B. L. Johnson.

OTHER PUBLICATIONS

*Geology of the Fort Bragg Reservoir Dam Site, by J. L. Stuckey. November 1940.

*Ground Water Investigations, Waynesville and Hendersonville District, by T. G. Murdock. November 1940.

*Mineral Resources of the Little Tennessee and Hiwassee River Basins, by T. G. Murdock. 1941. 8 p. (Report of Investigation No. 8).

*The Neuse, by B. D. MacNeill. 1952. 14 p.

*Ground Water Resources of the Charlotte Area, North Carolina, by H. E. LeGrand and S. D. Broadhurst. 1955. (Special Report).

*The Water-Power Situation in North Carolina, by T. Saville. 1922. 15 p. (Circular No. 2).

*Drainage Assessments: Their Imposition and Their Collection under the North Carolina Drainage Laws, by F. Nash. August 1922. 11 p. (Circular No. 4).

*Amendments to the North Carolina Drainage Law Passed by the General Assemblies of 1919, 1921, and 1923. April 1923. 11 p. (Circular No. 5).

*The Water-Power Situation in North Carolina, by T. Saville. 1923. 25 p. (Circular No. 6).

*North Carolina Drainage Law. 1923. 40 p. (Circular No. 8).

*The Power Situation in North Carolina: 1924, by T. Saville. 1924. 24 p. (Circular No. 10).

DEPARTMENT OF WATER AND AIR RESOURCES
P. O. Box 27048
Raleigh, North Carolina 27611

The reports issued by the Department of Water and Air Resources and its predecessor agencies are available for free distribution unless otherwise indicated. Those which are out of print may be examined at the offices of the Department. Some reports are limited in distribution and will not be released except to those with a demonstrated need. However, these and all other reports are available to any citizen at cost of reproduction.

The predecessor agencies from which selected responsibilities were transferred to the Board of Water Resources and Department of Water Resources were: Department of Conservation and Development – 1959; Board of Water Commissioners – 1959; and the Board of Health – 1959. Both the Stream Sanitation Committee and the Board of Water Resources supervised the Department of Water Resources from 1959 to 1967 and were then consolidated to form the present Board of Water and Air Resources.

ADMINISTRATIVE PROGRESS AND STATUS

*First Biennial Report of the North Carolina Board of Water Commissioners. October 15, 1956. Raleigh.

*Second Report of the North Carolina Board of Water Commissioners. November 12, 1958. Raleigh.

*First Biennial Report. July 1, 1959 – June 30, 1960. Department of Water Resources. Raleigh.

*Second Biennial Report. July 1, 1960 – June 30, 1962. Department of Water Resources. Raleigh.

*Third Biennial Report. July 1, 1962 – June 30, 1964. Department of Water Resources. Raleigh.

*Fourth Biennial Report. July 1, 1964 – June 30, 1966. Department of Water Resources. Raleigh.

*Fifth Biennial Report. July 1, 1966 – June 30, 1968. Department of Water and Air Resources. Raleigh.

Sixth Biennial Report. July 1, 1968 – June 30, 1970. Department of Water and Air Resources. Raleigh. (In preparation.)

*Civil Works Program for the State of North Carolina. Annual. 1959 to date. (Current year available for distribution, all preceding issues out of print).

*Minutes of the Board of Water Resources. State Stream Sanitation Committee, Board of Water and Air Resources. All years.

*Semi-Annual Reports. Director and Division of the Department of Water and Air Resources. All Years.

*Water and Air Resources Programs in North Carolina. Department of Water and Air Resources. (Brochure) Raleigh. 1970.

*Water and Air Resources Program. North Carolina Department of Water and Air Resources. Raleigh. June 1970.

BASIC DATA AND INVENTORY

*Chemical Character of Surface Waters of North Carolina, 1943-44. North Carolina Department of Conservation and Development. W. L. Lamar, 1945.

Chemical Character of Surface Waters of North Carolina, 1944-45. Bulletin 52, Vol. 1. Lamar. Prepared by the United States Geological Survey in cooperation with the North Carolina Department of Conservation and Development. Raleigh. 1947.

Chemical Character of Surface Waters of North Carolina, 1945-46. Bulletin 52, Vol. 2. Lamar. Prepared by the United States Geological Survey in cooperation with the North Carolina Department of Conservation and Development. Raleigh. 1948.

Chemical Character of Surface Waters of North Carolina, 1946-47. Bulletin 52, Vol. 3. Lamar and Joyner. Prepared by the United States Geological Survey in cooperation with the North Carolina Department of Conservation and Development. Raleigh. 1949.

Chemical Character of Surface Waters of North Carolina, 1947-48. Bulletin 52, Vol. 4. Pauszek and Joyner. Prepared by the United States Geological Survey in cooperation with the North Carolina Department of Conservation and Development. Raleigh. 1949.

Chemical Character of Surface Waters of North Carolina, 1948-49. Bulletin 52, Vol. 5. Pauszek. Prepared by the United States Geological Survey in cooperation with the North Carolina Department of Conservation and Development. Raleigh. 1950.

Chemical Character of Surface Waters of North Carolina, 1949-50. Bulletin 52, Vol. 6. Pauszek and Harris. Prepared by the United States Geological Survey in cooperation with the North Carolina Department of Conservation and Development. Raleigh. 1951.

Chemical Character of Surface Waters of North Carolina, 1950-51. Bulletin 52, Vol. 7. Pauszek. Prepared by the United States Geological Survey in cooperation with the North Carolina Department of Conservation and Development. Raleigh. 1952.

Chemical and Physical Character of Surface Waters of North Carolina, 1951-52. Bulletin 52, Vol. 8. Billingsley and Joyner.

Prepared by the United States Geological Survey in cooperation with the North Carolina Department of Conservation and Development. Raleigh. 1953.

Chemical and Physical Character of Surface Waters of North Carolina, 1952-53. Bulletin 52, Vol. 9. Billingsley and Joyner. Prepared by the United States Geological Survey in cooperation with the North Carolina Department of Conservation and Development. Raleigh. 1954.

Chemical and Physical Character of Surface Waters of North Carolina, 1953-54. Bulletin 52, Vol. 10. Harris and Joyner. Prepared by the United States Geological Survey in cooperation with the North Carolina Department of Conservation and Development. Raleigh. 1955.

Chemical and Physical Character of Surface Waters of North Carolina, 1954-55. Bulletin 52, Vol. 11. McAvoy and Harris. Prepared by the United States Geological Survey in cooperation with the North Carolina Department of Conservation and Development. Raleigh. 1956.

Chemical and Physical Character of Surface Waters of North Carolina. 1955-56. Bulletin 52, Vol. 12. McAvoy. Prepared by the United States Geological Survey in cooperation with the North Carolina Department of Conservation and Development. Raleigh. 1957.

Chemical and Physical Character of Surface Waters of North Carolina, 1956-57. Bulletin 1, Vol. I. Woodard & Thomas. Prepared by the United States Geological Survey in cooperation with the North Carolina Department of Conservation and Development and the North Carolina Department of Water Resources. Raleigh. 1959.

Chemical and Physical Character of Surface Waters of North Carolina, 1957-58. Bulletin 1, Vol. II. Woodard & Thomas. Prepared by the United States Geological Survey in cooperation with the North Carolina Department of Conservation and Development and the North Carolina Department of Water Resources. Raleigh. 1960.

Chemical and Physical Character of Surface Waters of North Carolina, 1958-59. Bulletin 1, Vol. III. Chemerys & Phibbs. Prepared by the United States Geological Survey in cooperation with the North Carolina Department of Water Resources. Raleigh. 1962.

Chemical and Physical Character of Surface Waters of North Carolina, 1959-60. Bulletin 1, Vol. IV. Woodard. Prepared by the United States Geological Survey in cooperation with the North Carolina Department of Water Resources. Raleigh. 1962.

Chemical and Physical Character of Surface Waters of North Carolina, 1960-61. Bulletin 1, Vol. V. Phibbs and Midgett. Prepared by the United States Geological Survey in cooperation with the North Carolina Department of Water Resources. Raleigh. 1963.

Chemical and Physical Character of Surface Waters of North Carolina, 1961-62. Bulletin 1, Vol. VI. Phibbs. Prepared by the United States Geological Survey in cooperation with the North Carolina Department of Water Resources. Raleigh. 1964.

Chemical and Physical Character of Surface Waters of North Carolina, 1962-63. Bulletin 1, Vol. VII. Woodard & Phibbs. Prepared by the United States Geological Survey in cooperation with the North Carolina Department of Water Resources. Raleigh. 1965.

Chemical and Physical Character of Surface Waters of North Carolina, 1963-64. Bulletin 1, Vol. VIII. Phibbs & Chemerys. Prepared by the United States Geological Survey in cooperation with the North Carolina Department of Water Resources. Raleigh. 1966.

Chemical and Physical Character of Surface Waters of North Carolina, 1964-65. Bulletin 1, Vol. IX. Phibbs. Prepared by the United States Geological Survey in cooperation with the North Carolina Department of Water Resources. Raleigh. 1966.

Chemical and Physical Character of Surface Waters of North Carolina, 1965-66. Bulletin 1, Vol. X. Phibbs. Prepared by the United States Geological Survey in cooperation with the North Carolina Department of Water Resources. Raleigh. 1967.

Chemical and Physical Character of Surface Waters of North Carolina, 1966-67. Bulletin 1, Vol. XI. Phibbs. Prepared by the United States Geological Survey in cooperation with the North Carolina Department of Water Resources. Raleigh. 1969.

Chemical and Physical Character of Municipal Water Supplies in North Carolina. Bulletin 2. Prepared by the United States Geological Survey in cooperation with the North Carolina State Board of Health and the North Carolina Department of Water Resources. Raleigh. 1961.

Chemical and Physical Character of Municipal Water Supplies in North Carolina. Bulletin 2. Supplement 1. Prepared by the United States Geological Survey in cooperation with the North Carolina Department of Water Resources. Raleigh. 1962.

Chemical and Physical Character of Municipal Water Supplies in North Carolina. Bulletin 2, Supplement 2. Prepared by the United States Geological Survey in cooperation with the North Carolina Department of Water Resources. Raleigh. 1964.

Chemical and Physical Character of Municipal Water Supplies in North Carolina. Bulletin 2, Supplement 3. Prepared by the United States Geological Survey in cooperation with the North Carolina Department of Water Resources. Raleigh. 1965.

Chemical and Physical Character of Municipal Water Supplies in North Carolina. Bulletin 3. E. J. Phibbs, Jr. Prepared by the United States Geological Survey in cooperation with the North Carolina Department of Water and Air Resources. Raleigh. 1969.

*Hydrologic Data on the Cape Fear River Basin. 1820-1945. Department of Conservation and Development. Prepared in cooperation with the United States Geological Survey and the United States Weather Bureau. Raleigh. 1947.

*Hydrologic Data on the Catawba and Broad River Basins. 1872-1945. Department of Conservation and Development. Prepared in cooperation with the United States Geological Survey and the United States Weather Bureau. Raleigh. 1949.

*Hydrologic Data on the French Broad River Basin. 1857-1945. Prepared by the United States Geological Survey and the United States Weather Bureau in cooperation with the North Carolina Department of Conservation and Development. Raleigh. 1950.

*Hydrologic Data on the Little Tennessee and Hiwassee Rivers. 1873-1945. Prepared by the United States Geological Survey in cooperation with the North Carolina Department of Conservation and Development. Raleigh. 1953.

*Hydrologic Data on the Neuse River Basin. 1866-1945. Prepared by the United States Geological Survey and the United States Weather Bureau in cooperation with the North Carolina Department of Conservation and Development. Raleigh. 1950.

*Hydrologic Data on the Roanoke and Tar River Basins. 1871-1945. Department of Conservation and Development. Prepared in cooperation with the United States Geological Survey and the United States Weather Bureau. Raleigh. 1952.

*Hydrologic Data on the Yadkin-Pee Dee River Basin. 1866-1945. Department of Conservation and Development. Prepared in cooperation with the United States Geological Survey and the United States Weather Bureau. Raleigh. 1948.

*Inventory of Municipal Sewage Facilities. State of North Carolina. Compiled by North Carolina Department of Water Resources. Division of Stream Sanitation and Hydrology. Raleigh. January 1962.

Low-flow Measurements of North Carolina Streams. North Carolina Department of Water and Air Resources Bulletin. W. L. Yonts. (In preparation.)

Register of Dams and Dam Sites in North Carolina. North Carolina Department of Water and Air Resources. Raleigh. 1969.

Summaries of Streamflow Records in North Carolina. North Carolina Department of Water and Air Resources Bulletin. N. O. Thomas. (In preparation.)

Surface Water Records of North Carolina. Prepared by the United States Geological Survey in cooperation with the State of North Carolina and Other Agencies. 1961.

Surface Water Records of North Carolina. Prepared by the United States Geological Survey in cooperation with the North Carolina Department of Water Resources and with Other State, Municipal, and Federal Agencies. 1962.

Surface Water Records of North Carolina. Prepared by the United States Geological Survey in cooperation with the North Carolina Department of Water Resources and with Other State, Municipal, and Federal Agencies. 1963.

Surface Water Records of North Carolina. Prepared by the United States Geological Survey in cooperation with the North Carolina Department of Water Resources and with Other State, Municipal, and Federal Agencies. 1964.

Water Quality Records in North Carolina. Prepared by the United States Geological Survey in cooperation with the North Carolina Department of Water Resources. 1964.

Water Resources Data for North Carolina. Part 1. Surface Water Records. Prepared by the United States Geological Survey in cooperation with the North Carolina Department of Water Resources and with Other State, Municipal, and Federal Agencies. 1965.

Water Resources Data for North Carolina. Part 2. Water Quality Records. Prepared by the United States Geological Survey in cooperation with the North Carolina Department of Water Resources and Federal Agencies. 1965.

Water Resources Data for North Carolina. Part 1. Surface Water Records. Prepared by the United States Geological Survey in cooperation with the North Carolina Department of Water Resources and with Other State, Municipal, and Federal Agencies. 1966.

Water Resources Data for North Carolina. Part 2. Water Quality Records. Prepared by the United States Geological Survey in cooperation with the North Carolina Department of Water Resources and Federal Agencies. 1966.

Water Resources Data for North Carolina. Part 1. Surface Water Records. Prepared by the United States Geological Survey in cooperation with the North Carolina Department of Water Resources and with Other State, Municipal, and Federal Agencies. 1967.

Water Resources Data for North Carolina. Part 2. Water Quality Records. Prepared by the United States Geological Survey in cooperation with the North Carolina Department of Water Resources and Federal Agencies. 1967.

Water Resources Data for North Carolina. Part 1. Surface Water Records. Prepared by the United States Geological Survey in cooperation with the North Carolina Department of Water Resources and with Other State, Municipal, and Federal Agencies. 1968.

Water Resources Data for North Carolina. Part 2. Water Quality Records. Prepared by the United States Geological Survey in cooperation with the North Carolina Department of Water Resources and Federal Agencies. 1968.

Water Resources Data for North Carolina. Part 1. Surface Water Records. Prepared by the United States Geological Survey in cooperation with the North Carolina Department of Water Resources and with Other State, Municipal, and Federal Agencies. 1969.

Water Resources Data for North Carolina. Part 2. Water Quality Records. Prepared by the United States Geological Survey in cooperation with the North Carolina Department of Water Resources and Federal Agencies. 1969.

Water Resources Investigations in North Carolina 1969. Conducted by the United States Geological Survey — Water Resources Division in cooperation with the North Carolina Department of Water and Air Resources and Other State, Municipal and Federal Agencies.

*Water Resources of North Carolina. North Carolina Department of Conservation and Development. Raleigh. 1955.

*Water Resources of North Carolina. Broad and Catawba River Basins. North Carolina Department of Conservation and Development. Raleigh. 1958.

*Water Resources of North Carolina. Cape Fear River Basin. North Carolina Department of Conservation and Development. Raleigh. 1955.

*Water Resources of North Carolina. Chowan River Basin. Department of Conservation and Development. Raleigh. 1955.

*Water Resources of North Carolina. Coastal Plain River Basins. North Carolina Department of Conservation and Development. Raleigh. 1959.

*Water Resources of North Carolina. French Broad River Basin. North Carolina Department of Conservation and Development. Raleigh. 1957.

*Water Resources of North Carolina. Hiwassee and Little Tennessee River Basins. North Carolina Department of Conservation and Development. Raleigh. 1959.

*Water Resources of North Carolina. Kanawha and Watauga River Basins. North Carolina Department of Conservation and Development. Raleigh. 1959.

*Water Resources of North Carolina. Neuse River Basin. North Carolina Department of Conservation and Development. Raleigh. 1955.

*Water Resources of North Carolina. Roanoke River Basin. North Carolina Department of Conservation and Development. Raleigh. 1956.

*Water Resources of North Carolina. Tar-Pamlico River Basin. North Carolina Department of Conservation and Development. Raleigh. 1958.

*Water Resources of North Carolina. Yadkin-Pee Dee River Basin. North Carolina Department of Conservation and Development. Raleigh. 1955.

Water Resources of North Carolina; an Inventory of Information and Data. By Frederick E. McJunkin, Mary J. Coe, and
Bruce A. Knarr of University of North Carolina, Chapel Hill
in cooperation with the Division of Planning, North Carolina
Department of Water and Air Resources. Raleigh, Water Resources Research Institute, 1968. (Report 22)

DESIGN GUIDES

Recommended Guide for the Design of Waste Stabilization
Lagoons. Adopted by State Stream Sanitation Committee, May
18, 1961. Raleigh, North Carolina Department of Water Resources.

The following Standard Plans are available from the Department for issue to County Health Departments:

Standard Plan "A" – Small Septic Tank. Issued December
                                  1959.

Standard Plan "C" – Septic Tank with Dosing Tank. (Single
                                  Siphon). Issued September 1962.

Standard Plan "D" – Septic Tank with Dosing Tank. (Double
                                  Siphon). Issued January 1961.

Standard Plan "E" – Surface Sand Filter. Issued August 1962.

Standard Plan "F" – Filtration Trench. Issued January 1961.

Standard Plan "G" – Nitrification Trench. Issued October
                                  1960.

Standard Plan "J" – Distribution Box. Issued October 1961.

EDUCATIONAL MATERIAL

Clean Water for North Carolina. North Carolina Department
of Water and Air Resources. Raleigh. Undated. 20 p. illus.

The Fight to Save North Carolina's Waters. A Mark Trail Ad-
venture in Public Health and Conservation. State Stream Sanitation Committee, North Carolina State Board of Health.
Raleigh. 1956.

The Neuse. Ben Dixon MacNeil. North Carolina Department
of Conservation and Development. Raleigh. 1952.

*Tar Heel Waters. State Stream Sanitation Committee. State
Board of Health. Raleigh. Undated.

GROUND WATER BULLETINS

1   Geology and Ground Water Resources of Wilmington-
    New Bern Area. Harry E. LeGrand. Prepared by United
    States Geological Survey in cooperation with the North
    Carolina Department of Water Resources. Raleigh. 1960.

2   Geology and Ground Water in the Goldsboro Area,
    North Carolina. Richard D. Pusey. Prepared by the
    United States Geological Survey in cooperation with the
    North Carolina Department of Conservation and Devel-
    opment and the North Carolina Department of Water
    Resources. Raleigh. 1960.

3   Geology and Ground Water of the Fayetteville Area,
    North Carolina. Robert G. Schipf. Prepared by the
    United States Geological Survey in cooperation with the
    North Carolina Department of Conservation and Devel-
    opment. Raleigh. 1961.

4   Geology and Ground Water Resources of the Swanquar-
    ter Area, North Carolina. Perry F. Nelson. Prepared by
    the North Carolina Department of Water Resources.
    Raleigh. 1964.

5   Geology and Ground Water Resources of the Monroe
    Area, North Carolina. Edwin O. Floyd. Prepared by
    the United States Geological Survey in cooperation with
    the North Carolina Department of Water Resources.
    Raleigh. 1965.

6   Reconnaissance of the Ground Water Resources of the
    Southport–Elizabethtown Area, North Carolina. Regi-
    nald G. Blankenship. Prepared by the United States
    Geological Survey in cooperation with the North Caro-
    lina Department of Water Resources. Raleigh. 1965.

7   Geology and Ground Water in the Durham Area, North
    Carolina. George L. Bain and J. O. Thomas. Prepared
    by the United States Geological Survey in cooperation
    with the North Carolina Department of Water Resources.
    Raleigh. May 1966.

8   Reconnaissance of the Ground Water Resources in the
    Waynesville Area, North Carolina. O. T. Marsh and R. L.
    Laney. Prepared by the United States Geological Survey
    in cooperation with the North Carolina Department of
    Water Resources. Raleigh. May 1966.

9   Ground Water Resources of Martin County. Granville G.
    Wyrick. Prepared by the United States Geological Sur-
    vey in cooperation with the North Carolina Department
    of Water Resources. Raleigh. November 1966.

10 Geology and Ground Water Resources of the Hertford-
    Elizabeth City Area, North Carolina. W. H. Harris and
    H. B. Wilder. Prepared by the United States Geological
    Survey in cooperation with the North Carolina Depart-
    ment of Water Resources. Raleigh. 1966.

11 Ground Water Resources of the Cleveland County Area,
    North Carolina. D. A. Duncan and R. R. Peace. North
    Carolina Department of Water Resources. Raleigh. De-
    cember 1966.

12 Geology and Ground Water Resources of the Morgan-
    ton Area, North Carolina. C. T. Sumsion and R. L.
    Laney. Prepared by the United States Geological Survey
    in cooperation with the North Carolina Department of
    Water Resources. Raleigh. March 1967.

13 Geology and Ground Water Resources of the Murphy
    Area, North Carolina. C. L. Dodson and R. L. Laney.
    North Carolina Department of Water and Air Resources.
    Raleigh. 1968.

14 Geology and Ground Water Resources of the Chowan
    County Area, North Carolina. Orville B. Lloyd. Pre-
    pared by the United States Geological Survey in cooper-
    ation with the North Carolina Department of Water and
    Air Resources. Raleigh. July 1968.

15 Geology and Ground Water Resources in the Raleigh
    Area, North Carolina. V. J. May and H. D. Thomas.
    Prepared by the United States Geological Survey in co-
    operation with the North Carolina Department of Water
    and Air Resources. Raleigh. 1968.

16 Geology and Ground Water Resources of the Asheville
    Area. Henry L. Trapp. Prepared by the United States
    Geological Survey in cooperation with the North Caro-
    lina Department of Water and Air Resources. Raleigh.
    April 1970.

17   Geology and Ground Water Resources of New Hanover County, North Carolina. George L. Bain. Prepared by the United States Geological Survey in cooperation with the New Hanover County Board of Commissioners and the North Carolina Department of Water and Air Resources. Raleigh. April 1970.

18   Geology and Ground Water Resources of Pitt County, North Carolina. Carl T. Sumsion. Prepared by the United States Geological Survey in cooperation with the Pitt County Board of Commissioners and the North Carolina Department of Water and Air Resources. Raleigh. March 1970.

GROUND WATER CIRCULARS

*1   Ground Water Conditions at Rutherford College. William E. Bright. North Carolina Department of Water Resources. Raleigh. 1963.

*2   Preliminary Report on Ground Water in Beaufort County with Special Reference to Potential Effects of Phosphate Mining. Perry F. Nelson and Harry M. Peek. North Carolina Department of Water Resources. Raleigh. 1964.

*3   Ground Water Conditions in the Clinton Area, North Carolina. Leland L. Laymond, and Robert G. Barksdale, North Carolina Department of Water Resources. Raleigh. 1964.

*4   Ground Water Conditions at Tanglewood Park, Clemmons, North Carolina. Richard R. Peace, Jr. North Carolina Department of Water Resources. Raleigh. 1964.

*5   Chemical and Physical Character of Ground Water in South School Area, Iredell County, North Carolina. Richard R. Peace, Jr. North Carolina Department of Water Resources. Raleigh. 1965.

*6   Ground Water Conditions in the Clyde Area, Haywood County, North Carolina. Donald A. Duncan. North Carolina Department of Water Resources. Raleigh. 1965.

*7   Ground Water Exploration at Surf City, North Carolina. Leland L. Laymon. North Carolina Department of Water Resources. Raleigh. 1965.

*8   Ground Water Conditions in the Liberty Area, Randolph County, North Carolina. Edward L. Berry. North Carolina Department of Water Resources. Raleigh. 1965.

*9   Geology and Ground Water Resources in the Hays Area, Wilkes County, North Carolina. Perry F. Nelson and Robert G. Barksdale. North Carolina Department of Water Resources. Raleigh. 1965.

*10   Interim Report on the Ground Water Resources of the Kinston Area, North Carolina. Perry F. Nelson and R. G. Barksdale. North Carolina Department of Water Resources. Raleigh. 1965.

*11   Geology and Ground-Water Resources in the Bostic Area, North Carolina. Donald A. Duncan. North Carolina Department of Water Resources. Raleigh. 1965.

*12   Geology and Ground Water Resources in the Broadway Area, Wilkes County, North Carolina (A Reconnaissance). Richard R. Peace, Jr. North Carolina Department of Water Resources. Raleigh. 1965.

13   Ground Water Levels in North Carolina in 1963-64. John K. Hunsucker and Joseph E. Shaffner, Jr. Prepared by the United States Geological Survey in cooperation with the North Carolina Department of Water and Air Resources. Raleigh. March 1970.

14   Well Records and Other Basic Ground Water Data Craven County, North Carolina. E. O. Floyd and A. T. Long. Prepared by the United States Geological Survey in cooperation with the North Carolina Department of Water and Air Resources. Raleigh. March 1970.

15   Ground Water Quality in Stanly County, North Carolina. Edward L. Berry. North Carolina Department of Water and Air Resources. Raleigh. 1970.

OTHER GROUND WATER

*Progress Report on Ground Water in North Carolina. Bulletin No. 47. M. J. Mundorff. Prepared by the United States Geological Survey in cooperation with the North Carolina Department of Conservation and Development. Raleigh. 1945.

*Ground Water in the Halifax Area, North Carolina. Bulletin No. 52. M. J. Mundorff. Prepared by the United States Geological Survey in cooperation with the North Carolina Department of Conservation and Development. Raleigh. 1946.

*Marls and Limestones of Eastern North Carolina. Bulletin No. 54. E. W. Berry. Prepared by the U. S. Geological Survey in cooperation with the North Carolina Department of Conservation and Development. Raleigh. 1947.

*Geology and Ground Water in the Greensboro Area, North Carolina. Bulletin No. 55. M. J. Mundorff. Prepared by the United States Geological Survey in cooperation with the North Carolina Department of Conservation and Development. Raleigh. 1948.

*Flood-Plain Deposits of North Carolina Piedmont and Mountain Streams as a Possible Source of Ground Water Supply. Bulletin No. 59. Preliminary Report by M. J. Mundorff. Prepared by the United States Geological Survey in cooperation with the North Carolina Department of Conservation and Development. Raleigh. 1950.

*Geology and Ground Water in the Charlotte Area, North Carolina. Bulletin No. 63. H. E. LeGrand and M. J. Mundorff. Prepared by the United States Geological Survey in cooperation with the North Carolina Department of Conservation and Development. Raleigh. 1952.

*Geology and Ground Water in the Statesville Area, North Carolina. Bulletin No. 68. H. E. LeGrand. Prepared by the United States Geological Survey in cooperation with the North Carolina Department of Conservation and Development. Raleigh. 1954.

*Ground Water Resources in North Carolina. Bulletin No. 69. H. E. LeGrand. Prepared by the United States Geological Survey in cooperation with the North Carolina Department of Conservation and Development. Raleigh. 1956.

*Well Logs from the Coastal Plain of North Carolina. Bulletin No. 72. P. M. Brown. Prepared by the United States Geological Survey in cooperation with the North Carolina Department of Conservation and Development. Raleigh. 1958.

*Geology and Ground Water Resources in the Greenville Area, North Carolina. Bulletin No. 73. P. M. Brown. Prepared by the United States Geological Survey in cooperation with the North Carolina Department of Conservation and Development. Raleigh. 1956.

Description of the Pungo River Formation in Beaufort County, North Carolina. Bulletin No. 79. J. O. Kimrey. Prepared by the United States Geological Survey in cooperation with the North Carolina Department of Conservation and Development and the Beaufort County Board of Commissioners. Raleigh. 1965. (This is not a Department of Water Resources publication, but it is as closely related to Department responsibilities as previously numbered reports relating to functions transferred to the Department. Not available for distribution.)

Ground Water Supply of Cape Hatteras National Seashore Recreational Area, North Carolina. Report of Investigations No. 1. Philip M. Brown. Prepared by United States Geological Survey in cooperation with the National Park Service and North Carolina Department of Water Resources. Raleigh. 1960.

Ground Water Supply of Cape Hatteras National Seashore Recreational Area, North Carolina. Report of Investigations No. 2. Part 2. Joel O. Kimrey. Prepared by the United States Geological Survey in cooperation with National Park Service and North Carolina Department of Water Resources. Raleigh. 1960.

Ground Water Supply for the Dare Beaches Sanitary District. Joel O. Kimrey. Report of Investigations No. 3. Prepared by United States Geological Survey in cooperation with North Carolina Department of Water Resources. Raleigh. 1961.

Ground Water Supply of Cape Hatteras National Seashore Recreational Area, North Carolina. Report of Investigations No. 4. Part 3. W. H. Harris and H. B. Wilder. Prepared by the United States Geological Survey in cooperation with the National Park Service and the North Carolina Department of Water Resources. Raleigh. 1964.

Ground Water Supply of Cape Hatteras National Seashore, North Carolina. Report of Investigations No. 5, Part 4. O. B. Lloyd and H. B. Wilder. Prepared by the United States Geological Survey in cooperation with the National Park Service and the North Carolina Department of Water and Air Resources. Raleigh. 1968.

Ground Water Supply of Cape Hatteras National Seashore Recreational Area, North Carolina. Report of Investigations No. 6. Part 5. G. G. Wyrick and R. B. Dean. Prepared by the United States Geological Survey in cooperation with the National Park Service and the North Carolina Department of Water and Air Resources. Raleigh. 1968.

Ground Water Supply of Cape Hatteras National Seashore Recreational Area, North Carolina. Report of Investigations No. 7. Part 6. O. B. Lloyd and R. B. Dean. Prepared by the United States Geological Survey in cooperation with the National Park Service and the North Carolina Department of Water and Air Resources. Raleigh. 1968.

Ground Water Resources of the Belhaven Area, North Carolina. Report of Investigations No. 8. O. B. Lloyd and E. O. Floyd. Prepared in cooperation with the Department of Water and Air Resources by the United States Geological Survey. Raleigh. 1968.

Evaluation of Potential Impact of Phosphate Mining on Ground Water Resources of Eastern North Carolina. Sayre, Dewiest, and Jacob, Consulting Board. North Carolina Department of Water Resources. Raleigh. January 1967.

*Public Ground Water Supplies in North Carolina. Progress Report No. 2. F. H. Pauszek. Prepared by the United States Geological Survey in cooperation with the North Carolina State Board of Health. Raleigh. 1949.

*Public Surface – Water Supplies in North Carolina. W. L. Lamar and F. H. Pauszek. Prepared by the United States Geological Survey in cooperation with the North Carolina State Board of Health. Raleigh. 1947.

LAWS, RULES AND REGULATIONS

*Classifications and Water Quality Standards Applicable to the Surface Waters of North Carolina. Adopted by Board of Water and Air Resources. Department of Water and Air Resources. Raleigh. January 30, 1968.

Engineering Criteria; Animal Waste Treatment Lagoons, North Carolina. Adopted by Board of Water and Air Resources. Raleigh. October 13, 1970.

The Use of Stream Channels to Deliver Stored Water: the Possibility of Interference by Third Parties. Water Resources Research Institute. Raleigh. 1969. (The Department of Water and Air Resources provided funds for this report.)

*The Law of Other States. Brochure Appendix G. Working Papers. Department of Water Resources. Raleigh. November 1965. (Note: This is a limited edition compendium prepared in connection with a study of water laws directed by the General Assembly.)

Laws of North Carolina Relating to Water and Air Resources. Issued by North Carolina Department of Water and Air Resources. Reprinted from General Statutes of North Carolina and 1967 Cumulative Supplement. The Michie Company. Charlottesville, Virginia. 1968. (Copies may be purchased from the Michie Company.)

Laws of North Carolina Relating to Water and Air Resources – 1969 Supplement. Issued by North Carolina Department of Water and Air Resources. Reprinted from 1969 Cumulative Supplement to General Statutes of North Carolina. The Michie Company. Charlottesville, Virginia. 1970.

North Carolina Well Construction Act of 1967. Interim Procedures and Requirements. North Carolina Department of Water and Air Resources.

Public Hearing Report. Broad River Basin. State Stream Sanitation Committee. North Carolina Department of Water Resources. Raleigh. July 12-13, 1962.

Public Hearing Report. Cape Fear River Basin. State Stream Sanitation Committee. North Carolina State Board of Health. Raleigh. September 10, 11, 12, 1958.

Public Hearing Report. Catawba River Basin. State Stream Sanitation Committee. North Carolina Department of Water Resources. Raleigh. July 13, 14, 1961.

Public Hearing Report. Chowan River Basin. State Stream Sanitation Committee. North Carolina State Board of Health. Raleigh. December 6, 1955.

Public Hearing Report. French Broad River Basin. State Stream Sanitation Committee. North Carolina State Board of Health. Raleigh. October 24, 1957.

Public Hearing Report. Hiwassee River Basin. State Stream Sanitation Committee. North Carolina Department of Water Resources. Raleigh. October 28, 1960.

Public Hearing Report. Little Tennessee and Savannah River Basins. State Stream Sanitation Committee. North Carolina Department of Water Resources. Raleigh. October 27, 1960.

Public Hearing Report. Lumber River Basin. State Stream Sanitation Committee. North Carolina Department of Water Resources. Raleigh. June 24-25, 1963.

Public Hearing Report. Neuse River Basin. State Stream Sanitation Committee. North Carolina State Board of Health. Raleigh. June 25-26, 1959.

Public Hearing Report. New River Basin. State Stream Sanitation Committee. North Carolina Department of Water Resources. Raleigh. October 26, 1962.

Public Hearing Report. Pasquotank River Basin. State Stream Sanitation Committee. North Carolina Department of Water Resources. Raleigh. July 15, 1960.

Public Hearing Report. Roanoke River Basin. State Stream Sanitation Committee. North Carolina State Board of Health. Public Hearing Report 16, 1957.

Public Hearing Report. Tar-Pamlico River Basin. State Stream Sanitation Committee. North Carolina Department of Water Resources. Raleigh. November 9-10, 1961.

Public Hearing Report. Watauga River Basin. State Stream Sanitation Committee. North Carolina Department of Water Resources. Raleigh. October 25, 1962.

Public Hearing Report. White Oak River Basin. State Stream Sanitation Committee. North Carolina State Board of Health. Raleigh. June 23-24, 1955.

Public Hearing Report. Yadkin River Basin. State Stream Sanitation Committee, North Carolina State Board of Health. Raleigh. June 8, 10, 18, 1954.

*Presentation of Water Quality Standards and Plan of Implementation for the Interstate and Coastal Waters of North Carolina Filed Pursuant to the Federal Water Quality Act of 1965. State Stream Sanitation Committee. Department of Water Resources. Raleigh. June 1967. (Note: Updating information has been supplied to F.W.Q.A. in 1968, 1969, and 1970 but not in report form).

Report of Proceedings at Public Hearing Concerning the Adoption of Proposed Amendments to the Classification and Water Quality Standards Applicable to Surface Waters of North Carolina. Department of Water and Air Resources. Raleigh. November 16, 1967.

Report of Proceedings at Public Hearing Concerning the Classification of Streams having Segments Heretofore Classified "E". Board of Water and Air Resources. Raleigh. January 7, 1971.

*Rules and Regulations and Classifications and Water Quality Standards Applicable to Surface Waters of North Carolina. Adopted by State Stream Sanitation Committee. North Carolina State Board of Health. Raleigh. November 19, 1953.

Rules, Regulations, Classifications and Water Quality Standards Applicable to the Surface Waters of North Carolina. Adopted by Board of Water and Air Resources. Raleigh, October 13, 1970.

Rules and Regulations Governing the Control of Air Pollution. Adopted by Board of Water and Air Resources. Raleigh. March 1970.

Rules and Regulations Relating to State Participation in Civil Works Projects. Adopted October 2, 1963. Amended March 3, 1964, and February 4, 1965. Board of Water Resources. Raleigh. 1965.

Schedules of assigned classifications are revised from time to time upon request followed by public hearing and a finding of necessity. When specific schedules are supplied upon request, the latest changes are always supplied.

Schedules of Assigned Classifications. Broad River Basin. State Stream Sanitation Committee. North Carolina Department of Water Resources. Raleigh. Adopted December 19, 1962. Effective March 1, 1963.

Schedules of Assigned Classifications. Cape Fear River Basin. State Stream Sanitation Committee. North Carolina State

Board of Health. Raleigh. Adopted January 20, 1959. Effective April 1, 1959.

Schedules of Assigned Classifications. Catawba River Basin. State Stream Sanitation Committee. North Carolina Department of Water Resources. Raleigh. Adopted December 15, 1961. Effective March 1, 1962.

Schedules of Assigned Classifications. Chowan River Basin. State Stream Sanitation Committee. North Carolina State Board of Health. Raleigh. Adopted March 7, 1956. Effective July 2, 1956.

Schedules of Assigned Classifications. French Broad River Basin. State Stream Sanitation Committee. North Carolina State Board of Health. Raleigh. Adopted January 30, 1958. Effective March 1, 1958.

Schedules of Assigned Classifications. Hiwassee River Basin. State Stream Sanitation Committee. North Carolina Department of Water Resources. Raleigh. Adopted May 17, 1961. Effective July 1, 1961.

Schedules of Assigned Classifications. Little Tennessee River Basin. State Stream Sanitation Committee. North Carolina Department of Water Resources. Raleigh. Adopted April 5, 1961. Effective July 1, 1961.

Schedules of Assigned Classifications. Lumber River Basin. State Stream Sanitation Committee. North Carolina Department of Water Resources. Raleigh. Adopted August 22, 1963. Effective December 16, 1963.

Schedules of Assigned Classifications. Neuse River Basin. State Stream Sanitation Committee. North Carolina Department of Water Resources. Raleigh. Adopted December 17, 1959. Effective April 1, 1960.

Schedules of Assigned Classifications. New River Basin. State Stream Sanitation Committee. North Carolina Department of Water Resources. Raleigh. Adopted February 8, 1963. Effective May 15, 1963.

Schedules of Assigned Classifications. Pasquotank River Basin. State Stream Sanitation Committee. North Carolina Department of Water Resources. Adopted January 6, 1961. Effective April 6, 1961.

Schedules of Assigned Classifications. Roanoke River Basin. State Stream Sanitation Committee. North Carolina State Board of Health. Raleigh. Adopted June 18, 1957. Effective September 1, 1952.

Schedules of Assigned Classifications. Tar-Pamlico River Basin. State Stream Sanitation Committee. North Carolina Department of Water Resources. Raleigh. Adopted April 6, 1962. Effective June 6, 1962.

Schedules of Assigned Classifications. Watauga River Basin. State Stream Sanitation Committee. Raleigh. Adopted February 8, 1963. Effective May 15, 1963.

Schedules of Assigned Classifications. White Oak River Basin. State Stream Sanitation Committee. Raleigh. Adopted February 9, 1956. Effective June 1, 1956.

Schedules of Assigned Classifications. Yadkin-Pee Dee River Basin. State Stream Sanitation Committee. North Carolina State Board of Health. Raleigh. Adopted December 14, 1954. Effective April 6, 1955.

*State and Federal Water Laws and Considerations Affecting Future Legislation. North Carolina Department of Conservation and Development. Raleigh. January 1956.

*Supplement to State and Federal Water Laws and Considerations Affecting Future Legislation. North Carolina Department of Conservation and Development. Raleigh. November 1957.

*State Laws, Policies and Programs Pertaining to Water and Related Land Resources – North Carolina. 1966. In Vol. XI, Appendix J of Ohio River Basin Comprehensive Survey. (Superseded by Chapter 1 – NCWP – Progress Report – Water Policy and Law 1971).

Water and Sewer Authorities Act – County Financing of Water and Sewerage Facilities. Issued by the North Carolina Department of Water Resources. Raleigh. May 1955. (Amended June 1961).

Well Construction Regulations and Standards. (Draft) Department of Water and Air Resources. Raleigh. 1971.

10 & 14 New (Kanawha) and Watauga River Basins.

11 Pasquotank River Basin.

12-1 Roanoke River Basin – 1.

12-2 Roanoke River Basin – 2.

13-1 Tar-Pamlico River Basin – 1 (Upper Basin).

13-2 Tar-Pamlico River Basin – 2 (Lower Basin).

15 White Oak River Basin.

16-1 Yadkin-Pee Dee River Basin – 1 (Upper Section).

16-2 Yadkin-Pee Dee River Basin – 2 (Middle Section).

16-3 Yadkin-Pee Dee River Basin – 3 (Lower Section).

MAPS AND CHARTS

The Department has on file chronoflex one-color positives of each of the following maps in two sizes, 17 x 34-inches and 8½ x 17-inches. Also available in each size are film negatives of four separation plates: streams, stream names, other map data, and associated names. Two-color prints of the maps in the 22 x 34-inch size are also available. Prints will be available on a limited basis for official use but not for general public release except when made up in reports or issued as Atlas sheets. Agencies having a valid use for any of these maps for reproduction should contact the Director, Department of Water and Air Resources, P. O. Box 27048, Raleigh, North Carolina 27611.

P-1 State of North Carolina.

P-1-2 (On the back of map no. P-1-2, is a numerical list of U.S.G.S. Quadrangles in North Carolina. There is also an attachment of an alphabetical list of U.S.G.S. Quadrangles in North Carolina. The map and attachment are available only in size 11 x 17 inches.)

17- Coastal Region of North Carolina.

01- Broad River Basin.

02-1 Cape Fear River Basin – 1 (Deep and Haw River Basins).

02-2 Cape Fear River Basin – 2 (Fayetteville Region, Northeast Cape Fear, and Associated Coastal Streams).

02-3 Cape Fear River Basin – 3 (Main Stem from Mouth to Fayetteville Region, South and Black Rivers, Coastal Areas).

03-1 Catawba River Basin – 1 (Upper Basin).

03-2 Catawba River Basin – 2 (Lower Basin).

04 Chowan River Basin.

05 French Broad River Basin.

06 Hiwassee River Basin.

07 Little Tennessee and Savannah River Basins.

08-1 Lumber River Basin – 1 (Lumber River and Minor Independent Tributaries).

08-2 Lumber River Basin – 2 (Waccamaw and Coastal Streams).

09-1 Neuse River Basin – 1 (Headwaters to Kinston Area).

09-2 Neuse River Basin – 2 (Kinston Area to Portsmouth Island).

PLANNING

*Development of Water Resources in Appalachia. North Carolina State Supplement. Detailed Report. 2 v. North Carolina Department of Water and Air Resources. 1968.

*Development of Water Resources in Appalachia. North Carolina State Supplement. North Carolina Department of Water and Air Resources. 1968. (Note: This is a condensation of the previously listed detailed report.)

Flood Damage Prevention in North Carolina. A Report Prepared for the Department of Water Resources by Milton S. Heath, Jr., Assistant Director, Institute of Government, UNC, Chapel Hill. Prepared in cooperation with the TVA. Raleigh. January 1963.

Map and Geographical Identification System to Facilitate Collection of Water and Related Resource Data. North Carolina Department of Water and Air Resources. Raleigh. 1967.

The North Carolina Water Plan; a Description and Progress Report. North Carolina Department of Water and Air Resources. Raleigh. November 1970.

*The North Carolina Water Plan and Associated Publications. Preliminary Edition. North Carolina Department of Water and Air Resources. Raleigh. October 1967.

North Carolina Water Plan Progress Report – Chapter 1 – Water Policy and Law. North Carolina Department of Water and Air Resources. Raleigh. February 1971.

North Carolina Water Plan Progress Report – Chapter 2 – Economic Data, Objectives and Economic Development. North Carolina Department of Water and Air Resources. Raleigh. August 1970.

North Carolina Water Plan Progress Report – Chapter 6 – Research. North Carolina Department of Water and Air Resources. Raleigh. December 1970.

North Carolina Water Plan Progress Report – Chapter 14A – Fish and Wildlife in North Carolina. North Carolina Department of Water and Air Resources. Raleigh. October 1970.

North Carolina Water Plan Progress Report – Chapter 19 – Power and Water. North Carolina Department of Water and Air Resources. Raleigh. November 1970.

North Carolina Water Plan Progress Report – Chapter 27 – Cape Fear River Basin. North Carolina Department of Water and Air Resources. Raleigh. (In preparation.)

North Carolina Water Plan Progress Report – Chapter 35 – New River Basin. North Carolina Department of Water and Air Resources. Raleigh. March 1970.

North Carolina Water Plan Progress Report — Chapter 44 — The Appalachian Region in North Carolina. North Carolina Department of Water and Air Resources. Raleigh. August 1970.

North Carolina Water Plan Progress Report — Appendix E — Publications Sponsored by the Department of Water and Air Resources and Selected United States Geological Survey Reports. North Carolina Department of Water and Air Resources. Raleigh. March 1971.

*Plan for Emergency Management of Resources. Part B. Resource Sections. Section XII Water. North Carolina Department of Water Resources. Raleigh. August 1966.

*Plan for Emergency Management of Resources. Part B. Resource Sections. Section XII Water. Reference Document No. 1. Current Assumptions. North Carolina Department of Water Resources. Raleigh. August 1966.

Plan for Emergency Management of Resources. Part B. Resource Sections. Section XII Water. Reference Document No. 3. Narrative Description and Selected Data on the Designated River Basins which Aggregate the State of North Carolina. North Carolina Department of Water Resources. Raleigh. August 1966.

Plan for Emergency Management of Resources. Part B. Resource Sections. Section XII Water. Reference Document No. 3A. Geographical Guide for Locational Reporting. North Carolina Department of Water Resources. Raleigh. November 1966.

Plan for Emergency Management of Resources. Part B. Resource Sections. Section XII Water. Reference Document No. 4. Federal Water Supplies by River Basin. North Carolina Department of Water Resources. Raleigh. September 1966.

Plan for Emergency Management of Resources. Part B. Resource Sections. Section XII Water. Reference Document No. 5. Federal Waste Disposal Facilities by River Basin. North Carolina Department of Water Resources. Raleigh. November 1966.

Plan for Emergency Management of Resources. Part B. Resource Sections. Section XII Water. Reference Document No. 6. State-owned Water Supplies by River Basins. North Carolina Department of Water Resources. Raleigh. October 1966.

Plan for Emergency Management of Resources. Part B. Resource Sections. Section XII Water. Reference Document No. 7. State-owned Waste Disposal Facilities by River Basins. North Carolina Department of Water Resources. Raleigh. November 1966.

Plan for Emergency Management of Resources. Part B. Resource Sections. Section XII Water. Reference Document No. 8. Summary Data on Municipal and Sanitary District Water Supplies. North Carolina Department of Water Resources. Raleigh. August 1966.

Population Data 1960 Census-Distribution by River Basin. North Carolina Department of Water and Air Resources. Raleigh. August 1970.

Water Resource Planning in North Carolina. Milton S. Heath, Jr. and David R. Godschalk. A report by the North Carolina Department of Water Resources. Prepared with the assistance of the Institute of Government, UNC, Chapel Hill. July 1964.

*Water Resources of North Carolina. 1900-1962 — 1962-1976. A Report prepared for Governor Terry Sanford. January 1, 1963. North Carolina Department of Water Resources. Raleigh. 1963.

*Water Resources of North Carolina. 1900-1964 — 1964-1976. A Report prepared for Governor Terry Sanford. October 1, 1964. North Carolina Department of Water Resources. 1964.

WATER QUALITY MANAGEMENT

*Comprehensive Pollution Abatement Plan. Broad River Basin. State Stream Sanitation Committee. North Carolina Department of Water Resources. Raleigh. Adopted March 12, 1963.

*Comprehensive Pollution Abatement Plan. Cape Fear River Basin. State Stream Sanitation Committee. North Carolina Department of Water Resources. Raleigh. Adopted May 8, 1959.

*Comprehensive Pollution Abatement Plan. Catawba River Basin. State Stream Sanitation Committee. North Carolina Department of Water Resources. Raleigh. Adopted May 31, 1962.

*Comprehensive Pollution Abatement Plan. Chowan River Basin. State Stream Sanitation Committee. North Carolina State Board of Health. Raleigh. Adopted April 30, 1956.

*Comprehensive Pollution Abatement Plan. French Broad River Basin. State Stream Sanitation Committee. North Carolina State Board of Health. Raleigh. Adopted July 25, 1958.

*Comprehensive Pollution Abatement Plan. Hiwassee River Basin. State Stream Sanitation Committee. North Carolina Department of Water Resources. Raleigh. Adopted September 7, 1961.

*Comprehensive Pollution Abatement Plan. Little Tennessee River Basin. State Stream Sanitation Committee. North Carolina Department of Water Resources. Raleigh. Adopted September 7, 1961.

*Comprehensive Pollution Abatement Plan. Lumber River Basin. State Stream Sanitation Committee. North Carolina Department of Water Resources. Raleigh. Adopted December 17, 1964.

*Comprehensive Pollution Abatement Plan. Neuse River Basin. State Stream Sanitation Committee. North Carolina Department of Water Resources. Raleigh. Adopted April 29, 1960.

*Comprehensive Pollution Abatement Plan. New River Basin. State Stream Sanitation Committee. North Carolina Department of Water Resources. Adopted July 9, 1963.

*Comprehensive Pollution Abatement Plan. Pasquotank River Basin. State Stream Sanitation Committee. North Carolina Department of Water Resources. Raleigh. Adopted April 5, 1961.

*Comprehensive Pollution Abatement Plan. Roanoke River Basin. State Stream Sanitation Committee. North Carolina State Board of Health. Raleigh. Adopted January 30, 1958.

*Comprehensive Pollution Abatement Plan. Tar-Pamlico River Basin. State Stream Sanitation Committee. North Carolina Department of Water Resources. Raleigh. Adopted July 24, 1962.

*Comprehensive Pollution Abatement Plan. Watauga River Basin. State Stream Sanitation Committee. North Carolina Department of Water Resources. Raleigh. Adopted July 9, 1963.

*Comprehensive Pollution Abatement Plan. White Oak River Basin. State Stream Sanitation Committee. North Carolina State Board of Health. Raleigh. Adopted April 30, 1956.

*Comprehensive Pollution Abatement Plan. Yadkin River Basin. State Stream Sanitation Committee. North Carolina State Board of Health. Raleigh. Adopted August 2, 1955.

Final Report of Investigation – Fish Kills – Yadkin River and High Rock Lake – June, July and August 1970. North Carolina Board of Water and Air Resources. Raleigh.

Interim Report on Chowan River. North Carolina Department of Water and Air Resources. Raleigh. June 1969.

Pollution Survey Report. Broad River Basin. State Stream Sanitation Committee. North Carolina Department of Water Resources. Raleigh. 1962.

Pollution Survey Report. Cape Fear River Basin. State Stream Sanitation Committee. North Carolina State Board of Health. Raleigh. 1957.

Pollution Survey Report. Catawba River Basin. State Stream Sanitation Committee. North Carolina Department of Water Resources. Raleigh. 1961.

*Pollution Survey Report. Chowan River Basin. State Stream Sanitation Committee. North Carolina State Board of Health. Raleigh. 1955.

Pollution Survey Report. French Broad River Basin. State Stream Sanitation Committee. North Carolina State Board of Health. Raleigh. 1957.

Pollution Survey Report. Hiwassee River Basin. State Stream Sanitation Committee. North Carolina Department of Water Resources. Raleigh. 1960.

Pollution Survey Report. Little Tennessee River Basin (including Savannah River). State Stream Sanitation Committee. North Carolina Department of Water Resources. Raleigh. 1960.

Pollution Survey Report. Lumber River Basin. State Stream Sanitation Committee. North Carolina Department of Water Resources. Raleigh. 1963.

Pollution Survey Report. Neuse River Basin. State Stream Sanitation Committee. North Carolina State Board of Health. Raleigh. 1959.

Pollution Survey Report. New River Basin. State Stream Sanitation Committee. North Carolina State Board of Health. Raleigh. 1962.

Pollution Survey Report. Pasquotank River Basin. State Stream Sanitation Committee. North Carolina Department of Water Resources. Raleigh. 1960.

*Pollution Survey Report. Roanoke River Basin. State Stream Sanitation Committee. North Carolina State Board of Health. Raleigh. 1956.

Pollution Survey Report. Tar-Pamlico River Basin. State Stream Sanitation Committee. North Carolina Department of Water Resources. Raleigh. 1961.

Pollution Survey Report. Watauga River Basin. State Stream Sanitation Committee. North Carolina Department of Water Resources. Raleigh. 1962.

*Pollution Survey Report. White Oak River Basin. State Stream Sanitation Committee. North Carolina State Board of Health. Raleigh. 1954.

*Pollution Survey Report. Yadkin River Basin. State Stream Sanitation Committee. North Carolina State Board of Health. Raleigh. 1953.

Report of Investigation of Fish Kills Hyde County, North Carolina. August 27 – September 2, 1970. North Carolina Department of Water and Air Resources. Raleigh.

Report of Investigation of the Surface Waters in Mecklenburg County. North Carolina Department of Water and Air Resources, North Carolina State Board of Health and Mecklenburg County Department of Public Health. Raleigh. December 1970.

NORTH CAROLINA GOVERNOR'S COMMITTEE ON WATER SAFETY
This Committee is no longer in existence.

*Safer Use of Water for Recreation in North Carolina. 1967. 53 p.

NORTH CAROLINA GOVERNOR'S CONFERENCE ON BEAUTIFICATION
c/o Governor's Office
State Capitol
Raleigh, North Carolina 27601

Scenic Waterways in North Carolina, by M. M. Hufschmidt. 1966. 3 p.

Seashore Enhancement. 1966. 2 p.

Stream Sanitation, by J. V. Whitfield. 1966. 5 p.

Water Rights Law as a Means for Resolving Conflicts in Water Use, by M. S. Heath, Jr. April 8, 1966. 4 p.

NORTH CAROLINA STATE PLANNING TASK FORCE
This Task Force is no longer in existence.

An Initial Outdoor Recreation Plan for North Carolina. March 1966. 92 p.

Upper French Broad River Basin: Regional Development and Investments Related to the Proposed Water Control System. Prepared for the Upper French Broad Economic Development Commission and Tennessee Valley Authority. October 1967. 53 p.

NORTH CAROLINA RECREATION COMMISSION
c/o Governor's Office
State Capitol
Raleigh, North Carolina 27601

*Water as Related to Recreation. March 1964.

*1965 Legislation Roundup. 1965. 18 p. (Recreation Leaflet).

*The Importance of Recreation Development to Water Resource Development and Economic Growth in North Carolina – a Policy Statement. June 1966.

*Inventory of Recreation Data, Alamance County.

NORTH CAROLINA SALT MARSH
MOSQUITO STUDY COMMISSION
This Commission is no longer in existence.

*Report of the North Carolina Salt Marsh Mosquito Study Commision. January 1959. 101 p. Raleigh, N. C.

STATE SOIL AND WATER CONSERVATION
COMMISSION
North Carolina State University
387 Williams Hall
Raleigh, North Carolina 27607

Long Range Program and Work Plan: Northhampton Soil and Water Conservation District, Jackson, North Carolina. 1964. 12 p.

1960 Conservation Progress Report. 15 p.

Program Objectives of Iredell Soil and Water Conservation District. Statesville, North Carolina. 1965. 15 p.

Small Watershed Act, an Amendment to the Soil and Water Conservation Districts Law of North Carolina, edited by B. R. Younts. August 1965. 25 p.

So You Are a Soil and Water Conservation District Supervisor? July 1966. 23 p.

Soil and Water Conservation District Laws of North Carolina as Amended, edited by H. A. Smith. May 1966. 15 p.

Soil Conservation Districts in Action. 1960. 14 p.

Soil Conservation Districts in Action. 1962. 15 p.

Watershed Protection and Flood Prevention. 1960. 15 p.

NORTH CAROLINA WILDLIFE RESOURCES
COMMISSION
Motor Vehicles Building
Raleigh, North Carolina 27603

Access to the Waters of North Carolina. 1966. 36 p.

Analyses of Accumulated Data, by W. D. Baker. 1963. 78 p. (Fishery Research Investigations — Power Reservoir Studies).

Analyses of Accumulated Data, Sandhills Project Lakes, by W. C. Carnes. 1966. 21 p. (Special Report).

Annual Report, Work Plan III, Federal Aid in Fish Restoration, Project F-16-R-1, Power Reservoir Investigations, by D. E. Louder. 1965. 16 p.

Biological Aspects of the Roanoke River Fish-Kill, April 21-28, 1963, by W. B. Smith and J. Bayless. 1963. 7 p.

Boating Access Areas. June 1967. 103 p.

Checklist of Fishes Collected from Lotic Waters of North Carolina, by H. M. Ratledge, W. C. Carnes and E. D. Collins. 1966. 13 p. (Special Publication).

Coastal Lakes I — 1965 Surveys, by J. D. Bayless. June 30, 1966. 11 p.

Coastal Lakes II — 1965 Surveys, by T. E. Crowell. June 30, 1966. 26 p.

Coastal Lakes III — 1965 Surveys, by W. B. Smith. June 30, 1966. 7 p.

Considerations of Estuarine Ecology, by J. H. Cornell. n.d.

Creel Census of High Rock Reservoir, by W. D. Baker. 1961-1963. (Fishery Research Investigations — Power Reservoir Studies).

Creel Census, Sandhill Lakes, by W. C. Carnes. 1966. 4 p. (Special Report).

Currituck Sound Investigations. 1963, 1966-   (Fishery Research Investigations).

The Distribution of Fishes in Relation to Water Quality, Fontana Reservoir, by C. D. Rael. 1966. 11 p. (Special Publication).

Effect of Coarse-Fish Removal from High Rock Reservoir, by W. D. Baker. 1961-1962. (Fishery Research Investigations — Power Reservoir Studies).

Effect of Fish Stocking on Sport Fishing in High Rock Reservoir. 1961-1963. (Fishery Research Investigations — Power Reservoir Studies).

Effect of Sea-Water Concentration on the Reproduction and Survival of Large-mouth Bass and Bluegill, by L. B. Tebo and E. G. McCoy. 1964. 8 p.

The Effects of Channelization Upon the Fish Populations of Lotic Waters in Eastern North Carolina, by J. Bayless and W. B. Smith. 1 vol. n.d.

Effects of Water Level Control on Muskrat Populations, by K. A. Wilson. 1955. 9 p. (Federal Aid in Wildlife Restoration, Project W-6-R).

Evaluation of Coarse Fish Removal from High Rock Reservoir, by W. D. Baker. 1963. 10 p. (Fishery Research Investigations — Power Research Studies).

Exotic Game Fish Stocking in High Rock Reservoir, by W. D. Baker. 1963. 3 p. (Fishery Research Investigations — Power Reservoir Studies).

Experimental Marsh Management near Currituck, North Carolina, by K. A. Wilson. 1955. 25 p. (Federal Aid in Wildlife Restoration Project W-6-R).

Farm Pond Studies, by W. C. Carnes. 1964. 20 p. (Fishery Research Investigations).

Farm Pond Studies; Fertilization, by W. C. Carnes. 1961. 3 p. (Fishery Research Investigations).

Farm Pond Studies; Physical, Chemical, and Biochemical Analyses as Indicators of Pond Fertility, by W. C. Carnes. 1963. 10 p. (Fishery Research Investigations).

Farm Pond Studies; Selection of Experimental Ponds, by W. C. Carnes. 1962-1963. (Fishery Research Investigations).

Fish Management in Municipal Water-Supply Lakes. 1966- (Special Report).

Impact of Pollution upon Sport-Fishing Waters. 1961-1963. (Statewide Fish Management Investigations).

Inventory of Fish Population in Lentic Waters. 1961. 317 p. (Job Completion Report for Job No. 1, Projects F-5-R and F-6-R).

Inventory of Fish Populations in Power Reservoirs and Natural Lakes. 1954-1955. (Warm Water Fish Management Investigations).

Investigations of Experimentally Stocked Farm Ponds, by W. C. Carnes. 1960. 49 p. (Warm Water Fish Management Investigations).

Investigations of Fish Populations and Investigations of Experimental Stockings in Farm Ponds, by E. B. Bradley. 1954-1955. (Warm Water Fish Management Investigations).

Laboratory Studies of Sedimentation Rates of Soil Samples Taken from the Proposed Oyster Shell Dredging Area in Eastern Albemarle Sound, by E. G. McCoy, G. M. Davis, and K. H. Johnston. April 1963.

Lake Lure; 1965 Surveys, by W. D. McNaughton. 1966.

Lake Waccamaw – 1965 Survey, by J. R. Davis. June 30, 1966. 9 p.

Limnological Studies of Badin and Mountain Island Reservoirs, by W. D. Baker. 1962-1963. (Fishery Research Investigations – Power Reservoir Studies).

Lower Yadkin and Lower Catawba River Reservoirs – 1965 Surveys, by H. A. Phillips. June 1966. 70 p.

The Management of Reclaimed Trout Streams, by F. F. Fish and H. M. Ratledge. 1963. 15 p.

The Minimum River Discharges Recommended for the Protection of the Roanoke River Anadromous Fishes, by F. F. Fish. December 1, 1960. 51 p.

Mountain Reservoirs – 1965 Surveys, by J. B. Messer. June 30, 1966. 60 p.

1962 Pre-Impoundment Study of the French Broad River Watershed; Anticipated Effects of the Presence of Ponds on Trout Streams in Transylvania and Henderson Counties, North Carolina, by H. M. Ratledge. 1962. 14 p.

North Carolina Wetlands; Their Distribution and Management, by K. A. Wilson. 1962. 169 p.

North Carolina's Boating Safety Law. April 1964. 14 p.

Power Reservoir Investigations, by W. D. Baker. 1966. 67 p. (Special Publications).

Quarterly Progress Reports. 1952-

Report, 1946/48 -

Salinity Variations in Currituck Sound (March 1955 – November 1955), by A. W. Dickson. n.d. 7 p. (Project F-5-R).

Small Lake Studies, by R. L. Humphries. 1961-1962, 1964. (Fishery Research Investigations).

Small Lakes Investigations, by W. C. Carnes. 1967. 9 p. (Special Report).

Small Watershed Developments in North Carolina, by F. B. Barick. 1966. 10 p.

Some Interesting Limnological Aspects of Fontana Reservoir. n.d. 9 p.

Special Investigations and Research on Wildlife Management Area Streams, by H. M. Ratledge. 1955-   (Project F-6-R).

Statewide Survey and Classification of Streams, by W. D. Baker. 1965. 61 p. (Statewide Fish Management Investigations).

Studies of Currituck Sound, by K. H. Johnston. 1961-1963. (Fishery Research Investigations – Brackish Water Investigations).

Survey and Classifications of the Broad River and Tributaries, North Carolina, by J. B. Messer, J. R. Davis, T. E. Crowell and W. C. Carnes. 1965. 87 p. Plus appendices. (Statewide Fish Management Investigations).

Survey and Classification of the Cape Fear River and Tributaries, North Carolina, by D. E. Louder. 1963. 15 p. Plus appendices.

Survey and Classification of the Cape Fear River Watershed, by D. E. Louder. 1963. 119 p. (Statewide Fish Management Investigations).

Survey and Classification of the Catawba River and Tributaries, North Carolina, by D. E. Louder. 1964. 97 p. Plus appendices. (Statewide Fish Management Investigations).

Survey and Classification of the Chowan River and Tributaries, North Carolina, by W. B. Smith. 1963. 15 p. Plus appendices.

Survey and Classification of the Deep-Haw Rivers and Tributaries, North Carolina, by W. C. Carnes, J. R. Davis and B. L. Tatum. 1964. 53 p. Plus appendices. (Statewide Fish Management Investigations).

Survey and Classification of the French Broad River and Tributaries, North Carolina, by F. R. Richardson. 1963. 51 p. Plus appendices. (Statewide Fish Management Investigations).

Survey and Classification of the French Broad River and Tributaries, North Carolina, by F. R. Richardson, H. M. Rutledge and J. B. Messer. 1963. 12 p.

Survey and Classification of the Hiwassee River and Tributaries, North Carolina, by J. B. Messer. 1965. 29 p. Plus appendices.

Survey and Classification of the Little Tennessee River and Tributaries, North Carolina, by J. B. Messer and H. M. Ratledge. 1963. 27 p. Plus appendices.

Survey and Classification of Lumber River and Shallotte River, North Carolina, by D. E. Louder. 1962. 124 p. Plus appendices. (Statewide Fish Management Investigations).

Survey and Classification of the Major Cooperative Wildlife Management Area Trout Streams, by H. M. Ratledge. June 30, 1966. 95 p.

Survey and Classification of the Neuse River and Tributaries, North Carolina, by J. D. Bayless and W. B. Smith. 1962. 33 p.

Survey and Classification of the New River and Tributaries, North Carolina, by F. R. Richardson and W. C. Carnes. 1964. 11 p. Plus appendices.

Survey and Classification of the New-White Oak-Newport Rivers and Tributaries, North Carolina, by J. R. Davis and B. G. McCoy. 1965. 12 p. Plus appendices.

Survey and Classification of the Northeast Cape Fear River and Tributaries, North Carolina, by J. D. Bayless. 1963. 11 p. Plus appendices.

Survey and Classification of the Pamlico River and Tributaries, North Carolina, by J. D. Bayless and E. H. Shannon. 1965. 95 p. Plus appendices. (Statewide Fish Management Investigations).

Survey and Classification of the Perguimans-Pasguotank-North Rivers and Tributaries, North Carolina, by W. D. Baker and W. B. Smith. 1965. 14 p. Plus appendices.

Survey and Classification of the Pigeon River and Tributaries, North Carolina, by J. B. Messer. 1964. 11 p. Plus appendices.

Survey and Classification of the Roanoke River and Tributaries, North Carolina, by W. C. Carnes. 1965. 71 p. Plus appendices. (Statewide Fish Management Investigations).

Survey and Classification of the Savannah River and Tributaries, North Carolina, by J. B. Messer. 1964. 16 p. Plus appendices.

Survey and Classification of the Scuppernong-Alligator Rivers and Tributaries, North Carolina, by W. B. Smith and W. D. Baker. 1965. 15 p. Plus appendices.

Survey and Classification of the Tar River and Tributaries, North Carolina, by W. B. Smith and J. Bayless. 1964. 19 p. Plus appendices.

Survey and Classification of the Toe River and Tributaries, North Carolina, by T. E. Crowell. 1965. 60 p. Plus appendices. (Statewide Fish Management Investigations).

Survey and Classification of the Watauga River and Tributaries, North Carolina, by F. R. Richardson. 1964. 8 p. Plus appendices.

Survey and Classification of the Yadkin River and Tributaries, North Carolina, by B. L. Tatum, W. C. Carnes, and F. Richardson. 1964. 40 p. Plus appendices.

Survey and Classification of the Yadkin River Watershed, by H. M. Ratledge, W. C. Carnes and F. R. Richardson. 1961. 35 p. (Statewide Fish Management Investigations).

Survey and Selection of Ponds, by D. F. Raver. 1955. 9 p. (Project F-3-R).

Tarheel Wildlife and Boating: Present and Future. March 1966. 67 p.

Upper Catawba and Upper Yadkin River Reservoirs – 1965 Surveys, by W. D. McNaughton. June 1966.

DIVISION OF INLAND FISHERIES

The Effects of Wind and Salinity Upon the Sedimentation Rates of Soils from Dredging Sites in Albemarle Sound, North Carolina, by E. G. McCoy and K. H. Johnson. n.d. 9 p.

A 'Fish Lock' for Passing Fishes Through Small Impoundment Structures, by W. D. Baker. 1966.

The Impact of Increasing Fishing Pressure upon Wild and Hatchery-Reared Trout Populations, by H. M. Ratledge. 1966.

Sport Fishery Statistics from the Inland Waters of North Carolina, by F. F. Fish. 1966.

WATER RESOURCES RESEARCH INSTITUTE
North Carolina State University
124 Riddick Building
Raleigh, North Carolina 27607

Unnumbered Plankton Heterotrophy in a North Carolina Estuary.

*Unnumbered Proceedings of Symposium on Estuarine Ecology Coastal Waters of North Carolina.

*1 Criteria for Evaluating the Quality of Water-Based Recreation Facilities. 1967. 88 p.

*2 Water Resources Problems and Research Needs of North Carolina. 1967. 43 p.

3 Water Resources Research Interests in the Colleges and Universities of North Carolina. 1970. 36 p.

4 Inventory of Active Water Resources Research Projects in North Carolina. 1970. 97 p.

5 Proceedings of Symposium on Hydrology of the Coastal Waters of North Carolina. 1967. 154 p.

*6 Current Studies in Pamlico River and Estuary of North Carolina.

*7 Solubility Equilibria Involving Metal Oxides and Corresponding Aqueous Metal Perchlorates. 1967. 16 p.

8 Groundwater Yields in the Raleigh Quadrangle. 1968. 61 p.

*9 Lake Oriented Subdivisions in North Carolina: Decision Factors and Policy Implications for Urban Growth Patterns – Part I – Developer Decisions. 1967. 177 p.

*10 As Above – Part II – Consumer Decisions. 1968. 88 p.

*11 Diffusion and Dispersion in Porous Media – Salt Water Mounds in Coastal Aquifers. 1968. 258 p.

12 Pigment Indices and Environmental Oxygen Stress. 1968. 41 p.

13 Current Study in the Neuse Estuary. 1969. 34 p.

*14 Color-Infrared Aerial Photographic Interpretation and Net Primary Productivity of a Regularly Flooded North Carolina Salt Marsh. 1968. 86 p.

15 Proceedings – Symposium on Better Water and Sewer Services for Small Communities in North Carolina. 1968. 113 p.

*16 Simulation of Regional Economic Impacts of Water Resources Development – An Exploratory Study. 1969. 16 p.

17 Streamflow Routing – With Application to North Carolina River. 1969. 72 p.

*18 Textile Wastes – Bibliography. 1969.

19 Water Monitoring System for Pesticides in North Carolina. 1970. 105 p.

20 A Field and Laboratory Study of Fluoride Uptake by Oysters. 1969. 13 p.

21 A Study of Water Pollution Control in the Textile Industry of North Carolina. 1970. 94 p.

22   Water Resources of North Carolina – An Inventory of Information and Data. 1968. 384 p.

23   Oxygenation of Iron (II) in Continuous Reactors. 1969. 53 p.

24   The Movement and Storage of Water in North Carolina Soils and the Role of the Soil in Determining Water Quality. 1969. 43 p.

25   Abatement of Pollution from Pulp and Paper Wastes by Modification and Utilization of Lignin Waste Products. 1970. 60 p.

26   The Effect of Different Low-Flow Hydrologic Regimes on Water Quality.

27   Workshop on Water Resource Problems and Research Needs Related to Agriculture in the Coastal Plains of North Carolina. 1969. 31 p.

28   Proceedings – Workshop on Flood Plain Management. 1969. 68 p.

29   The Role of Reservoir Owner Policies in Guiding Reservoir Land Development. 1969. 56 p.

30   Proceedings – Workshop on Water and Sewer Charges as Related to Water Use and Water Control. 1969. 120 p.

31   Neutron Activation Analysis in Water Resources Management in North Carolina. 1969. 142 p.

32   The Use of Stream Channels to Deliver Stored Water: The Possibility of Interference by Third Parties. 1969. 34 p.

33   Phosphorus Concentration in the Pamlico River Estuary of North Carolina. 1970. 47 p.

34   The Relative Significance of Phosphorus and Nitrogen as Algal Nutrients. 1970. 55 p.

35   Survey of Water Utilization and Waste Control Practices in the Southern Pulp and Paper Industry. 1970. 77 p.

36   Proceedings – Workshop on Mosquito Control in North Carolina. 1970. 144 p.

37   Quality of Stormwater Drainage from Urban Land Areas in North Carolina. 1970.

38   Public policy and shoreline landowner behavior. 1970. 126 p.

39   Hydrography of the Pamlico River Estuary, N. C. 1970. 69 p.

40   The Macrobenthos of the Pamlico River Estuary, North Carolina. 1970. 113 p.

41   An Economic Study of the Effect of Municipal Sewer Surcharges on Industrial Wastes. 1970. 122 p.

45   Proceedings Workshop on Stream Channelization and Wetland Drainage. 1971. 100 p.

47   Perception of Water Resource Information Sources and Educational Needs by Local Officials and Special Interest Groups. 1971. 27 p.

48   Water Quality Characteristics of the New Hope and Lower Haws Rivers July 1966 – February 1970 with Estimates of the Probable Quality of New Hope Lake. 1971. 139 p.

A Comparison of State Water Pollution Control Laws and Programs. (In preparation.)

Revision and Recodification of Drainage and Watershed Improvement Legislation in North Carolina. (In preparation.)

Recreational Capacity of Water Resources. (In preparation.)

Multivariate Hydrologic Simulation. (In preparation.)

The Relation of Estuarine Algae to Water Quality. (In preparation.)

NORTH DAKOTA

NORTH DAKOTA BUSINESS AND INDUSTRIAL DEVELOPMENT DEPARTMENT
State Office Building
Bismarck, North Dakota 58501

Comprehensive Area Sewer and Water Plans for North Dakota (copies on file with the State Planning Agency):

Barnes County C.A.P.	Completed
Bowman County C.A.P.	Completed
Burke County C.A.P.	Completed
Burleigh County C.A.P.	Under Study
Cass County C.A.P.	Completed
Dickey County C.A.P.	Application
Emmons County C.A.P.	Completed
Golden Valley County C.A.P.	Under Study
Grand Forks County C.A.P.	Completed
LaMoure County C.A.P.	Completed
McHenry County C.A.P.	Under Study
McIntosh County C.A.P.	Under Study
McLean County C.A.P.	Under Study
Mercer County C.A.P.	Under Study
Morton County C.A.P.	Under Study
Pembina County C.A.P.	Completed
Ramsey County C.A.P.	Completed
Renville County C.A.P.	Application
Richland County C.A.P.	Completed
Stark County C.A.P.	Under Study
Stutsman County C.A.P.	Completed
Traill County C.A.P.	Completed
Walsh County C.A.P.	Under Study
Ward County C.A.P.	Completed
Williams County C.A.P.	Under Study

Geology and Ground Water Studies (A joint effort by the State Water Commission and the North Dakota Geological Survey — copies on file in the BIDD files.) *Note: Only those studies not found under the Geological Survey Publication List are included here:*

    Logan and McIntosh Counties – 1962

    Southern Morton County – 1962

Feasibility of a Proposed Resort on the Garrison Reservoir. Midwest Research Institute. (Three back-up reports: site survey, financial analysis and summary, 1966.)

NORTH DAKOTA GEOLOGICAL SURVEY
University Station
Grand Forks, North Dakota 58201

Order publications from the above address. Cash, money order, or check, payable to the North Dakota Geological Survey, will be accepted.

ARTESIAN WATER PAPERS

This series was printed as a part of the Bulletin Series (see B-2, 3 and B 5-8).

BIENNIAL REPORTS

*BR-1 E. J. Babcock. This first biennial report deals with the topography and general geology of the state and presents three brief summaries of the information then available on clay, coal, and water. 103 p., 13 pls., 1901.

*BR-3 A. G. Leonard. This publication contains papers on the topography and geology of North Dakota, the lignite deposits west of the Missouri River, methods of stream measurement, and the run-off of the streams of North Dakota. 236 p., 33 pls., 1904.

The Biennial Reports, formerly issued by the North Dakota Geological Survey, have been combined with the report issued by the State Board of Higher Education, and are no longer being published by the North Dakota Geological Survey.

BULLETINS

B-2 Artesian Water Conditions, by Howard E. Simpson. This report includes the first Biennial Report of the State Water Geologist. 8 p., 1923. Rev. Ed. 1935. Free.

B-3 Methods of Reducing the Flow of Artesian Wells, by Howard E. Simpson. 4 p., 1924. Rev. Ed. 1932. Free.

B-5 The Conservation of Artesian Water, by Howard E. Simpson. This report includes the Second Biennial Report of the State Water Geologist. 24 p., 1926. Free.

B-6 A Method of Water Prospecting, by Howard E. Simpson. This report includes the Third Biennial Report of the State Water Geologist. 20 p., 1927. Free.

B-7 The Ground Waters of North Dakota, by Howard E. Simpson. This report includes the Fourth Biennial Report of the State Water Geologist. 26 p., 1932. Free.

*B-8 The Artesian Waters of North Dakota, by Howard E. Simpson. This report includes the Fifth and Sixth Biennial Reports of the State Water Geologist. 48 p., 2 pls., 1935.

B-9 The Fluoride Content of North Dakota Ground Waters as Related to the Occurrence and Distribution of Mottled Enamel, by G. A. Abbott. 16 p., 1937. Repr. 1959. Price: $0.25.

B-10 Change in Ground Water Levels in North Dakota, by Howard E. Simpson. 24 p., 1934. Printed 1937. Free.

B-11 The Municipal Ground Water Supplies of North Dakota, by G. A. Abbott and F. W. Voedisch. This bulletin is a study of the chemical nature of the ground water supplies of 295 of the 327 incorporated towns in North Dakota. 100 p., 2 pls., 1938. Repr. 1959. Price: $1.00.

B-12 Selected Deep Well Records, compiled by Wilson M. Laird. Records of 11 wells. 31 p., 1941. Price: $0.10.

B-17 The Geology and Ground Water Resources of the Emerado Quadrangle, by Wilson M. Laird. This report describes the surficial geology of the quadrangle located in Grand Forks County. 35 p., 3 pls., 1944. Repr. 1959. Price: $0.75.

B-20 A Reconnaissance of Possible Well Irrigation Areas, by W. C. Rasmussen. This report lists 15 areas investigated during the summer of 1940 for possible well irrigation areas. 6 p., 1945. Repr. 1959. Price: $0.25.

B-36 Part I—Geology and Ground Water Resources of Kidder County, North Dakota, Geology, by Jon L. Rau, and others. A colored map of Kidder County is provided to show the surficial geology which consists mainly of glacial deposits. The text is concerned chiefly with descriptions of the glacial landforms and interpretation of drainage features with a summary of the subsurface geology. 70 p., 1 pl., 1962. Price: $1.50.

B-36 Part II—Geology and Ground Water Resources of Kidder County, North Dakota, Ground Water Basic Data, by P. G. Randich, and others. This report presents data on wells, springs, and test drilling for water in Kidder County as well as chemical analyses of the water. Logs of test holes are also provided. 134 p., 1962. Price: $1.00.

B-36 Part III—Geology and Ground Water Resources of Kidder County, North Dakota, Ground Water and Chemical Quality of Water, by Edward Bradley, L. R. Petri, and D. G. Adolphson. This report describes the water-bearing characteristics of the bedrock and the unconsolidated glacial deposits, reports water-level fluctuations and aquifer tests. Chemical quality is analyzed in regard to irrigation, public supply, domestic use, and industry. 38 p., 1963. Price: $1.00.

B-41 Part I—Geology and Ground Water Resources of Stutsman County, North Dakota, Geology, by Harold A. Winters. This report provides descriptions of the glacial landforms and a glacial history of the area. It includes a colored landform map on a scale of 1/2 inch to the mile. 83 p., 4 pls., 1964. Price: $2.75.

B-41 Part II—Geology and Ground Water Resources of Stutsman County, North Dakota, Ground Water Basic Data, by C. J. Huxel, Jr., and L. R. Petri. This report contains ground water records, logs of test holes, chemical quality of water records, and related information. 339 p., 1964. Price: $2.00.

B-41 Part III—Geology and Ground Water Resources of Stutsman County, North Dakota, Ground Water and its Chemical Quality, by C. J. Huxel, Jr., and L. R. Petri. This report provides geologic cross sections and maps the areal extent of 18 known aquifers. 58 p., 1965. Price: $1.00.

B-42 Part I—Geology and Ground Water Resources of Burleigh County, North Dakota, Geology, by Jack Kume and Dan E. Hansen. This report describes the geology of the county with emphasis on the glacial landforms and glacial history. It includes a colored geologic map and a summary of the subsurface stratigraphy and detailed descriptions of formations which crop out in Burleigh County. 111 p., 7 pls., 1965. Price: $1.75.

B-42 Part II—Geology and Ground Water Resources of Burleigh County, North Dakota, Ground Water Basic Data, by P. G. Randich. This report consists of an inventory of water wells, logs of test holes, measured water levels, and chemical analyses of selected wells. 273 p., 1965. Price: $1.75.

B-42 Part III—Geology and Ground Water Resources of Burleigh County, North Dakota, Ground Water Resources, by P. G. Randich and J. L. Hatchett. This report is concerned with the availability, quality, and quantity of ground water of the county. 92 p., 1966. Price: $1.50.

B-43 Part I—Geology and Ground Water Resources of Barnes County, North Dakota, Geology, by T. E. Kelly and D. A. Block. This report describes the geology of the county with emphasis on the glacial landforms and glacial history. It includes a colored geologic map. 51 p., 4 pls., 1967. Price: $1.50.

B-43 Part II—Geology and Ground Water Resources of Barnes County, North Dakota, Ground Water Basic Data, by T. E. Kelly. This report consists of an inventory of water wells, logs of test holes, measured water levels, and chemical analyses of selected wells. 156 p., 1965. Price: $1.25.

B-43 Part III—Geology and Ground Water Resources of Barnes County, North Dakota, Ground Water Resources, by T. E. Kelly. This report describes the availability and quality of ground water of the county. 67 p., 1 pl., 1966. Price: $1.00.

B-44 Part I—Geology and Ground Water Resources of Eddy and Foster Counties, North Dakota, Geology, by John P. Bluemle. This report describes the geology of the county with the emphasis on the glacial landforms and glacial history. It includes a geologic map in color and a summary of the subsurface stratigraphy and economic geology. 66 p., 6 pls., 1965. Price: $1.25.

B-44 Part II—Geology and Ground Water Resources of Eddy and Foster Counties, North Dakota, Ground Water Basic Data, by Henry Trapp, Jr. This report contains ground water records, logs of test holes, chemical quality of water records, and related information. 243 p., 1966. Price: $1.25.

B-44 Part III—Geology and Ground Water Resources of Eddy and Foster Counties, North Dakota, Ground Water Resources, by Henry Trapp, Jr. This report describes the occurrence, quantity, and quality of water available to wells in these counties. 110 p., 6 pls., 1968. Price: $1.75.

B-45 Part I—Geology and Ground Water Resources of Divide County, North Dakota, Geology, by Dan E. Hansen. This report describes the geology of the county with the emphasis on the glacial landforms and glacial history. It includes a summary of the subsurface stratigraphy and maps of the formations that lie immediately below the glacial drift. The report contains a colored geologic map and a summary of economic geology. 100 p., 5 pls., 1967. Price: $2.00.

B-45 Part II—Geology and Ground Water Resources of Divide County, North Dakota, Ground Water Basic Data, by C. A. Armstrong. This report consists of an inventory of water wells, logs of test holes, measured water levels, and chemical analyses of selected wells. 112 p., 1965. Price: $0.75.

B-45 Part III—Geology and Ground Water Resources of Divide County, North Dakota, Ground Water Resources, by C. A. Armstrong. This report describes the occurrence, quantity, and quality of water available to wells from aquifers in the glacial drift. 56 p., 1967. Price: $1.00.

B-46 Part I—Geology and Ground Water Resources of Richland County, North Dakota, Geology, by Claud H. Baker, Jr. This report describes the geology of the county with emphasis on the glacial landforms and glacial history. It includes a map in color. 45 p., 4 pls., 1967. Price: $1.25.

B-46 Part II—Geology and Ground Water Resources of Richland County, North Dakota, Ground Water Basic Data, by Claud H. Baker, Jr. This report consists of an inventory of water wells, logs of test holes, measured water levels, and chemical analyses of selected wells. 170 p., 1966. Price: $1.25.

B-46 Part III—Geology and Ground Water Resources of Richland County, North Dakota, Ground Water Resources, by Claud H. Baker, Jr. and Q. F. Paulson. This report contains detailed information on all the major sources of ground water in the county. 45 p., 1 pl., 1967. Price: $1.25.

B-47 Part I—Geology and Ground Water Resources of Cass County, North Dakota, Geology, by Robert L. Klausing. This report describes the geology of the county with emphasis on the glacial landforms and glacial history. The report contains a colored geologic map. 39 p., 7 pls., 1968. Price: $1.50.

B-47 Part II—Geology and Ground Water Resources of Cass County, North Dakota, Ground Water Basic Data, by Robert L. Klausing. This report contains ground water records, logs of test holes, and chemical quality of water records. 158 p., 1966. Price: $1.00.

B-47 Part III—Geology and Ground Water Resources of Cass County, North Dakota, Hydrology, by Robert L. Klausing. This report describes the occurrence, quantity, and quality of water available from 6 glacial drift aquifers as well as the Dakota sandstone aquifer. 77 p., 2 pls., 1968. Price: $1.25.

B-48 Part I—Geology and Ground Water Resources of Williams County, North Dakota, Geology, by Theodore F. Freers. This report describes the geology of the county with emphasis on the glacial geology but includes discussion of the Tertiary and older stratigraphy. 55 p., 4 pls., 1970. Price: $2.00.

B-48 Part II—Geology and Ground Water Resources of Williams County, North Dakota, Ground Water Basic Data, by C. A. Armstrong. This report contains chemical analyses, inventory of water wells, logs of test holes, and measured water levels in the county. 132 p., 1967. Price: $1.00.

B-48 Part III—Geology and Ground Water Resources of Williams County, North Dakota, Hydrology, by C. A. Armstrong. This report describes the occurrence, quantity, and quality of water available from aquifers in the glacial drift, the Fort Union Group, and the Dakota Group. 82 p., 2 pls., 1969. Price: $1.50.

B-49 Part I—Geology and Ground Water Resources of Traill County, North Dakota, Geology, by John P. Bluemle. This report describes the geology of the county with the emphasis on the glacial landforms and glacial history. The report includes a geologic map in color. 35 p., 2 pls., 1967. Price: $1.25.

B-49 Part II—Geology and Ground Water Resources of Traill County, North Dakota, Ground Water Basic Data, by H. M. Jensen. This report consists of an inventory of water wells, logs of test holes, measured water levels, and other information. 103 p., 1967. Price: $1.25.

B-50 Part II—Geology and Ground Water Resources of Renville and Ward Counties, North Dakota, Ground Water Basic Data, by Wayne A. Pettyjohn. This report contains ground water records, logs of test holes, and chemical quality of water records. 302 p., 1 pl., 1968. Price: $2.00.

B-51 Part I—Geology and Ground Water Resources of Wells County, North Dakota, Geology, by John P. Bluemle, and others. This report describes the geology of the county with emphasis on the glacial landforms and glacial history. It includes a geologic map in color. 39 p., 3 pls., 1967. Price: $1.50.

B-51 Part II—Geology and Ground Water Resources of Wells County, Ground Water Basic Data, by Frank Buturla, Jr. This report contains data on 800 wells, springs, or test holes, water level observations, chemical analyses, and logs of selected test holes and wells. 118 p., 1 pl., 1968. Price: $1.00.

B-51 Part III—Geology and Ground Water Resources of Wells County, North Dakota, Ground Water Resources, by Frank Buturla, Jr. This report describes the occurrence, quantity, and quality of water available from aquifers which are primarily in the glacial drift. 57 p., 2 pls., 1970. Price: $1.50.

B-53 Part I—Geology and Ground Water Resources of Grand Forks County, North Dakota, Geology, by Dan E. Hansen and Jack Kume. This report describes the geology of the county with emphasis on the glacial geology and glacial history. 76 p., 4 pls., 1970. Price: $1.75.

B-53 Part II—Geology and Ground Water Resources of Grand Forks County, Ground Water Basic Data, by T. E. Kelly. This report contains data on 1,000 wells, springs and test holes, water level observations, chemical analyses, and logs of selected test holes and wells. 117 p., 1 pl., 1968. Price: $1.00.

B-55 Part II—Geology and Ground Water Resources of Burke and Mountrail Counties, Ground Water Basic Data, by C. A. Armstrong. This report contains data on about 2,100 wells, springs, and test holes, logs of 570 test holes and wells, 504 chemical analyses, and related information. 282 p., 2 pls., 1969. Price: $2.00.

COUNTY GROUND WATER STUDIES (see Bulletin Series B-36, 41-51, 53, 55)

MISCELLANEOUS SERIES

MS-16 Ground Water, a Vital North Dakota Resource, by Q. F. Paulson. This report is concerned with the occurrence and availability of ground water, types of wells, and quality of water in North Dakota. It reviews previous ground water studies, outlines how a ground water study is made, and reviews the cooperative study programs. 25 p., 1962. Free.

MS-35   The Flood Problem in Grand Forks—East Grand Forks, by Samuel S. Harrison. This report was written to explain for the laymen what causes floods, provides data on previous floods, and makes suggestions regarding planning and precautions which could reduce losses in future floods. 42 p., 1968. Price: $0.75.

OIL AND GAS PRODUCTION STATISTICS

The production reports give the amount of oil and water produced from each producing well in the state. The cumulative production of oil and water from each well is given as well as some GOR and BHP information. Statistics are also provided by pools and counties for cumulative oil, gas and water production. Yearly drilling statistics are also included.

1963	— First Half	$2.00
1963	— Second Half	$2.00
1964	— First Half	$2.00
1964	— Second Half	$2.00
1965	— First Half	$2.00
1965	— Second Half	$2.00
1966	— First Half	$2.50
*1966	— Second Half	$2.50
1967	— First Half	$2.50
1967	— Second Half	$2.50
1968	— First Half	$2.50
1968	— Second Half	$2.50
1969	— First Half	$2.50

REPORTS OF INVESTIGATIONS

RI-7   Additional Well Logs for North Dakota, compiled by Wilson M. Laird, Marjorie Ness, and Clarence Klipfel. A 137-page compilation of wells drilled for oil and water. 1952. Price: $1.00.

RI-25   Geology of the Lower Pipestem Creek Area, North Dakota, by Ronald J. Kresl. The area with which this report is concerned is located in Stutsman County, a few miles west of Jamestown, North Dakota. The glacial geology and ground water resources of the area are presented. A geologic map and a map showing water well data accompany the report. 1956. Price: $0.50.

UNCLASSIFIED MATERIAL AND LISTS

Bibliography of the Geology and Natural Resources of North Dakota. This volume contains a bibliography with indices of material published between 1814 and 1944, and two supplements, one for the period 1944-1948, and one for the period 1948-1951. The three works by Miss Chrissie E. Budge were first published separately as Bulletins 1, 4, and 6, of the North Dakota Research Foundation. 1959. Price: $3.00.

Circular Map. This map gives the location of all wells of which circulars have been printed by circular numbers. Price: $1.50.

STATE DEPARTMENT OF HEALTH
Division of Water Supply and Pollution Control
State Capitol Building
Bismarck, North Dakota 58501

Official Bulletin. A bimonthly periodical. Price: $3.00/year.

STATE OUTDOOR RECREATION AGENCY
State Office Building
Bismarck, North Dakota 58501

North Dakota Outdoor Recreation Plan — 1970. 144 p.

The 1970 North Dakota State Outdoor Recreation Plan. A Summary Document. 32 p.

STATE WATER CONSERVATION COMMISSION
State Office Building
Bismarck, North Dakota 58501

Publication Name:

Alexander Ground-Water Survey No. 35, 1961.

Amenia Ground-Water Survey No. 59. 1964.

Aneta Ground-Water Survey No. 7, 1947.

Ashley Ground-Water Survey No. 37, 1961.

Bank Stabilization Hearing Reports, 1966.

Barnes County Ground-Water Study No. 4 (Part 1 — Geology and Part 2 — Basic Data), by State Water Commission and North Dakota Geological Survey, 1966.

Benson-Pierce County Ground-Water Survey (Survey in progress — completion date 1971).

Berthold Ground-Water Survey No. 46, 1963.

Beulah Ground-Water Survey No. 40, 1962.

Biennial Report, 1968.

Bottineau Ground-Water Survey No. 52, 1963.

Bowbells Ground-Water Survey No. 42, 1962.

Burke-Mountrail County Ground-Water Survey (Survey in progress — completion date 1969).

Burleigh County Ground-Water Study No. 3 (Part 1 — Geology, Part 2 — Basic Data and Part 3 — Hydrology and Quality), by State Water Commission and North Dakota Geological Survey, 1966.

Cass County Ground-Water Study No. 8 (Part 1 — Geology and Part 2 — Basic Data), by State Water Commission and North Dakota Geological Survey, 1966.

Colorado State Water Well Laws (Information Series No. 25), 1968.

Columbus Ground-Water Survey No. 73, (Survey in Preparation).

Crosby-Mohall Ground-Water Survey No. 54, 1963.

Dam Construction Specifications, 1968.

*Devils Lake Ground-Water Survey No. 56, 1964.

Divide County Ground-Water Study No. 6 (Part 1 — Geology, Part 2 — Basic Data and Part 3 — Hydrology and Quality), by State Water Commission and North Dakota Geological Survey, 1967.

Drainage Area Data —

*Part I — Drainage Area for Cannonball Basin, 1966.

*Part II — Drainage Area for Heart River, 1965.

*Part III — Drainage Area for Knife River, 1966.

*Part IV — Drainage area for Little Missouri River Basin, 1966.

Drake Ground-Water Survey No. 31, 1961.

Eddy-Foster County Ground-Water Study No. 5 (Part 1 — Geology, Part 2 — Basic Data and Part 3 — Hydrology and Quality), by State Water Commission and North Dakota Geological Survey, 1968.

Ellendale Ground-Water Survey No. 61, 1965.

Facts of North Dakota (Brochure), by Economic Development Commission, 1967.

Fairmont Ground-Water Survey No. 22, 1953.

*Fargo-Moorhead Ground-Water Survey No. 11, 1949.

Flood Control Act of 1944, 78th Congress, 2nd Session, 1965.

Forest River Ground-Water Survey No. 28, 1961.

Frequency of Low Flows, Red River of the North, North Dakota and Minnesota, 1962.

Gackle Ground-Water Survey No. 33, 1961.

Garrison Dam-Lake Sakakawea (Brochure), U. S. Army Corps of Engineers, 1968.

Garrison Diversion Unit — Water Right Hearing, 1967.

Garrison Diversion Unit (Brochure), by the Garrison Diversion Conservancy District.

Grand Forks County Ground-Water Study No. 13 (Part 1 — Geology, Part 2 — Basic Data and Part 3 — Hydrology and Quality), by the State Water Commission and North Dakota Geological Survey, 1967.

Hatton Ground-Water Survey No. 39 and No. 66, 1962.

Hettinger Ground-Water Survey No. 24, 1956.

Hillsboro Ground-Water Survey No. 55, 1963.

Hoople Ground-Water Survey No. 49, 1962.

Hope Ground-Water Survey No. 9, 1948.

Hunter Ground-Water Survey No. 28, 1961.

Hydrologic Methods Applied to Small Watersheds, 1964.

International Joint Commission Hearings on Minot Water Supply, 1940.

Irrigation Districts and Related Organizations, 1962.

Irrigation Laws, 1964.

Kidder County Ground-Water Study No. 1 (Part 1 — Geology, Part 2 — Basic Data and Part 3 — Hydrology and Quality), by the State Water Commission and North Dakota Geological Survey, 1963.

*Lake Dakota Ground-Water Survey No. 4, 1947.

Lakota Ground-Water Survey No. 48, 1962.

Landa Ground-Water Survey No. 27, 1959.

Lansford Ground-Water Survey No. 64, 1966.

Leeds Ground-Water Survey No. 44, 1962.

Lehr Ground-Water Survey No. 38, 1962.

Linton Ground-Water Survey No. 50, 1963.

Maddock Ground-Water Survey No. 28, 1961.

Makoti Ground-Water Survey No. 72, 1968.

Max Ground-Water Survey No. 45, 1963.

McLean County Ground-Water Study (Study in progress, completion date 1970).

Michigan Ground-Water Survey No. 21, 1953.

Minnewaukan Ground-Water Survey No. 19, 1953.

Minot Recharge Ground-Water Survey No. 65, 1965.

Minto Ground-Water Survey No. 28, 1961.

Mountain Ground-Water Survey No. 2, 1946.

Mylo Ground-Water Survey No. 28, 1961.

Neche Ground-Water Survey No. 16, 1951.

Negative Impacts of Garrison and Oahe Reservoirs in the North Dakota Economy, by North Dakota State University, Agricultural Economics Experiment Station, 1962.

North Dakota Streamflow Data, by the State Water Commission and the U. S. Geological Survey, 1967.

North Dakota Water Laws, 1965.

Northwood Ground-Water Survey No. 34, 1961.

*Oakes Irrigation Project No. 4, 1947.

Oliver-Mercer County Ground-Water Study (Study in progress — Completion date 1970).

Parshall Ground-Water Survey No. 41, 1962.

Pierce-Benson County Ground-Water Study, (Study in progress — completion date 1971).

Powers Lake Ground-Water Survey No. 28, 1961.

Reynolds Ground-Water Survey No. 47, 1962.

Richland County Ground-Water Study No. 7 (Part 1 — Geology, Part 2 — Basic Data and Part 3 — Hydrology and Quality), by the State Water Commission and the North Dakota Geological Survey, 1967.

Rock Lake Ground-Water Survey No. 63, 1965.

Rolla Ground-Water Survey No. 28 and No. 57, 1961 & 1964.

Rugby Ground-Water Survey No. 62, 1965.

Ryder Ground-Water Survey No. 53, 1963.

St. John Ground-Water Survey No. 28 and No. 67, 1961 & 1967.

State Water Plan, 1968.

Appendix A – An Inventory of Water Storage and Retention Structures in North Dakota.

Appendix B – A State Wide Analysis of Soil Types by Major Drainage Basins and An Estimate of Irrigable Land in North Dakota.

Appendix C – An Inventory of Legal Drains in North Dakota.

Appendix D – An Economic Analysis of Water Resource Development for Irrigation in North Dakota.

Appendix E – North Dakota Wetlands Problem.

Sharon Ground-Water Survey No. 8, 1947.

Sheyenne Ground-Water Survey No. 60, 1964.

Soil, Water and Crop Management, by the U. S. Department of Agriculture, 1961.

Sprinkler Irrigation, by the Department of Interior, Bureau of Reclamation, 1949.

Stanley Ground-Water Survey No. 23, 1954.

Stark-Hettinger County Ground-Water Study (Study in progress – completion date 1970).

State Outdoor Recreation Agency Plan, by the State Outdoor Recreation Agency, 1968.

State Water Commission Project Index, 1967.

State Water Resources Development Map, 1963.

Strasburg Ground-Water Survey No. 50, 1963.

Streeter Ground-Water Survey No. 20, 1952.

Stutsman County Ground-Water Study No. 2 (Part 1 – Geology, Part 2 – Basic Data and Part 3 – Hydrology and Quality), by the State Water Commission and the North Dakota Geological Survey, 1965.

Tolley Ground-Water Survey No. 69, 1968.

Topographic Maps, by the U. S. Geological Survey.

Traill County Ground-Water Study No. 10 (Part 1 – Geology and Part 2 – Basic Data), by the State Water Commission and the North Dakota Geological Survey, 1967.

Walsh-Nelson County Ground-Water Study (Study in progress – completion date 1971).

Ward-Renville County Ground-Water Study No. 11, (Part 2 – Basic Data), by the State Water Commission and the North Dakota Geological Survey, 1968.

Water Brochure (Information Series No. 3), 1965.

Water Conservation Primer (Information Series No. 9), 1967.

Water Resources Planning Act – Public Law 89-80, 1966.

Wells County Ground-Water Study No. 12 (Part 1 – Geology, Part 2 – Basic Data and Part 3 – Hydrology and Quality), by the State Water Commission and the North Dakota Geological Survey, 1968.

Westhope Ground-Water Survey No. 27, 1959.

Williams County Ground-Water Study No. 9 (Part 2 – Basic Data), by the State Water Commission and the North Dakota Geological Survey, 1967.

Willow City Ground-Water Survey No. 70, 1968.

Wyndmere Ground-Water Survey No. 13, 1949.

Zeeland Ground-Water Survey No. 12, 1948.

WATER RESOURCES RESEARCH INSTITUTE
North Dakota State University
Fargo, North Dakota 58102

Pratt, George L., A Feasibility Study of a Livestock Waste Disposal System Involving the Reuse of Water, OWRR Project No. A-001-NDAK, December 1968, 24 p.

Fossum, Guilford O., and Cooley, Albert M., Water Pollution Abatement by Improved Coagulation and Effluents from Lye-Peel Potato Processing Plants, OWRR Project No. A-002-NDAK, January 1970, 29 p.

Vennes, John W., Microbiology of Sewage Lagoons – Role of Purple Sulfur Bacteria in the Stabilization of Industrial Wastes, OWRR Project No. A-003-NDAK, April 1970.

Peterka, John J., Water Quality in Relation to Productivity of Lake Ashtabula Reservoir in Southeastern North Dakota, OWRR Project No. A-004-NDAK, March 1969, 23 p.

Schroer, Fred W., A Study of the Effect of Water Quality and Management on the Physical and Chemical Properties of Selected Soils Under Irrigation, OWRR Project No. A-005-NDAK, February 1970, 48 p.

Hudson, J. C., Schwendemen, J. R., Jr., and Youngren, D. L., The Determination of Suitable Average Values of Meteorological Data for Use in Estimation of Evapotranspiration, OWRR Project No. A-008-NDAK, June 1970, 16 p.

Peterka, John J., Productivity of Phytoplankton and Quantities of Zooplankton and Bottom Fauna in Relation to Water Quality of Lake Ashtabula Reservoir, North Dakota, OWRR Project No. A-011-NDAK, February 1970, 79 p.

Peterka, John J., Selected Farm Ponds and Their Suitability for Fish, March 1970, 21 p.

Neel, Joe K., and Vennes, John W., The Limnobiochemistry of Devils Lake, North Dakota, OWRR Project No. A-014-NDAK, September 1969, 16 p.

Vennes, John W., Microbiology of Sewage Lagoons – Effects of Industrial Wastes on Coliform and Other Enteric Organisms, OWRR Project No. A-016-NDAK, August 1969.

Hertsgaard, Thor, Economic Impact of Water Resource Development, OWRR Project No. B-002-NDAK, March 1969, 31 p.

Stegman, E. C., Bauer, A., Anderson, D. O.; and Johnsgard, G. A., A Physical and Economic Analysis of Alternative Irrigation Methods in a Sub-humid Climate, OWRR Project No. B-007-NDAK, September 1968, 60 p.

D'Errico, T. R., and Skodje, M. T., The Use of Gravity Shafts for Ground Water Recharge – Phase I, OWRR Project No. B-008-NDAK, January 1970, 22 p.

OHIO

OHIO DEPARTMENT OF HEALTH
P. O. Box 118
Columbus, Ohio 43216

Report of Water Pollution Study of:

Miami River, January 1951, 38 p.

Maumee River Basin, April 1953, 90 p. (Prepared in co-operation with Indiana Stream Pollution Control Board and U. S. Department of Health, Education and Welfare.)

Mahoning River Basin, October 1954, 91 p.

Muskingum River Basin, January 1958, 116 p.

Cuyahoga River Basin, August 1960, 97 p.

Ohio's Health. Monthly Journal. Occasional issues deal with water. Available free of charge.

Ohio's Environment. 36 p.

OHIO DEPARTMENT OF HEALTH
Water Pollution Control Board
450 East Town Street
Columbus, Ohio 43216

Annual Report. To date.

Clean Waters for Ohio. A booklet usually of 16 pages, issued spring, summer and fall of each year.

OHIO DEPARTMENT OF NATURAL RESOURCES
Room 970 Ohio Departments Building
Columbus, Ohio 43215

Note: The code number indicates, by means of the first two numbers, the year, and by means of the second two numbers, the month in which the publication first appeared.

*What Water Means to Ohio. Code No. 6512A.

Developing Ohio Watersheds Through PL 566. Code No. 6910B. No charge in Ohio.

Guidelines for a Dynamic Water Program for Ohio. Code No. 6912B. No charge in Ohio.

The Wonderful World of Ohio Presents Past, Present and Future Water. Code No. 6912C. No charge in Ohio.

The Environmental Question. Code No. 705D. No charge in Ohio.

Water Resource Agencies of the Department of Natural Resources. Code No. 708F. No charge in Ohio.

How Can Northeast Ohio Have Clean Water. Code No. 711S. No charge in Ohio.

Ohio Water Resources Newsletter. Issued periodically. No charge in Ohio.

The Northwest Ohio Water Development Plan. January 1967. 299 p. (Report was prepared by Burgess and Niple, Limited, Columbus, Ohio.)

The Northeast Ohio Water Development Plan — Vol. 1: Program for Action, 1969. December 1968. (Prepared by Stanley Consultants, Cleveland, Ohio.)

OHIO DEPARTMENT OF NATURAL RESOURCES
Division of Geological Survey
1207 Grandview Avenue
Columbus, Ohio 43212

The publications listed, unless otherwise noted, may be purchased from the above address. Please make checks and money orders payable to the Division of Geological Survey.

A charge of 10% of the total cost of the order will be made for postage and handling. Please add that amount when sending money for publications listed here. Please send 10 cents when ordering free publications.

BULLETINS

B 19 Geology of Cincinnati and vicinity, by Nevin M. Fenneman. 207 p., 59 figs., 12 pls., 2 maps, 1916. $1.00.

*B 27 Geography of Ohio, by Roderick Peattie. 137 p., 28 figs., 8 pls., 1923.

*B 29 Industrial water supplies of Ohio, by C. W. Foulk. 406 p., 1925.

B 37 Brines of Ohio, by Wilber Stout, R. E. Lamborn, and Downs Schaaf. 123 p., 1 fig., 1 map, 1932. Reprinted 1952. $1.00.

B 44 Geology of water in Ohio, by Wilber Stout, Karl Ver Steeg, and G. F. Lamb. 694 p., 8 maps, 1 table, 1943. Reprinted 1968 in new format. $2.00.

B 48 Geology of Perry County, by Norman K. Flint. 234 p., 8 figs., 15 pls., 14 tables, colored geologic map, 1951.

$2.00 plus 8¢ tax in Ohio. Geologic map sold separately, $1.00.

B 60 Geology of Fairfield County, by Edward W. Wolfe, Jane L. Forsyth, and George D. Dove. 230 p., 63 figs., 3 pls., including bedrock geology map, colored glacial geology map, and ground-water resources map, 12 tables, 1962. $3.00 plus 12¢ tax in Ohio. Bedrock geologic map and glacial geology maps sold separately, each $0.75.

REPORTS OF INVESTIGATIONS

Free distribution except as noted.

RI 7 Shore erosion on Sandusky Bay, by Paul R. Shaffer. 5 p., 1 fig., 1951. Reprinted from Ohio Jour. Sci., vol. 51, p. 1-5, 1951. Reprinted 1968. $0.15.

*RI 9 1950 Investigation of Lake Erie sediments, vicinity of Sandusky, Ohio, by Howard J. Pincus, Marjorie L. Roseboom, and Curtis C. Humphris. 37 p., 25 figs., 2 tables, 1951.

RI 11 Additional analyses of brines from Ohio, by Raymond E. Lamborn. 56 p., 1 fig., 1952.

RI 18 1951 Investigations of Lake Erie shore erosion, edited by Howard J. Pincus. 138 p., figs., 1953. Limited distribution.

*RI 25 Bibliography of physical limnology, 1781 – 1954, by James L. Verber. 57 p., 1955.

RI 53 Effects of large structures on the Ohio shore of Lake Erie, by Robert P. Hartley. 30 p., 34 figs., 1964. $0.50.

RI 58 Synoptic survey of water properties in the western basin of Lake Erie, by Robert P. Hartley, Charles E. Herdendorf, and Myrl Keller. 19 p., 14 figs., 1966. $0.50.

RI 74 Water masses and their movements in western Lake Erie, by Charles E. Herdendorf. 7 p., 4 figs., 1969. $0.30.

RI 79 Lake Erie physical limnology cruise, midsummer 1967, by Charles E. Herdendorf. 77 p., 33 figs., 13 tables.

INFORMATION CIRCULARS

IC 13 Geology of Lake Hope State Park, by Mildred Fisher Marple. 30 p., 20 figs., 1954. Reprinted 1966. 25¢.

IC 34 Lake Erie bathythermograph recordings, 1952 – 1966, compiled by Charles E. Herdendorf. 36 p., 1 fig., 1 pl., 1967. $1.00.

OHIO COOPERATIVE TOPOGRAPHIC SURVEY

Final report in four volumes, by C. E. Sherman.

The Geological Survey has assumed responsibility for the distribution of the Final Report of the Ohio Cooperative Topographic Survey, which was active only until its last report was published.

OTS 4 Miscellaneous data. 327 p., 24 figs., tables, large map of Ohio streams and drainage areas, 1933. $1.00.

DIVISION OF SHORE EROSION PUBLICATIONS

Activities of the Division of Shore Erosion, Department of Natural Resources, were incorporated with those of other divisions of the Department by a revision of the State law, effective November 2, 1961. The Division of Geological Survey is now responsible for geological investigations of the Lake Erie shore and bottom, and published reports of activities will be available from this division as a part of its regular publication series.

Technical Reports

*TR 1 1950 Investigation of Lake Erie sediments, vicinity of Sandusky, Ohio, by Howard J. Pincus, Marjorie L. Roseboom, and Curtis C. Humphris, Jr. 37 p., 25 figs., 2 tables, 1951 (also published as Ohio Geol. Survey Rept. Inv. 9).

TR 2 1951 Investigations of Lake Erie shore erosion, edited by Howard J. Pincus. 138 p., figs., maps, 1953 (also published as Ohio Geol. Survey Rept. Inv. 18). Limited distribution.

*TR 3 Bibliography of physical limnology, 1781 – 1954, by James L. Verber. 57 p., 1955 (also published as Ohio Geol. Survey Rept. Inv. 25). Bibliography and subject index of literature relating to physical limnology, with emphasis on the Great Lakes.

TR 4 Bottom deposits of western Lake Erie, by Division of Shore Erosion staff. 4 p., 4 figs., 1957. Out of print. The map of bottom deposits that accompanied this report is available at $0.10 per copy.

TR 5 Sand dredging areas in Lake Erie, by Robert P. Hartley. 79 p., 13 figs., 26 pls., 5 tables, 1960. $0.97.

TR 6 Bottom deposits in Ohio waters of central Lake Erie, by Robert P. Hartley. 14 p., 7 pls., 1961. $0.50.

TR 7 Engineering geology of the Ohio shore line of Lake Erie, by Howard J. Pincus. 7 sheets, 1960. Each sheet $0.50.

Sheet A Area from 1¼ miles west of the west end of Lake Erie to 3 miles west of Port Clinton.

Sheet B Area from 3 miles west of Port Clinton to ½ mile west of Ceylon Junction.

Sheet C Area of Sandusky Bay.

Sheet D Area from Ceylon Junction to Avon Point.

Sheet E Area from 1 mile east of Avon Lake Village Park to ½ mile west of the Cuyahoga-Lake County line.

Sheet F Area from ½ mile west of the Cuyahoga-Lake County line to 1/8 mile east of the Lake-Ashtabula County line.

Sheet G Area from 1/8 mile east of the Lake-Ashtabula County line to the Ohio-Pennsylvania State line.

TR 8   Preliminary estimate of erosion or accretion along the Ohio shore of Lake Erie and critical erosion areas, by Division of Shore Erosion staff. 13 p., figs., table, 1961. Reprinted 1966. $0.25.

TR 9   Bottom sediments in the island area of Lake Erie, by Robert P. Hartley. 22 p., 10 pls., 3 tables, 1961. $0.97.

OHIO DEPARTMENT OF NATURAL RESOURCES

Division of Water
Room 815, Ohio Departments Building
65 South Front Street
Columbus, Ohio 43215

FOREWORD

The State of Ohio has had an agency since 1941 whose object is inventorying and investigating the water resources of the State and rendering assistance to other agencies and citizens of the State in obtaining water supplies. These functions rested with the Ohio Water Supply Board from 1941 to 1945 and with the Ohio Water Resources Board from 1945 through 1949. Chapter 1521 of the Ohio General Code established the Division of Water as a part of the Department of Natural Resources. This agency continues the functions of it's predecessors. Additionally, it is specifically charged with the duty of conducting comprehensive inventories of the water sources, uses, and future water plans for each of the major drainage basin systems of the State.

HOW TO OBTAIN PUBLICATIONS

Public Libraries may obtain Division of Water publications from the State Library, Room 1114, Ohio Departments Building, 65 South Front Street, Columbus, Ohio. There is no charge for the first copy to any public library in Ohio. Additional copies may be obtained as shown below for the general public.

Tax supported colleges and universities in Ohio, through their libraries, will automatically receive one copy of all publications as they come off the press, at no charge. Additional copies for department libraries within the larger institutions will be sent free upon certification by the college library that there is need for such additional copies. Publications for the libraries of individual faculty members or graduate degree candidates may be obtained at the prices indicated.

Libraries, both public and college, outside of Ohio may obtain publications at the indicated prices.

State officials, departments and agencies of the State of Ohio may obtain publications for their own use at no cost, upon request.

The Library of Congress will receive two copies of all publications, without charge, as they come off the press.

Agencies of the Federal government, states other than Ohio or local political subdivisions actively cooperating with the Department of Natural Resources will be supplied, gratis, such publications as may be required to implement their particular cooperative program.

The general public, persons, firms, or agencies not included in the foregoing may order publications directly from the Division of Water at the address given above. Policy as determined by the Auditor of State requires that all sales of publications under the above cited law must be on a cash basis. Therefore, all orders must be accompanied by cash, check, or money order. C. O. D. orders cannot be accepted. Purchase orders from public agencies will be accepted. Purchase orders from business and professional firms, when approved by the appropriate officer of the firm, will be accepted at the discretion of the Division of Water.

All publications, including those which are out of print, may be examined or purchased at the office of the Division of Water.

BULLETINS

Bulletins are the result of detailed, long-term studies, giving complete technical and non-technical discussion of the specified subject.

*BU-1   Records of wells in Montgomery County, by Ralph J. Bernhagen. 67 p., 1945.

*BU-2   The water resources of Fayette County, Ohio by Ralph J. Bernhagen, Earl E. Sanderson, and James W. Cummins. 54 p., 11 figs., 8 tables, 1946.

*BU-3   The ground-water resources of the glacial deposits in the vicinity of Canton, Ohio, by Edw. J. Schaefer, George W. White, and Donald W. Van Tuyl. 60 p., 6 pls., 7 figs., 4 tables, Appendix (approx. 13 p.), 1946.

*BU-4   The industrial utility of the surface waters of Ohio, by Walter F. White. Approx. 28 p., 2 figs., 13 tables, 1946.

*BU-5   Summary of ground-water conditions in Ohio, by Donald W. Van Tuyl and Ralph J. Bernhagen. 32 p., 18 pls., 19 tables, 1947.

*BU-6   The water resources of Tuscarawas County, Ohio, by James W. Cummins and Earl E. Sanderson. 52 p., 18 pls., 30 tables, 1947.

*BU-7   Floods in Ohio, magnitude and frequency, by William P. Cross, 154 p., 46 figs., 44 tables, 1946.

BU-8   Ground-water conditions in Butler and Hamilton Counties, Ohio, 1946, by Ralph J. Bernhagen and Edward J. Schaefer, 35 p., 11 tables, 13 pls., 13 illus., 1946. Price: $0.50.

*BU-9   The flood of June, 1946 in Wayne and Holmes Counties, by Wm. P. Cross. 44 p., 8 pls., 10 figs., 5 tables, 1947.

*BU-10   Ohio stream-flow characteristics, Part 1, flow duration, by William P. Cross and Ralph J. Bernhagen. 40 p., 186 tables, 19 pls., 19 illus., Appendix (Approx. 96 p.), 1949.

BU-11   Industrial ground-water pumpage in Ohio, by R. J. Bernhagen. 45 p., 3 pls., 1949. Price: $0.30.

*BU-12   The water resources of Montgomery County, Ohio, by Stanley E. Norris. 83 p., 31 tables, 51 pls., and appendix of well logs and climatological data, 1948.

*BU-13   Ohio stream-flow characteristics, Part 2, water supply and storage requirements, by Wm. P. Cross and Earl E. Webber. 13 p., 8 pls., 8 tables. Appendix (approx. 129 p.), 1950. Superseded by BU-31 and BU-37.

*BU-14 Local floods in Ohio during 1947, by Wm. P. Cross. 66 p., 29 tables, 13 pls., 1948.

*BU-15 The climatic factors of Ohio's water resources, by Earl E. Sanderson. 130 p., 77 pls., 19 tables, appendix (approx. 297 p.), 1950.

*BU-16 Ground-water levels in Ohio, 1947, by Donald W. Van Tuyl and Paul Kaser. 62 p., 30 pls., 20 tables, 1948.

*BU-17 Sedimentation of reservoirs in Ohio, by Earl E. Sanderson. 29 p., 8 pls., 4 tables, 1948.

*BU-18 Local floods in Ohio during 1948, by Wm. P. Cross. 45 p., 11 tables, 8 pls., 17 figs., 1949.

BU-19 The water resources of Greene County, Ohio, by Stanley E. Norris, Wm. P. Cross and Richard P. Goldthwait. 52 p., 23 pls., 8 tables, appendix (approx. 16 p.), 1950. Price: $1.75.

BU-20 Water in Ohio, summary and prospects, 1949, by C. V. Youngquist. 39 p., 1949. Price: $0.30.

*BU-21 Ground-water levels in Ohio, 1948, by Paul Kaser. 60 p., 32 pls., 44 tables, 1950.

*BU-22 The water resources of Clark County, Ohio, by Stanley E. Norris, Wm. P. Cross, Richard P. Goldthwait and Earl E. Sanderson. 82 p., 29 pls., 18 tables, 1952.

BU-23 Chemical character of surface waters of Ohio, 1946-1950, by Wm. L. Lamar and Merle E. Schroeder. 100 p., 3 pls., 30 tables, 1951. Price: $1.50.

BU-24 Reservoir sedimentation in Ohio, by Charles L. Hahn. 87 p., 42 pls., 7 tables, 1955. Price: $1.75.

*BU-25 Ground-water levels in Ohio, 1949 – 1950, by Paul Kaser. 103 p., 147 figs., 3 tables, 1952. Superseded by BU-28.

*BU-26 The water resources of Cuyahoga County, Ohio by John D. Winslow, Geo. W. White, Earl E. Webber. 123 p., 60 pls., 29 tables, 1953.

*BU-27 The ground-water resources of Summit County, Ohio, by Robert C. Smith and George W. White. 130 p., 22 pls., 6 tables, 1953.

*BU-28 Ground-water levels in Ohio, 1951 – 1952, by Paul Kaser. 95 p., 132 figs., 3 tables, 1954. Superseded by BU-29.

*BU-29 Ground-water levels in Ohio, 1953 –1954, by Paul Kaser. 92 p., 130 figs., 6 tables, 1956. Superseded by BU-34.

BU-30 The ground-water resources of Franklin County, Ohio, by James J. Schmidt. Glacial geology section by Richard P. Goldthwait. 97 p., 14 pls., 14 tables, 1958. Price: $2.50.

BU-31 Flow duration of Ohio streams, by William P. Cross and Richard E. Hedges. 152 p., 22 pls., 366 tables, 1959. Price: $2.00.

BU-32 Floods in Ohio, magnitude and frequency, by William P. Cross and Earl E. Webber. 325 p., 2 tables, 41 pls., 1959. Price: $5.00.

BU-33 The water resources of Madison County, Ohio by Stanley E. Norris. 63 p., 8 tables, 1 pl., 12 figs., 1959. Price: $2.50.

BU-34 Ground-water levels in Ohio, October 1954 – September 1959, by Paul Kaser. 132 p., 156 figs., 2 tables, 1961. Price: $1.25.

BU-35 Floods of January-February, 1959 in Ohio, by William P. Cross. 76 p., 127 figs., 6 tables, 1961. Price: $1.50.

BU-36 Water resources of Licking County, Ohio, by George D. Dove. 96 p., 17 tables, 35 pls., 1960. Price: $2.00.

BU-37 Low-flow frequencies and storage requirements for selected Ohio streams, by William P. Cross. 66 p., 68 tables, 13 pls., 1963. Price: $2.00.

BU-38 Floods of March 1963 in Ohio and the flash flood of June 1963 in the vicinity of Cambridge, by William P. Cross. 82 p., 9 tables, 23 pls., 1964. Price: $1.85.

*BU-39 Floods of March 1964 in Ohio, by William P. Cross. 58 p., 7 tables, 17 pls., 1964.

BU-40 Low-flow frequency and storage requirement indices for Ohio streams, by William P. Cross. 47 p., 2 tables, 23 pls., 1965. Supplemental to BU-37. Price: $1.00.

BU-41 Ground-water levels in Ohio, October 1959 – September 1964, by Paul Kaser and Leonard J. Harstine. (approximately – 140 p., 148 tables, 159 figs.), Price: $1.75.

BU-42 Flow duration of Ohio Streams, W. P. Cross, 1968 Library of Congress No. 6863365. Price: $1.25.

BU-43 Floods in Ohio, magnitude and frequency, a supplement to Bulletin 32, William P. Cross and R. I. Mayo, 1969, 203 p., 51 pls., 3 tables, 206 figs. Price: $4.50.

OHIO WATER PLAN INVENTORY REPORTS

Ohio water plan inventory reports are, like Bulletins, the result of detailed long-term studies. Each of them is a part of a systematic inventory of the water uses, resources, needs, and problems of the state and individual watershed areas. The most significant reports in this series are the water inventories by major river basin. These represent a comprehensive analysis of water supply, demand, and related subjects and supply the basis for planning and water management.

IR-1 Municipal water problems in Ohio, 11 p., 1959. Price: $0.25.

IR-2 Water inventory of the Cuyahoga and Chagrin River basins, Ohio, by Sherman L. Frost and Robert C. Smith. 90 p., 10 tables, 31 pls., 1959. Price: $2.75.

IR-2a Map supplement to IR-2, Water inventory of the Cuyahoga and Chagrin River basins, Ohio, 32 p., 21 color maps, 1959. Price: $3.25.

IR-3 Flow duration of Ohio streams, by William P. Cross and Richard E. Hedges. 152 p., 22 pls., 366 tables, 1959. (Same as Bulletin 31.) Price: $2.00.

IR-4   Floods in Ohio, magnitude and frequency, by
        William P. Cross and Earl E. Webber. 325 p., 2
        tables, 41 pls., 1959. (Same as Bulletin 32)
        Price: $5.00.

IR-5   Flood control in Ohio, by Miles M. Dawson. 130 p.,
        70 illus., 1959. Price: $1.00.

IR-6   Water use in Ohio, by Anthony R. Rudnick. 50 p.,
        10 tables, 6 pls., 1959. Price: $0.50.

IR-7   Irrigation and rural water use in Ohio, by Arthur F.
        Woldorf. 57 p., 10 figs., 6 pls., 8 tables, 1959.
        Price: $0.50.

IR-8   Industrial water use in Ohio, by Anthony R. Rud-
        nick. 113 p., 33 tables, 3 figs., 1960. Price: $1.00.

IR-9   Municipal water supply in Ohio, 1955 – 1957, by
        Anthony R. Rudnick. 88 p., 14 figs., 9 pls., 13
        tables, 1962. Price: $1.60.

IR-10   Buried river valleys in Ohio, by James W. Cummins.
        4 p., 2 large maps, 1959. Price: $0.50.

IR-11   Water inventory of the Maumee River basin, by Di-
        vision of Water staff. 112 p., 22 tables, 46 pls.,
        1960. Price: $3.85.

IR-12   Gazetteer of Ohio streams, by J. C. Krolczyk, 175
        p., first printing 1954. Revised edition in 1960 with
        appendix by O. H. Jeffers. Price: $2.65.

IR-12a Drainage areas of Ohio Streams, Supplement to
        Gazetteer of Ohio Streams, W. P. Cross, 1967.
        Price: $0.75.

IR-13   Hydrologic atlas, by Division of Water staff, 4 maps,
        1960. Price: $0.75.

IR-14   Quality of surface water in Ohio, 1946 – 1958, by
        J. H. Hubble and C. R. Collier. 317 p., 4 pls., 8
        tables, 2 figs., 1960. Price: $3.50.

IR-15   Water inventory of the Ohio Brush, Eagle, Straight
        and Whiteoak Creek basins, by the Division of Water
        staff. 50 p., 19 tables, 18 pls., 1960. Price: $1.30.

IR-16   Water inventory of the Mahoning and Grand River
        basins and adjacent areas in Ohio, by Division of
        Water staff, 86 p., 42 tables, 30 pls., 1961.
        Price: $3.50.

IR-17   Water inventory of the Scioto River basin, by Divi-
        sion of Water staff. 76 p., 26 tables, 36 pls., 1963.
        Price: $3.25.

IR-18   Water inventory of the Little Miami River and Mill
        Creek basins and adjacent Ohio River tributaries, by
        Division of Water staff. 106 p., 35 tables, 32 pls.,
        1964. Price: $3.25.

IR-19   Water inventory of the Hocking River basin, Shade
        River and Leading Creek basins and adjacent Ohio
        River tributary areas, by Division of Water staff.
        Price: $4.00.

IR-20   Water inventory of the Portage River and Sandusky
        River basins and adjacent Lake Erie tributary areas,
        by the Division of Water staff. Price: $4.00.

IR-21   Water Inventory of the Muskingum River Basin and
        Adjacent Ohio River Tributaries. 201 p., 41 tables,
        44 pls. Price: $5.00.

BURIED VALLEY REPORTS

*The permeable sand and gravel deposited by glaciers in
ancient river valleys provide the greatest potential source of
ground water in Ohio. These reports explore the geology and
hydrology of these aquifers as determined by research and
field survey. They will provide guidelines for future development of large ground water supplies for industry.*

BV-1   Ground water for industry in the Scioto River valley, by
        the Ground-Water Geology Section of the Division of
        Water. 29 p., 3 tables, 16 illus., 1965. Price: $0.50.

TECHNICAL REPORTS

*Technical reports are prepared for limited distribution
covering specific problems. They stress the technical approach
to hydrologic problems and may be considered contributions
to the science of hydrology.*

*TR-1   The hydraulic properties of a dolomite aquifer under-
        lying the village of Ada, Ohio, by W. C. Walton. 31 p.,
        20 figs., 4 tables, 1953.

TR-2   Vertical leakage through till as a source of recharge to a
        buried valley aquifer at Dayton, Ohio, by Stanley E.
        Norris. 16 p., 6 figs., 2 tables, 1959. Price: $0.50.

TR-3   Ground-water resources of the valley-train deposits in
        the Fairborn area, Ohio, by Wm. C. Walton and George
        D. Scudder. 57 p., 3 pls., 26 figs., 6 tables, 1960.
        Price: $1.00.

TR-4   A hydrologic study of the valley-fill deposits in the
        Venice Area, Ohio, by George D. Dove. 81 p., 55 figs.,
        6 tables, 1961. Price: $0.50.

TR-5   A statistical analysis of ground-water levels in twenty
        selected observation wells in Ohio, Marian Klein and
        Paul Kaser. 124 p., 91 tables, 89 illus., 1963.
        Price: $1.50.

TR-6   Graphical aides for the solution of formulas used in
        analyzing induced infiltration aquifer tests, by Edward
        J. Schaefer and Paul Kaser. 17 p., 12 pls., 1965.
        Price: $0.50.

INFORMATION CIRCULARS

*Information circulars are less detailed and less technical
than bulletins. They provide information on rapidly expanding
areas where there is an immediate need.*

IC-1   The water resources of Pike County, Ohio, by Robert
        C. Smith and James J. Schmidt. 15 p., 7 pls., 4 tables,
        appendix 10 p., 1953. Price: $0.50.

IC-2   The water resources of Scioto County, Ohio, by Alfred
        C. Walker and James J. Schmidt. 17 p., 8 pls., 3 tables,
        1953. Price: $0.50.

IC-3   The water resources of Jackson County, Ohio, by Alfred
        C. Walker. 15 p., 8 pls., 3 tables, 1953. Price: $0.50.

IC-4   The water resources of Ross County, Ohio, by James J.
        Schmidt. 25 p., 10 pls., 6 tables, 1954. Price: $0.50.

*IC-5   The ground-water resources of the areas in the vicinity
        of the interchanges on the east-west Ohio turnpike, by
        James J. Schmidt and Alfred C. Walker, 65 p., 16 pls.,
        16 tables, 1954.

IC-6 Ground-water levels in the vicinity of Leipsic, Ohio, by Paul Kaser. 15 p., 6 figs., 5 tables, 1958. Price: $0.50.

IC-7 Ground-water resources along State Route 1, between Harrisburg and Medina, Ohio, by Henry L. Pree. 16 p., 7 pls., 2 tables, 1962. Price: $0.50.

IC-8 Ground-water resources along Interstate Highway 71, between Cincinnati and Harrisburg, Ohio, by Henry L. Pree, Jr. 17 p., 2 tables, 6 pls., 1965. Price: $0.50.

MISCELLANEOUS REPORTS

MR-1 Lake Erie pollution survey, final report, by C. V. Youngquist and others. 201 p., 60 pls., 89 tables, 1953. Price: $2.00.

*MR-2 Lake Erie pollution survey, supplement to final report, by C. V. Youngquist and others. 125 p., 1953.

MR-3 The Crooksville area flood of June 16 – 17, by W. P. Cross. 12 p., 7 pls., 4 tables, 1950. Price: $0.50.

*MR-4 Regulations for the construction, operation, maintenance, and abandonment of water wells, by Ohio Division of Water. 25 p., 9 figs., 4 tables, 1958.

MR-5 Preliminary report of floods in Ohio, January – February 1959, edited by S. L. Frost. 125 p., 18 figs., 11 tables, 1959. Price: $1.00.

MR-6 Meteorology of floods in Ohio, January 1959, February 1959, by Paul Kaser. 55 p., 20 tables, 1959. Price: $1.00.

*MR-8 Some principles of water, its uses, behavior, problems and conservation, by S. L. Frost. 30 p., 1958.

MR-9 The conservancy district law. 65 p., 1959. (1963 – 64 addenda.) Price: $0.50.

*MR-10 Principles of water rights law in Ohio, by Charles C. Callahan, 34 p., 2 illus., 1957.

MR-11 Cisterns for rural water supply in Ohio, by Norman G. Bailey. 21 p., 4 illus., 5 tables, 1959. Price: $0.25.

MR-12 Water resources of southeastern Ohio, a preliminary report, edited by S. L. Frost. 55 p., 4 pls., 4 maps, 1959. Price: $0.30.

MR-13 Sediment discharges of Ohio streams during floods of January – February, 1959, by R. J. Archer. 16 p., 2 pls., 6 figs., 4 tables, 1960. Price: $0.25.

MR-14 Cable tool drilling, by Sanderson Cyclone Drill Co. 7 p., reprint from Tool & Drilling Manual of Sanderson Cyclone Drill Co., 1952. Free.

MR-15 Before you have a well drilled, by Richard K. Cash. 29 p., 8 figs., 1961. Facts a homeowner should know before hiring a well-drilling contractor. Free.

MR-16 Flood of July, 1965 in the vicinity of Hillsboro, by W. P. Cross. 10 p., 2 tables, 4 pls., 1966. Price: $0.50.

FREE PRINTED MATERIALS

These publications contain general non-technical discussions of, (1) The principles of water and the application of these principles to Ohio water problems, or

(2) Reports on the functions of Ohio water agencies. They are primarily intended for use by schools and service groups. Single copies can usually be provided at no cost, upon request. Requests for larger quantities will be considered on the basis of need and the stock available.

What water means to Ohio, by S. L. Frost, 37 p., fully illustrated, 1960.

The water cycle in Ohio, by Ohio Division of Water, 2 p.

The disposal of rainfall, by Ohio Division of Water, 1 p.

Before you have a well drilled, by Richard K. Cash, 29 p., 8 illus., 1961.

Multiple use lakes by Ned E. Williams and Frank C. Mohler; Highway lakes by Ned E. Williams. 4 p.

Ground-water for industry in Ohio, by A. C. Walker, 9 p., 1963.

The story of water supply, by the American Water Works Association, 15 pages, numerous illustrations, 1965.

OHIO WATER COMMISSION REPORTS

*OWC-1 Proceedings of the Ohio water management conference, 1960.

*OWC-2 Water policy and legislative recommendations, 1960.

*OWC-3 The 1960 hearings, what they revealed.

*OWC-4 The problem: floods in Ohio.

*OWC-5 Over-use of underground water supplies in upper Mill Creek valley.

*OWC-6 What water means to Ohio.

*OWC-7 Development of underground water supplies in the Sugar Creek area, Tuscarawas County (1960 hearing).

PERIODICALS

Index of conditions affecting water supply. *Approximately 8 pages of text, graphs, and charts showing monthly climatological data and water levels for selected lakes, streams and ground-water aquifers. All data is shown in relation to past record. Free*

CLIMATOLOGICAL SUMMARIES
(U. S. Weather Bureau Stations)

The summary for each station consists of a set of two sheets. The first contains a narrative summary of the climate of the station locality, monthly and period of record, mean precipitation and temperature, and associated data. The second sheet gives daily mean and extreme temperature and precipitation.

Eventually, summaries for all climatological stations in Ohio will be published. Data are prepared by the Weather Bureau, Environmental Science Services Administration and published by the Division of Water. Price, set of two sheets: $0.10.

Additional summaries are now available for the following stations in Ohio: Barnesville, Bellefontaine, Bucyrun, Cadiz, Carpenter, Chardon, Chippewa Lake, Dorset, Greenville, Hiram, Ironton, Kenton, Lancaster, Marietta, Millersburg, Millport, Napoleon, Norwalk, Oberlin, Steubenville, Tiffin, Upper Sandusky, Urbana, Wauseon, and Xenia.

REPORTS WHICH ARE NOT AVAILABLE FOR DISTRIBUTION, REPORTS OF OHIO WATER SUPPLY BOARD (1942 – 1945) AND OHIO WATER RESOURCES BOARD (1945 – 1949)

Reports listed here are either out of date and out of print or are those which were prepared for a specific purpose and were not published in quantity. Most are available for examination at the offices of the Ohio Division of Water.

The water resources of:
    *Mill Creek valley, 1942
    *Mansfield area, 1942
    *Perry (Lake County), 1942
    *Northwest of Shelby, 1942
    *West of Medina, 1942
    *North of Johnstown, 1942
    *Ashtabula, Lake, Geauga Counties, 1942
    *Clinton County, 1942
    *Jackson County, 1942
    *Highland County, 1942
    *Medina County, 1943
    *Preble County, 1943
    *Trumbull County, 1943
    *Clark County, 1943
    *Stark County, 1943
    *Franklin County, 1944
    *Summit County, 1944
    *Fulton County, 1945
    *Wood County, 1945
    *Record of Wells in Montgomery Co., 1945
    *Fayette County, 1945
    *First annual report, 1942
    *Second annual report, 1943
    *Third annual report, 1944
    *Fourth annual report, 1945

*Reconnaissance survey of ground-water resources:
  the valley of Little Miami River, Western Greene County, Ohio, 1947
  in southwestern Stark County, Ohio, 1947
  in Knox County, Ohio, 1947
  of the south fork of Licking River, 1947

OHIO DIVISION OF WATER

*Reconnaissance survey of ground-water resources in southwestern Stark County, Ohio, by James W. Cummins. 3 p., 1947.

*Memorandum of investigation of chloride contamination of ground water at Chathan, Ohio, by Paul Kaser, 10 p., 1949.

*Ground-water levels in the vicinity of Spencerville, Ohio, by Paul Kaser. Approx. 17 p., 1952.

*Preliminary investigation of ground-water resources of the Celeryville Marsh Conservancy District, by Robert C. Smith. 6 p., 1953.

*Water levels in an area north of Paulding, Ohio, by Paul Kaser. 17 p., 1953.

*Pilot study of the Black River basin, by the Division of Water. 11 p., 10 maps, 1954.

*Study of the Whiteoak Creek basin, by the Ohio Division of Water. 9 p., 8 maps, 1954.

*Report of a study of water well contamination, New Guilford, Ohio, 1959.

*Preliminary study of the East Rushville water well contamination problem. 4 p., 1959.

*Ground-water resources of Champaign County, Ohio. 142 p., 1960.

*Contamination of ground water in Ohio, Part I, Underground disposal of sewage, 11 p., 1960.

*Investigation of de-watered wells – The Plains, Athens County, Ohio. 5 p., 1960.

*Preliminary report of the ground-water supply at London Prison Farm, 7 p., 1960.

*City of Canton water-supply development along Sugar Creek in Tuscarawas County, a report to the Ohio Water Commission, by Paul Kaser with a summary and recommendations by C. V. Youngquist. 17 p., 1960.

*Geology and ground-water resources of Portage County, Ohio, 227 p., 1961.

*Contamination of underground water in the Bellevue area. 30 p., 1961.

*Preliminary study of the ground-water resources of a portion of the Miami River valley, 30 p., 1961.

*Ground-water levels in the vicinity of Eagle City, Clark County, Ohio (City of Springfield W. W.), a report to the Ohio Water Commission, by Paul Kaser. 82 p., 1962.

*Interim report on ground-water level observations in the vicinity of Strasburg, Ohio (City of Canton W. W.), a report to the Ohio Water Commission, by Paul Kaser. 10 p., 6 pls., 1962.

*Analysis of pumping test, railroad well, Hilliard, Ohio, by Paul Kaser. 18 p., 1963.

*A proposal for the replenishment of ground-water in the Mill Creek valley, Hamilton and Butler Counties, Ohio, by Paul Kaser. 19 p., 1963.

FLOOD PROFILE CHARTS

These are 24" x 36" black and white prints showing the high water elevation in feet above mean sea level of the January or February 1959 flood, for the below-listed streams. Also shown on the prints is the location of principal roads, railroads, corporate limits of towns or cities, and stream bottom or normal water elevation.
  (Scale: vertical, 1" = 5 feet; horizontal, 1" = 1 mile).

FP-1 Big Walnut Creek and Blacklick Creek from junction with Scioto River to Hoover Reservoir (1 sheet). $1.00.

FP-2 Alum Creek from junction with Big Walnut Creek to Delaware-Morrow County Line (2 sheets). $2.00.

FP-3 Blanchard River from Ottawa, Ohio through Findlay, Ohio to the Outlet (1 sheet). $1.00.

FP-4 Eagle Creek, Lye Creek, The Outlet and the Blanchard River at Findlay, Ohio (1 sheet). $1.00.

FP-5 Licking River, North Fork Licking River and Raccoon Creek from 5 miles above Outlet (Stadden Bridge) to State Route 157 (2 sheets). $2.00.

FP-6 St. Marys River from junction with Six Mile Creek to State Route 66, Beaver Creek from junction with Wabash

River to Lake St. Marys and Auglaize River from Wapakoneta, Ohio to Hengstler Road (1 sheet). $1.00.

FP-7 Buck Creek from junction with Mad River, through Springfield, Ohio to County Road No. 236 in Champaign County (1 sheet). $1.00.

FP-8 Mad River from Junction with the Miami River to Zanesfield, Ohio (2 sheets). $2.00.

FP-9 Kokosing River and North Branch Kokosing River from Mt. Vernon, Ohio to County Road No. 68, Dry Creek from junction with Kokosing River to State Route No. 229 (2 sheets). $2.00.

FP-10 Wolf Creek and Pigeon Creek, Barberton, Ohio area (1 sheet). $1.00.

FP-11 Tuscarawas River from U. S. No. 21 at Clinton, Ohio to Massillon Road, Barberton, Ohio (1 sheet). $1.00.

FP-12 Mill Creek and Mill Creek tributaries from junction with Scioto River to 6 miles above Marysville, Ohio (2 sheets). $2.00.

FP-13 Mill Creek, East Fork Mill Creek and West Fork Mill Creek, Cincinnati, Ohio area. Whitewater River from junction with the Miami River to 3 miles above the Ohio-Indiana State Line (2 sheets). $2.00.

FP-14 East Branch Nimishillen Creek, Nimishillen Creek, West Branch and Middle Branch Nimishillen Creek, Canton area (2 sheets). $2.00.

FP-15 Kokosing River, Center Run and Dry Creek, Mt. Vernon, Ohio area (2 sheets). $2.00.

FP-16 North and South Forks, Licking River and Raccoon Creek, Newark, Ohio area (2 sheets). $2.00.

FP-17 Scioto River, Lucasville to Columbus (4 sheets). $4.00.

FP-18 Scioto River, Columbus area (1 sheet). $1.00.

FP-19 Olentangy River, Columbus, Ohio area, Wilson Bridge Road to mouth (1 sheet). $1.00.

FP-20 Little Miami River, Milford, Ohio to Xenia, Ohio (2 sheets). $0.75.

FP-21 East Fork Little Miami River, Milford, Ohio to Fayetteville, Ohio (2 sheets). $2.00.

FP-22 Miami River, Ohio River to Russells Point, Ohio (5 sheets). $5.00.

FP-23 Mahoning River, Youngstown, Ohio area (3 sheets). $3.00.

FP-24 Hocking River and Rush Creek, Athens and Logan, Ohio area (2 sheets). $2.00.

FP-25 Chagrin River, Willoughby, Ohio area (1 sheet). $1.00.

FP-26 Cuyahoga River, Cleveland, Ohio area (1 sheet). $1.00.

URBAN FLOOD MAPS
(U. S. Geological Survey)

Following the 1959 floods in Ohio, flooded area maps for critical urban areas were prepared in cooperation with the U. S. Geological Survey as part of their Hydrologic Investigations Atlas series. These maps show on topographic bases (7.5 minute series) the approximate areas flooded in 1959. Additional flood information is included in the text. The following Hydrologic Atlases may be purchased from the Division of Water.

HA-40 Floods at Mount Vernon, Ohio. $0.75.

HA-43 Floods at Springfield, Ohio in 1915 and 1959. $0.75.

HA-44 Floods at Newark, Ohio. $0.75.

HA-45 Floods at Chillicothe, Ohio. $0.75.

HA-47 Floods at Fremont, Ohio. $0.75.

HA-48 Floods at Circleville, Ohio. $0.75.

HA-49 Floods at Barberton, Ohio. $0.75.

HA-50 Floods at Canton, Ohio. $0.75.

HA-51 Floods at Warren, Ohio. $0.75.

HA-52 Floods at Columbus, Ohio. $0.75.

HA-56 Floods on Crab Creek at Youngstown, Ohio. $0.75.

STREAM MAPS

Principal streams and their drainage areas, by John C. Krolczyk. Size 30" x 30", scale 1" = 10 miles. 4-color map. Free.

Principal streams in Ohio, by John C. Krolczyk. Size: 14" x 19", approximate scale 1" = 17 miles. 2-color map. Free.

UNDERGROUND WATER RESOURCES MAPS OF OHIO
A report series of The Ohio Water Plan Inventory

For purposes of detailed study and reporting, the State was divided into 108 areas, according to natural drainage boundaries. The Muskingum River area, for example, is divided into 19 numbered subordinate areas and the listed maps are available for these areas. When referring to these maps (as well as base maps of Ohio) please use the code number for your area.

These multicolored maps show estimated potential yield of underground water. Each map is 16" x 20", scale 2 miles per inch. Single copies $0.25. Complete set of 102 maps for Ohio $15.00.

The underground water resources maps are available for the following areas:

A-1 St. Marys River Basin

A-2 Little Auglaize River Basin

A-3 Upper Auglaize River Basin

A-4 Ottawa River Basin

A-5 Blanchard River Basin (lower)

A-6 Blanchard River Basin (upper)

A-7 Upper Maumee and Lower Auglaize River Basins

A-8 Tiffin River Basin

A-9 St. Joseph River Basin

A-10 Maumee River Basin (middle portion)

A-11 Maumee River Basin (part lower)

A-12 Lower Maumee River and Tenmile Creek Basins

B-1 Upper Portage River Basin

B-2 Lower Portage River and Muddy Creek Basins

B-3 Toussaint Creek Basin and Lake Erie tributaries

C-1	Tymochtee Creek Basin		M-7	Deer Creek Basin
C-2	Upper portion of Sandusky River Basin		M-8	Lower Darby Creek & portion Middle Scioto River Basin
C-3	Middle portion of Sandusky River Basin		M-9	Walnut Creek Basin
C-4	Lower portion of Sandusky River Basin		M-10	Salt Creek Basin
D-1	Pickerel Creek to Pipe Creek area and Lake Erie tributaries		M-11	Portion of Lower Scioto River Basin
D-2	Huron River Basin		M-12	Lower Paint Creek Basin
D-3	Vermilion River Basin and Lake Erie tributaries		M-13 & 14	Upper Paint Creek Basin
D-4	Black River Basin		M-15	Portion of Lower Scioto River Basin
D-5	Rocky River Basin and Lake Erie tributaries		M-16	Little Salt Creek Basin
E-1	Upper Cuyahoga River Basin		M-17	Scioto Brush Creek Basin & Ohio River tributaries
E-2	Lower Cuyahoga River Basin		N-1	Upper Raccoon Creek Basin
E-3	Chagrin River Basin		N-2	Lower Raccoon Creek Basin & Ohio River tributaries
F-1	Upper portion Grand River Basin		N-3 & 5	Symmes, Ice, and Indian Guyan Basins & Ohio River tributaries
F-2	Lower portion Grand River Basin		N-4	Little Scioto River & Pine Creek Basins & Ohio River tributaries
F-3	Ashtabula River & Conneaut Creek Basins & Lake Erie tributaries		O-1	Upper Portion Hocking River Basin
G	Ohio portion of Wabash River Basin		O-2	Middle Portion Hocking River Basin
H-1	Upper Miami River Basin		O-3	Lower Portion Hocking River Basin
H-2	Portion of Miami River Basin and Lower Mad River		O-4	Shade River & Leading Creek Basins
H-3	Upper Mad River Basin		P-1	Black & Clear Fork Basins
H-4 & 5	Portion of Middle Miami River Basin & Lower Mad River Basin		P-2	Lower Mohican River Basin
H-6 & 7	Stillwater River Basin		P-3	Upper Killbuck Creek Basin
H-8 & 11a	Twin Creek Basin & Ohio portion East Fork, Whitewater River		P-4	Part of Walhonding River Basin
H-9	Part Middle portion Miami River Basin		P-5	Middle Tuscarawas River & Sugar Creek Basins
H-10	Fourmile Creek Basin (Talawanda Creek)		P-6	Portion of Upper Tuscarawas River Basin
H-11	Lower portion Miami River Basin		P-7	Sandy Creek Basin
J	Mill Creek Basin & Ohio River tributaries		P-8	Conotton Creek Basin
K-1	Upper Little Miami River Basin		P-9	Stillwater Creek Basin
K-3	Todd Fork Basin		P-10	Part lower portion of Tuscarawas River Basin
K-4	East Fork Little Miami River Basin		P-11	Part upper portion of Muskingum River Basin
K-5	Portion of Lower Little Miami River Basin		P-12	Kokosing River Basin
K-6	Indian Creek Basin & Ohio River tributaries		P-13	Portion of Licking River Basin
L-1	Whiteoak Creek Basin		P-14	South Fork of Licking River Basin
L-2	Ohio Brush Creek Basin		P-15	Moxahala Creek Basin
L-3	Eagle & Straight Creek Basins & Ohio River tributaries		P-16	Part middle portion of Muskingum River Basin
M-1	Upper part of Upper Scioto River Basin		P-17	Lower Wills Creek Basin
M-2	Lower part of Upper Scioto River Basin		P-18	Upper Wills Creek Basin
M-3	Olentangy River Basin		P-19	Lower portion Muskingum River Basin & adjacent Ohio River tributaries
M-4	Big Walnut Creek Basin		R-1 & 2	Little Muskingum River and Duck Creek Basins
M-5	Mill Creek Basin & portion Middle Scioto River Basin		S-1	Little Beaver Creek Basin
M-6	Upper Darby Creek Basin		S-2	Yellow Creek & Cross Creek Basins
			S-3	Short Creek & Wheeling Creek Basins

S-4   McMahon, Captina & Sunfish Creek Basins

T-1   Upper portion Mahoning River Basin

T-2   Middle portion Mahoning River Basin

T-3   Lower portion Mahoning River Basin

T-4   Ohio portion of Pymatuning & Yankee Creek Basins

COMPOSITE BASE MAPS OF MAJOR WATERSHED STUDY AREAS

Base A   Maumee River Basin (Ohio portion). $0.50.

Base B   Portage River Basin and adjacent streams. $0.50.

Base C   Sandusky River Basin. $0.50.

Base D   Huron, Vermilion, Black, and Rocky River Basins. $0.75.

Base E   Cuyahoga and Chagrin River Basins. $0.50.

Base F   Grand River Basin and adjacent areas. $0.50.

Base F
& T   Mahoning and Grand River Basins. $0.50.

Base H
& G   Miami River and Upper Wabash River Basins. $0.50.

Base J
& K   Little Miami River and Mill Creek Basins. $0.50.

Base K   Little Miami River Basin. $0.75.

Base L   Eagle, Ohio Brush, Straight, and Whiteoak Creek Basins. $0.50.

Base M   Scioto River Basin. $0.75.

Base N   Raccoon Creek, Symmes Creek, Little Scioto River and Pine Creek Basins. $0.50.

Base O   Hocking River, Shade River and Leading Creek Basins. $0.50.

Base P   Muskingum River Basin. $0.75.

Base R   Little Muskingum River and Duck Creek Basins. $0.50.

Base R
& S   Ohio River tributaries between East Liverpool and Marietta. $0.50.

Base S₁   Little Beaver, Yellow and Cross Creek Basins. $0.50.

Base S₂   Short, Wheeling, McMahon, Captina and Sunfish Creek Basins. $0.50.

Base T   Mahoning River, Pymatuning Creek and Yankee Creek Basins. $0.50.

OHIO LEGISLATIVE SERVICE COMMISSION

State House
Columbus, Ohio 43215

Staff Research Report No. 67 – Comparative State Strip Mining and Reclamation Laws. January 1965. 38 p.

Staff Research Report No. 84 – Air and Water Pollution. February 1967. 86 p.

OHIO RIVER VALLEY WATER SANITATION COMMISSION
414 Walnut Street
Cincinnati, Ohio 45202

TECHNICAL AND RESEARCH REPORTS

*Acid-Mine Drainage, Principles and Guide to Practices. September 1963.

*Bacterial-Quality Objectives for the Ohio River. June 1951.

*Brine Contamination in the Muskingum River. August 1951. (Loan copy available.)

*Disposal of Spent Sulfate Pickling Solutions. October 1952. (Loan copy available.)

Dust Recovery Practice at Blast Furnaces. January 1958. Price: $1.00.

Fish-Kill Handbook. March 1956. Price: $0.50.

*Methods for Treating Metal-Finishing Wastes. January 1953. (Loan copy available.)

*Monongahela River Sewage-Treatment Considerations. January 1959. (Loan copy available.)

*Ohio River Pollution Patterns–1950. June 1951.

*Ohio River Pollution–Abatement Needs – Cincinnati Pool. January 1949. (Loan copy available.)

*Ohio River Pollution–Abatement Needs – Huntington to Cincinnati Stretch. February 1952.

Ohio River Pollution Abatement Needs – Pittsburgh to Huntington Stretch. March 1953. Limited supply.

Ohio River Pollution–Abatement Needs – Cincinnati to Cairo Stretch. November 1953. Limited supply.

*Oil Pipeline Breaks. September 1950. (Loan copy available.)

*Phenol Wastes Treatment by Chemical Oxidation. June 1951. (Loan copy available.)

Planning and Making Industrial Waste Surveys. April 1952. Price: $1.00.

Plating-Room Controls for Pollution Abatement. July 1951. Price: $0.50.

Procedures for Analyzing Metal-Finishing Wastes. August 1954. Price: $1.00.

Reducing Phenol Wastes from Coke Plants. January 1953. Price: $1.00.

*Regulatory Actions. January 1961 (revised January 1963).

*River-Quality Conditions During a 16-week Shutdown of Upper Ohio Valley Steel Mills. September 1961. (Loan copy available.)

Water Quality and Flow Variations in the Ohio River – 1951-55. March 1957. Price: $2.00.

Water Quality and Flow Variations – Ohio River and Tributaries – 1956-57. April 1959. Price: $2.00.

WATER RESOURCES CENTER

The Ohio State University
1791 Neil Avenue
Columbus, Ohio 43210

Annual Report Series:

Annual Report, Fiscal Years 1965 through 1970. The 1970 Report is available upon request.

Symposia Series:

Proceedings of the First Annual Symposium on Water Resources Research, June 24-25, 1965. Columbus: Ohio State University Water Resources Center, 1965. 218 p. Limited supply.

Proceedings of the Second Annual Symposium on Water Resources Research, June 15-16, 1966. Water Quality and Recreation in Ohio. Columbus: Ohio State University Water Resources Center, 1966. 308 p.

Proceedings of the Third Annual Symposium on Water Resources Research, September, 1967. Systems Approach to Water Quality in the Great Lakes. Columbus: Ohio State University Water Resources Center, 1968. 129 p.

Proceedings of the Fourth Annual Symposium on Water Resources Research, October, 1969. Systems Analysis for Great Lakes Water Resources. Columbus: Ohio State University Water Resources Center, 1970. 135 p.

Project Completion Report Series:

Smith, E. E. and Shumate, K. S. Development of a Natural Laboratory for the Study of Acid Mine Drainage. OWRR A-001-Ohio. Columbus: Ohio State University Water Resources Center, 1968. 37 p.

Dugan, P. R. and Randles, C. I. The Microbial Flora of Acid Mine Water and Its Relationship to Formation and Removal of Acid. OWRR A-002-Ohio. Columbus: Ohio State University Water Resources Center, 1968. 124 p.

Dambach, C. A. and Olive, J. H. Development of Biological Indices to Pollution Levels in Streams Affected by Acid Mine Drainage and Oil Field Brine Wastes. OWRR A-003-Ohio. Columbus; Ohio State University Water Resources Center, 1969. 90 p. 68 ref.

Lehr, J. H. A Study of Groundwater Contamination due to Saline Water Disposal in the Morrow County Oil Fields. OWRR A-004-Ohio. Columbus: Ohio State University Water Resources Center, 1969. 81 p. Limited supply.

Tybout, R. A. Alternative Economic Responses to the Acid Mine Drainage Problem in Appalachia. OWRR A-005-Ohio. 42 p. 1968.

Britt, N. W.; Skoch, E. J.; and Smith, K. R. Relationships Between Phosphate and Other Chemicals at the Water-Substrate Interface in Lake Erie. OWRR A-008-Ohio. 30 p. 33 ref. 1970.

Boyd, J. H. Pollution Charges, Waste Assimilative Capacity Investment, and Water Quality: The Public Costs of a Public Good. OWRR A-010-Ohio. 89 p. 1969. Limited supply.

Preul, H. C. and Laushey, L. M. Ground Water Basin Dynamics. OWRR A-012-Ohio. Cincinnati: University of Cincinnati; Department of Civil Engineering, Division of Water Resources and Hydraulics, 1968. 51 p. Limited supply.

Faure, G.; Jones, L. M.; Eastin, R.; and Christner, M. Strontium Isotope Composition and Trace Elements Concentrations in Lake Huron and Its Principal Tributaries. OWRR B-004-Ohio. 1967. 109 p.

Taylor, G. S. Well Drawdown in Unconfined Aquifers Under Non-Steady Conditions. OWRR B-006-Ohio. 1971. 21 p.

OKLAHOMA

OKLAHOMA DEPARTMENT OF HEALTH

3400 North Eastern Avenue
Oklahoma City, Oklahoma 73105

Clean Water is Everybody's Business, 1948. 26 p.

Washita River Basin; Water Use and Pollution Report, 1951. 66 p.

OKLAHOMA GEOLOGICAL SURVEY

The University of Oklahoma
830 Van Vleet Oval, Room 163
Norman, Oklahoma 73069

Prices include cost of mailing unless otherwise noted.

BULLETINS

*B 59 Geology and ground water resources of Texas County, Oklahoma, by S. L. Schoff. 1939.

*B 64 Geology and ground-water resources of Cimarron County, Oklahoma, by S. L. Schoff. 1943.

*B 69 Geology and mineral resources of Tulsa County, Oklahoma (includes parts of adjacent counties), by M. C. Oakes. Includes a chapter on Water Resources, by J. H. Warren. 1952.

B 72 Geology and ground-water resources of Ottawa County, Oklahoma, by E. W. Reed, S. L. Schoff, and C. C. Branson, 203 p., 14 tables, 14 figs. Colored geologic map; scale 1 inch equals 2 miles. February 9, 1955. Bound in blue cloth, $2.25; paper $1.75.

B 73 Geology and ground-water resources of Grady and northern Stephens Counties, Oklahoma, by L. V. Davis. 184 p. 15 tables, 14 figs. Colored geologic map; scale 1 inch equals 1 mile. July 8, 1955. Bound in blue cloth, $4.00; paper $3.40.

B 86 Geology and ground-water resources of southern McCurtain County, Oklahoma, by Leon V. Davis. 108 p., 1 pl., 19 figs. Colored geologic map. February 26, 1960. Cloth bound $2.75, paper $2.00.

B 87 Ground-water resources of Canadian County, Oklahoma, by J. L. Mogg, S. L. Schoff, and E. W. Reed. 112 p., 2 pls., 3 figs. April 7, 1960. Cloth bound $2.75, paper $2.00.

B 91 Geology and water resources of Okmulgee County, Oklahoma; Part I. Geology of Okmulgee County, by M. C. Oakes; Part II. Water resources of Okmulgee County,

by W. S. Motts. 164 p., 2 pls., including colored geologic map, 19 figs. April 17, 1963. Cloth bound $4.00, paper $3.00.

B 97 Ground-water resources of Beaver County, Oklahoma, by I. Wendell Marine and Stuart L. Schoff. 74 p., 12 figs., 2 pls., 11 tables. May 30, 1962. Cloth bound $5.00, paper $4.00.

CIRCULARS

C 25 Fluoride removal from drinking water, by A. L. Burwell, L. C. Case, and C. H. Goodnight. 1945. 41 p., 1 pl., 4 figs. $0.50.

C 28 Ground-water resources of the Arkansas River flood plain near Fort Gibson, Muskogee County, Oklahoma, by Stuart L. Schoff and Edwin W. Reed. 1951. 55 p., 12 pls., 1 fig. $0.60.

C 61 Ground-water resources of the Rush Springs Sandstone in the Caddo County area, Oklahoma, by Harry H. Tanaka and Leon V. Davis. 63 p., 11 figs., 2 pls., including colored geological map. May 6, 1963. $2.25.

C 71 Ground-water resources in Cleveland and Oklahoma Counties, Oklahoma, by P. R. Wood and L. C. Burton. 75 p., 8 figs., 2 pls., 9 tables. April 8, 1968. Paper bound $3.75.

MINERAL REPORTS

*MR 11 Geology of Oklahoma ground water supplies, by R. H. Dott. 1942.

*MR 18 Ground-water irrigation in the Duke area, Jackson and Greer Counties, Oklahoma, by S. L. Schoff. 1948.

MR 19 Ground water in Kingfisher County, Oklahoma by Stuart L. Schoff. 1949. 23 p., 1 pl. $0.05.

MR 20 Ground-water supplies in the Oklahoma City area, Oklahoma, by C. L. Jacobsen and E. W. Reed. 1949. 21 p., 2 pls. $0.05.

MR 21 Ground water in the Cherokee area, Alfalfa County, Oklahoma, by Stuart L. Schoff. 1950. 17 p., 1 pl. $0.05.

*MR 22 Ground water in the Pond Creek Basin, Caddo County, Oklahoma, by L. V. Davis. 1950.

DIRECTOR'S REPORT

Semi-Centennial Report. 1908-1958, by Carl C. Branson, Louise Jordan, and William E. Ham. 1958. 147 p., 5 maps. $0.50.

GUIDE BOOKS

Guide Book XIII. Sample descriptions and correlations for wells on a cross section from Barber County, Kansas, to Caddo County, Oklahoma, by W. L. Adkison and Mary G. Sheldon. 139 p., 2 figs. September 26, 1963. $3.50.

GEOLOGIC MAPS

Map GM-2. Map showing ground-water reservoirs of Oklahoma, by S. L. Schoff. Scale 1:750,000, in 2 colors. Accompanied by text describing ground-water conditions. November, 1955. $0.50.

HYDROLOGIC ATLASES

The Hydrologic Atlas series is to be the product of a 6-year cooperative investigation program between the Oklahoma Geological Survey and the U. S. Geological Survey for the State of Oklahoma on water resources. It is designed to provide reconnaissance appraisals of the State, exclusive of the Panhandle.

Hydrologic Atlas 1. Reconnaissance of the water resources of the Fort Smith quadrangle, east-central Oklahoma, by Melvin V. Marcher. Set of four maps at a scale of 1:250,000. October 27, 1969. $3.00 per set, folded in envelope.

EDUCATIONAL SERIES MAPS

Map 5. Ground-water reservoirs of Oklahoma. 9 inches by 11 3/4 inches. 1957. $0.10.

OKLAHOMA WATER RESOURCES BOARD

Dialex Building
2241 N. W. 40th Street
Oklahoma City, Oklahoma 73112

*1   Water, An Activity Report of the Oklahoma Resources Board.

*2   Oklahoma's Water Resources – 1960.

3   The Oklahoma Law of Water Rights, by Wells A. Hutchens. $2.00.

*4   Summary of Water Laws of Oklahoma and Rules and Regulations.

*5   Water for Oklahoma's Future.

*6   Oklahoma's Water Resources – 1963.

*7   Chemical Criteria for Water in Oklahoma.

*8   Rules and Regulations and Modes of Procedure.

*9   Ground Water in Oklahoma.

*10   Oklahoma's Water Resources 1965.

11   Caddo County Rush Springs Sandstone. $2.50.

12   Ground Water in Northern Arbuckles. $2.50.

13   Ground Water – Harmon, Jackson, Greer & Beckham Counties – 1966. $2.50.

14   Ground Water – Western Tillman County 1966. $2.50.

15   Ground Water – Caddo County Area 1966. $2.50.

*16   Oklahoma's Water Resources 1967.

*17   Appraisal of the Water and Related Land Resources Region I – 1968.

*18   Oklahoma's Water Resources 1968. Reported Water Use – 1966.

*19   Appraisal of the Water and Related Land Resources Region II – 1968.

20   Water Quality Standards – 1968. $1.75. (State Agencies, $1.50).

*21   Reported Water Use – Oklahoma – 1967.

*23   Appraisal of the Water and Related Land Resources Region III – 1968.

*24   Appraisal of the Water and Related Land Resources Region IV – 1969.

25   The Story of Oklahoma's Water (Information for Children – folder). No Chg.

26   Annual Report to the Governor and the 1st Session of the 32nd Legislature. No Chg.

Engineering Report for Arkansas-Oklahoma Compact (not available for general distribution).

27   Appraisal of the Water and Related Land Resources Regions V & VI – 1969. $5.00.

28   Reported Water Use 1968

29   Appraisal of the Water and Related Land Resources Region VII – 1970. $5.00.

30   Oklahoma's Water Resources 1970. No Chg.

31   Ozarks Report (not available for general distribution).

32   Rules, Regulations, and Modes of Procedure and Water Law References from the Oklahoma Statutes. No Chg.

33   Reported Water Use 1969. No Chg.

34   Appraisal of the Water and Related Land Resources Region VIII – 1970.

PUBLICATIONS BY THE OKLAHOMA WATER RESOURCES BOARD IN COOPERATION WITH OTHER AGENCIES

BULLETINS

1-4   Out of print and superseded by revised editions.

5   Chemical Character of Surface Water 1946-1948. $5.00.

6   Chemical Character of Surface Water 1949-1950. $5.00.

7   Chemical Character of Surface Water 1950-1951. $5.00.

*8   Chemical Character of Public Water Supplies 1953.

9   Ground Water Resources of Cimarron Terrace 1952. $2.50.

10   Chemical Character of Surface Water 1951-1952. $5.00.

11   Chemical Character of Surface Water 1952-1953. $5.00.

12   Ground Water Resources of Western Tillman County 1953. $2.50.

13   A Reconnaissance of Chemical and Physical Quality
      Pryor Creek – 1955. $1.50.

14   Chemical Character of Surface Water 1953-1954. $5.00.

15   Chemical Character of Surface Water 1954-1955. $5.00.

16   Chemical Character of Surface Water 1955-1956. $5.00.

17   Sandstone Creek Watershed 1951-1956. $1.50.

18   Chemical Character of Surface Water 1956-1957. $5.00.

19   Chemical Character of Surface Water 1957-1958. $5.00.

20.   Chemical Character of Surface Water 1958-1959. $5.00.

21   Woodward County – Ground Water. $2.50.

22   Chemical Character of Surface Waters of Oklahoma 1959-
      1960. $5.00.

23   Chemical Character of Surface Waters of Oklahoma 1960-
      1961. $5.00.

24   Chemical Character of Surface Water 1961-1962. $5.00.

25   Beckham County – Ground Water. $2.50.

26   Washita River – Ground Water in the Alluvium from
      Clinton to Anadarko. $2.50.

27   Ground Water in the Alluvium of Otter Creek Basin.
      $2.50.

28   Ground Water in the Alluvium of Elk Creek Basin.
      $2.50.

29   Ground Water Resources Harmon & parts of Greer and
      Jackson Counties, Okla. $2.50.

30   Chemical Character of Surface Waters of Oklahoma
      1962-1963. $5.00.

31   Water Quality Records in Oklahoma 1964 (same as Chem-
      ical Character). $5.00.

32   Water Quality Records in Oklahoma 1965 (same as Chem-
      ical Character). $5.00.

OKLAHOMA WATER RESOURCES
RESEARCH INSTITUTE

Oklahoma State University
Stillwater, Oklahoma 74074

Note: All publications are free of charge.

BROCHURES

Water Resources Research at Oklahoma State University. 1966.

Water Resources Research in Oklahoma, Oklahoma Water Resources Research Institute, Oklahoma State University. 1969.

Water Resources Research in Oklahoma: A Report to the Governor, Compiled and Edited by the Water Resources Research
Institute, Oklahoma State University. 1967.

TECHNICAL COMPLETION REPORTS

Water Resources Planning Study – Oklahoma and Arkansas,
OWR-006-July 1966 – June 1969, (Final Report) Don F.

Kincannon, A. F. Gaudy, Jr., M. Hamdy Bechir, Quinton B.
Graves, and Charles A. Rice, Principal Investigators, Project No.
B-006-OKLA. 1969.

Critical Review of the Oklahoma State Water Resources Qual-
ity Criteria, (Final Report) George Reid, Principal Investigator,
Bureau of Water Resources Research, University of Oklahoma,
Project No. B-004-OKLA. 1967.

Carbon Sources and Algal Community Structure and Metabolism in a Reservoir Undergoing Euthrophication by Domestic
and Industrial Effluents, (Final Report) Troy C. Dorris, Principal Investigator, Project No. B-008-OKLA. 1969.

Oxygen Diffusion in Semiquiescent Waters, Period: June 1965
– May 31, 1968, (Final Report) A. F. Gaudy, Jr., Principal Investigator, Project No. A-008-OKLA. 1968.

Ecological Factors Affecting Turbidity and Productivity in
Prairie Ponds in the Southern Great Plains, (Final Report) Dale
Toetz, Principal Investigator, Project No. A-001-OKLA. 1967.

Development of Design Criteria for Individual Domestic Water
Supplies from Surface Impoundments, (Final Report) Elmer R.
Daniel, Principal Investigator, Project No. A-003-OKLA. 1968.

Chemical and Thermal Characteristics of Keystone Reservoir,
(Final Report) Troy C. Dorris, Principal Investigator, Project
No. A-002-OKLA. 1968.

Reduction of Water Application Losses Through Improved Distribution Channel Design, (Final Report) James E. Garton,
Principal Investigator, Project No. A-004-OKLA. 1968.

Water Yield as Influenced by Watershed Characteristics and
Small Upstream Reservoirs, (Final Report) A. D. Barefoot,
Principal Investigator, Project No. A-005-OKLA. 1968.

The Mechanism of Direct Surface Runoff from Rainfall, (Final
Report) Charles E. Rice, Principal Investigator, Project No.
A-006-OKLA. 1968.

Measurement of Thermodynamic Properties of Saline Solutions,
(Final Report) David Knoebel, James C. Chou and Allen M.
Rowe, Jr., Principal Investigators, Project No. A-009-OKLA.
1968.

Application of Radioisotope Techniques to a Critical Water Resources Problem Area – Namely Nutritional Pollution, (Final
Report) George A. Reid, Robert A. Gearheart, James M. Robertson, Robert M. Sweazy, Project No. A-011-OKLA. 1969.

Carbon Sources in Algal Populations and Algal Community
Structure, (Final Report) Troy C. Dorris, Principal Investigator,
Project No. B-005-OKLA. 1967.

An Evaluation of Recent Approaches for the Design of Biological Waste Treatment, (Final Report) Quinton B. Graves, Principal Investigator, Project No. A-010-OKLA. 1969.

REPORTS

1968 Annual Report, Research Foundation, Oklahoma State
University. 1969.

Fourth Annual Report of the Oklahoma Water Resources Research Institute, July 1967 – June 1968, Part II. 1968.

Fourth Annual Report of the Oklahoma Water Resources Research Institute, July 1968 – June 1969, Part I. 1969.

Water Resources Planning Study Oklahoma and Arkansas,
OWR-006, July 1967 – June 1968, (Progress Report) M.
Hamdy Bechir and Anthony F. Gaudy, Jr., Principal Investi-
gators. 1968.

Overland Flow Analysis for a Simulated Vegetated Surface, (Termination Report) Charles E. Rice, Principal Investigator, Project No. A-016-OKLA. 1969.

Enzymes and Catalysts for Purification of Industrial Waste Water, (Termination Report) James W. Fulton, Principal Investigator, Project No. A-007-OKLA. 1966.

Water Resources Planning Studies Oklahoma and Arkansas, (Progress Report) M. H. Bechir, A. F. Gaudy, Jr., Q. B. Graves, and P. F. Johnson. 1967.

THESES

Organic Chemical Compounds in Keystone Reservoir, by Sterling L. Burks. 1969.

Chlorophyll and Carotenoid Distribution and Phytoplankton Ecology in Keystone Reservoir, Tulsa, Oklahoma, by Frederick L. Spangler. 1969.

Fish Distribution in Keystone Reservoir in Relation to Physicochemical Stratification, by Neil E. Carter, Candidate for Master of Science Degree. 1967.

Community Structure of Benthic Macroinvertebrates and Related Physicochemical Conditions in Keystone Reservoir Oklahoma, by John D. Ransom, Candidate for Master of Science Degree. 1969.

The Hydraulic Properties of Orifices and Circular Weirs with a 45 Degree Slope, by Armond D. Barefoot, Candidate for Master of Science Degree. 1968.

The Hydraulic Roughness of an Irrigation Channel with Decreasing Spatially Varied Flow, by John M. Sweeten, Jr. Candidate for Master of Science Degree. 1967.

Flood Routing on the Illinois River in Oklahoma, by Peter F. Johnson, Candidate for Bachelor of Science Degree, Project No. B-006-OKLA. 1967.

Analysis of Low Flows by Statistical Methods, by Lawrence E. Dunaway, Candidate for Bachelor of Science Degree, Project No. B-006-OKLA. 1968.

The Effects of Historical Record Lengths on Generating Synthetic Data Using a Stochastic Model of the Markov Chain, by Kenneth L. Perry, Candidate for Bachelor of Science Degree, Project No. B-006-OKLA. 1969.

Autocorrelation Analysis of Streamflow Sequences, by F. T. Painter, Candidate for Bachelor of Science Degree, Project No. B-006-OKLA. 1969.

A Statistical Study of the Relationship Between Inorganic Quality of River Water and Streamflow, by Wen-Hsiumg Kao, Candidate for Bachelor of Science Degree, Project No. B-006-OKLA. 1969.

The Criticality of the Nitrogen and Phosphorus Ratio to Aquatic Microorganisms, Namely Planktonic Algae, by Robert A. Gearheart, Candidate for Doctor of Philosophy Degree, Project No. A-011-OKLA. 1969.

OREGON

DEPARTMENT OF ENVIRONMENTAL QUALITY
P. O. Box 231
Portland, Oregon 97207

This Department was formerly the State Sanitary Authority.

BIENNIAL REPORTS

*First	2-25-39	to 6-30-40	7 p.
*Second	7-1-40	to 6-30-42	11 p.
*Third	7-1-42	to 6-30-44	14 p.
*Fourth	7-1-44	to 6-30-46	13 p.
*Fifth	7-1-46	to 6-30-48	21 p.
*Sixth	7-1-48	to 6-30-50	21 p.
*Seventh	7-1-50	to 6-30-52	27 p.
*Eighth	7-1-52	to 6-30-54	27 p.
*Ninth	7-1-54	to 6-30-56	48 p.
*Tenth	7-1-56	to 6-30-58	49 p.
*Eleventh	7-1-58	to 6-30-60	32 p.
*Twelfth	7-1-60	to 6-30-62	60 p.
*Thirteenth	7-1-62	to 6-30-64	18 p.
*Fourteenth (Summary)	7-1-64	to 12-31-65	9 p.

ANNUAL REPORTS

*1953 – 7 p.		1960 – 32 p.
*1955 – 17 p.		1961 – 38 p.
*1957 – 12 p.		1962 – 54 p.
*1958 – 25 p.		1963 – 66 p.
*1959 – 30 p.		

POLICIES AND REGULATIONS

*1   Standards of Purity for Waters of the State of Oregon and Requirements for the Disposal Therein of Sewage and Industrial Waste. November 1947. 2 p.

*2   Policies Governing the Preparation and Submission of Plans and Specifications for Sanitary Sewer Systems, Sewage Treatment Plants and Industrial Waste Disposal Works. 1949. 34 p.

*3   Minimum Requirements for the Disposal of Fruit and Vegetable Processing Wastes. May 1950. 1 p.

*4   Minimum Requirements for the Disposal of Certain Meat Processing and Animal Wastes. May 1950. 2 p.

*5   Waste Prevention Practices in the Dairy Industry. 1950. 2 p.

*6   Sewage and Industrial Waste Treatment Plant Operation (Regulation). June 1956. 1 p.

7   Rules of Procedure Before the Oregon State Sanitary Authority. December 1959. 5 p.

8   Oregon Administrative Rules, Chapter 334. December 1960. 18 p.

9   Laboratory Equipment for Small Sewage Treatment Plants. 1960. 6 p.

10   Policies Regarding Water Supplies in Sewage Treatment Plants and Pump Stations. June 1963. 1 p.

11   Criteria for Aerobic Digestion Sewage Treatment Plants. July 1964. 4 p.

12   Policies Regarding Sewage Lagoons or Stabilization Ponds. January 1965. 2 p.

*13   Criteria for Design and Utilization of Domestic Sewage Lagoons or Stabilization Ponds. July 1965. 6 p.

14   Criteria for Design and Utilization of Domestic Sewage Lagoons or Stabilization Ponds. (Revised). January 1966. 6 p.

15   Operating Manual for Small, Extended Aeration Activated Sludge Treatment Plants. March 1966. 20 p.

16   Sewer Design Criteria. January 1966.

17   Oregon State Sanitary Authority Requirements for Disinfection of Treated Sewage Effluent. March 1967. 1 p.

WILLAMETTE RIVER REPORTS

*1   Water Pollution Control in the Willamette River Basin – June 15, 1950. 48 p.

*2   Willamette River Survey – 1950. 6 p.

*3   Willamette River Stream Survey Report – 1951. 15 p.

*4   Willamette River Basin Stream Survey Data – 1952. 11 p.

*5   Willamette River Stream Survey Report – 1953. 24 p.

*6   Willamette River Survey in Vicinity of Salem – September 1953. 7 p.

*7   Interim Report on Status of Water Pollution Control in the Willamette River Basin – 1957. 50 p.

*8   Waste Disposal and Water Pollution Problems in the Willamette River Basin, June 1958. 21 p.

*9   Willamette River Harbor Pollution Survey – November 1963. 9 p.

*10   Water Quality and Waste Treatment Needs for the Willamette River – May 1964. 74 p.

*11   1964 Follow-up Report Willamette River Harbor Pollution Survey – January 1965. 8 p.

*12   Oregon's Program for Control of Water Quality in the Willamette River Basin – July 1965. 12 p.

*13   1965 Follow-up Report Willamette River Harbor Pollution Survey – December 1965. 18 p.

MISCELLANEOUS REPORTS

*1   Water Pollution Investigations of the Tualatin River. February 1940. 26 p.

*2   Report on Stream Pollution Investigations of Johnson Creek, Multnomah County, Oregon. October 1947. 14 p.

*3   Report on the Industrial Waste Disposal Problem at Hudson-Duncan Company, Dundee, Oregon. November 1947. 5 p.

*4   Sanitary Survey of Coos Bay Shellfish Growing Areas. March 1948. 5 p.

*5   Sanitary Survey of Yaquina Bay Shellfish Growing Areas. April 1948. 6 p.

*6   Sanitary Survey of Tillamook Bay Shellfish Growing Areas. April 1948. 5 p.

*7   Report on Sanitary Survey of Industrial Waste Disposal, Frontier Leather Company, Sherwood, Oregon. June 1948. 10 p.

*8   Water Pollution Control in the Deschutes River Basin. September 1950. 16 p.

*9   Report on Investigation of Sewage Collection System Serving West Moreland Addition, City of Eugene, Oregon. January 1951. 6 p.

*10   Report on Investigation of Ground Water Pollution in the Milton-Freewater Area. January 1951. 15 p.

*11   Stream Survey Report, Multnomah Channel Near St. Helens, Oregon. 1951. 7 p.

*12   Stream Survey Report, Rogue River and Bear Creek. 1952. 13 p.

13   Gold Dredge Siltation, Powder River, Oregon. 1953-1955. 9 p.

14   Interim Report on Water Quality Survey of Klamath Basin Waters in Oregon. February 1961. 28 p.

15   Established Water Sampling Stations. November 1961. 17 p.

16   An Engineering Report of the Pollution Conditions in Scappoose Bay and the Lower Multnomah Channel. March 1963. 17 p.

*17   Report on Houseboat Waste Disposal in the Vicinity of Portland, Oregon. December 1963. 15 p.

18   Stream Sanitation (an outline). Revised 1963. 14 p.

19   Sewage Disposal Practices in Oregon. February 1964. 8 p.

20   Final Report on Quality of Klamath Basin Waters in Oregon. June 1964. 30 p.

*21   Beaverton Creek Drainage Area Survey and Report. October 1964. 13 p.

22   Report on Pollution of the South Santiam River near Lebanon. April 1965. 15 p.

*23   Some Aspects of Water Pollution in Washington County. April 1965. 66 p.

*24   Notes on the Occurrence of Bacterial Slime, *Sphaerotilus*, and Waste Wood Fibers in the Lower Willamette River. 1965. 8 p.

*25   Oregon's Water Pollution Control Program, a Statement to the Legislative Interim Committee on Public Health. Oct. 1965. 24 p.

*26   A Report on the Frontier Leather Company at Sherwood, Oregon. December 1965. 18 p.

27   A Limnological Survey of Waldo Lake in Oregon. July 1966. 10 p.

*28   A Survey of Domestic Water Supply and Sewage Disposal Systems Wallowa Lake Basin. August 1966. 10 p.

29   Disposal of Domestic Wastes from Water Based Buildings and Structures. December 1966. 11 p.

REPORTS PUBLISHED JOINTLY WITH OTHERS

*1   Report on Investigation of Pollution in the Lower Columbia River. 1943. 143 p. (with Washington Pollution Control Commission).

*2   Basic Manual Sewage Works Operators, Part I. 1954. 116 p. (with Oregon State University and State Board of Health).

*3   Basic Manual Sewage Works Operators, Part II. 1954. 146 p. (with Oregon State University and Oregon State Board of Health.)

*4   Basic Course Sewage Works Short School. 1957. 105 p. (with Oregon State Board of Health, Oregon State University and League of Oregon Cities).

*5   A report of *Sphaerotilus* Growths in the Columbia River. October 1958. 72 p. (with Water Pollution Control Council and U. S. Public Health Service).

*6   Action Program to Control Pollution of the Lower Columbia River Between Bonneville Dam and Cathlamet, Washington. September 1958. 18 p. (with Water Pollution Control Council and U. S. Public Health Service).

*7   Present Status of the Action Program to Control Pollution on the Lower Columbia River Between Bonneville Dam and Cathlamet, Washington. September 1960. 13 p. (with Water Pollution Control Council and U. S. Public Health Service).

*8   Status Report No. 2 on the Action Program to Control Pollution on the Lower Columbia River Between Bonneville Dam and Cathlamet, Washington. September 1963. 19 p. (with Water Pollution Control Council and U. S. Public Health Service).

*9   Water Quality and Pollution Report, Middle Snake River, Adrian to Weiser. 1964. 48 p. (with Idaho State Department of Health).

*10   Water Quality Objectives, Pollution Control Council, Pacific Northwest Area, November 1966. 28 p.

PROPOSED WATER QUALITY STANDARDS

1 Water Quality Standards for Goose Lake, Lake County, Oregon. September 1966. 20 p.

2 Water Quality Standards for Grande Ronde River, Wallowa-Union Counties, Oregon and Walla Walla River, Umatilla County, Oregon. September 1966. 27 p.

3 Water Quality Standards for Snake River, Malheur, Baker, Wallowa Counties, Oregon. October 1966. 23 p.

4 Water Quality Standards for Columbia River, Oregon. October 1966. 34 p.

5 Water Quality Standards, Klamath River, Klamath County, Oregon. November 1966. 25 p.

*6 Water Quality Standards, Marine and Estuarine Waters of Oregon, January 1967. 32 p.

7 Water Quality Standards, Willamette River and Multnomah Channel, Oregon State Sanitary Authority, February 1967. 68 p.

OREGON DEPARTMENT OF GEOLOGY AND MINERAL INDUSTRIES
1069 State Office Building
Portland, Oregon 97201

BULLETINS

*19 Dredging of farmland in Oregon, 1939. F. W. Libbey.

*41 Ground-water studies in Umatilla and Morrow Counties, 1949. S. Wagner.

64 Mineral and water resources of Oregon, 1969. Price: $1.50.

G. M. I. SHORT PAPERS

*1 Preliminary report on Oregon saline lakes, 1939. O. R. Stafford.

MISCELLANEOUS PAPERS

14 Thermal springs and wells, 1970. R. G. Bowen and N. V. Peterson. Price: $1.00.

DEPARTMENT OF PLANNING AND DEVELOPMENT
560 State Office Building
Portland, Oregon 97201

Resources for Development. 1964. 144 p.

Water Pollution Control Policy in the Willamette Basin. 1965. 25 p. (Background paper No. 5, Willamette Basin Land Use Study).

Flood Plain Management Policy in the Willamette Basin. 1965. 30 p. (Background paper No. 7, Willamette Basin Land Use Study).

A Plan for Development of the Oregon Mid-Columbia River Waterfront. Prepared for Mid-Columbia Planning Council, by Joseph D. Meyers. 1966. 129 p.

STATE ENGINEER
1178 Chemeketa Street N. E.
Salem, Oregon 97310

GROUND WATER REPORTS

1 Records of wells, water levels and chemical quality of ground water in the French Prairie-Mission Bottom area, Northern Willamette Valley, Oregon, by Don Price. March 1961.

2 Records of wells, water levels and chemical quality of ground water in the Molalla-Salem Slope area, Northern Willamette Valley, Oregon, by E. R. Hampton. August 1963.

3 Records of wells and springs, water levels and chemical quality of ground water in the East Portland area, Oregon, by B. L. Foxworthy, G. M. Hogenson and E. R. Hampton. July 1964.

4 Ground-water levels – 1963, by Jack E. Sceva and Robert DeBow. July 1964.

5 Ground-water levels – 1964, by Jack E. Sceva and Robert DeBow. January 1965.

6 Records of wells, water levels and chemical quality of water in Baker Valley, Baker County, Oregon, by G. L. Ducret, Jr. and D. B. Anderson. March 1965.

7 Records of wells, water levels and chemical quality of ground water in the Eola Hills area, Polk and Yamhill Counties, Oregon, by Don Price and Nyra Johnson. November 1965.

8 The Champoeg Park demonstration well with a section on the design and testing of water wells, by Jack E. Sceva. January 1966.

9 Ground-water levels – 1965, by Jack E. Sceva and Robert DeBow. February 1966.

10 A reconnaissance of the ground-water resources of the Hood River Valley and the Cascade Locks area, Hood River County, Oregon, by Jack E. Sceva. April 1966.

11 A brief description of the ground-water conditions in the Ordnance area, Morrow and Umatilla Counties, Oregon, by Jack E. Sceva. May 1966.

12 Ground-water levels – 1966, by Wm. S. Bartholomew and Robert DeBow. May 1967.

13 Records of wells, water levels, and chemical quality of water in the lower Santiam River Basin, Middle Willamette Valley, Oregon, by D. C. Helm. May 1968.

14 Selected ground-water data in the Eugene-Springfield area, Southern Willamette Valley, Oregon, by J. F. Frank and Nyra A. Johnson. October 1970.

15 Ground-water levels – 1967-1968, by Wm. S. Bartholomew and Robert DeBow. May 1970.

OTHER PUBLICATIONS

*Biennial Report. 1905/06 – 1964/66.

*Bulletins 1-10. 10 vol. in 5. 1908-1946.

*The Columbia River Power Project near the Dalles, Oregon, by John H. Lewis. 1913. 56 p. (Bulletin No. 3).

*Deschutes Project. 1914. 147 p.

*Harney and Silver Creek Project, Irrigation and Drainage, by John T. Whistler and John H. Lewis. 1916. 91 p.

*John Day Project, Irrigation and Drainage, by John T. Whistler and John H. Lewis. 1916. 185 p.

*Malheur and Owyhee Projects, Irrigation and Drainage, by John T. Whistler and John H. Lewis. 1916. 201 p.

*Oregon's Opportunity in National Preparedness. A presentation of tentative plans and estimates of cost for the construction of a number of large water-power projects, by John H. Lewis (and others). 1916. 119 p. (Bulletin no. 5).

*Rogue River Valley Project and Willamette Valley Investigations, Irrigation and Drainage, by John T. Whistler and John H. Lewis. 1916. 111 p.

*Rules, Regulations, Forms and Practice of the Office of State Engineer and State Water Board Relative to the Control, Distribution and Use of the Water Resources of Oregon. Compiled by Percy A. Cupper. 1916. 70 p. (Bulletin no. 6).

*Silver Lake Project, Irrigation and Drainage, by John T. Whistler and John H. Lewis. 1915. 179 p.

*Warner Valley and White River Project (Irrigation and Drainage), by John T. Whistler and John H. Lewis. 1916. 123 p.

STATE WATER RESOURCES BOARD

500 Public Service Building
Salem, Oregon 97310

Note: Out of print material is available in the office of the State Water Resources Bd. On publications currently available, where no price is given it can be assumed a single copy is available free of charge.

BOARD MINUTES – PROGRAMS

Deschutes River Basin. 36 p., May 26, 1967.

Deschutes River Basin, Lower 6 p., Apr. 3, 1964.

Grande Ronde Basin. 40 p., April 3, 1964.

Hood Basin. 10 p., March 30, 1966.

John Day River Basin. 9 p., April 3, 1964.

McKenzie River Basin, Upper. 5 p., April 3, 1964.

Mid-Coast Basin. 17 p., July 12, 1966.

North Coast Basin. 8 p., April 3, 1964.

Rogue River Basin. 42 p., October 29, 1969.

Snake River Basin, Middle. 5 p., April 3, 1964.

South Coast Basin. 11 p., May 22, 1964.

Umatilla Basin. 6 p., February 13, 1964.

Umpqua River Basin. 30 p., April 3, 1964.

Willamette River Basin, Lower (incl. Sandy Basin). 26 p., August 26, 1968.

Willamette River Basin, Middle. 17 p., June 22, 1964.

Willamette River Basin, Upper. 37 p., June 22, 1964.

BASIN REPORTS

*Deschutes River Basin. 217 p., January 1961.

Grande Ronde Basin. 225 p., September 1960. Price: $2.50.

Hood Basin. 142 p., April 1965. Price: $2.50

John Day River Basin. 117 p., March 1962. Price: $2.50.

Malheur Lake Basin. 128 p., June 1967. Price: $2.50.

Mid-Coast Basin. 146 p., May 1965. Price: $2.50.

North Coast Basin. 166 p., June 1961. Price: $2.50.

Powder River Basin. 177 p., June 1967. Price: $2.50.

Rogue River Basin. 460 p., January 1959. Price: $2.50.

Rogue River Basin – Summary. 23 p., January 1959.

Snake River Study – Interim Report No. 1. 228 p., August 1958. Price: $2.50.

South Coast Basin. 149 p., January 1963. Price: $2.50.

Umatilla River Basin. 126 p., June 1963. Price: $2.50.

Umpqua River Basin. 221 p., July 1958. Price: $1.50.

Willamette River Basin. 106 p., June 1967. Price: $2.50.

Willamette River Basin, Lower (incl. Sandy Basin). 172 p., June 1965. Price: $2.50.

Willamette River Basin, Middle. 163 p., June 1963. Price: $2.50.

Willamette River Basin, Upper. 217 p., April 1961. Price: $2.50.

BIENNIAL REPORTS

*First. 67 p., January 1957.

Second. 96 p., January 1959.

Third. 82 p., January 1961.

Fourth. 33 p., January 1963.

*Fifth. 46 p., January 1965.

*Sixth. 47 p., January 1967.

*Seventh. 56 p., January 1969.

MISCELLANEOUS REPORTS

*Aggregate and Rock Sites. 22 p., July 1965.

Burns-Hines Flood Plain Study, Harney County, Oregon. 46 p. December 1968.

*Flood Plain Study of Ochoco Creek. 6 p., May 1967.

Irrigation Situation and Potential of the Mid-Columbia Region. 18 p., July 1965.

*Oregon's Long-Range Requirements for Water.

    Summary Report. 15 p., May 1969.

    Full Report. November 1969.

      Main Report. 397 p.

      Appendix I – General Soil Map Report by Drainage Basin:

        I-1, 16, 17 – North, Mid, and South Coast

I-2 – Willamette	I-10 – Malheur
I-4 – Hood	I-11 – Owyhee
I-5 – Deschutes	I-12 – Malheur Lake
I-6 – John Day	I-13 – Goose & Summer Lakes
I-7 – Umatilla	I-14 – Klamath
I-8 – Grande Ronde	I-15 – Rogue
I-9 – Powder	I-16 – Umpqua

      Appendix II – Irrigation and Food Products Projections. 134 p.

      Appendix III – Selected Major Water-using Industries and Population Projections. 299 p.

      Appendix IV – Forest Products Projections. 18 p.

      Appendix V – Recreation Projections. 46 p.

      Appendix VI – Water Quality Control Projections. 222 p.

      Appendix VII – Protection of Areas of Origin. 62 p.

Oregon's Water Problems and Future Needs. 197 p. December 1964.

Organization for Water Temperature Prediction and Control Study – Umpqua River Basin. 17 p., February 1963.

Organization for Water Temperature, Storage, Flow Correlation Study – Rogue River Basin. 20 p., May 1960.

Study of Water – Hood River County, Oregon. 28 p., June 1965.

The Flood Plain and Flood Damage Reduction. 8 p., November 1969.

Water Quality Data Inventory

    Bulletin No. 1. 129 p., June 1956.

    Bulletin No. 2. 71 p. June 1957.

Water Temperature Prediction and Control Study – Umpqua River Basin. 53 p., February 1964.

OTHER AGENCIES

Lincoln County Planning Commission

    Water Study – Lincoln County

      Summary. 22 p., December 1965.

      Volume I –– Economic Trends and Population Changes. 31 p., December 1965.

      Volume II – Water Sources, Supply and Quality. 47 p. December 1965.

      Volume III – Water Supply Plan. 159 p., December 1965.

Oregon State University

    Trends and Anticipated Changes in Water-use

      Practices for Irrigation in the Willamette Valley. 70 p., November 1965.

Water Resources Committee

    Report. 224 p., January 1955.

Willamette River Basin Commission

    *Final Report. 49 p., January 1955.

DATA SUMMARIES
Damsites

Deschutes Basin. 3 p., January 1961. Price: $0.15.

Grande Ronde Basin. 3 p., September 1960. Price: $0.15.

John Day Basin. 2 p., March 1962. Price: $0.10.

Mid-Coast Basin. 3 p., May 1965. Price: $0.15.

North Coast Basin. 3 p., June 1961. Price: $0.15.

Powder Basin. 1 p., June 1967. Price: $0.05.

*Rogue Basin. 1 p., April 1958.

South Coast Basin. 3 p., January 1963. Price: $0.15.

Willamette Basin (incl. Sandy Basin). 12 p., September 1965. Price: $0.60.

Geographic Names

Chetco Basin. 13 p., December 1961. Price: $0.65.

Coos-Coquille Basin. 14 p., August 1963. Price: $0.70.

Goose and Summer Lakes Basin. 8 p., 1964. Price: $0.40.

Grande Ronde Basin. 8 p., 1966. Price: $0.40.

Hood Basin. 8 p., 1964. Price: $0.40.

John Day Basin. 28 p., June 1964. Price: $1.40.

Malheur Lake Basin. 25 p., 1967. Price: $1.25.

Mid-Coast Basin. 11 p., 1964. Price: $0.55.

North Coast Basin. 14 p., 1960. Price: $0.70.

Powder Basin. 26 p., 1967. Price: $1.30.

Willamette Basin (incl. Sandy Basin). 32 p., 1964. Price: $1.60.

Recreation

Deschutes Basin. 16 p., January 1960. Price: $0.80.

John Day Basin. 2 p., March 1962. Price: $0.10.

Mid-Coast Basin. 3 p., May 1955. Price: $0.15.

North Coast Basin. 9 p., June 1961. Price: $0.45.

Powder Basin. 1 p., October 1965. Price: $0.05.

South Coast Basin. 2 p., January 1963. Price: $0.10.

Willamette Basin (incl. Sandy Basin). 10 p., December 1964. Price: $0.50.

Stream Miles

Mid-Coast Basin. 34 p., 1967. Price: $1.70.

North Coast Basin. 29 p., 1967. Price: $1.45.

South Coast Basin. 21 p. 1967. Price: $1.05.

Umpqua Basin. 29 p. 1967. Price: $1.45.

Willamette Basin (incl. Sandy Basin). 113 p., 1967. Price: $5.65.

Surface Areas of Lakes and Reservoirs

Deschutes Basin. 6 p., 1959. Price: $0.30.

Hood Basin. 1 p., 1967. Price: $0.05.

*Klamath Basin. 3 p., 1969.

*Mid-Coast Basin. 1 p., 1969.

North Coast Basin. 1 p., 1967. Price: $0.05.

*Powder Basin. 2 p., 1967.

*Rogue Basin. 3 p., 1969.

*South Coast Basin. 1 p., 1969.

*Umpqua Basin. 2 p., 1969.

Willamette Basin (incl. Sandy Basin). 8 p., 1967. Price: $0.40.

Surface Water Gaging Stations

Oregon. 40 p., 1968. Price: $2.00.

Hydrological Stations

Deschutes Basin. 44 p., June 1960. Price: $2.20.

John Day Basin. 2 p., March 1962. Price: $0.10.

Malheur Lake Basin. 3 p., 1966. Price: $0.15.

Mid-Coast Basin. 2 p., May 1965. Price: $0.10.

North Coast Basin. 23 p., May 1961. Price: $1.15.

Powder Basin. 4 p., September 1964. Price: $0.20.

South Coast Basin. 1 p., January 1963. Price: $0.05.

Willamette Basin (incl. Sandy Basin). 20 p., September 1964. Price: $1.00.

Literature

Coos-Coquille River Basin (South Coast Basin). 33 p., July 1961. Price: $1.65.

Goose & Summer Lakes Basin. 31 p., August 1968. Price: $1.55.

Hood Basin. 37 p., July 1963. Price: $1.85.

John Day Basin. 82 p., August 1960. Price: $4.10.

Klamath Basin. 23 p., July 1968. Price: $1.15.

Malheur Lake Basin. 49 p., May 1965. Price: $2.45

Malheur & Owyhee River Basins. 23 p., April 1967. Price: $1.15.

Middle Coast Drainage Basin. 58 p., April 1963. Price: $2.90.

North Coast Basin. 44 p., May 1960. Price: $2.20.

Powder River Drainage Basin. 76 p., February 1965. Price: $3.80.

Rogue River Basin. 22 p., July 1969. Price: $1.10.

South Coast Basin. 19 p., August 1969. Price: $0.95.

Umatilla River Basin. 69 p., January 1962. Price: $3.45.

Umpqua River Drainage Basin. 26 p., October 1968. Price: $1.30.

Willamette River Drainage Basin. 48 p., November 1969. Price: $2.40.

Precipitation Stations

Oregon. 44 p., 1968. Price: $2.20.

HEARINGS
Informational

Coos-Coquille and Chetco Basins. 217 p., November 16, 1961. Price: $1.00.

*Deschutes River Basin. 283 p., March 1, 1960.

Grande Ronde Basin. 122 p., April 22, 1958. Price: $1.00.

Hood Basin – Hood River County. 123 p., January 29, 1964. Price: $1.00.

Hood Basin – Wasco County. 95 p., January 29, 1964. Price: $1.00.

John Day River Basin. 121 p., May 9, 1961. Price: $1.00.

McKenzie River Basin, Upper – Volumes I and II. 170 p., December 2, 1957. Price: $1.00.

Malheur Lake Basin. 137 p., January 19, 1966. Price: $1.00.

Malheur and Owyhee River Basins. 165 p., March 9, 1967. Price: $1.00.

Mid-Coast Basin. 166 p., May 21, 1964. Price: $1.00.

North Coast Basin – Clatsop and Columbia Counties. 143 p., January 4, 1961. Price: $1.00.

North Coast Basin – Tillamook County. 133 p., January 5, 1961. Price: $1.00.

Powder Basin. 217 p., January 18, 1966. Price: $1.00.

Rogue River Basin – Curry County. 108 p., December 13, 1957. Price: $1.00.

Rogue River Basin – Jackson County. 117 p., December 11, 1957. Price: $1.00.

Rogue River Basin – Josephine County. 75 p., December 12, 1957. Price: $1.00.

Snake Basin, Middle. 119 p., February 10, 1958. Price: $1.00.

Snake River, Middle. 121 p., January 21, 1958. Price: $1.00.

Umatilla Basin. 136 p., January 30, 1962. Price: $1.00.

Umpqua River Basin. 126 p., October 15, 1956. Price: $1.00.

Willamette Basin, Lower (incl. Sandy Basin).
  Volume I – Clackamas and Multnomah Counties. 165 p., November 14, 1963. Price: $1.00
  Volume II – Washington County. 110 p., November 15, 1963. Price: $1.00.

Willamette Basin, Middle. 444 p., November 17, 1961. Price: $1.00.

Willamette Basin, Upper. 285 p., April 7, 1960. Price: $1.00.

Program

Deschutes, Grande Ronde and Upper Willamette. 36 p., October 26, 1961. Price: $1.00.

Deschutes, Lower Crooked River – Modification. 19 p., April 3, 1964. Price: $1.00.

Deschutes River Basin, Lower – Exception (Kaskela Ranch). 19 p., September 15, 1967. Price: $1.00.

Grande Ronde River Basin. 111 p., September 5, 1963. Price: $1.00.

Hood Basin. 32 p., November 19, 1965. Price: $1.00.

John Day River Basin. 28 p., October 31, 1962. Price: $1.00.

*McKenzie River Basin, Upper – Statement. 3 p., August 18, 1958.

Mid-Coast Basin. 126 p., November 19, 1965. Price: $1.00.

Mid-Coast Basin – Reconvened. 33 p., May 25, 1966. Price: $1.00.

Mid-Willamette Exception. 8 p., April 11, 1969. Price: $1.00.

*North Coast Basin. 17 p., May 24, 1962.

*River Basin Modifications:
Deschutes   McKenzie, Upper   Snake, Middle
Grande Ronde North Coast   Umpqua
John Day   Rogue   Willamette, Upper.
44 p., January 16, 1964.

River Basin Modifications and/or Exceptions:
Deschutes River Basin – Modification.
Mid-Coast Basin – Modification or Exception.
Willamette River Basin, Upper – Exception. 44 p., May 26, 1967. Price: $1.00.

Rogue River Basin. 25 p., July 23, 1959. Price: $1.00.

Rogue River Basin – Modification. 107 p., November 19, 1965. Price: $1.00.

Rogue River Basin – Modification. 52 p., December 10, 1968. Price: $1.00.

Rogue River Basin – Modification. 28 p., April 11, 1969. Price: $1.00.

South Coast Basin and Umatilla River Basin. 44 p., January 16, 1964. Price: $1.00.

South Coast Basin – Exception. 5 p., December 10, 1969. Price: $0.50.

South Coast Basin – Exception. 35 p., February 10, 1969. Price: $1.00.

*Umpqua River Basin – Comments. 13 p., November 24, 1958.

Umpqua River Basin – Exception. 10 p., October 12, 1967. Price: $0.50.

Willamette River Basin, Lower (incl. Sandy Basin). 43 p., March 30, 1966. Price: $1.00.

Willamette River Basin, Lower (incl. Sandy Basin) – Modification. 6 p., August 26, 1968. Price: $0.50.

Willamette River Basin, Middle – Modification (N. Santiam). 58 p., December 5, 1967. Price: $1.00.

Willamette River Basin – Exception. 8 p., April 11, 1969. Price: $0.50.

Willamette River Basin, Upper – Modification. 9 p., May 22, 1964. Price: $0.50.

Referral

*East Pine Creek, Snake River. 161 p., July 7, 1961.

High Mountain Sheep, Snake River – Volumes I – V. 560 p., January 5, 1960. Price: $1.00.

North Santiam River Project (Niagara). 129 p., March 4, 1960. Price: $1.00.

North Santiam River Project (Niagara) – Reconvened. 138 p., June 9, 1960. Price: $1.00.

Round Butte Project, Deschutes River – Volumes I – VI
Preliminary Permit. 1,190 p., October 12-16, 1959. Price: $1.00.

Reconvened. 156 p., November 19, 1959. Price: $1.00.

License. 200 p., September 9, 1960. Price: $1.00.

*Snake River – Application for Three Dams. 10 p., April 30, 1957.

Snake River – Application for Three Dams – Reconvened. May 22, 1957.

Snake River – Application for Three Dams – Reconvened. 56 p., August 26, 1957. Price: $1.00.

Withdrawal

Elk Creek, Rogue River. 107 p., November 19, 1965. Price: $1.00.

Dutchy Lake, Church Lake and Unnamed Lake and Creek. 22 p., March 24, 1965. Price: $1.00.

*Imnaha and Snake Rivers. 27 p., December 11, 1958.

*Roberts Creek, Umpqua River. 20 p., April 27, 1959.

*Willamette Falls, Willamette River. 25 p., June 28, 1965.

MAPS

The symbol † indicates maps are included in Basin Reports. †† indicates maps are included in Ultimate Needs Study Main Report. Size of maps given in inches.

Oregon

Drainage Basins. (Map No. 0.2) 1967. 8½ x 11.

Drainage Basins. (Map No. 0.4) 1967. 11 x 17.

Gross Irrigable Areas of Oregon†† (Map No. I-3) 1969. 20 x 27. Price: $0.50.

Oregon Land Forms and Average Annual Precipitation†† (Map No. I-1) 1969. 20 x 28. Price: $0.50.

Suggested Diversions NW to SW. (Map No. 0.27) 1964. 8½ x 11.

Water Use Programs. (Map No. 0.49) 1968. 11 x 17.

Chetco Drainage Basin

Drainage Basin.† (Map No. 17A.2) 1961. 8½ x 11. Price: $0.25.

Drainage Basin. (Map No. 17A.6) 1961. 21 x 27. Price: $0.50.

Stream Profile. (Map No. 17A.472) 1962. 11 x 22 Price: $0.25.

Water Rights. (Map No. 17A.63) 1962. 21 x 27. Price: $0.50.

Overprints on Map No. 17A.6:

Anadromous Fish Distribution.† 1961. 8½ x 11. Price: $0.25.

Damsites.† 1961. 8½ x 11. Price: $0.25.

Generalized Ground Water Geology. 1961. 8½ x 11. Price: $0.25.

Generalized Land Use. 1961. 8½ x 11. Price: $0.25.

Hydrological Stations and Average Annual Precipitation.† 1961. 8½ x 11. Price: $0.25.

Mineral Deposits. 1961. 8½ x 11. Price: $0.25.

Recreation Areas. 1961. 8½ x 11. Price: $0.25.

Water Rights.† 1962. 8½ x 11. Price: $0.25.

Coos-Coquille Drainage Basin

Drainage Basin.† (Map No. 17.6) 1961. 17 x 30. Price: $0.50.

Drainage Basin. (Map No. 17.8) 1961. 40 x 70. Price: $1.50.

Stream Profile. (Map No. 17.672) 1962. 17 x 30. Price: $0.50.

Water Rights. (Map No. 17.83) 1962. 40 x 70. Price: $1.50.

Overprints on Map No. 17.6:

Anadromous Fish Distribution.† 1961. 17 x 30. Price: $0.50.

Damsites.† 1961. 17 x 30. Price: $0.50.

*Generalized Ground Water Geology. 1961. 17 x 30.

Generalized Land Use. 1961. 17 x 30. Price: $0.50.

Hydrological Stations and Average Annual Precipitation.† 1961. 17 x 30. Price: $0.50.

*Mineral Deposits. 1961. 17 x 30.

Problem Areas. 1961. 17 x 30. Price: $0.50.

*Recreation Areas. 1961. 17 x 30.

Water Rights.† 1962. 17 x 30. Price: $0.50.

Deschutes Drainage Basin

Drainage Basin. (Map No. 5.2) 1967. 8½ x 11.

Drainage Basin. (Map No. 5.4) 1967. 11 x 17.

Drainage Basin.† (Map No. 5.6) 1960. 17 x 30. Price: $0.50.

Drainage Basin. (Map No. 5.8) 1960. 40 x 70. Price: $1.50.

Stream Profile.† (Map No. 5.672) 1960. 17 x 30. Price: $0.50.

Water Rights. (Map No. 5.83) 1960. 40 x 70. Price: $1.50.

Overprints on Map No. 5.6:

Chinook Salmon Spawning Areas. 1960. 17 x 30. Price: $0.50.

*Damsites.† 1960. 17 x 30.

Ground Water.† 1960. 17 x 30. Price: $0.50.

Hydrological Stations.† 1960. 17 x 30. Price: $0.50.

Irrigation Development.† 1960. 17 x 30. Price: $0.50.

Irrigation Lands.† 1960. 17 x 30. Price: $0.50.

*Mineral Deposits.† 1960. 17 x 30.

Problem Areas.† 1960. 17 x 30. Price: $0.50.

*Recreation Areas.† 1960. 17 x 30.

Resident Trout Spawning Areas.† 1959. 17 x 30. Price: $0.50.

Steelhead Trout Spawning Areas.† 1959. 17 x 30. Price: $0.50.

Water Rights.† 1960. 17 x 30. Price: $0.50.

Goose Lake Drainage Basin

Drainage Basin. (Map No. 13A.2) 1962. 8½ x 11.

Goose and Summer Lakes Drainage Basin

Drainage Basin. (Map No. 13.2) 1970. 8½ x 11.

Drainage Basin. (Map No. 13.4) 1970. 11 x 17.

Drainage Basin. (Map No. 13.6) 1961. 17 x 30. Price: $0.50.

Drainage Basin. (Map No. 13.8) 1961. 40 x 70. Price: $1.50.

Grande Ronde Drainage Basin

Drainage Basin. (Map No. 8.2) 1967. 8½ x 11.

Drainage Basin. (Map No. 8.4) 1967. 11 x 17.

Drainage Basin.† (Map No. 8.6) 1959. 17 x 30. Price: $0.50.

Drainage Basin. (Map No. 8.8) 1959. 40 x 70. Price: $1.50.

Stream Profile.† (Map No. 8.672) 1959. 17 x 30. Price: $0.50.

Water Rights. (Map No. 8.83) 1959. 40 x 70. Price: $1.50.

Overprints on Map No. 8.6:

Average Annual Precipitation.† 1959. 17 x 30. Price: $0.50.

Irrigation Development.† 1959. 17 x 30. Price: $0.50.

Irrigation Lands.† 1959. 17 x 30. Price: $0.50.

*Mineral Deposits.† 1959. 17 x 30.

Problem Areas.† 1959. 17 x 30. Price: $0.50.

Recreation Areas.† 1959. 17 x 30. Price: $0.50.

Stream Gages and Climatological Stations.† 1959. 17 x 30. Price: $0.50.

*Water Rights.† 1959. 17 x 30.

Hood Drainage Basin

Drainage Basin. (Map No. 4.2) 1967. 8½ x 11.

Drainage Basin. (Map No. 4.4) 1967. 11 x 17.

Drainage Basin.† (Map No. 4.6) 1964. 20 x 28. Price: $0.50.

Drainage Basin. (Map No. 4.8) 1964. 40 x 56. Price: $1.50.

Overprints on Map No. 4.6:

Hydrological Stations and Average Annual Precipitation.† 1964. 20 x 28. Price: $0.50.

Potential Development.† 1964. 20 x 28. Price: $0.50.

Recreation Areas.† 1964. 20 x 28. Price: $0.50.

John Day Drainage Basin

Drainage Basin. (Map No. 6.2) 1967. 8½ x 11.

Drainage Basin. (Map No. 6.4) 1967. 11 x 17.

Drainage Basin.† (Map No. 6.6) 1960. 17 x 30. Price: $0.50.

Drainage Basin. (Map No. 6.8) 1960. 40 x 70. Price: $1.50.

Stream Profile.† (Map No. 6.672) 1961. 17 x 30. Price: $0.50.

Water Rights. (Map No. 6.83) 1961. 40 x 70. Price: $1.50.

Overprints on Map No. 6.6:

Anadromous Fish Life.† 1960. 17 x 30. Price: $0.50.

Damsites.† 1960. 17 x 30. $0.50.

Generalized Ground Water Geology.† 1960. 17 x 30. Price: $0.50.

Hydrological Stations and Average Annual Precipitation.† 1960. 17 x 30. Price: $0.50.

Irrigated Land.† 1960. 17 x 30. Price: $0.50.

Mineral Deposits.† 1960. 17 x 30. Price: $0.50.

Recreation Areas.† 1960. 17 x 30. Price: $0.50.

Water Rights.† 1961. 17 x 30. Price: $0.50.

Klamath Drainage Basin

Drainage Basin. (Map No. 14.2) 1967. 8½ x 11.

Drainage Basin. (Map No. 14.4) 1967. 11 x 17.

Drainage Basin. (Map No. 14.6) 1968. 22 x 28. Price: $0.50.

Drainage Basin. (Map No. 14.8) 1968. 42 x 54. Price: $1.50.

Malheur Drainage Basin

Drainage Basin. (Map No. 10.2) 1967. 8½ x 11.

Drainage Basin. (Map No. 10.4) 1967. 11 x 17.

Drainage Basin. (Map No. 10.6) 1967. 22 x 28. Price: $0.50.

Drainage Basin. (Map No. 10.8) 1967. 41 x 42. Price: $1.00.

Overprints on Map No. 10.6:

Hydrological Stations. 1967. 22 x 22. Price: $0.50.

Potential Development. 1967. 22 x 22. Price: $0.50.

Malheur Lake Drainage Basin

Drainage Basin. (Map No. 12.2) 1970. 8½ x 11.

Drainage Basin. (Map No. 12.4) 1970. 11 x 17.

Drainage Basin. (Map No. 12.6) 1966. 22 x 30. Price: $0.50.

Drainage Basin. (Map No. 12.8) 1966. 42 x 58. Price: $1.50.

Overprints on Map No. 12.6:

Potential Development. 1966. 22 x 30. Price: $0.50.

Malheur-Owyhee Drainage Basin

Drainage Basin. (Map No. 10-11.4) 1968. 11 x 17.

Malheur Project Area. (Map No. 1011A.6) 1967. 22 x 33. Price: $0.50.

Malheur Project Area – Distribution System. (Map No. 10-11.57) 1968. 16 x 20. Price: $0.50.

Malheur Project Area – Land Ownership. (Map No. 10-11.526) 1968. 16 x 20. Price: $0.50.

Mid-Coast Drainage Basin

Drainage Basin. (Map No. 18.2) 1967. 8½ x 11.

Drainage Basin. (Map No. 18.4) 1967. 11 x 17.

Drainage Basin.† (Map No. 18.6) 1964. 20 x 34. Price: $0.50.

Drainage Basin. (Map No. 18.8) 1964. 40 x 68). Price: $1.50.

Overprints on Map No. 18.6:

Anadromous Fish.† 1964. 20 x 34. Price: $0.50.

Damsites and Flood Areas.† 1964. 20 x 34. Price: $0.50.

Hydrological Stations.† 1964. 20 x 34. Price: $0.50.

Recreation Areas.† 1964. 20 x 34. Price: $0.50.

North Coast Drainage Basin

Drainage Basin. (Map No. 1.2) 1967. 8½ x 11.

Drainage Basin. (Map No. 1.4) 1967. 11 x 17.

Drainage Basin.† (Map No. 1.6) 1960. 17 x 30. Price: $0.50.

Drainage Basin. (Map No. 1.8) 1960. 40 x 70. Price: $1.50.

Stream Profile.† (Map No. 1.672) 1960. 17 x 30. Price: $0.50.

Water Rights. (Map No. 1.83) 1960. 40 x 70. Price: $1.50.

Overprints on Map No. 1.6:

Anadromous Fish Spawning Areas.† 1960. 17 x 30. Price: $0.50.

Average Annual Precipitation.† 1960. 17 x 30. Price: $0.50.

Generalized Ground Water Geology.† 1960. 17 x 30. Price: $0.50.

Hydrological Stations.† 1960. 17 x 30. Price: $0.50.

Mineral Deposits.† 1960. 17 x 30. Price: $0.50.

Recreation Areas.† 1960. 17 x 30. Price: $0.50.

Storage Sites.† 1960. 17 x 30. Price: $0.50.

Water Rights.† 1960. 17 x 30. Price: $0.50.

Owyhee Drainage Basin

Drainage Basin (in Oregon). (Map No. 11.2) 1970. 8½ x 11.

Drainage Basin (in Oregon). (Map No. 11.4) 1970. 11 x 17.

Drainage Basin (in Oregon). (Map No. 11.6) 1967. 22 x 33. Price: $0.50.

Drainage Basin (in Oregon). (Map No. 11.8) 1967. 38 x 58. Price: $1.50.

Drainage Basin (Total Basin). (Map No. 11A.4) 1967. 11 x 17.

Overprints on Map No. 11.6:

Hydrological Stations. 1967. 22 x 33. Price: $0.50.

Potential Development. 1967. 22 x 33. Price: $0.50.

Powder Drainage Basin

Drainage Basin. (Map No. 9.2) 1970. 8½ x 11.

Drainage Basin. (Map No. 9.4) 1970. 11 x 17.

Drainage Basin.† (Map No. 9.6) 1965. 22 x 29. Price: $0.50.

Drainage Basin. (Map No. 9.8) 1965. 42 x 56. Price: $1.50.

Overprints on Map No. 9.6:

Arable Soils.† 1965. 22 x 29. Price: $0.50.

Hydrological Stations.† 1965. 22 x 29. Price: $0.50.

Potential Development.† 1965. 22 x 29. Price: $0.50.

Recreation Areas.† 1965. 22 x 29. Price: $0.50.

Rogue Drainage Basin

Drainage Basin. (Map No. 15.2) 1967. 8½ x 11.

Drainage Basin. (Map No. 15.4) 1967. 11 x 17.

Drainage Basin. (Map No. 15.6) 1958. 17 x 30. Price: $0.50.

Drainage Basin. (Map No. 15.8) 1970. 42 x 58. Price: $1.50.

Stream Profile.† (Map No. 15.472) 1958. 11 x 18. Price: $0.25.

Transportation Facilities. (Map No. 15.875) 1958. 40 x 70. Price: $1.50.

Water Rights. (Map No. 15.83) 1958. 40 x 70. Price: $1.50.

Sandy Drainage Basin — see Willamette Drainage Basin, or see Willamette Drainage Basin, Lower

South Coast Drainage Basin

Drainage Basin. (Map No. 17.2) 1967. 8½ x 11.

Drainage Basin. (Map No. 17.4) 1967. 11 x 17.

Umatilla Drainage Basin

Drainage Basin. (Map No. 7.2) 1967. 8½ x 11.

Drainage Basin. (Map No. 7.4) 1967. 11 x 17.

Drainage Basin.† (Map No. 7.6) 1962. 20 x 34. Price: $0.50.

Drainage Basin. (Map No. 7.8) 1962. 40 x 58. Price: $1.50.

Overprints on Map No. 7.6:

Hydrological Stations and Average Annual Precipitation.† 1962. 20 x 34. Price: $0.50.

Water Resource Development.† 1962. 20 x 34. Price: $0.50.

Umpqua Drainage Basin

Drainage Basin. (Map No. 16.2) 1967. 8½ x 11.

Drainage Basin. (Map No. 16.4) 1967. 11 x 17.

Drainage Basin. (Map No. 16.6) 1969. 22 x 28. Price: $0.50.

Drainage Basin. (Map No. 16.8) 1969. 42 x 54. Price: $1.50.

Willamette Drainage Basin
(includes Sandy Basin)

Drainage Basin. (Map No. 2.2) 1967. 8½ x 11.

Drainage Basin. (Map No. 2.4) 1967. 11 x 17.

Drainage Basin. (Map No. 2.6) 1964. 20 x 34. Price: $0.50.

Drainage Basin. (Map No. 2.8) 1964. 42 x 73. Price: $1.50.

Overprints on Map No. 2.6:

Damsites. 1964. 20 x 34. Price: $0.50.

Flooding. 1964. 20 x 34. Price: $0.50.

Hydrological Stations. 1964. 20 x 34. Price: $0.50.

Recreation Areas. 1964. 20 x 34. Price: $0.50.

Willamette Drainage Basin, Lower
(includes Sandy Basin)

Drainage Basin. (Map No. 2C.2) 1967. 8½ x 11.

Drainage Basin. (Map No. 2C.4) 1967. 11 x 17.

Drainage Basin.† (Map No. 2C.6) 1963. 20 x 28. Price: $0.50.

Drainage Basin. (Map No. 2C.8) 1963. 40 x 56. Price: $1.50.

Overprints on Map No. 2C.6:

Anadromous Fish.† 1963. 20 x 28. Price: $0.50.

General Land Use.† 1963. 20 x 28. Price: $0.50.

Legal Restrictions.† 1963. 20 x 28. Price: $0.50.

Willamette Drainage Basin, Middle

Drainage Basin. (Map No. 2B.2) 1967. 8½ x 11.

Drainage Basin. (Map No. 2B.4) 1967. 11 x 17.

Drainage Basin.† (Map No. 2B.6) 1961. 17 x 30. Price: $0.50.

Drainage Basin. (Map No. 2B.8) 1961. 40 x 70. Price: $1.50.

Stream Profile. (Map No. 2B.672) 1962. 17 x 30. Price: $0.50.

Water Rights. (Map No. 2B.83) 1962. 40 x 70. Price: $1.50.

Overprints on Map No. 2B.6:

Anadromous Fish.† 1961. 17 x 30. Price: $0.50.

Average Annual Precipitation. 1961. 17 x 30. Price: $0.50.

Generalized Land Use.† 1961. 17 x 30. Price: $0.50.

Ground Water Rights.† 1961. 17 x 30. Price: $0.50.

Irrigation. 1961. 17 x 30. Price: $0.50.

Surface Water Rights.† 1962. 17 x 30. Price: $0.50.

Willamette Drainage Basin, Upper

Drainage Basin. (Map No. 2A.2) 1967. 8½ x 11.

Drainage Basin. (Map No. 2A.4) 1967. 11 x 17.

Drainage Basin.† (Map No. 2A.6) 1960. 17 x 30. Price: $0.50.

Drainage Basin. (Map No. 2A.8) 1960. 40 x 70. Price: $1.50.

Stream Profile.† (Map No. 2A.672) 1960. 17 x 30. Price: $0.50.

Water Rights. (Map No. 2A.83) 1960. 40 x 70. Price: $1.50.

Overprints on Map No. 2A.6:

Anadromous Fish Spawning Areas.† 1960. 17 x 30. Price: $0.50.

Average Annual Precipitation.† 1960. 17 x 30. Price: $0.50.

Generalized Ground Water Geology.† 1960. 17 x 30. Price: $0.50.

Mineral Deposits.† 1960. 17 x 30. Price: $0.50.

Restricted Use Lands — Federal.† 1960. 17 x 30. Price: $0.50.

Water Rights.† 1960. 17 x 30. Price: $0.50.

AERIAL PHOTO MAPS

Burns-Hines Study Area. 1967. 31 x 40. Price: $1.00.

Old Indian Village Reservoir Site. 1967. 18 x 27. Price: $0.50.

Reservoir Site F. 1967. 18 x 27. Price: $0.50.

Reservoir Site G. 1967. 18 x 32. Price: $0.50.

Reservoir Site H. 1967. 18 x 28. Price: $0.50.

Ochoco Creek Flood Plain (2 sheets). 1966. 19 x 32. Price: $1.00.

WATER RESOURCES RESEARCH INSTITUTE
Oregon State University
Covell Hall 115
Corvallis, Oregon 97331

Note: Where available, single copies free of charge. Additional copies cost $1.00 each.

SEMINAR SERIES

*a Water Resources Planning and Development, July 1964.

*b Water Quality Control, January 1965.

*c Water Law, Politics, and Economics, July 1965.

*d Who's Responsible for Water Resources Research, January 1966.

*e Career Opportunities in Water Resources, July 1966.

*f The Use of Simulation in Water Research, January 1967.

*g Northwest-Southwest Water Diversion Issues, July 1967.

*h Water and Environmental Quality, January 1968.

i People and Water, July 1968.

j Reservoirs: Problems and Conflicts, January 1969.

k Snow, July 1969.

l Water Studies in Oregon, January 1970.

m Man and Aquatic Communities, July 1970.

SUMMARIES

a Water Research Summary, January 1966.

b Water Research Summary, March 1968, No. 2.

c Water Research Summary, March 1970, No. 3.

SPECIAL PUBLICATIONS

a Graduate Studies in Water Resources (descriptive brochure).

b Oregon's Water-Management Districts, by William L. Hallmark. Reprint from the *Oregon Law Review*, December 1967.

c Legal Aspects of Interregional Water Diversion, by Gary D. Weatherford, Reprint from the *UCLA Law Review*, September 1968.

*d Willamette River: River Lands and River Boundaries, WRRI-1, February 1970.

*e Waldo Lake, Oregon: A Special Study, WRRI-2, May 1970.

PENNSYLVANIA

BUREAU OF TOPOGRAPHIC AND GEOLOGIC SURVEY

130 Main Capitol Annex
Harrisburg, Pennsylvania 17120

Note: For ordering publications which are free, send requests to the above address. If there is a charge, send requests together with check payable to the Commonwealth of Pennsylvania, to Capitol Book Store, 54 Main Capitol Building, Harrisburg, Pennsylvania 17125. Out-of-print reports are available for study at the library of the Pennsylvania Geological Survey in Harrisburg, as well as in other large libraries in the state.

COUNTY REPORTS

C 39 Lehigh County, Geology and Geography, by B. L. Miller et al., 1942. 492 p., 17 figs., 39 pls., including 1 topographic and mine map and 1 geologic map. (Map scale 1:62,500). Price: $3.30.

C 48 Northampton County, Geology and Geography, by B. L. Miller, D. M. Fraser, and R. L. Miller, 1939; 2nd printing 1965. 496 p., 36 figs., 29 pls., including geologic map. (Map scale 1:62,500). Price: $5.10.

EDUCATIONAL SERIES

ES 3 Ground Water, by R. C. Bolger, 1962. 11 p., 7 figs. Free.

GENERAL GEOLOGY REPORTS

G 10 Recent Geological History of the Delaware Valley below the Water Gap, by Freeman Ward, 1938; 2nd printing 1962. 76 p., 13 figs., 10 pls. Price: $0.55.

G 23 Pleistocene Terraces of the Susquehanna River, by L. C. Peltier, 1949. 152 p., 49 figs. Price: $2.35.

INFORMATION CIRCULARS

IC 7 The Ground Water Program for Pennsylvania. 1956. 14 p. Free.

*IC 10 Ground Water. 1958 (replaced by ES 3).

IC 56 The Geography and Geology of Erie County, Pennsylvania, by J. C. Tomikel and V. C. Shepps, 1967. 64 p., 39 figs. Price: $0.95.

MINERAL RESOURCE REPORTS

M 33 Waterflooding in Pennsylvania, by Charles R. Fettke, 1950. 30 p., 16 figs. Price: $0.25.

M 44 Fuel Competition in Pennsylvania's Electric Generating Industry, by G. F. Deasy and P. R. Griess, 1961. 54 p., 21 figs. Price: $0.55.

M 47 The Occurrence of Brines in Western Pennsylvania, by C. W. Poth, 1962. 53 p., 11 figs. Price: $0.90.

PROGRESS REPORTS

PR 146 Ground-Water Resources of the Lansdale Area, by D. R. Rima, 1955. 25 p., 4 figs., 7 pls. Price: $0.40.

PR 171 Hydrology of the Carbonate Rocks of the Lancaster 15-minute Quadrangle, Pennsylvania, by Harold Meisler and A. E. Becher, 1966. 36 p., 7 figs., 1 pl. Price: $1.15.

WATER-RESOURCE REPORTS

W 1 Ground Water in Southwestern Pennsylvania, by A. M. Piper, 1933. 410 p., 40 figs. Price: $1.50.

W 2 Ground Water in Southeastern Pennsylvania, by G. M. Hall, 1934; 2nd printing 1967. 255 p., 7 figs., 7 pls. Price: $4.85.

W 3 Ground Water in Northwestern Pennsylvania, by R. M. Leggett, 1936; 2nd printing 1957. 215 p., 15 figs., 9 pls. Price: $3.20.

W 4 Ground Water in Northeastern Pennsylvania, by S. W. Lohman, 1937; 2nd printing 1957. 300 p., 18 figs., 7 pls. Price: $2.70.

W 5 Ground Water in South-Central Pennsylvania, by S. W. Lohman, 1938; 2nd printing 1968. 315 p., 11 figs., 19 pls. Price: $5.00.

W 6 Ground Water in North-Central Pennsylvania, by S. W. Lohman, 1939; 2nd printing 1967. 220 p., 13 figs., 11 pls. Price: $4.20.

W 7 Ground-Water Resources of Pennsylvania, by S. W. Lohman, 1941. 32 p., 11 figs., 1 pl. Price: $0.25.

W 8 Ground-Water Resources of the Valley-Fill Deposits of Allegheny County, Pennsylvania, by J. H. Adamson et al., 1949. 181 p., 9 figs., 5 pls. Price: $1.85.

W 9 Ground-Water Resources of Beaver County, Pennsylvania, by D. W. Van Tuyl and N. H. Klein, 1951. 84 p., 11 figs., 1 pl. Price: $1.50.

W 10 Ground Water for Air Conditioning at Pittsburgh, Pennsylvania, by D. W. Van Tuyl, 1951. 34 p., 9 figs. Price: $0.50.

W 11 Ground-Water Resources of Bucks County, Pennsylvania, by D. W. Greenman, 1955. 67 p., 1 fig., 2 pls., including geologic map of Bucks County. Price: $3.75.

W 12 Borehole Geophysical Methods for Analyzing the Specific Capacity of Aquifers in a Multiaquifer Well, by G. D. Bennett and E. P. Patten, 1960, 27 p., 8 figs. Price: $0.15.

W 13 Ground-Water Resources of the Coastal Plain Area of Southeastern Pennsylvania, by D. W. Greenman et al., 1961. 375 p., 27 figs., 22 pls. Price: $9.10.

W 14 Geology and Hydrology of the Stockton Formation in Southeastern Pennsylvania, by D. R. Rima, Harold Meisler, and Stanley Longwill, 1962. 11 p., 8 tables, 4 pls., including geologic map. Scale 1:24,000. Price: $4.45.

W 15 Geology and Hydrology of the Neshannock Quadrangle, Mercer and Lawrence Counties, Pennsylvania, by L. D. Carswell and G. D. Bennett, 1963. 98 p., 8 figs., 3 tables, 4 pls., including geologic map. Scale 1:24,000. Price: $4.00.

W 16 Geology and Hydrology of the Mercer Quadrangle, Mercer, Lawrence, and Butler Counties, Pennsylvania, by C. W. Poth, 1963. 149 p., 24 figs., 6 tables, 5 pls., including geologic map. Scale 1:48,000. Price: $4.95.

*W 17 Methods of Flow Measurement in Well Bores, by E. P. Patten, Jr. and G. D. Bennett, 1963. 28 p., 13 figs., 1 table. (Available as U.S.G.S. Water-Supply paper 1544C).

W 18 Hydrogeology of the Carbonate Rocks of the Lebanon Valley, Pennsylvania, by Harold Meisler, 1963. 81 p., 18 figs., 3 tables, 3 pls., including hydrogeologic map. Scale 1:24,000. Price: $3.55.

W 19 Application of Electrical and Radioactive Well Logging to Ground-Water Hydrology, by E. P. Patten, Jr. and G. D. Bennett, 1963. 60 p., 11 figs. Price: $0.25.

W 20 The Ground-Water Observation-Well Program in Pennsylvania, by C. W. Poth, 1963. 17 p., 8 figs. Price: $0.25.

W 21 Hydrology of the New Oxford Formation in Adams and York Counties, Pennsylvania, by P. R. Wood and H. E. Johnston, 1964. 66 p., 10 figs., and geologic map. Scale 1:62,500. Price: $2.15.

W 22 Hydrology of the Brunswick Formation in Montgomery and Berks Counties, Pennsylvania, by S. M. Longwill and C. R. Wood, 1965. 59 p., 13 figs., and geologic map. Scale 1:62,500. Price: $1.75.

W 23 Hydrology of the New Oxford Formation in Lancaster County, Pennsylvania, by H. E. Johnston, 1966. 80 p., 11 figs., and geologic map. Scale 1:62,500. Price: $1.50.

W 24 Geology and Hydrology of the Martinsburg Shale in Dauphin County, Pennsylvania, by L. D. Carswell, J. R. Hollowell, and L. B. Platt. Price: $2.30.

W 25 Hydrology of the Metamorphic and Igneous Rocks of Central Chester County, by Charles W. Poth, 1968. 84 p., 29 figs., 3 pls., including 2 geologic maps. Price: $4.50.

W 26 Hydrology of the Carbonate Rocks of the Lancaster 15' Quadrangle, by H. Meisler and A. E. Becher. Price not available.

DEPARTMENT OF ENVIRONMENTAL RESOURCES
P. O. Box 1467
Harrisburg, Pennsylvania 17120

WATER RESOURCES BULLETINS

1 Pennsylvania Streamflow Characteristics, Low-Flow Frequency and Flow Duration. Price: $1.90.

2 Water Resources Study – Neshaminy Creek Basin, Pennsylvania. Price: $1.90.

3 Water Resources of the Schuylkill River Basin. Price: $4.50.

4 Water Resources Survey – The Schuylkill River, Pennsylvania. Price: $3.50.

5 Dams, Reservoirs and Natural Lakes. (Price not available).

6 Pennsylvania Gazetteer of Streams, Part I. Price: $2.75.

TECHNICAL BULLETINS

1 Water Resources Investigations in the Upper Ohio River Basin.

2 Water Resources Investigations in the Susquehanna River Basin.

OTHER

Stream flow records. 1921/22 - 1940/41. (Annual except 1928-32 when a single report was issued for the four years. Preceding issues found in Annual Report of the Water Supply Commission.)

*The floods of March 1936 in Pennsylvania. (In cooperation with the U. S. Geological Survey.) 1936. 129 p.

*Natural water losses from Pennsylvania drainage basins. 1940. 73 p.

*Elevations of major floods along Pennsylvania rivers. (Prepared in cooperation with the U. S. Geological Survey.) 1942. 28 p.

*The floods of May 1942 in the Delaware and Lackawanna River basins. 1942. 29 p.

*The flood of July 1942 in the Upper Allegheny River and Sinnemahoning Creek basins. 1943. 35 p.

*Flood discharge records relating to Pennsylvania streams. 1950. 59 p.

*Hydraulic and hydrologic aspects of flood-plain planning, by Sulo W. Wiitala, Karl R. Jetter and Alan J. Sommerville. 1958. 92 p.

PENNSYLVANIA DEPARTMENT OF HEALTH
P. O. Box 90
Harrisburg, Pennsylvania 17120

Note: The publications listed here are largely of a pamphlet nature and are generally available free of charge.

SANITARY ENGINEERING

HSE-6020 P How to Improve your Fishing by Reporting Fishkills.

HSE-6039 P Stream Classification Manual.

HSE-6115 P Standard Conditions Relating to Silt-Laden Waste Water.

HSE-6116 P Industrial Wastes Manual.

HSE-6310 P Standard Conditions Relating to Sewerage.

HSE-6316 P Sewerage Manual.

HSE-6319 P Chlorination of Sewage Treatment Plant Effluent in Relation to Prevention of Disease.

HSE-6320 P Single Residence Sewage Treatment Manual.

HSE-6527 P Clean Water Is Wealth.

HSE-6528 P Everyone Benefits from Clean Streams.

HSE-6529 P Public Water Supply Manual.

HSE-6530 P Bathing Place Manual.

HSE-6760 P Mine Drainage Manual.

HSE-6761 P Standard Conditions Accompanying Permits Authorizing the Operation of Coal Mines.

HSE-6763 P Pennsylvania's Ten-Year Mine Drainage Pollution Abatement Program.

HSE-6766 P What We Can Do About Pollution From Abandoned Mines.

——   The Facts About Slippery Rock Creek.

SANITATION

HS-8042 P What is a Sanitary Landfill.

HS-8043 P Environmental Sanitary Survey.

HS-8053 P Model Sewage Ordinance.

HS-8059 P The Sanitary Landfill.

HS-8073 P Semi-Public Water Supply.

HS-8074 P Construction Standards for Individual Water Supplies.

HS-8078 P Mobilehome Park Sanitation.

GENERAL INTEREST

Chronology of Milestones — Pennsylvania's Clean Streams Program. 1970. 29 p.

Water Quality Management; Data Systems Guide. (Prepared by a Joint Committee on Water Quality Management Data.) 1969.

PENNSYLVANIA STATE PLANNING BOARD
Governor's Office
Harrisburg, Pennsylvania 17120

*10 Drainage Basin Study. 1937. 3 vols. 611 p.

17 Industrial Utility of Water in Pennsylvania; Chemical Character of Surface Water 1944-1946. 1947. 172 p.

23 Industrial Utility of Water in Pennsylvania; Chemical Character of Surface Water 1946-1949. 1951.

26 Industrial Utility of Water in Pennsylvania; Chemical Character of Surface Water 1949-1951. 1953.

OTHER

Project 70; A Plan for Pennsylvania's Outdoor Resources. 1963. 32 p.

The Delaware River Port, [prepared for the State Planning Board] by Hammer, Greene, Siler Associates and W. B. Saunders & Company, Washington, D. C. 1965. 137 p.

PENNSYLVANIA WATER RESOURCES COMMITTEE
This Committee is no longer in existence.

Report, February 1953; and Delaware River Basin Report [by] Pennsylvania Water Resources Committee Engineers' Study Committee, January 1953. 56 p.

PENNSYLVANIA WATER SUPPLY COMMISSION
This Commission is no longer in existence.

Annual Report. 1908-1922.

INSTITUTE FOR RESEARCH ON LAND & WATER RESOURCES
The Pennsylvania State University
108 Research Building A
University Park, Pennsylvania 16802

RESEARCH PUBLICATIONS

54 An Economic Analysis of Water Utilization in Pennsylvania, by J. Dean Jansma and Waldon R. Kerns. 1968.

55 A Pilot Plant Study of the Autopurification of Sewage Effluent-Acid Mine Drainage Mixtures, by Daniel M. Mclean and Joseph A. Wernham. 1968.

56 Microbiologic and *Escherichia coli* Serologic Tracing of Microbial Pollution, by Paul J. Glantz. 1968.

62 Hydrologic Behavior of Selected Watersheds in the Northern Appalachian Region, by W. E. Sopper, and others. 1969.

63 Flood Series for Gaged Pennsylvania Streams, by Brian M. Reich. 1969.

INFORMATION REPORTS

51 Proceedings of the Water Resources Law Colloquium. 1967.

60 Proceedings of the Northeast Water Resource Research Director's Meeting, College Park, Maryland, May 10, 1968. 1969.

62 Fiscal 1969 Annual Report of the Water Resources Center, by J. C. Frey and others. 1969.

64 Fiscal 1970 Annual Report of the Institute for Research on Land & Water Resources.

RHODE ISLAND

DEPARTMENT OF HEALTH
Division of Sanitary Engineering
State Office Building
Providence, Rhode Island 02903

Law, rules and regulations relating to the sanitation of food businesses. 1950. 10 p.

The Dept. of Health and its functions with respect to the prevention of the pollution of the waters of the State. Chapter 634 of the general law revision of 1938, amended to 1954.

Report to His Excellency, John O. Pastore, Governor of Rhode Island on pollution of the waters of the State. December 1946. 14 p. Maps.

Regulations regarding sanitation with reference to the conduct of a shellfish business. 13 p. Mimeographed.

DEPARTMENT OF HEALTH
Division of Water Supply and Pollution Control
State Office Building
Providence, Rhode Island 02903

Report for the 12-month period July 1, 1968 – June 30, 1969. Water Pollution Control. 82 p.

Report for the 12-month period July 1, 1969 – June 30, 1970. Water Supply Control, Water Pollution Control, and Industrial Wastes. 93 p.

Annual Report – 1970. Rhode Island Water Pollution Control Advisory Board. 5 p.

GOVERNOR'S CONFERENCE ON OIL POLLUTION
Governor's Office
State Capitol
Providence, Rhode Island 02903

Proceedings at preliminary conference called by Governor Christopher Del Sesto of the State of Rhode Island with advisors in regard to oil pollution of Narragansett Bay by "The Thirtle"; also as to the effect of marine life in the Bay. (1960 ?) 29 p.

Proceedings at public hearing of emergency conference called by Governor Christopher Del Sesto of the State of Rhode Island in regard to oil pollution of Narragansett Bay, Rhode Island by "The Thirtle" going aground at Jamestown. (1960 ?) 48 p.

GOVERNOR'S WATER RESOURCES TASK FORCE
This Task Force is no longer in existence.

Report of the Governor's Task Force on Water Resources Planning. 1967. 72 p.

INLAND WATERWAY COMMITTEE
This Committee is no longer in existence.

Progress Report. Joint Committee to study and report to the General Assembly upon the possibility of developing inland waterways within the State of Rhode Island. 1951. 10 p.

RHODE ISLAND WATER RESOURCES BOARD
265 Melrose Street
P. O. Box 2772
Providence, Rhode Island 02907

The publications listed below are available free of charge. However, due to the expense of mailing, the Board requires $0.18 in postage stamps for each publication ordered.

GROUND WATER MAPS

1   Wickford Quadrangle.

2   Slocum Quadrangle.

3   Crompton Quadrangle.

4   East Providence Quadrangle.

5   Narragansett Pier Quadrangle.

6   Hope Valley Quadrangle.

7   Fall River Quadrangle.

8   Coventry Center Quadrangle.

9   Carolina Quadrangle.

10   Oneco Quadrangle.

11   Quonochontaug Quadrangle.

12   North Sciutate Quadrangle.

13   Voluntown Quadrangle.

14   Watch Hill Quadrangle.

15   Chepachet Quadrangle.

*16   R. I. parts of Ashaway Quad. and Adjacent Areas of Connecticut.

17   Ground Water Map for Clayville Quadrangle.

18   R. I. Parts of Thompson and East Killingly Quadrangle.

19   R. I. parts of Attleboro, Franklin, Oxford, Uxbridge.

*20   Ground Water Map for Prudence Island-Newport Quadrangle.

*21   Tiverton, Sakonnet Point and R. I. portion of Westport.

GEOLOGICAL BULLETINS

1   Progress Report on Ground Water Resources of Providence.

2   Well & Test Hole Records of Providence.

3   Geology & Ground Water Resources of the Pawtucket Quadrangle.

4   Geology and Ground Water Resources of the Georgiaville Quadrangle.

5   Geology and Ground Water Resources of the Woonsocket Quadrangle.

6   Ground Water Resources of Rhode Island.

7   Ground Water Resources of Bristol Quadrangle, R. I., Mass.

8   Ground Water Resources of East Greenwich Quadrangle.

9   Ground Water Resources of Kingston Quadrangle.

10   Ground Water Resources of Providence Quadrangle.

11   Appraisal of the Ground Water Areas of Rhode Island.

12   Ground Water Resources in the Vicinity of Wallum Lake.

13   Geohydrological Data for the Upper Pawcatuck River.

14   Ground Water Resources of Block Island, Rhode Island.

HYDROLOGIC BULLETINS

1   Ground Water Levels in Rhode Island 1956.

2   Ground Water Levels in Rhode Island 1957.

2   Hydraulic Characteristics of Glacial Outwash in Rhode Island.

4   Ground Water Levels in Rhode Island 1958-1959.

5   Ground Water Levels in Rhode Island 1960-1962.

OTHER PUBLICATIONS

1   Inventory of Water Resources Reports.

2   Rhode Island Lakes and Ponds.

3   Rhode Island River Basins.

4   Rhode Island Public Water Systems.

5   Historical, Legal and Institutional Environment of Water and Related Land Resources in Rhode Island — (Section A — State Laws).

6   The Development of Basic Water Resources Laws and Policies in Rhode Island.

WATER RESOURCES POLICY COMMISSION

This Commission is no longer in existence.

*Report on the water resources of the State of Rhode Island, by Charles Maguire & Associates, Engineers. 1952. 330 p.

RHODE ISLAND WATER RESOURCES CENTER

University of Rhode Island
213 Crawford Hall
Kingston, Rhode Island 02881

Annual Report. October 1965 through October 1970. Various pagings.

Geophysical Resistivity Study of the Ground Water Characteristics of Glacial Deposits, Block Island, Rhode Island. 1967. 24 p.

SOUTH CAROLINA

DEPARTMENT OF PARKS, RECREATION AND TOURISM
Box 1358
Columbia, South Carolina 29202

South Carolina Recreational Guide. 1970. 127 p.

SOUTH CAROLINA STATE DEVELOPMENT BOARD
Division of Geology
P. O. Box 927
Columbia, South Carolina 29202

BULLETINS

*15   Progress Report on Ground-water Investigations in South Carolina.

*16B   Chemical Character of Surface Waters of South Carolina. (Revised 1956).

*16C   Chemical Character of Surface Waters of South Carolina. (Revised 1962).

*17   Surface Water Supply of South Carolina.

38   Ground Water Resources of Greenville County, South Carolina. $1.00.

MISCELLANEOUS REPORTS

MR-5 Ground Water Records of South Carolina. 1966.

SOUTH CAROLINA POLLUTION CONTROL AUTHORITY
1321 Lady Street
P. O. Box 11628
Columbia, South Carolina 29211

South Carolina Pollution Control Authority Rules and Regulations:

Regulation 1: Disposal Systems and Hearings Relating to Water Pollution Control. 1967. 2 p.

Regulation 2: A Regulation Requiring the Submission of Engineering Reports as a Part of Applications for the Discharge of Sewage and/or Industrial Wastes and for the Construction or Alteration of Treatment Works or Outlets or for the Increase of Load through Existing Treatment Works or Outlets. 1967. 3 p.

Water Classification-Standards System for the State of South Carolina. 8 p.

Twentieth Annual Report of the Pollution Control Authority, for the period ending June 30, 1969.

An Action Program for Clean Water. 1969. 80 p. This study was prepared cooperatively with the Federal Water Pollution Control Administration.

Roster of Certified Public Water and Wastewater Treatment Plant Operators. September 1969. 36 p. (South Carolina Board of Certification of Public Water and Wastewater Treatment Plant Operators.)

SOUTH CAROLINA WATER RESOURCES COMMISSION
2414 Bull Street
Columbia, South Carolina 29201

South Carolina Tidelands Report of 1970. 178 p. Price: $5.00.

High Resolution Seismic Survey of Port Royal Sound Area. 40 p.

Annual Report of State of South Carolina Water Resources Commission. Various pagings. (Last issue current.)

Proceedings, Governor's Conference on Water Resources. Issued annually. Various pagings. (last issue current.)

South Carolina Water Resources Supplemental Interim Report: Designated Appalachia Area. 150 p. Price: $5.00.

Index of Statutory Law: Ownership, Development, Management of the South Carolina Tidelands. 29 p.

Compilation of Tidelands Cases and Opinions — South Carolina. 38 p.

WATER RESOURCES RESEARCH INSTITUTE
Clemson University
Clemson, South Carolina 29631

REPORTS

1   First Annual South Carolina Governor's Conference on Water Resources. March 1967.

2   Prediction of the Rate of Soil Moisture Extraction by a Single Plant, by D. C. Kenyon and J. R. Lambert. February 1968. Based on Project B-001-SC.

3   South Carolina Law, Policies and Programs Pertaining to Water and Related Land Resources, by G. W. Dukes and J. M. Stepp. February 1968. Based on Project A-002-SC.

4   Conference Proceedings – Hydrology in Water Resources Management. March 1968.

5   Compilation of Water Resources Research in South Carolina. May 1968.

6   Bedrock Influence on Sediment Load of a Selected Hartwell Reservoir Tributary, by P. K. Birkhead and V. S. Griffin, Jr. July 1968. Based on Project A-004-SC.

7   Investigations of the Hydrology of the Root Zone, by J. T. Ligon, J. R. Lambert and R. Ahmed. Part A: Estimates of Field Infiltration into Layered Soils by Numerical Solutions of the Moisture Flow Equation. Part B: Evaluation of the Gamma Transmission Method for Determining Moisture Changes in the Root Zone. July 1968. Based on Project A-003-SC.

8   Water Use, Waste Treatment, Water Pollution and Related Economic Data on South Carolina Manufacturing Plants, by J. M. Stepp. August 1968.

9   Geology of Clemson Research Watershed, by J. R. Lambert, P. K. Birkhead, and T. V. Wilson. March 1969. Based on Project A-003-SC.

10   A Technique for Long Range Prediction of Streamflow, by Richard M. Greening and Albert G. Law. May 1969.

11   Feasibility Study of Electrical Geophysical Methods in the Determination of Subsurface Hydrogeologic Environments in the Piedmont Area of South Carolina, by Thomas L. Drake. July 1969. Based on Project A-011-SC.

12   Evaluation and Application of a Digital Hydrologic Simulation Model, by James T. Ligon, Albert G. Law and Donald H. Higgins. November 1969. Based on Project A-010-SC.

13   Interaction of Pesticide Pollutants and Aquatic Food-Chain Organisms, by John K. Reed. November 1969. Based on Project A-013-SC.

14   Physical, Meteorological, and Hydrologic Aspects of Evapotranspiration, by Jerry R. Lambert. March 1970.

15   Requirements and Costs of Alternative Systems for Treating Peach Cannery Wastes, by G. H. Liner and J. M. Stepp. April 1970. Based on Project A-002-SC.

16   Use of Taxes, Subsidies, and Regulations for Pollution Abatement, by Hugh H. Macaulay. June 1970. Based on Project B-004-SC.

SOUTH DAKOTA

SOUTH DAKOTA GEOLOGICAL SURVEY

Science Center
University of South Dakota
Vermillion, South Dakota 57069

The publications listed may be obtained by sending a request to the above address. Please make checks and money orders payable to the South Dakota Geological Survey.

Out of-print publications may be consulted in the office of the Geological Survey in Vermillion or Rapid City and in many public and technical libraries.

Notification of new reports and maps will be sent to anyone who requests to have his name placed on the announcement list. Include your zip code in all communications. Change of address should be reported promptly.

Add ten cents for packing and mailing for each order under $1.00. Add ten per cent for each order over $1.00.

Orders that are sent by special mail (first class, special delivery, etc.) at the request of the customer will be charged for at the prevailing rate for first-class mail or special delivery mail.

BULLETINS

Bulletins are detailed reports published to inform chiefly those persons in the geological sciences of the results and conclusions of field and laboratory studies which have been completed by the Geological Survey.

*5   Perisho, E. C., and Visher, S. S., 1912, A preliminary report upon the geography, geology, and biology of Mellette, Washabaugh, Bennett, and Todd Counties, south-central South Dakota, 152 p., 44 pls., 5 maps.

*8   Visher, S. S., 1918, Geography of South Dakota, 189 p., 52 figs.

16   U. S. Geological Survey, U. S. Bureau of Reclamation, and S. Dak. Geological Survey, 1964, Mineral and water resources of South Dakota, 295 p., 48 figs. Price: $1.00.

17   Steece, F. V., and Howells, L. W., Geology and ground-water supplies in Sanborn County, South Dakota.

   Part I: 1965, 182 p., 7 pls., 29 figs., 3 photos, 6 tables. Price: $2.00.

   Part II: 1968, Ground-water basic data, 203 p., 1 pl., 2 figs., 2 tables. Price: $2.00.

18   Hedges, Lynn S., Geology and water resources of Beadle County, South Dakota.

   Part I: 1968, Geology, 66 p., 12 figs., 5 pls., 2 photos, 3 tables. Price: $2.00.

   Part II: 1968, Water Resources, 58 p., 2 pls., 11 figs., 8 tables. Price: $2.00.

19   Christensen, Cleo M., and Stephens, Jerry C., Geology and hydrology of Clay County, South Dakota.

   Part I: 1967, Geology, 61 p., 4 pls., 16 figs., 5 tables. Price: $2.00.

   Part II: 1968, Water resources, 62 p., 4 pls., 11 figs., 4 tables. Price: $2.00.

20   Hedges, Lynn, and Koch, Neil C., Geology and Water Resources of Campbell County, South Dakota — Basic Data, Part III. Price: $2.00.

REPORTS OF INVESTIGATION

This series of reports is published to summarize the more important findings of field and laboratory work. These reports are issued because of their immediate interest for the public. The later detailed reports are published as bulletins.

4   Rothrock, E. P., 1936, Logs of some deep wells in western South Dakota, 107 p. Price: $0.75.

17   Rothrock, E. P., 1933, Water supplies and geology of Lake Kampeska, 11 p., 8 figs. Price: $0.75.

18   Rothrock, E. P., 1934, Water supplies of Fort Thompson, South Dakota, 10 p., 4 figs. Price: $0.75.

23   Rothrock, E. P., 1934, The geology of the Crow Creek Dam Site, 11 p., 5 figs. Price: $0.75.

*24   Rothrock, E. P., and Petsch, B. C., 1935, A shallow water supply for Huron, South Dakota, 13 p., 12 figs.

*25   Rothrock, E. P., 1935, The geology and water resources of Day County, South Dakota, 42 p., 10 figs., 2 maps.

*26   Rothrock, E. P., and Robinson, T. W., Jr., 1936, Artesian conditions in west-central South Dakota, 93 p., 3 maps.

30   Rothrock, E. P., and Ullery, Dorothy, 1938, Ground water fluctuations in eastern South Dakota, 29 p., 4 pls., 29 figs. Price: $0.75.

*32   Rothrock, E. P., 1939, Mineral products and Missouri River navigations in South Dakota, 10 p.

40   Rothrock, E. P., 1951, Sources of water supply for the city of Miller, South Dakota, 15 p., 3 pls., 1 fig. Price: $0.75.

*41   Rothrock, E. P., 1942, A hydrologic study of the White River valley, 32 p., 4 pls., 11 figs.

*56   Rothrock, E. P., and Otton, E. C., 1947, Ground water resources of the Sioux Falls area, South Dakota, Parts I and II, 110 p., 3 pls., 12 figs.

*59   Caddes, E. E., 1947, Ground water fluctuations in eastern South Dakota, 53 p., 15 figs.

71   Barkley, R. C., 1952, Artesian conditions in southeastern South Dakota, 71 p., 1 pl., 1 fig. Price: $0.75.

72 Barkley, R. C., 1953, Artesian conditions in the area surrounding the Sioux Quartzite Ridge, 68 p., 3 pls. Price: $0.75.

74 Erickson, H. D., 1954, Artesian conditions in east-central South Dakota, 116 p., 5 pls., 3 figs. Price: $0.75.

77 Erickson, H. D., 1955, Artesian conditions in northeastern South Dakota, 39 p., 3 pls. Price: $0.75.

78 Rothrock, E. P., 1955, Ground water reservoirs near Aberdeen, South Dakota, 47 p., 10 pls. Price: $0.75.

*80 Lee, K. Y., 1956, Geology and shallow water resources of the Blue Blanket Valley and Hoven Outwash, Potter County, South Dakota, 57 p., 3 pls., 12 figs.

81 Stoley, Aaron, 1956, A glacial outwash study in South Dakota (Delmont Outwash), 44 p., 5 pls., 1 fig. Price: $0.75.

*82 Tipton, M. J., 1957, Geology and hydrology of the Parker-Centerville Outwash, 52 p., 2 pls., 7 figs.

83 Lee, K. Y., 1957, Geology and shallow water resources between Hoven and Bowdle, South Dakota, 59 p., 3 pls., 4 figs. Price: $0.75.

84 Lee, K. Y., 1957, Geology and shallow ground water resources of the Brookings area, Brookings County, South Dakota, 62 p., 2 pls., 6 figs. Price: $0.75.

85 Steece, F. V., 1958, Geology and shallow ground water resources of the Watertown-Estelline area, South Dakota, 38 p., 2 pls., 6 figs. Price: $0.75.

86 Jorgensen, D. G., 1960, Geology and shallow ground water resources of the Missouri Valley between North Sioux City and Yankton, South Dakota, 59 p., 2 pls., 6 figs. Price: $0.75.

87 Lee, K. Y., and Powell, J. E., 1961, Geology and ground water resources of glacial deposits in the Flandreau area, 117 p., 3 pls., 3 figs. Price: $2.00.

89 Lum, Daniel, 1961, The resistivity method applied to ground water studies of glacial outwash deposits in eastern South Dakota, 24 p., 32 figs. Price: $1.50.

*90 Walker, I. R., 1961, Shallow ground water resources in the Wagner area, Charles Mix and Douglas Counties, South Dakota, 53 p., 2 pls., 12 figs.

CIRCULARS

This series of chiefly nontechnical reports provides scientific information about a subject of interest primarily for the lay reader.

16 Depts. of Geology, University of South Dakota and School of Mines, 1924, Natural resources of South Dakota, 28 p. Price: $0.25.

*29 Over, W. H., and Churchill, E. P., 1927, A preliminary report of a biological survey of the lakes of South Dakota, 18 p.

36 Schoon, R. A., 1968, Selected formation tops in water wells logged by the South Dakota Geological Survey to January 1, 1968, 28 p. Price: $1.00.

SPECIAL REPORTS

This series of reports is published to inform chiefly those people in city government of the results of water investigations made for them. The reports have limited distribution.

1 Steece, F. V., 1959, Water supply for the city of Eureka, 22 p., 1 pl., 4 figs. Price: $0.25.

2 Tipton, M. J., 1959, Geology of the shallow water supply at Madison, South Dakota, 11 p., 1 pl., 1 fig. Price: $0.25.

*3 Tipton, M. J., 1959, Shallow water supply for the city of Viborg, South Dakota, 4 p., 1 pl.

*4 Tipton, M. J., 1960, Shallow water supply near Huron, South Dakota, 15 p., 3 pls., 1 fig.

*5 Jorgensen, D. G., 1960, Geology and ground water resources at Ethan, South Dakota, 19 p., 5 figs.

*6 Jorgensen, D. G., 1960, Geology and ground water resources at Howard, South Dakota, 21 p., 6 figs.

*7 Wong, H. D., 1960, Shallow water supply for the city of Resholt, 16 p., 3 figs.

*8 Wong, H. D., 1960, Shallow water supply for the city of Clark, 13 p., 2 figs.

9 Wong, H. D., 1960, Shallow water supply for the city of Shelby, 19 p., 3 figs. Price: $0.25.

*10 Tipton, M. J., 1960, Shallow water supply for the city of Parker, 15 p., 3 figs.

*11 Tipton, M. J., 1960, Shallow water supply for the city of Ft. Pierre, 13 p., 3 figs.

*12 Tipton, M. J., 1960, Shallow water supply for the city of Sisseton, 22 p., 3 figs.

13 Bruce, R. L., 1962, Shallow water supply for the city of Tyndall, 23 p., 4 figs. Price: $0.25.

14 Christensen, C. M., 1962, Shallow water supply for the city of Faulkton, 23 p., 5 figs. Price: $0.25.

15 Hedges, L. S., 1962, Water supply for the city of Lake Preston, 24 p., 4 figs., Price: $0.25.

16 Bruce, R. L., 1962, Water supply for the city of Menno, 24 p., 5 figs. Price: $0.25.

17 Christensen, C. M., 1962, Water supply for the city of Miller, 23 p., 5 figs. Price: $0.25.

18 Christensen, C. M., 1962, Water supply for the city of Burke, 13 p., 3 figs. Price: $0.25.

19 Cox, E. J., 1962, Artesian water, Minnelusa and Pahasapa Formations, Spearfish-Belle Fourche area, 17 p., 2 pls., 3 figs. Price: $1.50.

20 Christensen, C. M., 1963, Water supply for the city of Scotland, 27 p., 6 figs. Price: $0.25.

21 Bruce, R. L., 1963, Water supply for the city of Vermillion, 30 p., 9 figs. Price: $0.25.

22 Baker, G. K., 1963, Water supply for the city of Beresford, 34 p., 5 figs. Price: $0.25.

23 Rukstad, L. R., 1963, Water supply for the city of Lesterville, 16 p., 3 figs. Price: $0.25.

24 Christensen, C. M., 1963, Water supply for the city of Redfield, 32 p., 4 figs., Price: $0.25.

25 Baker, G. K., 1963, Water supply for the city of Claremont, 23 p., 4 figs. Price: $0.25.

26 McMeen, J. A., 1964, Ground water supply for the city of Harrisburg, 27 p., 4 figs. Price: $0.25.

27 McMeen, J. A., 1964, Ground water supply for the city of Marion, 33 p., 5 figs. Price: $0.25.

28 Rukstad, L. R., and Hedges, L. S., 1964, Ground water supply for the city of Watertown, 32 p., 5 figs. Price: $0.25.

29 Wood, Allan, and Hedges, L. S., 1964, Ground water supply for the city of Langford, 27 p., 4 figs. Price: $0.25.

30 Rukstad, L. R., and Hedges, L. S., 1964, Ground water supply for the city of Bowdle, 28 p., 6 figs. Price: $0.25.

31 McMeen, J. A., 1965, Ground water supply for the city of Canton, 40 p., 4 figs. Price: $0.25.

32 Pottratz, S. W., 1965, Ground water supply for the city of Ipswich, 37 p., 5 figs. Price: $0.25.

33 McMeen, J. A., 1965, Ground water supply for the city of Britton, 34 p., 6 figs. Price: $0.25.

34 Jorgensen, D. G., 1965, Ground water supply for the city of Lake Norden, 37 p., 6 figs., 2 tables. Price: $0.25.

35 Jorgensen, D. G., 1965, Ground water supply for the city of Bryant, 33 p., 5 figs., 1 table. Price: $0.25.

36 Barari, Assad, 1965, Ground water supply for the city of Winner, 30 p., 6 figs., 2 tables. Price: $0.25.

37 Shurr, George W., 1966, Ground water supply for the city of Lake Andes, 23 p., 8 figs., 3 tables. Price: $0.25.

38 Steece, Fred V., and Shurr, George W., 1966, Ground water supply for the city of Wessington Springs, 15 p., 6 figs., 2 tables. Price: $0.25.

39 Barari, Assad, 1967, Ground water supply for the city of Dell Rapids, 21 p., 6 figs., 3 tables. Price: $0.25.

40 Beffort, J. D., and Hedges, Lynn S., 1967, Ground water supply for the city of Waubay, 20 p., 8 figs., 1 table. Price: $0.25.

41 Barari, Assad, 1967, Ground water supply for the city of Mission, 15 p., 5 figs., 2 tables. Price: $0.25.

42 Barari, Assad, 1967, Ground water supply for the city of Mitchell, 14 p., 4 figs., 1 table. Price: $0.25.

43 Beffort, J. D., and Christenson, C. M., 1968, Ground water supply for the city of Viborg, 44 p., 5 figs., 1 table. Price: $0.25.

44 [Water supply for the city of] Gettysburg. Price: $0.25.

45 Barari, Assad, 1968, Ground water supply for the city of Brookings, 51 p., 5 figs., 4 tables. Price: $0.25.

46 [Water supply for the city of] Lennox. Price: $0.25.

48 [Water supply for the city of] Colome. Price: $0.25.

49 [Water supply for the city of] Gregory. Price: $0.25.

50 [Water supply for the city of] Columbia. Price: $0.25.

BIENNIAL REPORTS

Report of the State Geologist. Biennial. 1913-1914, 1918-1920, 1922-1924 and to date (1968). Price: $0.10 each except for 1924-1926, 1930-1932, and 1957-1958 which are out of print.

BASIC DATA REPORTS

This series of reports, published in cooperation with the State Water Resources Commission and U. S. Geological Survey, presents the basic data of water investigations.

1 Hopkins, W. B., and Petri, L. A., 1962, Data on wells and test holes, and chemical analysis of ground water in the Lake Dakota Plain area, Brown, Marshall, and Spink Counties, South Dakota, 269 p. Price: $2.50.

2 McGuinness, C. L., 1962, Water in South Dakota, 33 p. Price: $0.20.

3 Adolphson, D. G., and Ellis, M. J., 1964, Basic hydro-geologic data, Skunk Creek-Lake Madison drainage basin, South Dakota, 70 p., 1 pl., 1 fig. Price: $1.00.

4 Pine Ridge Indian Reservation. Price: $1.00.

5 Big Sioux Drainage Basin, eastern South Dakota. Price: $1.25.

MISCELLANEOUS INVESTIGATIONS

This series of reports has been discontinued.

*4 Agnew, A. F., Tipton, M. J., and Steece, F. V., 1962, South Dakota's ground water needs and supplies, 9 p., 17 figs.

5 Hedges, L. S., 1962, Shallow water supply for the city of Wakpala, 17 p., 4 illus. Price: $0.20.

OTHER REPORTS

This series of reports has been discontinued.

2 Lee, K. Y., 1957, The water supply near Selby, Walworth County, South Dakota, 7 p., 2 pls., 2 figs. Price: $0.20.

3 Lee, K. Y., 1957, The water supply at Mound City, Campbell County, South Dakota, 15 p., 2 figs., Price: $0.20.

SOUTH DAKOTA STATE CONSERVATION COMMISSION
State Capitol
Pierre, South Dakota 57501

History of South Dakota's Conservation Districts. 1969. 230 p.

Biennial Report of the State Conservation Commission. 1936-1938, 1938-1940, etc., to 1968-1970.

Bi-monthly Newsletter. Published in cooperation with the State Association of Conservation Districts.

STATE DEPARTMENT OF HEALTH

Division of Sanitary Engineering
Pierre, South Dakota 57501

Sewage Stabilization Ponds in the Dakotas — An Evaluation of the Use of Stabilization Ponds as a Method of Sewage Disposal in Cold Climates. 1957. 87 p.

Sewage Stabilization Ponds in South Dakota. 1958. 19 p.

Laws Relating to Water Pollution. 1970. 4 p.

SOUTH DAKOTA STATE LEGISLATIVE RESEARCH COUNCIL

State Capitol
Pierre, South Dakota 57501

*Meandered Lakes. Staff Report No. 10. February 26, 1960. 8 p.

*Study of Parks and Recreational Facilities in South Dakota. (Background and Proposed Methodology). Staff Memorandum. October 6, 1961. 25 p.

*Study of Unification and Clarification of Certain Terms and Procedures Used in South Dakota's Conservation and Water Statutes. Staff Memorandum. January 9, 1962. 16 p.

*Study of Status of Any Possible Changes Needed in South Dakota Conservancy District Act. (Background and Proposed Methodology). Staff Memorandum. January 10, 1962. 9 p.

*Contract Approval Provisions of the South Dakota Conservancy District Act. Staff Memorandum. May 18, 1964. 14 p.

*Considerations Involving the Use of Ground Water in South Dakota. Staff Memorandum. November 1, 1969. 42 p.

SOUTH DAKOTA STATE PLANNING BOARD

Pierre
South Dakota 57501

*Water Resources of South Dakota. Brookings: The Board, Central Office. 1935. Mimeo. 69 p.

*Artesian Well Control. September 16, 1935. 26 p.

*Recommendations of the South Dakota State Planning Board to the Emergency Drouth Conference. November 15, 1936. 14 p.

*South Dakota Laws Pertaining to Irrigation and Irrigation Districts. May 5, 1937. 49 p.

*Supplementary Irrigation in Western South Dakota. June 30, 1937. 50 p.

*Artesian Well Flow in South Dakota. Brookings: The Board, Central Office. 1937. Mimeo. 138 p.

*Dams in South Dakota. Brookings: The Board, Central Office. 1937. Mimeo. 179 p.

*Stock Water in Western South Dakota. Brookings: The Board, Central Office. 1937. Mimeo. 18 p.

*Water Resources of the Bad River Drainage Basin. Brookings: The Board, Central Office. 1937. Mimeo. 58 p.

*Water Resources of the Big Sioux River Drainage Basin. Brookings: The Board, Central Office. 1937. Mimeo. 87 p.

*Water Resources of the Cheyenne River Drainage Basin. Brookings: The Board, Central Office. 1937. Mimeo. 108 p.

*Water Resources of the Grand River Drainage Basin. Brookings: The Board, Central Office. 1937. Mimeo. 50 p.

*Water Resources of the James River Drainage Basin. Brookings: The Board, Central Office. 1937. Mimeo. 129 p.

*Water Resources of the Keya-Ponca River Drainage Basin. Brookings: The Board, Central Office. 1937. Mimeo. 36 p.

*Water Resources of the Little Missouri River Drainage Basin. Brookings: The Board, Central Office. 1937. Mimeo. 44 p.

*Water Resources of the Minnesota River Drainage Basin. Brookings: The Board, Central Office. 1937. Mimeo. 44 p.

*Water Resources of the Missouri River Drainage Basin. Brookings: The Board, Central Office. 1937. Mimeo. 95 p.

*Water Resources of the Moreau River Drainage Basin. Brookings: The Board, Central Office. 1937. Mimeo. 53 p.

*Water Resources of the Vermillion River Drainage Basin. Brookings: The Board, Central Office. 1937. Mimeo. 53 p.

*Water Resources of the White River Drainage Basin. Brookings: The Board, Central Office. 1937. Mimeo. 69 p.

SOUTH DAKOTA WATER RESOURCES COMMISSION

State Office Building No. 2
Pierre, South Dakota 57501

Note: These publications are available at no charge, but the supply of each is limited.

Quality of Water in Selected Lakes of Eastern South Dakota, 55 p.

Observation Well Report, 1966, 45 p.

Water Resources Commission Biennial Reports for Years: 1958-1960; 1960-62; 1962-64; 1964-66; 1966-68; 1968-70.

State of South Dakota Water Laws pertaining to the following:
   Conservancy Districts, Water Rights, Watersheds, and Irrigation Districts.

1968 and 1969 Irrigation Questionnaire.

Map: Surface and Groundwater Source and Irrigation Development — 32 x 44 inches.

WATER RESOURCES
RESEARCH INSTITUTE
South Dakota State University
University Station
Brookings, South Dakota 57006

Methods for Rapid Identification and Enumeration of *Streptococcus Bovis* from Water, by L. Koupal, M.S. Thesis, 1969, 53 p. OWRR Project A-019-SDAK.

Survival of Fecal Coliforms and Fecal *Streptococci* in River Water, by J. Zerfas, M.S. Thesis, 1969, 84 p. OWRR Project A-019-SDAK.

An Investigation of the Pollutional Characteristics of Runoff from Two Feedlots, by Paul E. Thormodsgard, M.S. Thesis, 1970, 74 p. OWRR Project A-025-SDAK.

Automatic Irrigation: Sensors and Systems, by Herman Hamre, M.S. Thesis, 1970, 62 p. OWRR Project A-024-SDAK.

Digital Data Multiplexer for Irrigation Data Transmission, by Steve Schultz, Special Problem Report, 1970. OWRR Project A-024-SDAK.

Ecological Distribution of Pesticides in Lake Poinsett, South Dakota, by Yvonne A. Greichus, M. R. Hannon, R. L. Applegate, and A. C. Fox, Trans-American Fisheries Society, July 1970. 496-500 p. OWRR Project B-002-SDAK.

Feedlot Pollution: A Solvable Problem?, by James Dornbush and John Madden, South Dakota Farm & Home Research, Agricultural Experiment Station, Vol. XXI, No. 2, Spring 1970, p. 30-31.

Infiltration Lagoons as a Tertiary Treatment Device, by Terry L. Druyvestein, M.S. Thesis, 1970, 64 p. OWRR Project A-016-SDAK.

The Influence of an Unusually High Water Table on Groundwater Quality at a Refuse Disposal Site, by Charles Stock Johnson III, M.S. Thesis, 1970, 76 p. OWRR Project A-016-SDAK.

Irrigation Water Quality vs. Rate of Salt and Alkali Accumulation, by John Madden, ASAE Winter Meeting, December 1970. 15 p. OWRR Project A-020-SDAK.

Pollution Potential of Livestock Feeding Operations in South Dakota, by James N. Dornbush, proceedings from the South Dakota Agriculture and Water Quality Symposium on Water Pollution, March 17, 1970, p. 37-46. OWRR Project A-025-SDAK.

Redfield Soil Samples to SDSU for Research, by Maurice L. Norton, South Dakota Farm & Home Research, Vol. XXI, Winter 1970, p. 4-7. OWRR Project B-004-SDAK.

Role of Plant Canopies in Evapotranspiration, by M. L. Namken, and J. T. Ritchie, Proceedings of a Great Plains Evapotransporation Seminar, Bushland, Texas, March 23-25, 1970, 38 p. OWRR Project A-018-SDAK.

Seek Data in Feedlot Research, by James Dornbush and John Madden, South Dakota Farm & Home Research, Agricultural Experiment Station, Vol. XXI, No. 2, Spring 1970, p. 22-27. OWRR Project A-025-SDAK.

Sensitivity Analysis of the SDSU River Basin Model, by Kunjipalu Thoppil, M.S. Thesis, 1970, 69 p. OWRR Project A-014-SDAK.

Time of Base for Watersheds in Eastern South Dakota, by S. T. Chu and William F. Lytle, Winter Meeting of ASAE, December 1970, 13 p. OWRR Project A-023-SDAK.

Analysis of the Flow Variation of the Big Sioux River, by Kerwin L. Rakness, M.S. Thesis, 89 p. OWRR Project B-005-SDAK.

Dissolved Oxygen Concentration of the Big Sioux River Downstream from Sioux Falls, South Dakota, During Winter Conditions, by Bernard Poppenga, M.S. Thesis, 48 p. OWRR Project B-005-SDAK.

A Geologic Study of the Chemical Quality of Medicine Lake, by Merlin Tipton. Completion Report A-022-SDAK.

Influence of Low Rates of Water Application by Sprinklers on the Microclimate, by John L. Wiersma. Completion Report A-006-SDAK.

TENNESSEE

TENNESSEE DEPARTMENT OF CONSERVATION
Division of Geology
G5 State Office Building
Nashville, Tennessee 37219

Requests for publications should be directed to the above address. Remittance should accompany all orders.

Publications out of print are on file in many of the larger university libraries throughout the nation, at the Tennessee Division of Geology office in Nashville, and in libraries of state geological surveys in other states. Out-of-print reports can be reproduced by the Tennessee Division of Geology for $0.10 per page.

BULLETINS

*1 B Bibliography of Tennessee Geology, Soils, Drainage, Forestry, Etc., 117 p., by Elizabeth Cockrill (1911).

*3 A Drainage Problems in Tennessee, 10 p., by Geo. H. Ashley (1910).

* B Preliminary Report Upon the Drainage of the Lands Overflowed by the North and Middle Forks of the Forked Deer River and the Rutherford Fork of the Obion River in Gibson County, Tennessee, 26 p., by A. E. Morgan and S. H. McCrory (1910).

* C Drainage Law of Tennessee, 28 p. (1910).

*17 The Water Power of Tennessee (including a report on Doe River by A. H. Horton), 137 p., by J. A. Switzer (1914).

*20 The Larger Undeveloped Water-Powers of Tennessee, 35 p., by J. A. Switzer (1918).

30 A Study of Some of the Smaller Undeveloped Water Powers of Tennessee, 24 p., 36 pls., J. A. Switzer (1923). Price: $0.50.

34 Water Resources of Tennessee, 909 + xvi p., 31 pls., 6 figs., W. R. King (1925). Price: $0.50.

37 Geology and Mineral Resources of Hardin County, Tennessee, 117 p., 9 pls. (including geologic map), 3 figs., W. B. Jewell (1931). Price: $1.00.

40 Surface Waters of Tennessee, 165 + xii p., 28 tables, 21 pls., 35 figs., W. R. King (1931). Price: $0.50.

*42 Preliminary Report on the Artesian Water Supply of Memphis, Tennessee, 34 + iv p., by F. G. Wells (1931).

43 Ground Water in North-Central Tennessee, 238 + viii p., 9 pls., 7 figs., A. M. Piper (1932). Price: $0.50.

44 Ground-Water Resources of Western Tennessee, 319 + vii p., 16 pls., 18 figs., F. G. Wells (1933). Price: $0.50.

46 Ground Water in South-Central Tennessee, 182 + v p., 7 pls., 2 figs., C. V. Theis (1936). Price: $0.50.

58 pt 1 Ground-Water Resources of East Tennessee, 393 + x p., 15 pls., 1 fig., 83 tables, by G. D. DeBuchananne and R. M. Richardson (1956). Text and maps (not available separately). Price: $3.50.

61 Geology, Mineral Resources, and Ground Water of the Cleveland Area, Tennessee, 125 + v p., 8 figs., 5 pls., 6 tables, by George D. Swingle (1959). Price: $2.50.

62 Well Logs in Tennessee, 606 p., 1 pl., compiled by H. C. Milhous (1959). Price: $4.00.

REPORTS OF INVESTIGATIONS

1 Geologic Source and Chemical Quality of Public Ground-Water Supplies in Western Tennessee, 69 p., by C. R. Lanphere (1955). Price: $0.25.

4 Ground Water in the Central Basin of Tennessee, 81 + v p., by Roy Newcome, Jr. (1958). Price: $1.00.

7 Geology and Ground-Water Resources of the Dyersburg Quadrangle, Tennessee, 61 p., 10 figs., 3 pls., 5 tables, by Raymond L. Schreurs and Melvin V. Marcher (1959). Price: $1.50.

20 Well Sample Descriptions and Drillers' Logs, Morgan County, Tennessee, 175 p., by H. B. Burwell (1967). Price: $1.00.

21 Well Sample Descriptions and Drillers' Logs, Scott County, Tennessee, 201 p., by H. B. Burwell (1967). Price: $1.00.

26 Stratigraphy of the Fort Pillow Test Well, Lauderdale County, Tennessee, by Gerald K. Moore and Donald L. Brown (1969). Price: $1.00.

INFORMATION CIRCULARS

4 Irrigation in Tennessee in 1955. 7 p., by E. M. Cushing and R. M. Richardson (1957).

RESOURCES OF TENNESSEE (1st Series)

Volume I. 1911

*No. 1 The Utilization of the Small Water Powers in Tennessee, 18 p., by J. A. Switzer and G. H. Ashley.

 *Studies of Underground Water Supplies, 3 p.

*No. 5 The Watauga Power Company's Hydro-Electric Development, 6 p., by F. R. Weller.

Volume II. 1912.

*No. 1 The Utilization of Tennessee's Navigable Streams, 8 p., by G. H. Ashley.

*Tennessee to Have Another Great Water Power, 4 p., by George Byrne.

*No. 2 The Ocoee River Power Development, 6 p., by J. A. Switzer.

*No. 3 The Power Development at Hale's Bar, 14 p., by J. A. Switzer.

*No. 4 The Preliminary Consideration of Water Power Projects, 24 p., by J. A. Switzer.

*No. 6 On the Impounding of Waters to Prevent Floods, 5 p., by A. H. Purdue.

*Drainage Problems of Wolf, Hatchie, and South Fork of Forked Deer Rivers in West Tennessee, 19 p., by L. L. Hidinger and A. E. Morgan.

Volume III. 1913.

*No. 2 Conservation of the Water Powers of Tennessee, 6 p., by J. A. Switzer.

*Water Supply for Cities and Towns, 4 p., by A. H. Purdue.

*No. 3 The Relation of Water Supply to Health, 6 p., by J. A. Switzer.

Volume IV. 1914.

*No. 1 The Relation of Water Supply to Health, 12 p., by J. A. Switzer.

*No. 3 Recent Water Power Developments in Tennessee, 11 p., by J. A. Switzer.

Volume V. 1915.

*No. 1 The Operation of the Hydro-Electric System of Tennessee, 5 p., by J. A. Switzer.

MISCELLANEOUS CHARTS

1   Ground-Water Investigations – Subsurface Geologic Cross Section from Claybrook, Madison County to Memphis, Shelby County, Tennessee, by Robert Schneider and R. R. Blankenship (1950).

5   Ground-Water Investigations – Structure Contour Map on Top of the Knox Dolomite in Middle Tennessee, size 19 x 26 inches, by Roy Newcome, Jr. (1954). Contour interval 100 feet. Prepared in cooperation with the U. S. Geological Survey. Price: $0.25.

TENNESSEE DEPARTMENT OF CONSERVATION

Division of Water Resources
2611 West End Avenue
Nashville, Tennessee 37203

HYDROLOGIC ATLAS SERIES

HA-1 Summary of the Ground-Water Resources of Madison County, Tennessee: by Dale J. Nyman and Gerald K. Moore, 1963, 7 p.

HA-2 Well Water for Home Supplies in Montgomery County, Tennessee: by Roy H. Bingham, and Gerald K. Moore, 1963, 8 p.

HA-3 Well Water for Home Supplies in Lewis County, Tennessee: by Roy H. Bingham, 1964, 10 p.

HA-4 Water for Industry in Montgomery County, Tennessee: by W. J. Perry and Gerald K. Moore, 1965, 16 p.

MISCELLANEOUS PUBLICATIONS

MP-1 Public Water Policy in Tennessee: by Public Administration Service, 1956, 175 p.

MP-2 Interagency Report on Water Resources Activities in Tennessee: Edited by Edward Nave, 1962, 115 p.

MP-3 Tributary River Basins in Tennessee: by J. S. Cragwall, Jr., 1963, 8 p.

MP-4 Bibliography of Ground Water Investigations in Tennessee: by John M. Wilson, 1967, 18 p.

MP-5 Tennessee Water Well Contractors, Including The Tennessee Drillers Act: coordinated by Ollie Smith, Jr., 1970, 20 p.

WATER RESOURCES RESEARCH

WRR-1 Limestone Hydrology in the Upper Stones River Basin, Central Tennessee: by Gerald K. Moore, Charles R. Burchett, and Roy H. Bingham, 1969, 58 p.

WRR-2 Chemical Quality of Streams Draining the Central Basin of Tennessee: by Arthur L. Reesman and Andrew E. Godfrey, 1970, 74 p.

WRR-3 Hydrology, Geology and Erosion by Leaching in Skillman Basin on the Western Highland Rim, Lawrence County, Tennessee: by Richard G. Stearns and John M. Wilson, 1970, 60 p.

WATER RESOURCES SERIES

*WRS-1 Ground Water Resources of the Cumberland Plateau in Tennessee: by Roy Newcome, Jr., and Ollie Smith, Jr., 1958, 70 p.

*WRS-2 Tennessee's Water Resources: edited by Edward Nave, 1961, 128 p.

WRS-3 Impoundment of the Harpeth River: coordinated by Ollie Smith, Jr., 1961, 83 p.

*WRS-4 Ground Water Resources and Municipal Water Supplies of the Highland Rim in Tennessee: by Ollie Smith, Jr., 1962, 257 p.

WRS-5 Geology and Ground Water Resources of the Knox Dolomite in Middle Tennessee: by Roy Newcome, Jr., and Ollie Smith, Jr., 1962, 43 p.

WRS-6 Ground Water Resources and Geology of Cumberland County, Tennessee: by John M. Wilson, 1965, 56 p., 3 maps.

WRS-7 Geohydrology of Henry and Weakley Counties, Tennessee: by John M. Wilson and James H. Criner, 1969, 90 p., 1 pl.

WRS-8 Water Resources in the upper Stones River Basin, Tennessee: by Charles R. Burchett and Gerald K. Moore, 1970, 75 p.

WATER USE SERIES

WU-1 Irrigation in Tennessee, 1958: by Claiborne K. Mclemore, 1958, 16 p.

WU-2 Water Use in Tennessee: Part A–Agricultural Water Use: by A. M. F. Johnson, John M. Wilson, and H. B. Nichols, 1968, 34 p.

WU-3 Water Use in Tennessee: Part B–Industrial Water Use: by John M. Wilson, H. B. Nichols, and A. M. F. Johnson, 1969, 22 p.

WU-4 Water Use in Tennessee: Part C–Municipal Water Use: by A. M. F. Johnson and John M. Wilson, 1970, 64 p.

WU-5 Water Use in Tennessee: Part D–Summary: by John M. Wilson and A. M. F. Johnson, 1970, 28 p.

STATE LEGISLATIVE COUNCIL COMMITTEE

State Capitol
Nashville, Tennessee 37219

This Committee is no longer in existence

Tennessee's Water Resources and Related Lands: A Summary Report. 1962. 34 p. David H. Grubbs, Director of the Study. (No. FR 1962 – B13A).

Tennessee's Water Resources and Related Lands: Final Report. 1962. 219 p. David H. Grubbs, Director of the Study. (No. FR 1962 – B13).

TENNESSEE STATE PLANNING COMMISSION

C2-208 Central Services Building
Nashville, Tennessee 37219

Requests for publications or inquiries should include reference to the publication's number and title and should be directed to the above address. Xeroxed copies of out-of-print items will be prepared on request at $0.20 per page.

*5 Rutherford County: Location, Soils, Streams and Water. n. d. (1935?), 26 p., typed.

*18 Drainage Enterprises in the Obion River Watersheds and Suggestions for Study of Their Present Problem. June 1935, 10 p., typed, map.

*31 Obion River and Forked Deer River Watersheds. A Report on Drainage Enterprises and Land Conditions within the Area. March 1936, 17 p., maps.

*38 Comprehensive Report of the Cumberland River Drainage Basin. (Prepared for the National Resources Committee.) September 1936, 74 p., typed, tables.

*44 A Report Upon the Specific Drainage Problem of the South Fork of the Forked Deer River in Dyer and Lauderdale Counties. December 1936, 13 p., mimeo, 5 charts.

*59 Original Drainage Law of Tennessee. (With Amendments and Additions as Published in Williams and Shannon Code of 1932 and in Public Acts of Tennessee of 1933 and 1935.) February 1937, 49 p., mimeo.

*61 The Cumberland River. February 1937, 10 p., typed, tables.

*66 Water Resources of the Cumberland River Drainage Basin. April 1937, 68 p., mimeo, maps, tables.

*75 The Lakes of Tennessee. July 1937, 148 p., mimeo, map, bibliog.

*78 Park, Parkway and Recreational-Area Study of Tennessee. March 1938, 127 p., typed, maps, charts. (In cooperation with the Dept. of Conservation and the National Park Service.)

*85 Tennessee Electric Power Analysis, 1932-1937. (seven Major Companies') J. D. Goeltz, Bureau of Business Research, University of Tennessee in cooperation with Tennessee State Planning Commission. July 1938, 47 p., typed, tables, graphs.

*103 A Tentative and Preliminary Report on the Proposed Conversion of Portions of the West Tennessee Lowland into a National Forest. December 1938, 56 p., typed.

*120 The Park, Parkway and Recreational Area Study of Tennessee. A Preliminary Report. January 1939, 20 p., maps.

*130 Recreation Legislation of Tennessee. July 1939, 40 p., mimeo.

*144 County by County Compilation of Resources. (With a Preliminary Analysis of Industrial Opportunities for the Three Grand Divisions of Tennessee.) July 1943, 95 p., multilithed, maps.

*150 Towers of Power Back Industrial Opportunities in Tennessee, First Public Power State. 1944, 20 p., map. (In cooperation with Tennessee Department of Conservation.)

*153 Industrial Resources of Tennessee. May 1945, 224 p., maps, charts, tables.

*163 The Changing Geography of the Valley of the Tennessee. May 1946, 8 p., charts. (Reprinted from the Tennessee Planner, April 1946.)

*165 Planning Water and Sewerage Systems for the Small Community. October 1946, 37 p., multilithed.

*196 Water Supplies, Fuels, Electric Power and Transportation Facilities. Volume 3 of Industrial Resources of Tennessee. Revised edition, 1948. December 1948, 59 p.

*204 Sanitary Service Charges in Tennessee. Revised edition. July 1949, 83 p., multilithed.

*226 Sanitary Service Charges in Tennessee, 1950-51. September 1951, 113 p.

*233 Not Yet Too Late: A Study of Public Recreation and Needed Recreation Lands in the Chattanooga-Hamilton County Area. March 1952. 40 p. Price: $0.50.

*234 Master Plan for Recreation: Murfreesboro, Tennessee. February 1952, 56 p.

*241 A Guide to Community Growth: General Land Use Plan, Johnson City, Tennessee. September 1952, 29 p.

*243 State Parks – A Proposed Program for Tennessee. November 1952, 45 p.

*251 Sanitary Service Charges in Tennessee, 1953. May 1953 115 p.

*252 Planning for Recreation – A Guide for Tennessee Communities. June 1953, 37 p.

*260 Sanitary Service Charges in Tennessee, 1955. July 1955, 106 p.

262 Flood Problems and Their Solution Through Urban Planning Programs. September 1955, 48 p. Price: $1.00.

277 Flood Damage Prevention, Lewisburg, Tennessee. June 1957, 45 p. Price: $1.00.

*281 Sanitary Service Charges in Tennessee, 1957. December 1957, 162 p.

*286 A Recreation Plan for Lewis County, Tennessee. May 1958, 67 p.

*288 Reservoir Shore Line Development in Tennessee: A Study of Problems and Opportunities. August 1958, 77 p.

*291 Reelfoot Plan for Comprehensive Development. October 1958, 85 p.

*295 Report on the Effects of Barkley Reservoir and Cross Creeks National Wildlife Refuge on Stewart County, Tennessee. May 1959, 51 p.

*296 Sanitary Service Charges in Tennessee, 1959. July 1959, 96 p.

302 A Guide to Flood Damage Prevention. November 1959. Price: $1.00.

*309 Flood Damage Prevention for Tennessee. November 1960, 100 p.

*310 Melton Hill Reservoir: Comprehensive Plan for Land Use Development. December 1960, 92 p.

*311 The Tennessee River Gorge: Its Scenic Preservation. January 1961, 104 p.

— Final Report: Water Resources and Related Lands Study, 1962. State of Tennessee, Legislative Council Committee (200 p). Price: $0.20 per page or contact Legislations Council Librarian, State Capitol, Nashville, Tennessee 37219.

— A Program for the Preservation and Development of Industrial Areas along Tennessee's Waterways, May 1962. 20 p., available. (Published by State-Local Waterfront Industrial Site Committee).

*316 Sanitary Service Charges in Tennessee, 1961. September 1961, 50 p.

*320 Municipal and County Recreation in Tennessee, Part I. August 1962, 96 p.

*322 Public Outdoor Recreation Resources in Tennessee, Part II, Vol. I. October 1962, 17 p.

*323 Public Outdoor Recreation Resources in Tennessee, Part II, Vol. 2. October 1962, 251 p.

326 Sanitary Services in Tennessee, 1963. August 1963, 65 p. Price: $2.00.

331A Tennessee – Its Resources and Economy. Vol. I, The Tennessee Economy. February 1965, 43 p. Price: $2.00.

331B Tennessee – Its Resources and Economy. Vol. II, Tennessee's Natural Resources. September 1966, 76 p. Price: $2.00.

331C Tennessee – Its Resources and Economy. Vol. III, Tennessee's Outdoor Recreation Resources. April 1968, 56 p. Price: $2.00.

335 Nickajack Land Use Study. August 1965, 88 p. Price: $1.00.

339 Sanitary Services in Tennessee, 1965. December 1965, 70 p. Price: $2.00.

343 Comprehensive Plan for Development Vol. II, Kentucky Reservoir Region. October 1964, 153 p.

344 Comprehensive Plan for Development Vol. I, Kentucky Reservoir Region. October 1964, 469 p.

347 The Economic Geography of Tennessee Part A, Chapter I, A Statewide Population and Economic Base Study. December 1965, 65 p.

*349 Jellico Strip Mine Reclamation Project. May 1966, 24 p.

352 Beech River Watershed Development Plan and Program Proposals. March 1965, 143 p.

362 Sanitary Services in Tennessee, 1967. November 1967, 79 p.

383 Sanitary Services in Tennessee, 1970. December 1970, 96 p. Price: $2.00.

TENNESSEE STREAM POLLUTION CONTROL BOARD

621 Cordell Hull Building
Nashville, Tennessee 37219

Address all requests to the attention of the Executive Secretary.

Stream Pollution Control Law. 4 p.

General Regulations, Stream Pollution Control Board. 4 p.

General Water Quality Criteria. 7 p.

Water Pollution Control Policies of Tennessee. 1 p.

Regulations for the Control of Pollution from Boats and Floating Facilities. 3 p.

List of the Approved Types of Treatment Devices and Holding Tanks for Use on Boats and Floating Facilities. 1 p.

Fort Loudoun Reservoir Stream Investigation, 1963. 7 p.

Fresh-Water Coelenterates in Tennessee, 1962. 6 p.

Report of Stream Survey South Chickamauga Creek, Hamilton County, 1957. 14 p.

Occurrence of Bryozoa in Tennessee, 1963. 10 p.

Furthur Studies on the Introduced Asiatic Clam Corbicula in Tennessee, 1963. 75 p.

Stream Pollution Control in the Duck River Basin, 1964. 25 p.

Stream Pollution Control in the Hatchie River Basin, 1964. 28 p.

Stream Pollution Control Survey South Fork Holston River Kingsport Area, 1958. 66 p.

Stream Pollution Survey of the Chattanooga Area, 1964. 94 p.

Interstate Stream Pollution Survey, Chattanooga Area, 1965. 17 p.

Stream Pollution Control in the Upper Cumberland River Basin, 1965. 36 p.

Water Quality of Tennessee Surface Streams, 1960. 102 p.

Water Quality of Tennessee Surface Streams, 1961. 68 p.

Water Quality of Tennessee Surface Streams, 1962. 64 p.

Water Quality of Tennessee Surface Streams, 1963. 71 p.

Water Quality of Tennessee Surface Streams, 1960-1964. 309 p.

Water Quality of Tennessee Surface Streams, 1965. 46 p.

Water Quality of Tennessee Surface Streams, 1966. 122 p.

Water Quality Requirements for Elmid Beetles, 1964. 14 p.

Clean Streams in Tennessee (an information kit of publications).

Bacteriological Survey, Old Hickory Lake, 1962. 44 p.

Public Hearings on Policies and Water Quality Criteria for Tennessee. October, 1966. 155 p.

Notes on a Cladoceran (Leptodora kindtii) (Focke) 1844 — Water Fleas, 1963.

Ground Water Survey of Western Tennessee, 1964-65. 49 p.

Ground Water Survey of Middle Tennessee, 1965-66. 46 p.

Ground Water Survey of Northeastern Tennessee, 1966-67. 18 p.

Public Hearings on Water Uses, Stream Standards and Implementation Plans for Interstate Streams For Tennessee:

Volume I, Hearing No. 1, Paris Landing and Hearing No. 2, Savannah

Volume II, Hearing No. 3, Kingsport, 1967

Volume III, Hearing No. 4, Greeneville, 1967

Volume IV, Hearing No. 5, Knoxville, 1967

Volume V, Hearing No. 6, Chattanooga, 1967

Volume VI, Hearings No. 7, 8, and 9, Clarksville, Carthage, and Nashville, 1967

Volume VII, Hearing No. 10, Memphis, 1967

Catastrophic Fish Mortalities on Kentucky Lake, 1965. 6 p.

Investigation of Fish Kill on Cumberland River, August 2-5, 1968. 23 p.

Biological Evaluation of the Caney Fork River in the Tailwaters of Centerhill Reservoir, 1967. 18 p.

Implementation and Enforcement Plan for Interstate Streams of Tennessee.

Summary of progress to Obtain Sewage and Waste Treatment or Recovery. 2 p.

WATER RESOURCES RESEARCH CENTER
The University of Tennessee
1000 White Avenue
Knoxville, Tennessee 37916

1966

Proceedings Water Resources Seminar, Sponsored jointly by the University of Tennessee and the Tennessee Valley Authority, 114 p. 1966.

1968

Mangold, Therese and Marguerite Wagner. Comparison of Winter and Spring Algae in Selected Areas of Shelby County. (Journal of the Tennessee Academy of Science, Vol. 43, 1968) Sienna College (B-004-Tenn.)

Maskey, Karen. A Preliminary Study of Fresh-Water Diatoms in Shelby County. (Journal of the Tennessee Academy of Science, Vol. 43, 1968). Sienna College (B-004-Tenn.)

Nabholz, J. V. A Preliminary Report on Conditions of the Wolfe River at Thomas Street, Memphis, Tennessee. (Journal of the Tennessee Academy of Science, Vol. 43, 1968.) Christian Brothers College (B-004-Tenn.)

Sewell, J. I. Laboratory and Field Tests of Pond Sealing by Chemical Treatment. Bulletin 437, The University of Tennessee Agricultural Experiment Station, 25 p., 1968. (A-003-Tenn.)

Shelton, Curtis H. and Sewell, John I. Parameter Screening for Watershed Analyses. Paper No. 68-716, presented at Winter Meeting, American Society of Agricultural Engineers, 15 p. 1968. (A-002-Tenn.)

Sewell, John I. and Mote, Roland C. Liquid Limit Determinations as Indicators of the Effectiveness of Chemicals in Pond Sealing. Paper No. 68-713, presented at Winter Meeting, American Society of Agricultural Engineers, 12 p. 1968. (A-003-Tenn.)

Larson, F. C. Water Quality Investigation, Part I — Basic Data — Fort Loudoun Reservoir, April 1966 — June 1968. Technical Bulletin No. 1, Water Resources Research Center, The University of Tennessee. 89 p. 1968. (A-013-Tenn.)

1969

Chu, C. S. and Carl J. Remenyik, Turbulent Mixing in Submerged Two-Dimensional Wall Jets. University of Tennessee, Termination Report, 15 p., 1969. (A-016-Tenn.)

Stearns, Richard G. and John M. Wilson, Geochemistry and Hydrology of a Small Basin in the Upper Buffalo River Watershed, Tennessee. Vanderbilt University, Nashville, Tenn., 3 p., 1969. (A-011-Tenn.)

Staub, Robert B., J. W. Appling, A. M. Hofstetter, and I. J. Haas, Effect of Industrial Wastes of Memphis and Shelby County on Primary Planktonic Producers. University of Tennessee, Knoxville, Termination Report, 24 p. 1969. (B-004-Tenn.)

ANNUAL REPORTS

Annual Report to Office of Water Resources Research, The University of Tennessee Water Resources Research Center — 1966 through 1970.

TEXAS

TEXAS LEGISLATIVE COUNCIL

Box 2056 Capitol Station
Austin, Texas 78711

Staff Research Report No. 52-6: Inventory of Water Problems and Agencies in Texas. Price: $0.50.

TEXAS WATER DEVELOPMENT BOARD

P. O. Box 12386, Capitol Station
Austin, Texas 78711

Note: Includes publications of both the Texas Water Development Board and the Texas Water Rights Commission.

Out of print publications may be reviewed in the library of the Texas Water Development Board.

Direct all orders to the above address. Unless otherwise indicated in the numerical listings, all publications are free of charge with no postage required for shipment. Prepayment is required for priced publications. Checks and money orders should be made payable to the Texas Water Development.

A monthly newsletter Texas Water Conditions, not otherwise listed, is available on request.

REPORTS

1965

R1   Ground-Water Resources of Jackson County, Texas, by E. T. Baker, Jr. 229 p., 31 figs., 4 pls., Oct. 1965.

R2   Base-Flow Studies, Nueces River, Texas, Quantity and Quality, November 23-25, 1964, by W. E. Reeves, P. B. Rohne, J. F. Blakey, and C. R. Gilbert. 7 p., Oct. 1965.

*R3   Hydrologic Studies of Small Watersheds, Deep Creek, Colorado River Basin, Texas, 1951-61, by W. B. Mills, H. N. McGill, and M. W. Flugrath. 123 p., 11 figs., Nov. 1965.

*R4   Ground-Water Resources of Gonzales County, Texas, by G. H. Shafer. 93 p., 12 figs., 4 pls., Nov. 1965.

R5   Reconnaissance of the Chemical Quality of Surface Waters of the Neches River Basin, Texas, by L. S. Hughes and D. K. Leifeste. 64 p., 11 figs., 2 pls., Nov. 1965.

R6   Hydrologic Studies of Small Watersheds, Mukewater Creek, Colorado River Basin, Texas, 1952-60, by S. P. Sauer. 70 p., 18 figs., Nov. 1965.

R7   Chemical Composition of Texas Surface Waters, 1963, by L. S. Hughes and D. K. Leifeste. 168 p., 4 figs., 1 pl., Dec. 1965.

R8   Re-Use of Effluent in the Future, with an Annotated Bibliography, by G. A. Whetstone. 187 p., Dec. 1965.

R9   Use of Sewage Effluent for Production of Agricultural Crops, by Clark Harvey and Ronald Cantrell. 13 p., Dec. 1965.

R10   Studies of Playa Lakes in the High Plains of Texas. 17 p., Dec. 1965.

1966

R11   Importance of Irrigation Water to the Economy of the Texas High Plains, by H. W. Grubb. 54 p., 1 fig., Jan. 1966

*R12   Ground-Water Resources of Caldwell County, Texas, by C. R. Follett. 141 p., 18 figs., 3 pls., Jan. 1966.

R13   Reconnaissance of the Chemical Quality of Surface Waters of the San Jacinto River Basin, Texas, by L. S. Hughes and Jack Rawson. 46 p., 11 figs., 2 pls., Jan. 1966.

R14   Hydrologic Studies of Small Watersheds, Little Elm Creek, Trinity River Basin, Texas, 1956-62, by E. E. Schroeder. 59 p., 13 figs., Jan. 1966.

R15   Ground-Water Resources of Gaines County, Texas, by P. L. Rettman and E. R. Leggat. 186 p., 20 figs., 1 pl., Feb. 1966.

R16   Water-Level Data from Observation Wells in Culberson, Jeff Davis, Presidio, and Brewster Counties, Texas, by W. R. Muse. 62 p., 9 figs., 4 pls., Feb. 1966.

R17   Ground-Water Resources of Bee County, Texas, by B. N. Myers and O. C. Dale. 105 p., 11 figs., 4 pls., Feb. 1966.

R18   Ground-Water Resources of Houston County, Texas, by G. E. Tarver. 89 p., 21 figs., 3 pls., Mar. 1966.

R19   Ground-Water Resources of Guadalupe County, Texas, by G. H. Shafer. 95 p., 11 figs., 2 pls., Mar. 1966

R20   Ground-Water Resources of Lee County, Texas, by G. L. Thompson. 134 p., 22 figs., 3 pls., Mar. 1966.

R21   Water-Level Data from Observation Wells in the Southern High Plains of Texas, by S. W. Gammon and W. R. Muse. 537 p., 52 figs., Apr. 1966.

R22   Water-Delivery and Low-Flow Studies, Pecos River, Texas, Quantity and Quality, 1964 and 1965, by R. U. Grozier, H. W. Albert, J. F. Blakey, and C. H. Hembree. 23 p., 6 figs., 2 pls., May 1966.

*R23   A study of Some Effects of Urbanization on Storm Run-off from a Small Watershed, by W. H. Espey, Jr., C. W. Morgan, and F. D. Masch. 110 p., 27 figs., Aug. 1966.

R24   Effect of an Increased Heat Load on the Thermal Structure and Evaporation of Lake Colorado City, Texas, by G. E. Harbeck, Jr., J. S. Meyers, and G. H. Hughes. 37 p., 10 figs., Aug. 1966.

R25   Base-Flow Studies, Little Cypress Creek, Upshur, Gregg, and Harrison Counties, Texas, Quantity and Quality, January and June 1964, by J. T. Smith, J. H. Montgomery, and J. F. Blakey . 24 p., 7 figs., 1 pl., Aug. 1966.

R26   Base-Flow Studies, Big Elkhart and Little Elkhart Creeks, Trinity River Basin, Texas, Quantity and Quality, September 15-16, 1965, by W. B. Mills. 18 p., 5 figs., Aug. 1966.

R27   Ground-Water Resources of Harrison County, Texas, by M. E. Broom and B. N. Myers. 74 p., 11 figs., Aug. 1966.

R28   Analog Model Study of the Hueco Bolson near El Paso, Texas, by E. R. Leggat and M. E. Davis. 26 p., 13 figs., Sept. 1966.

R29   Base-Flow Studies, Upper Guadalupe River Basin, Texas, Quantity and Quality, March 1965, by H. L. Kunze and J. T. Smith. 34 p., 11 figs., Sept. 1966.

R30   Texas Droughts, Causes, Classification and Prediction, by J. T. Carr, Jr. 65 p., 27 figs., Nov. 1966.

*R31   Technical Papers on Selected Aspects of the Preliminary Texas Water Plan [Three technical papers presented at the October 1, 1966 meeting of the Texas Section, American Society of Civil Engineers]. 78 p., Sept. 1966.

R32   Ground-Water Resources of Atascosa and Frio Counties, Texas, by W. H. Alexander, Jr., and D. E. White. 219 p., 39 figs., Dec. 1966.

R33   Symposium on Consideration of Some Aspects of Storms and Floods in Water Planning [Eight technical papers presented at the October 7-9, 1965 meeting of the Texas Section, American Society of Civil Engineers]. 167 p., 49 figs., Nov. 1966.

R34   Ground-Water Resources of the San Antonio Area, Texas, A Progress Report on Studies, 1960-64, by Sergio Garza. 36 p., 11 figs., Nov. 1966.

R35   Quality of Water of Big Mineral Arm and Tributaries, Lake Texoma, Texas, January 18-20 and February 10-11, 1966, by H. B. Mendieta and P. W. Skinner. 20 p., 4 figs., Nov. 1966.

1967

R36   Comparative Results of Sediment Sampling With the Texas Sampler and the Depth-Integrating Samplers, and Specific Weight of Fluvial Sediment Deposits in Texas, by C. T. Welborn. 117 p., 32 figs., Jan. 1967.

R37   Ground-Water Resources of Sabine and San Augustine Counties, Texas, by R. B. Anders. 127 p., 16 figs., Jan. 1967.

R38   Additional Technical Papers on Selected Aspects of the Preliminary Texas Water Plan [Four technical papers presented at the February 6-9, 1967 Environmental Engineering Conference of the Americal Society of Civil Engineers]. 97 p., 19 figs., Feb. 1967.

R39   Hydrologic Studies of Small Watersheds, Escondido Creek, San Antonio River Basin, Texas, 1955-63, by F. W. Kennon, J. T. Smith, and C. T. Welborn. 129 p., 15 figs., Feb. 1967.

R40   Progress of Topographic Mapping in Texas, 1958-1966, by G. E. Blomquist. 27 p., 1 fig., 3 pls., Feb. 1967.

R41   Ground Water in the Flood-Plain Alluvium of the Brazos River, Whitney Dam to Vicinity of Richmond, Texas, by J. G. Cronin and C. A. Wilson. 230 p., 28 figs., Mar. 1967.

R42   Cost of Transporting Water by Pipeline, by Lockwood, Andrews and Newman, Inc. 146 p., 9 figs., Mar. 1967.

R43   A New Concept—Water for Preservation of Bays and Estuaries, by Lockwood, Andrews and Newnam, Inc. 47 p., 1 fig., Apr. 1967.

R44   Future Water Requirements for the Production of Oil in Texas, by P. D. Torrey. 53 p., 1 fig., Apr. 1967.

R45   Suspended-Sediment Load of Texas Streams, Compilation Report, October 1961-September 1963, by H. M. Cook. 67 p., 1 fig., Apr. 1967.

R46   Occurrence and Quality of Ground Water in Brown County, Texas, by D. R. Thompson. 150 p., 10 figs., May 1967.

R47   Occurrence and Quality of Ground Water in Crockett County, Texas, by H. H. Iglehart. 165 p., 22 figs., May 1967.

R48   Dams and Reservoirs in Texas, Historical and Descriptive Information, December 31, 1966, by C. L. Dowell and S. D. Breeding. 276 p., 21 photos, 1 pl., June 1967.

R49   Hurricanes Affecting the Texas Gulf Coast, by J. T. Carr, Jr. 68 p., 23 figs., June 1967.

R50   Ground-Water Resources of Mitchell and Western Nolan Counties, Texas, by V. M. Shamburger, Jr. 184 p., 23 figs., June 1967.

R51   Reconnaissance Investigation of the Ground-Water Resources of the Colorado River Basin, Texas, by J. R. Mount, F. A. Rayner, V. M. Shamburger, Jr., R. C. Peckham, and F. L. Osborne, Jr. 119 p., 11 figs., 17 pls., July 1967.

R52   Occurrence and Quality of Ground Water in Archer County, Texas, by D. E. Morris. 85 p., 12 figs., July 1967.

R53   The Climate and Physiography of Texas, by J. T. Carr, Jr. 35 p., 8 figs., July 1967.

R54   Hydrologic Studies of Small Watersheds, Pin Oak Creek, Trinity River Basin, Texas, 1956-62, by J. T. Smith and C. T. Welborn. 75 p., 26 figs., Aug. 1967.

R55   Study and Interpretation of Chemical Quality of Surface Waters in the Brazos River Basin, Texas, by Jack Rawson. 118 p., 10 figs., July 1967.

R56   Availability and Quality of Ground Water in Fayette County, Texas, by L. T. Rogers. 134 p., 17 figs., Aug. 1967.

R57   Occurrence and Quality of Ground Water in Coleman County, Texas, by L. E. Walker. 111 p., 12 figs., Sept. 1967.

R58   Occurrence and Quality of Ground Water in Montague County, Texas, by D. C. Bayha. 107 p., 13 figs., Aug. 1967.

R59 Ground-Water Resources of Jasper and Newton Counties, Texas, by J. B. Wesselman. 186 p., 31 figs., Sept. 1967.

R60 Ground-Water Resources of Kendall County, Texas, by R. D. Reeves. 108 p., 9 figs., Sept. 1967.

R61 Ground-Water Resources of Brooks County, Texas, by B. N. Myers and O. C. Dale. 102 p., 17 figs., Oct. 1967.

R62 Ground-Water Resources of Ellis County, Texas, by G. L. Thompson. 128 p., 17 figs., Oct. 1967.

R63 Development of Ground Water in the Houston District, Texas, 1961-65, by R. K. Gabrysch. 39 p., 19 figs., Oct. 1967.

R64 Monthly Reservoir Evaporation Rates for Texas, 1940 through 1965, by J. W. Kane. 121 p., 7 figs., Oct. 1967.

R65 Temperature of Texas Streams, by W. H. Goines. 242 p., 1 fig., Nov. 1967.

R66 Low-Flow Studies, Sabine and Old Rivers Near Orange, Texas, Quantity and Quality, April 12, October 31-November 4, 1966, by Jack Rawson, D. R. Reddy, and R. E. Smith. 27 p., 7 figs., Nov. 1967.

R67 Reconnaissance of the Chemical Quality of Surface Waters of the Trinity River Basin, Texas, by D. K. Leifeste and L. S. Hughes. 79 p., 12 figs., Dec. 1967.

R68 Ground-Water Resources of Austin and Waller Counties, Texas, by C. A. Wilson. 236 p., 27 figs., Dec. 1967.

R69 Characteristics of Tide-Affected Flow in the Brazos River Near Freeport Texas, March 29-30, 1965, by S. L. Johnson, Jack Rawson, and R. E. Smith. 77 p., 7 figs., Dec. 1967.

1968

R70 Water-Level Data From Observation Wells in the Northwestern Gulf Coastal Plain of Texas, by W. Howard. 212 p., 17 figs., Jan. 1968.

R71 Reconnaissance of the Chemical Quality of Surface Waters of the Colorado River Basin, Texas, by D. K. Leifeste and M. W. Lansford. 92 p., 13 figs., Mar. 1968.

R72 Ground-Water Resources of Liberty County, Texas, by R. B. Anders, G. D. McAdoo, and W. H. Alexander, Jr. 154 p., 20 figs., Apr. 1968.

R73 Ground-Water Resources of Nueces and San Patricio Counties, Texas, by G. H. Shafer. 143 p., 18 figs., May 1968.

R74 Ground-Water Resources of Tyler County, Texas, by G. R. Tarver. 106 p., 16 figs., May 1968.

R75 Water-Delivery Study, Lower Nueces River Valley, Texas, by Sergio Garza. 70 p., 12 figs., May 1968.

R76 Water-Delivery Study, Pecos River, Texas, Quantity and Quality, 1967, by R. U. Grozier, H. R. Hejl, Jr., and C. H. Hembree. 20 p., 6 figs., May 1968.

R77 Evaporation From Brine Solutions Under Controlled Laboratory Conditions, by Jaroy Moore and J. R. Runkles. 78 p., 24 figs., May 1968.

R78 Ground-Water Resources of Upton County, Texas, by D. E. White. 145 p., 21 figs., May 1968.

R79 Ground-Water Resources of Wood County, Texas, by M. E. Broom. 95 p., 20 figs., Aug. 1968.

R80 Ground-Water Resources of San Jacinto County, Texas, by W. M. Sandeen. 100 p., 21 figs., Aug. 1968.

R81 Major Hydroelectric Powerplants in Texas—Historical and Descriptive Information, by F. A. Godfrey and C. L. Dowell. 100 p., 28 figs., Aug. 1968.

R82 Ground-Water Resources of Polk County, Texas, by G. R. Tarver. 122 p., 16 figs., Aug. 1968.

R83 Floods From Hurricane Beulah in South Texas and Northeastern Mexico, September-October 1967, by R. U. Grozier, A. E. Hulme, E. E. Schroeder, and D. C. Hall. 206 p., 38 figs., Sept. 1968.

R84 Economic Evaluation of Water-Oriented Recreation in the Preliminary Texas Water Plan, by H. W. Grubb and J. T. Goodwin. 33 p., 4 figs., Sept. 1968.

R85 Quality of Water and Stratification of Possum Kingdom, Whitney, Hubbard Creek, Proctor, and Belton Reservoirs, by D. K. Leifeste and Barney Popkin. 122 p., 16 figs., Oct. 1968.

R86 Reconnaissance of the Chemical Quality of Surface Waters of the Canadian River Basin, Texas, by H. L. Kunze and J. N. Lee. 35 p., 9 figs., Dec. 1968.

R87 Reconnaissance of the Chemical Quality of Surface Waters of the Sulphur River and Cypress Creek Basins, Texas, by D. K. Leifeste. 40 p., 13 figs., Dec. 1968.

R88 Reconnaissance of the Chemical Quality of Surface Waters of the Guadalupe River Basin, Texas, by Jack Rawson. 45 p., 11 figs., Dec. 1968.

*R89 Laws and Programs Pertaining to Water and Related Land Resources, by D. B. Yarborough. 41 p., Dec. 1968.

1969

R90 Quantity and Quality of Low Flow in Sabine and Old Rivers Near Orange, Texas, September 12-15, 1967, by Jack Rawson, S. L. Johnson, and R. E. Smith. 21 p., 6 figs., Jan. 1969.

R91 Ground-Water Resources of Matagorda County, Texas, by W. W. Hammond, Jr., 180 p., 35 figs., Mar. 1969.

R92 Reconnaissance of the Chemical Quality of Surface Waters of the Lavaca River Basin, Texas, by H. L. Kunze. 27 p., 9 figs., Mar. 1969.

R93 Reconnaissance of the Chemical Quality of Surface Waters of the San Antonio River Basin, Texas, by Jack Rawson. 32 p., 9 figs., Apr. 1969.

R94 Ground-Water Resources of Johnson County, Texas, by G. L. Thompson. 95 p., 17 figs., Apr. 1969.

R95 Ground-Water Resources of Kimble County, Texas, by W. H. Alexander, Jr. and J. H. Patman. 106 p., 14 figs., May 1969.

R96 A Statistical Study of the Depth of Precipitable Water in Western Texas and Eastern New Mexico, by S. E. Baker. 87 p., 4 figs., June 1969.

R97 Base-Flow Studies, Leon and Lampasas Rivers, Texas, Quantity and Quality, January 16-17, 1968, by Jack Rawson and G. K. Schultz. 16 p., 2 figs., June 1969.

R98 Compilation of Results of Aquifer Tests in Texas, by B. N. Myers. 537 p., 4 figs., July 1969.

R99 Hydrologic Studies of Small Watersheds, Cow Bayou, Brazos River Basin, Texas, 1955-64, by W. B. Mills. 74 p., 12 figs., Oct. 1969.

R100 Occurrence and Quality of Ground Water in Shackelford County, Texas, by R. D. Preston. 75 p., 14 figs., Oct. 1969.

R101 Ground-Water Resources of Gregg and Upshur Counties, Texas, by M. E. Broom. 91 p., 16 figs., Oct. 1969.

R102 Ground-Water Resources of Kerr County, Texas, by R. D. Reeves. 71 p., 12 figs., Nov. 1969.

R103 Water-Level Measurements in Observation Wells in Harris County, Texas, by R. K. Gabrysch, W. L. Naftel, and Gene McAdoo. 257 p., 1 fig., Dec. 1969.

1970

R104 Water-Loss Studies of Lake Corpus Christi, Nueces River Basin, Texas, 1949–65. January 1970.

R105 Reconnaissance of Water Temperature of Selected Streams in Southeastern Texas. January 1970.

R106 Suspended-Sediment Load of Texas Streams, Compilation Report, October 1963–September 1965. January 1970.

R107 Quantity and Quality of Low Flow in the Pecos River Below Girvin, Texas, February 6-9, 1968. February 1970.

R108 Biochemical Oxygen Demand, Dissolved Oxygen, Selected Nutrients, and Pesticide Records of Texas Surface Water 1968. Feb. 1970.

R109 Ground-Water Resources of Bastrop County, Texas. March 1970.

R110 Ground-Water Conditions in Angelina and Nacogdoches Counties, Texas. March 1970.

R111 An Investigation of Clouds and Precipitation for the Texas High Plains. March 1970.

R112 Quantity and Chemical Quality of Low Flow in Cibolo Creek, Texas. March 4-8, 1968. April 1970.

R113 Occurrence and Quality of Ground Water in Throckmorton County, Texas. April 1970.

R114 Records of Water Levels and Chemical Analyses from Selected Wells in Parts of the Trans-Pecos Region, Texas, 1965–68. August 1970.

R115 Time of Travel of Translatory Waves on the Brazos, Leon and Little River, Texas. April 1970.

R116 Quantity and Chemical Quality of Low Flow on the Prairie Dog Town Fork Red River near Wayside, Texas February 6-9, 1968. May 1970.

R117 Chemical and Physical Characteristics of Water in Estuaries of Texas September 1967–September 1968. May 1970.

R118 Systems Simulation for Management of a Total Water Resource. May 1970.

R119 Ground-Water Resources of Collingsworth County, Texas. July 1970.

R120 Biochemical-Oxygen-Demand, Dissolved-Oxygen Selected Nutrients, and Pesticide Records of Texas Surface Waters, 1969 Water Year. Sept. 1970.

BIENNIAL REPORTS

First Report of the Texas Water Development Board Covering the Biennium September 1, 1964 through August 31, 1966. 118 p., 11 figs.

Second Report of the Texas Water Development Board Covering the Biennium September 1, 1966 through August 31, 1968. 134 p., 13 figs.

PLANNING SERIES

Published by the Texas Water Development Board. See Planning Series of the Texas Water Commission for earlier studies.

Water for Texas – A Plan for the Future. 37 p., 4 figs., 5 pls., May 1966. [The Preliminary Texas Water Plan].

23 Basin Summaries: Reports were published from June to August 1966 summarizing regional hydrology, water use, projected water needs, and the water-development projects tentatively proposed in the respective 23 major river and coastal basins of Texas. [The Preliminary Texas Water Plan].

The Texas Water Plan. 215 p., 37 figs., 4 pls., November 1968.

The Texas Water Plan – Summary. 53 p., 3pls., November 1968.

TEXAS WATER COMMISSION

BULLETINS

1950

*B5001 Geology and Ground-Water Resources of the Houston District, Texas, by J. W. Lang, A. G. Winslow, and W. N. White. 59 p., 15 figs., 3 pls., Oct. 1950.

*B5003 Geology and Ground-Water Resources of Walker County, Texas, by A. G. Winslow. 52 p., 4 figs., 2 pls., Oct. 1950.

*B5004 Development of Ground Water for Irrigation in the Dell City Area, Hudspeth County, Texas, by R. A. Scalapino. 41 p., 1 fig., 1 pl., Sept. 1950.

1951

B5101 Water Supply of the Houston Gulf Coast Region, by W. H. Goines, A. G. Winslow, and J. R. Barnes. 41 p., 23 figs., Jan. 1951.

*B5102 Summary of the Development of Ground Water for Irrigation in the Lobo Flats Area, Culberson and Jeff Davis Counties, Texas, by J. W. Hood and R. A. Scalapino. 29 p., 1 fig., 2 pls., Sept. 1951.

*B5103 Ground-Water Resources of Parker County, Texas, by G. J. Stramel. 58 p., 1 pl., Nov. 1951.

*B5104 Irrigation Wells and Water-Level Fluctuations in the High Plains of Texas to Jan. 1951, by E. R. Leggat. 29 p., 18 figs., Nov. 1951.

1952

*B5201 The Houston District, Texas, Pumpage and Decline of Artesian Pressure During 1950-51, by A. G. Winslow and T. R. Fluellen, Jr. 28 p., 17 figs., Jan. 1952.

B5202 Summary of Ground-Water Development in the Pecos Area, Reeves and Ward Counties, Texas, 1947-51, by J. W. Hood and D. B. Knowles. 13 p., 6 figs., Jan. 1952.

*B5203 Winter Garden District, Dimmit and Zavala Counties and Eastern Maverick County, Texas [Records of Wells], by D. E. Outlaw and others. 59 p., 1 pl., Mar. 1952.

*B5204 Ground-Water Resources in the Vicinity of Kenmore Farms, Kendall County, Texas, by W. O. George and W. W. Doyel. 17 p., 2 figs., June 1952.

*B5205 Texas Index of Surface Water Records, 1882-1951, Discharge, Sediment, Chemical Quality, and Water Temperature. 47 p., May 1952.

B5206 Results of Artificial Recharge of the Ground-Water Reservoir at El Paso, Texas, by R. W. Sundstrom and J. W. Hood. 21 p., 7 figs., July 1952.

*B5207 Geology and Ground-Water Resources of Lynn County, Texas, by E. R. Leggat. 76 p., 7 figs., 2 pls., Sept. 1952.

*B5208 Water Resources of Waller County, Texas, by T. R. Fluellen and W. H. Goines. 60 p., 8 figs., Sept. 1952.

*B5209 Ground-Water Resources of Starr County, Texas, by O. C. Dale. 50 p., 3 figs., 1 pl., Dec. 1952.

*B5210 Ground-Water Resources of Ector County, Texas, by D. B. Knowles. 117 p., 5 figs., 2 pls., Dec. 1952.

1953

*B5301 Ground-Water Resources of the Odell Sand Hills, Wilbarger County, Texas, by G. W. Willis and D. B. Knowles. 57 p., 12 figs., Jan. 1953.

*B5302 Records of Water-Level Measurements in Hale County, Texas, 1910-1953, by C. R. Follett. 44 p., map, Oct. 1953.

*B5303 Records of Water-Level Measurements in Lubbock County, Texas, 1936-1953, by C. R. Follett. 34 p., map, Oct. 1953.

*B5304 Records of Water-Level Measurements in Floyd County, Texas, 1913-1953, by C. R. Follett. 28 p., map, Nov. 1953.

*B5305 Records of Water-Level Measurements in Deaf Smith County, Texas, 1914-1953, by C. R. Follett. 23 p., map, Nov. 1953.

*B5306 Records of Water-Level Measurements in Lamb County, Texas, 1914-1953, by C. R. Follett. 21 p., map, chart, Dec. 1953.

*B5307 Records of Water-Level Measurements in Swisher County, Texas, 1914-1953, by C. R. Follett. 25 p., map, chart, Dec. 1953.

1954

*B5401 Pumpage of Ground Water and Decline of Artesian Pressure in the Houston District, Texas, During 1951 and 1952, by W. W. Doyel, A. G. Winslow, and W. L. Naftel. 31 p., 21 figs., Jan. 1954.

*B5402 Summary of Ground-Water Development in the Southern High Plains, Texas, by E. R. Leggat. 23 p., 10 figs., Feb. 1954.

*B5403 Ground-Water Resources of Cameron County, Texas, by O. C. Dale and W. O. George. 66 p., 4 figs., 1 pl., Feb. 1954.

*B5404 Records of Water-Level Measurements in Dallam, Hansford, Hartley, Hutchinson, Moore, Ochiltree, and Sherman Counties, Texas, compiled by C. R. Follett. 45 p., 7 maps, chart, Mar. 1954.

B5405 Records of Water-Level Measurements in Martin County, Texas, 1936-1953, compiled by C. R. Follett. 14 p., chart, Apr. 1954.

*B5406 Records of Water-Level Measurements in Bailey, Briscoe, Castro, Parmer, Potter, and Randall Counties, Texas, compiled by C. R. Follett. 59 p., 6 maps, 5 charts, Apr. 1954.

*B5407 Records of Water-Level Measurements in Cochran, Crosby, Gaines, Hockley, Lynn, and Terry Counties, Texas, compiled by C. R. Follett. 51 p., 6 maps, 6 charts, Apr. 1954.

B5408 Records of Water-Level Measurements in Loving and Ward Counties, Texas, compiled by C. R. Follett. 26 p., 2 maps, chart, May 1954.

*B5409 Salt Water and Its Relation to Fresh Ground Water in Harris County, Texas, by A. G. Winslow and W. W. Doyel. 40 p., 15 figs., June 1954.

B5410 Ground-Water Development in the Southern High Plains of Texas, 1953, by E. R. Leggat. 9 p., 2 figs., July 1954.

*B5411 Ground-Water Resources of Tom Green County, Texas, by G. W. Willis. 105 p., 12 figs., 2 pls., Sept. 1954.

*B5412 Ground-Water Resources of the San Antonio Area, Texas, A Progress Report of Current Studies, by J. W. Lang. 32 p., 6 figs., Aug. 1954.

*B5413 Records of Wells in Bastrop County, Texas, by G. M. Austin. 47 p., 1 pl., Sept. 1954.

*B5414 Records of Water-Level Measurements in Reeves County, Texas, compiled by C. R. Follett. 31 p., Sept. 1954.

*B5415 Records of Water-Level Measurements in Culberson, Hudspeth, and Jeff Davis Counties, Texas, compiled by C. R. Follett. 34 p., 3 maps, 4 charts, Nov. 1954.

*B5416 Records of Water-Level Measurements in Atascosa and Frio Counties, Texas, compiled by B. W. Swartz. 26 p., 2 maps, 2 charts, Dec. 1954.

*B5417 Records of Water-Level Measurements in El Paso County, Texas, compiled by C. R. Follett. 50 p., map, Dec. 1954.

*B5418 Ground-Water Resources of Jones County, Texas, by A. G. Winslow, W. W. Doyel, and C. H. Gaum. 32 p., 2 figs., 1 pl., Dec. 1954.

1955

*B5501 Records of Wells in Hays County, Texas, by K. J. DeCook and W. W. Doyel. 63 p., 1 pl., Feb. 1955.

B5502   Geology and Ground-Water Resources of Galveston County, Texas, by B. M. Petitt, Jr. and A. G. Winslow. 225 p., 33 figs., 3 pls., Oct. 1955.

B5503   Records of Water-Level Measurements in Haskell and Knox Counties, Texas, by C. R. Follett. 18 p., 2 maps, 2 charts, Sept. 1955.

1956

*B5601   Geology and Ground-Water Resources of Medina County, Texas, by C. L. R. Holt, Jr. 289 p., 15 figs., 14 pls., Aug. 1956.

B5602   Pumpage of Ground Water and Changes in Artesian Pressure in the Houston District and Baytown-LaPorte Area, Texas, 1953-55, by L. A. Wood. 41 p., 23 figs., Feb. 1956.

*B5603   Ground-Water Resources of the El Paso District, Texas, Progress Report No. 7, by R. E. Smith. 36 p., 6 figs., 1 pl., Feb. 1956.

*B5604   Ground-Water Resources of the Crane Sandhills, Crane County, Texas, by G. H. Shafer. 108 p., 7 figs., 1 pl., Mar. 1956.

*B5605   Basic Data and Summary of Ground-Water Resources of Chambers County, Texas, by W. W. Doyel. 91 p., 9 figs., 1 pl., Feb. 1956.

*B5606   Records of Water-Level Measurements in Bexar County, Texas, by C. R. Follett. 61 p., map, 2 charts, Mar. 1956.

B5607   Water-Level Decline Maps of 17 Counties, Southern High Plains, Texas, Jan. 1955 to Jan. 1956, by C. R. Follett. 20 p., 17 maps, Apr. 1956.

*B5608   Ground-Water Resources of the San Antonio Area, Texas, by B. M. Petitt, Jr. and W. O. George. Volume I, 85 p., 25 figs., 12 pls., July 1956 [Out of print]; Volume II, Part I, 255 p., 1 pl., July 1956; Volume II, Part II, 288 p., July 1956; Volume II, Part III, 231 p., 1 pl., July 1956.

B5609   Records of Water-Level Measurements in Medina County, Texas, 1930 to March 1956, by C. R. Follett. 25 p., map, 2 charts, Apr. 1956.

B5610   Records of Water-Level Measurements in Comal and Guadalupe Counties, Texas, 1933 to March 1956, by C. R. Follett. 34 p., map, 2 charts, Apr. 1956.

B5611   Records of Water-Level Measurements in Kinney, Uvalde, and Val Verde Counties, Texas, 1929 to March 1956, by C. R. Follett. 72 p., 3 maps, 5 charts, May 1956.

B5612   Records of Water-Level Measurements in Hays, Travis, and Williamson Counties, Texas, 1937 to May 1956, by C. R. Follett. 74 p., 3 maps, 5 charts, July 1956.

B5613   Records of Water-Level Measurements in Childress, Cottle, Hardeman, and King Counties, Texas, 1940 to Jan. 1956, by C. R. Follett. 28 p., 4 maps, 4 charts, July 1956.

B5614   Records of Water-Level Measurements in Foard and Wilbarger Counties, Texas, 1936 to Jan. 1956, by C. R. Follett. 32 p., 2 maps, 4 charts, Aug. 1956.

B5615   Ground-Water Resources of the Hueco Bolson, Northeast of El Paso, Texas, by D. B. Knowles and R. A. Kennedy. 270 p., 21 figs., 1 pl., Aug. 1956.

B5617   Records of Water-Level Measurements in Dimmit, Maverick, and Zavala Counties, Texas, 1920, 1928 to Sept. 1956, by C. R. Follett. 76 p., 3 maps, 4 charts, Dec. 1956.

1957

*B5701   Artificial-Recharge Experiments at McDonald Well Field, Amarillo, Texas, by E. A. Moulder and D. R. Frazor. 37 p., 15 figs., Jan. 1957.

*B5702   Records of Water-Levels in Bastrop and Caldwell Counties, Texas, 1937 through Dec. 1956, by B. W. Swartz. 24 p., 2 maps, 2 charts, Apr. 1957.

*B5703   Records of Water Levels in Aransas and San Patricio Counties, Texas, 1938 Through Dec. 1956, by B. W. Swartz. 26 p., 2 maps, 2 charts, Apr. 1957.

B5704   Geology and Ground-Water Resources of Lamb County, Texas, by E. R. Leggat. 187 p., 19 figs., 3 pls., Mar. 1957.

B5705   Water Level Decline Maps, 1956 to 1957, and Water Levels in Observation Wells in 20 Counties in the Southern High Plains, Texas, compiled by C. R. Follett. 44 p., 20 maps, Apr. 1957.

B5706   The Use of Ground Water for Irrigation in Childress County, Texas, by G. H. Shafer. 21 p., 3 figs., Mar. 1957.

*B5707   Water Level Maps and Water Levels in Observation Wells in the North High Plains, Texas, by C. R. Follett. 17 p., 7 maps, May 1957 (Revised Aug. 1957).

B5708   Records of Wells in Travis County, Texas, by Ted Arnow. 32 p., 1 fig., 1 pl., July 1957.

B5709   Geology and Ground-Water Resources of Tarrant County, Texas, by E. R. Leggat. 187 p., 26 figs., 9 pls., Sept. 1957.

*B5710   Ground-Water Geology of Wilson County, Texas, by R. B. Anders. 66 p., 9 figs., 3 pls., July 1957.

B5711   Ground-Water Resources of Goliad County, Texas, by O. C. Dale, E. A. Moulder, and Ted Arnow. 97 p., 8 figs., 3 pls., Sept. 1957.

*B5712   Ground-Water Geology of the Alpine Area, Brewster, Jeff Davis, and Presidio Counties, Texas, by R. T. Littleton and G. L. Audsley. 91 p., 9 figs., 2 pls., Sept. 1957.

1958

*B5801   Ground-Water Geology in the Vicinity of Dove & Croton Creeks, Stonewall, Kent, Dickens, and King Counties, Texas, with Special Reference to Salt-Water Seepage, by L. G. McMillion. 57 p., 11 figs., 2 pls., July 1958.

*B5802   Ground-Water Conditions in Carson County, Texas, by Chris Gard. 120 p., 6 figs., 2 pls., Aug. 1958.

*B5803   Ground-Water Geology of Real County, Texas, by A. T. Long. 50 p., 10 figs., 3 pls., Oct. 1958.

B5804   Records of Water-Level Measurements in Jackson, Matagorda, and Wharton Counties, Texas, 1934 to April 1958, by F. A. Rayner. 36 p., 3 maps, 3 charts, Dec. 1958.

*B5805   Pumpage of Ground Water and Fluctuations of Water Levels in the Houston District and Baytown-LaPorte Area, Texas, 1955-57, by L. A. Wood. 43 p., 27 figs., Dec. 1958.

*B5806   Records of Water Level Measurements in Collingsworth, Hemphill, Roberts, and Wheeler Counties, Texas, 1937 Through July 1958, by F. A. Rayner. 26 p., 4 maps, 3 charts, Dec. 1958.

B5807-A Compilation of Surface Water Records in Texas Through September 1957. 505 p., Sept. 1958. Price: $12.25.

*B5807-B Texas Index of Surface Water Records, Discharge, Sediment, Chemical Quality, and Water Temperature. 61 p., Nov. 1958.

B5807-C Summary of Peak Flood Flow Measurements and Other Measurements of Stream Discharge in Texas at Points Other Than Gaging Stations. 262 p., 4 pls., Feb. 1959. Price: $7.75.

B5807-D Channel Gain and Loss Investigations, Texas Streams, 1918-1958. 278 p., 31 figs., Apr. 1960. Price: $3.00.

*B5807-E Texas Stream-Gaging Program: Evaluation and Recommendations. 37 p., 4 figs., 2 pls., Oct. 1960.

*B5808   Pumpage of Ground Water and Changes in Water Levels in Galveston County, Texas, 1952-57, by L. A. Wood. 28 p., 13 figs., 1 pl., Dec. 1958.

1959

*B5901   Records of Water-Level Measurements in Chambers, Liberty, and Montgomery Counties, Texas, 1931 Through April 1958, by F. A. Rayner. 35 p., 3 maps, 3 charts, Jan. 1959.

*B5902   Records of Water-Level Measurements in Bell, McLennan, and Somervell Counties, Texas, 1930 Through 1957, by F. A. Rayner. 20 p., 3 maps, 3 charts, Feb. 1959.

*B5903   Records of Water-Level Measurements in Crockett, Glasscock, Reagan, Upton, Terrell Counties, Texas, 1937 Through 1957, by F. A. Rayner. 23 p., 4 maps, 3 charts, Mar. 1959.

*B5904   Records of Water-Level Measurements in Brazoria, Fort Bend, and Waller Counties, Texas, 1931 Through June 1958, by F. A. Rayner. 57 p., 6 figs., 3 maps, Feb. 1959.

*B5905   Chemical Composition of Texas Surface Waters, 1956. 59 p., Jan. 1959.

*B5906   Records of Water-Level Measurements in Crane and Midland Counties, Texas, 1937 Through 1957, by F. A. Rayner. 14 p., 2 maps, 2 charts, Mar. 1959.

*B5907   Records of Water-Level Measurements in Mitchell, Nolan, Sterling, and Tom Green Counties, Texas, 1938 Through 1957, by F. A. Rayner. 30 p., 3 maps, 3 charts, Mar. 1959.

*B5908   Water-Level Measurements and Maps, Southern High Plains, Texas, 1958 and 1959, by F. A. Rayner. 49 p., 23 maps, June 1959.

*B5909   Water-Level Measurements and Maps, Northern High Plains, Texas, 1958 and 1959, by F. A. Rayner. 19 p., 8 maps, Aug. 1959.

B5910   Water Requirements Survey for Texas [prepared by Bureau of Business Research, University of Texas]. 82 p., 1 pl., July 1959. Price: $1.25.

B5911   Ground-Water Geology of Bexar County, Texas, by Ted Arnow. 62 p., 13 figs., 4 pls., Oct. 1959. Price: $1.00.

B5912   Inventory and Use of Sedimentation Data in Texas [prepared by Soil Conservation Service. U.S.D.A.]. 89 p., 5 figs., 2 pls., Jan. 1959. Price: $1.25.

B5913   Texas Index of Meteorological Data [1885-1959]. 59 p., Oct. 1959. Price: $0.80.

*B5914   A Study of Droughts in Texas, by R. L. Lowry, Jr. 81 p., 1 fig., 11 pls., Dec. 1959. Price: $1.00.

B5915   Chemical Composition of Texas Surface Waters, 1957, by L. S. Hughes. 80 p., Nov. 1959. Price: $0.70.

B5916   Geology and Ground-Water Resources of Winkler County, Texas, by Sergio Garza and J. B. Wesselman. 216 p., 15 figs., 8 pls., Nov. 1959.

1960

*B6001   Surface Runoff from Texas Watersheds and Sub-Basins. 274 p., 2 figs., 2 maps, Feb. 1960. Price: $3.00.

*B6002   Brine Production and Disposal on the Lower Watershed of Chambers and Richland Creeks, Navarro County, Texas, by F. L. Osborne, Jr. and V. M. Shamburger, Jr. 73 p., 4 figs., 2 pls., Mar. 1960.

*B6003   Geology and Ground-Water Resources of Dimmit County, Texas, by C. C. Mason. 251 p., 10 figs., 13 pls., June 1960.

*B6004   Geology and Ground-Water Resources of Hays County, Texas, by K. J. DeCook. 170 p., 10 figs., 7 pls., Aug. 1960.

*B6005   Water-Level Measurements in Culberson, Hudspeth, and Jeff Davis Counties, Texas, by Jack Stearman. 9 p., 3 maps, Apr. 1960.

*B6006   Monthly Reservoir Evaporation rates for Texas, 1940 Through 1957. 95 p., 5 pls., May 1960. Price: $1.25.

*B6007   Ground-Water Geology of Karnes County, Texas, by R. B. Anders. 110 p., 10 figs., 4 pls., July 1960.

B6008   Water Levels in Observation Wells in Cameron, Hidalgo, and Starr Counties, Texas, 1950-1959, by Jack Stearman. 9 p., 3 maps. May 1960.

B6009   Water Levels in Observation Wells in Haskell and Knox Counties, Texas, 1956-1960, by Jack Stearman. 11 p., 2 maps, 2 charts, June 1960.

*B6010   Geology and Ground-Water Resources of Hale County, Texas, by J. G. Cronin and L. C. Wells. 158 p., 17 figs., 3 pls., Nov. 1960.

*B6011   Water Levels in Observation Wells, Southern High Plains, Texas, 1959 and 1960, by Jack Stearman. 49 p., 23 maps, July 1960.

*B6012   Water Levels in Observation Wells, Northern High
          Plains, Texas, 1958-1960, by Jack Stearman. 19 p.,
          8 maps, Aug. 1960.

*B6013   Geology and Ground-Water Resources of Grayson
          County, Texas, by E. T. Baker, Jr. 155 p., 19 figs.,
          1 pl., Sept. 1960.

B6014   Ground-Water Resources of the Lower Rio Grande
          Valley Area, Texas, by R. C. Baker and O. C. Dale.
          Volume I, 88 p., 10 figs., 14 pls., Feb. 1961; Volume
          II, 340 p., 1 pl., Feb. 1961.

*B6015   Water Levels in Observation Wells in Atascosa and
          Frio Counties, Texas, 1955-1960, by Jack Stearman.
          11 p., 2 maps, 2 charts, Sept. 1960.

*B6016   Reconnaissance Investigation of the Ground Water
          Resources of the Canadian River Basin, Texas. 33 p.,
          1 fig., 4 pls., Sept. 1960.

B6017   Ground-Water Geology of the Hickory Sandstone
          Member of the Riley Formation, McCulloch County,
          Texas, by C. C. Mason. 89 p., 14 figs., 1 pl., Feb.
          1961.

*B6018   Irrigation in Texas in 1958. 254 p., 2 pls., Nov.
          1960.

B6019   Consumptive Use of Water by Major Crops in Texas,
          by L. L. McDaniels. 51 p., Nov. 1960.

1961

*B6101   Water Levels in Observation Wells, Southern High
          Plains, Texas, 1960 and 1961, compiled by D. C.
          Draper. 56 p., 26 maps, Mar. 1961.

*B6102   Geology and Ground-Water Resources of Carson
          County and Part of Gray County, Texas, Progress
          Report No. 1, by A. T. Long, Jr. 49 p., 11 figs., Mar.
          1961.

B6103   Annual Water-Level Measurements in Observation
          Wells, Northern High Plains, Texas, 1960 and 1961,
          compiled by R. C. Lucas. 21 p., 9 maps, Mar. 1961.

*B6104   Chemical Composition of Texas Surface Waters, 1958,
          by L. S. Hughes and Wanda Jones. 88 p., 3 figs., 1
          pl., Apr. 1961. Price: $1.00.

*B6105   Ground-Water Geology of Live Oak County, Texas,
          by R. B. Anders and E. T. Baker, Jr. 128 p., 7 figs.,
          5pls., Apr. 1961.

*B6106   Geology and Ground-Water Resources of Pecos Coun-
          ty, Texas, by C. A. Armstrong and L. G. McMillion.
          Volume I, 250 p., 12 figs., 15 pls., Oct. 1961; Vol-
          ume II, 298 p., Oct. 1961.

*B6107   A Summary of the Occurrence and Development of
          Ground Water in the Southern High Plains of Texas,
          by J. G. Cronin. 110 p., 19 figs., Sept. 1961.

B6108   Silt Load of Texas Streams, A Compilation Report,
          June 1889-September 1959, compiled by I. M. Stout,
          L. C. Bentz, and H. W. Ingram. 242 p., 1 pl., Dec.
          1961.

*B6109   Geology and Ground-Water Resources of the Northern
          High Plains of Texas, Progress Report No. 1, by W. H.
          Alexander, Jr. 47 p., 5 figs., 4 pls., Nov. 1961.

*B6110   Ground-Water Reconnaissance of the Marfa Area,
          Presidio County, Texas, by M. E. Davis. 44 p., 4 figs.,
          Dec. 1961.

*B6111   A Reconnaissance of the Ground-Water Resources of
          the Marathon Area, Brewster County, Texas, by K. J.
          DeCook. 54 p., 3 figs., 2 pls., Dec. 1961.

1962

B6201   Recharge, Discharge, and Changes in Ground-Water
          Storage in the Edwards and Associated Limestones,
          San Antonio Area, Texas, A Progress Report on
          Studies, 1955-59, by Sergio Garza. 51 p., 16 figs.,
          3 pls., Jan. 1962.

*B6202   Ground-Water Resources of Victoria and Calhoun
          Counties, Texas, by R. F. Marvin, G. H. Shafer, and
          O. C. Dale. 161 p., 8 figs., 10 pls., Jan. 1962.

B6203   Ground-Water Resources of the Lower Mesilla Valley,
          Texas and New Mexico, by E. R. Leggat, M. E. Low-
          ry, and J. W. Hood. 199 p., 30 figs., 3 pls., Mar.
          1962.

*B6204   Development of Ground Water in the El Paso Dis-
          trict, Texas, 1955-60, Progress Report No. 8, by E. R.
          Leggat. 65 p., 12 figs., 5 pls., Mar. 1962.

*B6205   Chemical Composition of Texas Surface Waters, 1959,
          by L. S. Hughes and Wanda Shelby. 109 p., 3 figs.,
          1 pl., Apr. 1962.

B6206   Research in the Problem of Scaling of Electrodialysis
          Demineralizers, by D. A. Cowan. 40 p., 14 figs., Apr.
          1962.

*B6207   Water-Level Measurements through 1962 in Selected
          Observation Wells, Southern High Plains, Texas com-
          piled by the Staff of the Well Observation Program
          of the Ground Water Division. 158 p., 26 maps, 3
          charts, June 1962.

*B6208   Ground-Water Geology of Edwards County, Texas,
          by A. T. Long. 128 p., 9 figs., 1 pl., Apr. 1962.

B6209   Ground-Water Resources of Haskell and Knox Coun-
          ties, Texas, by William Ogilbee and F. L. Osborne, Jr.
          185 p., 6 figs., 7 pls., Aug. 1962.

*B6210   Ground-Water Geology of Bandera County, Texas,
          by R. D. Reeves and F. C. Lee. 78 p., 4 figs., 1 pl.,
          May 1962.

B6211   Pumpage of Ground Water and Fluctuation of Water
          Levels in the Houston District and the Baytown-La-
          Porte Area, Texas, 1957-61, by R. B. Anders and W.
          L. Naftel. 56 p., 26 figs., June 1962.

*B6212   Geology and Ground-Water Resources of Uvalde
          County, Texas, by F. A. Welder and R. D. Reeves.
          263 p., 11 figs., 5 pls., July 1962.

B6213   Annual Water-Level Measurements in Observation
          Wells, Northern High Plains, Texas, 1961 and 1962,
          compiled by the Staff of the Well Observation Section
          of the Ground Water Division. 21 p., 9 maps, July
          1962.

*B6214   Geology and Ground-Water Resources of Reeves
          County, Texas, by William Ogilbee, J. B. Wesselman,
          and Burdge Irelan. Volume I, 213 p., 10 figs., 13
          pls., Sept. 1962; Volume II, 248 p., Sept. 1962.

B6215   Chemical Composition of Texas Surface Waters, 1960,
          by L. S. Hughes and Wanda Shelby. 109 p., 3 figs.,
          Dec. 1962.

*B6216 Geology and Ground-Water Resources of Kinney County, Texas, by R. R. Bennett and A. N. Sayre. 176 p., 15 figs., 26 pls., Dec. 1962.

1963

*B6301 Availability of Ground Water from the Goliad Sand in the Alice Area, Texas, by C. C. Mason. 113 p., 17 figs., Mar. 1963.

B6302 Availability and Quality of Ground Water in Smith County, Texas, by J. W. Dillard. 124 p., 6 figs., 17 pls., May 1963.

B6303 Pumpage of Ground Water and Changes in Water Levels in Galveston County, Texas, 1958-62, by R. B. Anders and W. L. Naftel. 37 p., 12 figs., 1 pl., Mar. 1963.

*B6304 Chemical Composition of Texas Surface Waters, 1961, by L. S. Hughes and Wanda Shelby. 130 p., 4 figs., 1 pl., Sept. 1963.

*B6305 Reconnaissance Investigation of the Ground-Water Resources of the Gulf Coast Region, Texas, by L. A. Wood, R. K. Gabrysch, and Richard Marvin. 123 p., 18 figs., 15 pls., June 1963.

*B6306 Reconnaissance Investigation of the Ground-Water Resources of the Red River, Sulphur River, and Cypress Creek Basins, Texas, by E. T. Baker, Jr., A. T. Long, Jr., R. D. Reeves, and L. A. Wood. 137 p., 18 figs., 22 pls., July 1963.

B6307 Reconnaissance Investigation of the Ground-Water Resources of the Sabine River Basin, Texas, by B. B. Baker, J. W. Dillard, V. L. Souders, and R. C. Peckham. 63 p., 7 figs., 8 pls., Aug. 1963.

B6308 Reconnaissance Investigation of the Ground-Water Resources of the Neches River Basin, Texas, by B. B. Baker, J. W. Dillard, V. L. Souders, and R. C. Peckham. 63 p., 7 figs., 8 pls., Aug. 1963.

*B6309 Reconnaissance Investigation of the Ground-Water Resources of the Trinity River Basin, Texas, by R. C. Peckham, V. L. Souders, J. W. Dillard, and B. B. Baker. 120 p., 18 figs., 17 pls., Sept. 1963.

*B6310 Reconnaissance Investigation of the Ground-Water Resources of the Brazos River Basin, Texas, by J. G. Cronin, C. R. Follett, G. H. Shafer, and P. L. Rettman. 163 p., 24 figs., 11 pls., Dec. 1963.

B6311 Floods in Texas—Magnitude and Frequency of Peak Flows, by J. L. Patterson. 223 p., 19 figs., 2 pls., Dec. 1963.

*B6312 Ground-Water Resources of Refugio County, Texas, by C. C. Mason. 127 p., 15 figs., 5 pls., Oct. 1963.

1964

B6401 Research on Evaporation Retardation in Small Reservoirs, 1958-63, by W. W. Meinke and W. J. Waldrip. 89 p., 15 figs., Mar. 1964.

*B6402 Geology and Ground-Water Resources of Carson County and Part of Gray County, Texas, Progress Report No. 2, by G. D. McAdoo, E. R. Leggat, and A. T. Long. 30 p., 8 figs., Mar. 1964.

*B6403 Fifty Years of Water Development in Texas, by S. D. Breeding, P. B. Jones, R. W. Harden, H. M. Cook, and J. P. Dougherty. 35 p., 1 fig., Apr. 1964.

B6404 Conservation Storage Reservoirs in Texas, Some Aspects and Chronology of Surface-Water Resources Development, by L. L. McDaniels. 51 p., 1 fig., 1 pl., Apr. 1964.

B6405 Reconnaissance of the Chemical Quality of Surface Waters of the Sabine River Basin, Texas and Louisiana by L. S. Hughes and D. K. Leifeste. 74 p., 12 figs., 2 pls., May 1964.

B6406 Geology and Ground-Water Resources of Hardin County, Texas, by E. T. Baker, Jr. 199 p., 26 figs., 8 pls., June 1964.

B6407 Base-Flow Studies: Pedernales River, Texas, Quantity and Quality, April-May 1962, by P. H. Holland and L. S. Hughes. 19 p., 2 figs., 1 pl., June 1964.

*B6408 Dams and Reservoirs in Texas, Historical and Descriptive Information, by C. L. Dowell. 256 p., 19 photos, 1 pl., July 1964.

*B6409 Reconnaissance Investigation of the Ground-Water Resources of the Guadalupe, San Antonio, and Nueces River Basins, Texas, by W. H. Alexander, Jr., B. N. Myers, and O. C. Dale. 118 p., 19 figs., 14 pls, Aug. 1964.

B6410 Suspended-Sediment Load of Texas Streams, Compilation Report, October 1959-September 1961, by E. A. Adey and H. M. Cook. 56 p., 1 pl., Nov. 1964.

B6411 Chemical Quality of Surface Waters in the Hubbard Creek Watershed, Texas, Progress Report, September 1963, by C. H. Hembree and J. F. Blakey. 50 p., 23 figs., Nov. 1964.

B6412 Occurrence and Quality of Ground Water in Stephens County, Texas, by D. C. Bayha. 96 p., 6 figs., 3 pls., Sept. 1964.

B6413 Water-Supply Limitations on Irrigation from the Rio Grande in Starr, Hidalgo, Cameron, and Willacy Counties, Texas, by J. J. Vandertulip, L. L. McDaniels, and O. C. Rucker. 80 p., 19 figs., Nov. 1964.

B6413-A Appendices to Bulletin 6413, Water-Supply Limitations on Irrigation from the Rio Grande in Starr, Hidalgo, Cameron, and Willacy Counties, Texas, by J. T. Carr, Jr., I. G. Janca, R. T. Warzecha, R. B. Hendricks, A. E. Richardson, H. H. Porterfield, Jr., and P. T. Gillett. 137 p., 10 figs., Aug. 1965.

*B6414 Analysis of Unit Hydrographs for Small Watersheds in Texas, by W. L. Meier, Jr. 65 p., 21 figs., Aug. 1964.

B6415 Occurrence and Quality of Ground Water in Young County, Texas, by D. E. Morris. 106 p., 9 figs., 3 pls., Dec. 1964.

1965

*B6501 Chemical Composition of Texas Surface Waters, 1962, by L. S. Hughes and J. F. Blakey. 167 p., 4 figs., 1 pl., Jan. 1965.

*B6502 Reconnaissance Investigations of the Ground-Water Resources of the Rio Grande Basin, Texas [a 3-part report: (1) the Upper Basin by M. E. Davis and E. R. Leggat; (2) the Middle Basin by J. B. Brown, L. T. Rogers, and B. B. Baker; and (3) the Lower Basin by R. C. Baker]. 213 p., 43 figs., 17 pls., July 1965.

B6503 Base-Flow Studies, Guadalupe River, Comal County, Texas, Quantity, March 1962, by Pat H. Holland. 6 p., 1 fig., 1 pl., Mar. 1965.

B6504 The Current Status of Weather Modification, A Summary—1964, by J. T. Carr, Jr. 75 p., 8 figs., Apr. 1965.

B6505 Base-Flow Studies, Llano River, Texas, Quantity and Quality, by Pat H. Holland and H. B. Mendieta. 20 p., 4 figs., 1 pl., Mar. 1965.

B6506 Base-Flow Studies, Lampasas River, Texas, Quantity and Quality, June 3-6, 1963, by W. B. Mills and Jack Rawson. 16 p., 4 figs., 2 pls., Mar. 1965.

B6507 Water-Level Data from Observation Wells in Pecos and Reeves Counties, Texas, by W. R. Muse. 59 p., 8 figs., 2 pls., Apr. 1965.

B6508 Analog Model Study of Ground-Water in the Houston District, Texas, by L. A. Wood and R. K. Gabrysch [Contains a section on design, construction, and use of electric analog models, by E. P. Patton, Jr.]. 103 p., 43 figs., May 1965.

B6509 Water-Delivery Study, Nueces River, Texas, Quantity and Quality, August 1963, by S. P. Sauer and J. F. Blakey. 22 p., 6 figs., 5 pls., Apr. 1965.

B6510 Base-Flow Studies, San Gabriel River, Texas, Quantity and Quality, March 16-18, 1964, by D. K. Leifeste and J. T. Smith. 17 p., 8 figs., 1 pl., Apr. 1965.

B6511 Base-Flow Studies, Cibolo Creek, Texas, Quantity and Quality, March 5-7, 1963, by Pat H. Holland and C. T. Welborn. 13 p., 3 figs., 1 pl., Apr. 1965.

B6512 Symposium on Consideration of Droughts in Water Planning [A series of technical papers presented at the April 28-30, 1965 meeting of the Texas Section, American Society of Civil Engineers]. 178 p., 36 figs., Apr. 1965.

B6513 Availability and Quality of Ground Water in Leon County, Texas, by R. C. Peckham. 44 p., 8 figs., 11 pls., May 1965.

B6514 Development of Ground Water in the El Paso District, Texas, 1960-63, Progress Report No. 9, by M. E. Davis. 34 p., 9 figs., 6 pls., May 1965.

B6515 Inventory of Texas Irrigation, 1958 and 1964, by P. T. Gillett and I. G. Janca. 317 p., 6 pls., June 1965.

B6516 Geology and Ground-Water Resources of Orange County, Texas, by J. B. Wesselman. 112 p., 16 figs., 4 pls., July 1965.

B6517 Ground-Water Resources of Camp, Franklin, Morris, and Titus Counties, Texas, by M. E. Broom, W. H. Alexander, Jr., and B. N. Myers. 153 p., 13 figs., 3 pls., July 1965.

B6518 Ground-Water Resources of DeWitt County, Texas, by C. R. Follett and R. K. Gabrysch. 113 p., 10 figs., 4 pls., Aug. 1965.

B6519 Ground-Water Conditions in Menard County, Texas, by R. C. Baker, O. C. Dale, and G. H. Baum. 92 p., 6 figs., 2 pls., Aug. 1965.

B6520 Ground-Water Resources of La Salle and McMullen Counties, Texas, by H. B. Harris. 96 p., 16 figs., 5 pls., Aug. 1965.

B6521 Investigation of Ground-Water Contamination, Rhineland Area, Knox County, Texas, by H. D. Holloway. 39 p., 7 figs., 2 pls., Aug. 1965.

CIRCULARS

C62-01 The Present Reconnaissance Study Program of the Chemical Quality of Streams in Texas. 17 p., Apr. 1962.

C62-02 Drainage Areas of Texas Streams, Sabine River Basin and Sabine-Neches Coastal Area. 24 p., 2 figs., Oct. 1962.

C62-03 Drainage Areas of Texas Streams, Neches River Basin and Neches-Trinity Coastal Area. 15 p., 2 figs., Oct. 1962.

*C62-04 Texas Index of Surface Water Records, 1882-1961, Discharge, Sediment, Chemical Quality, and Water Temperature. 67 p., Nov. 1952.

C62-05 Drainage Areas of Texas Streams, San Jacinto River Basin and San Jacinto-Brazos Coastal Area. 15 p., 2 figs., Oct. 1962.

*C62-06 Publications of the Texas Water Commission. 36 p., map, Oct. 1962.

C63-01 Drainage Areas of Texas Streams, Trinity River Basin and Trinity-San Jacinto Coastal Area. 23 p., 2 figs., Feb. 1963.

*C63-02 Texas Gulf Coastal Industrial Water Survey, by Wilbur Meier. 28 p., 7 figs., Apr. 1963.

*C63-03 The Development of the Science of Hydrology, by P. B. Jones, G. D. Walker, R. W. Harden, and L. L. McDaniels. 37 p., fig., Apr. 1963.

C63-04 Annotated Bibliography of Surface-Water Publications and Open-File Reports of the Texas Water Commission and U. S. Geological Survey for Texas through June 1962, by W. B. Mills. 41 p., May 1963.

C63-05 Summary of the Ground-Water Aquifers in the Rio Grande Basin, by R. C. Peckham. 20 p., 3 figs., June 1963.

***C63-06** Publications of the Texas Water Commission, as of August 31, 1963. 39 p., map, Nov. 1963.

C63-07 Drainage Areas of Texas Streams, San Antonio River Basin. 13 p., 2 figs., Oct. 1963.

***C64-01** Water Levels and Chemical Analyses from Observation Wells in the Dell City Area, Hudspeth and Culberson Counties, Texas, 1948 Through January 1964, by J. W. Dillard and W. R. Muse. 26 p., 1 pl., Mar. 1964.

***C64-02** Annotated Bibliography of Ground-Water Publications and Open-File Reports of the Texas Water Commission and U. S. Geological Survey for Texas through August 1963, by R. C. Baker and J. B. Brown. 89 p., Dec. 1964.

***C64-03** Publications of the Texas Water Commission as of December 31, 1964. 39 p., index map, Dec. 1964.

C65-01 Drainage Areas of Texas Streams, Coastal Areas Between the Brazos River and the Rio Grande. 16 p., 2 figs., Apr. 1965.

MEMORANDUM REPORTS

MR 62-01 Ground-Water Conditions in the Vicinity of Burnet, Texas, by J. R. Mount. 65 p., 9 pls., Feb. 1962.

MR 62-02 Reconnaissance Survey of Salt Water Disposal in the Mexia, Negro Creek, and Cedar Creek Oil Fields, Limestone County, Texas, by S. C. Burnitt, H. D. Holloway, and J. T. Thornhill. 34 p., 2 figs., 2 pls., May 1962.

MR 63-01 Brazos River Basin Reservoir Studies, Progress Report, May 1962, Chemical Quality and Stratification of Belton, Whitney, and Possum Kingdom Reservoirs, by H. B. Mendieta and J. F. Blakey. 37 p., 9 pls., Feb. 1963.

***MR 63-02** Reconnaissance of Soil Damage and Ground-Water Quality, Fisher County, Texas, by S. C. Burnitt. 59 p., 7 figs., 2 pls., Sept. 1963.

MR 63-03 Investigation of Ground-Water Resources near Fredericksburg, Texas, by J. R. Mount. 119 p., 8 figs., Nov. 1963.

LIMITED-DISTRIBUTION REPORTS

These reports were printed in small quantities for limited distribution. Their content is similar to that of the Memorandum Reports (MR).

***LD-0162-MR** City of Hawkins, Wood County, Texas, Investigation of Ground-Water Contamination, by S. C. Burnitt. 28 p., fig., 2 pls., Aug. 1962 (revised Mar. 1963).

***LD-0262-MR** Henderson Oil Field Area, Rusk County, Texas, Investigation of Ground-Water Contamination, by S. C. Burnitt. 16 p., 2 figs., 1 pl., Oct. 1962.

***LD-0362-MR** City of Valera, Coleman County, Texas, Investigation of Ground-Water Contamination, by H. D. Holloway. 9 p., fig., Nov. 1962.

***LD-0163-MR** Bacteriological Pollution of Ground Water in the Big Spring Area, Howard County, Texas, by H. D. Holloway. 17 p., 4 figs., June 1963.

LD-0263-MR Ground-Water Availability at Whitney, Hill County, Texas, by J. R. Mount. 17 p., 4 figs., Dec. 1963.

***LD-0164-MR** Definitions and Use of the Terms "Flood," "Floodflow," and "Baseflow," and Use of Discharge Hydrographic Analyses to Separate These Components of Streamflow, by L. L. McDaniels, G. D. Walker, and J. J. Vandertulip. 16 p., Jan. 1964.

***LD-0264-MR** Summary of Recreation Facilities at Major Reservoirs in Texas, by L. B. Seward. 20 p., Jan. 1964. [Prepared for Governor's Statewide Water Recreation Study Committee].

***LD-0364-MR** Investigation of Ground-Water Contamination in the Juliana and West Jud Oil Fields, Haskell and Stonewall Counties, Texas, by R. L. Crouch, 25 p., 3 figs., 2 pls., Mar. 1964.

***LD-0464-MR** Investigation of Alleged Ground-Water Contamination, Tri-Rue and Ride Oil Fields, Scurry County, Texas, by R. L. Crouch. 23 p., 5 figs., 1 pl., Mar. 1964.

***LD-0564-MR** Investigation of Ground-Water Contamination, Coleto Creek Oil Field, Victoria County, Texas, by J. T. Thornhill. 25 p., 11 figs., 1 pl., Mar. 1964.

***LD-0664** Investigation of Alleged Ground-Water Contamination near Kilgore, Gregg County, Texas, by H. D. Holloway. 19 p., 2 figs., 1 pl., Apr. 1964.

***LD-0764** Investigation of Ground-Water Contamination, P. H. D., Hackberry, and Storie Oil Fields, Garza County, Texas, by S. C. Burnitt and R. L. Crouch. 101 p., 13 figs., 1 pl., June 1964.

***LD-0864** Investigation of Ground-Water Contamination by Cotton Seed Delinting Acid Waste, Terry County, Texas, by B. E. Fink. 29 p., 6 figs., 1 pl., Oct. 1964.

***LD-0165** Manual of Computing and Modeling Techniques and Their Application to Hydrologic Studies, by J. R. Mount. 53 p., Jan. 1965.

LD-0265 Investigation of Ground Water Contamination in the Vealmoor Oil Field, Howard and Borden Counties, Texas, by R. L. Crouch and S. C. Burnitt [Contains a design criterion for lined surface evaporation pits in the High Plains Region of Texas, by H. H. Porterfield]. 54 p., 23 figs., 1 pl., Jan. 1965.

***LD-0365** Investigation of Ground- and Surface-Water Contamination Near Harrold, Wilbarger County, Texas, by B. E. Fink. 22 p., 5 figs., 1 pl., Feb. 1965.

PLANNING SERIES

The Texas Board of Water Engineers was directed by the Texas Water Planning Act of 1957 "To prepare and submit to the Legislature a statewide report of the water resources of the State with a correlation and relationship of these resources and to make recommendations to the Legislature for the maximum development of the water resources of the State . . . . "Two ma-

jor planning reports were published by the Board of Water Engineers and the Water Commission in this series, and one brochure.

*Texas Water Resources Planning at the End of the Year 1958. 170 p., 4 figs., 21 pl., Dec. 1958.

A Plan for Meeting the 1980 Water Requirements of Texas. 228 p., 7 figs., 25 pls., May 1961.

*Texas Water Planning — A State Responsibility. 24 p., Oct. 1964.

MISCELLANEOUS PUBLICATIONS

The following listed publications were not issued as a series. They have been alphabetized by county, city, area or key subject word and assigned numbers and the letter prefix M for bibliographic identity.

Letter suffixes appear with the sequential reference numbers in instances where additions to the listing have been made subsequent to initial alphabetizing and numbering. The number sequence is thus maintained and also the alphabetical arrangement; generally, the letter suffix does not indicate a subjective relationship between individual publications.

*M1   Ground-Water Resources of the Area Southwest of Amarillo, Texas, by W. H. Alexander, Jr. and J. H. Dante. 45 p., map, Sept. 1946.

*M2   Artesian Water in the Elkhart Area, Southern Anderson County, Texas, by L. H. McMillion. 18 p., 4 figs., Nov. 1956.

*M3   Andrews County, Texas [Records of Wells, South Half], by S. F. Turner. 34 p., map, Dec. 1937.

*M4   Andrews County, Texas [Records of Wells]. 55 p., map, May 1940.

*M5   Aransas County, Texas [Records of Wells]. 47 p., map, Apr. 1940.

*M6   Armstrong County, Texas [Records of Wells]. 48 p., 2 maps, Sept. 1940.

*M7   Ground-Water Resources of Atascosa County, Texas, Progress Report. 55 p., 2 maps, Aug. 1945.

*M8   Austin County, Texas [Records of Wells]. 37 p., map, Feb. 1938.

*M9   Bailey County, Texas [Records of Wells, Northeast Part]. 17 p., map, June 1936.

*M10   Bailey County, Texas [Records of Wells]. 53 p., map, June 1937.

*M11   Ground-Water Resources of the Balmorhea Area in Western Texas, by W. N. White, H. S. Gale, and S. S. Nye. 102 p., 2 figs., 1 pl., Feb. 1938.

*M12   Bee County, Texas [Records of Wells]. 31 p., map, June 1940.

*M13   Ground-Water Resources of Bexar County, Texas, by Penn Livingston. 240 p., 2 figs., 2 pls., May 1947.

*M14   Blanco County, Texas [Records of Wells], by B. A. Barnes and J. C. Crumley. 56 p., map, Jan. 1942.

*M15a Brief of State Board of Water Engineers of Texas, in the matter of: Treaty between the United States of America and the Republic of Mexico respecting the division and diversion of waters of the lower Rio Grande between the

two countries, by J. E. Sturrock. 115 p., chart, Oct. 1938.

*M16   Ground-Water Resources of Borden County, Texas, by E. C. Ellis. 30 p., 2 figs., Sept. 1949.

*M17   Brazoria County, Texas [Records of Wells West of the Brazos River]. 45 p., 4 pls., Sept. 1937.

*M18   Brazoria County, Texas [Records of Wells East of the Brazos River], by S. F. Turner and Penn Livingston, 14 p., 2 maps, Apr. 1939.

*M19   Ground-Water Resources of Brazoria County, Texas, by C. R. Follett. 104 p., map, Nov. 1947.

*M20   Investigation of Contamination Complaint, Clemens Prison Farm, Brazoria County, Texas [Contamination Report No. 9], by R. C. Peckham. 10 p., 4 pls., Aug. 1960.

*M20a Quality of Water of Brazos River in Vicinity of Possum Kingdom Dam, Texas, by W. W. Hastings. 15 p., Feb. 1944.

*M21   Briscoe County, Texas [Records of Wells], by J. H. Dante. 26 p., Sept. 1946.

*M22   Brooks County, Texas [Records of Wells]. 64 p., map, 1940.

*M23   Brown County, Texas [Records of Wells]. 26 p., map, June 1938.

*M24   Ground Water in the Vicinity of Bryan and College Station, Texas, by S. F. Turner. 44 p., 2 figs., 1 pl., Jan. 1938.

*M25   Ground Water Supply of Bryan, Texas, by B. A. Barnes, C. P. Follett, and R. W. Sundstrom. 41 p., 8 figs., 1 pl., Aug. 1944.

*M26   Burleson County, Texas [Records of Wells]. 47 p., map, Aug. 1937.

*M27   Geology and Ground-Water Resources of Caldwell County, Texas, by W. C. Rasmussen. 62 p., 2 pls., May 1947.

*M28   Calhoun County, Texas [Records of Wells]. 71 p., map, May 1941.

*M29   Callahan County, Texas [Records of Wells]. 44 p., map, Nov. 1940.

*M30   Camp, Franklin, and Titus Counties, Texas [Records of Wells]. 42 p., map, Feb. 1943.

*M31   Results of Pumping Tests of Wells at Camp Hood, Texas, by W. F. Guyton and W. O. George. 31 p., 4 figs., Jan. 1943.

*M32   Carson County, Texas [Records of Wells]. 51 p., map, Apr. 1939.

*M33   Cass County, Texas [Records of Wells], by C. R. Follett and W. N. White. 44 p., 1 fig., map, Mar. 1942.

*M34   Castro County, Texas [Records of Wells], by L. J. Ruman, J. W. Lang, and W. L. Broadhurst. 61 p., map, Dec. 1939.

*M35   Chambers County, Texas [Records of Wells]. 97 p., 2 maps, Mar. 1942.

*M36   Chemical Composition of Texas Surface Waters, 1938-1944, by W. W. Hastings and J. H. Rowley. 170 p., Mar. 1945.

*M37   Chemical Composition of Texas Surface Waters, 1938-1945, by W. W. Hastings and J. H. Rowley. 235 p., Sept. 1946.

*M38   Chemical Composition of Texas Surface Waters, 1946, by W. W. Hastings and Burdge Irelan. 43 p., July 1947.

*M39   Chemical Composition of Texas Surface Waters, 1947, by Burdge Irelan and J. R. Avrett. 58 p., Sept. 1948.

*M40   Chemical Composition of Texas Surface Waters, 1948, by Burdge Irelan, and D. E. Weaver, and J. R. Avrett. 61 p., June 1949.

*M41   Chemical Composition of Texas Surface Waters, 1949. 72 p., Oct. 1950.

*M42   Chemical Composition of Texas Surface Waters, 1950. 107 p., Mar. 1952.

*M43   Chemical Composition of Texas Surface Waters, 1951. 66 p., Dec. 1954.

*M44   Chemical Composition of Texas Surface Waters, 1952. 64 p., Feb. 1956.

*M45   Chemical Composition of Texas Surface Waters, 1953. 63 p., July 1956.

*M46   Chemical Composition of Texas Surface Waters, 1954. 63 p., Dec. 1956.

*M47   Chemical Composition of Texas Surface Waters, 1955. 54 p., July 1957.

*M48   Review of Chemical Quality-of-Water Data Collection Program in the Brazos River Basin. 11 p., 1 pl., Jan. 1961.

*M49   Cherokee County, Texas [Records of Wells]. 105 p., map, Dec. 1936.

*M50   Childress County, Texas [Records of Wells], by W. O. George and C. V. Foster. 39 p., map, May 1942.

*M55   Coleman County, Texas [Records of Wells]. 65 p., map, Mar. 1938.

*M56   Collingsworth County, Texas [Records of Wells]. 63 p., map, Apr. 1939.

*M57   Colorado County, Texas [Records of Wells]. 25 p., map, Mar. 1938.

*M58   Comal County, Texas [Records of Wells]. 42 p., map, Aug. 1937.

*M59   Geology and Ground Water Resources of Comal County, Texas, by W. O. George, W. W. Hastings, and S. D. Breeding. 147 p., 7 figs., 5 pls., Feb. 1947.

*M59a   Coastal Area Water Conference at Houston, Texas, October 20, 1948 [Compilation of Papers Presented]. 72 p., 1948.

*M59b   South Texas Water Conference at Corpus Christi, Texas, August 13, 1948 [Compilation of Papers Presented]. 89 p., 1948.

*M59c   West Texas Water Conference at Big Spring, Texas. 67 p., Jan. 1948.

*M59d   East Texas Water Conference at Tyler, Texas. 93 p., May 1948.

*M59e   Central Texas Water Conference at Waco, Texas. 94 p., map, July 1948.

*M60   Underground Water Conservation Districts in Texas, by F. A. Rayner and L. G. McMillion [preliminary copies, subject to revision]. 66 p., 5 figs., Aug. 1960.

*M61   Water Requirements for Certain Irrigated Crops in Texas, by R. C. Garrett. 12 p., 1 fig., Aug. 1951.

*M62   Crosby County, Texas [Records of Wells]. 56 p., map, Aug. 1939.

*M63   Memorandum on Ground-Water Resources in the Vicinity of Crowell, Texas, by W. O. George and C. E. Johnson. 33 p., 5 figs., May 1941.

M64   Dallam County, Texas [Records of Wells]. 49 p., map, Aug. 1937.

*M65   Records of Wells Producing Water from the Travis Peak Formation in the Dallas Area, Texas, by Chris Gard. 13 p., 3 figs., Jan. 1957.

*M66   Dallas County, Texas [Records of Wells], by J. C. Cumley. 107 p., 2 pls., Dec. 1943.

*M67   Dawson County, Texas [Records of Wells], by J. C. Cumley. 41 p., map, Dec. 1938.

*M68   Deaf Smith County, Texas [Records of Wells], by J. W. Lang and C. R. Follett. 53 p., map, Nov. 1938.

*M69   Deaf Smith County, Texas [Records of Wells], by W. H. Alexander, Jr. 85 p., map, Oct. 1946.

*M72   DeWitt County, Texas [Records of Wells]. 44 p., map, June 1938.

*M73   Donley County, Texas [Records of Wells]. 45 p., map, June 1942.

*M74   The Influence of Natural Depletion of River Flow Upon the Quantity of Water Available for Diversion. 15 p., 6 figs., June 1951.

*M75   Occurrence of Ground Water in the Palangana Brine Field, Duval County, Texas, by A. M. Austin. 12 p., 2 pls., Apr. 1959.

*M76   Eastland County, Texas [Records of Wells]. 59 p., map, Dec. 1937.

*M77   Ector County, Texas [Records of Wells]. 34 p., map, Aug. 1937.

*M78   Edwards County, Texas [Records of Wells]. 30 p., map, July 1939.

*M79   Ground-Water Resources of the El Paso Area, Texas, Progress Report No. 6, by R. A. Scalapino and Burdge Irelan. 25 p., 10 figs., Oct. 1949.

*M80   Fayette County, Texas [Records of Wells]. 53 p., map, Feb. 1943.

*M82   Floyd County, Texas [Records of Wells], by W. L. Broadhurst, J. W. Lang, and G. H. Shafer. 50 p., map, June 1938.

*M83   Floyd County, Texas [Records of Wells], by C. R. Follett and J. H. Dante. 103 p., map, Apr. 1946.

*M84   Foard County, Texas [Records of Wells]. 61 p., map, May 1936.

*M85   Fort Bend County, Texas [Records of Wells, West of the Brazos River]. 52 p., 5 pls., Mar. 1937.

*M86   Fort Bend County, Texas [Records of Wells, East of the Brazos River], by Penn Livingston and S. F. Turner. 13 p., map, Apr. 1939.

*M87   Ground Water Resources of Fort Worth and Vicinity, Texas, by W. O. George and N. A. Rose. 25 p., map, Sept. 1942.

*M88   Freestone County, Texas [Records of Wells]. 87 p., map, June 1937.

*M89   Gaines County, Texas [Records of Wells], by G. H. Cromack. 27 p., map, Feb. 1946.

*M90   Report of Preliminary Investigation of the Occurrence of Ground Water in the Trinity Group near Gainesville, Cooke County, Texas, by R. W. Harden. 26 p., 6 figs., 5 pls., Oct. 1960.

*M91   Galveston County, Texas [Records of Wells], by Penn Livingston and S. F. Turner. 29 p., map, Apr. 1939.

*M92   Galveston County, Texas [Records of Wells], by B. A. Barnes. 157 p., map, Oct. 1941.

*M93   Gillespie County, Texas [Records of Wells]. 51 p., 5 pls., June 1937.

*M94   Glasscock County, Texas [Records of Wells]. 50 p., map, Nov. 1937.

*M95   Gonzales County, Texas [Records of Wells]. 59 p., map, May 1939.

*M96   Ground Water in the Greenville Area, Hunt County, Texas, by N. A. Rose. 8 p., map, June 1945.

*M97   Gregg County, Texas [Records of Wells]. 93 p., map, Feb. 1937.

*M98   Gregg County, Texas [Records of Wells]. 35 p., map, Apr. 1943.

*M99   Water Resources of Gregg County, Texas, by W. L. Broadhurst and S. D. Breeding. 51 p., 1 fig., map, Sept. 1945.

*M100   Grimes County, Texas [Records of Wells], by S. F. Turner. 6 p., Apr. 1939.

*M101   Grimes County, Texas [Records of Wells]. 40 p., map, Mar. 1943.

*M102   Estimated Use of Ground Water in Watersheds of Texas. 15 p., map, Jan. 1957.

*M103   Guadalupe County, Texas [Records of Wells]. 67 p., map, Oct. 1937.

*M104   Hale County, Texas [Records of Wells], by W. L. Broadhurst, C. R. Follett, J. W. Lang, B. G. Brigance, and G. H. Shafer. 73 p., map, Apr. 1938.

*M105   Hale County, Texas [Records of Wells], by R. B. Merritt and C. R. Follett. 179 p., map, July 1946.

*M106   Hansford County, Texas [Records of Wells]. 61 p., map, Sept. 1936.

*M107   Hardeman County, Texas [Records of Wells]. 82 p., 1 fig., Oct. 1936.

*M108   Hardin County, Texas [Records of Wells]. 36 p., map, Dec. 1942.

*M109   Harris County, Texas [Records of Wells], by Penn Livingston and S. F. Turner. 100 p., Apr. 1939.

*M110   Harrison County, Texas, Water Resources, by W. L. Broadhurst and S. D. Breeding. 55 p., 2 figs., map, May 1943.

*M111   Water Resources of Harrison County, Texas, by W. L. Broadhurst and S. D. Breeding. 58 p., 2 figs., map, Sept. 1943.

*M112   Harrison County, Texas [Records of Wells]. 43 p., 2 figs., map, Dec. 1942.

*M113   Hartley County, Texas [Records of Wells]. 43 p., map, July 1938.

*M114   Hays County, Texas [Records of Wells], by B. A. Barnes. 31 p., map, Nov. 1938.

*M115   Henderson County, Texas [Records of Wells]. 113 p., 9 pls., Sept. 1936

*M116   Hidalgo County, Texas [Records of Wells], by J. T. Lonsdale and S. S. Nye. 71 p., map, Sept. 1938.

*M117   Hidalgo County, Texas [Records of Wells]. 103 p., map, May 1941.

*M117a Ground Water in the Linn District, North-Central Hidalgo County, Texas, by W. O. George. 8 p., June 1947.

M118   Occurrence and Development of Ground Water in the Linn-Faysville Area, Hidalgo County, Texas, by C. R. Follett, W. N. White, and Burdge Irelan. 53 p., 1 fig., Sept. 1949.

*M119   Ground Water in the High Plains in Texas, by W. N. White, W. L. Broadhurst, and J. W. Lang. 59 p., 12 figs., Dec. 1940.

*M120   Progress Report on Ground Water in the High Plains in Texas, by W. H. Alexander, Jr., W. L. Broadhurst, and W. N. White. 35 p., 12 figs., Apr. 1943.

*M121   Progress Report on Ground Water in the High Plains in Texas, by W. L. Broadhurst and W. H. Alexander, Jr. 20 p., 7 figs., May 1944.

*M122   Ground Water in High Plains of Texas, Progress Report No. 5, by W. H. Alexander, Jr., and J. W. Lang. 41 p., 11 figs., May 1945.

*M123   Ground Water in High Plains in Texas, Progress Report No. 6, by W. L. Broadhurst. 44 p., 10 figs., Nov. 1946 (with addendum, Jan. 1947).

M124   Cost of Pumping Water for Irrigation, Texas High Plains: Field Investigations—1947 Irrigation Season, by W. F. Hughes. 28 p., 3 figs., Aug. 1951.

*M125   Geology and Ground Water in the Irrigated Region of the Southern High Plains in Texas, Progress Report No. 7, by J. R. Barnes, W. C. Ellis, E. R. Leggat, R. A. Scalapino, W. O. George, and Burdge Irelan, 56 p., 32 figs., 7 pls., map, Mar. 1949.

*M126   Hockley County, Texas [Records of Wells], by C. B. Mueller, J. W. Lang, and W. L. Broadhurst. 73 p., map, May 1940.

*M127   Hopkins County, Texas [Records of Wells]. 18 p., map, Mar. 1943.

*M128   Progress Report on the Ground-Water Resources of the Houston District, Texas, by W. N. White, S. F. Turner, and Penn Livingston. 64 p., 5 charts, 2 maps, Mar. 1937 (with postscript, June 1937).

*M129   Progress Report on the Ground-Water Resources of the Houston District, Texas, by W. N. White. 8 p., map, July 1938.

*M130   Ground-Water Resources of the Houston-Galveston Area and Adjacent Region, Texas, by W. N. White, Penn Livingston, and S. F. Turner. 304 p., 12 maps, 1939.

*M131   Progress Report on the Ground-Water Resources of the Houston District, Texas, by W. N. White. 18 p., Mar. 1939.

M132   Progress Report on the Ground-Water Resources of the Houston District, by W. N. White, N. A. Rose, and W. F. Guyton. 47 p., 10 figs., Nov. 1940.

*M133   Ground-Water Resources of the Houston District; Progress Report with Records of Wells, Pumpage, Water Level Fluctuations in Wells, and Well Water Analyses; Harris County and Adjoining Parts of Fort Bend and Waller Counties, Texas, by W. N. White, N. A. Rose, and W. F. Guyton. 191 p., 10 figs., Jan. 1942.

*M134   Progress Report on the Ground-Water Resources of the Houston District, by W. N. White, N. A. Rose, and W. F. Guyton. 33 p., 8 figs., Jan. 1942.

*M135   Pump Settings and Pumping Levels in Houston District, Texas, by N. A. Rose and W. T. Stuart. 25 p., May 1943.

*M136   Exploratory Water-Well Drilling in the Houston District, Texas, by N. A. Rose, W. N. White, and Penn Livingston. 44 p., 10 figs., June 1943.

*M137   Progress Report on the Ground-Water Resources of the Houston District, Texas, by N. A. Rose and W. H. Alexander, Jr. 40 p., 12 figs., Nov. 1944.

*M138   Ground-Water Resources of the Houston District, Texas, Progress Report for 1946, with Section on Results of Pumping Tests at New Southwest Pumping Plant, by J. W. Lang and R. W. Sundstrom. 51 p., 14 figs., Dec. 1946.

*M139   Memorandum on Multiple-Step Drawdown Tests, Southwest Well Field, Houston, Texas, February 1949, by M. I. Rorabaugh. 14 p., 4 figs., Sept. 1949.

*M140   Howard County, Texas [Records of Wells]. 97 p., map, Apr. 1937.

*M142   Irion County, Texas [Records of Wells]. 41 p., 2 maps, June 1941.

*M143   Chemical Quality Standards for Irrigation Waters. 7 p., 1 fig., Oct. 1956.

*M143a   General and Special Irrigation Laws of the State of Texas. 103 p., Dec. 1920.

*M144   Jackson County, Texas [Records of Wells], by C. R. Follett and J. C. Cumley. 45 p., map, Feb. 1943.

*M145   Jasper and Newton Counties, Texas [Records of Wells]. 53 p., map, Dec. 1942.

*M146   Jefferson County, Texas, Water Well Data. 69 p., 2 maps, Apr. 1942.

*M147   Northern Part of Jim Hogg County, Texas [Records of Wells]. 16 p., map, 1940.

*M148   Jim Wells County, Texas [Records of Wells]. 56 p., map, 1940.

*M149   Reconnaissance Report on Alleged Contamination of California Creek Near Avoca, Jones County, Texas [Contamination Report No. 5], by V. M. Shamburger, Jr. 15 p., 1 fig., Dec. 1958.

*M150   A Reconnaissance of Alleged Salt-Contamination of Soils Near Stamford, Jones County, Texas [Contamination Report No. 6], by V. M. Shamburger, Jr., 9 p., 1 fig., Jan. 1960.

*M151   Karnes County, Texas [Records of Wells]. 74 p., map, Oct. 1937.

*M152   Kendall County, Texas [Records of Wells]. 50 p., 2 maps, Aug. 1940.

*M153   Kenedy County, Texas [Records of Wells]. 57 p., map, 1940.

*M154   Kinney County, Texas [Records of Wells]. 38 p., map, 1940.

M155   Knox County, Texas [Records of Wells]. 60 p., map, Nov. 1937.

*M156   Investigation of Contamination Complaint in South-Central Knox County, Texas [Contamination Report No. 7], by D. C. Draper, 9 p., 4 pls., Jan. 1960.

*M157   Lamb County, Texas [Records of Wells]. 34 p., map, Jan. 1938.

*M158   Lavaca County, Texas [Records of Wells]. 62 p., map, June 1936.

*M159   Lee County, Texas [Records of Wells]. 29 p., map, Nov. 1937.

*M160   Leon County, Texas [Records of Wells]. 75 p., map, Oct. 1937.

*M161   Ground-Water Resources of Liberty County, Texas, by W. H. Alexander, Jr. and S. D. Breeding. 73 p., 4 figs., pl., Oct. 1945.

*M162   Live Oak County, Texas [Records of Wells]. 16 p., map, 1940.

*M163   A Reconnaissance Investigation of Alleged Contamination of Irrigation Wells Near Lockett, Wilbarger County [Contamination Report No. 8], by Jack Stearman. 12 p., 4 figs., Mar. 1960.

*M164   Duty of Water on the Lower Rio Grande Valley, Season 1914-1920, by R. G. Hemphill. 52 p., 12 figs., Nov. 1920.

*M165   WPA Proj. 1759-Water Table Survey in the Lower Rio Grande Valley, Part 9, Sec. 1—Cameron County W.I.D. No. 6. 145 p., 1937.

*M166   WPA Proj. 1759-Water Table Survey in the Lower Rio Grande Valley, Part 8—Cameron County W.I.D. No. 1 and Cameron County W.I.D. No. 15. 119 p., 1937.

*M167   WPA Proj. 1759-Water Table Survey in the Lower Rio Grande Valley, Part 7, Sec. 2—Hidalgo and Cameron Counties W.C. & I.D. No. 9. 129 p., 1937.

*M168   WPA Proj. 1759-Water Table Survey in the Lower Rio Grande Valley, Part 7, Sec. 1—Hidalgo and Cameron Counties W.C. & I.D. No. 9. 125 p., 1937.

*M169   WPA Proj. 1759-Water Table Survey in the Lower Rio Grande Valley, Part 6—Cameron County W.C. & I.D. No. 5. 193 p., 1937.

*M170   WPA Proj. 1759-Water Table Survey in the Lower Rio Grande Valley, Part 5–Hidalgo County W.I.D. No. 2. 21 p., 1937.

*M171   WPA Proj. 1759-Water Table Survey in the Lower Rio Grande Valley, Part 4–LaFeria W.C. & I.D. Cameron County No. 3. 47 p., 1937.

*M172   WPA Proj. 1759-Water Table Survey in the Lower Rio Grande Valley, Part 3–Donna Irrigation District, Hidalgo County No. 1. 91 p., 1937.

*M173   WPA Proj. 1759-Water Table Survey in the Lower Rio Grande Valley, Part 2–Cameron County W.I.D. No. 2. 144 p., 1937.

*M174   WPA Proj. 1759-Water Table Survey in the Lower Rio Grande Valley, Part 1–Willacy County, Texas. 199 p., 1937.

*M175   Lubbock County, Texas [Records of Wells]. 50 p., map, Oct. 1937.

*M176   Lubbock County, Texas [Records of Wells]. 128 p., map, Apr. 1945.

*M177   Water Resources of the Lubbock District, Texas, by J. W. Lang and Trigg Twichell. 168 p., 9 figs., 2 pls., July 1945.

*M179   Marion County, Texas [Records of Wells]. 18 p., 1 fig., map, Feb. 1943.

*M180   Water Resources of the Marion County, Texas, by W. L. Broadhurst and S. D. Breeding. 34 p., 3 figs., map, Sept. 1943.

*M181   Martin County, Texas [Records of Wells]. 84 p., map, Dec. 1936.

*M182   Mason County, Texas [Records of Wells]. 50 p., 2 pls., July 1940.

*M183   Matagorda County, Texas [Records of Wells]. 32 p., map, May 1944.

*M184   Ground-Water Resources of Matagorda County, Texas, by R. W. Sundstrom, G. H. Cromack, and N. N. West. 44 p., 2 figs., Apr. 1949.

*M185   Memorandum Report of Mathematical Method of Comparing Chemical Analyses, by F. A. Rayner. 13 p., Apr. 1960.

*M186   Ground-Water Conditions in the Memphis Area, Texas, by J. W. Lang. 45 p., 4 figs., June 1943.

*M187   Midland County, Texas [Records of Wells]. 42 p., map, Jan. 1938.

*M188   Milam County, Texas [Records of Wells]. 58 p., map, Mar. 1937.

*M189   Memorandum on Ground-Water Irrigation in Mitchell County, Texas, by O. C. Dale and W. L. Broadhurst. 14 p., 1 fig., July 1953.

*M190   Ground-Water Resources in the Vicinity of Nocona, Montague County, Texas, by W. L. Broadhurst and C. R. Follett. 16 p., 1 fig., Dec. 1944.

*M191   Montgomery County, Texas [Records of Wells], by Penn Livingston. 15 p., map, Apr. 1939.

*M192   Montgomery County, Texas [Records of Wells]. 31 p., 2 charts, map, Apr. 1943.

*M193   Pumping Costs, Selected Pumping Plants in Moore and Hansford Counties, Texas, by W. F. Hughes, 8 p., Mar. 1955.

*M194   Morris County, Texas [Records of Wells], by C. R. Follett. 20 p., map, June 1942.

*M195   Nacogdoches County, Texas [Records of Wells]. 54 p., map, Feb. 1937.

M196   Ground Water in Northwestern Nolan County, Texas [Records of Wells], by D. B. Knowles. 9 p., 1 fig., June 1947.

*M197   Nueces County, Texas [Records of Wells], by W. A. Lynch. 29 p., map, 1934.

*M198   Ochiltree County, Texas [Records of Wells]. 45 p., map, June 1939.

*M199   Oldham County, Texas, [Records of Wells]. 51 p., map, Nov. 1938.

*M200   Orange County, Texas, Water Wells, by Penn Livingston and G. H. Cromack. 44 p., map, Mar. 1942.

*M201   A Review of the Proposed Sunday Canyon Reservoir Project, Palo Duro State Park, Texas [Prepared for the Texas State Parks Board]. 35 p., 9 figs., Oct. 1961.

M202   Panola County, Texas [Records of Wells]. 46 p., map, Apr. 1938.

*M203   Parmer County, Texas [Records of Wells]. 46 p., map, Apr. 1938.

*M208   Records of Wells and Springs in Northern Pecos County, Texas, by J. H. Dante. 89 p., 1 pl., July 1947.

M209   Reconnaissance of Ground-Water Development in the Fort Stockton Area, Pecos County, Texas, by G. L. Audsley. 70 p., 4 figs., 1 pl., Sept. 1956.

*M209a Water Resources of the Pecos River Basin. Volume I [Pecos River Joint Investigation–Part III, Report B, Geology and Ground Water, by staff of the U. S. Geological Survey]. 99 p., 6 figs., 7 pls., Mar. 1941; Volume II [Records of Wells], by P. E. Dennis and J. W. Lang, 177 p., 1 pl., Mar. 1941; Volume III [Records of Auger Holes], by P. E. Dennis and J. W. Lang, 198 p., 2 figs., 2 pls., Feb. 1941.

*M210   Reconnaissance Report of the Bishkin-Meyers Well Near Pierce, Wharton County, Texas [Contamination Report no. 4], by V. M. Shamburger, Jr. 15 p., 3 figs., Dec. 1958.

*M211   Potter County, Texas [Records of Wells]. 53 p., map, Jan. 1938.

*M212   Ground-Water Conditions in Premont-LaGloria-Falfurrias District, Texas, by G. H. Cromack. 15 p., May 1944.

*M213   Public Water Supplies in Central and North-Central Texas, by R. W. Sundstrom, W. L. Broadhurst, and Mrs. B. C. Dwyer. 250 p., map, July 1947.

*M214   Public Water Supplies in Eastern Texas, by R. W. Sundstrom, W. W. Hastings, and W. L. Broadhurst. Volume I, 250 p., Feb. 1945; Volume II, 229 p., Feb. 1945.

*M215 Public Water Supplies in Southern Texas, by W. L. Broadhurst, R. W. Sundstrom, and J. H. Rowley. 190 p., July 1946.

M216 Public Water Supplies in Western Texas, by W. L. Broadhurst, R. W. Sundstrom, and D. E. Weaver. 284 p., June 1949.

*M217 List of Ground Water Publications [Board of Water Engineers and U. S. Geological Survey]. 22 p., Feb. 1954.

*M218 List of Ground Water Publications [Board of Water Engineers and U. S. Geological Survey, with list of open-file reports]. 57 p., Nov. 1955.

*M219 List of Ground-Water Publications [Board of Water Engineers and U. S. Geological Survey, with list of open-file reports]. 88 p., July 1957.

*M220 List of Publications [Board of Water Engineers]. 23 p., May 1960 (Revised Dec. 1960).

*M221 List of Available Publications [Board of Water Engineers]. 17 p., June 1961.

*M223 Rains County, Texas [Records of Wells]. 14 p., map, Feb. 1943.

*M224 Randall County, Texas [Records of Wells]. 32 p., map, Feb. 1938.

M226 Preliminary Report on the Geology and Ground-Water Resources of Reeves County, Texas, by D. B. Knowles and J. W. Lang. 92 p., 1 fig., 2 pls., July 1947.

*M227 Refugio County, Texas [Records of Wells]. 46 p., 5 maps, June 1936.

*M228 Refugio County and Part of Goliad County, Texas [Records of Wells]. 92 p., 2 pls., June 1938.

*M231 Roberts County, Texas [Records of Wells]. 65 p., 2 maps, Nov. 1940.

*M232 Robertson County, Texas [Records of Wells]. 62 p., map, Feb. 1942.

*M236 Reconnaissance of Water Well Pollution and the Occurrence of Shallow Ground Water, Runnels County, Texas, by V. M. Shamburger, Jr. 30 p., 2 figs., Mar. 1959.

*M236a Water Supply in the Sandflat Area and Adjacent Territory in Rusk, Nacogdoches and Shelby Counties, Texas, by W. L. Broadhurst and Trigg Twichell. 34 p., 1 fig., 1 pl., Apr. 1942.

*M237 Rusk County, Texas [Records of Wells]. 87 p., map, Sept. 1937.

*M238 Rusk County, Texas [Records of Wells, Northwestern Part]. 58 p., Sept. 1943.

*M239 Sabine and San Augustine Counties, Texas [Records of Wells]. 43 p., 2 maps, Apr. 1943.

*M240 A Few Interesting Facts Regarding the Natural Flow From Artesian Well 4 owned by The San Antonio Public Service Company, San Antonio, Texas, by P. P. Livingston. 10 p., map, June 1942.

*M241 Ground-Water Resources of San Jacinto County, Texas, by W. H. Alexander, Jr. 34 p., 2 figs., 1 pl., Feb. 1947.

*M242 San Patricio County, Texas [Records of Wells]. 64 p., 2 pls., Oct. 1939.

*M243 San Saba County, Texas [Records of Wells]. 50 p., map, Aug. 1939.

*M244 Water Supply for the City of San Saba, Texas, by W. O. George. 10 p., June 1944.

*M245 Scurry County, Texas [Records of Wells, Snyder Area and Southeastern Part]. 34 p., 2 figs., Oct. 1946.

*M246 Seepage Losses from Canals in Texas. 103 p., 6 figs., July 1946.

M247 Shelby County, Texas [Records of Wells]. 33 p., map, Mar. 1938.

*M248 Memorandum Report of Preliminary Ground-Water Investigation of Shelby County, Texas, by J. W. Dillard. 9 p., 4 figs., May 1960.

*M249 Ground-Water Resources of Sherman, Texas, by Penn Livingston. 21 p., 2 figs., 1 pl., Nov. 1945.

*M250 Investigation of Salt Water Contamination in a Woodbine Well Near Sherman, Grayson County, Texas [Contamination Report No. 10], by J. W. White. 12 p., 2 figs., Apr. 1961.

*M251 The Silt Load of Texas Streams (Progress Report as of Sept. 20, 1939), compiled by D. W. Bloodgood and A. C. Cook. 102 p., map, Sept. 1940.

*M252 The Silt Load of Texas Streams—Part II (A Progress Report as of October 1, 1939 to September 30, 1940), compiled by D. W. Bloodgood and A. A. Meador. 25 p., Dec. 1941.

*M253 The Silt Load of Texas Streams—Part III (A Progress Report as of October 1, 1940 to September 30, 1941), compiled by D. W. Bloodgood and A. A. Meador. 44 p., May 1943.

*M254 The Silt Load of Texas Streams—Part IV (A Progress Report as of October 1, 1941 to September 30, 1942), compiled by D. W. Bloodgood and A. A. Meador. 44 p., May 1943.

*M255 The Silt Load of Texas Streams—Part V (A Progress Report as of October 1, 1942 to September 30, 1943), compiled by D. W. Bloodgood and A. A. Meador. 51 p., 1 fig., map, May 1944.

*M256 The Silt Load of Texas Streams—Part VI (A Progress Report as of October 1, 1943 to September 30, 1944), compiled by D. W. Bloodgood and A. A. Meador. 51 p., 1 fig., map, Dec. 1945.

*M257 The Silt Load of Texas Streams—Part VII (A Progress Report as of October 1, 1944 to September 30, 1945), compiled by D. W. Bloodgood and A. A. Meador. 62 p., 1 fig., map, Sept. 1946.

*M258 The Silt Load of Texas Streams—Part VIII (A Progress Report as of October 1, 1945 to September 30, 1946), compiled by D. W. Bloodgood and I. M. Stout. 60 p., 1 fig., map, July 1947.

*M259 The Silt Load of Texas Streams—Part IX (A Progress Report as of October 1, 1946 to September 30, 1947), compiled by D. W. Bloodgood and Ivan Stout. 58 p., map, Aug. 1948.

*M260   Progress Report No. 10 of Silt Load of Texas Streams (1947-1948), by D. W. Bloodgood. 63 p., map, Aug. 1949.

*M261   Progress Report No. 11 of Silt Load of Texas Streams (1948-1949), by D. W. Bloodgood. 63 p., map, Aug. 1950.

*M262   Progress Report No. 12 of Silt Load of Texas Streams (1949-1950), by D. W. Bloodgood and J. E. Mortensen. 63 p., map, Aug. 1951.

M263   Progress Report No. 13 of Silt Load of Texas Streams (1950-1951), by D. W. Bloodgood and J. E. Mortensen. 55 p., map, Aug. 1952.

*M264   Fourteenth Annual Report of the Silt Load of Texas Streams, 1951-1952, and A Summary of Silt Studies Made in Texas, by D. W. Bloodgood and J. E. Mortensen. 95 p., map, Aug. 1953.

M265   Fifteenth Annual Report of the Silt Load of Texas Streams for Water Year, 1952-1953, by D. W. Bloodgood. 61 p., Oct. 1954.

*M266   Sixteenth Annual Report of the Silt Load of Texas Streams for Water Year, 1953-54, by D. W. Bloodgood. 61 p., map, Oct. 1955.

*M267   Smith County, Texas [Records of Wells]. 68 p., map, Sept. 1937.

*M268   A Study of the Movement of Moisture in Soils, by W. L. Rockwell. 52 p., 19 figs., Oct. 1948 [3rd Ed.].

*M269   A Report on Model Spillway Studies. 26 p., 11 figs., Sept. 1954.

*M270   Stephens County, Texas [Records of Wells]. 38 p., map, June 1937.

*M271   Sterling County, Texas [Records of Wells], by W. O. George and J. C. Dalgarn. 60 p., 2 maps, May 1942.

*M272   Surface Water Reservoirs of Texas. 59 p., Dec. 1956.

*M273   An Inventory of the Surface Water Resources of Texas, by R. L. Lowry. 63 p., 23 figs., Aug. 1956.

*M274   Swisher County, Texas [Records of Wells], by C. R. Follett. 36 p., map, Apr. 1938.

*M275   Swisher County, Texas [Records of Wells]. 92 p., May 1946.

*M276   Taylor County, Texas [Records of Wells], by H. A. Smith. 38 p., map, Jan. 1940.

*M277   Terry County, Texas [Records of Wells], by G. H. Cromack. 29 p., Nov. 1944.

M278   Texas Floods, April-May-June 1957. 118 p., 18 figs., Oct. 1957.

*M279   Tom Green County, Texas [Records of Wells]. 82 p., 2 pls., Sept. 1941.

*M280   Results of Pumping Test of Municipal Wells at Tyler, Texas, by W. L. Broadhurst. 32 p., 3 figs., Oct. 1944.

*M281   Survey of Underground Waters of Texas, by W. N. White and O. E. Meinzer. 34 p., 3 maps, Feb. 1931.

*M282   Travis County, Texas [Records of Wells]. 102 p., map, Aug. 1941.

*M282a The Unit Hydrograph—Its Construction and Uses, by R. C. Garrett and A. H. Woolverton. 21 p., 11 figs., Aug. 1951.

*M283   Upshur County, Texas [Records of Wells]. 16 p., map, Dec. 1942.

*M284   Relationship of Ground Water to the Discharge of the Leona River in Uvalde and Zavala Counties, Texas, by Penn Livingston. 81 p., 4 figs., 2 pls., Apr. 1947.

*M285   Val Verde County, Texas [Records of Wells]. 51 p., map, Mar. 1940.

*M286   Ground Water Resources in the Vicinity of Vernon, Texas, by C. R. Follett, R. W. Sundstrom, and W. N. White. 46 p., map, Feb. 1944.

*M287   Victoria County, Texas [Records of Wells]. 34 p., map, 1940.

*M288   Results of Tests on Wells at Waco, Texas, by W. O. George and B. A. Barnes. 22 p., 2 figs., Apr. 1945 (Revised Aug. 1945, reprinted Dec. 1952).

*M289   Waller County, Texas [Records of Wells], by S. F. Turner and Penn Livingston. 22 p., map, Apr. 1939.

*M290   Washington County, Texas [Records of Wells]. 47 p., map, Apr. 1943.

*M291   Report to Water Resources Committee. 104 p., Apr. 1954.

*M292   Results of Pumping Tests on the City Wells at Waxahachie, Texas. 9 p., 1 fig., May 1948.

M293   Historical Ground-Water Uses by Municipalities for the Years 1955 Through 1959 for Selected Areas in Texas. 51 p., 9 pls., Jan. 1961.

*M294   Water Use Reported by Municipalities and Industries in Texas. 44 p., June 1958.

*M296   Wharton County, Texas [Records of Wells]. 54 p., map, 1940.

*M297   Ground-Water Resources of Wharton County, Texas, by J. R. Barnes. 86 p., 1 fig., 3 pls., Nov. 1948.

*M298   Williamson County, Texas [Records of Wells], by J. C. Cumley, G. H. Cromack, and C. R. Follett. 95 p., map, Jan. 1942.

*M299   Wilson County, Texas [Records of Wells]. 73 p., map, Aug. 1936.

*M300   Memorandum Report on Water Well Contamination in the Saspamco Area, Wilson County, Texas [Contamination Report No. 3], by V. M. Shamburger, Jr. 15 p., 1 fig., Sept. 1958.

*M301   Winkler County, Texas [Records of Wells]. 36 p., map, May 1941.

*M302   Winter Garden District in Dimmit and Zavala Counties and Eastern Maverick County, Texas [Records of Wells]. 125 p., 3 pls., 1940.

*M303   Wood County, Texas [Records of Wells], by C. R. Follett. 43 p., map, June 1942.

*M304   Yoakum County, Texas [Records of Wells], by G. H. Cromack. 30 p., map, May 1945.

*M305   Contamination of Surface and Ground Water in Southeast Young County, Texas, by R. T. Littleton. 15 p., 1 fig., June 1956.

STATE RECLAMATION DEPARTMENT REPORTS

Next listed is a report of the State Levee and Drainage Commissioner and numerous bulletins that were published by successive State Reclamation Engineers, which are now distributed by the Texas Water Development Board. Publications that are priced are so indicated in this list only if distribution stocks are available.

The office of State Reclamation Engineer was created by an act of the Thirty-third Legislature in 1913. An earlier act had created a State Levee and Drainage Board with comparable duties. In 1939, the functions of the State Reclamation Engineer were transferred to the Commissioner of the General Land Office and the office of State Reclamation Engineer was abolished. Under the provisions of Senate Bill 398 of the Fifty-second Legislature in 1962, the Board of Water Engineers was assigned the powers and duties of the State Reclamation Engineer; the Water Development Board now distributes these reports.

*1   The First Technical Report of the State Levee and Drainage Commissioner on the Reclamation of the Overflowed Lands. 78 p., 1912.

*2   Levee and Drainage Laws of Texas. 61 p., Dec. 1913.

*3   Amendments and Other Levee and Drainage Laws of Texas [To accompany Bulletin No. 2]. 23 p., Apr. 1914.

*4   Levee and Drainage Laws of Texas. 91 p., June 1915.

*5   Tables of Cubic Contents of Levee Embankments. 216 p., June 1917.

*5-A   Factors for Obtaining Cubic Yards on Sloping Cross Sections from Cubic Yards on Level Cross Sections—Base Widths and Vertical Heights on Level Cross Sections with Zero Crowns [Supplement to Bulletin No. 5]. 26 p., Oct. 1918.

*6   Tables of Velocity of Water in Open Channels, Derived from Kutter's Formula. 135 p., Aug. 1917.

*9   Report of the State Reclamation Engineer for the Two Years Ending August 31, 1918. 25 p., Sept. 1918.

*10   Levee and Drainage Laws of Texas: Digest of 1919 [with amendments to the drainage laws down to 1925]. 139 p., Dec. 1919.

*12   Levee Laws of Texas: Digest of 1925. 73 p., July 1925.

*13   Biennial Report of the State Reclamation Engineer, August 31, 1926, with a List of Levee Improvement Districts. 38 p., Sept. 1926.

*15   Forms for Use in Creating a Levee District Under the Act of 1925, Based on Court Records. 60 p., June 1928.

*16   Biennial Report of the State Reclamation Engineer, August 31, 1928, with a List of Levee Improvement Districts. 49 p., Sept. 1928.

*18   A Study of Rainfall in Texas: Charts and Diagrams. 170 p., Aug. 1929.

*19   Biennial Report of the State Reclamation Engineer, August 31, 1930, with Lists of Levee Districts and Drainage Districts. 48 p., Sept. 1930.

*22   Biennial Report of the State Reclamation Engineer, August 31, 1932, with Lists of Levee Districts and Drainage Districts. 47 p., Sept. 1932.

*24   Biennial Report of the State Reclamation Engineer, August 31, 1934, with Lists of Levee Districts and Drainage Districts. 44 p., map, Oct. 1934.

25   Excessive Rainfall in Texas [Revision of Bulletin 18]. 157 p., 115 figs., Nov. 1934. Price: $2.00.

*27   Practical Aspects of Flood Control and Reclamation of Overflowed Lands. 87 p., 38 figs., Dec. 1935.

*28   Biennial Report of the State Reclamation Engineer, August 31, 1936, with Lists of Levee Districts and Drainage Districts. 68 p., map, Oct. 1936.

31   Biennial Report of the State Reclamation Engineer, August 31, 1938. 38 p., map, Dec. 1938.

*----   Levee Report No. 1, Levee Improvement Districts of Texas. 60 p., 4 maps, Jan. 1937.

*----   Report of Colorado River Flood of July-August, 1938, Submitted to Senate Investigating Committee, 45th Legislature. 12 p., 3 charts, Sept. 1938.

TEXAS WATER QUALITY BOARD
1108 Lavaca Street
Austin, Texas 78701

*"Rules of the Texas Water Quality Board", 1970. 143 p.

*"Water Quality Standards Summary".

"Texas Water Quality Requirements (Coastal Waters)". Price: $2.09.

"Texas Water Quality Requirements (Inland Waters)". Price: $2.09.

"Livestock Industry in Texas as it is Related to Water Quality", by Dwight Pittman. A booklet.

*"First Reader on Water Quality", by Joseph Teller. A booklet designed to supply non-technical explanations of water treatment and water quality.

*"Second Reader on Water Quality", by Joseph Teller.

*"Biennial Report".

River Basins: (copies at $0.53 each)

| Canadian River | Brazos-Colorado Coastal |
| Red River | Colorado River |

Sulphur River   Colorado-Lavaca Coastal

Cypress Creek   Lavaca River

Sabine River   Lavaca-Guadalupe Coastal

Neches River   Guadalupe River

Neches-Trinity Coastal   San Antonio River

Trinity River   San Antonio-Nueces Coastal

Trinity-San Jacinto Coastal Nueces River

San Jacinto River   Nueces-Rio Grande Coastal

San Jacinto-Brazos Coastal   Rio Grande

Brazos River

WATER RESOURCES CENTER

Texas Tech University
P. O. Box 4630
Lubbock, Texas 79409

WRC-68-1   Summary of Current Water Resources Research at Texas Technological College.

WRC-69-1   Ogallala Aquifer, Rich Lake Area, Terry County, Texas.

*WRC-69-2   Aerobic Decomposition of Solid Wastes from Cattle Feedlots.

*WRC-69-3   The Effect of Feed, Design, and Management on the Control of Pollution from Beef Cattle Feedlots.

WRC-69-4   Project Completion Report – "Alternate Methods of Mosquito Control to Reduce Chemical Pollution of Waters for Recharge of the Ogallala Formation" – OWRR Project No. B-007-TEX.

WRC-69-5   Project Completion Report – "Development of Systems for Ground Water Recharge into the Ogallala Formation" – OWRR Project No. B-016-TEX.

WRC-69-6   A Checklist and Annotated Bibliography of the Subterranean Aquatic Fauna of Texas.

WRC-69-7   Interim Report Number 1 – Cattle Feedlot Pollution Study.

*WRC-70-1   Summary of Current Water Resources Research at Texas Tech University.

WRC-70-2   Interbasin Diversions: Annotated Bibliography.

WRC-70-3   Interim Report Variation of Urban Runoff with Duration and Intensity of Storms.

WATER RESOURCES INSTITUTE

Texas A&M University
College Station, Texas 77843

Note: Where available, single copies may be obtained free of charge.

TECHNICAL REPORTS

*Glass, Larry Joe, "The Effect of Rainfall on the Velocity Distribution in Shallow Channel Flow." Technical Report No. 1, January 1965. 92 p.

Nail, Frank M., "Flume Studies of Sediment Transportation in Shallow Flow with Simulated Rainfall." Technical Report No. 2, January 1966. 90 p.

*Hudlow, Michael D., "Techniques for Hydrograph Synthesis Based on Analysis and Data from Small Drainage Basins in Texas." Technical Report No. 3, May 1966. 79 p. (Based on Project A-002-TEX).

McBrayer, Michael A., "Shallow Seismic Investigation and Hydrogeologic Problems in the Brazos River Alluvium, Texas A&M Plantation, Burleson County, Texas." Technical Report No. 4, July 1966. 73 p.

*Clark, William J., "Publications, Personnel and Government Organizations Related to the Limnology, Aquatic Biology, Ichthyology of the Inland Waters of Texas." Technical Report No. 5, November 1966. 102 p. (Based on Project A-005-TEX).

*Wixson, Bobby G., "Studies on the Ecological Impact of Evaporation Retardation Monolayers." Technical Report No. 6, December 1966. 101 p. (Based on Project A-003-TEX).

*Hudlow, Michael D., "Streamflow Forecasting Based on Statistical Applications and Measurements Made With Rain Gage and Weather Radar." Technical Report No. 7, August 1967. 110 p. (Based on Project A-002-TEX).

*Pearson, John A., "A Study of the Economic Impact of Water Impoundment Through the Development of a Comparative–Projection Model." Technical Report No. 8, August 1967. 200 p., (Based on Project B-001-TEX).

*Amad, Mohamad T. and Reynolds, Tom D., "The Effect of an Evaporation Suppressant Upon Liquid Film Oxygen Transfer Coefficient." Technical Report No. 9, August 1967. 76 p. (Based on Project A-003-TEX).

*Runnels, Robert C., "On the Feasibility of Precisely Measuring the Properties of a Precipitating Cloud With A Weather Radar." Technical Report No. 10, December 1967. 118 p.

*Barfield, Billy J., "Studies of Turbulence in Shallow Sediment Laden Flow with Superimposed Rainfall." Technical Report No. 11, January 1968. 106 p.

*Canion, Robert Larry and Trock, Warren L., "Input-Output as a Method of Evaluation of the Economic Impact of Water Resources Development." Technical Report No. 12, May 1968. 82 p.

Wilke, Otto C., "A Hydrodynamic Study of Flow in Irrigation Furrows." Technical Report No. 13, July 1968. 95 p.

Machemehl, Jerry L., "Sediment Transport in Shallow Subcritical Flow Distributed by Simulated Rainfall." Technical Report No. 14, September 1968. 137 p.

*Clark, Robert A., "Research on the Morphology of Precipitation and Runoff in Texas." Technical Report No. 15, December 1968. 96 p.

Clark, Robert A., Iehle, W. O., and Powers, R. J., "Meteorological Tables for Determination of Precipitable Water, Temperatures, and Pressure Aloft for a Saturated Pseudoadiabatic Atmosphere – in the Metric System." Technical Report No. 16, December 1968. 35 p.

*Hann, Roy W., "Development of Optimization Systems Analysis Technique for Texas Water Resources." Technical Report No. 17, February 1969. 220 p.

*Davis, W. B., and Reynolds, Tom D., "Influence of Fatty Alcohols and Acids on the Clarity and Biota of Impounded Reservoirs." Technical Report No. 18, February 1969. 84 p.

Schmer, Fred A., "Investigation of a Linear Model to Describe Hydrologic Phenomenon of Drainage Basins." Technical Report No. 19, December 1969. 115 p.

Pearson, John A., "A Study of the Economic Impact of Water Impoundment Through Validity Testing of a Comparative-Projection Model." Technical Report No. 20, August 1969. 192 p.

Trock, W. L., and Casbeer, T. J., "A Study of Institutional Factors Affecting Water Resource Development in the Lower Rio Grande Valley, Texas." Technical Report No. 21, September 1969. 168 p.

Schmer, Fred A., and Trock, Warren L., "Evaluation of Resource Use and Economic Effects Due to Irrigation Water Availability in Texas." Technical Report No. 22, August 1969. 84 p.

Herbich, J. B., Smith, E. B., and Benson, J. D., "Requirements for Effective Use of the Water Resources Scientific Information Center (WRSIC) – Determined by Field Evaluation." Technical Report No. 23, November 1969. (3 volumes)

Wendt, Charles W., "Water Transfer From Soil to the Atmosphere as Related to Climate and Soil Properties." Technical Report No. 24, February 1970. 99 p.

Conner, James Richard, "Incorporation of Agricultural Risk into Water Resource Planning Models." Technical Report No. 25, January 1970. 114 p.

Baldauf, R. J., "A Study of Selected Chemical and Biological Conditions of the Lower Trinity River and the Upper Trinity Bay." Technical Report No. 26, February 1970. 177 p.

Gerard, C. J., "Influence of Transpiration Suppressants, Sprinkler Irrigation and Moisture Levels on Transpiration and Evapotranspiration." Technical Report No. 27, May 1970.

Clark, Robert A., "A Hydrometeorological Study Related to the Distribution of Precipitation and Runoff over Small Drainage Basins – Urban Versus Rural Areas." Technical Report No. 28, June 1970.

Langley, W. D., "Intermediate Products in the Bacterial Decomposition of Hexadecanol and Octadecanol." Technical Report No. 29, June 1970.

Meier, W. L., "Application of Specialized Optimization Techniques in Water Quantity and Quality Management with Respect to Planning for the Trinity River Basin." Technical Report No. 30, July 1970.

Hiler, E. A. and Lyle, W. M., "Electrophoretic Clarification of Water". Technical Report No. 31, August 1970.

MISCELLANEOUS PAPERS

Smerdon, Ernest T., "Research Needs in Long Range Water Resource Planning." Presented at joint meeting of the Southeast and Southwest Sections of the American Society of Agricultural Engineers, Dallas, Texas. February 1, 1965.

*Smerdon, Ernest T., "The Water Resources Institute at Texas A&M University." Presented at West Texas Water Conference, Lubbock, Texas. February 5, 1965.

*Smerdon, Ernest T., "Agricultural Engineering in Water Resources." Paper No. 65-585, ASAE, Chicago, Illinois, December, 1965.

*Schmer, Fred A. and Keese, Carrol W., "Agricultural Water Considerations in Developing State Water Plans." Presented to Southwest Section Meeting and ASAE, Little Rock, Arkansas. April 1, 1966. (Based on Project A-001-TEX).

Smerdon, Ernest T., "Texas Water Resources." Presented at Natural Resources Institute, Ohio State University, March, 1965.

Smerdon, Ernest T., "The Impact of Evapotranspiration on Water Resources". Presented at the ASCE Environmental Engineering Conference. February, 1967.

Schmer, Fred A. and Wistrand, Glen L., "Projection of Agricultural Water and Land Use for Long Range Water Resources in Texas." Presented at the 3rd Annual American Water Resources Conference, San Francisco, California, 1967.

*Smerdon, E. T. and Smith, E. B., "Developments in Storage, Retrieval and Dissemination of Water Information." Presented at the Texas Section, American Society of Civil Engineers, San Antonio, Texas. October 1968.

BROCHURES

"Water for Texas" a 12 page brochure on Texas water problems and the Texas A&M University program in water resources. This brochure is available in quantity from the Water Resources Institute.

PROCEEDINGS, CONFERENCE ON WATER FOR TEXAS

*First Conference, September 19-20, 1955. Theme – "Knowledge Necessary for Intelligent Management of Water."

*Second Conference, September 17-19, 1956. Theme – "Phases of Management."

Third Conference, September 16-18, 1957. Theme – "What is Happening to Our Water."

*Fourth Conference, September 15-17, 1958. Theme – "Watershed Management and Water Supply."

*Fifth Conference, September 9-11, 1959. Theme – "Water for Industry and Agriculture."

*Sixth Conference, September 7-9, 1960. Theme – "Future Water Needs."

Seventh Conference, September 6-8, 1961. Theme – "Technical Conservation, Reclamation and Economic Projections."

Eighth Conference, November 18-20, 1963. Theme – "Education and Research Programs Needed for Water in Texas."

Ninth Conference, November 23-24, 1964. Theme – "Water Quality and Chemicals – Industrial and Agricultural."

Tenth Conference, November 22-23, 1965. Theme – "Creative Thinking and Practical Planning."

Eleventh Conference, November 21-22, 1966. Theme – "Challenges of the Present."

Twelfth Conference, November 20-21, 1967. Theme – "Aspects of Water Management."

Thirteenth Conference, November 25-26, 1968. Theme —
"Meeting Texas Water Needs."

ANNUAL REPORTS

*1965 Annual Report, Water Resources Institute, August 1965.

*1966 Annual Report, Water Resources Institute, August 1966.

1967 Annual Report, Water Resources Institute, August 1967.

1968 Annual Report, Water Resources Institute, August 1968.

1969 Annual Report, Water Resources Institute, July 1969.

1970 Annual Report, Water Resources Institute, July 1970.

SPECIAL REPORTS

"Current Water Resources Research at and in Cooperation with
Texas A&M University." August 1964, 155 p.

*Runkles, Jack R. and Smerdon, Ernest T. (Editors). "Agricul-
tural Resources Related to Water Development in Texas." Preliminary Report to the Texas Water Development Board, September 1965, 167 p. (Based on Project A-001-TEX).

Wells, Dan M. Smerdon, Ernest T. and Gloyna, Earnest F.
"The Galveston Bay Work Plan." A special report to the Fed-
eral Water Pollution Control Administration, USDI, and the
Texas Water Pollution Control Board prepared jointly by the
Texas Technological College, The University of Texas and Tex-
as A&M University, October 1966, 13 p.

Wells, Dan M., Smerdon, Ernest T. and Gloyna, Earnest F. (Editors). "The Galveston Bay Work Plan — Appendices." October 1966, 219 p.

BUREAU OF ECONOMIC GEOLOGY

The University of Texas
University Station
Box X
Austin, Texas 78712

*The Bureau of Economic Geology is a research bureau of
the University of Texas at Austin and functions as the Texas
State Geological Survey. Its director fills the position of State
Geologist.*

*Address all orders to the above address. Remittance should
be made payable to the Bureau. Most of the publications
which are out of print are available on a loan basis for a period of two weeks. A deposit of $20.00 per publication is re-
quired by separate check made payable to the Bureau of Economic Geology. These loan copies are sent, and should be returned, by insured mail. Deposit is returned to the borrower
when the insured publication is received by the Bureau.*

BULLETINS

*57   Geology and Underground Waters of the Northern Llano
      Estacado, by C. L. Baker. 1915. 225 p., 3 maps.

2234   Report on Texas Alkali Lakes, by C. C. Meigs, H. P. Bas-
      sett, and G. B. Slaughter. 1923. 59 p., (Deals with the
      practicability of recovering potash from various lakes.)
      Price: $0.40.

*2327 Investigations on the Red River Made in Connection
      with the Oklahoma-Texas Boundary Suite, by E. H.
      Sellards, B. C. Tharp, and R. T. Hill. 1923. 174 p.,
      6 colored maps.

3138   Underground Waters and Subsurface Temperatures of
      the Woodbine Sand in Northeast Texas, by F. B. Plum-
      mer and E. C. Sargent. 1931. 178 p., map. Price:
      $1.00.

4301   Texas Mineral Resources. 1943 [1946]. 390 p. (A
      volume containing twenty-seven papers, some available
      separately.) Price: $1.50.

      (y) Texas Water Resources, by F. B. Plummer.
           Price: $0.10.
      (z) Earth Temperatures and Oil Field Waters of
           North-Central Texas, by V. E. Barnes. Price:
           $0.20.

SYMPOSIA

Oil and Water-Related Resource Problems of the Southwest. A
Symposium. Contains eight papers presented at meeting of
Southwestern Federation of Geological Societies, Austin, Tex-
as. January 19, 1965. 64 p. Price: $0.50.

MINERAL RESOURCE SURVEY CIRCULARS

Based on results of work under W.P.A. project sponsored
by Bureau of Economic Geology, 1936-1943.

4   Report on a Shallow Water Investigation as Part of a
      Mineral Resource Survey in Clay County, Texas, by G.
      L. Evans. Free on request.

UTAH

DEPARTMENT OF NATURAL RESOURCES

Division of Fish & Game
1596 West North Temple
Salt Lake City, Utah 84116

Note: A number of these publications are now out of print. Write to the Division for more specific information on availability.

60-2 Investigations of Specific Problems of Utah's Fisheries: Fish Lake, Scofield, Strawberry, Deer Creek Reservoirs and Provo River, by Arnold Bangerter.

60-3 Pre-Impoundment Investigations of the Green River and Colorado River Developments, by Phil Dotson.

60-7 Life History Notes on the Walleye in a Turbid Water, Utah Lake, Utah, by Arnold Bangerter.

61-9 General Survey of Water Pollution in Utah, by Norm Chamberlain.

62-4 Relationship of Carp to Waterfowl Food Plants on a Western Marsh, by Bob Robell and Don Smith.

63-3 High Uinta Lakes Booklets.

63-4 High Uinta Lakes Booklets.

63-5 High Uinta Lakes Booklets.

63-9 Utah Fishing and Hunting Guide.

63-13 The Effects of Beaver on Stream Flow, by James W. Bates.

64-5 Popular Utah Fishing Waters, by Arnold Bangerter.

64-8 Lakes of the High Uintas.

64-9 Lakes of the High Uintas.

64-12 Economic Value of Fishing and Hunting in Utah (updating), by Ed Rawley.

65-4 Ten Year Management Guide for the Utah State Department of Fish and Game, by Temple A. Reynolds.

65-5 The Effects of Water Development Upon Populations of Gambel's Quail in Southwestern Utah, by Darrell H. Nish.

66-2 Cattail Control Methods in Utah, by N. F. Nelson and R. H. Dietz.

66-11 The Pollutional Degradation of the Jordan River as Shown by Aquatic Invertebrates, by Russell N. Hinshaw.

67-3 Spawning Ecology of White Bass in Utah Lake, by Fred Vincent.

67-6 Plankton Periodicity as Related to the Chemical, Physical and Biological Environment of Flaming Gorge Reservoir, Utah-Wyoming.

67-11 Bear River Investigations, Cache and Box Elder Counties, 1962-65, by Arnold Bangerter.

69-1 Ecology of Waterfowl in the Uinta Mountains, by S. R. Peterson.

69-7 Fish Lake Research Project.

69-9 Water Requirements for Waterfowl Marshlands in Northern Utah.

69-13 Fish Harvest Inventory 1968, by Arnold Bangerter.

70-5 Fish Lake Research Project 1969, by Arnold Bangerter.

DEPARTMENT OF NATURAL RESOURCES

Division of Water Resources
435 State Capitol
Salt Lake City, Utah 84114

Note: Also included here are the publications of the predecessor agency, the Utah Water and Power Board.

NUMBERED COOPERATIVE REPORTS
WATER PLAN

Developing A State Water Plan — A Basic Water Resource Data Program for Utah — Cooperative Investigations Report No. 1, October 1964. 23 p. (Prepared by the U. S. Geological Survey and published by the Utah Water and Power Board.)

Developing A State Water Plan — Ground-Water Conditions in Utah, Spring of 1964. — Cooperative Investigations Report No. 2. November 1964. 104 p. (Prepared by the U. S. Geological Survey and published by the Utah Water and Power Board.)

Developing A State Water Plan — Ground-Water Conditions in Utah, Spring 1965. — Cooperative Investigations Report No. 3. (Prepared by the U. S. Geological Survey and published by the Utah Water and Power Board.) 99 p., Illus., maps, December 1965.

*Developing A State Water Plan — Ground-Water Conditions in Utah, Spring 1966. Cooperative Investigations Report No. 4. (Prepared by the U. S. Geological Survey and published by the Utah Water and Power Board.) 95 p., illus., maps.

Developing A State Water Plan — Ground-Water Conditions in Utah, Spring 1967. Cooperative Investigations Report No. 5. (Prepared by the U. S. Geological Survey and published by the Utah Water and Power Board.) 89 p., illus., maps. November 1967.

*Developing A State Water Plan — Ground-Water Conditions in Utah, Spring 1968. Cooperative Investigations Report No. 6. (Prepared by the U. S. Geological Survey and published by the Division of Water Resources.) 104 p., maps, illus. October 1968.

*Developing A State Water Plan — Ground-Water Conditions in Utah, Spring of 1969. Cooperative Investigations Report No. 7. (Prepared by the U. S. Geological Survey and published by the Division of Water Resources.) 61 p., maps, illus.

Developing A State Water Plan — Ground-Water Conditions in Utah, Spring of 1970. Cooperative Investigations Report No. 8. (Prepared by the U. S. Geological Survey and published by the Division of Water Resources.) 71 p., maps, illus.

STAFF REPORTS ON THE STATE WATER PLAN

*1   Appraisal of Water Supply and Depletions Colorado River Basin. February 1965. 11 p. and appendices.

2   Developing A State Water Plan — Hydrologic Study of Great Salt Lake. January 1966. 17 p., illus.

*3   Report on Goals, Objectives and Planning Principles. June 1967. 11 p.

*4   Review of State Water Planning Activities. January 1968. 20 p.

*5   Utah's Ground Water Resources, Brief Appraisals — Parts I and II. February 1968. 28 p.

*6   Interim Report on State Water Plan. June 1969.

*7   Interim Report on State Water Plan. Revised March, 1970. 44 p. plus Appendices A and B.

SPECIAL PUBLICATIONS, STATE WATER PLAN.

*Developing A State Water Plan, Status of Water Planning In Utah, April 1, 1966, Special Publication No. 1, Utah Water and Power Board Publication, Proceedings of a symposium on State and Federal Water Planning in Utah Sponsored by the Water and Power Board Staff, June 1966. 135 p., map.

*Preliminary Assessment of Desalting and Electric Power and Process Steam Production for The Wasatch Front Area of Utah, prepared jointly by the Atomic Energy Commission, Office of Saline Water and Utah Division of Water Resources, Draft completed June, 1968. 213 p., maps, illus. December 1968.

*State of Utah Plan for Emergency Management Water Resources, February 1968, E. B. Haycock.

Report on the Ute Indian Unit of the Central Utah Project, February 1968. 28 p., map, Staff of Division of Water Resources.

*Report on the Uintah Unit of the Central Utah Project, March 1968, 17 p., Division of Water Resources publication.

1971 Action Program for the Utah State Water Plan. December, 1970. Unnumbered. Maps, illus. Staff of the Division of Water Resources.

UNNUMBERED REPORTS PREPARED UNDER COOPERATIVE ARRANGEMENTS, WATER PLAN.

*Developing A State Water Plan — Summary and Recommendations. November 1962. 19 p. (Issued jointly with Utah State University.)

*Developing A State Water Plan — Utah's Water Resources, Problems and Needs — A Challenge. March 1963. 122 p., maps, illus. (Issued jointly with Utah State University.)

*Developing A State Water Plan — Summary of Surface Water Records in Utah. September 1963. 30 p. (Issued jointly with Utah State University.)

Reconnaissance of Water Resources of a Part of Western Kane County, Utah by Harry D. Goode, Department of Geology, University of Utah. Prepared by the Utah Engineering Experiment Station — University of Utah. Published by the Utah Geological and Mineralogical Survey and the Utah Water and Power Board. Water Resources Bulletin 5. August 1964. 63 p. illus.

*Developing A State Water Plan — Water Yields in Utah. Special Report 18, Utah Agricultural Experiment Station. September 1964. 65 p. (Prepared by Utah State University and published by Utah Water and Power Board.)

Mineralized Springs in Utah — prepared by Utah Water Research Laboratory in Cooperation with the Utah Water and Power Board, Sept. 1966. 50 p., maps, illus.

*Reconnaissance of Water Resources of a Part of Western Kane County, Utah, No. 8, by Harry D. Goode, Department of Geology, University of Utah. Prepared by the Utah Engineering Experiment Station — University of Utah. Published by the Utah Geological and Mineralogical Survey and the Utah Water and Power Board. Water Resources Bulletin No. 8. August 1966. 44 p., illus.

*Arable Land Resources of Utah, prepared by Utah Agricultural Experiment Station in cooperation with the U. S. Soil Conservation Service and the U. S. Bureau of Reclamation, February 1948. 33 p., maps, illus.

*Water Related Land Use in the Utah Lake Drainage Area, prepared by the Utah Water Resources Laboratory, Utah State University in cooperation with the Utah Division of Water Resources, February 1968. Maps, illus.

*The Economics of Water Allocation in Utah (An Input-Output Analysis), December 1968. 81 p. In cooperation with the University of Utah.

*Hydrologic Atlas of Utah, November 1968. 306 p. In cooperation with Utah State University.

*Water Related Land Use in the Bear River Drainage Area. In cooperation with Utah State University.

Hydrologic Inventory of the Uintah Study Unit. March, 1970. 181 p. (Issued jointly with Utah State University.)

Hydrologic Inventory of the Utah Lake Drainage Area. November, 1969. 137 p. (Issued jointly with Utah State University.)

*Water Related Land Use in the Weber River Drainage Area. February, 1970. (Issued jointly with Utah State University.)

ACCOMPLISHMENT FOLDERS AND ACHIEVEMENT FOLDERS OF THE DIVISION OF WATER RESOURCES AND THE UTAH WATER AND POWER BOARD.

Available for reference in files of the Division of Water Resources.

Accomplishments of the Utah Water and Power Board for Period of May 12, 1947 to June 30, 1953. 8 p.

Accomplishments of the Utah Water and Power Board for Period of May 12, 1947 to October 31, 1954. 6 p.

Accomplishments of the Utah Water and Power Board for Period of May 12, 1947 to July 31, 1956. 6 p.

Accomplishments of Utah Water and Power Board from May 12, 1947 to June 30, 1958. Folder.

Achievements of the Utah Water and Power Board from May 12, 1947 to June 30, 1960. Folder.

Achievements of the Utah Water and Power Board from May 12, 1947 to June 30, 1962. Folder.

Achievements of the Utah Water and Power Board from May 12, 1947 to June 30, 1964. Folder.

Achievements of the Utah Water and Power Board from May 12, 1947 to June 30, 1966. Folder.

Achievements of the Division of Water Resources from May 12, 1947 to June 30, 1968. Folder.

MINUTES

Available for reference in Water Resources Library. No. 110 W.

Minutes of the meeting of the Utah Water and Power Board from May 1947 to June 1967. Minutes of the Board of Water Resources (formerly the Utah Water and Power Board) from July 1967 to present. Meetings held once a month.

BIENNIAL REPORTS — UTAH WATER AND POWER BOARD

Available for reference in Water Resources Library.

Progress Report of the Utah Water and Power Board to the Governor of Utah — For the Period of May 12, 1947 to November 1, 1948. 59 p., maps.

Second Biennial Report of the Utah Water and Power Board to the Governor of Utah — For the Period of July 1, 1948 to June 30, 1950. 68 p.

Third Biennial Report of the Utah Water and Power Board to the Governor of Utah — For the Period of July 1, 1950 to June 30, 1952. 47 p.

Fourth Biennial Report of the Utah Water and Power Board, to the Governor of Utah — For the Period of July 1, 1952 to June 30, 1954. 31 p.

Fifth Biennial Report of the Utah Water and Power Board to the Governor of Utah — For the Period of July 1, 1954 to June 30, 1956. 69 p.

Sixth Biennial Report of the Utah Water and Power Board to the Governor of Utah — for the Period of July 1, 1956 to June 30, 1958. 58 p., maps.

Seventh Biennial Report of the Utah Water and Power Board to the Governor of Utah — For the Period of July 1, 1958 to June 30, 1960. 79 p.

Eighth Biennial Report of the Utah Water and Power Board to the Governor of Utah — For the Period of July 1, 1960 to June 30, 1962. 64 p., maps.

Ninth Biennial Report of the Utah Water and Power Board to the Governor of Utah — For the Period of July 1, 1962 to June 30, 1964. 96 p., maps, illus.

Tenth Biennial Report of the Utah Water and Power Board to the Governor of Utah — For the Period of July 1, 1964 to June 30, 1966. 81 p., maps, illus.

BIENNIAL REPORTS
DIVISION OF WATER RESOURCES

Available for reference in Water Resources Library.

Eleventh Biennial Report of the Division of Water Resources to the Governor of Utah — For the Period of July 1, 1966 to June 30, 1968. 73 p., maps, and illus.

OTHER PUBLICATIONS — LEAFLETS

*Historical Background on Utah Water & Power Board and Predecessor Organizations, published by the Utah Water and Power Board, 1964. 28 p.

Laws of Utah as Related to the Board of Water Resources and the Division of Water Resources, prepared by the Division of Water Resources, April 1969.

*Scofield-Gooseberry Chronology. Compiled by the Utah Water and Power Board staff. 1965. 26 p.

Guidelines of Policy for use of Revolving Construction Fund published by Division of Water Resources, Jan. 2, 1968. 6 p.

*The County's Role in Water Development, prepared by the Utah Water and Power Board Staff for presentation to County Regional Schools held in 1966.

*Revised Chronology Document File, Scofield-Gooseberry, 1965.

*Revised Chronology, Scofield-Gooseberry Project, 1964. 23 p.

COLORADO RIVER PROJECT LEAFLETS

*Colorado River News Report. Issued July 1957; September 1957; November 1958; Fall 1960; December 1962; April 1964.

*It's Time to Call a Spade a Spade, by George D. Clyde, Commissioner of Interstate Streams and Director of the Utah Water and Power Board. 5 p. No date.

*The Case of the Upper Colorado River Storage Project and Its Participating Projects by George D. Clyde, Sept. 1954. 11 p.

*The Echo Park Dam — Neither an Invasion nor a Precedent by George D. Clyde. Abstract, 4 p., no date.

*Echo Park Dam by William R. Wallace, Chairman, Utah Water and Power Board, no date.

*Utah's Interest in the Echo Park Dam by George D. Clyde, no date. 2 p.

*Brief Summary of Colorado River Storage Project and Its Participating Projects by George D. Clyde. June 1954. 4 p.

*Utah's Last Waterhole — The Colorado River — Cooperative Report by Greater Utah Valley, Inc., Uintah County Colorado River Development Committee and Utah Water and Power Board, Colorado River Development Association, no date.

*Questions and Answers — The Central Utah Project and What it Means to the Duchesne River Area, published by the Utah Water and Power Board, no date.

*The Central Utah Project published by Committee for Development of Colorado River, no date.

*Questions and Answers — The Central Utah Project and What it Means to the Uintah Basin Area, prepared by Utah Water and Power Board and the Uintah Water Conservancy District.

*What Does it Mean to Utah — The Colorado River Storage Project, prepared by Utah Committee for Development of the Colorado River, no date.

*The Dixie Project, published by Utah Water and Power Board — maps and report. Revised Edition published later, no date.

*The Dixie Project Deserves Your Support Because: published by Utah Water and Power Board, no date.

*The Dixie Project, published by the Utah Water and Power Board, 1965.

*News Report Concerning the Central Utah Project, December 1965, published by the Utah Water and Power Board.

*Recreation — New Opportunities for Utah — A bonus from the Colorado River Project, no date.

*Utah's Last Waterhole — The Colorado River, map and report. Cooperative Report with Greater Utah Valley, Inc. and the Utah Water and Power Board, Uintah County Colo. Dev. Committee, Colorado River Dev. Association.

OTHER PUBLICATIONS — BOOKLETS

*Water For Utah — For Full Development of Utah's Resources. July 1, 1948. 129 p., maps, illus.

*Water for Utah — For Full Development of Utah's Resources. 20 p., maps, illus.

*Proposed Irrigation Projects in Utah. December 1948. 196 p., maps.

Water Conservancy Act — Utah Code Annotated, 1943. Replacement Volume Seven, Chapter 9 As Amended by the Thirty-Fourth Legislature of the State of Utah. 1961. 37 p.

*Utah's Ground-Water Reservoirs by Ray E. Marsell. Reprinted from Seventh Biennial Report of the Utah Water and Power Board 1958-1960. 14 p., illus.

Utah's Ground-Water Reservoirs by Ray E. Marsell. Reprinted from Eighth Biennial Report of the Utah Water and Power Board 1960-62. 12 p., illus.

*Ground-Water in Bedrock in Utah by Ray E. Marsell. Reprinted from Ninth Biennial Report of the Utah Water and Power Board 1962-1964. 33 p., illus.

*Developing A State Water Plan — Summary of Progress by Edwin B. Haycock. 12 p., maps, illus.

*Water Conservation Agencies of the State of Utah. December 1965. 115 p., maps. Prepared by the Utah Water and Power Board.

Water Conservation Agencies of the State of Utah, prepared by the Div. of Water Resources, June 1968. 119 p., maps.

Water Resources Law prepared by the Division of Water Resources — Water Laws of Utah, Title 73 as now in Force Relating to the Board of Water Resources and the Division of Water Resources Under the New Department of Natural Resources. A Statement of Policy of the Utah Water and Power Board and Information on Committees. 1967. 30 p.

*Relevant Data Regarding the Proposal to Establish a National Monument on Antelope Island, compiled by Div. Of Water Resources Staff. 57 p., illus.

*Comments Relating to the Colorado River Storage Project and Participating Projects, 1947-1952, published by Utah Water and Power Board.

*Grouse Creek Water Plan, Box Elder County, 1962. 25 p. with illustrated maps, published by Utah Water and Power Board.

*House of Representatives Bills and Correspondence Relating to Reclamation, compiled by Utah Water and Power Board. Library Card No. 110.8 W.

*Little Dell Dam Project. Preliminary Report, February 1962. With illustrated maps.

*Miscellaneous File Regarding House of Representatives Bills and Correspondence compiled by Utah Water and Power Board.

*Miscellaneous File Regarding U. S. Senate Bills compiled by Utah Water and Power Board.

*Reports to Executive Secretary of Utah Water and Power Board on Feasibility, Economics, Adequacy, and Security Furnished on Various Utah Water and Power Board Project constructed and under construction. Unpaged. Published by Utah Water and Power Board. Prepared by Wallace R. Wayman. 1949.

*Inspection Reports of the Utah Water and Power Board from May 17, 1947 to September 10, 1959, prepared by Elvon L. Bay.

DEPARTMENT OF NATURAL RESOURCES
Division of Water Rights
State Capitol
Salt Lake City, Utah 84114

Note: Many of these studies were prepared with the cooperation of the U. S. Geological Survey, while several of the Information Bulletins were cooperative efforts involving the U. S. Department of Agriculture.

TECHNICAL PUBLICATIONS

1 Underground leakage from artesian wells in the Flowell area, near Fillmore, Utah, by Penn Livingston and G. B. Maxey, USGS, 1944.

2   The Ogden Valley artesian reservoir, Weber County, Utah, by H. E. Thomas, USGS, 1945.

*3   Ground water in Pavant Valley, Millard County, Utah, by P. E. Dennis, G. B. Maxey, and H. E. Thomas, USGS, 1946.

*4   Ground water in Tooele Valley, Tooele County, Utah, by H. E. Thomas, USGS, in Utah State Eng. 25th Bienn. Rept., p. 91-238, pls. 1-6, 1946.

*5   Ground water in the East Shore area, Utah: Part I, Bountiful District, Davis County, Utah, by H. E. Thomas and W. B. Nelson, USGS, in Utah State Eng. 26th Bienn. Rept., p. 53-206, pls. 1-2, 1948.

*6   Ground water in the Escalante Valley, Beaver, Iron, and Washington Counties, Utah, by P. F. Fix, W. B. Nelson, B. E. Lofgren, and R. G. Butler, USGS, in Utah State Eng. 27th Bienn. Rept., p. 107-210, pls. 1-10, 1950.

7   Status of development of selected ground-water basins in Utah, by H. E. Thomas, W. B. Nelson, B. E. Lofgren, and R. G. Butler, USGS, 1952.

*8   Consumptive use of water and irrigation requirements of crops in Utah, by C. O. Roskelly and Wayne D. Criddle, 1952.

8   (Revised) Consumptive use and water requirements for Utah, by W. D. Criddle, K. Harris, and L. S. Willardson, 1962.

9   Progress report on selected ground water basins in Utah, by H. A. Waite, W. B. Nelson, and others, USGS, 1954.

*10 A compilation of chemical quality data for ground and surface waters in Utah, by J. G. Connor, C. G. Mitchell, and others, USGS, 1958.

*11 Ground water in northern Utah Valley, Utah: A progress report for the period 1948-63, by R. M. Cordova and Seymour Subitzky, USGS, 1965.

12   Reevaluation of the ground-water resources of Tooele Valley, Utah, by Joseph S. Gates, USGS, 1965.

*13 Ground-water resources of selected basins in southwestern Utah, by G. W. Sandberg, USGS, 1966.

*14 Water-resources appraisal of the Snake Valley area, Utah and Nevada, by J. W. Hood and F. E. Rush, USGS, 1966.

*15 Water from bedrock in the Colorado Plateau of Utah, by R. D. Feltis, USGS, 1966.

16   Ground-water conditions in Cedar Valley, Utah County, Utah, by R. D. Feltis, USGS, 1967.

*17 Ground-water resources of northern Juab Valley, Utah, by L. J. Bjorklund, USGS, 1968.

18   Hydrologic reconnaissance of Skull Valley, Tooele County, Utah, by J. W. Hood and K. M. Waddell, USGS, 1968.

19   An appraisal of the quality of surface water in the Sevier Lake basin, Utah, by D. C. Hahl and J. C. Mundorff, USGS, 1968.

20   Extensions of streamflow records in Utah, by J. K. Reid, L. E. Carroon, and G. E. Pyper, USGS, 1969.

21   Summary of maximum discharges in Utah streams, by G. L. Whitaker, USGS, 1969.

22   Reconnaissance of the ground-water resources of the upper Fremont River valley, Wayne County, Utah, by L. J. Bjorklund, USGS, 1969.

23   Hydrologic reconnaissance of Rush Valley, Tooele County, Utah, by J. W. Hood, Don Price, and K. M. Waddell, USGS, 1969.

24   Hydrologic reconnaissance of Deep Creek valley, Tooele and Juab Counties, Utah, and Elko and White Pine Counties, Nevada, by J. W. Hood and K. M. Waddell, USGS, 1969.

25   Hydrologic reconnaissance of Curlew Valley, Utah and Idaho, by E. L. Bolke and Don Price, USGS, 1969.

26   Hydrologic reconnaissance of the Sink Valley area, Tooele and Box Elder Counties, Utah, by Don Price and E. L. Bolke, USGS, 1969.

27   Water resources of the Heber-Kamas-Park City area, north-central Utah, by C. H. Baker, Jr., USGS, 1970.

28   Ground-water conditions in southern Utah Valley and Goshen Valley, Utah, by R. M. Cordova, USGS, 1970.

29   Hydrologic reconnaissance of Grouse Creek valley, Box Elder County, Utah, by J. W. Hood and Don Price, USGS, 1970.

30   Hydrologic reconnaissance of the Park Valley area, Box Elder County, Utah, by J. W. Hood, USGS, 1970.

31   Water resources of Salt Lake County, Utah, by Allen G. Hely, R. W. Mower, and C. Albert Harr, USGS, 1971.

32   Geology and water resources of the Spanish Valley area, Grand and San Juan Counties, Utah, by C. T. Sumsion, USGS, 1971.

33   Hydrologic reconnaissance of Hansel Valley and northern Rozel Flat, Box Elder County, Utah, by J. W. Hood, USGS, 1971.

34   Summary of water resources of Salt Lake County, Utah, by Allen G. Hely, R. W. Mower, and C. Albert Harr, USGS, 1970.

35   Ground-water conditions in the East Shore area, Box Elder, Davis, and Weber Counties, Utah, 1960-69, by E. L. Bolke and K. M. Waddell, USGS, 1971.

WATER CIRCULARS

1   Ground water in the Jordan Valley, Salt Lake County, Utah, by Ted Arnow, USGS, 1965.

2   Ground water in Tooele Valley, Utah, by J. S. Gates and O. A. Keller, USGS, 1970.

BASIC-DATA REPORTS

*1   Records and water-level measurements of selected wells and chemical analyses of ground water, East Shore area, Davis, Weber, and Box Elder Counties, Utah, by R. E. Smith, USGS, 1961.

*2   Records of selected wells and springs, selected drillers' logs of wells, and chemical analyses of ground and surface waters, northern Utah Valley, Utah County, Utah, by Seymour Subitzky, USGS, 1962.

*3   Ground water data, central Sevier Valley, parts of San-
      pete, Sevier, and Piute Counties, Utah, by C. H. Carpen-
      ter and R. A. Young, USGS, 1963.

*4   Selected hydrologic data, Jordan Valley, Salt Lake
      County, Utah, by I. W. Marine and Don Price, USGS,
      1963.

*5   Selected hydrologic data, Pavant Valley, Millard County,
      Utah, by R. W. Mower, USGS, 1963.

*6   Ground-water data, parts of Washington, Iron, Beaver,
      and Millard Counties, Utah, by G. W. Sandberg, USGS,
      1963.

7   Selected hydrologic data, Tooele Valley, Tooele County,
      Utah, by J. S. Gates, USGS, 1963.

8   Selected hydrologic data, upper Sevier River basin, Utah,
      by C. H. Carpenter, G. B. Robinson, Jr., and L. J. Bjork-
      lund, USGS, 1964.

9   Ground-water data, Sevier Desert, Utah, by R. W. Mower
      and R. D. Feltis, USGS, 1964.

*10   Quality of surface water in the Sevier Lake basin, Utah,
      by D. C. Hahl and R. E. Cabell, USGS, 1965.

*11   Hydrologic and climatologic data, collected through
      1964, Salt Lake County, Utah by W. V. Iorns, R. W.
      Mower, and C. A. Horr, USGS, 1966.

12   Hydrologic and climatologic data, 1965, Salt Lake Coun-
      ty, Utah, by W. V. Iorns, R. W. Mower, and C. A. Horr,
      USGS, 1966.

13   Hydrologic and climatologic data, 1966, Salt Lake Coun-
      ty, Utah, by A. G. Hely, R. W. Mower, and C. A. Horr,
      USGS, 1967.

14   Selected hydrologic data, San Pitch River drainage basin,
      Utah, by G. B. Robinson, Jr., USGS, 1968.

15   Hydrologic and climatologic data, 1967, Salt Lake Coun-
      ty, Utah, by A. G. Hely, R. W. Mower, and C. A. Horr,
      USGS, 1968.

16   Selected hydrologic data, southern Utah and Goshen Val-
      leys, Utah, by R. M. Cordova, USGS, 1969.

17   Hydrologic and climatologic data, 1968, Salt Lake Coun-
      ty, Utah, by A. G. Hely, R. W. Mower, and C. A. Horr,
      USGS, 1969.

18   Quality of surface water in the Bear River basin, Utah,
      Wyoming, and Idaho, by K. M. Waddell, USGS, 1970.

19   Daily water-temperature records for Utah streams, 1944-
      68, by G. L. Whitaker, USGS, 1970.

20   Water quality data for the Flaming Gorge area, Utah and
      Wyoming, R. J. Madison, USGS, 1970.

21   Selected hydrologic data, Cache Valley, Utah and Idaho,
      L. J. McGreevy and L. J. Bjorklund, USGS, 1970.

INFORMATION BULLETINS

*1   Plan of work for the Sevier River Basin (Sec. 6, P. L.
      566), U. S. Department of Agriculture, 1960.

*2   Water production from oil wells in Utah, by Jerry Tuttle,
      Utah State Engineer's Office, 1960.

*3   Ground-water areas and well logs, central Sevier Valley,
      Utah, by R. A. Young, USGS, 1960.

*4   Ground-water investigations in Utah in 1960 and reports
      published by the U. S. Geological Survey or the Utah
      State Engineer prior to 1960, by H. D. Goode, USGS,
      1960.

*5   Developing ground water in the central Sevier Valley,
      Utah, by R. A. Young and C. H. Carpenter, USGS, 1961.

*6   Work outline and report outline for Sevier River basin
      survey, (Sec. 6, P. L. 566), U. S. Department of Agricul-
      ture, 1961.

7   Relation of the deep and shallow artesian aquifers near
      Lynndyl, Utah, by R. W. Mower, USGS, 1961.

*8   Projected 1975 municipal water-use requirements, Davis
      County, Utah, by Utah State Engineer's Office, 1962.

9   Projected 1975 municipal water-use requirements, Weber
      County, Utah, by Utah State Engineer's Office, 1962.

*10   Effects on the shallow artesian aquifer of withdrawing
      water from the deep artesian aquifer near Sugarville, Mil-
      lard County, Utah, by R. W. Mower, USGS, 1963.

11   Amendments to plan of work and work outline for the
      Sevier River basin (Sec. 6, P. L. 566), U. S. Department
      of Agriculture, 1964.

*12   Test drilling in the upper Sevier River drainage basin,
      Garfield and Piute Counties, Utah, by R. D. Feltis and
      G. B. Robinson, Jr., USGS, 1963.

*13   Water requirements of lower Jordan River, Utah, by Karl
      Harris, Irrigation Engineer, Agricultural Research Service,
      Phoenix, Arizona, prepared under informal cooperation
      approved by Mr. William W. Donnan, Chief, Southwest
      Branch (Riverside, California) Soil and Water Conserva-
      tion Research Division, Agricultural Research Service,
      U.S.D.A., and by Wayne D. Criddle, State Engineer,
      State of Utah, Salt Lake City, Utah, 1964.

*14   Consumptive use of water by native vegetation and irri-
      gated crops in the Virgin River area of Utah, by Wayne
      D. Criddle, Jay M. Bagley, R. Keith Higginson, and Dav-
      id W. Hendricks, through cooperation of Utah Agricul-
      tural Experiment Station, Agricultural Research Service,
      Soil and Water Conservation Branch, Western Soil and
      Water Management Section, Utah Water and Power
      Board, and Utah State Engineer, Salt Lake City, Utah,
      1964.

*15   Ground-water conditions and related water-administration
      problems in Cedar City Valley, Iron County, Utah, Feb-
      ruary, 1966, by Jack A. Barnett and Francis T. Mayo,
      Utah State Engineer's Office.

*16   Summary of water well drilling activities in Utah, 1960
      through 1965, compiled by Utah State Engineer's Office,
      1966.

17   Bibliography of U. S. Geological Survey Water Resources
      Reports for Utah, compiled by Olive A. Keller, USGS,
      1966.

18   The effect of pumping large-discharge wells on the
      ground-water reservoir in southern Utah Valley, Utah
      County, Utah, by R. M. Cordova and R. W. Mower,
      USGS, 1967.

19   Ground-water hydrology of southern Cache Valley, Utah,
      by L. P. Beer, 1967.

20   Fluvial sediment in Utah, 1905-65, A data compilation
      by J. C. Mundorff, USGS, 1968.

OTHER PUBLICATIONS
(Utah State Engineer's Office)

Biennial Report, 1897/1898 – 1956/1958. Vol. 1-31. (No longer published.)

Report of Distribution of Water Supply, Duchesne River. 1934-1935.

Report of Distribution of Water Supply, Lakefort and Uintah Rivers. 1934-1935.

DEPARTMENT OF SOCIAL SERVICES
Division of Health
44 Medical Drive
Salt Lake City, Utah 84113

Utah Air & Water Newsletter. A monthly newsletter.

First Annual Report – Water Quality Section.

UTAH GEOLOGICAL AND MINERALOGICAL SURVEY
103 Utah Geological Survey Building
University of Utah
Salt Lake City, Utah 84112

Note: Payment should accompany all requests for publications. Quantity discounts are available on Utah Geological and Mineralogical Survey Bulletins, Special Studies and Water-Resource Bulletins, and Utah Geological Society publications. Contact the Survey for further information. Out-of-print material may be consulted in a number of larger college libraries.

BULLETINS

*5   Measurement of Flowing Streams.

73   Mineral and Water Resources of Utah, 1969 (reprinted from 1964 edition). Price: $1.00.

SPECIAL STUDIES

*4   Hydrothermal Alteration in the Southeast Part of the Frisco Quadrangle, Beaver County, Utah, by Bronson Stringham, 1963, 20 p., 2 figs., 3 colored maps.

6   Geology and Hydrothermal Alteration in Northwestern Black Mountains and Southern Shauntie Hills, Beaver and Iron Counties, Utah, by M. P. Erickson and E. J. Dasch, 1963, 32 p., 9 pls. Price: $1.75.

12   Hydrothermal Alteration and Mineralization in the Staats Mine and Blawn Mountain Areas, Central Wah Wah Range, Beaver County, Utah, by J. A. Whelan, 1965, 31 p., 3 figs. Price: $1.50.

13   Concentrated Subsurface Brines in the Moab Region, Utah, by E. J. Mayhew and E. B. Heylmun, 1965, 28 p., 7 figs. Price: $1.50.

14   Geothermal Power Potential in Utah, by E. B. Heylmun, 1966, 28 p., 2 pls., 5 figs. Price: $1.25.

16   Hydrothermal Alteration Near the Horn Silver Mine, Beaver County, Utah, by Bronson Stringham, 1966, 34 p., 2 pls., 11 figs., 1 table. Price: $2.00.

24   Part I – Mineral Resources, San Juan County, Utah, and Adjacent Areas: Petroleum, Potash, Groundwater, and Miscellaneous Minerals, by Howard R. Ritzma and Hellmut H. Doelling, 1969, 125 p., 2 pls., 24 figs., 14 tables, 10 maps. Price: $3.50.

30   Subsurface Brines and Soluble Salts of Subsurface Sediments, Sevier Lake, Millard County, Utah, by J. A. Whelan, 1969. Price: $1.00.

WATER-RESOURCES BULLETINS

1   Water Production from Oil Wells of the Uinta Basin, Uintah and Duchesne Counties, Utah, by H. D. Goode and R. D. Feltis, 1962, 32 p., 3 pls., 4 figs., 2 tables. Price: $1.00.

2   Ground-Water Conditions in the Southern and Central Parts of the East Shore Area, Utah, 1953-1961, by R. E. Smith and J. S. Gates, 1963, 48 p., 2 pls., 8 figs., 4 tables. Price: $1.75.

3   Dissolved-Mineral Inflow to Great Salt Lake and Chemical Characteristics of the Salt Lake Brine, Part I: Selected Hydrologic Data, by D. C. Hahl and C. G. Mitchell, 1963, 40 p., 1 illus., 7 tables. Price: $1.75.

3   Dissolved-Mineral Inflow to Great Salt Lake and Chemical Characteristics of the Salt Lake Brine, Part II: Technical Report, by D. C. Hahl and R. H. Langford, 1964, 25 p., 9 illus., 9 tables. Price: $1.25.

4   Hydrogeologic Reconnaissance of Part of the Headwaters Area of the Price River, Utah, by R. M. Cordova, 1964, 25 p., 5 illus., 8 tables. Price: $1.75.

5   Reconnaissance of Water Resources of a Part of Western Kane County, Utah, by H. D. Goode, 1964, 64 p., 3 pls., 13 figs., 7 tables. Price: $1.00.

6   Evaporation Studies, Great Salt Lake, by E. L. Peck, D. R. Dickson, and C. McCullom, 1965, 36 p., 10 figs., 4 tables. Price: $2.50.

7   Geology and Ground-Water Resources of the Jordan Valley, Utah, by I. W. Marine and Don Price, 1964, 68 p., 30 figs., 9 tables. Price: $3.00.

8   Second Reconnaissance of Water Resources in Western Kane County, Utah, by H. D. Goode, 1966, 44 p., 11 pls., 10 figs., 6 tables. Price: $1.00.

9   Reconnaissance of the Chemical Quality of Water in Western Utah, Part I: Sink Valley Drainage Basins of Skull, Rush, and Government Creek Valleys and the Dugway Valley – Old River Bed Area, by K. M. Waddell, 1967, 15 p., 6 figs., 3 tables. Price: $1.50.

10   Dissolved-Mineral Inflow to Great Salt Lake and Chemical Characteristics of the Salt Brine: Summary for Water Years 1960, 1961, and 1964, by D. C. Hahl, 1968, 35 p., 17 figs., 15 tables. Price: $2.00.

11   Reconnaissance Appraisal of the Water Resources Near Escalante, Garfield Cty., Utah. H. D. Goode. Price: $2.00.

12 Great Salt Lake, Utah. Chemical and Physical Variations
    of the Brine, 1963-1966. Hahl & Handy, USGS. Price:
    $2.00.

13 Major Thermal Springs of Utah. J. C. Mundorff & USGS.
    Price: $3.00.

14 Effects of a Causeway on the Chemistry of the Brine in
    Great Salt Lake. R. J. Madison & USGS. Price: $2.50.

MAPS

27 Wasatch Fault Zone – Salt Lake City Aqueduct System,
    City Creek Canyon to Provo River, Salt Lake and Utah
    Counties, Utah, 1969. Price: $0.25 (over the counter),
    $0.35 (mailed).

CIRCULARS

*21 The Natural Resources and Chemical Industries of Utah.

OPEN-FILE REPORTS

These materials may be reviewed in the office of the Survey on the campus of the University of Utah.

FIELD REPORTS

Report on Water Supplies for Bryce Canyon Lodge, by A. C.
Boyle, Jr., June 1928.

REPORTS OF INVESTIGATION

These materials may be reviewed in the office of the Survey on the campus of the University of Utah.

3   Reconnaissance Report on Great Salt Lake with a Dis-
    cussion of the Disposal of Mill Tailings from Kennecott
    Copper Corporation Concentrators into Great Salt Lake,
    by R. E. Cohenour, A. J. Eardley, W. P. Hewitt and H.
    R. Bradford, June 1963; 49 p.

4   Mineral Appraisal and Valuation of Lands of the Glen
    Canyon Withdrawal Involved in Litigation – State of
    Utah vs. United States of America, by R. E. Cohenour,
    A. J. Eardley, and W. P. Hewitt, June 1963, 52 p.

12 Producing Wells Adjacent to State Lands in which there
    are no Wells Present.

29 Tailings Drift – Morton Salt Inlet, prepared at the re-
    quest of the Great Salt Lake Authority, Oct. 1966, 15 p.

35 Bonneville Salt Flats Hydrogeological Study near Wend-
    over, Utah, by B. N. Kaliser, June 1967, 16 p.

38 Engineering Geology of the Victory Road Reservoir Site,
    Salt Lake City, Utah, by B. N. Kaliser, June 1968, 16 p.

UTAH GEOLOGICAL SOCIETY GUIDEBOOKS

*1   Guidebook to the Geology and Geography of the Henry
     Mountain Region, by C. B. Hunt, 1946.

20   The Great Salt Lake, W. L. Stokes (ed.), 1966, 173 p.,
     38 figs., 8 tables. Price: $4.50.

UTAH WATER RESEARCH LABORATORY
College of Engineering
Utah State University
Logan, Utah 84321

Publications which are out of print may be obtained on a short-time loan basis from the UWRL library.

PROJECT REPORTS

These are preliminary, continuing, and final reports of projects being studied, developed, and investigated by the staff. Some project reports are also designated as student theses sponsored in full or part by the laboratory and supervised by laboratory personnel (indicated as in PRWG17-1T).

PROJECT WG17

*PRWG17-1T The Dynamics of Turbulent Flow in Steep, Rough,
            Open Channels. P. K. Mohanty. 1959.

*PRWG17-2   Flume Studies of Flow in Steep, Rough, Open
            Channels. D. F. Peterson, Jr., and P. K. Mohanty.
            1960.

*PRWG17-3T A Study of Bed Characteristics in Relation to
            Flow in Rough, High-Gradient Natural Channels.
            Harl E. Judd. 1963.

*PRWG17-4T Relation Between the Bed Pavement and the Hy-
            draulic Characteristics of High Gradient Channels
            in Non-cohesive Sediments. Davoud Hariri. 1964.

*PRWG17-5T Flume Study of the Effect of Concentration and
            Size Roughness Elements on Flow in High-gradient
            Natural Channels. M. W. Abdelsalam. 1965.

PRWG17-6   Hydraulics of Large Bed Element Channels. Harl
            E. Judd and Dean F. Peterson. August 1969.
            ($2.50).

PROJECT WG18

*PRWG18   Water Requirements for Waterfowl Areas near the
            Great Salt Lake. In cooperation with Utah Fish
            and Game Department and USU Cooperative Wild-
            life Research Unit. (Please see next five project
            reports for contents.)

*PRWG18-1   January 1960. J. E. Christiansen. Part I.

*PRWG18-2   June 1960. J. E. Christiansen. Part II.

*PRWG18-3   December 1960. J. E. Christiansen, J. B. Low,
            and M. C. Tsai. Part III.

*PRWG18-4   June 1961. J. E. Christiansen, M. C. Tsai, Jack
            Keller, J. B. Low, J. W. Teeter, and D. K. Kaushik.
            Part IV.

*PRWG18-5   November 1961. J. E. Christiansen and M. C.
            Tsai. Part I-II.

*PRWG18-6   The Influence of Salinity on the Growth and Re-
            production of Marsh Plants. D. K. Kaushik, J. B.
            Low, and J. W. Teeter. November 1961.

*PRWG18-7 Evapotranspiration Studies at Howard Slough Refuge and Salinity Measurements at all State and Federal Waterfowl Refuges for 1962. J. E. Christiansen. April 1963.

*PRWG18-8 Evapotranspiration Studies at Howard Slough Refuge and Salinity Measurements at all State and Federal Waterfowl Refuges for 1963. J. E. Christiansen. February 1964.

*PRWG18-9T Water Consumptive Use Studies at Howard Slough Refuge, Weber County, Utah. M. C. Tsai. 1962.

*PRWG18-10T The Influence of Salinity on the Growth and Reproduction of Marsh Plants. D. K. Kaushik. 1963.

*PRWG18-11T The Influence of Sodium Chloride on the Growth and Reproduction of the Sago Pondweed (Potamogeton Pectinatus L.). James W. Teeter. 1963.

*PRWG18-12T Consumptive Use of Water at Howard Slough Refuge in 1962. E-Chiang Lee. 1964.

PROJECT WG19

*PRWG19-1 Prefabricated Irrigation Structures Design, Development, and Field Evaluation. C. Earl Israelsen and Guy O. Woodward. October 1961.

*PRWG19-2 Interim Pictorial Report of Research and Development of Prefabricated Irrigation Structures. C. Earl Israelsen, Fred Haroldsen, and Gordon H. Flammer. August 1960.

PROJECT WG21

*PRWG21-1 Soil Test and Stability Analysis for Porcupine Dam. Gordon H. Flammer. Prepared for Utah Water and Power Board. May 1961 and June 1961.

*PRWG21-2 Woodruff Narrows Dam. Model Analysis of Spillway and Outlet Works. Gordon H. Flammer and C. Earl Israelsen. Prepared for the Utah Water and Power Board. August 1961.

PROJECT WG22

*PRWG22-1 Hexadecanol Monolayer Films on Storage Reservoirs Applied by Aerial Spraying Equipment. Glen E. Stringham. August 1961.

*PRWG22-2 Aerial Spraying Equipment, Feasibility Study Applying Hexadecanol Monolayer Films on Storage Reservoirs. Glen E. Stringham and Vaughn E. Hansen. September 1961.

*PRWG22-3 Aerial Application of Evaporation-Reducing Chemicals. C. Earl Israelsen and Vaughn E. Hansen. July 1963.

PRWG22-4 Equipment and Techniques for Aerial Application of Evaporation-Reducing, Monolayer-forming Materials to Lakes and Reservoirs. Gaylord V. Skogerboe and Vaughn E. Hansen. December 1964.

PROJECT WG23

*PRWG23-1 Developing a State Water Plan, Summary and Recommendations. Jay M. Bagley et al. Joint publication, Utah Water and Power Board and Utah State University. November 1962.

*PRWG23-2 Developing a State Water Plan. Utah's Water Resources – Problems and Needs – A Challenge. Jay M. Bagley et al. Joint publication, Utah Water and Power Board and Utah State University. March 1963.

*PRWG23-3 Summary of Surface Water Records in Utah. Jay M. Bagley et al. Joint Publication, Utah Water and Power Board and Utah State University. September 1963.

*PRWG23-4 Water Yields in Utah. Jay M. Bagley, Roland W. Jeppson, Cleve H. Milligan. Joint publication, Utah Water and Power Board and Utah State University. 1964.

PRWG23-5 Graphical Solutions to Frequently Encountered Fluid Flow Problems. Roland W. Jeppson. June 1965.

PRWG23-6 Mineralized Springs in Utah and Their Effect on Manageable Water Supplies. James H. Milligan, Ray E. Marsell, and Jay M. Bagley. Cooperative publication, Utah Water and Power Board and Utah State University. September 1966.

PROJECT WG24

*PRWG24-1 Calibration of Irrigation Headgates by Model Analysis. Gaylord V. Skogerboe and Vaughn E. Hansen. March 1964.

*PRWG24-2T Design, Calibration, and Evaluation of a Trapezoidal Measuring Flume by Model Study. M. Leon Hyatt. 1965.

*PRWG24-3 Design, Operation, and Calibration of the Canal 'A' Submerged Rectangular Measuring Flume. Gaylord V. Skogerboe, W. R. Walker, and L. R. Robinson. March 1965.

*PRWG24-4 Modifications to Gate-flume Structures on the Weber-Davis Canal. Gaylord V. Skogerboe and M. Leon Hyatt. February 1966.

PRWG24-5 Rating Flow Regulation Structures in the Bear River Canal System. Gaylord V. Skogerboe, Winford M. Barrus, and Lloyd H. Austin. November 1966.

PROJECT WG25

*PRWG25-1 Hydrologic Instrumentation and Telemetering. Duane G. Chadwick. Report for 1965-66. July 1966.

PROJECT WG26

*PRWG26-1T Analysis of Drag Forces on a Hemisphere with Free Surface Effects. Earl Sewell Mason. 1965.

PROJECT WG28

*PRWG28-1 Evaluation of Chemical Composition and Particle Size Gradation of Evaporation-reducing Monolayer-forming Materials. Summary to Proctor and Gamble Company. Vaughn E. Hansen and Gaylord V. Skogerboe. August 1965.

PROJECT PRWG30

PRWG30-1 Brief Abstracts of Some Papers on Seeding Agents. Jay D. Schiffman and Joel E. Fletcher. February 1967.

*PRWG30-2 Reliability of Can-type Precipitation Gage Measurements. C. Earl Israelsen. July 1967.

*PRWG30-3 The Reliability of USU Telemetered Precipitation Data—1., The Counter Precision Factor of 8" x 36" Gages. George W. Reynolds and Duane G. Chadwick. July 1967.

PRWG30-4 Atomic Absorption as an Index of the Silver Concentration in Precipitation. Silver Iodide Plume Studies, Part 1. Joel E. Fletcher and Harvey C. Millar. January 1968.

*PRWG30-5 Determination of Silver Using P-Dimethylamino-benzylidenerhodanine Dissolved in Dimethylformamide as a Chromophore. Reaction Carried Out on Filter Paper, Part 1. H. C. Millar and Joel E. Fletcher. January 1968.

*PRWG30-6 USU Remote Total Precipitation Telemetry Station. Duane G. Chadwick. July 1968.

PRWG30-7 USU Telemetering Precipitation Gage Network. C. Earl Israelsen and Don Griffin. May 1969.

PRWG30-8 Telemetry System Modifications and 1968-69 Operation. Duane G. Chadwick. June 1969.

*PRWG30-9 Supplemental Final Report, Wasatch Weather Modification Project. George W. Reynolds. June 16, 1968 to June 15, 1969.

PROJECT WG31

*PRWG31-1T Effects of Boundary Geometry on Critical and Subcritical Flow through Measuring Flumes. Keith O. Eggleston. 1967.

PRWG31-2 Design and Calibration of Submerged Open Channel Flow Measurement Structures. Part 1, Submerged Flow. Gaylord V. Skogerboe, M. Leon Hyatt, and Keith O. Eggleston. February 1967.

PRWG31-3 Design and Calibration of Submerged Open Channel Flow Measurement Structures. Part 2, Parshall Flumes. Gaylord V. Skogerboe, M. Leon Hyatt, Joe D. England, J. Raymond Johnson. March 1967.

PRWG31-4 Design and Calibration of Submerged Open Channel Flow Measurement Structures. Part 3, Cutthroat Flumes. Gaylord V. Skogerboe, M. Leon Hyatt, Ross K. Anderson, Keith O. Eggleston. April 1967.

PRWG31-5 Design and Calibration of Submerged Open Channel Flow Measurement Structures. Part 4, Weirs. Gaylord V. Skogerboe, M. Leon Hyatt, Lloyd H. Austin. May 1967.

PROJECT WG32

*PRWG32-1 Application of Electronic Analog Computer to Solution of Hydrologic and River Basin Planning Problems: Utah Simulation Model II. J. Paul Riley, Duane G. Chadwick, and Jay M. Bagley. October 1966.

PROJECT WG34

*PRWG34-1T The Structure of Turbulence in an Open Channel with Large Spherical Roughness Elements. Farooq Nazir. 1967.

*PRWG34-2T Two Dimensional Flow Resistance over a Bed of Spherical Roughness Elements. Robert Pi-Chang Yu. January 1969.

PROJECT WG35

PRWG35-1 Hydrologic Atlas of Utah. Roland W. Jeppson, Gaylen L. Ashcroft, A. Leon Huber, Gaylord V. Skogerboe, Jay M. Bagley. November 1968. Price: $10.00.

*PRWG35 Mass Curve Analysis of Streamflow for Determining Reservoir Storage Requirements. Part 1. Roland W. Jeppson. April 1967.

*PRWG35 Frequency and Magnitude of Monthly and Annual Flow Rates. Part 2. Roland W. Jeppson. April 1967.

*PRWG35 Frequency Analyses and Probable Storage Requirements by Frequency and Mass Curve Methods. Roland W. Jeppson. May 1967.

PRWG35a-1 Estimating Water Yields in Utah by Principal Component Analysis. Leei-Luoh Wang and A. Leon Huber. June 1967.

PRWG35a-2 Consecutive Streamflow Averages for 90 Utah Stations. A. Leon Huber. June 1967.

PROJECT WG38

*PRWG38-1 Application of an Electronic Analog Computer for the Simulation of Hydrologic Events on a Southwest Watershed. J. Paul Riley, Duane G. Chadwick, Eugene K. Israelsen. February 1967.

PRWG38-2 Analog Computer Solution of the Unsteady Flow Equations and Its Use in Modeling the Surface Runoff Process. Roger A. Amisial, J. Paul Riley, Kenneth G. Renard, Eugene K. Israelsen. May 1969.

PROJECT WG39

*PRWG39-1T Effects of Effluent and Influent Seepage on the Hydro-dynamic Forces Acting on an Idealized Non-cohesive Sediment Particle. M. V. P. Rao. June 1969.

PROJECT WG40

PRWG40-1 Water Related Land Use in the Utah Lake Drainage Area. M. Leon Hyatt, Gaylord V. Skogerboe, and Frank W. Haws. February 1968.

PRWG40-2 Water Related Land Use in the Bear River Drainage Area. Frank W. Haws. April 1969.

PRWG40-3 Hydrologic Inventory of the Utah Lake Drainage Area. M. Leon Hyatt, Gaylord V. Skogerboe, Frank W. Haws, Lloyd H. Austin. November 1969. Price: $2.50.

PRWG40-4 Water Related Land Use in the Weber River Drainage Area. Frank W. Haws. February 1970.

PRWG40-5 Hydrologic Inventory of the Uintah Study Unit. Lloyd H. Austin and Gaylord V. Skogerboe. March 1970. Price: $2.50.

PRWG40-6 Hydrologic Inventory of the Weber Study Unit. Frank W. Haws. August 1970. Price: $2.50.

PROJECT WG41

*PRWG41-1 Feasibility Study of a Capacitance-type Electronic Sediment-sensing Device. Progress Report. C. Earl Israelsen and Duane G. Chadwick. December 1967.

*PRWG41-2 Feasibility Study of a Capacitance-type Electronic Sediment-sensing Device. Final Report. C. Earl Israelsen and Duane G. Chadwick. June 1968.

PROJECT WG42

*PRWG42-1T A Procedure for Determining the Feasibility of Planned Conjunctive Use of Surface and Ground Water. Barry C. Saunders. 1967.

*PRWG42-2T Linear Programming with Random Requirements. Nak Je Kim. March 1969.

PRWG42-4T (Supersedes PRWG42-3T) Optimizing Conjunctive Use of Groundwater and Surface Water. James H. Milligan. June 1970. Price: $3.00.

PROJECT WG46

*PRWG46-1T Application of an Electronic Analog Computer to the Problems of River Basin Hydrology. J. Paul Riley. 1967.

*PRWG46-2T Mathematical Simulation of Small Watershed Hydrologic Phenomena. V. V. Dhruva Narayana and Jay M. Bagley. December 1967.

PROJECT WG51

PRWG51-1 Feasibility of Rating Current Meters in a Velocity Field. Gaylord V. Skogerboe, Lloyd H. Austin, Roland W. Jeppson, and Chi-Yuan Wei. January 1968.

PROJECT WG52

*PRWG52-1 Finite Difference Solutions to Free-surface Flow through Nonhomogeneous Porous Media. Roland W. Jeppson. September 1967.

*PRWG52-2 Solutions to Axisymmetric Seepage from Ponds through Homogeneous and Nonhomogeneous Porous Media. Roland W. Jeppson. May 1968.

PROJECT WG53

*PRWG53-1 Water Quality Telemetry. Duard S. Woffinden and Allen D. Kartchner. August 1968.

PRWG53-2 Water Quality Telemetry, Final Progress Report. Duard S. Woffinden and Allen D. Kartchner. August 1969.

PROJECT WG55

PRWG55-1 Analysis of Small Water Management Structures in Irrigation Distribution Systems. Gaylord V. Skogerboe, Wynn R. Walker, Brent B. Hacking, Lloyd H. Austin. June 1969.

PROJECT WG56

PRWG56-1 Analog Computer Simulation of the Runoff Characteristics of an Urban Watershed. V. V. Dhruva Narayana, J. Paul Riley, Eugene K. Israelsen. January 1969. Price: $2.50.

PROJECT WG59c

*PRWG59c-1 Numerical Solution of the Steady-State Two-Dimensional Flow System Resulting from Infiltration on a Watershed. Roland W. Jeppson. June 1969.

PRWG59c-2 Transient Flow of Water from Infiltrometers — Formulation of Mathematical Model and Preliminary Numerical Solutions and Analyses of Results. Roland W. Jeppson. July 1970.

PRWG59c-3 (Supplement to PRWG59c-2) Formulation and Solution of Transient Flow of Water from an Infiltrometer Using the Kirchhoff Transformation. Roland W. Jeppson. July 1970.

PRWG59c-4 Determination of Hydraulic Conductivity — Capillary Pressure Relationship from Saturation — Capillary Pressure Data from Soils. Roland W. Jeppson. July 1970.

PRWG59c-5 Solution to Transient Vertical Moisture Movement Based upon Saturation — Capillary Pressure Data and a Modified Burdine Theory. Roland W. Jeppson. December 1970.

PROJECT WG60

PRWG60-1 A Theoretical Study of Infiltration into Range and Forest Soils. Joel E. Fletcher and Yehia Z. El-Shafei. July 1970.

PROJECT WG61

*PRWG61-1 Evaluation of the Adequacy of Stream Flow Operational Hydrology in Duplicating Extended Periods of High and Low Flows. Roland W. Jeppson and Calvin G. Clyde. May 1969.

PRWG61-2 Optimum Operation of Desalting Plants as a Supplemental Source of Safe Yield. Calvin G. Clyde and Wesley H. Blood. July 1969. Price: $2.50.

PROJECT WG62

*PRWG62-1   Bacterial Adsorption on Soils — Thermodynamics. David W. Hendricks, Frederick J. Post, Deorao R. Khairnar, and Jerome J. Jurinak. July 1970.

PROJECT WG64

PRWG64-1   Electronic Analog Computer Simulation of the Paez-Pedraza Region of Venezuela. J. Paul Riley, V. V. Dhruva Narayana, and Kousoum S. Sakhan. May 1969.

PROJECT WG67

PRWG67-1   Developing a Hydro-quality Simulation Model. Neal P. Dixon, David W. Hendricks, A. Leon Huber, and Jay M. Bagley. June 1970.

PROJECT WG71

PRWG71-1   Subcritical Flow at Open Channel Structures — Open Channel Expansions. Lloyd H. Austin, Gaylord V. Skogerboe, and Ray S. Bennett. August 1970.

PRWG71-2   Subcritical Flow at Open Channel Structures — Bridge Constrictions. Gaylord V. Skogerboe, Lloyd H. Austin, and Kuan-Tao Chang. September 1970.

PROJECT WG73

*PRWG73-1   Formulation of a Mathematical Model for the Allocation of Colorado River Waters in Utah. Rick L. Gold, James H. Milligan, and Calvin G. Clyde. September 1969.

PROJECT WG75

PRWG75-1   Influence of Mountain Groundwater on Streamflow. Bi-Huei Wang and Roland W. Jeppson. September 1969.

PROJECT WG76

PRWG76-1   Finite Difference Solutions to Free Jet and Confined Cavity Flows Past Disks with Preliminary Analyses of the Results. Roland W. Jeppson. November 1969.

PROJECT WG81

PRWG81-1   An Examination of Approximately Simultaneous Salt Lake Valley and Cache Valley Clearing (Ventilation) Indexes. George W. Reynolds, William McNeill, Floyd Johnson, and Janet Cleary. August 1970.

PROJECT WR4

*PRWR4-1T   Construction, Instrumentation, and Preliminary Verification of a Physical Hydrologic Model. Donald L. Chery, Jr. 1965.

PROJECT WR6

*PRWR6-1   Submerged Parshall Flumes of Small Size. Gaylord V. Skogerboe, M. Leon Hyatt, J. Raymond Johnson, and Joseph D. England. July 1965.

*PRWR6-2   Submergence in a Two-foot Parshall Flume. Gaylord V. Skogerboe, M. Leon Hyatt, J. Raymond Johnson, and Joseph D. England. August 1965.

*PRWR6-3   Flow Rate Measurement of Logan Outfall Effluents. M. Leon Hyatt, J. Raymond Johnson, and Joseph D. England. October 1965.

*PRWR6-4   Measuring Water with Parshall Flumes. Gaylord V. Skogerboe, M. Leon Hyatt, Joseph D. England, J. Raymond Johnson, and Richard E. Griffin. Joint publication, Utah Water Research Laboratory and Utah State University Extension Services. December 1965.

*PRWR6-5   Evaluation of Free and Submerged Flow Data for Large Parshall Flumes. M. Leon Hyatt, Gaylord V. Skogerboe, Keith O. Eggleston. January 1966.

*PRWR6-6   Laboratory Investigation of Submerged Flow in Selected Parshall Flumes. M. Leon Hyatt, Gaylord V. Skogerboe, Keith O. Eggleston. January 1966.

*PRWR6-7   Stagefall Discharge Relations for Flood Flows over Highway Embankments. Gaylord V. Skogerboe, M. Leon Hyatt, Lloyd H. Austin. March 1966.

*PRWR6-8   Subcritical Flow over Various Weir Shapes. M. Leon Hyatt, Gaylord V. Skogerboe, Lloyd H. Austin. June 1966.

PROJECT WR7

PRWR7-1   State Organizational Patterns for Comprehensive Planning of Water Resources Development. Daniel H. Hoggan. June 1969. Price: $5.00.

PROJECT WR8

*PRWR8-1   Water Vapor Measurements Using Infrared Adsorption. Duard S. Woffinden. 1964.

PROJECT WR11

*PRWR11-1   Techniques of Border Irrigation by a Hydrologic Method of Routing. Cheng-lung Chen. November 1965.

*PRWR11-2   Mathematical Hydraulics of Surface Irrigation. Cheng-lung Chen. June 1966.

*PRWR11-3T   Effect of the Free Surface on the Resistance to Flow over Schematic Dunes in Open Channels. K. E. Israelsen. 1966.

PROJECT WR13

*PRWR13-1   A Rational Approach to the Estimation of Evapotranspiration from Climatological Data. J. E. Christiansen. June 1961.

*PRWR13-2T   New Formula for the Evaluation of Evaporation. Bal. B. Patil. March 1963.

*PRWR13-3   A Bibliography on Evaporation and Evapotrans- piration. J. E. Christiansen and Nella W. Laurit- zen. 1963.

*PRWR13-4T   Comparison of Four Methods of Computing Evap- oration. A. C. Patel. March 1963.

*PRWR13-5T   The Use of Climatological and Related Factors for Estimating Evaporation. Kenneth Jose Mathi- son. 1963.

*PRWR13-6T   Estimation of Evapotranspiration from Climatic Formulas. Carlos Julian Grassi. 1964.

*PRWR13-7T   Evaporation and Potential Evapotranspiration in Central Iraq. Ala H. Al-Barrak. 1964.

*PRWR13-8T   Estimation of Pan Evaporation and Potential Evapotranspiration of Rice in the Central Plain of Thailand by Using Various Formulas Based on Climatological Data. Paitoon Palysoot. 1965.

*PRWR13-9T   Estimation of Pan Evaporation from Climatologi- cal Data. Ashwin D. Mehta. 1965.

*PRWR13-10   Estimating Evaporation and Evapotranspiration from Climatic Data. J. E. Christiansen. Present- ed at Annual Meeting of the Rocky Mountain Section, ASAE, Fort Collins, Colo. April 1966.

*PRWR13-11   A Procedure for Estimating Pan Evaporation and Evapotranspiration from Climatic Data. J. E. Christiansen. Paper presented at the 48th Annual Meeting of the American Geophysical Union. Washington, D.C., April 1967.

*PRWR13-12T Hydraulic Characteristics of a Modified Venturi Section. Muhammad Aslam Rasheed. 1967.

PROJECT PRCWRR12

PRCWRR12-1   Instrumentation and Development of Tech- niques to Measure and Evaluate Meteorological Problems Important to Hydrology. Duane G. Chadwick. November 1970.

PROJECT PREC30

PREC30-1   The Effect of Sediment Properties of an Ultrason- ic Plane Wave. G. H. Flammer, N. E. Stauffer, Jr., and E. Y. Liu. September 1969.

PREC30-2   Ultrasonic Measurement of Sediment Size Distrib- ution and Concentration. Gordon H. Flammer and Ernest Y. Liu. November 1969.

PROJECT EC51

*PREC51-1   Report on Feasibility of an Electronic Analog Ap- proach to Sevier River Basin Investigations for Wa- ter Resource Development and Conservation Plan-

ning. Jay M. Bagley, Duane G. Chadwick, Robert B. Hickok, and Marvin Rosa. August 1963.

PROJECT CSC 6810

*CSC 6810-1 Theoretical and Experimental Aspects of Water- shed Infiltration in Terms of Basic Soil Properties. Roland W. Jeppson. Northwest Operations, Com- puter Science Corporation, Richland, Washington. October 1968.

OCCASIONAL PAPERS

These are papers worthy of publication prepared for presen- tation at a symposium or conference, but not published in a proceedings of that symposium or conference. They might also be papers of general information about certain aspects of the Utah Water Research Laboratory program.

OP1   Engineering for the Human Environment. Senator Frank E. Moss. June 1967.

OP2   Water Resources Research — A Challenge to the Social Scientists. Dean F. Peterson. June 1968.

OP3   A Perspective of Contemporary Water Planning and Man- agement Problems in Utah. Jay M. Bagley. August 1969.

OP4   Attitudes for Environmental Design for the 1970's. Dean F. Peterson. June 1970.

OP5   Computer Simulation of Water Resource Systems at Utah State University. J. Paul Riley. August 1970.

PROCEEDINGS

These are papers presented at symposiums or conferences sponsored entirely or in part by the Utah Water Research Lab- oratory.

*1   Groundwater Development in Arid Basins. Proceedings of a Symposium. Utah State University. March 1967.

*2   Pollution Control of Industrial Wastewaters. Proceedings of a Symposium. Utah State University. August 1967.

*3   Air Pollution Control and Abatement. Proceedings of a Symposium. Utah State University. September 1968.

*   Proceedings of a Summer Institute in Water Resources. Edited by Jay M. Bagley.
       Volume 1 — Philosophical, Institutional, and Legal As- pects of Water Resources.
       Volume 2 — The Economics of Water Resource Devel- opment and Conservation.
       Volume 3 — Water Quality Control and Management.
       Volume 4 — General Principles of Water Resources Plan- ning.

       April 1966.

VERMONT

AGENCY OF ENVIRONMENTAL CONSERVATION

Department of Water Resources
State Office Building
Montpelier, Vermont 05602

BULLETINS

These studies were prepared cooperatively with the U. S. Geological Survey.

1   Ground Water Favorability Map of the Batten Kill, Walloomsac River and Hoosic River Basins, by Arthur L. Hodges, Jr. (USGS). 1966.

2   Ground Water Favorability Map of the Otter Creek Basin, Vermont, by Arthur L. Hodges, Jr. (USGS). 1967.

3   Ground Water Favorability Map of the Winooski River Basin, Vermont, by Arthur L. Hodges, Jr. (USGS), assisted by David Butterfield. 1967.

4   Ground Water Favorability Map of the Lamoille River Basin, Vermont, by Arthur L. Hodges, Jr. (USGS), assisted by David Butterfield. 1967.

5   Ground Water Favorability Map of the Missisquoi River Basin, Vermont, by Arthur L. Hodges, Jr. (USGS), assisted by David Butterfield. 1967.

6   Ground Water Favorability Map of the Lake Memphremagog Basin, Vermont, by Arthur L. Hodges, Jr. (USGS), assisted by David Butterfield. 1967.

7   Ground Water Favorability Map of the Nulhegan – Passumpsic River Basin, Vermont, by Arthur L. Hodges, Jr. (USGS), assisted by David Butterfield. 1967.

8   Ground Water Favorability Map of the Wells – Ompompanoosuc River Basin, Vermont, by Arthur L. Hodges, Jr. (USGS), assisted by David Butterfield. 1968.

9   Ground Water Favorability Map of the White River Basin, Vermont, by Arthur L. Hodges, Jr. (USGS), assisted by David Butterfield. 1968.

10 Ground Water Favorability Map of the Ottauquechee – Saxtons River Basin, Vermont, by Arthur L. Hodges, Jr. (USGS), assisted by David Butterfield, 1968.

11 Ground Water Favorability Map of the West – Deerfield River Basin, Vermont, by Arthur L. Hodges, Jr. (USGS), assisted by David Butterfield. 1968.

OTHER PUBLICATIONS

Cleaner Streams for Vermont, by the Vermont Dept. of Water Resources. 8 p. (Pamphlet).

Cleaner Streams for Vermont Requires Rural Sewage Disposal, by the Vermont Dept. of Water Resources. 8 p. (Pamphlet).

A Preliminary Biological Survey of Selected Lakes and Ponds in Vermont, by Carl F. Baren. 1967.

Algae and Weeds in Farm Ponds, by the Extension Service, University of Vermont and the Vermont Dept. of Water Resources. 1968. 11 p. (Pamphlet).

Canoeing on the Connecticut River, by the Vermont State Board of Recreation and the Vermont Dept. of Water Resources. 1968. 34 p. (Pamphlet).

Vermont Laws Relating to Water Resources, by the Vermont Dept. of Water Resources. 1969. 115 p.

Effects of Industrial Wastes on the Upper Connecticut River, by James W. Morse and P. Howard Flanders. 1969.

CENTRAL PLANNING OFFICE

118 State Street
Montpelier, Vermont 05602

*Quality of Land Water Supplies. 1964.

Status of Outlets and Control Structures of Lakes and Ponds Over Twenty Acres in Vermont. 1964.

*Comprehensive Plan for Outdoor Recreation. 1967.

Vermont Natural Areas. 1969. 30 p. (Report 2).

VERMONT STATE DEVELOPMENT COMMISSION

This Commission is no longer in existence.

Effects in Vermont of the Comprehensive Plan for Flood Control of the Connecticut River. A report to the Vermont State Water Conservation Board. Montpelier, 1947. 104 p.

VERMONT STATE GENERAL ASSEMBLY – COMMITTEE TO INVESTIGATE FLOOD DAMAGE IN THE UPPER VALLEY OF THE CONNECTICUT RIVER

This Committee is no longer in existence.

*Report. Issued annually, 1944-1947.

VERMONT GEOLOGICAL SURVEY
University of Vermont
Burlington, Vermont 05401

Note: Order publications from Vermont Department of Libraries, Montpelier, Vermont 05602. Payment must accompany order, with checks payable to Vermont Department of Libraries.

BULLETINS

4   A Study of Lakes in Northeastern Vermont, by John Ross Mills. 1951. Price: $2.00.

OTHER

The Physical Features of Vermont, by Elbridge Churchill Jacobs. 1950. Price: $1.00.

VERMONT RESOURCES RESEARCH CENTER
The University of Vermont
Burlington, Vermont 05410

REPORTS

1   Natural Areas in Vermont — Some Ecological Sites of Public Importance.

3   The Outdoor Recreation Industry in Vermont.

12   Vermont Resources — Extent, Management, and Development Potential.

16   Recreation Potential of Vermont.

*17   Role of Basin Physiography on the Runoff from Small Watersheds.

18   Scenery Classification.

20   Goals for Natural Resources Planning.

OTHER REPORTS

1   Parameterization of Observed Hydrographs. December 1970. 57 p.

VIRGINIA

VIRGINIA ADVISORY COUNCIL ON THE VIRGINIA ECONOMY — COMMITTEE ON WATER RESOURCES

This Committee is no longer in existence.

*Water Resources of Virginia. 1952. 142 p.

COMMISSION OF OUTDOOR RECREATION

Eighth Street Office Building
803 East Broad Street
Richmond, Virginia 23219

Virginia's Common Wealth. Statewide Outdoor Recreation Plan, 1965. Virginia Outdoor Recreation Study Commission. 96 p. Copies available.

Virginia's Scenic Rivers. 1969. Commission of Outdoor Recreation. 24 p. Copies available.

DEPARTMENT OF CONSERVATION AND ECONOMIC DEVELOPMENT

Division of Mineral Resources
Box 3667
Charlottesville, Virginia 22903

Payment is to accompany all requests for publications. Those items marked by an asterisk may be consulted in the library maintained by this Division or in many public and college libraries.

BULLETINS

3   Hydrography of Virginia, by N. C. Grover and R. H. Bolster. 233 p., 10 pls., 1 fig., 1906. Price: $0.25.

5   Underground Water Resources of the Coastal Plain Province of Virginia, by Samuel Sanford. 361 p., 1 pl., 8 figs., 11 tables, 1913. Price: $0.50.

10   Surface Water Supply of Virginia, by G. C. Stevens. 247 p., 5 pls., 1916. Price: $0.25.

31   Water Resources of Virginia, by J. J. Dirzulaitis and G. C. Stevens. 510 p., 9 pls., 1927. Prepared in cooperation with the United States Geological Survey. Distributed only by the Division of Water Resources, P. O. Box 5184, Barracks Road Station, Charlottesville, VA 22903.

*36   Thermal Springs of Virginia, by Frank Reeves. 56 p., 8 pls., 4 figs., 7 tables, 1932.

41   Preliminary Report on Ground-Water Resources in Northern Virginia, by R. C. Cady. 48 p., 1 pl., 3 figs., 17 tables, 1933. Price: $0.25 (Clothbound edition; add $1.00).

45   Ground-Water Resources of the Shenandoah Valley, Virginia, by R. C. Cady, with Analyses, by E. W. Lohr. 137 p., 5 pls., 2 figs., 22 tables, 1936. Price: $0.25 (Clothbound edition; add $1.00).

*50   Ground-Water Resources of Northern Virginia, by R. C. Cady. 200 p., 7 pls., 5 figs., 42 tables, 1938.

58   Chloride in Ground Water in the Coastal Plain of Virginia, by D. J. Cederstrom. 36 p., 4 pls., 5 figs., 14 tables, 1943. Price: $0.25.

63   Geology and Ground-Water Resources of the Coastal Plain in Southeastern Virginia, by D. J. Cederstrom. 384 p., 38 pls., 31 figs., 50 tables, 1945. Price: $0.75.

68   Chemical Character of Ground Water in the Coastal Plain of Virginia, by D. J. Cederstrom. 62 p., 10 figs., 6 tables, 1946. Price: $0.25.

69   Public and Industrial Ground-Water Supplies of the Roanoke-Salem District, Virginia, by B. F. Latta. 53 p., 6 pls., 3 figs., 5 tables, 1956. Price: $0.25 (Clothbound edition; add $1.00).

75   Geology and Ground-Water Resources of Pittsylvania and Halifax Counties, Virginia, by H. E. LeGrand. 87 p., 1 pl., 6 figs., 11 tables, 1960. Price: $1.25. (Map available separately.)

MINERAL RESOURCES REPORTS

9   Ground-Water Resources of Accomack and Northampton Counties, Virginia, by Allen Sinnott and G. Chase Tibbitts, Jr. 113 p., 4 pls., 7 figs., 8 tables, 1968. Price: $1.25.

INFORMATION CIRCULARS

2   Water-Well Data, Western Part of Albemarle County, by Whitman Cross, II. 18 p., 1960. Price: $0.15.

MINERAL RESOURCES CIRCULARS

2   Summary of Geology and Ground-Water Resources of the Eastern Shore Peninsula, Virginia. A Preliminary Report, by Allen Sinnott and G. C. Tibbitts, Jr., 18 p., 1954. Price: $0.50.

4   Summary of Geology and Ground-Water Conditions in the Fredericksburg District, Eastern Spotsylvania County,

Virginia. A Preliminary Report, by Seymour Subitzky. 32 p., 1955. Price: $0.15.

MISCELLANEOUS PUBLICATIONS

Cederstrom, D. J., 1941, Ground-Water Resources of the Southeastern Virginia Coastal Plain: 11 p. Price: $0.15.

Mathews, E. B., and Nelson, W. A., 1928, Report on the Location of the Boundary Line Along the Potomac River Between Virginia and Maryland: Baltimore, 48 p., 6 maps. Price: $0.25.

DEPARTMENT OF CONSERVATION AND ECONOMIC DEVELOPMENT

Division of Water Resources
7th Floor, 911 East Broad Street
Richmond, Virginia 23219

In-print publications are available free of charge upon request directed to the above address.

BULLETINS

1 Springs of Virginia, by W. D. Collins, 1930, 55 p.

3 Chemical Character of Surface Waters of Virginia, 1929-1931, by W. D. Collins, 1932, 148 p.

4 Surface Water Supply of Viginia: Potomac, Rappahannock, and York River Basins, 1927-1942, by D. S. Wallace, 1944, 293 p.

5 Surface Water Supply of Virginia: James River Basin, 1927-1942, by D. S. Wallace, 1944, 442 p.

6 Surface Water Supply of Virginia: Chowan and Roanoke River Basins, 1927-1942, by D. S. Wallace, 1944, 341 p.

7 Surface Water Supply of Virginia: New, Big Sandy, and Tennessee River Basins, 1927-1942, by D. S. Wallace, 1944, 298 p.

8 Chemical Character of Surface Waters of Virginia, 1945-1946, by William L. Lamar, 1947, 46 p.

9 Major Storage Reservoirs of Virginia.

10 Flood of June 1949 in Stokesville-Bridgewater Area, by Orville D. Mussey, 1950, 20 p.

11 Chemical Quality of Surface Waters of Virginia, 1946-1948, by G. W. Whetstone, 1952, 38 p.

*12 Surface Water Supply of Virginia: Potomac, Rappahannock, and York River Basins, 1942-1950, by D. S. Wallace, 1952. 372 p.

13 Surface Water Supply of Virginia: James River Basin, 1942-1950, by D. S. Wallace, 1952, 394 p.

14 Surface Water Supply of Virginia: Chowan and Roanoke River Basins, 1942-1950, by D. S. Wallace, 1953, 333 p.

15 Surface Water Supply of Virginia: New, Big Sandy, and Tennessee River Basins. 1942-1950, by D, S. Wallace, 1953, 296 p.

16 Surface Water Supply of Virginia: Potomac, Rappahannock, and York River Basins, 1951-1955, by H. B. Holmes, Jr., 1957, 364 p.

17 Surface Water Supply of Virginia: James River Basin, 1951-1955, by H. B. Holmes, Jr., 1957, 281 p.

18 Surface Water Supply of Virginia: Chowan and Roanoke River Basins, 1951-1955, by H. B. Holmes, Jr., 1957, 277 p.

19 Surface Water Supply of Virginia: New, Big Sandy, and Tennessee River Basins, 1951-1955, by H. B. Holmes, Jr., 1957, 239 p.

20 Chemical and Physical Character of Surface Waters of Virginia, 1948-1951, by J. G. Connor, 1957, 107 p.

21 Chemical and Physical Character of Surface Waters of Virginia, 1951-1954, by M. E. Schroeder, 1957, 199 p.

22 Chemical and Physical Character of Surface Waters of Virginia, 1954-1956, by S. F. Kapustka, 1957, 161 p.

23 Chemical Character of Surface Waters of Virginia, August 1958-February 1960, by H. B. Holmes, Jr., 1960, 59 p.

24 Surface Water Supply of Virginia: Potomac, Rappahannock, and York River Basins, 1956-1960, by H. B. Holmes, Jr., 1961, 340 p.

25 Surface Water Supply of Virginia: James River Basin, 1956-1960, by H. B. Holmes, Jr., 1961, 278 p.

26 Surface Water Supply of Virginia: Chowan and Roanoke River Basins, 1956-1960, by H. B. Holmes, Jr., 1961, 306 p.

27 Surfacc Water Supply of Virginia: New, Big Sandy, and Tennessee River Basins, 1956-1960, by H. B. Holmes, Jr., 1961, 232 p.

31 Water Resources of Virginia. (Records of discharge prior to Sept. 30, 1927). [This bulletin was published by the Virginia Geological Survey (now Virginia Division of Mineral Resources) as Bulletin 31 in their series of publications but is obtained through this office.]

BASIC DATA BULLETINS

33 Flow Characteristics – North Atlantic Slope Basin.

34 Flow Characteristics – South Atlantic Slope Basin.

35 Flow Characteristics – Ohio River Basin.

INFORMATION BULLETINS

501 Notes on Virginia Water Laws and Agencies. 1969, 32 p.

502 Ground Water in Virginia. Revised 1969, 86 p.

504 Computer Programming and Math Modeling in Water Resources Planning.

PLANNING BULLETINS

New River Basin Comprehensive Water Resources Plan:

201 Vol. I Introduction. 1966, 78 p.

202 Vol. II Economic Base Study. 1967, 139 p.

203   Vol. III   Hydrologic Analysis. 1967, 170 p.

        Vol. IV   Water Resources Requirement. 1967, 142 p.

        Vol. V   Engineering Development Alternatives. 1967, 131 p.

206   Vol. VI   Implementation of Development Alternatives. 1967, 30 p.

Potomac-Shenandoah River Basin Comprehensive Water Resources Plan:

207   Vol. I   Introduction. 1969, 157 p.

        Vol. II   Economic Base Study. 1969, 96 p.

        Vol. III Hydrologic Analysis. 1969, 294 p.

        Vol. IV   Water Resource Requirement. 1969, 195 p.

        Vol. V   Engineering Development Alternatives.

James River Basin Comprehensive Water Resources Plan:

213   Vol. I   Introduction. 1969, 193 p.

        Vol. II   Economic Base Study. 1970. 98 p.

        Vol. III Hydrologic Analysis. 1970, 369 p.

        Vol. IV   Water Resource Requirement & Problems.

Rappahannock River Basin Comprehensive Water Resources Plan:

219   Vol. I   Introduction.

        Vol. III Hydrologic Analysis.

York River Basin Comprehensive Water Resources Plan:

225   Vol. I   Introduction.

        Vol. III Hydrologic Analysis.

261   **Ground Water of Southeastern Virginia.**

OTHER

*Index of the Surface Waters of Virginia, 1960, 66 p.

Notes on Surface Water in Virginia, 1965. 88 p.

Virginia Water (irregular periodical):

        Vol. I   Nos. 1 & 2 (1966).
        Vol. II   Nos. 1-3 (1967).
        Vol. III Nos. 1-3 (1968).
        Vol. IV   Nos. 1-4 (1969).
        Vol. V   Nos. 1 & 2 (1970).

VIRGINIA DEPARTMENT OF HEALTH
1314 East Grace Street
Richmond Virginia 23219

*Water Quality Survey of Hampton Roads Shellfish Area, 1949-1950. 1950. 122 p.

GOVERNOR'S OFFICE
Division of Industrial Development
1010 State Office Building
Richmond, Virginia 23219

Virginia Facts and Figures — 1971. Revised annually and available free of charge. (Contains a brief summary of ground and surface water resources in the State.)

VIRGINIA (STATE) GOVERNOR'S SPECIAL COMMITTEE ON WATER RESOURCES
This Committee is no longer in existence.

*Report. 1965. 39 p.

VIRGINIA INSTITUTE OF MARINE SCIENCE
Gloucester Point
Virginia 23062

SPECIAL SCIENTIFIC REPORTS

*2   References bearing on the hydrography of Chesapeake Bay and its tributaries, by W. A. Van Engel. 1948. 12 p.

*6   A biological survey of the Rappahannock River, Virginia, by William H. Massmann, Ernest C. Ladd and Henry N. McCutcheon. 1952. Parts I and II, 221 p.

*12   Investigations of the effects on oyster culture of the dredging for the Hampton Roads Bridge-Tunnel, by Jay D. Andrews, Dexter S. Haven, and J. L. McHugh. 1957. 21 p. (An investigation conducted by the Virginia Fisheries Laboratory for the Virginia State Department of Highways).

*14   Present status of the Rappahannock River for oyster culture, by J. L. McHugh and J. D. Andrews. 1956. 7 p.

*15   Status of pollution and oyster culture in the York River, by J. L. McHugh and J. D. Andrews. 1958.

*16   Maximum-minimum water temperatures, York River, Virginia, 1952-1958 (with annual supplement), by J. L. McHugh. 1959.

22   Summary of data from productivity experiments in the York River, Virginia, June 1960 — June 1961, by Bernard C. Patten and Ernest Warinner. 1961.

25   Distribution of ammonia and nitrate nitrogen in the lower York River, Virginia, by Bernard C. Patten and John R. Lacey. 1961.

27   Water temperatures and salinities, and fishes collected during Chesapeake Bay, York and Pamunkey river trawl surveys, 1957-1959, by William H. Massmann. 1962.

30   Diatoms from Virginia tidal waters, 1960 and 1961, by Richard A. Mulford. 1962.

31   Data on coastal currents off Chesapeake Bay, by J. J. Norcross, W. H. Massmann and E. B. Joseph. 1962.

*34   Bibliography of the physical, chemical, and geological oceanography of Chesapeake Bay, by Maynard M. Nichols. 1962.

*36   The aquatic phycomycetous flora of marine and brackish waters in the vicinity of Gloucester Point, Virginia, by William Scott. 1962.

*38   Phytoplankton diversity in the lower York River, Virginia, June 1960 – June 1961, by B. C. Patten. 1962.

*39   Dark and light bottle studies in the lower Chesapeake region, summer 1961, by B. C. Patten et al. 1963.

*40   Diffusion in a low-velocity, inshore tidal current off Virginia Beach, Virginia, by Wyman Harrison. 1963.

41   Shelf observations – Hydrography, (Cruise of August 21-26, 1962), by M. M. Nichols and M. P. Lynch. 1964.

*43   The net phytoplankton taken in Virginia tidal waters, January – December 1962, by R. A. Mulford. 1963.

44   Suspended particulate material in the lower York River, Virginia, June 1961 – July 1962, by Bernard Patten, Dave Young and Morris Roberts. 1963.

*45   Dark and light bottle studies in the lower York River, Virginia, June 1961 – August 1962, by Bernard Patten, Dave Young and Charles Rutherford. 1963.

48   Shelf observations – Hydrography, (Cruises of January 22-25, July 15-19, 1963), by M. M. Nichols and M. P. Lynch. 1964.

53   Characteristics of sediments in the James River estuary, Virginia, by Richard Moncure and Maynard Nichols. 1968.

DATA REPORTS

(This series has been established to present data with little or no interpretation.)

1   Bay observations – Hydrography (Cruises of Nov. 27, 1961 and Nov. 20, 1962), by M. M. Nichols. 1965.

5   Hydrographic data collection for "Operation James River – 1964", by J. K. Shidler and W. G. MacIntyre. 1967. Maps, 155 p.

MARINE RESOURCES ADVISORY SERIES

2   James River Hydraulic model, by Lawrence W. Mason and Fred C. Biggs. 1969. 7 p.

SPECIAL REPORTS IN APPLIED MARINE SCIENCE AND OCEAN ENGINEERING

1-5   (Not yet available.)

6   A biological and chemical study of the tidal James River, by Morris L. Brehmer and Samuel O. Haltiwanger. 1966. 32 p. Appendix A-E.

7   Final report on Operation James River (an evaluation of the physical and biological effects of the proposed James River navigation project), by William J. Hargis, Jr. 1966. 73 p.

8   A study of the effects of dredging and dredge spoil disposal on the marine environment. (A cooperative study between the Institute and the U. S. Army Corps of Engineers). 25 p. Appendix.

9   A biological and chemical study of the Nansemond River, Virginia, by Morris L. Brehmer, Samuel O. Haltiwanger and Willard I. Simmonds. 1967. 10 p. Appendix A-D.

10   Coastal wetlands of Virginia, interim report to the Governor and General Assembly, by Marvin L. Wass and Thomas D. Wright. 1969. 154 p.

Coastal wetlands of Virginia; interim report, summary and recommendations, by Marvin L. Wass and Thomas D. Wright. 1969. 18 p.

VIRGINIA STATE PLANNING BOARD — RIVER BASIN COMMITTEE

This Committee is no longer in existence.

*Report on the Proposed Development of the Roanoke River Basin. 1947. 161 p.

VIRGINIA SOIL AND WATER CONSERVATION COMMISSION
P. O. Box 1163
Richmond, Virginia 23209

Water Resources of Virginia: the Story of Water Conservation in Virginia, 1959. 111 p.

A Report of Erosion, Flooding and Sedimentation in Fairfax County, Virginia, by The Northern Virginia Soil Conservation District, 1964. 24 p.

Erosion and Sediment Control Technical Handbook, by The Northern Virginia Soil and Water Conservation District, 1970. 37 p.

Water and Land for You. A brochure.

23 Reasons Why Soil and Water Conservation is Your Business. A brochure.

Reclaiming the Land, Restoring the Waterways – An Act of Cooperation. A brochure.

STATE WATER CONTROL BOARD
P. O. Box 11143
Richmond, Virginia 23230

This information is available free upon request directed to the above address.

State Water Control Law
Publication includes:
    State Water Control Law
    Regulations and Requirements (established by State Water Control Board)
    Miscellaneous Offenses (Code of Virginia)
    Accelerated Amortization Rate (Tax relief on certain facilities designed to control pollution)

Water Quality Standards
Publication includes:
Rules and General Statewide Application
Stream Section Descriptions
Key to Special Standards

Information to be submitted in applying for certificates to discharge industrial wastes.

Municipal waste (sewage) treatment facility grants (procedure for application).

Water pollution control (Virginia state water control board).

Virginia water quality (periodic bulletin).

Miscellaneous – pamphlets, reports, maps, charts and graphs.

WATER RESOURCES RESEARCH CENTER

Virginia Polytechnic Institute
Blacksburg, Virginia 24061

BULLETINS

*1 Water Resources of Virginia – An Inventory of Printed Information and Data, by Frederick E. McJunkin and William R. Walker.

*2 Multidisciplinary Research as an Aid to Public Policy Formation. Papers presented at a Seminar sponsored by the Water Resources Research Center.

*3 Stochastic Model for Pollution and Dissolved Oxygen in Streams, by Richard P. Thayer and Richard G. Krutchkoff.

*4 Water Resources Programs in Virginia. Papers presented at a Symposium sponsored by the Water Resources Research Center.

*5 Translocation of Growth Regulators in *Chara Vulgaris,* a Non-Vascular Aquatic Plant Found in Virginia's Waters, by Thomas O. Evrard and William E. Chappell.

*6 Annual Report – Fiscal Year 1966. Water Resources Research Center.

7 Lime Treatment for Removal of Phosphate from Digester Supernatant Liquor, by William A. Parsons, H. H. Yeh, and J. M. Glennon, Jr.

*8 Annual Report – Fiscal Year 1967. Water Resources Research Center.

*9 Water Resource Laws in Virginia, by William R. Walker.

10 Flood Damage Abatement Study for Virginia, by William R. Walker. (In press.)

11 Multicomponent Mass Transport in Aqueous and Membrane Systems, by George B. Wills.

*12 Analysis of Hydrologic System, by James M. Wiggert.

13 The Effect of Water Quality on the Metabolism of the Lactic Streptococci, by Robert E. Benoit.

14 Hydrologic Aspects of No-Tillage Versus Conventional Tillage Systems for Corn Production, by Vernon O. Shanholtz and James H. Lillard.

15 Instantaneous Unit Hydrograph Response by Harmonic Analysis, by John Phillippe and James H. Lillard.

16 Computer System for the Reduction and Analysis of Soil Moisture Data, by Vernon O. Shanholtz.

17 Water Resources Research Interests in the Colleges and Universities of Virginia, by William R. Walker.

18 Water Resources Research in Virginia, by William R. Walker.

19 Annual Report – Fiscal Year 1968. Water Resources Research Center.

20 Probability Forecasts of 30-Day Precipitation, by John W. Philpot and Richard G. Krutchkoff.

21 The Effects of Pumped Storage Reservoir Operation on Biological Productivity and Water Quality, by Stuart E. Neff and George Simmons.

22 Stochastic Models for Biochemical Oxygen Demand and Dissolved Oxygen in Estuaries, by Richard G. Krutchkoff and Stephen W. Custer.

23 Some Water Quality Aspects of the Upper Roanoke River Basin with Special Emphasis on Temperature, by Kenneth B. Cumming.

*24 Prediction Models for Investment in Urban Drainage Systems, by John W. Knapp and Walter J. Rawls.

25 Geologic Control of Rainfall-Runoff Relations in the Peak Creek Watershed, Pulaski and Wythe Counties, Virginia, by Byron N. Cooper.

*26 Economics of Air and Water Pollution. Papers presented at a Seminar sponsored by the Water Resources Research Center. William R. Walker, Editor.

27 Water Evaporation and Suppression, by John L. Gainer, J. Taylor Beard and Robert T. Thomas.

28 Generalized Initial Conditions for the Stochastic Model for Pollution and Dissolved Oxygen in Streams, by Richard H. Moushegian and Richard G. Krutchkoff.

29 Public Perception of Water Resource Problems, Charles A. Ibsen and John A. Ballweg.

30 The Influence of Solar Radiation Reflectance on Water Evaporation, by J. Taylor Beard and David K. Hollen.

31 Annual Report – Fiscal Year 1969. Water Resources Research Center.

32 Removal of Selected Contaminants from Water by Sorption on Coal, by Paul H. King, Francis R. McNeice and Pierre S. Warren.

33 Temperature and Turbulence Effects on the Parameter Δ in the Stochastic Model for BOD and DO in Streams, by Joseph R. Bosley, John J. Cibulka and Richard G. Krutchkoff.

34 Treatment of Disperse Textile Dye Wastes by Foam Fractionation, by Donald L. Michelsen and Tom B. Fansler. (In press).

35 The Effect of Detergents on Gas Absorption, by Jerry A. Caskey, Ralph F. Herbert and Yan Pui To. (In press).

36 The Release of Soluble Phosphate in the Activated Sludge Process, by Clifford W. Randall, Bruce S. Hulcher and Paul H. King. (In press).

37 Legal Aspects of Water Supply and Water Quality Storage, by William R. Walker and William E. Cox. (In press).

38 Digital Simulation of the Soil Water Content in Two Contrasting Systems of Corn Production – No Tillage and Conventional Tillage, by Vernon Odell Shanholtz. (In press).

WASHINGTON

DEPARTMENT OF COMMERCE AND ECONOMIC DEVELOPMENT

Economic & Planning Analysis Division
Olympia, Washington 98501

The following Climatological Summaries are arranged alphabetically by city or town and summary number:

Aberdeen	R59-2	Laurier	R65-5
Anacortes	R59-6	Leavenworth	R64-5
Anatone	R65-6	Longview	R61-5
Battle Ground	R62-8	Metaline Falls	R63-4
Bellingham	R60-12	Monroe	R61-14
Bickleton	R65-5	Moses Lake	R61-8
Blaine	R62-1	Mount Adams	R65-16
Bremerton	R62-2	Mount Baker	R61-10
Buckley	R65-11	Mount Rainier	R60-18
Bumping Lake	R64-3	Newport	R63-6
Centralia	R59-1	Northwest Olympic	
Chelan	R59-7	Peninsula	R63-9
Chewelah	R64-7	Oakville	R65-1
Clarkston	R62-3	Ocean Beaches	R63-7
Cle Elum	R62-9	Odessa	R64-4
Colfax	R61-11	Olga (Orcas Island)	
Colville	R60-9	Olympia	R60-17
Crescent Bar	R65-9	Omak	R61-16
Cushman Dam		Oroville	R65-13
(Hoodsport)	R65-14	Othello	R61-7
Darrington	R64-1	Parkway Crystal Crk	R62-10
Davenport	R61-17	Pomeroy	R63-3
Dayton	R61-15	Port Angeles	R60-5 (Rev.)
Deer Park	R63-5	Port Townsend	R59-3
Diablo Dam	R64-2	Pullman	R60-21
Ellensburg	R60-22	Puyallup	R61-9
Ephrata	R65-17 (Rev.)	Quilcene	R65-4
Everett	R59-5	Quincy	R61-6
Forks	R60-1	Republic	R60-16
Goldendale	R61-13	Rimrock Dam	R65-8
Grand Coulee	R62-7	Ritzville	R61-2
Grapeview	R67-1	Rosalia	R64-6
Greenwater	R66-1	Seattle	R62-4
Holden	R63-1	Sedro Woolley	R60-15
Inchelium	R65-12	Sequim	R60-4
Kennewick	R60-14	Shelton	R60-10
Kosmos	R62-5	Snoqualmie Falls	R65-2
		Snoqualmie Pass	R60-20
		Spirit Lake	R64-8
		Spokane	R60-7 (Rev.)
		Stampede Pass	R60-19
		Stehekin	R63-2
		Stevens Pass	R65-7
		Sunnyside	R60-6

Tacoma	R61-1
Tri-City Area (Pasco, Richland, Kennewick)	R63-8
Vancouver	R60-11
Vashon Island	R62-6
Walla Walla	R60-8
Waterville	R65-10
Wenatchee	R59-4 (Rev.)
Whidbey Island	R61-4
Wilbur	R64-9
Willapa Harbor	R60-13
Wind River	R65-15
Winthrop	R61-12
Yakima	R61-3

DEPARTMENT OF ECOLOGY

335 General Administration Building
Olympia, Washington 98501

The following are reports of the Department of Ecology or its predecessors, the Department of Water Resources or the Department of Conservation. They represent technical and professional papers in geology, water quality, water quantity, snow surveys and other disciplines which compose the complex field of hydrology. Some of the reports were prepared by Department personnel. Others were prepared by several federal agencies with which the Department of Ecology carries on a continuing cooperative program designed to inventory the quantity and quality of the state's water resources.

Copies of the reports which are available may be ordered from the above address, at the prices shown in the list. When ordering, please make check payable to the Department of Ecology. Prices include all mailing and handling charges. Those reports unavailable for distribution may be examined at the Department of Ecology office. Many of the reports also may be consulted at the U. S. Geological Survey, 1305 Tacoma Avenue South, Tacoma, Washington, or at public libraries in the area to which the individual reports refer.

WATER SUPPLY BULLETINS

*1-5   Incorporated in Water Supply Bulletin 6.

6   Monthly and Yearly Summaries of Hydrographic Data in the State of Washington to September 1953, 1955. No charge.

7   Artificial Recharge of a Well Tapping Basalt Aquifers, Walla Walla Area, 1960, by Charles E. Price. Price: $0.50.

8   Geology and Ground Water Resources of the Columbia Basin Project Area, Washington, Volume 1, 1960, by Kenneth L. Walters and Maurice J. Grolier. Price: $1.50.

*9   Geology and Ground Water Resources of Clark County, Washington, 1964, by M. J. Mundorff.

10   Geology and Ground Water Resources of Thurston County, Washington, Volume 1 and 2, 1961, 1966, by Eugene F. Wallace, Dee Molenaar, and John B. Noble. Price: Volume 1, $1.50; Volume 2, $2.00.

11   A Preliminary Report on the Geology and Ground Water Resources of the Sequim-Dungeness Area, Clallam County, Washington, 1960, by John B. Noble Price: $0.50.

12   Water Resources of the Nooksack River Basin and Certain Adjacent Streams, 1960, by M. E. Garling, Dee Molenaar and others. Price: $2.00.

13   Summary of Snow Survey Measurements in the State of Washington, 1915 – 1960 Inclusive. No charge.

14   Lakes of Washington, Volume 1, Western Washington, 2d ed, 1965, by E. E. Wolcott. Price: $3.50.

*14   Lakes of Washington, Volume 2, Eastern Washington, 1964.

15   Monthly and Yearly Summaries of Hydrographic Data in the State of Washington, October 1953 to September 1960, 1962. No Charge.

*16   Flowing Artesian Wells in Washington State, 1961, by Dee Molenaar.

17   Geology and Ground Water Resources of West-Central Lewis County, Washington, 1962, by J. M. Weigle and B. L. Foxworthy. Price: $2.00.

18   Water Resources and Geology of the Kitsap Peninsula and Certain Adjacent Islands, 1965, by M. E. Garling, Dee Molenaar and others. Price: $2.00 (Includes Pls. 1 through 5). (Bulletin – out of print. Pls. – still available.)

*19   Water Resources of the Tacoma Area, Washington, 1962, by W. C. Griffin, J. E. Sceva, H. A. Swenson and M. J. Mundorff.

20   Geology and Ground Water Resources of Northwestern King County, Washington, 1963, by Bruce A. Liesch, Charles E. Price and Kenneth L. Walters. Price: $2.00.

21   Geology and Ground Water Resources of the Walla Walla River Basin, Washington-Oregon, 1965, by R. C. Newcomb. Price: $2.50.

22   Ground Water Occurrence and Stratigraphy of Unconsolidated Deposits of Central Pierce County, Washington, 1968, by Kenneth L. Walters and Grant E. Kimmel. Price: $5.00.

23   Miscellaneous Streamflow Measurements in Washington 1890 – 1961, 1964. No Charge.

24   Ground Water in Washington: Its Chemical and Physical Quality, 1965, by A. S. VanDenburgh and J. S. Santos. Price: $1.50.

25   Pleistocene Stratigraphy and Ground Water Resources of Island County, Washington, 1968, by Don J. Easterbrook and H. W. Anderson, Jr. Price: $5.00.

26   A Reconnaissance Report on the Geology and Ground Water Resources of Whitman County, Washington, 1969, by Kenneth L. Walters and P. A. Glancy. Price: $4.00.

27   Ground Water Resources and Related Geology, North-Central Spokane and Southeastern Stevens Counties of Washington, 1969, by Denzel R. Cline. Price: $4.00.

28   Geology and Ground Water Resources of Southwest King County, Washington, 1969, by James Luzier. Price: $4.00.

29   Geology and Ground Water Resources of Southeastern Mason County, Washington, 1970, by Dee Molenaar and John B. Noble. Price: $4.00.

30 Geology and Ground Water Resources of Lower Chehalis River Valley and Adjacent Areas, 1966, by Paul A. Eddy. Price: $1.00.

31 Ground Water Withdrawal in the Odessa Area, Adams, Grant and Lincoln Counties, Washington, 1968, by A. A. Garrett. Price: $2.00.

32 Reconnaissance of Sea Water Encroachment by K. L. Walters and others. (In Progress.)

33 Ground Water Hydrology and Development in East Central Washington. (In Progress.)

34 Quantitative Ground Water Study, Columbia Basin Irrigation Project, Washington. (In Progress.)

35 Availability of Ground Water in Cowlitz County, Washington, 1970, by Dave Meyers. Price: $2.00. (Not yet published.)

36 Ground Water Survey, Odessa-Lind Area, Washington, 1969, by J. E. Luzier, J. W. Bingham and others. Price: $2.00.

37 Reconnaissance of Geology and Ground Water Resources of the Developed Areas of Okanogan and Contiguous Counties. (In Progress.)

38 Quantitative Study of Water Resources of the Walla Walla Basin. (In Progress.)

MONOGRAPHS

1 A Geohydrologic Reconnaissance of Northwestern Walla Walla County, Washington, 1968, by Dee Molenaar. Price: $1.00.

2 Ground Water Data for the Goldendale-Klickitat County Area, 1969, by Paul A. Eddy.

DIVISION OF
POWER RESOURCES BULLETINS

JT. 1 Potentials of Irrigation in the Pacific Northwest, 1960, by Charles McGinnis.

1 Weather Modification – A Power Potential, 1959, by Truman P. Price.

*6 Pacific Northwest Regional Planning – A Review, 1963, by Roy F. Bessey. No Charge.

9 The Public Issues of Middle Snake River Development, 1964, by Roy F. Bessey. No Charge.

MISCELLANEOUS REPORTS

Biennial Reports of the Department of Conservation. (A predecessor agency of the Department of Ecology.) 1920/22 through 1962/1964.

23rd Biennial Report of the Department of Conservation: 1964/1966. Also included here are the reports of the Columbia Basin Commission, the State Soil and Water Conservation Committee and the Weather Modification Board. (These were not included in earlier biennial reports of the Dept. of Conservation.) No charge.

1st Biennial Report of the Department of Water Resources: 1966/1967 and 1967/1968. No charge.

Quality of Surface Water: June 1959 – July 1960. 1961. 97 p. No charge.

Washington State Surface and Ground Water Codes, Chapter 90.03. 100 p. No charge.

Water Pollution Control Laws, Chapter 90.48 RCW.

Department of Ecology Chapter 43.21A. 12 p.

Implementation and Enforcement Plan for Water Quality Regulations, Surface Waters, State of Washington. September 1970. 95 p.

Sewage Drainage Basin and Urban Area Planning Guide for Water Pollution Control and Abatement, 2nd Edition. September 1970.

Effects of Aerial Forest Fertilization on Water Quality for Two Streams in the Capitol Forest, by Merley McCall. October 1970. 20 p.

Ground Water Occurrence in the Goldendale Area Klickitat County, Washington, by J. E. Luzier. 1969. No charge. (A cooperative study with the U. S. Geological Survey.)

WASHINGTON STATE DEPARTMENT OF FISHERIES
Room 115, General Administration Building
Olympia, Washington 98501

Note: Many of the out-of-print articles can be xeroxed at a nominal fee.

ANNUAL REPORTS

1897 – to date. All preceeding 1960 out of print.

RESEARCH BULLETINS

*1 Toxic effects of sulfite waste liquor on young salmon. Fall 1953. R. W. Williams, E. M. Mains, W. E. Eldridge, J. E. Lasater. Edited by Gil A. Holland.

*3 Investigations of mortalities to downstream migrant salmon at two Dams on the Elwha River. By Dale E. Schoneneman and Charles O. Junge. 1954.

5 Toxic effects of organic and inorganic pollutants on young salmon and trout. G. A. Holland, J. E. Lasater, E. D. Neumann, W. E. Eldridge (Chemish, Poll. Cont. Comm.) Sept., 1960.

*6 Reports on sulfite waste liquor in a marine environment and its effect on oyster larvae. Cedric Lindsay, Ron E. Westley, Charles E. Woelke. December, 1960. 161 p.

8 Economic valuation of the 1965-1966 saltwater fisheries of Washington. James A. Crutchfield, Dougald MacFarlane.

FISHERIES RESEARCH PAPERS

*Vol. 1, No. 1 July, 1953

Stream flow and silver salmon production in Western Washington. William A. Smoker p. 5-12.

Vol. 1, No. 3 February, 1955.

Logging dams on coastal Washington stream, Henry O. Wendler and Gene Deschamps. p. 27-38.

Estimating the contribution of a salmon production area by marked fish experiments. Charles O. Junge and William H. Bayliff. p. 51-58.

*Vol. 1, No. 4 March, 1956.

Retention of Pacific oyster larvae in an inlet with stratified waters. Ronald E. Westley. p. 25-31.

A proposed correction of migratory fish problems at box culverts. W. R. McKinley and R. D. Webb. p. 33-45.

Tests on hauling as a means of reducing downstream migrant salmon mortalities on the Columbia River. C. H. Ellis. p. 46-48.

Vol. 2, No. 1 June, 1957.

The vertical and horizontal distribution of seaward migrant salmon in the forebay of Baker Dam. William H. Rees. p. 5-18.

Downstream migrant salmon survival in free fall from a Ski-jump spill-way. Albert F. Regenthal. p. 19-24.

Vol. 2, No. 2 April, 1959.

Survival of downstream migrant salmon passing Alder dam in an open flume. Dale E. Schoneman. p. 31-37.

Effects of stream dredging on young silver salmon, *Oncorhynchus kisutch*, and bottom fauna. William H. Rees. p. 53-65.

A study of localized predation on marked chinook salmon fingerlings released at McNary dam. Richard B. Thompson. p. 81-83.

Measurements of water transport through Swinomish Slough, Washington. William R. McKinley, D. C. Brooks, R. E. Westley. p. 84-87.

Vol. 2, No. 3 March 1964.

The distribution, size, time and current preferences of seaward migrant chinook salmon in the Columbia and Snake Rivers. Edward M. Mains and John M. Smith. p. 5.

*Vol. 2, No. 4 — Out of stock.

The effect of artificial circulation on production of a thermally stratified lake. Ray C. Johnson. p. 5.

A shipping and spreading bag for rotenone when used as a fish toxicant. Russell D. Webb. p. 16.

Floating salmon smolt collectors at Baker River dams. Elmer Quistorff. p. 39.

Vol. 3, No. 1.

Diet and growth of juvenile salmon in an estuarial impoundment. Robert Engstrom-Heg. p. 5.

Scuba diving observations on lingcod spawning at a Seattle breakwater. Earle D. Jewell. p. 27.

Economic criteria for division of catch between sport and commercial fisheries with special reference to Columbia River chinook salmon. Stephen B. Mathews and Henry O. Wendler. p. 93.

DEPARTMENT OF NATURAL RESOURCES

Division of Mines and Geology
P. O. Box 168
Olympia, Washington 98501

In ordering publications, please give both the series designation, as Bulletin 37, Part 1, and the title. Payment must accompany orders. Many of the out-of-print items are available for consultation in the larger public and educational institution libraries.

WASHINGTON GEOLOGICAL SURVEY, 1901-1921, ANNUAL REPORTS

*Vol. 1. Annual Report for 1901. 6 parts.

Part 5 The water resources of Washington. Potable and mineral water, by H. Byers. Artesian water, by C. A. Ruddy. Water power, by R. E. Heine. 1902. 37 p. 7 pls.

WASHINGTON GEOLOGICAL SURVEY, 1901-1921, BULLETINS

*14 A preliminary report on the Quincy Valley irrigation project, by Henry Landes, A. W. Mangum, H. K. Benson, E. J. Saunders, and Joseph Jacobs. 1912. 49 p. 7 pls.

DIVISION OF GEOLOGY, 1921-1945, BULLETINS

26 Underground water supply of the region about White Bluffs and Hanford, by Olaf. P. Jenkins. 1922. 41 p. 3 pls. 1 fig. Price: $0.50.

DIVISION OF MINES AND GEOLOGY REPRINTS

Mineral and water resources of Washington, prepared by the U. S. Geological Survey in cooperation with the Washington Department of Conservation, Division of Mines and Geology; Washington Department of Highways; U. S. Bureau of Reclamation; and Bonneville Power Administration. 1966. 436 p. 90 figs. Price: $2.00.

OCEANOGRAPHIC COMMISSION OF WASHINGTON

312 First Avenue North
Seattle, Washington 98109

The following publications are available from the Oceanographic Commission of Washington at the above address:

1 Report to the Legislature — 1969, 1970, and 1971. Summarizes the activities of the Oceanographic Commission during each year.

2 Pacific Northwest Sea. A quarterly newsletter distributed free of charge to the circulation list.

The following publications are available from the Oceanographic Institute of Washington at the above address:

1 Oceanographic Resources of the Pacific Northwest. Seattle: University of Washington Press, 1967. 263 p. Price: $9.95.

2 A Proposal for a Washington State Commission on Oceanography. Battelle-Northwest, 1966. 62 p. Price: $4.95.

WASHINGTON STATE POLLUTION CONTROL COMMISSION

Succeeded by Department of Ecology in 1970

TECHNICAL BULLETINS

*1 Investigation of sulfite waste liquor pollution in Fidalgo and Padilla Bays, by Walter W. Saxon and Albert Young. (1949 ?). 25 p.

*2 A survey of Puget Sound pollution Seattle metropolitan area, by Robert O. Sylvester and others. (1950 ?). 32 p.

*3 An investigation of pollution in Port Gardner Bay and the Lower Snohomish River, by Gerald T. Orlob, M. D. Anderson, and Dale L. Hansen. 1950. 25 p.

*4 Pea processing wastes from five major flood-processing plants in Southeastern Washington, by Walter W. Saxton. 1951. 14 p.

5 (Title not available).

*6 An investigation of domestic and industrial waste pollution in the lower Chehalis River and Grays Harbor, by Gerald T. Orlob, Kenneth R. Jones and Donald R. Peterson. 1951. 36 p.

7 (Title not available).

*8 An investigation of pollution in Commencement Bay and the Puyallup River system, by Gerald T. Orlob, Donald R. Peterson and Kenneth R. Jones. 1950. 26 p.

*9 An investigation of pollution in the Yakima River Basin, by Robert O. Sylvester and others. 1951. 47 p.

*10 An investigation of pollution in the vicinity of the Fort Lewis sewer outfall, by Donald R. Peterson, Gerald T. Orlob and Kenneth R. Jones. 1951. 10 p.

*11 A reinvestigation of pollution in Port Gardner Bay and the lower Snohomish River by Gerald T. Orlob, Donald R. Peterson and Kenneth R. Jones. 1951. 11 p.

*12 An investigation of pollution in the lower Columbia River Basin, by Kenneth R. Jones, Donald R. Peterson and Gerald T. Orlob. 1951. 53 p.

*13 The sewage disposal problem in the Seattle metropolitan area; a study and recommendations. 1952. 28 p.

*14 An investigation of pollution in Lake Washington, by Donald R. Peterson, Kenneth R. Jones and Gerald T. Orlob. With contributions by the Seattle-King County Health Department and Seattle Engineering Department. 1952. 29 p.

15 (Title not available).

*16 Sewage pollution in the estuarial river areas of Grays Harbor. 1953. 17 p.

17 (Title not available).

*18 An investigation of pollutional effects in Lake Washington (1952-1953). 1955. 18 p.

*19 Pulp and paper mill waste disposal problems, by Alfred T. Neale. 1955. 16 p.

*20 An investigation of pollution in the Green-Duwamish River, by Donald R. Peterson, Alfred Livingston and James H. Behlke. 1955. 22 p.

*21 A re-investigation of pollution in the lower Chehalis River and Grays Harbor (1956-57), by Donald R. Peterson, Richard A. Wagner and Alfred Livingston III. 1957. 51 p.

*22 An investigation of pollution in Northern Puget Sound, by R. A. Wagner, Charles D. Ziebell, and Alfred Livingston III. 1957. 27 p.

*23 An investigation of pollution in the vicinity of Port Angeles, by Donald R. Peterson and Charles V. Gibbs. 1957. 35 p.

*24 An investigation of water quality conditions in the Chambers Creek estuary, by R. A. Wagner, A. Livingston and C. D. Ziebell. 1958. 67 p.

*25 The development and operation of sewage lagoons. 1960. 16 p.

69-1 A preliminary investigation of the low dissolved oxygen concentrations that exist in Long Lake located near Spokane, Washington. 1969.

69-2 Limnological studies of selected Washington State lakes, by R. Lee. 1969.

70-1 A report on the water quality of the Little Spokane River, by Burkhalter, Cunningham and Tracy. 1970. 26 p.

MISCELLANEOUS

Report investigation of pollution in the lower Columbia River, by John H. Lincoln and Richard F. Foster. 1943. 143 p.

Oyster and sulfite waste liquor, a special consultant's report, by Gordon Gunter and Jack McKee. 1960. 93 p.

Implementation and enforcement plan for interstate and coastal waters. 1967. 146 p.

Water Pollution Control Plant Manual. Laboratory Equipment Testing Schedule Procedures, 1969 (2nd printing).

Bacteriological effects of primary treatment plant discharge at Bremerton, Washington. 1970. 60 p. (Together with the FWPCA – NW Region).

Rules and regulations for development, submission and adoption of water pollution control and abatement plans for sewage drainage basins. 1970.

WASHINGTON WATER RESEARCH CENTER
Washington State University
Pullman, Washington 99163

Note: The copying charge for articles which are out of print is $0.10 per page.

*Adams, John A., et al., A first estimate of future demands for water in the State of Washington. February 1967. Approx. 300 p. D of E Report No. 2, Volume 1.

Agnew, Allen F., A third approximation. October 14, 1969. 17 p. Address: Inland Empire Waterways Ass'n.

*Agnew, Allen F., et al., A water planning concept for the State of Washington. June 30, 1970. 72 p. Open File Report No. 7.

Agnew, Allen F., et al., A water planning concept for the State of Washington. June 30, 1970. 78 p. D of E Report No. 6.

Allan, G. G., et al., Enhancement of water quality using forest-derived coagulating systems. July 20, 1970. 33 p. A-019-Wash.

*Barkley, P. W., et al., Guidelines for establishing economic and engineering flood criteria. June 1970. 103 p. D of E Report 4A.

*Bender, Donald L., Determination of flows for ungaged streams. September, 1969. 10 p. A-009-Wash.

Bender, Donald L., Water resources research needs in the State of Washington. D of E Report No. 1. 103 p. October, 1967.

Brown, Gardner L., et al., Public utility pricing and output under risk. 23 p. Based on A-015-Wash.

Brown, Gardner, Selection of the optimum method for estimating the demand for nonmarket water resources with incomplete information. August 18, 1968. 8 p. A-015-Wash.

Buss, Irven O., Effects of water impoundments on reproduction and population number of waterfowl on the Snake River, Washington. July 15, 1970. 19 p. A-005-Wash.

*Butcher, Walter R., et al., Irrigation atlas of the State of Washington. Feb. 1967. Approx. 100 p. D of E Report No. 2, Volume 3.

Carlson, Dale A., et al., Improvement in treatment design for enhancing waste water quality. July 11, 1968. 32 p. A-016-Wash.

Carlson, Dale A., Nitrate removal from activated sludge systems. July 15, 1970. 38 p. A-026-Wash.

*Crosby, James W., III, Ground-water research in the Pullman-Moscow basin. October, 1967. 21 p. A-007-Wash.

Crosby, James W., III, Migration of pollutants in a glacial outwash environment. October 1968. 20 p. (reprint). Based on: B-005-Wash.

Crutchfield, J. W., et al., Summary – commentary in improving the flood-associated activities of the State of Washington Department of Water Resources. June 1970. 18 p. D of E Report 4.

Drake, Charles, Ecology of Selected aquatic bacteria in the Snake River. December 5, 1969. 14 p. A-018-Wash.

Eberhart, D. R. (moderator), Access – its effect on area growth and environmental quality. May 15, 1970. 78 p. Proceedings of a conference partially sponsored by Water Research Center.

Faulkner, Lindsey R., et al., Occurrence of large nematode populations in irrigation canals of south central Washington. Reprint from *Nematologica*. 11 p. A-011-Wash.

Flaherty, David C., (editor), Washington and its water. March 1969, issue of *Quest*. 21 p.

Garvey, M. D., et al., An analysis of the law governing six selected Washington water-oriented special districts. June, 1970. 378 p. D of E Report 4B.

*Gladwell, John S., et al., A study of certain aspects of the water resources of the State of Washington. December 10, 1966. 60 p. Water Research Center Open File No. 1.

*Gladwell, John S., et al., Some applications of order-statistics in hydrology. 36 p.

Gladwell, John S., Runoff generation in western Washington as a function of precipitation and watershed characteristics. June 1970. 353 p. A-028-Wash.

*Gladwell, John S., et al., Water resources atlas of the State of Washington. Approx. 325 p. D of E Report No. 2, Volume 2.

Hammond, Kenneth A., et al., A beginner's guide to research in environmental legislation and policy. December 1969. 92 p. Based on B-019-Wash. Available from Central Washington State College (Ellensburg) Bookstore. Price: $2.05.

Hammond, Kenneth A., et al., The impact of federal water legislation at the state and local level. October, 1970. 335 p. B-019-Wash.

Harms, Archie A., et al., An extension to the Thomas-Fiering model for the sequential generation of streamflow. September 1967, Reprint from Water Resources Research. 10 p. A-017-Wash.

*Hastay, Millard, et al., A statistical evaluation of the effects of the 1963-64 cloud seeding program on runoff from the Skagit River Watershed. April 1968. 176 p. Water Research Center Open File No. 5.

Higgins, David T., et al., The storage coefficient as a function of water table celerity. August 1970. 46 p. A-029-Wash.

Iulo, William, The role of industrial process changes in affecting water requirements. January 31, 1969. 27 p. A-013-Wash.

*Jensen, Max C., et al., Drainage theory for removal of excess water from irrigated lands and lateral movement above the water table. December 31, 1968. 50 p. A-006-Wash.

Kraft, Gerald F., et al., Factors affecting the movement of water and organisms within a regulated multipurpose lake. July 29, 1970. 21 p. B-011-Wash.

LaRock, Robert G., Infiltration beneath a forest floor. February 1967. 25 p. A-001-Wash.

Lenarz, William H., Simulation of a water resource system. February 5, 1969. 12 p. A-003-Wash.

*Lin, Chang-Lu, Factors affecting ground-water recharge in the Moscow Basin, Latah County, Idaho. October 1967. 95 p. A-007-Wash.

Mar, Brian W., et al., Water quality aspects of the State of Washington. D of E Report 3B. 211 p. June 1970.

Martig, Kenneth W. Jr., et al., Serial correlation in annual stream runoff. June 1968. 53 p. A-020-Wash.

*Mueller, August C., Catalog of water resources research projects in the State of Washington. November 1967. 133 p. Water Research Center Open File No. 4.

Nece, R. E., Stream temperature study, North Fork Snoqualmie River, Washington. January 1968. 55 p. A-012-Wash.

Nunnallee and Mar, A quantitative compilation of industrial and commercial wastes in the State of Washington. July 1, 1969. Project Study 3F.

*Proctor, Donald L., Evaluation of factors affecting stream self-purification. 1969. 45 p. A-008-Wash.

*Rambow, Carl A., et al., Water quality in the State of Washington. D of E Report No. 2 Volume 4. Approx. 270 p.

Richey, E. P., Fluid mechanics of downstream fish passage structures. September 1967. 10 p. A-004-Wash.

Rittall, Walter F., et al., Internal currents resulting from intermediate density inflows into stratified reservoirs. June 1970. 42 p. A-023-Wash.

Salo, Ernest O., et al., Water quality as related to the survival of salmon eggs and larvae. August 8, 1968. 5 p. B-004-Wash.

Schreiber, David L., Optimization techniques for water resource systems. November 16, 1968. 52 p. Open File Report No. 6.

Schreiber, David L., Overland flow simulation by a nonlinear distributed parameter model. 1970. 205 p. A-009-Wash.

Seabloom, Robert W., Bacteriological effect of small boat wastes on small harbors. July 1969. 26 p. A-024-Wash.

Sjolseth, D. E., et al., Studies of juvenile salmon in the Nooksack River system and Bellingham Bay. February 7, 1969. 54 p. B-003-Wash.

Stolte, William J., et al., Flow serial correlation & related streamflow generation models. June 1970. 162 p. A-035-Wash.

Stolte, William J., et al., Physical influences on flow serial correlation. June 1969. 105 p. A-020-Wash.

*Tinney, E. Roy, An initial study of the water resources of the State of Washington; digest. February 1967. 30 p. D of E Report 2 – Digest.

Van Ness, William, Uncertainty in Washington water rights. February 1967. 95 p. A-002-Wash.

*Van Ness, William, Washington water law, a survey. February 1967. 93 p. Open File Report No. 2.

State of Washington Water Research Center, Proceedings of the state-wide water resources forum. Held in Seattle, December 12-13, 1966. 144 p.

State of Washington Water Research Center, Introducing the Water Research Center, Washington State University. 18 p.

State of Washington Water Research Center, First annual report. September 1965. 35 p.

*State of Washington Water Research Center, Second annual report. 1966. 67 p.

*State of Washington Water Research Center, Third annual report. 1967. 147 p.

State of Washington Water Research Center, Fourth annual report. September 1969. 146 p.

State of Washington Water Research Center, Fifth annual report. July 1969. 161 p.

Wenatchee Daily World (pub.), Proceedings of the seminar on the continental use of Arctic flowing rivers. December 20, 1968. 180 p. (Seminar held April 1 – May 20, 1968). Can be purchased from Wenatchee Daily World. Price: $5.00.

Wooldridge, David, Effects of forest cover manipulation on water yield as studied by an electric analog. January 1970. 16 p. A-027-Wash.

Wooldridge, David W., et al., Analog computers for forest hydrology research. September, 1970. 39 p. A-037-Wash.

SUPPLEMENTAL LIST

Flaherty, David C. (editor), water enough for all? The State of Washington Water Research Center. March 1965, issue of *Quest,* 13 p.

Universities Council on Water Resources (publisher), graduate studies in water resources, 1970. 33 p.

Universities Council on Water Resources (publisher), hydrology (pamphlet).

Universities Council on Water Resources (publisher), career opportunities in water resources. 10 p.

Rosenow, Beverly J., a study of various procedures utilized by selected water-oriented special districts which are common to all of them. July, 1970. 157 p. A-030-Wash.

Warren, Robert, et al., a comparative analysis of American and Canadian governmental arrangements for the development of regional water policy in the Columbia River Basin. September 1970. 306 p. A-031-Wash.

WEST VIRGINIA

WEST VIRGINIA CONSERVATION COMMISSION

This Commision is no longer in existence.

*Principal Springs of West Virginia. 1948. 50 p.

WEST VIRGINIA STATE CONSERVATION NEEDS COMMITTEE

This Committee is no longer in existence.

*West Virginia Soil and Water Conservation Needs Inventory. 1961. 129 p.

WEST VIRGINIA STATE DEPARTMENT OF HEALTH

1800 Washington Street, East
Charleston, West Virginia 25311

*Public Water Supplies in West Virginia. 1956. 45 p.

DEPARTMENT OF NATURAL RESOURCES

Division of Water Resources
Charleston, West Virginia 25305

Annual Report. 1929/30, 1957/58 – . (Before 1960/61 the report was issued by predecessor agencies: State Water Resources Board; State Water Commission; and State Water Resources Commission. Beginning with 1961/62 the report was issued in the December issue of *West Virginia Conservation* as the annual report of the Division. No report appeared during period 1930 - 1957.)

West Virginia Water Quality Network 1960/61 (55 p.), 1962 (50 p.), and 1963 (50 p.).

*Little Kanawha River Survey, July 9 to July 20, 1962. 30 p.

*Water Resources of West Virginia, by W. L. Doll, Gerald Meyer, and R. J. Archer. 1963. 134 p.

An Annotated Bibliography of Water Resource Papers Pertaining to the State of West Virginia, by John Cha-Hong Tsai and Jerry C. Burchinal. 1963. 132 p.

*Design of Water Resources Plan for West Virginia, Project Director: James C. Kellogg. 1967. 62 p.

*Comprehensive Water Resources Study of the Greenbrier River Sub-basin, by J. Raymond DePaulo and M. S. Baloch. 1968.

*Comprehensive Survey of Elk River Sub-basin. 1969. 2 vols.

*Flow Characteristics of Greenbrier River, by M. S. Baloch, E. N. Henry and W. H. Dickerson. 1969. 95 p.

Streamflow Characteristics of the Elk River, by M. S. Baloch, E. N. Henry, and W. H. Dickerson. 1970. 96 p.

West Virginia Water Resources Study Information Bulletin. 5 p. (no date listed).

Cooperative Studies with either the U. S. Army Corps of Engineers (USACE) or the U. S. Geological Survey (USGS):

Water Resources of West Virginia, by Warwick L. Doll, Gerald Meyer, and Roger J. Archer. 1963. 134 p. (USGS cooperative study).

Water Resources of the Monongahela River Basin, West Virginia, by E. A. Friel, B. M. Wilmoth, P. E. Ward, and J. W. Wark. 1967. 118 p. (USGS cooperative study).

Flood Plain Information, Mud River in Vicinity of Milton, West Virginia. 1968. 39 p. (USACE).

Flood Plain Information, Little Kanawha River, Glenville, West Virginia. January 1970. 39 p. (USACE).

Flood Plain Information, Little Coal River, Madison, West Virginia. January 1970. 43 p. (USACE).

*Flood Plain Information, Little Kanawha River, Grantsville, West Virginia. January 1970. 41 p. (USACE).

WEST VIRGINIA GEOLOGICAL SURVEY

P. O. Box 879
Morgantown, West Virginia 26505

Please enclose cost of publication with order. Checks or money orders should be made payable to the West Virginia Geological Survey.

VOLUMES

VI   Springs of West Virginia, by Paul H. Price, J. B. McCue, and H. A. Hoskins. 1936. 146 p., 37 pls., 1 map (in pocket). Price: $2.25.

VIII   Salt Brines of West Virginia, by Paul H. Price, C. E. Hare, J. B. McCue and H. A. Hoskins. 1937. 203 p., 23 pls., 18 figs. Price: $2.50.

*X   Geology and Natural Resources of West Virginia, by Paul H. Price, R. C. Tucker, and O. L. Haught. 1937. 462 p., 231 pls., 61 figs.

XXII Geology and Economic Resources of the Ohio River Valley in West Virginia, by A. T. Cross and others. 1955-56. 409 p., 2 pls., 199 figs., 19 tables, 4 maps. In three parts:
Part I: "Geology", by A. T. Cross and M. P. Schemel. 150 p., 93 figs.
Part II: "Economic Resources", by A. T. Cross and M. P. Schemel with a chapter by O. L. Haught. 135 p., 68 figs.
Part III: "Ground-Water Resources", by C. W. Carlston and D. G. Graef, Jr., 131 p., 2 pls., 38 figs., 19 tables.
Price: Three parts bound in one volume – $7.00. Parts available separately, paperbound – $1.25 each. Maps available separately – $1.00 per sheet.

XXIII West Virginia Geological and Economic Survey – Its Accomplishments and Outlook, edited by I. S. Latimer, Jr., and others. 1963. 207 p., 65 figs., 7 tables. Price: $2.50.

BULLETINS

B 4 Bibliography and Index of Geology and Natural Resources of West Virginia, by J. B. Lucke. 1937. 84 p. Price: $1.25.

B 5 Surface Water Supply of West Virginia, by H. M. Erskine. 1942. 54 p. Price: $0.50.

B 8 Permeability, Porosity, Oil and Water Content of Natural Gas Reservoirs, Kanawha-Jackson and Campbell Creek Oriskany Wells, by A. J. W. Headlee and J. S. Joseph. 1945. 12 p., 4 figs. Price: $0.50.

B 10 Ground-Water Conditions Along the Ohio Valley at Parkersburg, West Virginia, by R. M. Jeffords. 1945. 57 p. 19 figs., 11 tables. Price: $0.75.

B 14 Ground-Water Resources of Harrison County, W. Va., by R. L. Nace and P. P. Bieber. 1958. 55 p., 2 figs., 11 tables. Price: $2.00.

B 15 Ground-Water Resources of Monongalia County, W. Va., by C. W. Carlston. 1958. 42 p., 2 pls., 8 figs., 3 tables. Price: $2.00.

B 20 Water Resources of Kanawha County, W. Va., by W. L. Doll and others. 1960. 180 p., 4 pls., 29 figs., 30 tables. Price: $2.25.

B 21 Ground-Water Features of Berkeley and Jefferson Counties, W. Va., by P. P. Bieber. 1961. 81 p., 2 pls., 7 figs., 10 tables. Price: $2.25.

B 27 Occurrence and Availability of Ground Water in Ohio County, W. Va., by T. M. Robison. 1964. 57 p., 8 figs., 7 tables. Price: $2.00.

B 28 Appalachian Connate Water, by E. R. Heck, C. E. Hare and H. A. Hoskins. 1964. 42 p., 10 figs., 3 tables. Is in two parts: "Ocean Salt" and "Geochemistry". Price: $0.75.

B 32 Ground Water in Mason and Putnam Counties, W. Va., by Benton M. Wilmoth. 1966. 162 p., 16 figs., 3 pls., 16 tables. Price: $2.25.

RIVER BASIN BULLETINS

RBB 1 Ground-Water Hydrology of the Monongahela River Basin in West Virginia, by Porter E. Ward and Benton M. Wilmoth. 1968. 54 p., 22 figs., 6 tables. Price: $2.25.

REPORTS OF INVESTIGATIONS

*RI 1 Analyses of West Virginia Brines, by H. A. Hoskins. 1947. 22 p. Supplements Vol. VIII with analyses made since 1937.

*RI 2 Ground-Water Conditions at Charleston, W. Va., by R. M. Heffords and R. L. Nace. 1947. 6 p.

RI 7 The Geomorphic History of the New-Kanawha River System, by H. M. Fridley. 1950. 12 p., 4 pls., 4 figs., 1 table. Price: $0.75.

RI 13 Relation of Geology to Drainage, Floods, and Landslides in the Petersburg Area, W. Va., by V. T. Stringfield and R. C. Smith. 1956. 19 p., 3 pls., 2 figs., 1 table. Price: $0.75.

BASIC DATA REPORTS

BDR 1 Records of Wells, Springs, and Test Borings, Chemical Analyses of Ground Water and Selected Driller's Logs from the Monongahela River Basin in West Virginia, by Porter E. Ward and Benton M. Wilmoth. 1968. 73 p., 2 figs., 4 tables. Price: $1.75.

EDUCATIONAL SERIES

Natural Resources of West Virginia, by Paul H. Price. 2nd edition – 1957. 19 p., 35 figs. Price: $0.50.

STATE MAPS

Drainage Map of West Virginia. 1912. Scale 1:500,000, size 33 inches x 38 inches. (Published by U. S. Geological Survey). Price: $2.00 rolled.

Relief Map of West Virginia. 1967. Scale 1:500,000, size 33 inches x 37 inches. (Includes streams and reservoirs.) Price: $3.00.

COUNTY MAPS

Drainage Maps of Each County. Scale 1:62,500. Price: $0.50 rolled.

WEST VIRGINIA STATE PLANNING BOARD
This Board is no longer in existence.

*Water Resources of West Virginia. 1954. 57 p.

WEST VIRGINIA STATE WATER COMMISSION
This Commission is no longer in existence.

*Report on Pollution Survey of Cheat River Basin. 1930. 46 p.

*Stream Conditions in the Weston Area. 1946. 4 p.

*Slaughter House Waste Treatment Guide. 1946. 22 p.

*Kanawha Basin Zoning Report. 1947. 39 p.

*Potomac Basin Zoning Report. 1948. 40 p.

*Stream Conditions in the Berkeley Springs Area. 1949. 5 p.

*Stream Conditions in the Clarksburg Area and Pollution Affecting Same. 1949. 10 p.

*The West Virginia Water Commission's Program of Stream Pollution Control. 1949. 10 p.

*Zoning Report, Little Kanawha, Guyandot, Big Sandy Basin. 1949. 38 p.

*Stream Conditions in the Charleston Area. 1950. 13 p.

*Shame of our Streams. 1951. 31 p.

*Methods of Financing Sewers and Sewage Treatment Works in West Virginia. 1952. 54 p.

*Planning and Constructing Sewage Disposal Facilities. 1953. 35 p.

*Water Pollution Control Law. 1953. 13 p.

*A Guide to the Clarification of Coal Washery Wastes Water. 1955. 35 p.

*"West Virginia Waters". No. 1, 1955 -   . (Quarterly news bulletin; after March 1959, issued by State Water Resources Commission).

WEST VIRGINIA WATER RESOURCES COMMISSION

This Commission is no longer in existence.

*Drainage Map of West Virginia, showing principal streams and their drainage areas. Compiled in cooperation with the U. S. Geological Survey. 1959 edition.

WATER RESEARCH INSTITUTE
17 Grant Avenue
West Virginia University
Morgantown, West Virginia 26506

Bennett, Herald D., 1969, Algae in Relation to Mine Water: Morgantown, Water Research Institute, Appalachian Center, West Virginia University, Journal Report 1. (Available from National Technical Information Service, U. S. Dept. of Commerce, Springfield, Virginia 22151, as PB 188906).

Dodson, Chester L. (editor and compiler), 1963, West Virginia Water Research Symposium Proceedings 1963: Morgantown, Water Research Institute, Office of Research and Development, Appalachian Center, West Virginia University, 101 p.

Grafton, C. R., and Dickerson, W. H., 1969, Influence of Topography on Rainfall in West Virginia: Morgantown, Water Research Institute, Appalachian Center, West Virginia University, Bulletin 1, 45 p.

Kralovic, Raymond C., and Wilson, H. A., 1969, Survival and Activity of Sewage Microorganisms in Acid Mine Water: Morgantown, Water Research Institute, Appalachian Center, West Virginia University, Research Report 1, 30 p.

Lugar, Marlyn E., 1967, Water Rights Law and Management in West Virginia — Future Needs and Alternatives: Morgantown, Office of Research and Development, Appalachian Center, West Virginia University, Public Affairs Series No. 4, 50 p.

Tsai, John Cha-Hong, and Burchinal, Jerry C., 1963, Water Resources of West Virginia (An Annotated Bibliography): Morgantown, Office of Research and Development, Appalachian Center, West Virginia University, 132 p.

WISCONSIN

COMMITTEE ON WATER POLLUTION
Madison, Wisconsin 53701

Cooperative state-industry studies of Wisconsin rivers in 1965, published jointly with the Sulphite Pulp Manufacturers' Research League, March 1, 1966. 24, 22 p. (Bulletin WP-111).

Report on an investigation of the pollution in the lower Wisconsin River drainage basin made during 1965.

Water pollution control program, January 1, 1966. 8 p.

Report on an investigation of the pollution in the Lake Superior drainage basin made during 1965 and early 1966. (1966).

DEPARTMENT OF NATURAL RESOURCES
Box 450
Madison, Wisconsin 53701

Note: Loan copies for some of the out-of-print reports are available upon request.

RESEARCH REPORTS
This series will be discontinued after report number 75 is issued.

*7 History of Beaver in Wisconsin, by George J. Knudsen. 1963.

*12 Limnology of a Borrow-Pit Lake, by Ronald J. Poff and Oscar M. Brynildson. 1965.

*21 Survival of Walleyes from Eggs of Known DDT and Dieldrin Residues in Three Southeastern Wisconsin Lakes, by Stanton J. Kleinert. 1967.

22 Limnological Changes Resulting from Artificial Destratification and Aeration of an Impoundment, by Thomas L. Wirth and Russell C. Dunst. 1967.

23 DDT and Dieldrin Residues Found in Wisconsin Fishes, by Stanton J. Kleinert, Paul Degurse, Thomas Wirth and Linda Hall. 1967.

*25 The Control of Aquatic and Marginal Weeds – Notes and Abstracts from the 7th Annual Meeting of the Weed Science Society of America, by Leon D. Johnson. 1967.

*27 A List of Fishes of Lake Winnebago, by Gordon R. Priegel. 1967.

*31 Effects of Habitat Alteration on Production, Standing Crops and Yield of Brook Trout in Lawrence Creek, Wisconsin, by Robert L. Hunt. 1968.

*33 Bibliography of Freshwater Wetlands, Ecology and Management, by Linda C. Hall. 1968.

*34 The Control of Aquatic and Marginal Weeds, by Leon D. Johnson. 1968.

37 Survival of Walleye Eggs and Fry of Known DDT Residue Levels from Ten Wisconsin Waters in 1967, by Stanton J. Kleinert and Paul E. Degurse. 1968. 30 p.

*39 Aquatic Plant Survey of Major Lakes in the Fox River (Illinois) Watershed, by Brian J. Belonger. 1969. 60 p.

40 Experimental Management of Spruce Lake, a Small Bog in Northeastern Wisconsin, by J. Kempinger. 1969. 15 p.

*41 Economic Incentives and Water Quality Management Programs, by Ved Prakasl and Robert H. Morgan. 1969. 74 p.

42 Fecal and Total Coliform Tests in Water Quality Evaluation, by Duane Schuettpelz. 1969. 25, [3] p.

43 Impact of an Overwinter Drawdown on the Aquatic Vegetation in Murphy Flowage, by Thomas D. Beard. 1969. 16 p.

45 Techniques for Wetland Management, by Arlyn F. Linde. 1969. 15 p.

47 Cox Hollow Lake: The First 8 Years of Impoundment, by Russell Dunst. 1969. 19 p.

50 Private Outdoor Recreation Businesses – Picnicking Enterprises, by Melville H. Cohee. 1970.

51 Private Outdoor Recreation Businesses – Swimming Enterprises, by Melville H. Cohee. 1970.

52 Aquatic Vegetation Survey of Milwaukee River Watershed Lakes, by Richard F. Modlin. 1970. 45 p.

53 Private Outdoor Recreation Businesses – Pondfishing Enterprises, by Melville H. Cohee. 1970. 21 p.

55 Private Outdoor Recreation Businesses – Their Composition, Operation and Stability, by Melville H. Cohee. 1970.

57 Wisconsin's Wetland Soils – A Review, by John Phillips. 1970.

58 Wild Rivers Fish Populations (Pine, Popple and Pike), by John W. Mason and Gerald D. Wegner. 1970. 42 p.

60 Private Outdoor Recreation Businesses – Camping Enterprises, by Melville H. Cohee. 1970.

62 Manipulation of Reservoir Waters for Improved Quality and Fish Population Response, by Thomas L. Wirth et al. 1970. 23 p.

63   Recommendations for a Scattered Wetlands Program of Pheasant Habitat Preservation in Southeast Wisconsin, by John M. Gates. 1970.

64   Private Outdoor Recreation Businesses — Boat Rental Enterprises, by Melville H. Cohee. 1971. 36 p.

65   Regulations to Reduce Conflicts Between Recreation Water Uses, by Jon A. Kusler. 1970. 283 p.

68   Water Quality and Trophic Condition of Lake Superior (Wisconsin Waters), by Donald R. Winter. 1971.

69   Ground Water Pollution from Sanitary Landfills and Refuse Dump Grounds, by A. E. Zanoni. 1971.

73   Mercury Levels in Fish From Selected Wisconsin Waters (A Preliminary Report), by Stanton J. Kleinert and Paul E. Degurse. 1971. 16 p.

74   Mercury Content of Various Bottom Sediments, Sewage Treatment Plant Effluents and Water Supplies in Wisconsin, by John G. Konrad. 1971.

OTHER REPORTS

Surface water resources of Barron County, by LaVerne M. Sather and C. W. Threinen. 1964. 135 p.

Preliminary report, water evaluation program. 1965. 1 vol., various pagings.

Surface water resources of Dodge County. 1966. 63 p.

Land Water Conservation Fund Act. 1966.

Surface water resources of Door County. 1966. 66 p.

Surface water resources of Adams County, by Thomas A. Klick and C. W. Threinen. 1966. 70 p.

Surface water resources of Wood County, by Thomas A. Klick and C. W. Threinen. 1967. 93 p.

Surface water resources of Oneida County, by Lloyd M. Andrews and C. W. Threinen. 1967. 284 p.

Surface water resources of Kewaunee County. 50 p.

Surface water resources of Jackson County, by Thomas A. Klick and C. W. Threinen. 1968. 133 p.

Surface water resources of Sheboygan County. 1968. 81 p.

Wisconsin's Outdoor Recreation Plan. 1968. Publication no. 802. vars. p.

Water resource management in Wisconsin. 1968. 49 p.

Water use conflicts — possible solutions (a review of Jon A. Kusler's "Regulations to Reduce Conflicts Between Recreation Water Uses"). 1970. 8 p.

1970 Status report on wild rivers. 1970. 14 p. (Compiled by the Fish Management Bureau as part of its role coordinating wild river programs.)

GENERAL PUBLICATIONS AVAILABLE IN QUANTITY

Fish Management and Biology

Wisconsin Trout Streams. Complete listing of all streams containing various species of trout. Pub. No. 213. Price: $0.25.

Wisconsin Lakes. Lists the lakes of Wisconsin, with each lake entered under the appropriate county. 36 p. Pub. No. 218. Price: $0.25.

Smallmouth Bass Streams. Information on all of the state's smallmouth bass streams. 11 p. Pub. No. 224. Price: $0.25.

Commercial Recreation

Recreation Land Development. A report to guide the commercial recreation developer. 88 p. Price: $0.75.

Recreation Site Evaluation. This report illustrates a step-by-step development plan analysis for a totally new lake. Price: $0.35.

Water Pollution

Quest for Clean Waters. History of Wisconsin's fight for clean water, standards, surveys, enforcement, industrial and sewage treatment information. Pub. No. 1101. Price: $0.15.

Miscellaneous

Wisconsin Water Trails. Describes 48 canoe or small boat trips on 36 Wisconsin rivers and lakes, with maps and text. Pub. No. 104. Price: $0.25.

Wisconsin Motorboat Trails. A guide to areas providing motorboat recreation. Designed for 2-day outings. Pub. No. 113. Price: $0.25.

Guidelines for Citizen Action on Environmental Problems. Ideas for individual action to protect the environment. Price: $0.02.

The Parade of Plants Series: I. Wetlands. Price: $0.15.

SURFACE WATER RESOURCE PUBLICATIONS
Listed by county and year published.

Adams	1966
Ashland	1966
Barron	1964
Burnett	1966
Chippewa	1963
Clark	1965
Columbia	1965
*Dane	1962
Dodge	1965
Door	1966
Dunn	1962
Eau Claire	1964
Fond du Lac	1969
*Green	1961
Iowa	1969
Jackson	1968
Jefferson	1969
Juneau	1969
Kenosha	1961
Kewaunee	1966
Lafayette	1967
Manitowoc	1969

Marquette	1963
*Menominee	1963
*Milwaukee	1964
Monroe	1969
Oneida	1966
Ozaukee	1964
*Polk	1961
Racine	1961
Rock	1970
St. Croix	1961
Sawyer	1969
Shawano	1968
Sheboygan	1968
Taylor	1970
Vilas	1963
Walworth	1961
Washington	1962
Waukesha	1963
Waushara	1970
Wood	1967

LAKE USE REPORT SERIES FOR LAKES IN THE FOX RIVER WATERSHED

Listed by report number, followed by lake, county and year published.

FX No.	
41	Army: Walworth – 1969.
40	Benedict: Kenosha & Walworth – 1969.
7	Beulah: Walworth – 1969.
3	Big Muskego: Waukesha – 1971.
25	Bohner: Racine – 1969.
31	Booth: Walworth – 1969.
15	Browns: Racine – 1968.
12	Camp: Kenosha – 1969.
27	Center: Kenosha – 1969.
4	Como: Walworth – 1969.
35	Cross: Kenosha – 1969.
23	Denoon: Waukesha – 1969.
45	Dyer: Kenosha – 1969.
9	Eagle: Racine – 1969.
19	Eagle Spring: Waukesha – 1969.
42	Echo: Racine – 1970.
7	Elizabeth: Kenosha – 1969.
1	Geneva: Walworth – 1969.
32	Kee Nong Go-Mong: Racine – 1969.
17, 18 & 20	Lauderdale Lakes (Green, Middle & Mill): Walworth – 1969.
34	Lilly: Kenosha – 1969.
10	Little Muskego: Waukesha – 1969.

29	Long: Racine – 1969.
14	Lower Phantom: Waukesha – 1969.
39	Lulu: Walworth – 1969.
17	Marie: Kenosha – 1970.
21	North: Walworth – 1970.
37	Pell: Walworth – 1969.
43	Peters: Walworth – 1969.
2	Pewaukee: Waukesha – 1970.
25	Pleasant: Walworth – 1969.
24	Potters: Walworth – 1967 (on cover).
13	Powers: Kenosha – 1969.
11	Silver: Kenosha – 1968.
38	Silver: Walworth – 1970.
34	Spring: Waukesha – 1969.
33	Upper Phantom: Waukesha – 1969.
45	Voltz: Kenosha – 1970.
30	Wandawega: Walworth – 1969.
6	Waterford Impoundment & Tichigan Lake: Racine – 1970.
26	Waubeesee: Racine – 1969.
5	Wind: Racine – 1969.

LAKE USE REPORTS FOR LAKES IN THE MILWAUKEE RIVER WATERSHED

Listed by report number, followed by lake, county and year published.

MI No.	
9	Auburn: Fond du Lac – 1970.
10	Crooked: Sheboygan-Fond du Lac – 1970.
7	Ellen: Sheboygan – 1970.
21	Forest: Fond du Lac – 1970.
14	Green: Washington – 1970.
13	Lucas: Washington – 1970.
12	Mauthe: Fond du Lac – 1970.
18	Mud: Fond du Lac – 1970.
11	Smith: Washington – 1970.
17	Spring: Ozaukee – 1970.
19	Twelve: Washington – 1970.
20	Wallace: Washington – 1970.

*WISCONSIN WETLAND INVENTORIES BY COUNTIES

Note: loan copies of these reports may be obtained from the Bureau of Research.

Columbia – 1960.

Dane – 1961.

Dodge – 1961.

Fond du Lac – 1961.

Green – 1963.

Green Lake – 1963.

Jefferson – 1961.

Marguette – 1963.

Racine and Kenosha – 1960.

Rock – 1959.

Walworth – 1959.

Waukesha – 1960.

Winnebago – 1962.

Upper Wisconsin River pollution investigation survey. July 1970.

State of Wisconsin public water supply data. 1970. 101 p.

Suggestions for prospective buyers of waterfront property in rural Wisconsin. (folder).

Investigation of alleged pollution of the surface waters in the Upper Wisconsin River basin in Vilas, Oneida, Price, Taylor, Lincoln, Langlade, Clark, Marathon, Wood, Portage, Juneau, Adams and Waushara Counties, Wisconsin.

Lower Rock River pollution investigation survey. 27 p.

Sheboygan River pollution investigation survey.

DEPARTMENT OF NATURAL RESOURCES
Division of Environmental Protection
Madison, Wisconsin 53701

Pollution abatement progress in Wisconsin, 1968-69. 14 p.

Report of an investigation of the pollution in the Black River Drainage Basin made during 1968. 17, [26] p.

Report of an investigation of the pollution in the Manitowoc River Drainage Basin, made during 1968. 29, [5] p.

Report on an investigation of the pollution in the Oconto River Drainage Basin made during 1968. 19, [5] p.

Report on an investigation of the pollution in the Upper Rock River Drainage Basin made during 1967-1968. 55, [4] p.

Report on an investigation of the pollution of the Menominee River and its tributaries in Wisconsin made during 1968. 21, [8] p.

Report on an investigation of the pollution of the Milwaukee River, its tributaries, and Oak Creek, made during 1968 and 1969. 43, [5] p.

Report on an investigation of the pollution of the Peshtigo River and its tributaries made during 1968. 20, [6] p.

Des Plaines-Pike River Drainage Area. [8] p. (Env. 3:Dr/3/-1968/2A-8A).

Investigation of alleged pollution of the surface water in the Black River Basin in Clark, Jackson, La Crosse, Marathon, Monroe, Taylor, Trempealeau and Wood Counties, Wisconsin. [35] p. (Env. 3:Dr/23/1970/1-28).

Investigation of alleged pollution of the surface waters in the Upper Rock River Basin in Fond du Lac, Dodge, Jefferson, Columbia, Dane, Washington, and Waukesha Counties, Wisconsin. [7] p. (Env. 3:Dr/1U/1970/1-53).

Investigation of alleged pollution of the surface waters of the Milwaukee River, its tributaries, and Oak Creek in Milwaukee County, Wisconsin. [10] p. (Env. 3:Dr/5/1970/1-8).

Lower Fox River Drainage Basin. [26] p. (Env. 3:Dr/11a/-1968/2A-70AA).

Root River Drainage Area. [22] p. (Env. 3:Dr/4/1968/3A-26A).

Upper Milwaukee River Drainage Area. [27] p. (Env. 3:Dr-/5/1968/1A-25A).

DEPARTMENT OF NATURAL RESOURCES
Division of Resource Development
Madison, Wisconsin 53701

Report on an investigation of the pollution in the Des Plaines and Pike Basin made during 1966 and 1967. 12, A-9, 3 p.

Report on an investigation of the pollution in the Fox (Illinois) River drainage basin made during 1966 and 1967. 19, A-15, 4 p.

Report on an investigation of the pollution in the Root River basin made during 1966 and 1967. 17, A-11, 4 p.

Report on an investigation of the pollution in the upper Fox River basin made during 1966 and early 1967. 21, A-28, [2] p.

In the matter of the alleged pollution of the lower Wisconsin River and its tributaries in Columbia, Dane, Sauk, Iowa, Grant, Crawford, Richland, Vernon, and Monroe counties, Wisconsin. 1968.

In the matter of the alleged pollution of the Pecatonica River and its tributaries in Dane, Iowa, Lafayette and Green counties, Wisconsin. 1968. 2 p.

In the matter of the alleged pollution of the surface waters in Des Plaines River and Pike Basin in Kenosha and Racine counties, Wisconsin. 1968. 9 p.

In the matter of the alleged pollution of the surface waters in the lower Fox River Basin downstream from Lake Winnebago in Brown, Calumet, Outagamie and Winnebago counties, Wisconsin, and in Green Bay. 1968. [52] p.

In the matter of the alleged pollution of the surface waters in the Root River Drainage Basin in Kenosha, Milwaukee, Racine and Waukesha counties, Wisconsin. 1968. [34] p.

In the matter of the alleged pollution of the surface waters in the Upper Fox River Basin, exclusive of the Wolf River, in Adams, Calumet, Columbia, Fond du Lac, Green Lake, Marquette, Waushara and Winnebago counties, Wisconsin. 1968. [65] p.

Town of Albion, Dane County, Town of Fulton, Rock County (Newville), Town of Koshkonong, Jefferson County, Town of Milton, Rock County, Town of Sumner, Jefferson County; findings of fact. 1968. [2] p.

The second wave; a biennial report (1966-1968) of the Wisconsin Resource Development Board. 1968. 29 p.

Report on an investigation of the pollution in the Lower Fox River and Green Bay made during 1966 and 1967. 1968.

Report on an investigation of the pollution in the Milwaukee River Basin made during 1966 and 1967. 1968.

GEOLOGICAL AND NATURAL HISTORY SURVEY

The University of Wisconsin
1815 University Avenue
Madison, Wisconsin 53706

Note: Publications listed as out of print may be obtained from the Survey on temporary inter-library loan; second-hand copies are occasionally available for library purchase.

BULLETINS

*V. Educational Series No. 1. The Geography of the Region about Devil's Lake and the Dalles of the Wisconsin with some notes on its surface geology. Rollin D. Salisbury and Wallace W. Atwood. 1900.

VIII. Educational Series No. 2. The Lakes of Southeastern Wisconsin. N. M. Fenneman, Professor of General and Geographic Geology, University of Wisconsin. 1902. 178 p., 36 pls., 38 figs. A second edition was issued in 1910. Price: $1.50.

*XII. Scientific Series No. 3. The Plankton of Lake Winnebago and Green Lake. Dwight March. 1903.

XVII. Scientific Series No. 5. The Abandoned Shore-Lines of Eastern Wisconsin. J. W. Goldthwait, Assistant Professor of Geology, Northwestern University. 1907. 134 p., 38 pls., 37 figs. Price: $1.50.

*XX. Economic Series No. 13. The Water Powers of Wisconsin. L. S. Smith. 1908.

*XXII. Scientific Series No. 7. The Inland Lakes of Wisconsin; the Dissolved Gases of the Water and Their Biological Significance. Edward A. Birge and Chancey Juday. 1911.

*XXVI. Educational Series No. 3. The Geography and Industries of Wisconsin. R. H. Whitbeck. 1913.

XXVII. Scientific Series No. 9. The Inland Lakes of Wisconsin. Hydrography and Morphometry. C. Juday, 1914. 137 p., 29 maps, 3 figs. Cloth bound. Restricted distribution.

XXXV. Economic Series No. 17. The Underground and Surface Water Supplies of Wisconsin. Samuel Weidman, of the Wisconsin Geological and Natural History Survey; and A. R. Schultz, of the U. S. Geological Survey. 1915. 664 p., 72 figs., 5 pls., and a colored geological map of the state. Scale: 1 inch equals 16 miles. Cloth bound. Price: $3.50.

XXXVI. Education Series No. 4 Second Edition. The Physical Geography of Wisconsin. Lawrence Martin, formerly Associate Professor of Physiography and Geography, University of Wisconsin. 1932. 608 p., 211 figs., 36 pls. Includes relief map of Wisconsin. Cloth bound. Restricted distribution.
Note: A reprint of this publication, without the relief map, may be purchased from the Univ. of Wisconsin Press, Box 1379, Madison, Wis. 53701. Paper backed edition $3.00. Cloth, $7.50.

*XLII. Educational Series No. 5. Geography of the Fox-Winnebago Valley. R. H. Whitbeck. 1915.

51. Scientific Series No. 11. Inland Lakes of Wisconsin. Temperatures. E. A. Birge. Not published.

*57. Scientific Series No. 12. The Phytoplankton of the Inland Lakes of Wisconsin. Gilbert M. Smith, Part I. 1920. Part II. 1924.

58. Educational Series No. 6. Geography of Southeastern Wisconsin. R. H. Whitbeck, Associate Professor of Geography, University of Wisconsin. 1920. 160 p., 3 pls., 100 figs. Restricted distribution.

64. Scientific Series No. 13. The Inland Lakes of Wisconsin. The Plankton. 1. Its Quantity and Chemical Composition. Edward A. Birge and Chancey Juday. 1922. 222 p., 40 figs. Paper bound. Price: $2.00. Cloth $4.00.

65. Educational Series No. 8. The Geography of Southwestern Wisconsin. W. O. Blanchard, Professor of Geography, University of Illinois. (Formerly with Department of Geography, University of Wisconsin.) 1924. 105 p., 1 pl., 81 figs. Cloth bound. Price: $1.50.

*67. Educational Series No. 9. A brief Outline of the Geology, Physical Geography, Geography, and Industries of Wisconsin, by W. O. Hotchkiss and E. F. Bean. 1925. 60 p. Paper bound.

*70. Scientific Series No. 14. The Fresh Water Mollusca of Wisconsin, Part I. Gastropoda. Part II. Pelecypoda. Frank Collins Baker, Curator, Museum of Natural History, University of Illinois. 1928.

INFORMATION CIRCULARS

I Some Effects of Precipitation on Ground Water in Wisconsin. William J. Drescher. 1955. 17 p., 5 figs. Price: $0.20.

III Ground Water in Wisconsin. William J. Drescher. 37 p., 5 figs., 4 tables. 1956. Price: $0.75.

IV Water Levels in Observation Wells in Wisconsin through 1957. R. E. Audini, C. F. Berkstresser, Jr., and D. B. Knowles. 1959. 192 p., 164 figs., 4 tables. Price: $1.25.

V A Preliminary Study of the Distribution of Saline Water in the Bedrock Aquifers of Eastern Wisconsin. Roy W. Ryling. 23 p., 1961. Price: $0.50.

IX Trends in Ground-Water Levels in Wisconsin through 1966 by Robert W. Devaul, 1967. 109 p., 16 figs., 2 tables, 220 hydrographs. Price: $2.00.

XVII Field Trip Guidebook to the Hydrogeology of the Rock-Fox River Basin of Southeastern Wisconsin, by C. L. R. Holt, Jr., R. D. Cotter, J. H. Green and P. G. Olcott. 47 p., 18 figs., 1 table. Price: $1.50.

SPECIAL REPORT

1. Preliminary Report on the Irrigation Potential of Dunn County, Wisconsin. Perry G. Olcott, Francis D. Hole and G. F. Hanson. 1967. 17 p., 4 figs., 4 tables. Price: $0.50.

HYDROGRAPHIC MAPS

Madison area lakes. A hydrographic map in shaded relief showing the depths of lakes Mendota, Monona and Wingra is available for $0.50.

Note: Hydrographic maps of other Wisconsin lakes are available from the following commercial agencies. Star Map Service, P. O. Box 3007, Milwaukee, Wisconsin 53218 and the Clarkson Map Company, 724 Desnoyer Street, Kaukauna, Wisconsin 54130.

MISCELLANEOUS

Ground-water Supplies in Wisconsin and Illinois Adjacent to Lake Michigan by R. E. Bergstrom and G. F. Hanson. 1962. Reprinted from Great Lakes Basin, American Association for the Advancement of Science, p. 251-268. Price: $0.10.

COOPERATIVE PUBLICATIONS OF THE UNITED STATES GEOLOGICAL SURVEY

The following publications of the U. S. Geological Survey have been prepared as a result of cooperative studies with the Wisconsin Geological and Natural History Survey. They are not available for purchase from the Wisconsin Geological Survey unless specifically stated. Circulars must be secured from U. S. Geological Survey, Washington, D. C. 20242. Orders for Water-Supply Papers must be directed to the U. S. Superintendent of Documents, U. S. Government Printing Office, Washington, D. C. 20402.

USGS CIRCULARS

274. Water resources of the Milwaukee area, Wisconsin, by W. J. Drescher, F. C. Dreher, and P. N. Brown. 1953. 42 p. Free.

USGS WATER-SUPPLY PAPERS

*1190. Ground-water conditions in artesian aquifers in Brown County, Wis., by W. J. Drescher. 1953. 49 p.

*1229. Ground-water conditions in the Milwaukee-Waukesha area, Wisconsin, by F. C. Foley, W. C. Walton and W. J. Drescher. 1953. 96 p.

*1294. Ground-water conditions in southwestern Langlade County, Wis., by A. H. Harder and W. J. Drescher. 1954. (1955). 39 p.

*1421. Geology and ground-water resources of Outagamie County, Wis., by E. F. LeRoux. 1957. 57 p.

*1604. Geology and ground-water resources of Fond du Lac County, Wis., by Thomas G. Newport. 1962. 52 p.

*1499-G. Water Resources of the Green Bay Area, Wis., by D. B. Knowles, F. G. Dreher, and G. Whetstone, 1964. 6 p.

*1619-X. Geology and Ground-water Resources of Rock County, Wis., by E. F. LeRoux, 1963. 50 p.

*1669-C. Hydrology of Upper Black Earth Creek Basin, Wis., by D. R. Cline with a section on surface water by M. W. Busby, 1963. 27 p.

*1669-J. Ground-Water conditions in the Green Bay Area, Wis., 1950-1960, by D. B. Knowles, 1964. 37 p.

*1669-U. Geology and Ground-water Resources of Waupaca County, Wis., by C. F. Berkstresser, Jr., 1964. 38 p.

*1779-U. Geology and Water Resources of Dane County, Wis., by D. R. Cline, 1965. 64 p.

*1796. Geology and Water Resources of Portage County, Wis., by C. L. R. Holt, Jr., 1965. 77 p.

1809-B. Geology and Ground-water Resources of Waushara County, Wis., by W. K. Summers, 1965. 32 p. Price: $2.00.

1809-I. Ground-water Pumpage and Water-level Changes in the Milwaukee-Waukesha Area, Wis., 1950-1961, by J. H. Green and R. D. Hutchinson, 1965. 19 p. Price: $1.00.

1811. Hydrology of the Little Plover Basin, Portage County, and the Effects of Water Resource Development by E. P. Weeks, D. W. Ericson, and C. L. R. Holt, Jr., 1965. 78 p. Price: $1.25.

1814. Geology and Water Resources of Winnebago County, Wis., by Perry G. Olcott, 1966. 61 p. Price: $3.50. (Available from Wis. Geol. Surv.)

1878. Water Resources of Racine and Kenosha Counties, Southeast Wisconsin, by R. D. Hutchinson, 1970. 63 p.

HYDROLOGIC ATLASES

This series is designed to show the hydrologic systems in the major river basins of the state by colored maps, figures and diagrams. Contents include the general physical setting, the availability and natural quality of ground water and surface water, stream flows, water use and other pertinent hydrologic facts.

The atlases may be purchased either from the Wisconsin Geological and Natural History Survey, University Extension, 1815 University Ave., Madison, 53706 or the U. S. Geological Survey, Washington, D. C., 20242. Remittances must cover all orders payable to the agency addressed.

HA-321   Water Resources of Wisconsin, Fox-Wolf River Basin, by Perry G. Olcott, 1968. 4 sheets. Price: $2.00.

HA-360   Water Resources of Wisconsin, Rock-Fox River Basin, by R. D. Cotter.

HA-367   Water Resources of Wisconsin, Central Wisconsin River Basin, by R. Devaul.

NATURAL RESOURCES COMMITTEE OF STATE AGENCIES
Madison, Wisconsin 53701

Natural Resources of Wisconsin. 1967. 157 p. (Reprint from 1964 Wisconsin Blue Book).

State of Wisconsin state laws, policies and programs pertaining to water and related land resources. 1967. 103 p.

SOIL CONSERVATION BOARD
Soils Building, University of Wisconsin
Madison, Wisconsin 53706

Guidelines for Inter-Agency Cooperation in Wisconsin Watershed Projects. 1968. Copy available upon request.

WATER RESOURCES CENTER

The University of Wisconsin

Hydraulics & Sanitary Laboratory

Madison, Wisconsin 53706

Should you desire a copy of a particular publication listed below, please contact the Center for information as to the availability, source, cost (if any), etc. Several of the publications are followed by a PB (Publication Board) number enclosed in brackets. For a copy of any such publication, you should write directly to: U. S. Department of Commerce, National Technical Information Service, 5285 Port Royal Road, Springfield, Virginia 22151.

The price schedule is (for publications announced after 1/1/69): 1 to 300 p. Price: $3.00. 301 to 600 p. Price: $6.00. 601 to 900 p. Price: $9.00. Over 900 p. Exception Price.

Documents announced prior to 1/1/69 have a service charge of $3.00 added to the announcement price.

Microfiche reproduction of documents on a demand basis are priced at $0.95 per document.

REPORTS AND PAPERS

Bahnick, Donald A.; Horton, J. W.; and Roubal, R. K. Comparison of the Water Quality of the Bois Brule and Poplar Rivers, Wisconsin — Both Tributary to Lake Superior. Contribution No. 16, Center for Lake Superior Environmental Studies. 16 p. OWRR A-023-Wis. 1970. [PB 194030].

Berg, Ronald J.; and Magnuson, John J. Variability of Winter-kill Survival in Fishes. Technical Report, 44 p. OWRR A-024-Wis. 1970. [PB 194031].

Burris, Robert H. Biological N_2 Fixation in Lakes. Technical Report, 7 p. OWRR B-020-Wis. 1969. [PB 189163].

Burris, R. H. Measurement of Biological N_2 Fixation. Paper presented at Meeting of IBP on Microbial Production, Leningrad, May, 1969, 9 p. OWRR B-020-Wis.

Byrne, Frank. The Geological and Hydrological Characteristics of the Whitewater Area, Wisconsin. Technical Report, 92 p. OWRR A-013-Wis. 1970.

Cain, John M. A Critical Analysis of the Use of Soil Survey Information in Preparation and Implementation of Land Use Plans. Report. OWRR B-002-Wis. 1967.

Carlson, R. F.; Watts, D. G.; and MacCormick, A. J. Linear Random Models of Annual Streamflow Series. Report. 1968.

Carlson, R. F.; Watts, D. G.; Stadler, G. J.; and MacCormick, A. J. Hydrology and Reservoir Control of the Wisconsin River Basin. Report. 1968.

Chesters, G. Insecticide Adsorption by Lake Sediments as a Factor Controlling Insecticide Accumulation in Lakes. (Terminal report on Phase I). 30 p. OWRR B-008-Wis. 1967.

Cottam, Grant and Nichols, Stanley A. Changes in Water Environment Resulting from Aquatic Plant Control. Technical Report, 27 p. OWRR B-019-Wis. 1970.

Crabtree, Koby T. Nitrate Variation in Ground Water. Technical Report, 65 p. OSW UI-00556-01, DNR 133-6451, and OWRR B-004-Wis. 1970. [PB 193707].

Csanady, G. T. The Interaction of the Atmosphere and Oceanic Ekman Layers. Department of Meteorology, University of Wisconsin. OWRR A-004-Wis. 1966.

Davidson, D. W. The Forest Vegetation of the Brule River Basin, Wisconsin, Tributary to Lake Superior. Technical paper presented before Minnesota Academy of Science, May 3, 1969. OWRR A-023-Wis. 1969.

Davidson, Donald W. Inter-Relationship of Certain Biological, Chemical, and Geological Parameters of the Bois Brule and Poplar River Watersheds, Douglas County, Wisconsin. Paper presented at 13th Annual Meeting of the International Assoc. for Great Lakes Research, Buffalo, New York, 5 p. OWRR A-023-Wis. 1970.

Davidson, Donald W. The Upland Forest Vegetation of the Bois Brule River Basin, Tributary to Lake Superior. Contribution No. 17, Center for Lake Superior Environmental Studies. Paper presented at 13th Annual Meeting of the International Association for Great Lakes Research, Buffalo, New York, April 3, 1970. 14 p. OWRR A-023-Wis. 1970.

Day, John C. An Activity Analysis of Non-Structural Flood Plain Management Alternatives. Technical Report, 127 p. OWRR B-002-Wis. 1969. [PB 189525].

Dickas, Albert B. Depositional Environments of Lake Superior Sands Through Grain Size Analysis. Contribution No. 15, Center for Lake Superior Environmental Studies, 11 p. OWRR A-023-Wis. 1970. [PB 194029].

Dickas, Albert B., and Tychsen, Paul C. Importance of the Bois Brule River to Recent Sedimentation History of Western Lake Superior. Preliminary report on Sediments and Geology of Bois Brule River, Western Lake Superior. 31 p. OWRR A-023-Wis. 1969.

Dickas, Albert B., and Tychsen, Paul C. Sediments and Geology of Bois Brule River, Western Lake Superior. Reprint from Proceedings, 12th Conf. Great Lakes Research., International Assoc. Great Lakes Res., p. 161-169. OWRR A-023-Wis. 1969.

Dunst, R. C. Cox Hollow Lake: The First Eight Years of Impoundment. Research report No. 47, Wisconsin Dept. of Natural Resources. OWRR B-013-Wis. 1969.

Dunst, Russel C. I'm Forever Blowing Bubbles (Deals with Lake Aeration). Technical paper, Wisconsin Conservation Department Bulletin, Vol. 3, No. 32, p. 16-17. OWRR B-013-Wis. 1967.

Fox, I. K. Policies for Effective and Economic Control of the Environment. Paper presented at the Executive Management Seminar, Washington, D. C., February 7-9, 1969, 22 p. OWRR C-1228/Title II. 1969.

Fox, I. K. Some Political Aspects of Large Scale Inter-Basin Transfers. Paper presented at the Annual Meeting of the American Association for the Advancement of Science, Dallas, Texas, December 30, 1968, 22 p. OWRR C-1228/Title II.

Fox, I. K.; Gotzman, Hans; Smith, S. C.; and Torti, T. U. Administration of International Rivers. Paper presented at the United Nations Panel of Experts on Legal and Institutional Implications of International Water Resources Development, December 9-14, 1968, Vienna, Austria, 48 p. OWRR C-1228/-Title II.

Governor's Conference on Water Resources Management in Wisconsin. Selected papers and a summary of the Proceedings of the Governor's Conference on Water Resources Management held at the State Capitol, Madison, Wisconsin, October 14-15, 1965, 81 p. 1966.

Gratz, R. L., and Villemonte, J. R. Acquisition and Analysis of Turbulent Water Velocities. Presented at ASCE Annual Hydraulics Conference, Logan, Utah, August 1969. OWRR B-012-Wis.

Gratz, R. L., and Villemonte, J. R. Characteristics of Liquid Turbulence in a Circular Pipe as Measured by a Magnetohydrodynamic Probe. Technical paper presented at the American Society of Civil Engineering Meeting on Environmental Engineering at Chattanooga, Tennessee, May 10, 1968. OWRR B-012-Wis.

Harrison, Samuel S. Magnitude of Waves on Lake Butte Des Morts and Their Effect on Lake Depth and Sediment Distribution. Technical Report, 45 p. OWRR A-027-Wis. 1970.

Hasler, A. D.; Terraguchi, M.; and Wall, J. P. Biological Aspects of Eutrophication in Lakes Mendota, Crystal, Trout, and Green. Report. OWRR A-002-Wis. 1969.

Higgins, D. T., and Monkmeyer, P. L. Unsteady Drawdown in an Unconfined, Two-dimensional Aquifer. Technical paper presented at the Water Resources Engineering Meeting, American Society of Civil Engineers, New Orleans, Louisiana, 40 p. February 1969. OWRR B-021-Wis.

Hoopes, J. A. Wind-driven Circulation in a Two-layer Lake. Paper presented at the Seventh National Fall Meeting of American Geophysical Union, San Francisco, California, December 2-4, 1968. OWRR B-009-Wis.

Hoopes, J. A.; Lien, S. L.; and Mitchell, J. W. Model Studies and Numerical Solutions of the Circulation in Lake Superior. Technical paper presented at the 12th Conference on Great Lakes Research, Ann Arbor, Michigan, May 5-7, 1969. OWRR B-009-Wis.

Institutional Design for Water Quality Management: A Case Study of the Wisconsin River Basin. OWRR C-1228/Title II, 9 Volumes. (This study was supported, in part, by the Office of Water Resources Research, Washington, D. C.)

Volume I   Summary. (Not yet available).

     II   Hydrology. 50 p. (Available from U. S. National Technical Information Service.)

     III   The Development of a Predictive Water Quality Model. (Not yet available.)

     IV   Cost Functions for Influencing Water Quality – Relation of Participation in Outdoor Recreation and Public Attitudes Toward Water Quality. 140 p. (Available from U. S. National Technical Information Service.)

     V   Systems Analysis of Hydropower Production on the Wisconsin River. 318 p. (Available from U. S. National Technical Information Service.)

     VI   The Nature of Minimum Cost Systems for Water Quality Management on the Wisconsin River. (Not yet available.)

     VII   Five Legal Studies on Water Quality Management in Wisconsin. 425 p. (Available from U. S. National Technical Information Service.)

     VIII   The Economic and Fiscal Aspects of a Regional Water Quality Management System. (Not yet available.)

     IX   An Analysis of Alternative Institutional Patterns for Managing Water Quality on a Regional System Basis. 251 p. (Available from U. S. National Technical Information Service.)

Interagency Water Resources Research and Data Collection Program. Dept. of Natural Resources; Geological and Natural History Survey, The University of Wisconsin-Extension; and, Water Resources Center, 58 p. State of Wisconsin Laws of 1965, Chapter 502 (6-S Program). 1968.

Interagency Water Resources Research and Data Collection Program. Dept. of Natural Resources; Geological and Natural History Survey, The University of Wisconsin-Extension; and, Water Resources Center. State of Wisconsin Laws of 1965, Chapter 502 (6-S Program). (1970-In press).

Kalter, Robert J. Estimating Local Secondary Impacts of Water-based Recreation Investment Using Interindustry Analysis. Report No. 2, June 1967, 85 p. OWRR A-007-Wis.

Kapoor, Vinod K. On the Validation of Simulation Experiments: A Review of Existing Techniques and a Proposed Technique for the Wisconsin River Water Quality Simulation Model. An independent study paper, 28 p. plus figures, May 1968. OWRR C-1228/Title II.

Kerrigan, J. E., ed. Proceedings of the National Symposium on Data and Instrumentation for Water Quality Management. Symposium held at The University of Wisconsin, Madison, Wisconsin, July 21-23, 1970, xi plus 521 p. Price: $5.00.

Kerrigan, James E., and Rohlich, Gerard A. General Water Quality Requirements. Technical paper presented at Special Lecture Series on Advances in Water Quality Improvement – Physical and Chemical Processes, University of Texas, Austin, Texas, March 31, 1969.

Law, Albert G., and Monkmeyer, Peter L. Ground Water Flow Toward a Clogged Streambank. Technical paper presented at ASCE Water Resources Engineering Conference, Denver, Colorado, 25 p. OWRR A-005-Wis. 1966.

Livermore, D. F.; Bruhn, H. D.; and Pollock, B. W. Processing Characteristics of Subsurface Macrophytes of Madison, Wisconsin Lakes in Relation to Mechanical Harvesting Systems. Paper presented at IBP/UNESCO Meeting on Production, Ecology, and Hydrological Implications of Aquatic Macrophytes, September 1-10, 1970, Rumania, 14 p. OWRR B-018-Wis.

MacCormick, A. J. A., and Watts, D. G. Behavior of the Autocorrelation Function of Mixed Autoregressive Moving Average Models. Technical Report No. 223, Department of Statistics, February 1970. OWRR C-1228/Title II.

Madary, James V. Studies on Flow-Through Electromagnetic Turbulence Indicators. An advanced independent study. Report of the Department of Civil Engineering, January 1969. OWRR B-012-Wis.

Malhotra, S. K. Metabolic Storage of Phosphorus in the Activated Sludge Floc. Technical Completion Report, 80 p. OWRR A-015-Wis. 1970.

McCoy, E. Lagooning of Liquid Manure (Bovine)-Bacteriological Aspects. Presented at the Winter Meeting of the American Society of Agricultural Engineers, Chicago, Illinois, December 1966. OWRR B-004-Wis.

McCoy, E., and Iwami, M. The Fate of Pathogens in Animal Waste Lagoons and Soil. OWRR B-004-Wis. (date unknown).

McCoy, E., and Sarles, W. B. Bacteria in Lakes: Population and Functional Relations. International Proceedings, Symposium on Eutrophication, June 1967. OWRR B-004-Wis.

McQuillam, Charles E. Stochastic Programming: A Survey. Technical Report, 66 p. OWRR C-1228/Title II. 1969. [PB 189535].

Mermin, Samuel. The Fox-Wisconsin Rivers Improvement – An Historical Study in Legal Institutions and Political Economy. 250 p. 1968. Price: $4.50.

Milfred, C. J.; Parker, Dale E.; and Lee, G. B. Remote Sensing for Resource Management and Flood Plain Delineation. Paper presented at the 24th Midwestern States Flood Control and

Water Resources Conference, May 21-22, 1969, Milwaukee, Wisconsin, 17 p. OWRR B-002-Wis.

Misaka, Y., and Polkowski, L. B. Filtration of Activated Sludge Secondary Effluents Through Sand and Anthracite-Sand Beds. Technical Report, 110 pages plus approximately 150 pages of figures. OWRR A-006-Wis. 1969. [PB 189162].

Misra, H. C., and Monkmeyer, P. L. On the Response of Sound Waves to the Permeability of a Porous Medium. Presented at ASCE Hydraulics Division Conference, Madison, Wisconsin, August 1966. OWRR A-005-Wis.

Monkmeyer, P. L., and Murray, W. A. Unsteady Unconfined Ground-water Flow Toward a Well. Technical paper presented at the Irrigation and Drainage Division Specialty Conference, American Society of Civil Engineers, Phoenix, Arizona, November 1968. OWRR B-021-Wis.

Polkowski, L. B.; Gramms, L. C.; and Witzel, S. A. Lagooning of Liquid Manure (Bovine) — Material Balance and Design Aspects. Presented at the Winter Meeting of the American Society of Agricultural Engineering, Chicago, Illinois, December 1966. OWRR B-004-Wis.

Prakash, Ved, and Morgan, R. H., Jr. Economic Incentives and Water Quality Management Programs. Department of Natural Resources, Division of Environmental Protection, and The University of Wisconsin, Madison, Wisconsin. Research Report No. 41, 74 p. OWRR C-1228/Title II. 1969.

Ragotzkie, Robert A., and Hoopes, John A. Circulation and Mixing Processes in Lakes. Technical Completion Report, 17 p. OWRR A-004-Wis. 1968.

Ragotzkie, R. A. Infra-red and Hydrographic Studies of Lake Superior. Proceedings of Ninth Conference on Great Lakes Research, Great Lakes Research Division, Institute of Science and Technology, University of Michigan. OWRR A-004-Wis. 1966.

Ragotzkie, R. A. The Keweenaw Current: A Regular Feature of the Summer Circulation of Lake Superior. Technical Report No. 29, 30 p. OWRR A-004-Wis. 1966.

Schlough, S. E. Processing Lake Weeds, A Research Project in Agricultural Engineering. A student project report. OWRR B-018-Wis. 1969.

Shen, M. C., and Shih, S. M. Asymptotic Nonlinear Wave Motion of a Viscous Fluid in an Inclined Channel of Arbitrary Cross Section. Report No. 1047, 30 pages. U. S. Army Contract No. DA-31-124-ARO-D-462 and OWRR A-037-Wis. 1970.

Te Kippe, R. J., and Ham, R. K. Coagulation Testing: A Comparison of Techniques. Technical Report, 58 p. OWRR A-028-Wis. 1970.

Tews, Leonard L. Microfungi in the Water, Mud, and Litter of a Cattail Marsh. Proceedings, 13th Conference International Association for Great Lakes Research. OWRR A-025-Wis. 1970.

Uttormark, Paul D. Some Effects of Continual Hypolimnion Discharge Upon a Downstream Channel. Presented at 31st Annual Midwest Fish and Wildlife Conference, St. Paul, Minnesota, December 1969. OWRR B-013-Wis. 1969.

Uttormark, Paul D.; Nunnele, L. J.; and Utter, L. C. Selected Water Resources Index for Wisconsin. July 1969. [PB 187312].

Uttormark, Paul D. Some Effects of Hypolimnitic Discharges on Temperatures in the Stream Below. Technical Report, 34 p. OWRR B-013-Wis. 1970.

Vierbicher, J. A. A Model of Lake Superior. OWRR A-004-Wis. 1967.

Water Resources Center. Abstracts — Eutrophication Program. Published monthly. (Available upon request).

Wilke, John. Nutrient Losses on the Fennimore Watersheds. OWRR B-004-Wis.

Williams, J. D. H.; Armstrong, D. E.; Syers, J. K.; and Harris, R. F. Sediment Properties Affecting Retention and Release of Phosphorus. Presented before American Chem. Society, New York. OWRR B-022-Wis. 1969.

Williams, J. D. H.; Syers, J. K.; Armstrong, D. E.; Harris, R. F.; and Spyridakis, D. E. Forms of Inorganic P in Non Calcareous Lake Sediments. Presented before Amer. Soc. of Limnology and Oceanography, August 1969. OWRR B-022-Wis.

Williams, J. D. H.; Syers, J. K.; Armstrong, D. E.; Harris, R. F.; and Spyridakis, D. E. Fractionation of Inorganic Phosphorus in Lake Sediments: I. Release and Resorption of Phosphorus During Fractionation. 12 p. OWRR B-022-Wis. 1969.

Williams, J. D. H.; Syers, J. K.; Armstrong, D. E.; Harris, R. F.; and Spyridakis, D. E. Fractionation of Inorganic P in Lake Sediments: II. Forms and Amounts of Inorganic p. 13 p. OWRR B-022-Wis. 1969.

Wirth, J. L. Effect of Impoundment on Fisheries. Water Chemistry Seminar, University of Wisconsin, November 1966. OWRR B-013-Wis.

Wirth, T. L., and Dunst, R. C. Limnological Changes Resulting from Artificial Destratification and Aeration of an Impoundment. Research Report No. 22 (Fisheries), Wisconsin Conservation Department, Research and Planning Division, 16 p. OWRR B-013-Wis. 1967.

Wirth, T. L.; Dunst, Russel C.; Uttormark, P. D.; and Hilsenhoff, William. Manipulation of Reservoir Waters for Improved Quality and Fish Population Response. Report No. 62, Department of Natural Resources, 23 p. OWRR B-013-Wis. 1970.

Witzel, S. A.; McCoy, E.; Attoe, O. J.; and Nichols, M. S. Physical, Chemical and Bacteriological Properties of Farm Wastes (Bovine Species). Proceedings of National Symposium on Animal Waste Management, Michigan State University, East Lansing, ASAE Publication No. SP-0366. OWRR B-004-Wis. 1966.

Witzel, S. A.; Attoe, O. J.; McCoy, E.; Polkowski, L. B.; and Crabtree, K. A Study of Farm Waste (Farm Animal Waste: Characterization, Handling, Utilization). Technical Completion Report, Department of Health, Education and Welfare, Office of Solid Wastes, 150 p. OSW UI-00556-01 to -04 and OWRR B-004-Wis. 1969. [PB 193708].

Witzel, S. A.; McCoy, E.; Attoe, O. J.; Polkowski, L. B.; and Crabtree, K. The Nitrogen Cycle in Surface and Subsurface Waters. Technical Completion Report, 69 p. OWRR B-004-Wis. 1968.

Zanoni, A. E. Eutrophic Evaluation of a Small Multi-Land Use Watershed. Technical Completion Report, 100 p. OWRR A-014-Wis. 1970.

WYOMING

DEPARTMENT OF HEALTH AND SOCIAL SERVICES

Sanitary Engineering Services
State Office Building
Cheyenne, Wyoming 82001

Water Quality Standards for Interstate Waters in Wyoming.

*Standards for Sewerage & Sewage Works.

Minimum Standards for Private or Semi-Public Water Supplies.

Minimum Standards for Private Sewage Disposal Systems.

GEOLOGICAL SURVEY OF WYOMING

University of Wyoming
Box 3008, University Station
Laramie, Wyoming 82070

Publications distributed without charge unless otherwise noted. Those out of print may be borrowed through Loan Librarian, University of Wyoming Library, Laramie, Wyoming.

BULLETINS

*19   Mineral hot springs of Wyoming: A. B. Bartlett, 1926.

*30   Underground water resources of Horse Creek and Bear Creek valleys, southeastern Wyoming: W. L. Dockery, 1940.

*32   Underground water resources of Chugwater Creek, Laramie River and North Laramie River Valleys, Wyoming: A. R. Edwards, 1941.

REPORTS OF INVESTIGATIONS

*R.I. 1   The Saline Lake deposits of Wyoming, Part I, the Downey Lakes, Albany County, Wyoming: S. H. Knight, 1934.

*R.I. 2   The Saline Lake deposits of Wyoming, Part II, the Rock Creek Lakes, Albany County, Wyoming: S. H. Knight, 1939, reprinted 1943.

WYOMING STATE ENGINEER

State Office Building
2001 Central Avenue
Cheyenne, Wyoming 82001

"Official Record, Upper Colorado River Basin Compact Commission," published in three volumes, in limited quantity, July 1946 to August 1949.

"Official Record, Upper Colorado River Commission," published in limited quantity. Vol. I - 1949 through Vol. VII - 1955.

"Wyoming Water and Irrigation Laws," 1969. 83 p.

Wyoming State Engineer's Office Biennial Report. Vol. 1 (1891/92) through Vol. 39 (1966/68).

"Water Laws": 5th biennial report, 1899-1900, p. 165-171.

Seventh biennial report, 1902/04 has supplement: The Irrigation Laws of Wyoming, June 1905.

1936/38 and following include the report of the State Water Conservation Board.

Supplement A, 1918/20 and following include "Tabulation of permits issued, arranged according to water division."

Supplement B, 1918/20 and following include "Surface Waters of Wyoming."

Supplement C, 1930/32 and following include "Adjudications and other proceedings of the State Board of Control."

WYOMING WATER PLANNING PROGRAM

1   Leaflet – The Wyoming State Water Plan, Fall of 1968, State Water Planning staff.

2   State Water Plan Report No. 1 – Computerized System For Wyoming Surface Water Records. September 1968, Wyoming Water Resources Institute, University of Wyoming.

3   Wyoming Water Planning Program Report No. 2 – Objectives and Policies of the State Water Plan. October 1968, Revised 1970, Wyoming Water Planning Program staff.

*4   Wyoming Water Planning Program Report No. 3 – (Preliminary) Water and Related Land Resources of the Green River Basin, Wyoming. January 1969, Wyoming Water Planning Program staff. (Printed in limited copy. The report is being rewritten.)

5   Wyoming Water Planning Program Report No. 4 – Tabulation of Existing Wyoming Reservoirs Over 500 Acre-Feet Capacity. March 1970, Wyoming Water Planning Program staff.

6 Wyoming Water Planning Program Report No. 5 – Consumptive Use of Irrigation Water in Wyoming. July 1970, by Frank J. Trelease, Theodore J. Schwartz, Paul A. Rechard, and Robert D. Burman.

7 Wyoming Water Planning Program Report No. 6 – An Approach To the Selection of a Streamflow Base Period. July 1970, by Wm. N. Embree.

8 The Wyoming Water Rights Information Storage and Retrieval System. September 20, 1968, Auerbach Corporation.

*9 Proposal for Development of the State of Wyoming Water Rights Information System. December 1968, Ernst & Ernst.

*10 Report on Wyoming's Water Supplies and Needs in the Bear River Basin. December 1968, J. T. Banner & Associates.

*11 Wind-Bighorn-Clarks Fork River Basin, Plan of Work, Type IV Survey. April 1969, Revised July 1970, U. S. Department of Agriculture, Soil Conservation Service, Economic Research Service, Forest Service.

*12 Selected Methods of Estimating Consumptive Use For Mountain Meadows in Wyoming. June 1969, Ronald C. Rickenbaugh. (Thesis submitted to the University of Wyoming for M. S. Degree in Water Resources, funded by Wyoming Water Planning Program.)

*13 Report on Preliminary Reconnaissance of Potential Reservoirs, Green River Basin, Wyoming. July 1969, submitted to the Department of Economic Planning & Development and the Wyoming Water Planning Program, State Engineer's Office, Cheyenne, Wyoming, by J. T. Banner & Associates, Consulting Engineers.

*14 Wyoming Mineral Industries – Review and Forecast. A report prepared for the Wyoming Natural Resource Board and the Wyoming Water Planning Program, September 1969, by Cameron Engineers, Denver, Colorado.

15 Demographic Study of Wyoming – Population and Transition. December 1969, by William E. Morgan, Margaret W. Pearl, Florence P. Barker, Division of Economic and Business Research, University of Wyoming. This may be obtained from the University of Wyoming, Laramie, Wyoming 82070.

16 Wyoming: Comprehensive Economic Studies to Facilitate Development Through Planning. January 1970, by William E. Morgan, Robert D. Schriner, and Merlin H. Hackbart, prepared for the Wyoming Department of Economic Planning & Development and the Wyoming State Engineer by the Division of Business and Economic Research, College of Commerce and Industry, University of Wyoming. This may be obtained from the University of Wyoming, Laramie, Wyoming 82070.

WYOMING LEGISLATIVE RESEARCH COMMITTEE
Cheyenne, Wyoming 82001

Severance of Water Rights from Wyoming Lands, by Frank J. Trelease. 1960. 54 p. (Research Report No. 2.)

WYOMING NATURAL RESOURCES BOARD
210 West 23rd Street
Cheyenne, Wyoming 82001

*Report on Development and Utilization of Wyoming's Colorado River Basin Water Resources, by J. T. Banner and Associates, Laramie, Wyoming. January 1955.

*Report on Proposed Methods for Augmenting Laramie River Basin Water Supplies, by J. T. Banner & Associates, Laramie, Wyoming. December 1955.

Wyoming's Water Resources. Edwin R. Lang, editor. 1956. 76 p.

Selected Bibliography on Water Resources, State of Wyoming. 1956. 15 p.

Ground Water Reconnaissance Study of the State of Wyoming, by George F. Dana. 1962. 7 parts in 1 volume.

Water for Industry in Wyoming. 1968. 30 p.

NATURAL RESOURCES RESEARCH INSTITUTE
The University of Wyoming, College of Engineering
P. O. Box 3038, University Station
Laramie, Wyoming 82070

Xerox copies may be obtained from the Institute for any report the supply of which is exhausted. There will be a minimum charge of $0.07 per page copied.

INFORMATION CIRCULARS

11 Bellamy, John C., Kinds of Natural Resources Research, December 1960, 15 p.

14 Bellamy, John C., Requirements for High Altitude Meteorology, 1965-1975. June, 1961, 13 p.

16 Hoyt, Philip M., and John C. Bellamy, Periods of Records of Stream Gages in Wyoming, August, 1962, 8 p. and map.

18 Williams, Merlin C., and Leonard B. Baldwin, Jr., Informatic Precipitation Gage Data, September, 1962, 14 p. and 2 maps.

20 Bellamy, John C., Aerodetic Aspects of Altimetry, February, 1963, 21 p.

21 Bellamy, John C., and Staff, Weather Modification Research, March, 1963, 25 p.

24 Smith, Verne E., Informatic Stream Gage Data, August, 1963, 36 p.

26 Bellamy, John C., and Staff, Summary Report Weather Modification Research, U. S. Bureau of Reclamation, Contract 14-06-D-4857. April, 1964, 21 p.

32 Bellamy, John C., and Anton C. Munari, 'SIPLIC' Forms of Hourly Precipitation Data, August, 1965, 25 p.

33 Killam, Everett H., A Watershed Treatment Technique for Subalpine Runoff, August, 1965, 65 p.

35　　Veal, Donald L., Informatic Portrayals Utilizing Uadic Numerals of Snow Pillow Data, August, 1965, 6 p.

40　　Williams, Merlin C., Weather Modification Research – Summary Report – U. S. Bureau of Reclamation – 1963–1964 and 1964–1965 Winter Seasons, February, 1, 1966, 79 p.

51　　Auer, August, and Donald L. Veal, Characteristics of the Cloud within the N-car Ice Nucleus Counter. September, 1967, 18 p.

52　　Hoffman, E. J., Water Requirements for Coal Conversion. October, 1967, 8 p.

54　　Auer, August, D. L. Veal and J. D. Marwitz. Plume Tracking and Mass Flow Studies Within the Elk Mountain Water Resource Observatory and Western South Dakota. Paper presented at the Third Project Skywater Planning Conference of the Bureau of Reclamation, Fort Collins, Colorado. February, 1967, 22 p.

55　　Veal, Donald L., Atmospheric Resources Research. College of Engineering, University of Wyoming. Presented at the Bureau of Reclamation Skywater Conference No. 4, May 21-22, 1968, Denver, Colorado, 9 p.

59　　Veal, Donald L., August H. Auer, and John D. Marwitz, Atmospheric Resources Research, April, 1969. Presented at the 3rd Annual Meeting of the Western Snow Conference, Salt Lake City, Utah, April 15-17, 1969, 27 p.

60　　Veal, Donald L., Prediction and Verification of Airflow Over 3-D Mountain. June, 1969, 26 p.

61　　Bellamy, John C., Final Summary Report, Environmental Data Format Study, August, 1969, 29 p.

MISCELLANEOUS PUBLICATIONS

1　　Fisk, Henry G., Progress and Work of the Natural Resources Research Institute, University of Wyoming, 1943-1946. 1947, 14 p.

*3　　Anonymous, Wyoming's Natural Resources. June 7, 1949, 1 p.

16　　Everybody Talks About the Weather – Now They are Doing Something About It. *The Wyoming Alumnews,* September - October, 1962.

ANNUAL REPORTS

Annual Reports covering the work of the Institute from January, 1945, through the current fiscal year are available for reference at the Library of the University of Wyoming. The latest reports covering the periods of July, 1960, through the current fiscal year are available for free distribution at the Institute.

ANNUAL PROGRESS REPORTS

Annual Progress Report for July, 1963 - June, 1965 is available for free distribution at the Institute.

ALSO AVAILABLE

Wyoming Natural Resource Board, Cheyenne, "Wyoming Weather Facts." June, 1966, 47 p.

WYOMING STATE PLANNING AND WATER CONSERVATION BOARD

Succeeded by Natural Resources Board in 1951

*Thermopolis Hot Springs, a Resource of National Importance. 1940. 15 p.

WATER RESOURCES RESEARCH INSTITUTE

The University of Wyoming
P. O. Box 3038, University Station
Laramie, Wyoming 82070

Note: Publications listed under Water Resources Series and under Other Publications are available free of charge by writing to the above address.

WATER RESOURCES SERIES

1　　Glossary of Selected Hydrologic Terms, by Paul A. Rechard and Richard McQuisten (compilers). 1966, Revised 1968. 43 p. Funded in part by OWRR-A-001-WYO.

2　　Progress Report on the Effects of Varying Land and Water Use on Streamflow Regimen, by Paul A. Rechard and Frederick R. Potter. 1966. 41 p. Funded in part by OWRR-A-001-WYO.

3　　Snow Water Acidity in Wyoming, by Pierre Clement. 1966. 41 p. Funded in part by OWRR-A-001-WYO.

4　　Population Trends in the Green and Platte River Basins of Wyoming: 1890-2010, by Raymond K. Kenney and John W. Birch. 1967. 41 p. Funded in part by OWRR-A-001-WYO.

5　　Projected Gross Residential Water Requirements in the Green and Platte River Basins of Wyoming: 1970-2010, by James C. Kildebeck, Orman H. Paananen, and John W. Birch. 1967. 50 p. Funded in part by OWRR-A-001-WYO.

6　　Psychrometric Tables for Wyoming (High Elevations), by Paul A. Rechard. 1967. 31 p. Funded in part by OWRR-A-001-WYO.

7　　Confluence Analyses of Land Surfaces, by M. R. McGaw. 1967. 49 p. Funded in part by OWRR-A-001-WYO.

8　　Water Resource Observatory Climatological Data – Water Year 1966 and Prior, compiled under the direction of Paul A. Rechard. 1967. 323 p. Funded in part by OWRR-A-001-WYO.

9　　Municipal Water and Sewage Systems in Wyoming – A Source Book of Data, compiled by Keith R. Schwer. 1968. 124 p. Funded in part by OWRR-A-001-WYO.

10　　The Effects of Varying Land and Water Use on Streamflow Regimen, by Paul A. Rechard and John E. Lane. 1968. 64 p. Funded in part by OWRR-B-001-WYO.

11　　Legal Aspects of Weather Modification – Snowpack Augmentation in Wyoming, by John M. Pierce. 1968. 61 p. Funded in part by OWRR-A-001-WYO.

12   Water Resource Observatory Climatological Data – Water Year 1967, compiled under the direction of Paul A. Rechard. 1968. 391 p. Funded in part by OWRR-A-001-WYO.

13   Computerized System for Wyoming Surface Water Records, by William N. Embree, Lee W. Larson, and Paul A. Rechard, (compilers). 1968, revised 1970. 73 p. Funded in part by Wyoming Water Planning Program and OWRR-A-001-WYO.

14   Water Resources Observatory Climatological Data – Water Year 1968, compiled under the direction of Paul A. Rechard. 1969. 391 p. Funded in part by OWRR-A-001-WYO.

15   Snowy Range Water Resource Observatory (A Progress Report), by Paul A. Rechard, editor. 1969. 34 p. Funded in part by OWRR-A-001-WYO.

16   Water Resource Observatory Solar Radiation Data – Water Year 1969 and Prior, compiled under the direction of Paul A. Rechard. 1969. 39 p. Funded in part by OWRR-A-001-WYO.

17   Water Resource Observatory Climatological Data – Water Year 1969, compiled under the direction of Paul A. Rechard. 1970. 343 p. Funded in part by OWRR-A-001-WYO.

18   Surface Water System – Operational Handbook, by William N. Embree. 1970. 67 p. Funded in part by Wyoming Water Planning Program and OWRR-A-001-WYO.

19   Consumptive Use of Irrigation Water in Wyoming, by Frank J. Trelease, J. Swartz, Paul A. Rechard, Robert D. Burman. 1970. 21 p. Funded in part by Wyoming Water Planning Program and OWRR-B-003-WYO.

20   An Approach to the Selection of a Streamflow Base Period, by William N. Embree. 1970. 99 p. Funded in part by Wyoming Water Planning Program and OWRR-A-001-WYO.

LAND AND WATER LAW REVIEW

A semi-annual journal edited in the College of Law, University of Wyoming through the Land and Water Law Center, funded in part by OWRR-A-001-WYO. Vol. I, Nos. 1 & 2 - 1966 through Vol. V, Nos. 1 & 2 - 1970. (Subscription available at $6.00 per year).

OTHER PUBLICATIONS

Annual Reports
   First through Fourth – August 1965 through August 1968.
   Fifth through Sixth   – July 1969 through July 1970.

Wyoming Weather Facts. 1966. Compiled by the Natural Resources Research Institute – University of Wyoming, for the Wyoming Natural Resource Board. 47 p.

State Water Planning Recommendations. 1966. Prepared by Water Resources Research Institute – University of Wyoming, for the Wyoming Natural Resource Board. 20 p.

   Supplement: Availability of Funds under Federal Legislation. 21 p.

   Supplement: Other States' Planning Programs and State Planning Organizations. 35 p.

   Supplement: Planning Example – North Platte River Basin. 38 p.